Marketing Africa's High-Value Foods:

Comparative Experiences of an Emergent Private Sector

Steven Jaffee, The World Bank

John Morton, Overseas Development

Administration, U.K.

Editors

KENDALL/HUNT PUBLISHING COMPANY
4050 Westmark Drive   P.O. Box 1840   Dubuque, Iowa 52004-1840

The opinions and recommendations presented in this book are the result of research supported by the World Bank; however, they are solely those of the respective authors, and do not necessarily represent the position or policies of the World Bank, its affiliated organizations, members of its Board of Executive Directors, or the countries they represent.

To our wives Gilat and Diana,
and our children Danielle, Elan, and Helena.

Table of Contents

Acknowledgements

The preparation of this book and most of the research upon which it is based was jointly funded by the World Bank and the Overseas Development Administration. The sponsoring departments within the World Bank were the Agriculture and Natural Resources Department and the Africa Technical Department. The sponsoring department within ODA was the Africa Regional Desk. The opinions and recommendations presented in the book are solely those of the editors and respective authors, and do not necessarily represent the position or policies of the World Bank, ODA, or their affiliated organizations.

For their support in launching this project and providing continued guidance through its various stages, we would like to thank Gershon Feder, Graeme Donovan, Kevin Cleaver, Brian Grimwood, and Felicity Proctor. For their time, advice, and support in accessing relevant literature, we thank Alex Duncan (Food Studies Group), Mary Tiffen (ODI), Anthony Ellmann and Nick Hetherington (CDC), Helen Wedgewood (ITDG), Ingrid Vanore-Speirs and colleagues (ITC), Laurens van der Laan and colleagues (African Studies Centre), Nicolas Bricas and colleagues (CIRAD), Richard Roberts, Andrew Shepherd, Marc Bral and colleagues (FAO), John Holtzman (Abt Associates), Caroline Moser, Yvan Grouitch, Tyler Biggs, Jim Coates, Eduardo Loayza, and others (World Bank/IFC), and members of the Social Sciences Group and Food Science and Crop Utilization Division of the Natural Resources Institute. For superb editorial assistance and production support, thanks to Annette Bickel and Marianne Sabers. Special thanks are extended to the many African entrepreneurs and business executives whose cooperation and insights have made this book possible.

I.

Introduction

Agriculture dominates the economies of most of sub-Saharan Africa's forty-seven countries. For the region as a whole, agriculture accounts for 70% of total employment and 40% of total merchandise exports, with these shares considerably higher in some countries.[1] Although agriculture accounts for only 32% of recorded GDP in sub-Saharan Africa (SSA), in most countries one- to two-thirds of manufacturing value added is based on agricultural raw materials, and many services are linked to agriculture.[2]

Over the past two decades, SSA's overall agricultural performance has been poor, and the weakness of this sector is an important factor in the region's wider economic stagnation. Even with increased food imports, the decline in per capita food production has resulted in a decline in per capita daily caloric intake since the mid-1970s.[3] Table 1.1 highlights the low or negative growth rates for different indicators of production and trade. Both the volume and value of African agricultural exports have declined since the mid-1970s and this is reflected in SSA's loss of part of its share of the market for many of its most important agricultural exports (see Table 1.2). The region's agricultural trade is now more concentrated among these same commodities than it was a quarter century ago.[4] Due to stagnant or declining crop production, weak incentives and inefficient raw material procurement systems, a considerable proportion of the region's formal sector agricultural processing capacity remains underutilized.

---

[1] Data from World Bank (1991) and (1992).

[2] Food processing, beverage, tobacco, and textile industries are among those dependent on agricultural raw materials. Agricultural input supply and food marketing services are among the leading service activities in many African countries.

[3] From 2059 calories over the 1976–80 period to 2027 calories over the 1986–90 period (World Bank (1993a).

[4] In 1961–63, six commodities—cotton, coffee, cocoa, sugar, tobacco, and tea—accounted for 53% of the region's agricultural exports. By 1984–86, the share of these commodities was 75.4%, with coffee and cocoa alone accounting for over 54% (Akiyama and Larson 1989).

TABLE 1.1: **Agricultural Performance Indicators for SSA**
(Average Growth Rates)

Indicator	1975–1980	1980–1985	1986–1990
Value Added in Agriculture	+1.9	+0.4	+1.5
Agricultural Production	+0.5	+1.0	+1.6
Per Capita Food Production	–2.3	–2.1	–1.5
Volume of Agricultural Exports	–0.8	–2.9	–2.5
Value of Agricultural Exports	+9.6	–2.9	–3.1
Value of Food Exports	+9.9	–2.0	–6.7
Value of Food Imports	+19.8	–5.7	+3.2

SOURCE: World Bank (1992).

This gloomy aggregate picture obscures the progress which has been achieved by some countries in obtaining higher rates of agricultural growth, in expanding or adding value to traditional exports, and in diversifying their trade into higher value commodities with favorable world market trends. Between 1986 and 1991, Nigeria, Uganda, Tanzania, Chad and Botswana each achieved agricultural growth rates exceeding 4% per year. Moreover, there are now signs of recovery in industries which had previously faltered, such as Ghanaian cocoa, Ugandan coffee and Tanzanian cashew nuts. Among non-traditional exports, both Kenya and Côte d'Ivoire have become significant competitors in the world horticultural products trade.

External or unavoidable factors, including declining world prices for major export commodities, frequent drought and civil strife, have undoubtedly contributed to the poor agricultural performance of some African countries. But they do not explain everything. Since the early 1980s there has been a growing consensus that various forms of **institutional failure,** particularly within the public sector, have been a central factor in Africa's agricultural and more general economic stagnation.[5] According to this view, African agriculture and agro-industry have been strongly and adversely affected by misguided macroeconomic and pricing policies and by excessive government intervention in factor and commodity markets. These interventions, together with the imposition and maintenance of inefficient, and frequently monopolistic, state-

---

[5] A World Bank study published in 1981, *Accelerated Development in Sub-Saharan Africa*, linked Africa's economic problems to misguided macroeconomic and sectoral policies and to the overextension and weak performance of public institutions. Although controversial at the time, within a few years analysts from across the political spectrum were extending or echoing its analysis and major findings. They include Bates (1981), Ellis (1982), Hart (1982), Hyden (1983), de Wilde (1984), Arhin, Hesp and van der Laan (1985), and Ghai and Smith (1987).

owned or state-sponsored processing and marketing organizations, are held to have undermined producer incentives and crowded out private investment in most of the region's important agro-industries. Despite sizeable amounts of state aid and international donor financial and technical assistance, parastatal agribusiness enterprises have largely been deficient in providing support services to farmers and in managing the logistics of trade. Their record of anticipating opportunities and responding to changes in world markets has been even worse.

The policy prescriptions following from this analysis have been straightforward, even if the implementation by specific country or sector has proven to be complex and problematic. Over the past decade, the agenda pursued by African governments and international donors has centered around macroeconomic reforms, trade and domestic market liberalization, and public sector restructuring. More recently, measures have been geared toward expanding the role of the private sector.[6] Attention has been directed at improving the enabling environment for business (through legal and regulatory means), at reforms which strengthen domestic financial systems and at privatizing selected public enterprises. In many countries the agricultural sector has been the subject of far-reaching proposals and programs of structural reform.

A curious feature of much of the recent literature discussing new policies (and even of the programmed reforms) is the abstract nature of recommendations regarding 'private sector development' and greater reliance upon 'mar-

TABLE 1.2: **World Market Shares of sub-Saharan Africa for Major Agricultural Commodities** (% of World Export Value)

Commodity	1969–71	1989–91
Coffee	27.3	17.8
Cocoa	77.9	67.1
Cotton	16.0	13.9
Sugar	8.6	8.6
Tobacco	7.7	13.5
Tea	12.5	15.3
Combined	20.8	16.3

SOURCE: Data from FAO *Trade Yearbook,* various issues.

---

[6] These have been the focal areas of the many structural and sectoral adjustment programs implemented within the region. For reviews of this experience, see Helleiner (1992), Jaeger (1992) and World Bank (1994).

ket forces'. Despite the widespread advocacy of agricultural market liberalization and privatization in Africa, the actual forms which competitive markets and private enterprises might take in the African context and the speed and direction of their development are rarely examined. Lele (1988) argues that the abstract nature of the recommended institutional reforms stems from the fact that so little is known about 'non-state' marketing institutions. Although it is true that there have been few detailed studies on private processing and trading activity, even the empirical evidence that is available has rarely been introduced into policy discussions.[7]

Significant policy reforms are now being implemented in many African countries. Yet there is growing recognition that such reforms alone are unlikely to bring about the desired supply response from farmers, private traders and processors.[8] This is leading both African governments and international donors to move toward more direct measures to promote private sector agribusiness development. In a large number of countries—including but not limited to Uganda, Kenya, Guinea, Madagascar, Malawi, Burundi, Ghana, Zambia, Cameroon and Mali—donor-funded projects geared toward promoting private agribusiness are already being implemented or are in preparation. Many additional projects have been proposed. To intervene successfully in this area, both African governments and donor agencies must acquire a greater understanding of the private sector in Africa, the constraints it faces, its modes and strategies of operation and its varied responses to trade and market liberalization. This improved understanding will facilitate the design of interventions which are consistent with private sector strategies while also promoting broader development objectives.

---

[7] Social science research on African domestic food markets conducted during the 1960s and 1970s found that many of the prerequisites for efficient trading relations—including effective transport and communication systems, functioning capital markets, physical security, and consistently enforced laws—were either weak or absent in African economies. This gave rise to high logistical and transaction costs in trade dominated by the private sector. Partly as a result of these conditions, long distance trade occurred most often within oligopolistic market structures. It was dominated by particular ethnic groups who had developed specialized information and financial arrangements (see Cohen 1969; Meillassoux 1971; Jones 1972 and van der Laan 1975). Contemporary research on export-oriented agribusiness in Africa has also emphasized significant efficiency and income distribution problems (Kaplinsky 1979; Mackintosh 1980; and Dinham and Hines 1983). It is not surprising that advocates of privatization tend to compare the inefficiencies or ineffectiveness of *actual* public enterprises operating in real world political economies with the *theoretical* merits of a competitive and dynamic private sector.

[8] See Platteau (1990) for an insightful analysis of technical and environmental barriers to agricultural growth in Africa.

Investigation should consider the following structural features of African private enterprise.

Characteristics of Private Entrepreneurs/Enterprises

Which private entrepreneurs and firms are able to take advantage of market opportunities and liberalization? How can they be characterized with respect to ethnicity, gender, ownership, management, sources of finance and operational size? What is the relative importance of indigenous, ethnic minority, joint venture and foreign companies in different markets?

Operational Strategies of Private Sector

What are the operational strategies adopted by private firms and individuals in response to the market, regulatory, infrastructural, and social environment in which they operate? What patterns of commodity, functional and market specialization or diversification can be distinguished? What preferences are shown between different types of technology and between domestic and export market orientations?

Crop/Raw Material Procurement Strategies

How do private firms and individuals organize their supplies of raw materials or commodities? Do they simply buy on a spot market basis and have little or no linkage to the production system? Or do they maintain contractual ties with suppliers or engage in direct primary-level production? How do the techno-economic characteristics of commodities influence these patterns?

Organization of Private Trading

What is the structure of private marketing channels and privately-dominated markets? What institutional arrangements govern long distance and export trading? What is the competitive structure of these markets and what forms of competition occur? How do the characteristics of particular commodities and the demand for them influence such patterns?

Performance of the Private Sector

How have private processors and traders performed as measured by their cost efficiency, profitability, capacity utilization, market and product development, and innovativeness in applying processing and marketing technologies? Have these agents effectively supported primary producers (for instance farmers, herders, fishermen) through provision of technical, marketing and other services?

Role of Government in Private Sector Development

What has been the role of government in fostering private agribusiness development? What public goods (such as research and infrastructure) have been essential in the development of private markets and industries? What types of regulatory frameworks have best aided—or most hindered—private sector development? How has government reduced the risks and transaction costs faced by private firms—or has it increased them?

OBJECTIVE AND FOCUS OF THE STUDY

The objective of this study is to expand the knowledge base on private agro-processing and marketing activity in Africa. It seeks to enrich the on-going policy discussions and program initiatives directed toward private agribusiness development. The study addresses the empirical issues identified above through a systematic review of existing studies on food marketing and processing in Africa and six detailed case studies of commodity systems in particular countries.

COMMODITY FOCUS: Most prior research on agricultural marketing and processing in Africa has centered on either grain and other staple food marketing, or the processing and trade of 'traditional' export commodities like cocoa, coffee, cotton, tobacco and tea. The reasons for this research focus are easy to understand. While cereals and starches feature prominently in African diets and in concerns about food security, beverage crops and other traditional industrial crops have for many years accounted for a large proportion of agricultural foreign exchange earnings in most African countries. Prior research focus is also related to and implicated in longstanding policy discussions. Throughout Africa, governments have intervened heavily in the markets for staple foods and in the pricing and marketing of traditional export crops. Finally, pragmatic considerations have contributed to the concentration of researcher attention on staple food and traditional industrial crop marketing: in many countries, the only official data on the structure and performance of production, processing and marketing that has readily been available was that collected for these crops by public marketing boards and crop development authorities.

This book has a different focus and therefore seeks to complement the broader literature on African agricultural marketing. It examines private processing and marketing of **high-value food products and raw materials** which are defined here to include:

- Fresh and Processed Fish Products
- Live Animals
- Fresh and Processed Meat Products
- Milk and other Dairy Products
- Fresh Fruit and Vegetables
- Processed Fruit and Vegetable Products
- Tree Nuts (e.g. cashews)
- Oilseeds and Vegetable Oils
- Spices and Flavorings

Individually or in aggregate, these commodity groups have an important though under-recognized role in African economies in terms of household expenditures, agricultural and manufactured product value added and foreign trade. High-value foods account for approximately one-fourth of total household cash expenditures and nearly two-thirds of food-related cash expenditures in sub-Saharan Africa.[9] As Table 1.3 indicates, for African countries with above-average rates of urbanization and higher levels of per capita GNP, the share of high-value foods in total and food-related expenditures is even higher.

Over the 1980–1991 period, Africa's urban population grew at an average annual rate of 5.8%, compared with a 3.1% per annum increase in total population. By 1991, 29% of Africa's population was urban.[10] With continued rapid rates of urban population growth and future income growth, demand for high value foods is likely to increase significantly in Africa.

---

[9] In most analyses of the food situation in Africa, it is generally assumed that cereals are the mainstay of the diet. However, for the region as a whole, cereals account for only 47% of total caloric consumption and a lower proportion of protein and fat consumption (FAO 1991). While roots and tubers account for a large share of caloric consumption in much of Central and Western Africa, items such as fish, meat, dairy products, fruits, vegetables and vegetable oils figure prominently in protein and fat consumption throughout much of SSA. Given their relatively high value, and given that only a small minority of producers are self-sufficient in their supply, cash outlays for the latter commodities tend to be quite significant.

[10] World Bank, 1993a, Table 31.

TABLE 1.3: **High-Value Foods in Total Expenditures**[1]

Country	Per Capita GNP ($)	% of Population Urban	Share of Food in Total Household Expenditure (%)	Share of HVF in Total Household Expenditure (%)	Share in HVF in Food Expenditures (%)
Tanzania	100	34	64	32	50
Ethiopia	120	13	49	25	51
Madagascar	210	25	59	33	56
Kenya	340	24	38	22	58
Sierra Leone	210	33	56	34	61
Mali	280	20	57	35	61
Nigeria	340	36	48	30	63
Rwanda	270	8	29	19	66
Côte d'Ivoire	690	41	39	26	67
Benin	380	38	37	25	68
Senegal	720	39	49	34	69
Malawi	230	12	30	21	70
Cameroon	850	42	24	17	71
Mauritius	2410	41	24	17	71
Zimbabwe	650	28	40	31	78
Zambia	—	51	36	28	78
Simple Average	—	—	42	27	65
Weighted Average All SSA	350	29	—	—	—

[1] Food expenditure data are from 1980 or 1985. Per capita GNP and urbanization rates are for 1991. Higher-value foods are defined here as foods other than cereals, roots and tubers.

SOURCE: Data compiled from World Bank, *World Development Report 1993*.

The available evidence suggests that expenditures on high-value foods are not confined to the relatively wealthy income groups in Africa and that even among the poorest groups, cash expenditures on high value foods as a group are as high or higher than those for staple foodstuffs. These patterns demonstrate that the efficiency of processing and marketing for high-value foods is important not only for middle or upper class consumers, as sometimes believed, but also for the relatively poor both as consumers and as producers.

High value foods figure prominently within sub-Saharan Africa's agricultural trade. Although much attention has been given to Africa's growing cereal imports and their adverse effect on national balance of payments positions, cereals in fact account for less than one-third of the value of sub-Saharan Africa's food and beverage imports (Table 1.4).

In contrast, the high-value foods considered in this study account for more than one-half of such imports. Except in years of major drought over large parts of the continent, the value of imports of livestock products (that is, animals, meat and dairy products) alone approximate those for cereals.

Although no single high-value food commodity is as important as either coffee or cocoa in Africa's food exports, as a group high-value foods register larger annual exports than either of the major beverage commodities. African exports of coffee and cocoa were valued at $2.4 and $1.9 billion respectively in 1988 whereas African exports of high value foods totaled $2.9 billion for that unexceptional year. Among high value foods, African exports are largest for fresh fruit and vegetables (especially citrus fruit, pineapples and bananas) and for various fish products (especially frozen shrimp and fish). Official exports of livestock (and livestock products), oilseeds/oils, and nuts and spices are considerably lower, although unofficial exports of both livestock and oilseeds are probably quite substantial (see Table 1.5).

The vast majority of African countries have markets or industries for these

TABLE 1.4: **Composition of sub-Saharan Africa's Food and Beverage Imports** ($ Millions; 1988)

Commodity (Group)	Value	Share of Total(%)
Cereals	1754	32.1
High-Value Foods		
Fish + Products	700	12.8
Dairy + Eggs	566	10.3
Meat + Products	533	9.7
Vegetable Oils	461	8.4
Live Animals	333	6.1
Vegetables/Fruit/Nuts[1]	222	4.1
Sub-total	2815	51.4
Other		
Sugar	272	5.0
Wine, Beer, Tea	262	4.8
Other Items[2]	368	6.7
Sub-Total	902	16.5
Total	5471	100.0

[1] Includes fruit and vegetable juices, but not other processed products.

[2] Including roots/tubers, legumes, spices, canned fruit/vegetables, and other items.

SOURCES: USDA World Agricultural Statistics; FAO Fisheries Commodity Yearbook.

commodities. Insights from private sector experiences in particular countries are thus potentially relevant over large parts of the region. Contrast this situation with that of tea, cocoa or tobacco where only a handful of countries feature significant export-oriented development and minimal local market development.[11] In addition, marketing and processing activities for most of the focal commodities have traditionally been dominated by the private sector, whether on a formal or an informal level. This differs greatly from the common pattern for beverage crops which has been one of single-channel marketing systems dominated by parastatals.[12]

TABLE 1.5: **African Exports of High-Value Food Products (1988)**

Product Group	Export Value ($ Million)	% of HVF Exports
Fruit/Vegetables	**1217.0**	**41.6**
Fresh	930.6	
Processed	286.6	
Fish Products	**957.0**	**32.7**
Shell Fish	481.2	
Other	475.8	
Livestock	**313.2**	**10.7**
Live Animals	163.7	
Meat	138.0	
Dairy	11.5	
Oilseed/Oils	**270.3**	**9.2**
Oilseeds	112.3	
Oils	158.0	
Nuts/Spices	**165.0**	**5.6**
Nuts	58.6	
Spices	106.4	
Totals	**2922.5**	**100.0**
Items:		
Total African Food Exports	8160.6	
Coffee Exports	2436.3	
Cocoa Exports	1883.5	

SOURCES: TARS Data Base (World Bank).

---

[11] Only five African countries had exports of tea or cocoa exceeding $10 million in 1989. Only four countries had similarly large export-oriented industries for tobacco. By contrast, in that same year there were thirteen countries with sizable (e.g.>$10 million) exports of fish products and nine countries with sizeable horticultural product exports, with significant domestic market development in these commodities as well (data from FAO Trade Yearbook and FAO Fisheries Statistics).

[12] Varangis et al. (1990) highlight recent structural changes in some of the region's beverage crop industries.

Due to certain market characteristics and other properties that these high-value foods share, the prospects are favorable for expanded future trade and value-adding activities by the private sector in Africa. First of all, these commodity groups feature relatively *high income elasticities of demand* in comparison with staple food crops.[13]

Second, these commodities offer greater *potential for the development of domestic markets and of intra-regional trade* than do most of the region's traditional major export commodities (especially beverage crops). Third, many of these commodity groups have exhibited very *favorable international market trends* which contrast with the patterns for the major traditional exports (See Tables 1.6 and 1.7). Fourth, each of these commodities offers very *wide scope for new product development and value-adding activities*, frequently without requiring the use of large-scale, sophisticated technologies. Most of the commodities that Africa has traditionally exported do not offer the scope for horizontal diversification that is possible with tomatoes, fish, groundnuts and the other items included in our focal commodity set.

ENTERPRISE FOCUS: The private sector that is engaged in marketing and processing high-value food products is highly varied, ranging from individual traders to large-scale corporations. In a few industries, most activities are conducted within an 'informal sector' by individuals who are not registered or licensed. Much of this activity is unrecorded and undocumented. Although there are many empirical studies on African micro-enterprises in general, such as those done through USAID's GEMINI[14] project, few of them examine systematically the activities of food traders and processors. Primary research on informal activity was not possible within the present study, with the partial exception of the case studies in Somalia and Ghana, and the subject is covered here mainly through a literature review.

This study concentrates on formal sector processing and trading activities because these play a predominant role in the high quality domestic markets and intraregional and international trade. Formal sector enterprises have also been the focus of much government and international donor attention through programs to privatize public enterprises and promote private sector

---

[13] Cross-country analyses by Sarma and Young (1985) and Islam (1990) found that among developing countries, the income elasticities of demand for cereals, vegetables, meat, fruit and eggs were 0.16, 0.61, 0.63, 0.68 and 1.00, respectively.

[14] Growth and Equity through Microenterprise Investments and Institutions.

TABLE 1.6: **Comparative Export Values and Growth Rates** (Export Values for 1988/89; Average Annual Growth Rates, 1980–1989)

High-Value Food Commodities				Cereals and Traditional Exports			
Commodity	World Trade ($ Billions)	World Export Growth (%)	Developing Country Export Growth (%)	Commodity	World Trade ($ Billions)	World Export Growth (%)	Developing Country Export Growth (%)
Fresh/Frozen Meat	23.8	5.1	3.9	Wheat	15.6	0.4	2.9
Fresh Fruit + Nuts	15.8	4.4	4.1	Sugar	11.3	−3.0	−3.3
Fresh Vegetables	15.8	6.8	4.0	Coffee	11.0	−2.1	−3.1
Fresh/Frozen Fish	11.6	9.6	8.5	Maize	9.1	−1.9	−6.4
Oilseeds (Soft)	9.8	0.8	4.8	Cotton	8.1	0.5	−0.3
Live Animals	7.3	6.3	12.2	Cocoa	4.4	−0.5	−0.8
Processed Fruit	7.2	7.2	8.9	Rice	4.1	0.2	2.1
Processed Fish	5.0	6.9	11.4	Tea	2.3	4.2	1.7

SOURCE: UNCTAD (1991) Handbook of International Trade and Development Statistics.

TABLE 1.7: **Recent Commodity Price Trends** (Indices of Unit Values of Imports for OECD Countries) (1976–80 = 100; Current Prices)

Commodity	1976–1980	1981–1984	1985–1988
Beverage Crops/Sugar			
Cocoa	100	66	75
Coffee	100	79	87
Tea	100	107	110
Sugar	100	107	93
Meat/Fish			
Canned Meat	100	106	114
Beef	100	111	121
Shell Fish	100	115	137
Fresh Fish	100	112	147
Fruit/Vegetables/Nuts			
Tomato	100	106	111
Oranges	100	106	126
Bananas	100	130	157
Groundnuts	100	123	104
Cashew Kernels	100	128	153

SOURCES: Data from World Bank (1993) Commodity Trade and Price Trends; Gill and Duffus Edible Nut Reports, various years.

development. Analysis of the experience of formal sector high-value food processing and trading thus has direct public policy relevance. This formal sector features a diverse array of private operators from small, family-owned units through to medium- and large-scale domestic and foreign owned firms.

In contrast to much of the earlier work, the present study places private traders and processors in the center of its analysis and examines the functional and temporal relations structuring their actions, their relationship to public regulatory and support agencies, and their perceptions of the environment in which they operate. Relatively little attention is given to the primary production of raw materials, except in the context of the procurement strategies which bring these traders and processors into contact with farming, herding and fishing communities.

Methodology

The study combines a series of detailed commodity case studies with a broader review of private agribusiness experience within the sub-Saharan region. The case studies focus on sub-sectors where the private sector has long played a dominant role or where it has already started to respond to recent market reforms involving the decontrol of prices and trade. Some of the focal commodity sub-sectors have been export-oriented; others have been oriented partly or primarily to the domestic market. The case studies are based on recent field work where the researchers conducted structured interviews with samples of private traders and processors and met with government officials, research institutes, banks and other local institutions.[15] They were selected in order to provide a cross section of countries, commodities, types of private sector development experiences, and degrees of success or failure. Each case highlights the empirical issues listed earlier, setting patterns within the historical context of the particular commodity sub-sector and the wider context of African trade in the focal commodity.

The case studies presented in this study relate to the following sub-sectors:

- Cashew Nuts in Tanzania
- Dairy Products in Kenya
- Vanilla in Madagascar

---

[15] Three of the case studies (Tanzania cashews, Kenya dairy and Ghana fisheries) are based on field work conducted in 1992 or 1993 specifically for this study. Field work for the Kenyan horticultural case was undertaken in 1985/86, with updated information coming from a brief 1992 field visit. Field work for the Madagascar case study was undertaken in 1991 as part of a sectoral analysis for the World Bank. Field work for the Somalia livestock case was undertaken in 1987/88 as part of work funded by USAID. Studies completed previously were revised or completely redrafted to follow the conceptual approach and to focus on the main themes of this study.

- Fresh and Processed Horticultural Products in Kenya
- Fish and Fish Products in Ghana
- Livestock (Cattle) in Somalia

The analysis seeks to relate the organization and performance of private sector processing and marketing to the distinctive techno-economic characteristics of the individual commodities. These characteristics—which relate to the commodities themselves as well as to their production, processing and handling—are expected to influence the nature and significance of operating risks, entry and transaction costs, and the skill requirements for those active in processing and trade.[16] Systematic relationships between the techno-economic characteristics of commodities and forms of organization in private marketing channels will be hypothesized.[17] In general terms, it will be posited that the range of feasible institutional arrangements for commodities which pose inherent problems for quality control and vertical coordination and which are associated with economies of scale in production and/or processing will be limited to vertically-integrated systems or contract-based systems. In contrast, for commodities with less demanding techno-economic characteristics and lower investment requirements, decentralized, small-scale trading and processing operations could well be the efficient institutional norm. Similarly, where fixed investment costs and operating risks are very high, one would expect that private sector investment in Africa would be limited, at least for certain types of firms.[18]

This type of analysis offers insights relevant to policy formulation. It can point to a range of commodities where private sector response to market liberalization is likely to be rapid and broadly-based. It can also indicate commodities for which technical and economic entry barriers are likely to be high and where the expected private response will be slow and limited to a

---

[16] Examples of techno-economic characteristics include: the rate of perishability and degree of quality variability of the commodity, its value/bulk ratio, the timing of harvest, storage and transport characteristics, the specificity of processing equipment, economies of scale in processing, the fixed costs in plant and equipment, and packaging/display requirements.

[17] Such analysis parallels the work of Binswanger and Rosensweig (1986) which relates properties of productive assets (e.g. land, trees, animals) to patterns of organization in agricultural production. It also corresponds to work by Williamson (1979, 1985) and others operating under the rubric of 'transaction cost economics' which seeks to link organizational or contractual arrangements with technical, competitive and other variables in the market environment.

[18] For some commodities, foreign investment or joint venture investment and management arrangements may be necessary, at least in the short- to medium-term.

few larger firms. The need for and types of appropriate public sector regulatory support will differ considerably between these two scenarios. In these ways, a commodity orientation can provide specificity and nuance to policies and programs promoting private sector agribusiness development in Africa.

Complementing the case studies is a broader review of the existing literature dealing with marketing and agro-industrial development in the focal commodities in Africa. Cross-cutting themes related to private sector characteristics (gender, ethnicity, nationality, size), raw material procurement (for example, contract farming), food processing (both artisanal and larger-scale), and marketing (marketing channels, credit, product diversification) are explored. A variety of vignettes from throughout the region provide specific applications of the broad themes identified.

Structure of the Study

Chapter II presents the *conceptual framework for the study*. This framework positions private processing and marketing activity within wider commodity systems which integrate producers and consumers. The study examines both generic and commodity-specific barriers to entry and organizational effectiveness in processing and marketing and outlines a range of alternative institutional responses to such barriers. Emphasis is given to problems of risk and transaction costs in commodity systems and to the ways in which private actors can reduce or spread their risks and costs. This microeconomic perspective is necessary to fully understand the constraints facing private ventures in Africa as well as the nature and effectiveness of private organizational and technical responses.

Chapter III provides a *synthesis of regional experience* in private sector processing and marketing of high-value foods. The chapter reviews adverse features of the trading environment facing private agents, characterizes types of private high-value food operators and examines major patterns in private sector raw material procurement, food processing and marketing operations. It also touches on recent experience in the privatization of public food processing enterprises. The chapter draws on an extended array of academic, consultancy and project documents in addition to the case studies in order to provide a region-wide perspective on the issues.

Chapters IV through IX are case studies examining the development of and private sector role and performance in particular commodity systems. Chapter IV examines the development of *Tanzania's cashew nut industry*,

emphasizing the nature and impact of recent policy changes which have liberalized the market and permitted private firms to participate. The case study
delineates the role of policies in the long-term decline of the industry and the
confusing nature of the recent reform process that was designed to reverse
this decline. It provides insights into the nature of private sector responses to
policy reforms in a still uncertain policy and market environment.

Chapter V examines the development of the private sector role in *Kenya's
dairy sub-sector*. While smallholder dairy production in Kenya has been a
success, marketing has been dominated by a government-controlled cooperative which has used the powers of the state and donor financing to marginalize truly private and cooperative dairies. The case study examines the precarious position of these private and cooperative dairies and their prospects
under a liberalized market.

Chapter VI deals with *Madagascar's vanilla sub-sector*. It provides a case
in which processing and trade functions are conducted exclusively by private
firms and individuals within a highly controlled framework set by government. In the 1960s and early 1970s, the government and private sector collaborated effectively to organize what had been a chaotic market. This produced a boom in exports. Starting in the mid-1970s, the government has
increased its control over management in the sub-sector. Excessive market
controls and a short-sighted commercial policy have dulled producer and trader
incentives and channeled private entrepreneurship into rent-seeking modes.
This in turn has undercut the country's international competitiveness and
former dominant market share. The case of the vanilla industry is illustrative of circumstances in Africa where private firms have been forced to serve
as agents for the state.

Chapter VII deals with the case of *Kenyan horticulture*, one of Africa's
major success stories in export diversification. In sharp contrast to Kenya's
other agricultural export industries, private firms and individuals have played
a leading role in the horticultural industry throughout its sixty year history.
The case study highlights the diverse forms which private enterprises take
and their varied links with producers and overseas markets. Kenya's experience offers important lessons for other African countries aspiring to diversify
into the high-value horticultural trade.

Chapter VIII examines the case of *Ghana fisheries*, one of West Africa's
largest and most influential fishery sub-sectors. The case highlights the importance of artisanal fishing and processing activities for domestic markets

and the adverse effects which structural adjustment has had on both artisanal and industrial components of the sub-sector.

Chapter IX deals with the case of *cattle marketing in Southern Somalia* prior to the breakdown of civil order in the country. The case study illustrates the importance of informal, kinship-based trading networks in Africa's long distance and cross-border trade in live animals, and the responsiveness of traders to wider economic and political instability.

Chapter X offers further reflections on private sector processing and marketing activity in Africa, including suggested initiatives to facilitate its future development, which may be useful to policy-makers.

PART
A

II.

Transaction Costs, Risk and the Organization of Private Sector Food Commodity Systems

Steven Jaffee

This chapter provides a conceptual framework for examining private sector processing and marketing of high-value foods in Africa. It provides both systems and micro-level perspectives on marketing. After reviewing several generic barriers to private sector entry and effectiveness which are specific to high-value foods, the chapter presents a range of technical and institutional measures that can be adopted to overcome such barriers.

MARKETING HIGH-VALUE FOOD COMMODITIES: A SYSTEMS PERSPECTIVES

A high-value food product represents the outcome of a sequential series of investments, activities and decisions. This process begins with the articulation of consumer demand and leads to decisions by farmers and fishermen to produce, raise or catch particular crops, animals and fish. It continues through a series of activities which produce and subsequently transform the crop or animal product in form, time and place to match consumer demand (Breimyer 1976).

Food marketing is the physical and economic bridge which links raw material production and consumer food purchases. It involves a set of **interdependent** decisions, investments, institutions, resource flows and physical and business activities (Kohls and Uhl 1985). As the bridge between

producers and consumers, food marketing must fulfill several functions
simultaneously:

a) **stimulate and support raw material production**—Food marketing
plays a critical role in stimulating, orienting and facilitating raw material production at the farm level. This requires the communication of information to farmers regarding what and when to produce,
the provision of financial and other incentives to produce food items
for sale, the facilitation of farmer access to those production resources
(for example, credit and material inputs) needed to respond to such
incentives and the reduction of transaction costs between producers
and consumers.

b) **balance commodity supply and demand**—Food marketing institutions
provide the organizational framework for coordinating production and
consumption. This framework balances the supply and demand for food
raw materials and commodities, not only in quantitative terms, but
also in terms of quality, time and place. This coordination entails logistical and informational tasks, transactions for current or future supplies, quality control measures and physical transformation of the raw
materials/commodities themselves.

c) **stimulate demand and enhance consumer welfare**—Food marketing
promotes increased demand, consumption and consumer welfare by introducing new products, improving product quality, reducing consumer
costs, making foods available on a more consistent basis and educating
consumers on the merits and alternative uses of products. These tasks
will require the dissemination of information, the development and application of processing and logistics technologies, and efficient mechanisms for the exchange of goods.

The process of marketing high-value food products transcends several different industries and markets and may cross international borders (Marion
et al. 1986). In this process, the physical commodity can be conceived of as
'flowing' from one value-adding stage to another. Each of these stages is associated with a particular industry as conventionally defined (transport, food
processing, packaging and retailing). The product gains value as its form is
changed and it is graded, stored, packaged and transported in order to more
closely match consumer demand. Other important 'flows' precede, accompany
and follow upon the flow of the physical product. These include (i) informa-

tion flows pertaining to products, markets and technologies between consumers and traders, producers and traders, and among both traders and producers; (ii) financial flows to finance production and remunerate participants which are channeled backward from the consumer through the production chain and occur between financiers, producers and marketing entities; and (iii) ownership flows whereby the right or title to the product accompany its physical movement and transformation.

Food marketing involves several essential activities. Some are physical activities, such as grading, handling, transporting, storing and numerous forms of processing. Others are activities which relate specifically to the transfer of ownership or possession of the commodities. These are the exchange functions of buying and selling. Still other activities facilitate these physical and exchange functions. They include risk bearing, financing, standardization of quantities and qualities, and information collection, interpretation and dissemination.

There is a high degree of technical and economic interdependence among many of these activities. Storage and transport functions are interconnected as what timing and modes of transport are feasible depend upon the scope and methods for storing a product or raw material. Sorting and grading are of little value if the subsequent storage and transport of a crop do not maintain its quality. Efficient processing operations require sufficient quantities and quality of raw materials, which in turn are at least partly a function of effective input supply, production financing and raw material transport activities.

In the marketing of high-value food products, many of the pertinent production, post-harvest and distribution activities require specialized technical or market knowledge, skills or assets and the presence of participants in particular locations. This suggests possible gains from a division of labor whereby many different individuals and organizations specialize in the performance of one or relatively few physical and business activities. Given the nature of food marketing, a strong degree of interdependence among these various individuals and organizations will remain, which must be reflected in the effective coordination of participant decisions and activities, whether through market, administrative or other means (Davis and Goldberg 1957).

Once we recognize that production and food marketing activities are interdependent, that those individuals and organizations performing these activities are themselves interdependent, and that all of these are linked through a network of exchange relations and additional coordinating mechanisms, it becomes useful to view them as elements of a comprehensive system (Arthur et al.1968). Faced with enormous problems in the conceptualization and empirical study of national food systems, analysts in agribusiness and agricultural marketing have focused their attention on individual commodity systems[1], defined by Marion et al. (1986) as: "small economic systems . . . incorporating an interdependent array of organizations, resources, laws and institutions involved in producing, processing and distributing an agricultural commodity." Commodity systems may involve the production, processing and marketing of a single commodity or a set of very closely related commodities (as in dairy product, poultry, oilseed or citrus fruit systems).[2]

Individual commodity systems exhibit widely different *organizational characteristics,* both within and among countries. Some commodity systems derive all of their raw materials from domestic sources, whereas others rely wholly or substantially on imported supplies. Some commodity systems are exclusively export-oriented, while others are focused entirely on the domestic market or service multiple markets. Some systems generate only a single or very few types of products for consumers, while others yield dozens or hundreds of products, some of which have little observable connection with the initial farm level raw materials.

Most commodity system studies by agricultural economists and agribusiness specialists describe both horizontal and vertical structural elements. The former relate to entry and competitive conditions prevailing at each industry stage (for instance processing or retailing); the latter to the location/timing/ clustering of marketing functions, inter-stage differences in size, seasonality, etc., the number of parallel marketing channels, and the incidence and forms of contractual or ownership integration. Other institutional elements of the commodity system landscape are government programs which affect the

---

[1] Agricultural economists have tended to use the term commodity sub-sectors. This is an inappropriate term since there is nothing 'sub' about them, except that they include particular sub-components of agriculture. A more appropriate term would be trans-sector since the focal system cuts across several sectors, markets or industries. The term *filière*, widely used in French language literature (with a literal meaning of 'channel'), also conveys this characteristic well (see Griffon 1989).

[2] As with industries or markets, commodity systems are conceptual artifacts. The borders between one commodity system and another may be quite hazy. This is especially true where highly processed foods are concerned. Many individual foods are the product of several commodity systems. For example, the manufacturer of prepared soups and ready-to-eat meals frequently draws upon raw materials from the vegetable, grain, and meat sectors. Technological change enables greater substitution among agricultural raw materials, and this blurs even further the distinctions between traditional commodity systems.

commodity's production and marketing,[3] and institutions such as banks, auctions, trade associations and insurance companies which perform specific trade facilitation functions.

In commodity system analysis, the central focus is on the problems and mechanisms for *coordination* (Goldberg 1968; Marion 1976). Coordination is a general problem of arranging interdependent activities which requires linking the decisions and actions of different technical and ownership units when collective or overlapping tasks are performed. Vertical coordination poses a major challenge to food systems. Vertical coordination is the process of harmonizing the decisions and actions of input suppliers, farmers, processors and traders so as to match the supply and demand for food raw materials and products (in terms of quantity, quality, timing, and location) at the various value-adding stages (Mighell and Jones 1963).[4] This process entails significant flows of information and other resources which define and shift incentives. It also entails the definition and redefinition of required, permissible and impermissible patterns of behavior for system participants. In a food marketing context, the absence of effective vertical coordination is likely to result in resource misallocation, technical inefficiency and greater production and marketing risks.[5]

Closely related to coordination is the issue of food system control, namely, the ability to exercise influence over key variables in the environment of others. Conventional industrial organization analysis focuses on horizontal control or market power—the ability to influence prices, incomes and other results in particular markets as a result of one's large market share and/or product differentiation. Vertical control is also important. It is the right or ability to make strategic decisions which will influence the activities and welfare of participants at different stages in the commodity system. Such decisions may be associated with what is produced and by whom, how it is marketed and how returns and risks are distributed. As will be discussed below,

---

[3] Studies by Goldberg (1974), Morissey (1974) and Marion et al. (1986) typify this type of analysis.

[4] As will be discussed below, there are certain techno-economic features of the commodities and of the relevant production and processing functions which render vertical coordination especially difficult in food systems.

[5] For example, where the quantity of a commodity supplied exceeds the quantities purchased, extra storage costs will be incurred or part of the crop will be wasted. Where the quantity falls short of that demanded, the commodity buyer may not be able to fully utilize his processing or other marketing facilities (thus raising unit costs) and may not be able to meet demand further 'downstream'. On these and other inefficiencies and resource misallocations in food markets, see Lang (1977).

coordination and control within food marketing systems can be achieved through a wide range of institutional measures through market, administrative or regulative means.

MARKETING HIGH-VALUE FOOD COMMODITIES: A MICRO PERSPECTIVE

Viewing the marketing process in this way, it is not difficult to see why many past 'marketing' interventions involving the construction or rehabilitation of physical infrastructure (for example, marketplaces, processing plants, storage facilities) have had only limited beneficial impact. The marketing process, and market development more generally, depends upon effective flows of information and financial resources, and efficient exchange relationships. Market development entails the development of exchange networks since it is within the context of (potential) trading relationships that individuals are stimulated to invest in specialized production and marketing activities. Exchange networks enable individuals to transfer needed information and resources and capture the benefits of a division of labor and functional specialization.

To properly understand markets and market development, one needs to examine patterns of exchange among existing and potential market participants. Each transaction between food system participants can be viewed as a process, entailing a series of stages from the time when potential transactors make initial contact until the time when the terms of the ensuing agreement have been carried out and enforced.[6] Important stages in the exchange process are those of:

—**searching** for exchange opportunities and partners,

—**screening** information about the products/parties one wishes to deal with,

—**bargaining** over the terms of trade,

—**transferring** the goods, services, titles, cash, etc.,

—**monitoring** the exchange to assess whether the agreed terms are complied with,

—**enforcing** the stipulated terms.

---

[6] Both Commons (1934) and Coase (1960) discussed exchange as a process.

The centrality of information within the process of exchange is evident from this formulation. Exchange does not occur without the collection, processing and transfer of information regarding preferences, products and transactor behavior. It involves a two-way transfer of goods, services and money as well as the transfer of property rights associated with these assets. These are the rights to control the use, alteration or further transfer of assets. Finally, it is evident that exchange is always a rule-bound process, whether by private or social restraints on decisions and actions. Transacting parties offer one another certain benefits, but these are conditional upon certain patterns of behavior which the parties either explicitly agree to or they assume under the prevailing system of laws, norms and conventions.[7]

There are several generic problems that are associated with information, property rights and conflict of interest between self-interested parties that are well-known to social scientists, regulators and business people. The acquisition and processing of information can be a very costly activity, requiring investments in personal time and in the purchase of materials containing market intelligence or technology. The actual cost and effectiveness of 'searching' and 'screening' will depend upon a variety of factors including (i) the nature (for example, complexity) of the good, service or asset being considered, (ii) the similarity of new information to established knowledge, (iii) the physical and cultural proximity to the sources of information, and (iv) the overall skills, assets and experience of the searcher.[8]

The second generic problem concerns information which may be unevenly distributed with different transactors having different levels and qualities of exchange-relevant information. This situation creates opportunities for one or both parties to pursue individual gains by misrepresenting their actual intentions, capabilities and products and by manipulating information in a strategic manner. This behavior has been referred to as 'opportunistic behavior' (Williamson 1975).

Third, the property rights accorded to individuals may be incomplete in terms of either imperfect excludability or non-transferability. Imperfect excludability arises when ownership is conferred upon a group rather than an individual, or when an individual asset owner is unable to detect or punish unauthorized use or alteration of the asset. Even where individuals do have

---

[7] Leblebici (1985) stresses the importance of working rules for trade.
[8] Arrow (1974); Nelson and Winter (1981).

exclusive property rights and can in fact exclude others from asset use, they may be restricted or lack altogether the right or ability to transfer assets to others. This may stem from trade regulations or from physical properties of the assets which render their transfer highly risky.

Fourth, even though there is some mutuality of interests in any trading relationship, at least some degree of conflict over the distribution of benefits, costs and risks will be inevitable. Conflicting interests may provoke a lengthy and costly bargaining process or prevent agents from arriving at a mutually satisfying agreement. Conflicts of interest will also create problems in exchange monitoring and enforcement, typically discussed under the heading of *agency* problems. Self-interested parties may behave in ways which violate the letter, if not the spirit of agreements, and in so doing, undermine the interests of their transacting partner. With information asymmetry, the principal cannot detect whether the outcomes derive from the agent's opportunism or whether some exogenous factors were more important. Agent opportunism reduces the principal's gains from exchange and requires the latter to make expenditures in monitoring the agent's behavior.[9] Many of the institutions which emerge in commodity systems are geared toward modifying or constraining self-interested acts so that some balance is achieved in the cooperative and competitive motivations of the participating parties.

These generic problems of information, property rights and conflicts of interest can create direct barriers to mutually beneficial exchange and greatly increase the costs associated with trade. These lost opportunities and expenditures fall under the general heading of *transaction costs*. In a food marketing setting, transaction costs are the whole array of costs associated with buying, selling and transferring ownership of goods and services. They are the information costs incurred in identifying and screening different trading opportunities, outlets and partners, the costs of negotiating trading agreements, the costs of actually transferring goods, services, and ownership rights, the costs of monitoring trade conditions to determine whether the agreed terms are complied with, and the costs of enforcing stipulated terms through legal, social or other means. Table 2.1 below distinguishes between different types of transaction costs, identifies their origins and indicates various tangible forms which these costs may take. Despite their considerable impor-

---

[9] See, for example, Jensen and Meckling (1976).

tance, transaction costs other than for transport, storage and handling have rarely been examined in studies of food marketing in developing countries. The vast majority of these costs either are not considered at all or are lumped together under the category of overhead costs.

What factors influence the level of transaction costs in any particular trading context? According to Williamson (1979, 1985), the level of transaction costs is a function of three main dimensions in the trading environment:

1) *asset specificity:* the extent to which physical and other assets required for production and exchange are durable and specialized for a particular product or trading relationship;

2) *uncertainty:* the overall degree of uncertainty surrounding the exchange (pertaining to the availability and quality of products, the assurance of market outlets, the operating 'rules of the game');

3) *competitive market structure:* particularly the number of alternative buyers and sellers.

Transaction cost economics places greatest emphasis on asset specificity problems. For any particular production and trading operation, individuals may undertake general or specialized investments. Certain types of plant, equipment, materials and knowledge have potentially generalized use across a broad range of products or trades. Other assets are highly specialized and therefore have little or no alternative use or value should a production scheme fail or a trade relationship break down. Making investments in specialized assets thus exposes the investor to potentially severe bargaining and contractual enforcement problems since the investor will be locked into particular activities and encounter pressure from trading partners to improve the terms of trade. Examples of asset-specificity in agriculture include tree crops with extended gestation periods, large-scale specialized processing and post-harvest facilities and use of highly specialized production inputs and technical knowledge.

The relationship between uncertainty and transaction costs is apparent in Table 2.1. Much of the effort and expenditure to gather information, structure terms of trade and monitor behavior is done to counter various forms of uncertainty. Fewer alternative buyers or sellers may lower screening costs while increasing bargaining and enforcement costs. When there are relatively few alternative trading partners, one might expect (i) less complete disclosure of interests to trade and less disclosure of product information, (ii) better

TABLE 2.1: **Transaction Costs in a Commodity Trading Setting**

Type of Transaction Cost	Source/Origin of Costs	Tangible Forms of Transaction Cost
Search Costs	Lack of knowledge about opportunities (e.g. products, prices, demand, supply, trading rights, market outlets)	Personal/Personnel Time Travel Expenses Communication Costs
Screening Costs	Uncertainty about the reliability of potential suppliers/buyers Uncertainty about the actual quality of goods/ services offered	Consulting Service Fees Advertising/Promotion Costs Costs of Credit Rating Checks
Bargaining Costs	Conflicting objectives and interests of transacting parties Uncertainty about the willingness of others to trade on certain terms Uncertainty over transactor rights and obligations	Licensing Fees Insurance Premiums
Transfer Costs	Legal, extra-legal or physical constraints on the movement/transfer of goods	Handling/Storage Costs Transport Costs Bribery and Corruption Expenses
Monitoring Costs	Uncertainty about transactor compliance with specified terms Uncertainty about possible changes in the quality of goods and services	Auditing Fees Product Inspection Charges Investments in Measurement Devices
Enforcement Costs	Uncertainty about the level of damages/ injury to a transacting party arising from contractual non-compliance Problems in exacting penalties through bilateral arrangements or through use of third parties.	Arbitration, Legal, Court Fees Costs to Bring Social Pressure

opportunities for strategic bargaining, and (iii) more transaction enforcement problems since threats to terminate trade and deal with competitors will be less credible.

BARRIERS TO PRIVATE SECTOR ENTRY AND COORDINATION IN FOOD COMMODITY SYSTEMS

Food products, raw materials, production, marketing infrastructure and marketing services have intrinsic technical and economic properties which frequently cause severe problems that are related to risk, inadequate information, transaction costs, logistics and overall marketing costs. These occur frequently in developing countries. Each can constitute a major barrier to coordination in commodity systems. In this section, we refine our analysis by discussing problems intrinsic to food marketing—problems which will arise even in favorable policy environments.

The discussion reviews some of the generic technical and economic characteristics of food products, commodity production, production support services and downstream marketing functions. It points out their possible implications for the risks and transaction costs faced by producers and marketing enterprises. In the subsequent section, this analysis is applied specifically to a sample of high-value foods commonly produced in Africa.

Food Product Technical Characteristics

Compared with most other products, food products and raw materials are bulkier and more perishable. Bulky commodities have relatively low values per unit weight or volume. They generate physical handling and transport problems related to the development and utilization of infrastructure capacities and are associated with potentially high unit logistical costs. For very bulky goods, it may be necessary to establish processing facilities (and attendant power and water supply) in close proximity to farm production areas. Perishability limits the period of time during which a product can be marketed as a fresh commodity and used as raw material in processing.[10] It greatly limits the marketing flexibility of producers and increases their market risks and has the potential to place them in an unfavorable bargaining position vis-a-vis buyers who have alternative supply sources.

Commodity perishability enhances risk of product loss or decline in value during transport and storage. It may necessitate investment in highly specialized and 'lumpy' transport and storage facilities and equipment. It also limits the role of storage in balancing supply and demand over time, and raises the risk of contamination in food processing. In addition to these losses and special costs, rapid perishability raises transaction costs because it requires raw materials to be repeatedly screened and graded for quality at each point in the commodity system.[11]

---

[10] The perishability of a crop or commodity stems from its own physiological properties, its stage of maturity at harvest, the storage and handling procedures used, and the post-harvest environmental conditions.

[11] Selling highly perishable commodities 'on description' poses risks for both sellers and buyers since their quality may deteriorate in the interim period before actual delivery.

While agricultural commodities are often regarded as relatively homogeneous, food commodities and raw materials do exhibit considerable variability in quality from unit to unit and from one supply period to another. This stems from several factors including: (i) the wide range of different biological varieties or species of crops, livestock and fish; (ii) the strong influence of environmental conditions and changes on production; and (iii) variations in the production and post-harvest practices used. Food commodities and raw materials tend to have multiple quality attributes, some of which are difficult to measure (or observe). Most of these attributes are valued and weighted differently by specific groups of users and consumers. These features limit the scope for informative grading, create information asymmetries related to quality and reduce the likelihood that market prices will signal complete information about the quality of these goods.[12]

Food Commodity Production Characteristics

The physical production of many food commodities and raw materials has features which render it inherently risky, heighten transaction costs in a market setting and inhibit effective coordination of production with downstream operations and consumption. When compared to manufactured products, food products tend to be produced over a more dispersed geographical area and by individual producers who are smaller in scale and less specialized. This is because of the immobility of land, the absence of significant economics of scale in primary production, and the risks of specialized agricultural production. This production pattern may result in high costs for crop intelligence and transmission of information to producers regarding consumer preferences. It also contributes to potentially high transportation costs for the collection of raw materials or animals, thus interrupting physical commodity flows. The output from each individual producer may be insufficient for him/her to invest in a transport vehicle (a 'lumpy' investment) or for a buyer to conduct a procurement run specifically for one or a few farms. The output of a small producer may be insufficient to warrant investment in proper storage facilities or standardized containers, and this may lead to additional han-

---

[12] Since the quality of food directly affects human health, informational asymmetries are potentially quite serious. In the absence of labels which indicate the true contents of food products, their nutritional value and other health implications, consumer choice may be poorly informed (Caswell and Padberg 1992).

dling activities and require additional quality inspection. All of these imply higher transaction costs.[13]

At the same time, small, dispersed producers can face a situation of monopsonistic competition with only one or very few active buyers in their area. Often, the most efficient scale of operation at the farm level does not match that of subsequent processing operations. In this instance, hierarchical market structures featuring one relatively large processor and multiple small suppliers may emerge with asymmetric information and considerable inequality of bargaining power. The mismatch in efficient operating scales serves as a barrier to forward integration among un-organized producers and requires the processor to develop multiple supply sources to enable it to utilize its full capacity. A coordination problem arises because production schedules for different suppliers must be spread out over time. Otherwise, processors would operate at well below their full capacities or incur higher costs by purchasing raw materials during a short period of time and storing them in a raw or semi-processed condition.

A second common set of food production characteristics concerns the yield lag, yield uncertainty and seasonality of production. The production of most food crops and animal products is dependent upon the life cycle of plants and animals. In some cases (for example, tree crops, beef cattle), this life cycle involves an extended gestation period before commercial yields are attained. This in turn creates a need for medium-term financing and presents a potentially considerable commercial risk for the producer. Agricultural production is inherently highly risky due to the important influence of weather and the possible incidence of plant diseases or pests. Adverse natural events or social incidents can undermine total supply or the supply from one geographical area, resulting in farmer losses, un(der)-utilized marketing and processing facilities and unmet consumer demand.[14] The seasonality of crop and animal production creates problems for cost-efficient utilization of transport and processing facilities. For perishable commodities, processing requirements may make it necessary to extend planting and harvest activities into riskier periods of production.

---

[13] From the point of view of marketing agents, such added transaction costs are at least partly counterbalanced by the reduced risk of total supply failure (due to weather, disease, or pests) when production is geographically dispersed.

[14] These unplanned variations in annual production levels may result in similarly wide swings in producer and consumer prices. If either producer incomes or consumer purchases are narrowly based, such price variations can have major welfare implications.

Production Facilitation Functions

Food marketing enterprises can play an important role in stimulating and directly supporting raw material production. Food marketing enterprises can support production in various ways, including the supply of market and technical information, financing and material inputs (seeds, chicks, fertilizers). The ability of these enterprises to capture the benefits from such services will be influenced by the nature of the services themselves as well as the competitive environment. The incentives for marketing enterprises to provide services will depend upon their ability to appropriate the benefits deriving from them, benefits such as increased output, enhanced product quality and output better timed to marketing or processing requirements.[15]

The dissemination of technical and market information has the properties of a public good: such information is non-rival in its consumption, and it is very difficult to exclude individuals who benefit from the information without contributing to its cost. The marketing enterprise is unlikely to capture the full benefit from its supply of information since in a competitive environment, producers can utilize the information and then sell their product to a competing buyer. Where such 'free-riding' is widespread, there will be little incentive for private firms to provide more than minimal market or technical information.

The provision of information may also be associated with what have been termed 'moral hazard' problems: the directed message may be biased toward the particular needs of the buyer rather than properly informing the producer about the wider range of technical and market options. The provision of technical information and the direct supply of production inputs can also give rise to negative externalities as when the recommended practice (for example, heavy chemical use) adversely affects neighboring farmers or residents. Firms might benefit in the short term from supplying low quality seeds, breeding stock, etc. but those companies active in the purchasing and sale of the farm product would have an incentive to supply high quality inputs. In these circumstances where private and social benefits and costs diverge, there may be a justification for government intervention.

With respect to production financing, barriers arise due to limited collateral and asymmetric information. The producer is generally better informed

---

[15] See Umali et al. (1992) and Jaffee and Srivastava (1992) for more detailed analysis of the incentives for private sector supply of selected agricultural inputs and services.

than the marketing enterprise about his/her creditworthiness. The firm's ability to recover the loan may be better in a non-competitive situation than in a competitive market, since in the former case producers will have little or no alternative market outlet. This enables the lender to deduct the loan amount from payments due for the commodity.

Processing and Distribution Functions

Several types of infrastructure, information and other resources needed for efficient food processing and distribution functions have characteristics which may inhibit private investment in specialized activities and weaken the competitiveness of a commodity system. For example, certain types of infrastructure necessary for marketing have either properties of a public good or are subject to such great economies of scale as to result in natural monopolies in all but very large countries. Roads are an example of the former and rail and port facilities of the latter. Private firms engaged in food marketing will generally lack the capacity to invest in such facilities, yet their absence (or poor quality) will reduce producer incentives, raise marketing costs and restrain trade.

Although other types of marketing infrastructure do not exhibit economies of scale as significant as for rail and port facilities, they do nonetheless entail 'lumpy' investments which can serve as a major barrier to entry. Investments in modern processing, storage, transport and trading facilities can provide the investor, at least initially, with an operational capacity far in excess of current supplies or supplies expected within a few years. The large unit operating costs in these initial years, together with uncertainty about future raw material and commodity supplies, may inhibit many private firms from undertaking such investments.[16] These markets may be perceived as 'non-contestable' by those not currently active.[17] In the absence of a well functioning stock or financial market, there may be few local means to pool the risk associated with such investments. Hence, in certain cases, private firms may

---

[16] The problem may be circular: farmers may not expand production to levels which would make the marketing investment cost-effective without first seeing tangible evidence of facility development.

[17] According to Baumol et al. (1982), a 'perfectly contestable market' is one which is subject to potential entry by firms that have no disadvantage relative to incumbents. This is generally associated with circumstances where sunk costs are not incurred and where entry is easily reversible. Pressures felt by the incumbent from unimpeded potential entrants are expected to impose efficiency on the incumbent.

not be able to perform the necessary risk-bearing function. For some types of infrastructure, there are also possible negative externalities such as the environmental effects of marketplaces and slaughterhouses.

Risks will be especially high for a new or highly specialized product which requires specialized processing, facilities or equipment. In the short run, while supplies of the targeted product are being built up, the specialized equipment may not be applicable to other currently available raw materials and commodities. Under such a condition of asset specificity, the processor/storer/transporter is locked into a certain type of operation and becomes vulnerable to bargaining pressure from raw material suppliers and product buyers who possess alternative production, trading or consumption options.

The processing, transport and storage of raw materials and commodities takes time. The ability to participate in these activities depends on access to finance, both to pay for raw materials/commodities purchased and to cover interest and costs of goods held in storage or transit. Thus, the availability and cost of credit is an important factor in the entry and viability of firms and individuals in the marketing system. Many private financial institutions have limited experience in lending for agricultural marketing and processing. Limited recognized collateral and information asymmetries are again a potential problem.

Several additional processing and development functions are associated with economies of scale that may inhibit entry and therefore result in concentrated market structures. Crop intelligence and market research feature economies of scale and scope due to certain 'lumpy' investments in assets (for instance, computers and databases), and the advantages that accrue to those with multiple, diverse sources of information and those trading in several commodities simultaneously. Product promotion is also associated with economies of scale or scope, and a certain threshold level of trade and supply capability is necessary for such promotion to be worthwhile. There are both large sunk costs and large commercial risks associated with launching a new product. These represent potential barriers to entry and sustained competitiveness.

Additionally, product promotion may give rise to externalities, though this may depend on the specificity of the promotion. Promotion of generic products (as opposed to individual brands) presents 'free rider' problems since some producers/traders will benefit from the promotion without contributing to its costs. Related to this is the promotion of an overall industry or country within international markets. It too features economies of scale and externalities.

For some product groups, especially fresh produce, there are potential advantages in promoting a national image for quality. This image or reputation is a public good: all firms in the industry are associated with it and new entrants into the trade inherit it. Yet, the reputation needs to be protected. The supply of substandard produce by one producer/exporter can jeopardize the reputation of a whole commodity system with adverse effects on market access and realized prices. Measures will need to be adopted to internalize these positive or negative externalities.

Economies of scale are also associated with international transport of food products since minimum quantities are needed to fill individual pallets and containers and utilize the full freight capacity of a ship, train or plane. A certain minimum level of trade on a consistent basis may be necessary to attract those who provide international freight services in the first place. The supply of such services tends toward oligopoly (air carriers, ship conference lines) or localized monopoly (train services), which raises potential bargaining problems when the export trade is fragmented among many small firms.

In an international context, transaction costs alone may be a major barrier to trade for many individuals and firms. In setting up a trade, exporters are likely to incur higher search and bargaining costs than domestic market traders. Physical distance to the target market constrains access to information about trading opportunities, and thinner information networks yield less complete information regarding the capabilities and financial solvency of buyers and agents. Physical distance and language barriers may prevent face-to-face negotiations and contribute to an extended bargaining process. International traders may be unfamiliar with the standard trading practices in the target country and this may contribute to misperceptions about respective bargaining positions and tactics. Large geographical distances between traders increase logistical costs and risks and limit the scope for direct monitoring of trade partner performance. Enforcement of international contracts may prove difficult and costly due to weak legal integration of trading countries and to the more limited scope for social group or trade association to pressure contract defaulters.

Table 2.2 summarizes the economic properties of major marketing infrastructure and functions. The table indicates that while relatively few of the facilities and services have properties of public goods, many are associated with externalities, economies of scale/scope and 'moral hazard' problems. Together with the important problems of risk, transaction costs and logistics management, these features inhibit private investment in specialized produc-

TABLE 2.2: **Economic Properties of Infrastructure and Functions Associated with Food Marketing**

Facilities/Function	Public Good Properties	Externality	Economies of Scale/Scope	Moral Hazard
Overhead Infrastructure				
Roads	X	X		
Rail and Port Facilities		X	Large	
Marketplaces		X	Some	
Power and Water Services		X	Large	
Production Support Services				
Inputs Supply		X	Some	X
Production Finance				X
Technical Info Supply	X	X		X
Market Info Supply	X			X
Post-Harvest Assessment / Transformation				
Crop/Production Intelligence			Some	
Initial Grading/Selection		X		X
Product Assembly				
Storage			Some	
Quality Control		X		X
Processing			Varied	
Marketing and Distribution				
Local/International Transport			Some/Large	
Wholesaling/Retailing			Some	
Market Research/Intelligence			Some	
Product Promotion			Some	X
Standardization	X		Some	
Country/Industry Promotion	X		Some	

tion and marketing activities and reduce the degree to which such investments are privately and socially efficient. Table 2.3 summarizes the discussion in an alternative way by identifying possible gaps or bottlenecks in the flow of physical commodities, information and financial resources within commodity systems that might stem from the inherent technical and economic characteristics of food products, production, processing and marketing.

Risk and Transaction Costs in the Processing and Marketing of High-Value Foods

The above discussion has been very general in nature, pointing out characteristics of commodities, production, infrastructure, processing and marketing activities that pose barriers to entry, create risks and increase transaction costs for commodity system participants. These features differ significantly

TABLE 2.3: **Generic Barriers to Commodity System Flows**

Problem/Barrier	Physical Product Flows	Informational Flows	Financial Flows
Commodity Characteristics			
Bulkiness	X		
Perishability	X		
Heterogeneity		X	
Production (Support) Characteristics			
Geographical Dispersion	X	X	
Unstable Production	X	X	
Extended Gestation Period	X		X
Public Goods Nature of Market/Technical Information		X	
Information Asymmetry in Credit			X
Processing/Distribution Characteristics			
Scale Economies/Public Goods Nature of Transport Infrastructure	X		
Scale Economies/Public Goods Nature of Communication Infrastructure		X	
Asset Specificity in Processing	X		X
Information Asymmetry in Credit		X	X
Scale Economies in Crop Intelligence and Market Research		X	

by commodity and also by the prevailing regulatory and competitive environment. Here we discuss commodity-specific factors that inhibit investment and trade, leaving points about the African operating environment to Chapter III.

In order to operationalize the insights of transaction cost economics in the study of high-value food processing and marketing, it is necessary to identify quantitative or proxy qualitative indicators for uncertainty and asset-specificity, and then to evaluate different commodities according to these indicators. This will enable us to develop hypotheses later on regarding the expected organization of privately-based commodity systems for high-value foods. Three dimensions of uncertainty and four dimensions of asset-specificity are explored here. All of these pertain to the linkage between production and marketing or to post-harvest and processing activities themselves, rather than to primary production.

These indicators are:

UNCERTAINTY:

1) degree or rate of perishability of the raw material in its harvested, caught, or slaughtered state,

2) specificity of quality standards required for the raw material or commodity,

3) seasonal variability of raw material supply;

ASSET-SPECIFICITY:

1) technical sophistication and equipment specialization in post-harvest activities,[18]

2) level of fixed costs and scope for economies of scale in post-harvest activities,

3) technical sophistication and equipment specialization in processing operations,

4) level of fixed costs and scope for economies of scale in processing operations.

Table 2.4 rates these variables for selected high-value food commodities and products. It is assumed that the traded commodity or processed product is destined for export markets or to a segment of the domestic market that is quality-conscious and "up-scale". This assumption biases upward the quality of raw material required as well as the degree of sophistication and costs of equipment involved in post-harvest and processing operations.

Quantitative measures have been used to provide ratings of 'high', 'medium' and 'low'. For *perishability*, a high rating signifies that the raw material loses its value or ability to be processed in less than two weeks after harvest, slaughter or catch. A medium rating allows a period of two to four weeks before deterioration. A low rating signifies that the product keeps its quality for longer than one month if storage conditions are favorable.

For *seasonality of raw material supply*, a high rating signifies that the raw material is available only during a very brief harvesting period (less than four months). A medium rating signifies that raw materials are produced virtually year-round with well defined seasonal patterns. A low rating signifies limited seasonal change in raw material supplies even in the absence of sophisticated production technologies.

For *levels of fixed costs* (in plant and equipment) for post-harvest and processing operations, a high rating has been assigned where costs exceed $50,000, a medium rating for costs of between $10,000 and $50,000, and a low rating for costs below $10,000.

---

[18] Such as milk cooling, animal slaughter, fish icing, fruit and vegetable packing and nut drying.

TABLE 2.4: Techno-Economic Characteristics of Selected High-Value Foods

Commodity	Elements of Uncertainty			Elements of Asset-Specificity			
	Perishability of raw material	Quality specificity in raw material or commodity	Seasonal variability of raw material supply	Degree of technical sophistication and equipment specialization in post-harvest activities	Fixed cost or scale economies of post-harvest activities	Technical sophistication and equipment specialization in processing	Fixed cost or scale economies in processing
Milk (Pasteurized)	High	Med	Med	Low–Med	Med	Med	Med
Cheese/Yogurt	High	High	Med	Low–Med	Med	Med	Med
Beef (Canned)	High	Low–Med	Med	Low	Med	Low	High
Poultry (Frozen)	High	Med	Low	Low	Med	Med–High	High
Fish (Dried)	High	Low	Med	Low	Low	Low	Low
Fish (Frozen)	High	Med–High	Med	Low	Low	Low	High
Fish (Canned)	High	Med	Med	Low	Low	Low–Med	High
Banana	Med	Med	Low	Low–Med	Med	Na.	Na.
Mango	Low	Med	High	Low	Low–Med	Na.	Na.
Pineapple (Fresh)	Med	High	Low	Low	Low	Na.	Na.
Pineapple (Canned)	Med	Med	Low	Low	Low	Med	High
French Beans (Fresh)	High	Med–High	Med	Low	Low–Med	Na.	Na.
French Beans (Canned)	High	High	Med	Low	Low–Med	Low	Med–High
Cashew Nuts	Low	Med	High	Low	Low	Med	Low–Med
Vanilla Beans	High	Med–High	High	Low	Low	High	Low–Med
Oil Palm	High	Med–High	Med	Low–Med	Low–Med	High	High

Na. Not applicable.

SOURCES: Brown (1991); Hyman (1990); Keddie and Cleghorn (1980); Manchester (1983); Case Studies.

For the other indicators, qualitative measures have been used. For *quality specificity*, a high rating signifies very exacting standards below which trade and processing are not profitable. A medium rating signifies significant premiums or discounts for high (or low) grades. A low rating signifies that quality standards are not tightly defined and simple minimum standards must be met.

For the *technical sophistication and equipment specialization*, a high rating implies highly specialized skills are required and/or that certain pieces of equipment are designed only for the processing of the raw material in question. A medium rating signifies that skilled workers with close supervision are needed and that major pieces of equipment have limited alternative food processing uses. A low rating signifies that unskilled workers with minimal supervision can perform the function and that major pieces of equipment have widespread alternative uses.

As Table 2.4 indicates, if we use these definitions, most of the listed high-value foods are highly perishable in their raw state and require rapid sale to retain their value or rapid processing to prevent deterioration or contamination. Few of these raw materials can remain with the primary producer for more than a few weeks after harvest (or slaughter or catch). Cashew nuts are a major exception since they can be stored for a year or more once properly dried. Moderate to high levels of quality-specificity also apply in all cases except to fish which will be dried. Hence, significant price premiums or discounts will be associated with effective inducements of high-quality raw material supplies (and the subsequent maintenance of quality levels). Only a few of the commodities exhibit a very narrow seasonal yielding pattern. Yet most experience at least some seasonal variation in supplies, suggesting possible pressures on or sporadic underutilization of transport, processing and other infrastructure. In general, moderate to high levels of uncertainty will tend to surround the procurement of raw materials related to high-value foods.

Turning to asset specificity, the table shows generally low levels of technical sophistication or equipment specialization required for post-harvest activities and generally low to moderate fixed costs involved in undertaking these activities. This suggests that the technical or economic barriers to entry by firms or individuals in such activities may not be significant, and fairly broad patterns of participation would be expected where market licensing and other rules permit. Food processing is generally less technically sophisticated than other manufacturing fields and there are a variety of different processing technologies for most food product groups. Nevertheless, for some food product lines various pieces of specialized equipment have been designed to consistently meet international standards for quality. The same applies to the many technical innovations related to materials handling, product development, and packaging which food processors require to achieve and retain international competitiveness. While most of these innovations are developed outside of the food processing industry (indicating the importance of local institutions to conduct or transfer results from basic and applied research), large food manufacturers may benefit from in-house research, especially in the realm of new product development. Such large firms may have a strong competitive advantage in countries where overall research capabilities in food technology are weak.

Among high-value foods, higher stage processing operations more commonly feature significant fixed cost elements (and economies of scale) than they do technical sophistication or specialization. This applies to meat and fish canning and freezing and certain types of vegetable oil extraction and fruit and vegetable processing. This feature increases the costs of entry and intensifies the challenge of obtaining a reliable source of raw materials. Illustrative examples of fixed costs incurred in the start-up of high-value food processing and trading operations are indicated in Table 2.5.

TABLE 2.5: **Indicative Fixed Costs for Starting Food Processing Operations**
(Costs of Buildings, Civil Works, Equipment, and Installation Services)

Unit	Description	Fixed Costs ($)
Stall for Street Foods (e.g. kebabs, fritters)	urban Senegal, 1984	15
Open-air Restaurant	urban Senegal, 1984	90
Food Wholesaling Business	urban Senegal, 1984	2,500
Small Fermented Milk Unit	500 liters/day capacity, rural Kenya, 1992	13,670
Pig Slaughterhouse	7500 head/year capacity, urban Kenya, 1991	87,000
Small Meat Processing Unit	25 pig + 2 beef carcasses/week capacity, urban Kenya, 1991	190,000
Small Cashew Nut Factory	500 tons/year capacity, rural Tanzania, 1993	464,000
Small Fish/Shrimp Processing Facility	235 tons/year capacity, urban Benin, 1991	552,000
Medium-Scale Vegetable Processing/ Freezing Plant	6000 tons/year capacity, urban Cameroon, 1992	2,000,000
Large-Scale Fish Processing/ Freezing Facility	13,000 tons/year capacity, rural Uganda, 1992	3,900,000

SOURCES: Various Feasibility Studies; Also Bricas (1984).

Technologies, Institutions, and Other Solutions to Generic Food Marketing Problems

A wide range of technical and institutional measures can be adopted to facilitate the flow of information, goods, money and product ownership rights in commodity systems. These same measures can also facilitate economies of scale, reduce risks and transaction costs, internalize externalities, and provide those public goods necessary for efficient market development. Many of these measures are essentially market or quasi-market responses on the part of private firms and individuals, while others entail government intervention to stimulate, re-direct or supplement private activity. This section examines a representative sample of such measures, noting their potential for promoting improved efficiency and coordination.

Technological Measures[19]

Technologies can be introduced at the production level which have strong marketing implications. For example, crop varieties have been developed which can be harvested earlier or over a longer period of time and whose harvested product has improved storage, taste and aesthetic properties. Cultivation practices and chemicals can induce or delay crop maturity. Production under controlled irrigation, temperature, lighting and other conditions can influence the timing of production as well as the quality of raw material output. These and many other production technologies reduce production risks, enable producers to diversify their crop/livestock mix and facilitate closer coordination between production and subsequent processing or distribution activities.

There is also a wide range of well-established technologies and new ones are emerging that facilitate the post-harvest flow of food products and raw materials by countering their perishability and bulkiness, thereby lowering the risks and costs of commodity storage and transport. These include controlled atmosphere storage and transport, advanced mechanical handling tech-

---

[19] Only a brief discussion is provided here on the many production, processing, storage, transport, and other technologies which can be adopted to facilitate more efficient food marketing and commodity system coordination. For more detailed coverage, readers are referred to the Economic Development Institute (1990–91) working paper series on agricultural processing technologies (edited by Brown) and the papers by Greeley (1991), the Economic Commission for Europe (1991), and Peters (1992) dealing with post-harvest technologies, food processing machinery, and logistics management, respectively.

niques, vacuum and polyethylene packaging, wax coating, irradiation and containerization in internal and international transport. Computerized warehousing and computer monitoring of goods in transit can improve physical commodity and informational flows, plus provide early warning regarding product quality deterioration.

Technologies can be introduced to more effectively measure the quality of raw materials before processing. They provide improved information and incentive to producers. Uniform measures enable processors to better sort raw materials for production of different types of products. Examples of such technologies include those which enable more accurate measurement of the fat content of meat, the color, sizing and chemical make-up of fruit and vegetables, the kernel out-turn of raw cashew nuts and the moisture content of grains and raw sugar.

Processing and related food technologies can facilitate improved physical product flows, counter the uncertainties and costs of raw material procurement and enhance consumer demand. Many processing functions directly reduce the bulk and perishability of raw materials. The use of ultra-high temperature processing, together with aseptic packaging, can extend the market life of commodities which are ordinarily highly perishable (for example, 'long-life' milk). Technologies enable the replacement of natural raw materials with tailor-made fat-, sugar- and beverage-substitutes. These obviate the need to coordinate processing with farm production. New processing technologies can promote greater uniformity of output and better hygiene and lower unit costs of production.

Information technologies can improve monitoring of demand and communications between commodity system participants. Laser scanners at retail locations are an example of the former. Scanning not only speeds up retailer inventory management, but provides detailed information about the buying patterns of consumers, information which can be very valuable both to the retailer and to food manufacturers. Improved communications via facsimile, computer networks and other electronic devices can lower the costs of doing business and keep suppliers and buyers in up-to-the-minute contact regarding available suppliers, delivery times and prices. The investment costs and the skills required to utilize each of the above technologies vary enormously, thereby influencing who will be in a position to adopt them and to gain a competitive advantage from their use.

Laws, Rules, and Standards

All commodity systems operate within an institutional environment consisting of a set of fundamental political, social and legal ground rules. These ground rules establish the basis for production, exchange and distribution. According to Ruttan and Hayami (1984, p. 204), these rules:

> . . . facilitate coordination among people by helping them form expectations which each person can reasonably hold in dealing with others . . . [They] provide assurance respecting the actions of others and give order and stability to expectations in the complex and uncertain world of economic relations.

The institutional environment governing a commodity system consists of several different types of rules. The most important are (1) **rules defining, allocating and enforcing property rights** (for example, property and bankruptcy laws), and (2) **rules and conventions defining permissible and non-permissible forms of cooperation and competition** (for example, standards, licensing rules, laws of contract and liability, company and cooperative laws and 'fair trading' conventions).

A well articulated and consistently enforced system of property rights is a fundamental precondition for efficient exchange within commodity systems. Clarity over ownership and the rights to use, trade and alter assets is vital to market development since this assigns to individuals the right to benefits (and the burden of losses) from specialized production and marketing activities (Bromley 1986). The general system of property laws places boundaries on participant behavior and expectations, and in doing so, increases the scope for coordination. As we will see later in Chapter III, in many African countries there is a lack of clarity regarding 'the rules of the game' for private trading activity which deters private investment in marketing and processing facilities where significant fixed costs must be incurred.

Rules and conventions specifying entry conditions and boundaries on co-operative and competitive practices may also facilitate exchange and coordination. The establishment and enforcement of standards can reduce transaction costs by increasing the available information to buyers and consumers.[20] Standards, which may include basic weights, measures and quality grades, provide farmers and marketing agents with a more exact language to com-

---

[20] On standards and grades, see Kindleberger (1983), Bowbrick (1983), and Rottenberg and Yandle (1988).

municate offers, a norm to compare actual with expected behavior, and a more detailed and objective view of the actual outcome. Quality standards may be mandatory or voluntary; they may be minimum standards or include multiple grades. They are especially important when trade takes place over long distances and among strangers because standardized goods can more easily be traded 'on description'. The development of appropriate standards and grades is not an easy task, especially when the commodity has numerous valued characteristics. Standards can also be abused when designed to serve as a major barrier to entry for smaller, less well-capitalized firms.

The licensing of producers and marketing agents can also assist trade by reducing transaction costs. This would occur where the criteria for licensing centers around the asset holdings, past experience, financial solvency and other proxies for competence of the enterprise in question. In this case, a public or collective authority provides the initial screening of the capabilities and credibility of alternative suppliers and buyers. Performance incentives are built in since suppliers of substandard produce would risk revocation of license. Of course, if licensing is based on criteria other than capability and competence (such as ethnicity or payment of bribes), then arrangements will provide misleading information and inefficient restraints on trader behavior. In addition, licensing increases the cost of entry and may generate economic rents if only a limited number of parties are permitted to trade.

As food products become more complex and varied, consumers cannot be expected to have full knowledge about the choices available to them and the quality of products which are offered. The food supplier has the incentive to supply just enough information to differentiate its product from its competitors, but no more. In order to enable consumers to make more informed decisions and to protect themselves from potentially harmful products and practices, regulations may be established requiring tests or inspections of products, certain handling or processing procedures, nutritional or other labels and truth-in-advertising. For such regulations to maintain credibility in the eyes of consumers and other buyers, those implementing the regulations must be immune to financial inducements to 'look the other way' if proffered.[21]

---

[21] The definition and enforcement of each of the above sets of rules generally involves both government and private sector participation. Quality standards may be set by government, participating firms or prevailing (international) competition. Both licensing and food safety and labeling procedures and criteria are normally determined by governments in consultation with (or at the behest of) participating firms.

Spot Marketing Trading

The conception of market exchange found in most textbooks is one of an impersonal, one-time encounter between a buyer and seller of a standardized good or service. In such transactions, goods, services, money and titles are transferred simultaneously 'on the spot'. Goods which have already been produced are traded and their market prices serve as the primary source of information, constraints and incentives. In this type of trade, each of the participating parties make independent decisions based on its own conditions and preferences and on the information available about the preferences and behavior of others.

There are several potential advantages of spot market trading over more elaborate trading or organizational ties (Hayek 1945; Williamson 1985). The market price system offers clear and powerful incentives. Prices automatically meter and reward productive effort. Unlike the case of many alternative institutional arrangements, the distribution of costs and benefits from spot market exchange are not complicated by past or future considerations or by the provision of non-measured services. Spot market trade offers wide scope for flexibility to respond to changes in market conditions as it is generally easier to negotiate an adjustment in price levels alone than to agree upon and implement changes in trading rules or lines of command. Market prices place clear and powerful constraints on individual behavior. Factor prices generate budgetary constraints, while final goods prices limit purchasing options. In contrast, under alternative institutional arrangements, most behavioral constraints must be negotiated and supervised. Finally, in a competitive environment, spot market trading provides economies in information with market prices 'summarizing' all or most of the information which trading parties require to conduct trade.

Spot market transactions can occur across several different types of markets, including auctions, private treaty and posted price (Cassady 1974; Marion et al. 1986). Auction markets are common in agricultural trade. They feature an impersonal competitive bidding process which 'discovers' the market price. Auctions carry very low transaction costs when large quantities of standardized products are traded. They also allow for great flexibility of prices which tend to change from minute to minute. If the auction is well supplied, trading may provide up-to-date information on supply and demand conditions. Auction markets generally feature standardized procedures for the exchange of payments and title to goods.

There are several potential drawbacks to reliance on auction trading. The volatility of auction prices makes it difficult for suppliers and buyers to properly plan their transactions. In circumstances where trade through auctions is small, market prices may not reflect overall supply and demand conditions very well, therefore sending misleading signals. Auction prices may provide only weak signals about the product attributes which buyers prefer and which suppliers are capable of delivering. Where the number of buyers in the auction is very limited (or where active collusion takes place), suppliers may not receive competitive prices.

Reputations, Brand Names, and Advertising

Reputations are one means of signaling competence and credibility. The reputation of an individual (or firm) will incorporate perceptions about the quality of the goods and services offered, the trustworthiness of words and actions, competence, and various other real or mythical aspects of character and behavior (Casson 1982). Good reputations reduce the costs of arms-length trade as buyers and sellers will have greater confidence in one another, permitting them to lower their initial screening efforts and subsequent monitoring of product quality. In contrast, when a firm or individual has a 'bad name', this is a signal to other parties to pass up potential trades. The alternative is to monitor closely product quality, ask for prepayment for goods and employ other defensive techniques. Reputations, both good and bad, provide a proxy for a large amount of information which may not be readily available to potential trading partners. A good reputation may facilitate entry into new markets and can carry over onto other goods and services which its bearer may provide.

One means of encouraging this spillover is to develop and promote a brand name, which can be done for a company or a country. Where the link between producers and ultimate consumers is weak or non-existent, the reputation of the seller and brand name may serve as an effective proxy for quality. The brand name establishes responsibility for the product, thus increasing the scope for compensation should quality be substandard (Demsetz 1964). Branding not only helps in the introduction of new products: it inhibits the consumer from substituting cheaper items for the product.

Advertising is another direct means of providing information to buyers and consumers and persuading them of the merits of generic or branded products. Advertising can support the growth of firms and markets and therefore can contribute to the realization of economies of scale. Because of these economies of scale/scope in branding and advertising, their practice can weaken the competitive position of smaller firms.

Personalized Trading Networks

Actual market relations frequently differ from spot market trading in that each established buyer and seller frequently develops groups of suppliers or customers with whom they are more inclined to deal than anyone else. Through experience, each market participant locates specific parties in whom they have confidence and with whom personalized, recurrent trading relationships develop under the aegis of unwritten, informal understandings. This repeated trading helps to reduce information costs—and with the development of norms and the establishment of trust—the costs of bargaining, monitoring and enforcement (Wilson 1980). In examining the 'bazaar economy' Geertz (1978) notes the importance of 'clientization', or the pairing of buyers and sellers in recurrent transactions, in reducing information costs in an uncertain trading environment. Richardson (1964) notes a similar process whereby buyers and sellers who are loyal to one another may obtain favorable attention or services, such as priority in times of product scarcity.

In those environments where formal (legal) procedures for monitoring and enforcing agreements are absent or inadequate, the generation of trust and the establishment of relationships based on reciprocity are likely to be crucial factors in the development of trade; they serve as a proxy for laws (Posner 1980). Trust can allow transactors to build flexibility into their trading relationships since adjustments can be made sequentially with less risk of each party bringing false or incomplete information to the bargaining table (Macauley 1963). The parties are aware that opportunistic behavior can undermine the basis of trust and therefore threaten the privileged trading status that each party holds vis-a-vis the other. Trust and reciprocity enable trade to take place, even in a very uncertain and unstable economic environment.[22]

---

[22] Some analysts, particularly in socio-anthropological studies of marketing, have observed the development of 'insider trader networks' based on ethnicity, kinship, or other personal or corporate ties. In such cases, mutual conceptions of fairness and reciprocity exist. Within the group, there are extensive flows of information, favored access to credit and marketing channels, and the availability of risk-spreading measures. See for example Cohen (1969), Barton (1974), and Kilby (1983). Landa (1981) provides a theoretical analysis of such 'insider' trading groups.

Personalized, long-term trading arrangements present several potential limitations. First, these arrangements may inhibit adaptation in the face of rapid or major market changes. Market changes may require fundamental changes in the nature of the trading relationship, which one or both parties may resist. Mutual inclinations to 'work things out' may not be adequate. Second, given the open-ended and unmeasurable aspect of reciprocity, there is little scope for third-party arbitration of disputes. Third, transaction cost advantages may come at the expense of production cost disadvantages since the preferences given to a particular supplier may leave undeveloped or unexplored alternative, less expensive market sources. Finally, while 'insider trader networks' reduce the transaction costs faced by insiders, they provide potentially significant barriers to entry from outsiders.

Brokerage

Brokers are intermediaries who link suppliers and customers but who do not take title over the commodities traded. They are commonly found in agricultural markets and in all forms of international trade. Brokered trade can be less costly for suppliers and customers for several reasons. As regular players in the market, brokers are likely to be better informed about market conditions than the buyers, sellers or both.[23] Brokers can assist buyers and sellers in sifting through and selecting the relevant data for them to make proper decisions. A broker may also have the social standing, experience and bargaining skills to effectively bring together buyers and sellers from different locations, clans or social settings. A broker who cultivates the trust of both buyer and seller can impart a more personal tone to trades between parties which do not know or directly communicate with one another. Finally, brokers can achieve economies of scale in deal-making by accumulating small supplies/offers from many parties and selling to many other parties.[24] Use of a broker may enable a supplier (or buyer) to stabilize their sales (or purchases) given the plethora of market outlets (and supply sources) which the

---

[23] Information relevant to marketing decisions is generated as a by-product of trading activities and is thus more easily and readily acquired by those actors continuously engaged in trade.

[24] Many individual suppliers and customers may not conduct levels of trade which are sufficient to warrant investment in the skills, contacts, and data needed to identify and negotiate deals with others.

broker can offer. Brokers may thus provide buyers and sellers with a wider array of market sources and outlets, as well as lower the transaction costs of trade, especially international trade.

The possible agency costs of reliance on intermediaries must be set against the above advantages. The interests of the principals (namely, suppliers and customers) will not fully overlap with those of the agent. Since the agent is generally better informed than either of the principals, there is scope for shirking or opportunistic behavior, which results in higher costs and lower returns for the principals. Additional costs will be incurred in monitoring the agent's activities.

Contract Coordination

Contract coordination represents an intermediate institutional arrangement between spot market trading and the vertical integration of production and marketing functions (Mighell and Jones 1963; Macneil 1975; Goldberg 1976). It can provide many of the benefits of integration, while enabling its participants to retain at least some degree of autonomy. Market and production contracts which cover a production cycle, a marketing season or a longer time period formalize a degree of continuity or futurity in trading relationships. In contrast with spot market exchange, the agreed exchange is in *promised* goods and services rather than in *already produced* goods and services. Contractual details can vary enormously as can the overall intensity of the contractual relationship.

Two generic types of contracts can be identified, namely:

a) **forward market contracts** involving future commitments by sellers and buyers to sell and purchase a particular commodity at or over a stated time period. Such contracts specify either particular weights or volumes of the commodity to be exchanged or else some minimum or maximum quantities. Specifications are also generally made regarding quality attributes. Pricing arrangements vary, although agreements are generally made on the basis of fixed prices or a formula for determining price upon delivery.[25] Forward market contracts are commonly made between farmers and first-handlers, between exporters and importers, and between wholesalers or manufacturers and retailers.

---

[25] One variant is futures market contracts where actual deliveries of the commodities are rare and where one contractual obligation can be countered by another one for the same commodity.

b) **forward resource/management contracts** which combine forward market sale and purchase commitments with stipulations regarding the transfer and use of specific resources and managerial functions. In these cases, the exchange of the raw material/commodity is made contingent upon the application of specified inputs and/or methods. The buyer or seller may act to advise, supervise or take over the management of particular production or trading activities. Such arrangements, which internalize some though not all product and factor transactions, are found in many sub-contracting (Mead 1984), franchising, distributorship, and marketing/management agreements (Casson 1987) and many contract farming schemes in agriculture (Wilson 1986; Watts et al. 1988; Glover and Kusterer 1990).

Both of these arrangements can serve as effective vehicles for buyers to transfer complex information to sellers regarding their future delivery time, location and quality preferences. This can be done through direct specifications or by erecting price schedules according to timing, quality, etc. By creating a forward market, contracts reduce the uncertainty of buyers regarding access to supplies and the uncertainty of sellers regarding access to markets. Such arrangements can also reduce the price and income risks of one or both parties, although this will depend upon the pricing methods used and the actual sources of price instability. Management contracts can serve as a means of transferring complex technical information, production inputs and credit despite prevailing market imperfections in these areas (Minot 1986). Moreover, production contracts can sometimes be used as a form of collateral by farmers seeking credit from third parties.

There are several potential drawbacks or limitations to contractual coordination. First, widespread contractual coordination may render spot markets very 'thin', raising price volatility in the market and reducing or distorting the information supplied by such prices. Contractual terms may not be well known beyond the direct participants. Second, contractual coordination may result in significant barriers to entry as when the contractor limits its suppliers to those who can plant or deliver certain minimum quantities or meet very exacting standards. Third, contract coordination may involve a highly asymmetric bargaining situation in which a single or few buyers can largely determine the terms of trade from a position of localized monopsony. Finally, contract provisions may be costly or impossible to enforce, given acts of nature, participant opportunism, incompetence and the prevailing legal system.

Cooperatives/Associations/Voluntary Chains

A cooperative enterprise, association or voluntary chain of stores is formed by a group of economic entities who agree to act collectively in order to further their joint and individual private interests. These associations can be formed by farmers, processors, wholesalers, retailers or exporters, in order to undertake joint investments, common practices, or collective self-regulation of competition. The members essentially enter into a series of explicit and implicit contracts with one another and agree to membership terms and standard operating procedures (Staatz 1984; Zusman 1989).

Voluntary cooperation can support commodity system investment and coordination because:[26]

a) It can **counter the problem of 'lumpy' investments** in marketing infrastructure and services since the fixed costs of such investments can be shared among the group members.

b) It can serve to **internalize certain externalities** and allow for private provision of certain public goods. One area for this is in product promotion, which may not be worthwhile for an individual producer or trader, but can be profitable for a group since costs can be spread and benefits internalized. An association can also promote and protect an industry's reputation for quality and reliability by monitoring its members and penalizing (perhaps through loss of membership) those parties which provide substandard service to buyers/consumers.

c) It can **reduce or pool member risks** by guaranteeing commodity purchases and sales on behalf of members and by providing insurance and/or credit to members. When selling on behalf of the cooperative, the group will pool the market price and access risks of members. Cooperatives or associations may be better placed to provide insurance and credit to members because of having more detailed and reliable information about their risks and creditworthiness.

d) It can **lower transaction costs** for members and for non-members trading with members by settling disputes and by obtaining, interpreting and disseminating information about production, markets, and farmer/trader competence and creditworthiness. A trade association can be an

---

[26] This discussion is based on Staatz (1984), Shaffer (n.d.), Coleman (1987), Schneiberg and Hollingsworth (1990), and Smith and Thomson (1991).

important 'first stop' for a prospective buyer and can provide a channel for consumer/buyer complaints. A farmers' cooperative can synthesize information about its members' production and function as a low-cost channel for information from processors or traders.

e) It can **exercise or counter market power** for its members through collective negotiations with suppliers or buyers, by controlling/withholding member supply into the market, and by informing members about prevailing terms of trade.[27]

There are several types of generic problems associated with voluntary co-operation. One of these is the 'free-rider' problem. In some instances, members outside of the group are able to capture part of the benefits from a cooperative effort without contributing to the costs. This might occur in areas related to product promotion, industry reputation or the provision of crop intelligence and market information. If group membership did not also imply additional services whose benefits can be fully internalized by members, economic entities may be unwilling to contribute to cooperative costs. Group members may also be able to free ride through measures which yield them benefits above their proper share or reduce their contribution to group costs.

The size of the group may be important in determining the level of benefits and costs from voluntary cooperation. Small-sized groups have certain advantages over larger groups. In small groups, each member is likely to receive a large share of the total benefits and contribute significantly to total costs. This promotes commitment to the group while also giving each member bargaining power. Members of small groups will have detailed information about one another. Mutual trust is more easily maintained and transaction costs are lower. However, small groups may facilitate very limited mobilization of capital and do not allow for specialized management functions, such as marketing or finance. Among small groups engaged in a particular activity, there is likely to be a high covariance of risk, limiting the potential for cooperative insurance and credit supply.

Large groups enable the achievement of economies of scale with more limited investments per member and provide greater scope for pooling or spreading risks. Yet, as group size increases, so will transaction costs. In

---

[27] The former two methods are most effective when the organization accounts for a large proportion of total supply—the organization provides a means of implementing cartel arrangements, thereby raising or stabilizing profits and shifting the burdens of adjustment on to other parties.

larger groups there is likely to be more divergent interests with different sub-groups lobbying for different policies. Each member will have less information about other members, providing greater problems for monitoring behavior and detecting free-riding by members. Large groups may be run by a leadership group whose private interests conflict with those of the total group. Asymmetric information and power may prevail within the group.

Vertical Integration

Vertical integration involves the combination of two or more separable stages of production or marketing under common ownership and management. It can take place via simultaneous investment in multiple, interrelated activities or through investments forward or backward to existing activities. Vertical integration can be complete or partial. The latter involves at least some sales (or purchases) of the focal intermediate products to (or from) outside parties. The economics literature stresses four major rationales for vertical integration, each relevant to our discussion of food commodity systems.

   a) **Production/logistical economies:** Vertical integration may reduce logistical costs associated with the procurement of raw materials and the sale of finished products. Where vertical integration involves bringing together in one location formerly distinct operating units, transport costs can be saved, particularly for bulky and perishable raw materials. Consolidating under one management the suppliers and users of a raw material or other intermediate input can reduce the level of required inventory because internal planning allows for a better match of supply and demand in terms of quantity and location.

   b) **Transaction cost economies:** With vertical integration, the firm can save on the cost of information because it becomes the sole or predominant supplier to itself for certain goods and services (Coase 1937; Williamson 1979). Bargaining costs are saved because the firm engages in relatively few long-term employment contracts, instead of numerous short-term hiring and supply agreements. Streamlined information systems provide ample scope for transmitting complex instructions within the firm. Centralized decision-making provides scope for rapid adjustments to changing technical or market conditions. Adaptations can be made without having to consult, revise or renegotiate agreements with other firms.

c) **Risk-bearing advantages:** Vertical integration may be a very effective institutional means of overcoming problems of risk and uncertainty (Arrow 1975). By internalizing flows of intermediate inputs, the firm may be able to eliminate certain risks such as variability of supplies, outlets and quality and the unauthorized use of technical information. More direct control over goods and assets can be exercised than under any arms-length or voluntary cooperation scheme. This reduced uncertainty may render the integrated firm better able to invest in highly specialized processing and marketing facilities and to take advantage of potential economies of scale. Partial integration may provide an even better combination of flexibility and reduced risk (Carlton 1979).

d) **Advantages in the presence of market imperfections:** In the early stages of market development when certain production or marketing functions lag behind, vertical integration of multiple stages may be necessary to stimulate consumer demand and guarantee the availability of the commodity (Stigler 1951). In the presence of taxes, price and exchange controls and other regulations, the mere act of internalizing transactions may provide pecuniary gains to the firm. Governments treat market transactions differently from those that occur within firms. Vertically integrated firms may thus be able to bypass or minimize the effects of taxes and market controls.[28] Finally, vertical integration may enable the firm to increase its market share and its leverage vis-a-vis suppliers and customers.[29]

As the above discussion implies, vertical integration may generate certain social costs due to reduced tax revenues and increased market concentration. There are also additional private costs to consider. For example, where adjacent stages of production/trading are not scale-compatible, it is likely that the production and logistical costs of integrated firms will be higher than those of non-integrated firms. There may be economies of scale in processing, yet diseconomies of scale in primary production. Large sunk costs in its own

---

[28] Invoice or transfer prices within the firm can be used to minimize the impact of fiscal interventions such as exchange controls on capital, ad valorem tariffs, and sales or company taxes. On the pecuniary gains from vertical integration, see Koutsoyiannis (1982) and Casson (1984).

[29] An integrated firm may be able to exclude others from segments of a market, exercise substantial leverage over non-integrated competitors, suppliers, and customers, raise the amount of capital needed to enter a market, and/or facilitate product differentiation and price discrimination (Comanor 1967).

production facilities will bias the firm toward internal supply, even where external supply sources are cheaper or of better quality.

Government Intervention

In circumstances where the private supply of goods and services remains below the social optimum and where market, contractual and cooperative mechanisms fail to effectively coordinate production and marketing activities, there may be justification for government intervention. State interventions can reduce the risks and transaction costs faced by private firms and individuals. It can also compensate for missing or deficient markets and influence the organization and performance of commodity systems so as to enhance benefits to the country or to particular interest groups (for example, consumers, farmers or manufacturers).[30] Government intervention need not entail direct government provision of goods and services. Regulation, taxation and subsidization are alternative modes of intervention. Since relatively few food marketing activities have the properties of a public good, these alternative types of intervention are usually more appropriate than direct government participation.[31]

The government has certain fundamental roles to play when only a sovereign body has the legitimacy or capability to act and when, for economic or technical reasons, the private sector has insufficient incentive to provide a good or service at socially optimal levels. One of these roles is the definition and consistent enforcement of a reasonable set of property rights and regulations pertaining to acceptable and non-acceptable competitive and cooperative actions. Property rights and regulations not only facilitate production

---

[30] In theory, governments have certain advantages over private or cooperative entities when it comes to investment and coordination (North 1986). Governments possess the unique powers of taxation and legitimate coercion. Such powers, together with certain economies of scale in utilizing these powers, potentially enable governments to better control against 'free riders', internalize externalities and constrain individual behavior. Governments also have a better capacity to bear economic or financial risk since they can spread risks over a larger number of people and over a broad range of sectors or investments. Nevertheless, governments operate in the same uncertain environment as do private entities and their capacity to obtain and interpret the relevant information may not be better. Governments face potentially large political risks. Their powers of taxation and coercion are constrained by the threat of competition from internal contenders, dissent and private and corporate evasion of controls and taxation.

[31] Our objective here is merely to highlight a series of fundamental roles for government and examine several additional common government interventions which affect food commodity systems, not to provide a comprehensive treatment of the roles and alternative modes of intervention in food marketing and commodity system development.

and trade, but also protect consumers against misleading claims and health-threatening foods.

A second fundamental role of government is to negotiate and define the rules for international trade and market entry. Governments can negotiate, either in bilateral or multilateral forums, to facilitate a particular commodity transaction (for instance, a deal with a state importing company) or to arrange longer-term access for national firms to foreign markets on terms equal or superior to those accorded to competitive suppliers. At the same time (and usually under the influence of domestic interest groups), governments must determine the general rules for foreign entry into domestic financial, production input and commodity markets. These rules will influence the competitiveness of food commodity systems vis-a-vis imported products as well as the availability and costs of production and other resources.

A third fundamental role of government is to directly undertake or support the provision of goods and services which have public good properties, give rise to significant externalities or feature economies of scale which are so significant as to result in natural monopolies. Several forms of physical and social infrastructure, including roads, rail and port facilities, power and water systems, technical research and training, and selected quality control and market information services fall into this category of publicly desirable but indivisible goods. Because of the inherent economic properties of these goods and services, private supply may not be profitable or at least may not result in a socially optimal level of supply. While many governments have chosen to provide them directly, other options are to subsidize private supply, contract out supply to the private sector (thus assuring payment for services), or provide particular private or cooperative organizations with exclusive supply rights (e.g. on utility supply) or coercive powers (e.g. on quality control).

There are still other common types of government intervention in commodity systems. Though of a less fundamental nature, these interventions serve to counter market imperfections, reduce or alter the distribution of risks, influence the volume and price of traded products, and influence the distribution of opportunities and income.

Governments sometimes attempt to compensate for missing or deficient markets. This is particularly common in the area of credit, where risk factors and major information imperfections are at play. Weak credit markets result in limited funds available to small-scale farmers, cooperatives and commodity traders. Farmers and firms seeking to invest in assets carrying long gestation periods or being 'lumpy' in character are also disserved by insufficient credit opportunities. Because governments are less risk-averse (for reasons noted earlier), they may be better positioned to extend credit to these and other commodity system participants. An 'infant industry' argument for government support may be applicable in the early stages of development of particular commodity systems.

Another service commonly provided by governments is price stabilization. Stabilized prices can be regarded as a public good for farmers, consumers, processors and other commodity system participants. Price stabilization—involving instruments such as price controls, floor prices, buffer stocks, variable taxes and quantity controls—is ostensibly undertaken in order to lower the risks and stabilize the incomes of producers and/or consumers.[32] However, price stabilization is most often costly to undertake, generates allocative distortions, and can adversely affect producer or trader incentives.[33] Instead of stabilizing prices with large-scale interventions and controls, it may be more efficient for governments to support strategies which reduce risks to producers (for example, crop diversification, non-farm employment, irrigation development) through credit, technical support and other programs, and to provide targeted food subsidies to vulnerable consumer groups (such as children).

Additional forms of government intervention are geared toward influencing the competitive structure of markets, which affects the volume and value of trade and the distribution of income. Regulations may be geared toward promoting or protecting a competitive market structure or conversely, toward promoting the concentration or monopolization of trade. The former would be more common in a domestic market setting—in the relations between farmers and processors or at wholesale or retail levels. The latter is more common in export-oriented industries where economies of scale and improved bargaining power can be achieved through some degree of trade concentration.

When voluntary cooperation fails to control 'free riders', capture the benefits from scale economies or enable suppliers to exercise market power, governments can institute schemes for compulsory cooperation. The most common and well-documented forms of compulsory cooperation are one channel

---

[32] See *World Development Report 1986*, pp. 87–94.

[33] In circumstances where supply variability is considerable, price stabilization may further destabilize producer, trader, and/or consumer incomes. See Newberry and Stiglitz (1981).

procurement and sales through marketing boards, and supply and pricing controls through marketing orders (Jesse 1979; Hoos 1979). Both marketing boards and marketing orders can be used to control physical commodity flows, enforce quality standards and pool market risks.

Monopoly export marketing boards can make an entire commodity system 'behave' like a single firm vis-a-vis the world market by regulating the mix and quality of products going to different markets and negotiating with transporters and buyers with a single voice. While export marketing boards can achieve certain economies of scale, pool risks and assert international market power, they can easily become a major barrier in the flow of information between foreign buyers and local producers and processors. In addition, export marketing boards can become the tool of certain vested interest groups (for example, the political leadership, influential farmers or processors) or an unstable arena in which various interest groups battle over policies and the spoils of trade (Bates 1981; Arhin et al. 1985). In either case, marketing board policies may result in reduced production incentives and a processing and marketing strategy which is not demand-oriented, and thus is not sustainable, in a competitive world market.

Table 2.5 summarizes this discussion by indicating whether the noted technologies or institutional mechanisms facilitate improved commodity and other flows, reduce raw material procurement and market risks, internalize externalities, and so on. These are, of course, their *theoretical* roles. As mentioned above, there are circumstances in which these instruments will fail to deliver the desired benefits and/or give rise to private or social costs which might match or exceed benefits. The analysis of actual institutional arrangements within commodity systems must thus take into account the specific operating context as influenced by the prevailing market structure and relevant socio-economic, political and historical factors.

TABLE 2.5: **Technological/Institutional Measures to Facilitate Commodity System Coordination, Efficiency, and Market Power**

Technology or Institution	Improve Info Flow	Improve Product Flow	Improve Money Flow	Improve Flow of Title	Reduce Raw Material Procurement Risks	Reduce Market Risks	Internalize/Counter Externalities	Achieve Economies of Scale	Gain or Counter Market Power
Technologies									
Production Technologies: Varieties, Irrigation, etc.		Yes			Yes	Yes			
Refrig. Storage/Transport		Yes			Yes				
Containerization		Yes							
Quality Meas. Techniques	Yes	Yes			Yes				Yes
Laser Scanning	Yes	Yes						Yes	Yes
Market/Quasi-Market Measures									
Auctions	Yes	Yes	Yes	Yes					
Reputation/Brand Names	Yes				Yes	Yes			Yes
Advertising	Yes		Yes					Yes	Yes
Personal Trade Networks	Yes				Yes	Yes			
Brokerage	Yes	Yes			Yes	Yes		Yes	
Forward Contracts	Yes	Yes	Yes	Yes	Yes	Yes	Yes	Yes	Yes
Cooperative Marketing	Yes	Yes	Yes			Yes	Yes	Yes	Yes
Trade Associations	Yes					Yes	Yes		Yes
Vertical Integration	Yes	Yes	Yes	Yes	Yes	Yes	Yes	Yes	Yes
Laws/Rules/Regulations									
Property Rights	Yes		Yes	Yes	Yes	Yes	Yes		
Standards/Grades	Yes	Yes			Yes	Yes			Yes
Licensing	Yes			Yes		Yes			Yes
Government Interventions									
Infrastructure Investments	Yes	Yes			Yes	Yes			
Credit Scheme		Yes	Yes		Yes			Yes	
Price Stabilization Scheme						Yes	Yes		
Export Marketing Board	Yes	Yes	Yes	Yes	Yes	Yes	Yes	Yes	Yes

III.

Private Sector High-Value Food Processing and Marketing: A Synthesis of African Experiences

Steven Jaffee and John Morton

This chapter provides a synthesis of the literature pertaining to private sector processing and marketing of high-value foods (HVFs) in sub-Saharan Africa. It applies insights of institutional economics from the previous chapter to better understand the nature of private sector high-value food activity in the region. It is organized into three main sections. The first section examines the environment in which private enterprises typically must operate in Africa. Although improvements are evident in some countries, the discussion shows how the persistence of macroeconomic instability, policy uncertainty and infrastructural and financial market weaknesses raise the risks and transaction costs associated with private investment and trade in the region.

The second section addresses the question of which types of private entrepreneurs and firms are able to take advantage of HVF market opportunities in African settings. It examines the respective roles of foreign, ethnic minority and 'indigenous' firms and individuals, and highlights the role of women in the focal activities. The third and largest section examines the operations of private HVF processors and traders. It focuses on their strategies for raw material procurement, product choice and development, marketing, and overcoming financial and bureaucratic obstacles. These observed strategies are discussed using the conceptual framework developed in Chapter II.

GENERAL PROBLEMS IN THE OPERATIONAL ENVIRONMENT

The literature on agricultural marketing and market liberalization in Africa highlights various dimensions of the operating environment that constrain the activities of traders and processors and increase the risks which they face and the costs which they incur. Several common and prominent dimensions of the operating environment are discussed here and we point out their implications for private investment and trading activity. First, we examine selected operating conditions which influence the incentives for private agents to undertake investments and engage in trade. These relate to macroeconomic instability, foreign exchange shortages and controls, overall policy uncertainty, and the persistence of official and unofficial restraints on trade. We then look at two major areas in which deficient investments or institutions constrain the ability of private agents to respond to market opportunities and raise their risks and costs. These relate to the inadequate and poorly maintained physical infrastructure in the region and the relatively weak development of its formal financial markets.

Macroeconomic Instability and Foreign Exchange Shortages

Over the past two decades, a combination of external shocks, economic policies and the narrow structural base of many African economies have contributed to significant macroeconomic instability as evidenced by large fiscal and balance of payments deficits, high rates of inflation and severe shortages of foreign exchange. Although many countries have instituted macroeconomic reform programs, inflation rates remain high by world standards and currencies continue to be overvalued. Macroeconomic instability has deterred private investment generally. Investments which are relatively irreversible, for example, in food processing facilities and cold stores, have suffered the greatest.

Exchange rate misalignment (and overvaluation) inhibit trade for several reasons. First, currency overvaluation serves as an implicit tax on exports and other tradeable commodities, inducing shifts of resources into the production of non-tradeables. Second, significant currency misalignment engenders uncertainty among economic agents. Future production and trading plans are affected by expectations of sudden, potentially large devaluations. Incentives to maintain external accounts of foreign currency will be strong, setting in motion a continued battle between exporters, central banks and other officials in charge of monitoring export transactions and associated financial flows. When, as in recent years, major devaluations have been implemented, substantial increases in the real cost of capital goods have followed and short term investments have fallen. Third, currency misalignment distorts opportunities for intra-regional trade and may negate real opportunities associated with differences in production and transport costs.

Shortages of foreign exchange have frequently resulted in the imposition of strict licensing and foreign exchange allocation systems, administered by inter-ministerial government agencies. Imports are restricted to particular products and firms. Private investors who require imported equipment or materials are faced with the choice of delaying their investment or incurring additional costs while lobbying for licensing and foreign exchange. In many countries, an imposed policy of import contraction has contributed to severe shortages of spare parts, raw materials and equipment needed by food processors and traders, as well as by those industries providing inputs into agricultural production. Some high-value food industries, such as the poultry industry in Nigeria, have virtually collapsed as a result of import controls.

The implementation of import licensing and foreign exchange allocation systems entails an implicit or explicit prioritization of import needs by government officials. When ranked, high-value food products have often been regarded as inessential. This has undoubtedly inhibited efforts by traders and processors to develop local markets for these products. In a number of cases, it has also hindered intra-regional trade. For example, during the 1980s there were wide year-to-year fluctuations in trade among Southern African countries in commodities such as beef, fish, oilseeds and vegetable oils which corresponded to shifting import control policies. Local firms developed a preference for foreign suppliers who could send products through foreign aid programs or who could provide extended payment terms. Typically, such suppliers were located outside the region.

The lag between the initiation of a stabilization program and the occurrence of significant new private investment has been considerable in several countries. Domestic stabilization programs, centering around improved budgetary control, increased taxes, and sometimes, massive layoffs of public employees, have had negative effects, at least initially, on many traders and processors. Tight monetary policies, layoffs and other measures have decreased overall consumption expenditures, particularly for high-value foods.[1] Thus,

---

[1] This comes out strongly in the case of the Ghanaian fish industry. Structural adjustment has also affected the Tanzanian cashew nut trade through the tightening of credit availability and it set in motion a series of developments which have encouraged food processors in Nigeria to utilize soybeans as a raw material.

processors and traders have had difficulty passing on their rising costs for fuel and packaging that are associated with devaluation.[2] They have been squeezed from the other side as growing concern for cost recovery has led governments to increase the licensing fees and local taxes paid by traders.[3]

Policy Uncertainty, Residual Market Controls and Corruption

The majority of African countries have adopted structural adjustment programs which, in addition to macroeconomic policy reforms, have included measures to broaden agricultural and industrial market competition and to increase private sector participation in trade. Overall, the reform process has been uneven across both countries and sectors. A recent review of the structural adjustment experience in twenty-six African countries concluded that only six of the countries experienced a strong improvement in macroeconomic policies, nine countries a small improvement, and the remaining eleven countries a deterioration.[4] In general, the reform of markets for domestic food staples has progressed further than has the reform of export crop marketing, although a few export marketing boards have been abolished (for coffee in Madagascar, groundnuts in Niger and a range of crops in Nigeria), and there are a number of cases in which producer prices have been more closely linked to international prices. While parastatals have lost their monopoly trading status in a number of countries, in most of them various forms of official and unofficial restrictions on private sector participation remain. Both in the context of market liberalization programs and in the more general pronouncements of government officials, there remains an element of deep suspicion towards private trader activities.

In practice, it has not often been clear just how and where to liberalize and what the legal status of private traders should be. In Tanzania in the mid-1980s, policy changes for staple foods marketing were transmitted through ministerial statements and as answers to questions put forward within the parliament. However, they were not formally incorporated into legislation. This may have worked out for the best since the government subsequently changed its policies regarding prices, crop movements and participants on an almost yearly basis. Their vacillation created considerable confusion and de-

---

[2] This point was made by Meagher (1990) for Uganda and by the FAO (1992) for Zambia.
[3] Chapter IV illustrates how this has affected the movement of cashew nuts in Tanzania.
[4] World Bank (1994).

terred any additional private investment in storage and transport facilities. In the end, many of the restrictions were unenforceable and traders in what had been a parallel market continued with their business.[5] More recently, the Tanzanian government made new, initial announcements of policy changes in the cashew nut trade over the radio and via press releases. Yet, it did not direct formal correspondence to regional officials who were supposed to implement the policy changes. For nearly an entire export season, private traders were uncertain as to their rights to procure and trade nuts, and regional officials used their own discretion in implementing the vaguely communicated policies.

Variations in the interpretation and implementation of policy reforms by regional and local officials appear to be a common feature of reform programs. Local government officials may have vested interest in retaining control over important resources such as crop taxes and transport contracts with the local parastatal. Ranking officials can exploit poorly informed traders by adding fictitious fees or regulations to their own advantage.[6] They may also be under pressure to protect local cooperatives from the impending competition by private traders. Finally, there are local officials who have yet to be converted to the reformist creed and who maintain their belief that government should control markets.[7]

One residual form of market control has been licensing. While licensing has been restrictive in some countries, in most places it has functioned as a means for governments to monitor private activity and a source of supplemental income for poorly paid civil servants. In Madagascar, local officials continue to impose a wide range of restrictions on traders, limiting their numbers and requiring them to issue regular reports on purchases and stocks.[8] In Tanzania, the initial licensing of private cashew nut traders was done without undermining the operations of cooperative unions and was used as a revenue-raising exercise by certain local officials. In Kenya, many prospective milk processors have received no answer on their license applications, ostensibly to protect the market of a parastatal whose restructuring has been imminent for several years. In contrast, most processors of higher value dairy

---

[5] See Thompson (1992) and Coulter and Golob (1992).
[6] Holtzman et al. (1992).
[7] For example, in Mozambique, while price controls on most commodities have been formally lifted at the national level, in many localities such controls have been retained (Sahn and Sarris 1994).
[8] See for example Berg (1989).

products regularly obtain license approvals and renewals, though informal payments are essential to prevent delay.[9] Such policy uncertainty and residual market controls deter private investment, especially in costly processing and trading facilities which are specialized for handling 'decontrolled' commodities. Investors are more inclined to lease facilities or use general purpose warehouses and equipment until the direction and end of policy reforms are clearer.

Although present in all societies, problems of bureaucratic delays and official corruption are especially severe in many African countries and contribute to the obstacles facing private sector development. While from a purely economic standpoint they provide some redress to unsustainably low civil service pay scales, corruption functions as a major impediment to private processing and trading activity, raising its costs considerably.

Several different forms of corruption are common.[10] One involves the issue of payments to officials in order to reduce the time for them to complete the procedures for issuing licenses, certificates, and other trade or financial documentation. The trader may face a trade-off between the direct costs of such payments and the opportunity costs associated with a delay. A second form involves payments for illicit services such as official sanctioning of extra-legal activities. This would apply to official disregard for faulty and overloaded vehicles, unsanitary processing and trading facilities, mislabeling of products, and 'loss' or falsification of trading and financial documents. A third form of corruption is outright extortion where payments are needed to prevent arrest, confiscation of goods or other severe penalties due to trumped up charges.

The actual payments and opportunity costs incurred by processors and traders will vary by country and type of activity. Kulibaba and Holtzman (1990) found such costs to be particularly high for the trade in live animals between Sahalian and Coastal West African countries. They estimated aggregated corruption costs to be CFA 2500–7000 per head of cattle and CFA 1500–2500 per small ruminant. These figures represent 10–20% of market-

---

[9] The literature on grain market reform mentions the continuation of quantitative restrictions on trade. This appears to be less common for high value food commodities, although (unenforceable) limitations have been placed on the volume of trade which Kenyan dairies and Tanzanian cashew nut traders can handle.

[10] This discussion is based on Kulibaba and Holtzman (1990). The analytics of this issue are also covered by Klitgaard (1988).

ing costs. They found that traders have adopted three, non-mutually exclusive strategies to reduce corruption-related costs and delays. One approach has been to explicitly build estimates of such costs into one's marketing strategy, making adjustments in market destinations and transport modes in order to maximize total returns. A second approach has been to cultivate official patronage through gift-giving as a shield against excessive abuse by minor officials. A third and particularly interesting approach has been the formation of private companies—*sociétés de convoyage*—whose function is to facilitate the movement of goods by negotiating fixed rates of payment to customs, veterinary and other control point officials. Several firms of this type have developed and competition among them has effectively bid down the payments issued to officials.[11]

Infrastructural Constraints

Private processors and traders endure substantial risks, incur considerable costs, and face more general constraints in market development as a result of the inadequate, underdeveloped and sometimes dilapidated state of transport and communications infrastructure in Africa. Infrastructural problems are a major constraint on physical commodity movements and on trader communications within their own country, with neighboring countries and with major trading partners abroad.

The level of physical infrastructure development and the availability of associated assets and services is considerably lower in Africa than in other developing regions. This can be seen in Table 3.1 below, which compares several indicators of infrastructure development and access for selected African and Asian countries. The African countries selected include many of the region's most commercialized economies. Infrastructural indicators for other African countries are considerably worse.

With the exception of Zimbabwe, the African countries listed exhibit far lower rail and road densities, far fewer motorized vehicles, far poorer access to telephone and postal services, dramatically less rural electrification, substantially fewer international flights, and much less international airfreight traffic. Africa's limited road and rail network, together with shortages of ve-

---

[11] While savings on corruption costs are estimated to have declined by 40% per truckload of animals, the conveyers have yet to negotiate standardized rates with uniformed officials (police, army, etc.).

TABLE 3.1: **Comparative Indicators of Infrastructure Development and Access**

Country	Rail and Road Mileage Per 100 Persons (1989/90)	# of Motorized Vehicles per Mile of Paved Road (1989/90)	# of Telephone Main Lines per 1000 Persons (1991)	Average Number of People Served by One Post Office (1986–88)	Percent of Villages with Electricity	Int'l Scheduled Aircraft Departures (000s) (1991)	Int'l Freight Loaded + Unloaded (000 Tons) (1989/90)
Cameroon	Na.	Na.	3.16	33,800	Na.	3	13.7
Côte d'Ivoire	Na.	Na.	5.35	8600	Na.	2	29.7
Kenya	0.30	19.2	7.37	20,900	3	5	54.2
Nigeria	0.73	23.7	2.65	28,400	Na.	6	30.0
Senegal	0.44	12.2	6.05	Na.	4	2	Na.
Tanzania	0.15	14.2	2.80	30,300	Na.	3	5.6
Zimbabwe	1.09	35.7	13.70	24,300	5	3	Na.
Bangladesh	0.07	47.5	1.83	13,200	12	6	Na.
India	0.68	49.0	6.14	4700	61	16	282.5
Indonesia	0.77	Na.	5.22	9900	Na.	24	97.1
Pakistan	0.73	42.5	7.76	8100	62	16	120.7
Philippines	1.65	51.8	10.87	Na.	52	9	Na.
Sri Lanka	1.01	Na.	7.13	4300	Na.	8	38.8

Na. Not available.

SOURCES: Siemens (1992); Civil Aviation Statistics of the World (1991); International Road Transport Union (1990); UNDP Human Development Report (1993); Ahmed and Donovan (1992).

hicles, spare parts and fuel, pose considerable constraints on traders in reaching production areas and market outlets, and in doing so on a timely basis. The direction of roads and especially rail lines reflect colonial trading patterns and biases against certain forms of trade. This is especially true in Southern Africa where most rail lines lead either to South Africa or the sea, and there are no direct rail links between Harare and either Lusaka or Blantyre. Most of the investment earmarked for improving that region's rail systems has gone to corridors used for trade to European and other international destinations. In West Africa, transport links are relatively poor between Anglophone and Francophone countries.

Limited (and frequently unreliable) telephone services and congested mail services are likely to impede long-distance trade and raise trader transaction costs by necessitating alternative, more expensive communication methods (for example, private couriers, CB radio) or more frequent direct visits to producing areas and markets. Communication bottlenecks hinder the responsiveness of traders to new market opportunities and changes in trade partner requirements. Lack of rural (and in some cases urban) electrification places constraints on where processing and storage activities can be located, or else necessitates additional investment in power generators. Breaks in electrification weaken local market demand for highly perishable commodities which require refrigeration and add difficulty and cost to maintaining cold chains for intra-regional trade in meat and fish and for export-oriented horticultural operations.[12]

Compared with Asian countries, most African countries have relatively limited international air carrier traffic, implying barriers or delays in business-related travel and far lower availability of air-freight space for the exportation of high-value perishables. Nigeria, a country with nearly 100 million people and a GDP exceeding $35 billion, has fewer international flights and a lower volume of inward and outward international air freight than Sri Lanka, a country with 17 million people and a GDP one-fifth that of Nigeria. Even with its highly successful tourist industry, Kenya has fewer international scheduled departures than does Bangladesh.

The problem facing African traders and processors is not simply the limited extent of infrastructural development. Difficulties are also caused by its often low or uncertain quality. In most African countries, less than 20% of the

---

[12] On cold chain barriers to increased West African trade in fish and meat, see Infopeche (1990) and Kulibaba and Holtzman (1991).

road area is paved. This proportion is considerably lower in some countries. Where rural roads exist, they are often in extremely poor condition due to inadequate maintenance or initially faulty construction. One study has suggested that about half of Africa's rural road network requires "substantial rehabilitation".[13] Many rural roads are impassable, except perhaps by tractor, during rainy seasons. Yet, these periods often correspond to peak raw material availability (for example, in Kenya's dairy industry and Tanzania's cashew nut industry). Delays in raw material procurement result in waste and reduced efficiency in factory use.

Many African rail lines and services are in a poor state. Holtzman et al. (1992) indicate that declining rail services in Côte d'Ivoire and Burkina Faso are forcing traders to use more expensive transport modes. Similarly in Southern Africa, lack of equipment and spare parts, shortages of locomotive power, lack of maintenance and past sabotage have severely weakened rail freight services. Port facilities in countries such as Angola, Mozambique and Tanzania have lacked the infrastructure, management and freedom from physical attack to operate anywhere near their capacity. Port congestion is a common feature of African ports, as is the risk of product damage or theft during handling and storage.[14] Stories abound about poor airport freight handling and the frequent off-loading of high-value produce onto airport landing tarmacs.

In many countries, government policies have exacerbated the transport bottlenecks faced by agricultural traders and processors. Complex regulations, rate-setting (below market rates), restrictions on how commodities can be transported, obligatory use of parastatal transport services, restrictions on or high landing fees for foreign carrier or charter landings, and other interventions have reduced the availability of passenger and freight services and rendered trader access to such services highly uncertain.

Furthermore, transport costs are higher for African traders and processors than is the case elsewhere. This applies for road, rail and airfreight traffic. Delgado (1992) indicates that due to agricultural transport and other transfer costs, the economic cost of a ton of grain at inland points of consumption in West Africa is frequently twice that at the landed point of entry.

---

[13] Riverson et al. (1991).

[14] Traders in land-locked countries are likely to encounter even greater problems of bureaucracy, delay, and losses in the ports which they use to import or export products. On the major problems of port operations and sea freight logistics in one country (Côte d'Ivoire), see TransExpert (1993).

Russike (1988) reports on a case in which containerized cargo was sent from the United Kingdom to Dar es Salaam at a cost of $80/metric ton, while the cost of transporting the cargo from Dar es Salaam to Lusaka was $103/metric ton. High unit transport costs stem from the high cost of spare parts and fuel, administrative costs and fees for vehicle registration, and very high transaction costs in the form of bribes, extortion and similar behavior on the part of uniformed personnel located at checkpoints, rail stations, marketplaces and borders. These latter payments are especially high for cross-border trade.[15] High transport and associated transaction costs may thus inhibit intra-regional trade.

Air freight rates from African countries to Western Europe are generally higher than those from equally or more distant countries. For example, in early 1992 freight rates per kilogram for floricultural products to Northern European destinations were $1.85 for South Africa, $1.59–$2.00 for Kenya, and $2.54 for Zimbabwe. Compare these to those of Israel ($1.48), the United States-Miami ($1.69), and much more distant Thailand ($2.35).[16]

Weak Financial Market Services

Financial systems in sub-Saharan Africa have traditionally been characterized by weak resource mobilization, low credit repayment rates, high transaction costs and extensive political interference. In many countries, the formal financial sector—comprising commercial, cooperative, development and savings banks—is not well developed. Most African countries have fewer than ten banks and only four countries (Kenya, Nigeria, Zambia and Côte d'Ivoire) have more than five private banks. Together with stringent interest rate controls, sectoral allocations and quantitative prescriptions made by government, this has tended to stifle competition. In some countries, the formal financial sector is but an extension of the fiscal system. Government has a major ownership share in most of the banks, and public sector enterprises receive a large proportion of bank loan funds. It is not difficult to see how private sector lending might be crowded out in such systems.

African governments have attempted to use financial markets to promote targeted activities, frequently through subsidized credit programs. Political patronage has been a common feature of these programs; loans have been

---

[15] See Kulibaba and Holtzman (1990) for examples in the West African livestock trade.

[16] These and other rate differentials stem in part from the lower competition on some African-European routes and the interventions to protect less efficient, parastatal national carriers.

allocated or rationed using non-financial criteria.[17] Most of these programs have been unsuccessful, reaching only a small minority of the intended beneficiaries and not contributing to the development of sustainable financial systems. The artificially low (or negative) interest rates imposed under these programs have distorted financial markets and often weakened the capacity of the participating institutions to perform other services.

Lack of access to formal credit on affordable terms is widely cited as a constraint on private enterprise development, both small and large, within Africa. To take Ghana as an example, one author recently stated that, "Virtually all industrial or small-enterprise surveys have reported high proportions of firms citing lack of access to credit as a major constraint."[18] In a survey of over 10,000 micro-, small- and medium-scale enterprises in Malawi, only 1.2% were found to have taken out loans from formal credit institutions.[19] For Southern Africa generally, a series of recent surveys found that problems of working capital and other financial matters were perceived to exist for a majority of micro- and small enterprises during their initial start-up and later phases of growth.[20]

There are a number of reasons why small enterprises have particular difficulty obtaining formal credit or find the cost not worth the effort. Small processing and trading enterprises are frequently unable to provide the collateral required by credit organizations, since most are 'asset-poor' and unable to use as collateral land held under traditional land tenure systems. The requirement for collateral is itself a product of the risks, real or perceived, and the high transaction costs of lending to small enterprises. For the prospective borrower, the transaction costs of acquiring a bank loan may be very high relative to the actual size of the loan. One study estimated that it would cost a Ugandan firm 200,000 Ugandan shillings to prepare the paperwork in order to qualify for a 500,000 shilling overdraft. Understandably, this firm and ones in similar circumstances would choose to refrain from investing or to raise credit from informal sources rather than engaging an expensive bank loan.[21]

---

[17] See for example von Pischke (1991) and Thillairajah (1994).

[18] Cuevas et al. (1993). Their own argument is different from that of the studies mentioned. More generally, see Terpend (1992) and Marsden (1990).

[19] Daniels and Ngwira (1993).

[20] Liedholm and Mead (1993). The 'problems of working capital' generally scored higher than 'credit and finance', and tend to point towards different policy responses. An informal sector analogue of the findings on Ghana is reviewed below.

[21] ODA/World Bank (1991).

For larger enterprises, a major weakness of African financial markets is the extremely limited availability of long term finance, especially in local currency. This applies even in countries such as Zimbabwe and Kenya whose financial markets are relatively well developed. The imposition of interest rate ceilings and stringent liquidity requirements on commercial and merchant banks, together with the short term nature of most bank liabilities, are some of the reasons for the limited availability of medium to long term loans. Two additional factors working against agro-industrial entrepreneurs are the perceived high risk of their activities and the limited skills to appraise and advise agribusiness ventures that are generally found in financial institutions.[22] The above weaknesses in formal financial markets inhibit private agribusiness investment in Africa and the ability of individual firms to respond to market opportunities both at home and abroad.

Lack of formal credit has to be put into the context of the overall financial arrangements of enterprises. There are distinct and highly visible forms of informal credit, such as rotating savings and credit associations, consisting of members with social, ethnic, employment or other bonds. Research in Cameroon suggests that these associations handle more deposits than do commercial banks.[23] It is common for ethnic minorities (for example, Asians in Kenya)[24] to form them in order to finance even large business ventures. Still, few such associations are able to provide term finance. Hence, risk capital for small and medium-scale enterprises must generally come from the personal savings of entrepreneurs and their families, and funds for expansion or facility modernization typically come from the same personal savings and retained earnings.

CHARACTERISTICS OF PRIVATE TRADERS AND PROCESSORS IN AFRICA

The private sector in Africa displays great diversity. Categories which structure and organize this experience help us grasp the range and variety of endeavors in all their complexity. Thus, private enterprises can be placed along a continuum from informal to formal. The concept of the 'informal sec-

---

[22] While offshore hard currency loans might be available, the exchange rate risks are considerable.

[23] Schreider (1989).

[24] The term ethnic minorities is used here to denote any identifiable group trading outside its home area, even if they form the largest single ethnic group in the country (e.g. Sudanese Arabs, Kenyan Kikuyu).

tor' has been widely used since its enthusiastic adoption by the International Labor Organization in the 1970s, but has rarely been satisfactorily defined, certainly not as a discrete entity.[25] By treating 'formality-informality' as a continuum, the problem of definition is largely avoided, and much of the literature does this. Enterprises will be placed near the informal end of the continuum if: (1) they are not registered or licensed by any government department, (2) their activity is unrecorded in official statistics, (3) they operate at a low or artisanal level of technology, and/or (4) if they have few employees or hold limited assets.[26]

Private sector activities after primary agricultural production take many forms. These will be grouped for analytic purposes under four categories:

- Simple trade (e.g. trade in raw milk, fresh fruit, landed fish)
- Intermediate activities (e.g. icing of fish, refrigerated transport, packing of fruit)
- Artisanal processing (e.g. fish salting and smoking, cheese-making, sun-drying of fruit)
- Industrial processing (e.g. fish and fruit canning, milk pasteurization)

In this section we examine selected characteristics of private traders and processors. The discussion points up the importance of foreign and ethnic minority companies in certain lines of formal trade and the predominance of women in small-scale trading and artisanal processing in certain parts of the region. These very features of African high-value food processing and trade have brought strong social and political considerations into the discussion about market liberalization and private sector support. While analysis of market liberalization and privatization is usually couched in terms of enhancing economic efficiency, the real concerns about privatization relate to class, gender, ethnicity and the related political questions of ownership, authority and control.

Local vs Foreign Ownership

In the period prior to World War II, much of Africa's external trade in primary agricultural commodities was handled by European trading companies

---

[25] See Hart (1987) for a discussion.

[26] Obviously, an enterprise may be formal in the light of some of these characteristics and informal in regard to others. Enterprises can comply with all legal regulations, but still be small in scale. They can operate on a large-scale but use simple technology, or the reverse. It is also possible that enterprises be regarded as legal by one branch of government, but not by another.

which operated with the support and protection of metropolitan and colonial governments.[27] In countries featuring a sizable European settler population, the colonialists were often successful in using the powers of the colonial state to control the domestic marketing of cereals and dairy products in order to limit competition from indigenous producers and traders.[28] In some countries a business class which had come originally from overseas, such as the Lebanese in West Africa and the Indians and Arabs in East and Southern Africa, played an important role in export and domestic agricultural trade, frequently as an intermediary between European companies and African producers and consumers.

During World War II and up through the early years of African independence, marketing boards and other parastatal organizations were created. Official efforts to promote the development of cooperatives, and licensing and credit measures to promote the indigenization of trade and services (for example, 'Kenyanization', 'Nigerianization'), counterbalanced and diminished the relative importance of foreign agricultural trading and processing companies. The specific ownership and ethnic composition of private enterprises remain important concerns in Africa and come up frequently during discussions of market liberalization and privatization. At issue both within and beyond African governments is whether market liberalization will result in renewed dominance of foreign companies and particular ethnic groups (both African and non-African) in agricultural trade with the corresponding undesirable economic and political consequences associated with inequality, non-representation and lack of accountability.[29]

In almost all African countries, a large proportion of processing and trade geared toward the domestic food market is currently undertaken by indigenous firms and individuals. This segment of the private sector predominates in small-scale and informal activities which service the majority of local consumers (especially rural consumers). In Nigeria, Sudan, Ghana and Malawi, there are numerous indigenous firms among medium-to-large-scale food processors and non-traditional agricultural exporters, though in Nigeria and Ghana the largest private firms tend to be subsidiaries of multinational corporations.[30] In most other countries, foreign or non-indigenous ethnic minor-

---

[27] See Bauer (1954) and van der Laan (1987) for West Africa, and Martin (1973) and Swainson (1980) for East Africa.

[28] For the experiences in Zimbabwe and Kenya, see Mosley (1983).

[29] This issue is discussed by Abbott (1987), Berg (1987), and Schatz (1987).

[30] In Nigeria, the permissible foreign ownership share in many food processing industries is limited to 40–60%.

TABLE 3.2: **Foreign Ownership, Management, and Employment in the Food Processing Industry of Côte d'Ivoire (1985)**

Sub-Sector	% Foreign Ownership	% Foreign Senior Management	% Foreign Skilled Workers	% Foreign Unskilled Workers
Edible Oils	7	30	18	36
Food Preparations	74	}		
		}		
Fish Processing	69	} (for all sub-sectors combined)		
		} 34 23 76		
Meat Processing	52	}		
		}		
Fruit/Vegetable Processing	29	}		
		}		

SOURCE: République de Côte d'Ivoire, Ministre d'Industrie (1988).

ity firms are generally the largest private exporters and processors of high value foods. This is reflected in both ownership and senior managerial patterns (see Table 3.2 for the case of Côte d'Ivoire). In a number of countries, large multi-product and multi-sectoral conglomerates with interlocking directorates account for large shares of trade, manufacturing activities and employment (Box 3.1). A portion of these conglomerates are locally owned; others feature a mixture of foreign and local interests.

Over the past decade, foreign investment has generally been stagnant or declining in sub-Saharan Africa. Net flows of private capital (in 1980 US$) into the region averaged only $363 million over the 1986–90 period, down from $482 million in 1981–85 and from $694 million in the previous decade. Only a few individual countries have experienced an increase in foreign investment (for example, Mauritius and Lesotho and more recently, Uganda), whereas many more have experienced negative net foreign direct investment in recent years.[31] Investment data specific for agro-processing and trade are not available, though they are unlikely to differ significantly from the broader trends.[32]

---

[31] Ghana is one country which has experienced an increase in foreign investment since the mid-1980s. However, the food, beverage and tobacco industries have been the target of little of this investment. While these industries account for some 38% of manufactured value added, they represent only 18% of approved foreign investment over the 1986–90 period (Lall et al., 1993).

[32] Rhee et al. (1993).

Box 3.1: MULTI-SECTORAL CONGLOMERATES

Examples of conglomerates playing important roles in local food processing industries are found throughout the region. Some of these conglomerates are publicly owned, e.g. ZIMCO in Zambia and the Agricultural Development Authority in Zimbabwe. Others are entirely private.

A Ghanaian mining company initially invested in agriculture in order to feed its workers and their families. Facing declining mineral prices, the firm subsequently diversified into commercial production of maize, vegetables, cattle, poultry and fish, as well as the production and export of pineapples. In Uganda, one firm combines industrial good distribution operations (for petroleum products, vehicles, tractors) with extensive agribusiness activities. The latter include dairy, spices, fruit, and oilseed production, grain milling, tea and coffee processing/packing, and fish processing and export. In Mozambique, multi-sectoral firms play major roles in certain agro-industries. For instance, one firm has sizeable interests in automobile distribution, cashew nut processing, vegetable oil production, forestry products and cotton.

The large physical assets of such firms, their well-developed distribution channels and their favorable access to finance (including offshore finance) provide them with considerable advantages over their competitors in individual markets.

Despite macroeconomic reforms and adjustments in investment codes in many African countries, potential foreign investors continue to have negative images of and imperfect information on the business environment in Africa.[33] The majority of the foreign companies now operating food processing and marketing subsidiaries in Africa have been located there since the 1960s or earlier. The experience within our case study industries as well as wider anecdotal evidence suggests that much of the new agribusiness investment over the past decade by foreign companies has been made by firms which have already been established for a long time within the countries where they are operating. Investments have been geared toward expanding existing capacity and trade or toward diversifying product lines away from commodities facing adverse market trends. For example, Kenya has witnessed the

---

[33] Rhee et al. (1993).

diversification of foreign-owned tea, coffee and sisal companies into horticul-tural production and trade. In Ghana, several mining companies have in-vested in pineapple production and exports.

Much of the incremental involvement of foreign companies in the process-ing and marketing of high-value foods in Africa has not occurred through conventional investments in subsidiaries. It has taken other forms including: (1) management and marketing contracts with existing public and private companies, (2) equipment supply, consultancy services and technical contracts, frequently under the aegis of donor-funded projects, and (3) joint ventures with parastatal or local private enterprises (see Box 3.2). These arrangements have enabled foreign firms to profit from their own technical experience, mar-keting expertise and linkages, while incurring considerably lower risk than that associated with a 'green field' direct investment. In many recent export-oriented ventures, European import and distribution firms have entered into partnerships with local entrepreneurs, assuming a minority equity stake and making arms-length arrangements for marketing.

Ethnicity

Ethnicity is a very visible and much discussed characteristic of actors in food marketing and processing. Private traders may be ethnically distinct from the mass of the population because they are:

(a) *settlers identified with the former colonial power*, such as 'Europeans' in Kenya and Zimbabwe;

(b) *members of other non-African minorities*: the Asians in East Africa and the Lebanese in West Africa are the best known examples.[34] These communities occupied an intermediate position in the colonial economic and social structure between the Africans and the colonial power.

(c) *members of ethnic groups from other African countries*: this category includes traders from the Sahelian countries active in the livestock trade in coastal West Africa, Yoruba in Ghana; and Mauritanians in Senegal until their forcible removal in 1989.[35]

---

[34] Greeks in the Nile Valley and Central Africa, and Yemenis on the East African coast (see Le Guennec-Coppens 1989) are two other examples.

[35] Associated with this category but not traders or processors in a strict sense, are Somali trans-porters elsewhere in East Africa, and Ghanaian and Senegalese migrant fishing communities else-where in West Africa.

Box 3.2: CAMEROON: YES, WE NOW HAVE BANANAS!

Technical and marketing contracts between parastatal agricultural enterprises and foreign capital can under certain conditions amount to the virtual privatization of the enterprise. This has happened with the production of bananas by the Cameroon Development Corporation (CDC). Production on CDC's Ekona estate had fallen to 10,000 tons per year in 1987 from a peak of 16,000 eight years earlier. This was symptomatic of the decline of banana production in the whole country due to the failure of the state marketing board, the Office Camerounais de la Banane, to organize export opportunities and to provide effective crop protection services. As a result, Cameroon was at risk of losing its share of the French banana market.

The solution adopted by CDC was to enter into a technical and marketing contract with the Del Monte Group to cover the operation of a new plantation over the period 1987–1994. Under the contract, Del Monte agreed to buy the entire production, subject to quality, for CDC's cost price FOB, plus a bonus of CFA 15/kg. Del Monte also agreed to provide an interest-free loan of $12 million, to be repaid by withholding CFA 7.5 per kg. of bananas. Del Monte was to provide technical assistance entirely at its own cost. Its interests in this contract were to diversify its own sources of production and to use existing agreements between Cameroon and France to penetrate European markets. The contract enabled it to do this without direct investment and without becoming involved in the bureaucratic problem of registering as a Cameroonian company and acquiring land. By contracting to buy from a new plantation, it also avoided any involvement in reducing the workforce at Ekona.

The company's interest in reducing costs quickly transformed its 'technical assistance' into a complete management service, including total control of loaned funds, though this was not foreseen in the contract. In particular, it introduced computerized control systems and used Cameroonian private firms, rather than CDC, for construction work, transport and maintenance. The contract has been successful in improving quality and reducing costs of Cameroonian bananas. The Cameroon government has adopted a procedure that avoids some of the political and administrative problems of outright privatization, but still sees its share of the profits subsidizing other CDC losses. It has been suggested that similar contracts elsewhere could involve the sale of assets to the foreign partner after a certain period of successful operation.

SOURCE: Grouitch (1992).

d) *members of ethnic groups originating within the country concerned, but conspicuously successful in trading outside their home areas:* the Bamileke in Cameroon, Chagga in Tanzania, Kikuyu in Kenya and Gurage in Ethiopia are all good examples.

Members of the first three categories are defined by some sense of 'outsider' status to the countries in which they live and trade, even though some or all the members of these communities may be born in those countries and be citizens of them. This differs from case to case, according to the history of the community and the politics of the host country. For instance, many Lebanese in Senegal now hold Senegalese nationality exclusively, whereas no Lebanese in Sierra Leone (except for those of mixed parentage) have Sierra Leonean nationality.[36] Nor does a long history of settlement and national status necessarily relate to how these groups are perceived by the majority population or by governments. Malawian Asians, for example, are generally thought of as Malawian citizens, but are still subject to specific legal restrictions on their economic activity.

There is ample evidence that ethnic minorities are particularly active in many sector markets. In Lagos' main livestock market in 1991, for example, 41% of the traders were Hausa, either from Northern Nigeria or neighboring countries, and a further 49% were from other identifiably Moslem ethnic groups.[37] In the early 1980s Bamileke made up 50% of food traders in Yaounde's Mokolo market and 36% of an aggregate sample from the city's five major markets.[38] The seventh chapter discusses the prominent role of Kenyan Asians in that country's fruit and vegetable export trade over the past thirty years. The continuing ability of Tanzanian Asians to find new economic opportunities is documented in Chapter IV.

There can be no single explanation for the success of such diverse groups, and many of the explanations advanced by concerned politicians and disgruntled competitors are little more than prejudices. The success in trade of certain ethnic minorities can be related to their development of mutual credit and information sharing institutions (see Box 3.3), their capacity for innovation, their association with specific commodities, the conditions in their region of origin, and resistance to extra-economic pressures.

---

[36] Boumedouha (1990), van der Laan (1975).
[37] Kulibaba (1991).
[38] Dongmo (1983).

One of the most important advantages of belonging to an ethnic minority is the tendency of members to give each other mutual support through pooling market information, providing credit and informally contracting to secure supplies and markets. Moreover, these arrangements are enforceable through community pressure.[39] Traders outside their home areas have an additional advantage in being able to resist extra-economic demands that a trader from the area would accede to: demands for loans—perhaps interest-free—gifts, lower prices, etc. Yemeni retailers in northeast Sudan are a good example of this.[40] Ethnic minorities who have left their home regions are also likely to depart from their traditional economic and social patterns. They may be willing to experiment with new commodities, techniques and ways of doing business. The Lebanese who settled in Sierra Leone are a good example. They fulfilled a vital function by developing a new unwritten law of business practice that was neither traditional nor colonial.[41]

A simple explanation for the concentration of some ethnic minorities in certain sub-sectors is that the commodities are produced by the same group, or that the group has particular handling or processing skills. This is especially marked with livestock where people from pastoralist societies are most likely to have the skills needed for herding and handling. The success of Kenyan Asians in the trade of 'Asian vegetables' (for example, okra, bitter gourd and chilies) is not surprising given their detailed knowledge of the quality, storage and consumption properties of these vegetables.

A common but by no means universal factor is that successful trading minorities come from agriculturally poor and/or land-hungry areas. Members of these groups were forced at some point to seek careers away from home and then graduated from petty trade into larger-scale trade. The Bamileke, for whom land-hunger is exacerbated by primogeniture, fit this paradigm well as do the Chagga in Tanzania and the Kikuyu in Kenya.[42]

Beyond these generalizations, there are further specific reasons for each minority's success: links to political power (for example, white settlers, Arabs

---

[39] These characteristics are described for a long-distance trading network in Cohen's classic study of Hausa livestock traders in Ibadan (1969).

[40] Morton (1989).

[41] van der Laan (1975).

[42] Brenner et al. (1990). The Gurage of Ethiopia present a variation on this theme. Their particular cultivation system based on the 'false-banana' could support high population densities, but did not produce any marketable commodities. Thus, they were pushed towards urban wage-labor, and from there, moved on to trade (Baker 1992).

Box 3.3: SUDAN: A TRADITIONAL MERCHANT CLASS

Sudan's position on the Nile Valley trade route between sub-Saharan Africa and the Mediterranean world, and its peculiar colonial history, have led to the continued domination of a traditional merchant class associated with the dominant ethnic group, the Arabs, and the relative absence of the public sector in agricultural marketing.

While long-distance trade was practiced in a variety of forms by the pre-colonial states of Central and Western Sudan and by nineteenth-century Egyptian and European adventurers, the present trading system experienced its critical development during the Condominium period (1898–1956). As rural production systems became more integrated into the cash economy, and as transport across the huge and varied country became easier, family trading enterprises from Northern Sudan spread out into the rest of the country as agents and beneficiaries of these integrating trends. These traders have been referred to since the seventeenth century as *jellaba*, a term connoting both an occupation and an ethnic identity.

Condominium policies were not, on the face of it, beneficial to the *jellaba*. British trading houses, and a tier of smaller Greek and Syrian enterprises, were allowed to dominate official import and export, and much wholesaling. *Jellaba* access to many more remote areas was administratively blocked to prevent the spread of Islam and Arabic culture, and out of a paternalistic concern to protect rural people from the 'over-sophisticated' traders.

Nevertheless, during this time *jellaba* traders were spreading all over the country, setting up small shops to buy agricultural produce and sell consumer goods. Typically, expansion was by junior family members being given credit, or agency contracts with the family business, to set up new trading posts. In the peripheral areas, *jellaba* maintained an ethnic exclusiveness and solidarity. Services such as credit and the forwarding of goods were exchanged on a less than strictly commercial basis within the community (credit was also given to farmers but in the form of crop-mortgage contracts concealing high interest rates). Primary loyalty, however, was to the family and its trading concern, reinforced by continuous personal links to the home village in the North.

The Condominium government intervened remarkably little in agricultural marketing, though it was heavily involved in production of cotton, the major export crop. The gum arabic, livestock, and oilseed trades were significant (Sudan is the world's leading producer of both gum arabic and sesame) and wholly in the hands of the private sector. Through these trades, some Sudanese, either themselves from *jellaba* backgrounds, or taking advantage of *jellaba* collection networks, were able to establish themselves among the country's wealthiest men. Camel-drawn sesame presses producing a crude oil for refining in Britain gave very high returns for low investment and were a key pathway for agricultural traders to diversify into industry.

Independence and the early policies of the Nimeiri regime in 1969–1971 led to the departure of many foreign businesses, and *jellaba* businesses expanded and diversified to fill the gap. *Jellaba* had in fact been diversifying into agricultural production for decades, but were quick to seize new state-sponsored opportunities in mechanized cotton and sorghum production. It was also business of *jellaba* origin that invested in and became licensed collecting agents for the new semi-public monopoly companies that were founded to control the gum arabic and oilseed trades.

While an important minority of Sudanese businessmen are of Middle-Eastern or Greek origin, and while foreign, particularly Gulf Arab, capital is investing in the agricultural and agro-industrial sectors, the *jellaba* tradition and *jellaba* networks are still vitally important. Tradition is seen in continuing patterns of expansion and vertical integration through family and ethnic ties, and a widespread preference, even before they were imposed by law, for financial practices that avoid the form of fixed-rate interest. The Sudanese private sector historically has seen far fewer restrictions than in many other countries, and even where the state does intervene, the ethnic groups from which the *jellaba* have sprung are those that dominate the government. There is therefore an important political dimension; domination of trading networks by *jellaba* has helped fuel Sudan's explosive ethnic tensions.

SOURCES: Manger (1984); Mahmoud (1984).

in Sudan, Kikuyu in Kenya[43]) and links to export markets (whites and Asians in East Africa). During the colonial period, Asians and Lebanese using family labor penetrated to remote areas and performed a labor-intensive collection function which Europeans were not prepared to do. These minorities also had the trading skills that rural Africans did not at that time possess.[44]

The dominance in certain sectors of ethnic minorities, particularly those from outside the country in question, raises concerns and fears among gov-

---

[43] Some governments may actively favor a business class that is 'foreign' and therefore politically powerless: the Asians in Kenya (under Moi) and the Lebanese in Senegal (Boumedouha 1990) were so encouraged.

[44] Bryceson (1993), van der Laan (1975).

ernments and local populations. The mutual trust and information-pooling within minorities are interpreted as collusion and price-fixing, and the opening of markets in remote areas as exploitation, though there is little evidence that ethnic minorities *per se* are more (or less) guilty of these charges than other traders.[45] At a national level, non-African minorities are often accused of illegal export of capital, yet again there is little evidence that they indulge in this more than indigenous elites. Governments may feel that non-African minorities do not cooperate with official pricing policies, but this may be because the policies are inconsistent with prevailing conditions of supply and demand.

Yet, even if these fears are unfounded, they may still have real effects on government policy. The whole drift to state-controlled trade in British East Africa is partially explicable by fears that Asians would dominate an open market[46], and these fears are still an influence, largely unacknowledged, on government views of liberalization in East Africa. Some attempts at positive discrimination towards indigenous (that is, non-Asian) businesses have been made by East African governments (see Chapter VII), but these tend to favor political elites rather than genuine entrepreneurs.

Gender

Throughout Africa, women are responsible for a great deal of informal sector activity in food marketing and processing. Given their predominant role in food production and in domestic food preparation, this is hardly surprising. Women's involvement is most visible in West Africa. In Ghana, trading is considered to be part of everyday life for 80% of urban women. The central market in Kumasi, the country's largest and the key to national food distribution, has over 15,000 traders, 70% of whom are women.[47] This is a phenomenon repeated on a smaller scale across Ghana and West Africa.[48] One important feature of West African women traders is the degree to which they are organized among themselves by hierarchies which culminate in the 'market

---

[45] Bryceson (1993) gives the example of a colonial administrator in Tanganyika who considered food prices charged by Asians in a remote area as excessive and as evidence of collusion, but was unable to match them using government transport on a no-profit basis. Haaland (1984) provides useful counter-arguments to charges brought against Sudanese *jellaba*.

[46] Bryceson (1993).

[47] Clark (1988, 1992).

[48] Dongmo (1983) found that 67% of traders on the Yaounde food markets were women.

queens' (see Chapter VIII). Women also have a virtual monopoly on a range of artisanal processing activities.

Women do not dominate marketplace trade in the same way in Eastern and Southern Africa; their involvement in food marketing and processing is less visible and is assumed to be more related to recent economic and social trends.[49] It is nonetheless diverse and very significant, both in simple trade and in artisanal processing. Women traders assure supplies of camel milk for Mogadishu and are well represented in food markets in Zambia. As sellers of cooked offal, they are an important source of food for urban workers in Cape Town.[50] In Tanzanian towns a large proportion of low-income and middle-income women engage in some cash-earning activity, many of which involve high value food commodities. A similar pattern is found in rural areas. A review of recent studies of micro-enterprises shows the importance of female ownership (Table 3.3).

Women's activities in food marketing and processing vary according to the commodities available and cultural patterns, but several sectors stand out. For example, artisanal processing of fish—salting, sun-drying and smoking—is associated with women throughout Africa. In many areas, women process fish caught by male family members, but they may also buy, process and sell in their own right, and loan money to their husbands and other men for boats and equipment. Some may graduate to become wholesalers or transporters. Women are also quick to become involved in new activities of clam and oyster collection.[51]

TABLE 3.3: **Ownership of Micro-Enterprises in Eastern and Southern Africa by Gender**

Gender of Proprietors (%)	Botswana	Kenya	Lesotho	Malawi	S. Africa	Swaziland	Zimbabwe
Female	75	43	73	46	62	84	67
Male	19	53	25	52	32	12	32
Mixed	6	4	2	3	6	4	2

SOURCE: Liedholm and Mead (1993).

---

[49] Tovo (1991).
[50] Herren (1990), Due and White-Jones (1989), Karaan and Myburgh (1992).
[51] Randall (n.d.), Cormier-Salem (1992).

The palm oil sector in West Africa is sharply separated into industrial and artisanal sub-sectors. Artisanal processing is done by women throughout the region.[52] Although manioc lies outside the definition of high-value foods adopted in this study, artisanal processing of this tuber, principally into the roasted granules known as *gari* in Ghana and Nigeria, is a major female activity across West Africa. Where mechanized (but still small-scale) techniques have been introduced, there has been some move into the sub-sector by men, but women are still dominant in every stage of processing and selling.[53]

The small-scale sale of milk and dairy products is a female activity in many areas, especially since managing the milk supply for the family's own consumption is a female role in many pastoral and agro-pastoral societies.[54] In some countries, men are equally involved, particularly in itinerant, urban milk sales on donkey or bicycle.

Women's participation in informal processing and trade depends largely on cultural traditions which vary throughout Africa—social restrictions on movement, the ability of women to keep separate budgets from their husbands, and the extension of domestic tasks. These economic activities have gained the importance they have because they serve the needs of society at large. One advantage of female marketing networks is their flexibility. Women traders in Ghana cultivate contacts among producers in different areas, deal in small quantities and in different crops as the year progresses, and will move into processing quickly if the supply of fresh produce is interrupted.[55] Such flexibility derives primarily from the long hours women are prepared to work for relatively low returns.[56] This in turn probably reflects their lack of access to more lucrative employment or investment opportunities.

Women make up a much smaller proportion of entrepreneurs in the formal sector than in the informal sector. To some extent this is definitional: women's enterprises, even if large in scale and with substantial fixed assets, risk being labeled as informal because they are women's. There is also a shortage of information, other than anecdotal, on women in the formal sector (see Boxes 3.4 and 3.5).

---

[52] Ay (1990), Devautour (1990).

[53] NRI (1992).

[54] Kerven (1987), Waters-Bayer (1985).

[55] Clark (1992). See also Ali-Gaye et al. (1989).

[56] Due and White-Jones (1989) show that market women in Zambia spend longer hours at their trade than farming women do in the fields, although their overall working day is shorter.

Box 3.4: SMALL-SCALE FOOD PROCESSING BY WOMEN:
***DADDAWA* IN NIGERIA**

Throughout the West African savanna, *daddawa* (also known as *soumbara*) is regularly used as a protein-rich seasoning in soups, stews and porridge. Traditionally made from locust beans, in Nigeria *daddawa* is now derived primarily from soybeans. While soybean cultivation is done both by men and women, the processing of soybeans into *daddawa* and its subsequent distribution is performed almost entirely by middle-aged women.

Processing technologies are relatively simple and low cost, involving the frying, mashing and boiling of the bean. While in some villages, processing and marketing are undertaken by groups, in others, these activities are done by individuals alone. Some *daddawa* production is for home use, 75% or more is sold commercially. Periodic market days have been set up at the village level, plus sales are made in the main towns of central Nigeria. From there, *daddawa* is transported to the main towns in the south and north of the country and even as far as Niger, Cameroon and Chad. Even though *daddawa* processing and trade provides an important source of income for several thousand women in parts of Kwara and Kaduna States, this cottage industry is largely unrecorded in official statistics.

SOURCES: Chuke et al. (1985); Mebrahtu and Hahn (1986); Waters-Bayer (1988).

The flourishing informal sector in certain West Africa countries provides a basis for some women to move on to more formal trade and processing. In Ghana, several women fish traders have become lorry owners, and a number now own one or more ocean going vessels with foreign captains.[57] At least one industrial fish processing plant in Ghana is owned by a woman. Cameroon also has a relatively high proportion of women entrepreneurs, but those in the formal sector are concentrated in small- and medium-scale enterprises. As entrepreneurs, they gain only a small proportion of government loans targeted at that sector.[58] Several of Kenya's small, peri-urban dairy processing firms are owned and/or managed by women, including one that is considered to be the most dynamic single company.

---

[57] Randall (n.d.); Marsden (1990).
[58] UNECA (1987).

Box 3.5: A MULTI-PURPOSE PRIVATE COOPERATIVE IN MOZAMBIQUE

The Union of Cooperatives (UGC) is a private enterprise. Started in 1980 with the support of foreign NGOs, the UGC bought and rehabilitated farms and facilities formerly owned by state enterprises. The UGC now manages its own feed mill, hatchery, broiler breeding houses, and equipment workshop, while providing input supply, extension, and marketing services to 181 cooperatives and some 6000 smallholder farmers located in the green zones around Maputo.

While the Union's initial activities centered around pig and horticultural production and marketing, since 1988, poultry production, processing, and sales have been the backbone of its operations. Union sales of poultry increased from zero in 1988 to 1200 tons of meat in 1991. While for several years (including critical food shortage years, 1984–1987) the cooperative movement played a major role in the supply of food to Maputo, more recently it has taken the lead in responding to more liberal market policies on the part of government and to the improved security situation.

The UGC is led by an Italian priest, working full-time on a voluntary basis. Its board of directors and most of its 960 workers are women, as are most of the smallholders whom it serves. The UGC's recent financial results have been very favorable. Profits have been used to invest in social programs, including some 35 infant nurseries attached to the cooperatives and a secondary school (for 1200 students) for the benefit of families in the cooperatives.

SOURCE: FAO (1991) "Women's Cooperative Development in Maputo Green Zone".

Women entrepreneurs face many problems in surviving in the market and in expanding and formalizing their businesses. A problem frequently cited is the availability of credit. Women may have problems negotiating with credit agencies entirely staffed by men. They may be specifically prohibited from applying for credit in their own right. Or they may not have the necessary collateral for loans, especially in societies where they cannot own land. There are donor-funded credit programs targeted at women both for the formal and informal sectors, but much work needs to be done before women in sectors such as food processing will have generalized access to sustainable credit institutions.

Another problem is the possibility, as mechanical technology is introduced, that women will lose control to men of their roles in processing. Men may also gain control of niche markets targeted at expatriates and the middle classes.[59]

A broader problem is overtly political, and it is a combination of the physical vulnerability of women traders and a lack of understanding among decision-makers of their role. There is a widespread assumption that simple trade is a parasitic activity. Yet, this ignores the risk-bearing, collection and de-bulking functions of petty traders. This assumption becomes more potent when held by men about women, particularly in societies where petty trade is primarily associated with women. Thus, there have been repeated calls by Cameroonian academics for the suppression of the female petty traders known as *buy'em sell'em*.[60] Such calls have been translated into action in Tanzania and Ghana. Militants of the first Rawlings regime in Ghana attacked women traders in 1979 and subsequently proved unable to negotiate respectfully with women's leaders, causing serious disruption to food supply all over the country. Such occurrences are only particularly extreme examples of the widespread incomprehension of and hostility towards women's trading roles.

TRADER AND PROCESSOR RAW MATERIAL PROCUREMENT ARRANGEMENTS

One of the major challenges facing private traders and processors lies in the procurement of raw materials in the quantity and quality required at the necessary time and at a cost that enables the firm to profit from its own value-adding services. Failure to properly manage this interaction with the primary productive sector will limit the ability of traders and processors to operate efficiently and develop markets.[61]

Failure to stimulate increased raw material production and to coordinate it with processing and trading requirements is a severe and widespread problem in sub-Saharan Africa. It is one of the major reasons why most of the region's medium- to large-scale food processing facilities have operated at

---

[59] As with Congolese vegetable traders (Ali-Gaye et al. 1989).

[60] Dongmo (1983) makes such a proposal.

[61] An evaluation of the experience of the International Finance Corporation in agricultural processing and storage emphasized the significance of raw material supply problems in undermining the performance of numerous ventures. Raw material availability, price, quality and unpredictability were all problems, especially in ventures relying on 'non-captive' sources, that is, where suppliers could sell to alternative buyers (IFC 1987).

well below their rated capacity, and as a result, incurred relatively high unit processing costs.

Many factors have contributed to this pattern. Some are not enterprise- or industry-specific, but simply part of the overall environment in which African agribusinesses commonly operate. These include the frequent incidence of drought, the impassability of many rural roads, the limited availability of bank finance for crop purchases, and restrictions on imports and land ownership. Others may be specific to a firm or sub-sector, as are price controls, crop movement restrictions, regulations requiring raw material purchases solely from parastatals, the non-availability of key inputs and the poor management of integrated production operations.

Private trader and processor strategies to procure raw materials have taken several, non-mutually exclusive forms. One strategy has been to *import raw materials* rather than organize supplies locally. This approach predominates in the dairy industries in much of West Africa. A combination of ecology, geography and policy has rendered it easier and less costly to import powdered milk and butter oil for local reconstitution, rather than organize local raw milk collection systems. Overvalued currencies, the availability of milk powder through aid programs or at subsidized rates, donor financing of reconstitution plants, and the failure of programs to promote local milk delivery have all contributed to this pattern. Imports of fish, beef and oilseeds are also important for the food processing industries in many African countries, although to a lesser extent than for dairy industries. In Nigeria and Côte d'Ivoire, imports accounted for 35% and 25%, respectively, of the raw materials used in their food and beverage processing sectors during the mid-1980s.[62]

When firms are highly dependent upon imported raw materials, they face risks associated with sudden and prolonged bans or restrictions on imports, controls on access to foreign exchange and sharp currency movements. This happened in Nigeria during the 1980s. When it does, in order to maintain access to imported raw materials, frequently firms resort to smuggling and remunerating licensing and customs officials. Port congestion and other difficulties related to physical logistics are also common problems encountered by firms reliant upon imported raw materials.

---

[62] Data for Nigeria are from a UNIDO study cited by Stevens (1990). Data for Côte d'Ivoire are from Ministrie de l'Industrie studies cited by Riddell (1990).

The second common approach is to procure raw materials and commodities locally through *open market transactions* direct with suppliers or at established market places. This might involve buying runs through production areas, purchases at village market places, or purchases from intermediaries who themselves are in contact with primary producers. While there may be some regularity in buying patterns or in the suppliers they deal with, traders and processors pay current market prices and have no involvement in the primary production process. This approach is commonly used by firms which trade on a part-time or highly seasonal basis, firms for whom raw material quality need not meet very high standards, and firms which operate on too small a scale to warrant making 'investments' in longer-term trading relationships. It is also found among fruit and vegetable processing firms geared toward African domestic markets, which tend to buy during periods of seasonal glut (at low market prices) and then store raw materials in a semi-processed state for use over a longer period.

A variant of market-based procurement is the trader's or processor's use of agents who are either based in the major production areas or have extensive experience and social ties within these areas. The agents act to recruit suppliers (for instance, farmers, fishermen, cooperatives), screen quality, bulk up supplies and manage physical logistics all the way through to delivery to the buyer. The latter is never in direct contact with primary producers.

This type of arrangement operates in the export-oriented cattle marketing channels in Somalia and among private exporters in Tanzania's recently liberalized cashew nut market. In the first case, exporters rely upon a limited number of agents to procure animals from herders and small local traders and to arrange the trekking of those animals to a collection point or to the port for export. The agents partially pay the herders and then incur costs for labor, water, veterinary supplies, etc. during the trek, which they only recover later from the exporters. Without utilizing agents who have in-depth knowledge of producing areas and herders, exporters would be hard pressed to organize their shipments of large numbers of animals on a timely basis. Family and clan-based ties between exporters and agents are common.

In the Tanzanian case, cashew nut exporters have relied upon local trading firms to manage crop procurement in the main production areas and the logistics of preparing the crop for shipment. The exporter indicates the quantities needed and the price which the agents should pay to farmers or cooperatives. Each agent deals exclusively with one exporter, although low grade nuts are sold by the agents to other buyers. In contrast with the Somalia pattern, these agents work on a commission basis. The exporters provide them with large sums of cash in order to pay farmers at the time of purchase. Again, it is not surprising to find that several of the agents are linked to exporters through family ties, or at least have had long-standing trading relationships for other commodities. Cash (in)security is likely to be an important barrier to potential exporters who lack strong ties with traders within the region who are well equipped with transport and other facilities.

Recurrent trading linkages, based on kinship, common origin, habit or simply shared interests are common between primary producers and traders. For example, in the Brazzaville vegetable trade, village-level wholesalers will regularly buy from two or three producers, usually their relatives, and then sell to an urban woman originating from the village. Such a choice of partners is natural within a village setting. The enhanced trust involved also counteracts the effects of distance. A special case of trade between kin occurs widely in artisanal fisheries where fishermen habitually sell to their wives who then process the fish. It should not be assumed that this is anything but strictly commercial—in these communities husbands and wives tend to keep their own budgets. In Ghana the system has the additional feature that wives (or other unrelated women traders) may claim a share of the catch against equity they hold in the fishing boat or unpaid loans for equipment. Recurrent farmer-trader market ties whereby particular traders are given the right of first access to or refusal of supplies are also commonly found in the fresh produce export trades of Kenya and Senegal.[63]

Another common strategy is procurement through *formal contractual ties* with producers. Contract farming is widespread in African agro-industry. A mid-1980s review of the literature on African agriculture and agribusiness identified eighty-eight contract farming schemes in twenty-one countries. Most likely this underestimates its incidence since little information on small-scale, privately organized contracting schemes has been collected. In Kenya and Cameroon, major contract farming schemes have been developed for a half-dozen or more commodities that occupy a central role in these countries' agro-industrial sectors. In at least five African countries (Kenya, Cameroon, Burkina Faso, Senegal and Mali), contract farming schemes involve the participation of over 75,000 smallholder farmers.

Table 3.4 shows the incidence and selected characteristics of documented

---

[63] Jaffee (1990); Horton (1987).

contract farming schemes in Africa as of the mid-1980s. Nearly two-thirds of the schemes have involved the focal commodities of this study, with schemes for fruits and vegetables being the most numerous. Contract farming has also been an important institutional framework in traditional agro-industries for sugar, cotton, tobacco and tea, and indeed, some of the largest individual schemes have been for such crops. The commodities which have commonly been procured through contract farming share certain technical and economic

TABLE 3.4: **Documented Contract Farming Schemes in Africa (Mid-1980s)**

Commodity	# of Schemes	# of Countries	Ave. # of Farmers	Market Orientation	Ownerships Patterns (% of Schemes)		
					Private	Public	Joint Venture
Fresh Fruit/ Vegetables	25+	6	<100	Mostly Export	90	5	5
Sugar	12	6	5000	Domestic/ Export	33	33	33
Processed Fruit/ Vegetables	9	7	3000[a]	Export/ Domestic	33	22	45
Palm Oil	8	5	2000	Domestic/ Export	0	75	25
Cotton	7	7	64000[b]	Domestic/ Export	0	57	43
Tea	7	5	26000	Export/ Domestic	28	72	0
Tobacco	6	6	5500	Domestic	17	33	50
Dairy	3	3	4000	Domestic	0	100	0
Rubber	2	2	1250	Export	0	50	50
Poultry	2	2	Na.	Domestic	50	0	50
Rice	2	2	2000	Domestic	0	100	0
Spices	2	2	Na.	Export	100	0	0
Oilseeds	2	1	Na.	Domestic	50	0	50
Gari	1	1	141	Domestic	100	0	0
Totals	88	21			41	33	26

[a] Based on information on seven schemes only.
[b] Based on information on four schemes only.
Na. Not available.

SOURCES: Watts et al. (1988); Jaffee (1987).

characteristics that ordinarily contribute to high levels of risk for producers and processor/traders. These commodities are generally (a) highly perishable in their raw form, (b) valuable per unit weight or volume, and (c) heterogenous in quality. They also require specialized skills and inputs to produce, have extended production cycles or gestation periods, and feature economies of scale in processing, though not in farm-level production. Under these circumstances, farmers are likely to require specialized services and they especially value market assurances. Processors and traders themselves seek greater security in raw material supplies and can appropriate significant benefits (for example, improved quality) from providing production support services.

In contrast, there have been relatively few contract farming schemes in Africa for livestock and dairy products. This differs from patterns in North America, Western Europe and Latin America where contracting of such commodities is common. In the case of livestock products, the reason may stem from the still limited effective demand for high-quality meat and the limited availability of refrigeration and other technology to maintain the quality of high-priced meat.[64] Where contracting does occur, it commonly involves hotels, restaurants and upscale retailers or else processing companies which serve this type of establishment (Box 3.6).

For dairy products, contracting has not occurred because of the widespread reliance on imported raw materials and the common presence of price and milk movement controls in industries based on local raw materials. Chapter V examines the experience of private dairies in Kenya. Until 1992, these firms were legally prevented from dealing directly with farmers. They had to rely upon supplies from the dominant parastatal firm, *ad hoc* extra-legal purchases from farmers or cooperatives, or the production from their own cows. With market liberalization, there are likely to be efforts by the dairies to contract supplies and to provide inputs and technical services to farmers.[65] Cases of formal contracting between fishermen (or fisherman groups) and

---

[64] This is discussed by Kane (1987).

[65] There are relatively few cases of contract farming for staple grains in Africa. Food grains lack most of the technical and market characteristics that would lead to a demand for and supply of market and production contracts. They have low value per unit weight or volume, their markets and prices are widely controlled, they do not require specialized inputs, have relatively short production cycles, and readily identifiable quality variations. Carney (1987) documents an interesting case in the Gambia.

**Box 3.6: RATIONING CONTRACTS IN A GLUTTED MARKET—
PERI-URBAN POULTRY PRODUCTION AND TRADE IN SENEGAL**

Following a 1980 ban on imported poultry products, a local poultry industry developed rapidly in Senegal. Though initially serving the small resident European and Lebanese communities, the market expanded to include the larger middle-class urban population. By 1986, there were some 300 enterprises using imported chicks, producing nearly 1000 tons of meat and 360,000 dozen eggs per year. With the encouragement of agricultural officials, large numbers of additional growers invested in broiler production, using local, unimproved stock. The result was a severe market glut, dominated by low quality produce.

Producers sought market security through informal agreements with buyers which gave the latter first option at a price negotiated at the time of sale. In this buyers' market, any forward commitments were at prices below spot market levels and left buyers with discretionary judgement over quality.

More enduring contractual ties have been developed by a limited number of medium-to-large-scale producers—producing at least 500 broilers a week or owning 5000 layers—with institutions such as hotels, restaurants, and 'up market' retailers which have special quality requirements. Even these are largely sales agreements, as it has been very rare for buyers to provide producers with inputs, credit, or technical assistance.

Among the larger producers, there have been a few cases of more formal vertical integration as with one firm developing an integrated feed mill/poultry/processing operation and with a ship chandler integrating backward into poultry production and processing.

SOURCE: Billings (1987).

---

downstream processors and traders are not well documented although see Box 3.7.[66]

Contract farming has taken many different forms, incorporating different numbers and combinations of smallholder and larger farmers and varying allocations of rights, responsibilities and decision-making control between farmers, contractors and third parties such as government agencies, farmer

---

[66] See also van der Hoeven and Budeba (1993) for the incidence of contractual ties between fisherman and joint venture fish processing enterprises in Tanzania.

associations and financial institutions. Enormous differences in size, ownership and management of contracting schemes are also apparent. Although
the vast majority of schemes organized by private traders and processors
have involved less than 1000 contract farmers, several public sector programs
have included 50,000 or more farmers. The KTDA tea scheme (Kenya) and
several of the West African cotton schemes are prominent examples.

Most contracting enterprises have established criteria for restricting entry
into their schemes. Such criteria normally relate to location, landholding and
other assets. Although there have been exceptions, these provisions have restricted the poorest farmers and the least favorable areas in most countries
from participating in contract farming schemes.[67] Landless persons and poorer
farmers have migrated in significant numbers to work in many contracting
schemes. Successful programs have enabled better resource-endowed commercial smallholders to diversify their income sources and production operations, or to move into more specialized production of more contracted crops.

**Box 3.7: BACKWARD INTEGRATION FOR HIGH-QUALITY SHRIMP
EXPORTS FROM CÔTE D'IVOIRE**

Over the past decade, a few firms in Côte d'Ivoire have built up a successful
export trade in frozen shrimp. The largest exporting company was established
in 1980, focusing initially on processing imported fish and selling in the local
market. Within a few years, it diversified into shrimp processing, targeting the
high-quality segments of the French and Belgian markets. A Marseille-based
subsidiary was set up to market the product. To procure shrimp, the firm
organized some 2000 fishermen into cooperatives, providing them with working capital, fishing gear, ice, and collection/transport facilities. The cooperatives provided the firm with most of their catch from off-shore lagoons at pre-
agreed prices. To supplement this supply and to extend its product mix to
include larger sea-caught shrimp, the firm leased several trawlers, the catch
of which accounted for about 30% of procured supplies by 1990. The firm
has subsequently spread its net wider by entering into a joint venture shrimp
project in Benin, the output of which will be marketed through the firm's
existing European channels.

---

[67] Jaffee (1987) discusses a case in western Kenya where more than 20,000 resource-poor farmers,
70% of which are women, have been contracted to grow french beans for subsequent processing and
export to Europe.

As Table 3.4 indicates, the public sector has been heavily involved in contract farming in Africa, especially for traditional industrial crops. Many government-initiated schemes have involved financial, managerial and technical assistance from international financial institutions, in particular the Commonwealth Development Corporation and the World Bank. A large proportion of these schemes, including most of those involving sugar or tree crops and the construction of large processing facilities, have also featured the development of nucleus estates. This has been done in order to guarantee minimum throughput into the factories, undertake technical research and develop high-quality planting materials. Another common feature of government-initiated contract farming schemes has been the participation of multinational corporations in technical and managerial capacities, and who have frequently taken on a minority shareholding. There are a great number of these hybrid institutions combining government ownership, donor financing and private management, and they belie the stark analytical dichotomy of the public and private sectors found in most of the literature on African agribusiness.

Private sector involvement is widespread via joint ventures and management contracts. Only for horticultural crops and some minor, specialty commodities (for example, spices, high-quality poultry) have there been many cases where private traders and processors have initiated and managed contracting schemes on their own. In examining the history of horticultural development of countries such as Kenya, Côte d'Ivoire, Senegal and Zimbabwe, one finds that most of the formal contracting schemes have been undertaken by the larger firms in the industry. More often than not, these latter are owned and managed by foreign companies or by non-African local minorities since, for the most part, smaller indigenous horticultural exporters have lacked the technical capacity and financial resources to organize significant contract farming schemes and to extend inputs and credit to farmers.

The effectiveness of contract farming schemes has varied by country, subsector and venture, calling for caution in drawing generalized conclusions. Advocates of contract farming have viewed it as a salvation for African agriculture, which involves a "dynamic partnership [between] agribusiness and the small farmer."[68] While contract farming has proven to be an effective institutional framework in a number of African agro-industries, it is not a viable model for many crops and types of farmers and firms. Where it has worked, contract farming has served to reduce the technical and market risks

---

[68] Williams and Karen (1985).

faced by farmers, processors and traders and to better coordinate their activities in operating environments generally characterized by poorly functioning input and commodity markets and limited agricultural support services.

Yet, many individual schemes, including a majority of those initiated and run by private firms, have either failed entirely or not been sustainable over time. In contrast with the (generally larger) public sector schemes, few private schemes have benefited from preferential access to land, finance and improved roads, protection against competitive imported goods, and, perhaps most importantly, protection against competing buyers of the contracted crop. As a result, contractual enforcement problems have been extremely common in private schemes, in turn resulting in the non-sustainability of most of them (see Box 3.8). Unlike the case of many state-run schemes—where the contractor has de jure or de facto monopsony powers and where alternative, artisanal processing is either discouraged or banned outright (the case with both Kenyan tea and palm oil from Côte d'Ivoire)—private contractors often face competition and experience the 'leakage' of the crop into alternative marketing channels. Competing firms can afford to make higher cash payments to farmers because they haven't invested in inputs, technical services, etc. The 'leakage' of the crop not only undercuts raw material supplies to the contractor, but also accentuates problems in the recovery of input loans. Legal remedies to contract default have been costly or near impossible to implement since government officials have typically sided with farmers in disputes. Other frequent problems of private contractors include: (a) opportunism and inefficiency on the part of intermediaries (for instance, cooperatives), (b) poor quality in the technical assistance provided, (c) difficulty in gaining access to inputs, and (d) interference from government officials.

Box 3.8: BROKEN PROMISES: CONTRACT ENFORCEMENT PROBLEMS IN UGANDA AND KENYA

Beginning in 1990, Shell Uganda Ltd. began a campaign to encourage farmer production of dried chilies which Shell would then export to Europe. The firm sponsored several media programs which outlined appropriate production techniques. It then contracted a local cooperative to supply an agreed quantity of chilies, providing the cooperative with seeds, tractors, ploughs, and crop pre-financing to pass on to its members. While drought wiped out the first crop, Shell persisted and supplied additional inputs for renewed planting. This time, the cooperative management misused the supplied funds/ inputs and paid farmers only half of the originally agreed purchase price. Farmers withheld their crop or sold it elsewhere, leaving Shell with unrecovered loans and with a crop far to small to meet its export commitments. The foreign buyer placed a claim of $200,000 against Shell for failure to meet its own contract commitment. In the aftermath to this episode, Shell moved to develop its own network of buyers and input suppliers for chili producers.

Kenya Horticultural Exporters (KHE), Kenya's largest trader in fresh produce, had a longer, yet similarly disappointing experience with smallholder contract farming. In the early 1980s, KHE was contacted by a farmers group in Matuu (Machokos District) which sought a reliable outlet for its produce. KHE entered into a contractual relationship with the group, providing its members with seeds, technical advice and a commitment to purchase various types of vegetables in particular quantities at particular prices over an extended period. For two years this scheme functioned relatively well, with KHE expanding its trade and injecting large amounts of money into the local economy. Still, farmers were apparently using the KHE contract as a safety net, planting speculatively, selling some supplies to other traders, and providing the remainder to KHE. On an individual commodity basis, the Matuu supplies did not match KHE's requirements.

During the third year, the scheme totally collapsed. A drought in other parts of the country had resulted in a substantial increase in market prices. In order to meet their downstream commitments, many exporters came to the Matuu area and offered cash prices several times those of KHE's contract price, even though they would sustain a loss of their exports. The Matuu farmers concluded that KHE must have been "exploiting" them all along. They abandoned the firm and refused to repay their input loans. In subsequent seasons, export-oriented vegetable production continued to expand rapidly in Matuu, yet to the benefit of KHE's competitors. Drawing negative lessons from its experience, KHE moved to secure much of its commodity requirements by leasing and managing its own farms.

SOURCES: Herlehey (1993); Jaffee (1987).

Kenya's experience with contract farming is the most extensive in Africa and illustrates the mixed record of private companies in organizing such schemes. Contract farming in Kenya dates to World War II when the colonial government organized a smallholder vegetable scheme to produce dehydrated vegetables for the Allied forces based in East Africa. Since then, formal contracting schemes have been developed by public, joint venture or fully private enterprises for a wide range of crops, including tea, tobacco, sugar, oilseeds, barley, seeds and a broad range of horticultural commodities. In 1991, nearly 350,000 smallholder farmers were registered in contract farming schemes. Assuming that about 10% of such smallholders produce more than one crop under contract, then some 315,000 smallholders, representing about 16% of Kenya's two million smallholder families, were growing crops under contract.[69]

Contract farming in Kenya has generally been most successful in generating raw supplies of materials and commodities for processors and traders, in raising smallholder incomes and in raising farmer productivity. An illustration of the latter is provided in Table 3.5 which compares long-term trends in yield patterns for three types of operations: (1) smallholders growing crops under contract, (2) smallholders growing other crops within the framework of general support services and marketing board procurement, and (3) large-scale, plantation-based agribusiness operations. The table makes visible the

TABLE 3.5: **Comparative Long-Term Yield Patterns in Kenyan Agriculture**

System Category Commodity	Time Period	Average Annual Rate of Change (%)
Contract Farming[a]		
Sugar[b]	1966–85	6.7
Tea[c]	1971–86	2.7
Tobacco[b]	1966–85	13.8
French beans[d]	1982–86	37.9
General Support/Marketing Board[a]		
Cashew Nuts[b]	1961–84	−1.6
Coffee[e]	1971–86	2.1
Cotton[f]	1965–86	−1.3
Maize[b]	1966–87	1.3
Vertical-Integration Agribusiness		
Pineapple[g]	1973–86	2.5
Sisal[b]	1961–84	2.7
Estate Tea[h]	1971–82	5.6

[a] Smallholders only.
[b] FAO Production Yearbook, various years.
[c] KTDA Annual Reports, various years.
[d] Njoro Canners Ltd. Production Farmer Records.
[e] Coffee Board of Kenya, Annual Reports
[f] Lele et al. (1989), Table 3.
[g] Kenya Canners Ltd., personal communication.
[h] Kenya Tea Board as reported in Lamb and Mueller (1982).

---

[69] On the origins and development of contract farming in Kenya, see Jaffee (1990).

fact that over an extended period, smallholder productivity under contractual schemes has been far greater than when support services were limited to the general official system of extension and credit. Smallholders under contract have also matched or exceeded the productivity gains achieved by relatively high-input, large-scale agribusiness. The expansion and improved productivity in smallholder tea, tobacco, sugar and french bean production has been directly linked to the dedicated support and supervisory system for these crops[70], while inefficient support systems and payment delays have been major factors in the weaker performance of smallholder coffee, cotton, maize and cashew nut production.[71]

Yet, success within the private sector is not universal and many contracting schemes have failed or proved to be unsustainable. Several programs run by private processors to encourage production of sunflower and sesame seed were unsustainable due to the 'leakage' of the contracted crop to competing firms or to artisanal processing activities. Jaffee (1994) has documented the rocky road of contract farming in Kenya's horticultural sub-sector, where private firms have experienced general problems related to competition, farmer and intermediary opportunism and maintenance of high quality standards. Even so, contract farming has proven to be an important basis for the initial development and subsequent expansion of trade and processing operations for many of the leading firms in that sub-sector.

A final organizational mode for raw material procurement is own production, that is, *vertical integration of primary production and processing and/or trade*. In Africa, both complete and partial vertical integration have occurred. Partially integrated firms continue to rely upon 'non-captive' sources for part of their supplies or else sell part of their own crop, herd or catch to other traders or processors. Many agro-industrial ventures have combined nucleus estates and outgrower programs.

Vertical integration in African agribusiness has taken three main forms. One form involves small farmers who process or directly retail their own production. The woman farmer who brings to market and sells her chickens, eggs and tomatoes undertakes vertical integration on a tiny scale. A second form of vertical integration involves medium-to-large-scale farmers (or farmer

---

[70] See Lamb and Mueller (1982) for tea, Allen (1983) for sugar, Buch-Hansen and Kieler (1983) for tobacco, and Jaffee (1987, 1994) for french beans. The latter two are privately-initiated and -run schemes, while the major sugar schemes are privately-managed.

[71] Schluter (1984); Ommeh (1984); Lele et al. (1989).

cooperatives) who integrate their activities with processing and trade. By making investments in marketing and processing infrastructure, and by undertaking sales direct to retailers, consumers and overseas buyers, these farmers seek to add greater value to their produce and bypass intermediaries. During the colonial period, groups of European settler farmers in Kenya, Zimbabwe and Malawi took this route, frequently obtaining protection by government from competition from other firms. The third common form of vertical integration involves relatively large companies, which make simultaneous investments in estates and processing infrastructure, or which integrate backward due to dissatisfaction with alternative raw material procurement arrangements (see Box 3.9).

Box 3.9: RIDING PIGGY-BACK—PRIVATE SECTOR REVIVAL OF KENYA'S PIG INDUSTRY

Kenya's pork product industry is relatively small, accounting for less than 1% of agricultural GDP. Domestic consumption has historically been limited by high prices relative to those of beef, religious constraints (for the local Muslim population), and the general absence of a traditional consumption pattern. However, the industry has strong links to the domestic tourism industry and it was historically a significant earner of foreign exchange through exports.

From 1906 until the early 1980s, the pork products industry was dominated by a single firm—Uplands Bacon Factory. Originally a private company, Uplands Bacon was brought under majority government ownership during the late 1950s. At that time, over 85,000 pigs were slaughtered per year and export trade flourished. Although production levels declined somewhat, export sales remained significant through the 1960s. By the mid-1970s, however, the factory's performance was declining. Mismanagement, high employee turnover, declining factory repair, maintenance and hygienic conditions, and burgeoning financial losses were among the ills. Exports ceased and an increasing proportion of pigs were sold by farmers to small butcheries. Supplies of high-quality meat were inadequate to serve the country's expanding tourist trade. Facing severe liquidity problems and encountering frequent factory breakdowns, Uplands Bacon Factory pig slaughters fell to 40,000 in 1979 and all the way to 6000 by 1985. Facing a huge debt, the company was liquidated in 1986 and some of its assets were auctioned off.

The Uplands Bacon Factory was never the sole processor of pork products, although it long dominated the market. Several private firms had produced pig meat, serving local markets or particular market niches (such as supplies to the airlines). It was not until the late 1980s that a major private company stepped in to fill the vacuum created by the demise of Uplands Bacon. The company Farmer's Choice Ltd. was initially established in 1975 in order to supply fresh meats and produce to the hotels and restaurants of its parent company Block Hotels. Later on it developed a marketing and distribution system to service the country's retail outlets catering to middle- and upper-income residents. In 1989 Farmer's Choice was acquired by the local subsidiary of Lonrho, providing it with additional resources and with closer links to Lonrho's local farming operations.

The pig meat processing and marketing operations of Farmer's Choice have increased substantially since the mid-1980s. The number of pigs slaughtered by the company increased from about 22,000 in 1984 to 35,000 in 1988 (when a large, modern processing facility was constructed) to an average of more than 46,000 during the 1991–1993 period. Much of the recent expansion in processing has been facilitated by the development of highly-efficient, large-scale pig-raising units on farms owned by the company and by another Lonrho affiliate. In 1992, nearly half of the company's supply of pigs was from affiliated farming operations.

Farmer's Choice currently accounts for about 85% of the domestic pig meat market. Approximately 70% of its sales are directed to hotels, restaurants, and institutions. The company has also made a considerable effort to promote consumption among the local middle-class population, conducting in-store promotions, advertising through various media, and taking "mobile kitchens" into shopping and residential areas to offer samples, promote products, and conduct market research. A successful export trade has also been redeveloped, and is expected to grow in the future.

The incidence of the last form of vertical integration is strongly influenced by government policies pertaining to access to land, land taxes, etc. Sometimes, company access to land is restricted or is otherwise frowned upon politically. To circumvent this, firms have entered into joint ventures or technical and management contracts with prominent landowners, at times guaranteeing the latter a certain level of revenue or profit per hectare. There have also been cases where governments have leased or sold large tracts of land to companies as part of their encouragement of agro-industrial investment.

Nigeria provides an example of this. During the mid-1980s, the government encouraged vertical integration by agro-industrial firms through the sale or lease of large land areas to them. It adopted an import licensing system which gave preference to processors who could demonstrate that they sought to increase local raw material supplies through the development of their own farms. Many of the country's largest conglomerates and food and beverage processors took this route, developing large farms for grains, vegetables, oilseeds, soybean and dairy production. The Kenyan government has also supported vertical integration in certain industries (Box 3.10).

More generally, vertical integration of primary production and processing and trade has been relatively common in Africa in oil palm processing and fish freezing operations and in export-oriented horticulture. Less common have been cases of vertical integration for tree nuts, oilseeds and meat processing. Among our case study industries, vertical integration has featured prominently only in certain segments of Kenya's horticultural industry, but there are indications that larger firms may take this route in the future for Tanzanian cashew nuts and Kenyan dairy products.

Despite much-touted statistics giving a favorable impression of the productivity (yet not the resource use efficiency) of large-scale estates by comparison with smallholdings, the actual record of vertical integration in Africa is quite mixed. For the most part, farmers have not been particularly adept at food processing or export marketing because they lack the skills, contacts and time to be effective (see Box 3.11 for an example). There are exceptions of course.[72] At the same time, many processors and traders who have tried to integrate production into their activities have experienced major problems with regard to land acquisition, farm management, labor, and input and spare part availability. Traditional plantation companies have generally fared better.

Financial Strategies

Lack of access to credit (and foreign exchange) is perceived as a constraint on private enterprise, both informal and formal. Without minimizing the need for reform and expansion of credit institutions, our discussion now turns to the strategies enterprises have developed for obtaining capital which may or may not be defined as credit.

In the informal sector, the most common source of start-up capital is the entrepreneur's own resources saved from previous employment together with loans or gifts from relatives and inheritances. For many micro-enterprises in

---

[72] For example, since the mid-1980s, several dozen (locally-owned) integrated farming/trading operations have built up a successful export trade in Ghana for fresh pineapples.

Box 3.10: VERTICAL INTEGRATION WITH GOVERNMENT SUPPORT: THE PINEAPPLE CANNING INDUSTRY OF KENYA

Kenya's canned pineapple industry dates to the late 1940s when two firms built processing facilities and organized raw material supplies from European settler farmers. As such raw material supplies were inadequate, the firms began to buy the surplus pineapple crop of smallholder farmers, then growing for the local fresh market. By the mid-1950s, government launched a pineapple support program in order to expand the industry and enhance the incomes of smallholder farmers. Inputs, technical advice, credit, and minimum price guarantees were provided. The scheme and the processors encountered major technical, logistical, and competitive problems and the industry survived only because of government subsidies.

After independence, one of the processors—Kenya Canners—entered into a management and marketing contract with Del Monte. With an investment made to expand Kenya Canner's processing capacity, the Kenyan government offered to expand the smallholder production program and to purchase and lease to the firm an estate of 5000 acres for it to assess the feasibility of developing a nucleus estate.

Raw material supply problems persisted in the subsequent two years as a result of drought and the rapid expansion and better returns to coffee in the main pineapple growing areas. Faced with this situation and having Del Monte's prior experience in plantation agriculture, Kenya Canners proposed that the further expansion of the industry be based on estate production. The government agreed to a proposed program, purchasing and leasing to Kenya Canners (then under majority Del Monte ownership) an additional 15,000 acres. The smallholder production program was phased out, with the government writing off outstanding loans. By 1974, Kenya Canners' operation was fully vertically integrated.

The development of a large estate by Kenya Canners and the linkage of the Kenyan operation into the international marketing and distribution system of Del Monte were key factors in the huge expansion of the industry. Between 1974 and 1977, canned pineapple exports increased fivefold, from 8,678 to 45,327 tons. Since then, Kenya's exports have generally remained within the range of 40,000 to 50,000 tons/year, placing the country among the five largest exporters worldwide and keeping canned pineapple ranked first among Kenya's manufactured product exports.

SOURCE: Jaffee (1994).

the food sector, no fixed investment in the true sense is necessary, merely expenditure on the first stock. For itinerant micro-retailers in Dakar in 1984, this could be equivalent to as little as twelve hours work at the formal sector minimum wage.

There are many informal credit institutions, most notably the rotating credit associations known as *susus* in Ghana, *tontines* in Francophone Africa, and *sanaadig* in Sudan. While these share a common form, their scale and content are very diverse. Some are purely social, others have welfare or insurance rather than credit functions. Many are organizations for disciplined saving and at a certain scale can provide useful capital for informal economic activity. In some countries, rotating credit associations are large in scale and may include formal-sector entrepreneurs as participants. In Cameroon there is a system of bidding for use of the funds that introduces an element of real

---

Box 3.11: LEARNING BY DOING: HARD LUCK IN UGANDA

In the mid-1980s, a group of commercial farmers and businessmen formed the Ntangauzi and Vegetable Growers Association (NVGA). By 1989, the group sent samples of fresh and dried ginger to Europe and the Middle East. Exports during 1989/90 were small, yet the product quality was sufficient to secure larger orders to the next year. The NVGA quickly organized an outgrower scheme (with 500 farmers) and borrowed a sizable sum from a commercial bank in order to modify a coffee-drying factory for the purpose of drying ginger. The factory modifications and additional investments were made without consulting with ginger specialists.

The firm was not in close contact with its outgrowers, most of whom had no prior ginger-growing experience. The quality of production varied and was exacerbated by delays in crop collection and grading. Factory operations were also problematic as the diesel powdered driers could not lower the moisture content of the ginger to international standard levels. As a result of these quality problems, the NVGA's main foreign buyer deducted 60% from the originally quoted price. Now starved of cash, NVGA ceased its buying operations and sought to renegotiate its loans. This being unsuccessful, NVGA was closed down.

SOURCE: Herlehy (1993).

interest.[73] A development from these in both Ghana and Cameroon are *susu* collectors or *tontiniers*, small operators who collect daily savings and return them at the end of the month. Again these are savings rather than credit systems, and clients accept a small negative interest rate (the collector's commission) for the convenience involved. In Ghana some of these operators have attempted to formalize their businesses as 'savings and loans companies' with mixed results.[74] In many countries there are money-lenders, either legal or illegal, who usual charge high interest rates.[75]

Less visible and more amorphous habits of savings and patterns of informal credit may be just as significant. *Susu* collectors in Ghana were found to be important for market women and traders, but not for urban small or medium enterprises. Of 103 small and medium enterprises recently surveyed, none had used *susus* and only two had used *susu* collectors.[76]

One other common form of credit consists of traders deferring payments to producers until they themselves have realized a profit, a widely accepted practice, especially in the livestock trade. In the formal sector this is referred to as 'trade credit' and is increasingly seen as an important part of the business strategy of the enterprise. Even near the formal end of the spectrum, credit from banks may be inaccessible, expensive or simply less convenient than trade credit. In a study of small and medium formal Ghanaian enterprises, 71% of investment in capital stock by enterprises in the food sector was financed from internal sources and only 17% from banks. Of the total debt portfolio of food enterprises, 31% was with banks, 37% with suppliers, 15% with clients and 17% with family and friends.[77] Of the ten small to medium scale commercial cheese and yogurt producers in Kenya interviewed for this study, only three have utilized loans from commercial banks for investments or working capital. Similarly, only a small minority of firms which have entered Tanzania's liberalized cashew nut market at the primary level

---

[73] Henry et al. (1991).

[74] Duggleby, Aryeetey and Steel (1992).

[75] Indicative figures of 30% per month for short term loans, and 50–100% per year for long term loans are given by Duggelby, Aryeetey and Steel (1992).

[76] Duggleby, Aryeetey and Steel (1992).

[77] Cuevas et al. (1993). The sub-sample for the food sector is extremely small, but figures are comparable with a larger sample including other sectors (43 for source of capital, 33 for composition of debt portfolio).

have relied upon (or been able to obtain) credit from commercial banks for crop purchasing.

While access to formal credit will obviously be greater for larger-scale traders, the overall picture even for the formal sector is for a preponderance of informal credit in agricultural trade which is only now beginning to diminish. Terpend (1992) gives thumbnail sketches of the credit situation in agricultural trade in six francophone countries. In Congo, despite an apparently active government-sponsored Credit Union in rural areas, the flow of credit is from producers to traders through differed payments.[78] In Mali, village associations which engage in marketing can obtain credit from the Agricultural Bank, while large and small wholesalers organized into groups borrow from commercial banks. The bank loans are secured against stocks, which has necessitated a state-sponsored storage capacity. Retailers and village-level purchasers are not reached by either channel. In Burkina Faso up to 1990, government views on private agricultural trade were so negative that no formal credit was available.

In Guinea-Bissau there was no private banking system until 1989, and the entire rice-cashew trade (cashews are grown in grain-deficit areas so cashew traders also deal in rice for consumption) was financed informally. Until 1986 debts could not even be repaid in cash. Traders are happy with the current modified informal system. Credit for domestic food marketing in Guinea has been almost entirely informal, apart from pilot projects of government credit institutions. Food importers could receive short-term loans from private banks. In Niger credit is advanced down the hierarchy of traders from the half-dozen large scale merchants to wholesalers, small wholesalers and village-level purchasers.

A variety of donor-supported initiatives to remedy the lack of access to credit have been tried. These can be targeted at enterprises of particular scales or degrees of formality, at particular sub-sectors, or special target groups such as women. They can be highly concessional or approximate to varying degrees market rates and conditions on collateral. They can operate through special structures, government institutions or commercial banks.[79] In Ghana,

---

[78] Terpend sees this as a source of abuse. Micro studies of informal domestic agricultural marketing in Congo see it rather as part of the prevailing trust relations (Ma-Mfuka 1989).

[79] The SME Credit Program in Ghana is a good example of the latter, see Duggleby, Aryeetey and Steel (1992).

there are presently at least ten projects or institutions involved or potentially involved in credit to small-scale agribusiness (see Box 3.12).[80] In Malawi, there are at least two government institutions and seven donor programs as well as a multitude of NGO initiatives geared toward the supply of credit to small-scale, off-farm, rural enterprise. Despite these initiatives, a recent survey found that only 1.2% of Malawi's small enterprises have taken loans from formal credit institutions and projects.[81]

Informal means of obtaining foreign exchange are also prevalent. These include the practices of over- and under-invoicing, delaying the repatriation of foreign exchange, mislabeling of goods for export, and offering inducements to bank officials to disregard missing currency forms and other trade documentation. Such measures are a response to overvalued exchange rates, strict controls on access to foreign exchange, expectations about future devaluations and overall uncertainty about one's future economic (and perhaps civil) rights. In countries where macroeconomic stability has been restored, where exporters have been permitted to retain at least part of their foreign exchange earnings, and where auctions or other mechanisms for the legal purchase or sale of foreign exchange have been created, private firms have had significantly less need to employ informal mechanisms.

FORMAL AND INFORMAL FOOD PROCESSING

Food processing is the largest single component of the manufacturing sector of most African countries. The discussion here first focuses on formal medium-to-large-scale activities and then on artisanal and small-scale activities. These components feature quite different actors and results. It must again be noted that the statistical and wider information base for examining private processing activities in Africa is extremely poor. Most industrial censuses are now quite dated and few surveys make a distinction between public and private enterprises.[82]

---

[80] RIO (1993).
[81] Daniels and Ngwira (1993).
[82] Under the research program Africa Regional Program on Enterprise Development, which is coordinated by the World Bank, an effort is being made to systematize the available data on manufacturing industries in selected countries and to gather survey data on private firms in a number of industries.

Box 3.12: GHANAIAN ENTREPRENEURS: CHOOSE YOUR CREDIT LINE

Small-scale rural entrepreneurs can be offered a great variety of credit opportunities and related schemes, reflecting the diverse and overlapping interests of donors and their chosen counterparts within the government.

This is illustrated by Ghana's recent experience. The largest initiative is the Bank of Ghana's Fund for Small and Medium Enterprise Development which has a $25 million credit line from the World Bank. $0.5 million is earmarked for enterprises with assets below $20,000. These funds are to be used indirectly in mutual savings schemes that can then serve as collateral for commercial bank loans. The World Bank is also involved in the development of small-scale palm oil processing through the Agricultural Development Bank and Technoserve (an American NGO), the strengthening of rural banks, a credit line for small-scale enterprises through the National Board for Small-Scale Industries (which makes loans of up to $4000), and training and credit through Women's World Banking.

The European Community's Micro Projects Program includes some funding of market infrastructure and cooperative agro-industrial enterprise. It is about to begin loans to small and medium enterprises under the GRATIS scheme. UNDP funds the Central Region Development Program with credit, training, marketing and technical assistance components. Most loans are between $83 and $417. UNDP also provides credit to women's groups through the National Board for Small Scale Industries and two national women's organizations. IFAD's Smallholder Credit and Marketing Project, implemented by the Ministry of Agriculture, the Ghana Food Distribution Corporation and the Association of People for Practical Life Education, includes a credit component for marketing activities.

The initiatives listed above include only those active in rural areas of two of Ghana's nine regions. Many of these projects target cooperative-style groups rather than individual entrepreneurs. What is less clear is how entrepreneurs and would-be entrepreneurs actually make use of these diverse opportunities.

SOURCE: RIO (1993).

Medium-to-Large-Scale Processing

After independence and up through the mid-1980s, the policies and direct investments of African governments favored relatively large-scale industrial units in the food industries and elsewhere. The objectives of industrial policy were to generate employment in urban areas, save or earn foreign currency, and meet short-to-medium-term goals of financial viability. Most manufacturing activities, including food and beverage manufacturing ventures, were geared toward import-substitution which was encouraged through high levels of nominal protection. In many countries, overvalued exchange rates enhanced an anti-export bias. Government attention to food processing centered around the establishment and operation of parastatal enterprises.

African governments received extensive support from multilateral and bilateral donor activities in this import-substitution, parastatal-led industrialization strategy. A World Bank review of its own experience in supporting agricultural processing ventures found that over the 1974–1985 period, parastatals were the focal institutions in 84% of its projects in East Africa and 66% of its projects in West Africa in which there were agricultural marketing/processing components.[83] Parastatals were also the focus of most support efforts in African food processing by the FAO and by bilateral agencies.

Where new investments were supported, this typically involved turnkey factories based on imported plant and equipment. These factories were capital-intensive and required well developed infrastructure, strong maintenance and repair capabilities, and skilled labor to operate them on an efficient basis. Precisely these resources and capabilities were lacking in many African countries. Nonetheless, initial investments were high. Other common features included the following:

OVERSTAFFING AND INAPPROPRIATE STAFFING: Hiring and wage policies were determined by government and were subject to outside interference. The manual workforce was likely to be paid more than its counterparts in the private sector and traditional agriculture. The size of the workforce could be increased for political reasons, but reduced only with difficulty, and there was little flexibility to hire seasonal or part-time workers. Management was drawn from the ranks of generalist civil servants without commercial or industrial backgrounds and was subject to sudden transfer elsewhere. Appointments became a form of patronage.

---

[83] World Bank (1990), p. 29.

POOR OVERALL MANAGEMENT: Management was of low quality not only because of the individuals recruited as managers, but also because of unnecessary procedural rules (for example, cumbersome requirements to tender and restrictions on the purchase of second-hand equipment, requirements to buy from or sell to other parastatals, fixed prices, lack of flexibility in product development and confused objectives). Government protection meant that there was little pressure to rectify poor decisions.

COSTLY PURSUIT OF NON-COMMERCIAL OBJECTIVES: Some agro-industrial parastatals also had social or development functions with mandates to provide a variety of services to rural populations. Several performed both these and their primary functions well,[84] and the extra services if worth performing should not be regarded in the same light as commercial losses. There is, however, reasonable doubt as to whether agro-industrial enterprises were the most suitable organizations to fulfill these functions.

As a result of these structural weaknesses, many of the investments were failures. They were sustained only through government subsidies, additional donor resources (for enterprise rehabilitation), and restrictions or outright bans on competitive activities by other firms. To some extent, private agro-industries of the same scale experienced similar problems, but there is direct evidence, particularly vivid for Cameroon, that private enterprises operating in the same sub-sector and in geographical proximity to parastatals outperformed them by a considerable degree.[85] There is more general evidence that private firms have achieved higher levels of capacity utilization than have public enterprises.

Table 3.6 provides a list of some of the many government and donor-supported high-value food processing enterprises which have experienced severe operational problems over the past decade. It can be argued that the failures of these firms have been far more costly than simply the low (if not negative) return on initial investment and additional funds subsequently injected for working capital and coverage of losses. The dominance of these firms in their respective industries crowded out private investment.

At the same time, parastatal illiquidity contributed to a decline in production support and raw material procurement services and prevented the para-

---

[84] For example SODECOTON, the Cameroon Cotton Development Organization, see Schiavo-Campo et al. (1983).

[85] Grouitch (1992).

TABLE 3.6: **Illustrative Cases of Problematic (Donor-Supported) Food Processing Parastatals**

Country	Enterprise	Activity	Experience
Kenya	Kenya Cooperative Creameries	Dairy Processing	Expanded production, yet capacity under-utilization Large financial losses Restricted private competition
	Kenya Meat Commission	Meat Processing	Capacity under-utilization Loss of domestic + export markets Large financial losses
Zambia	Zamhort	Fruit/Veg. Processing	'White Elephant' Inadequate raw materials Poor location Lack of operating capital
	Dairy Produce Board	Dairy Processing	Weak procurement system Capacity under-utilization
Tanzania	Tanzania Cashew Nut Board	Cashew Nut Processing	Extremely low capacity utilization Negative processing margins Poor processing efficiency Poor product quality Decline of procurement system
Gambia	Gambia Produce Marketing Board	Groundnut Processing	Capacity under-utilization Negative processing margins Large financial losses
Guinea	Salguidia	Pineapple Processing	Capacity under-utilization Loss of markets
Burkina Faso	O.N.E.R.A.	Meat Slaughter Cold Storage	High unit costs Large subsidies required

SOURCES: FAO (1992); Holtzman (1990); World Bank (1990); Woodward et al. (1989); Case Studies.

statals from increasing producer prices for raw materials. Parastatal inefficiencies thus undercut the incentives for producers to develop the focal high-value commodities and may have presented an additional burden on any new private investor. Such an investor would have had to overcome the disillusioned attitude among producers which the parastatal nurtured during its waning years of operation.

Among our case studies, these problems were borne out in the development of Tanzania's cashew nut industry and Kenya's dairy industry. In the former case, a multilateral donor supported a major government effort during the 1970s to build up local cashew processing facilities in order to add value to nuts formerly being exported in raw form. State-of-the-art, capital-intensive processing technologies were to be adopted, since there were concerns about insufficient labor for industrial activities in the main cashew nut growing areas in the southern part of the country. Cost overruns in factory construction were significant, leading to a cutback in technical assistance and cashew research and extension.

By the time the factories came on line, raw material production had declined to less than one-third of peak levels. Of the ten new factories that were completed by the early 1980s, two never opened and four others operated infrequently. On a national level, cashew factory capacity utilization never exceeded 13% during the 1980s due to raw material shortages, power and water supply problems, shortages of spare parts, and overall liquidity problems for the parastatal enterprise which forced it to sell raw nuts rather than process the nuts and wait several months for final sale and payment.

If these problems were not enough, the highly mechanized processing technology that was employed resulted in very poor technical results in terms of the yield of whole nut kernels. The technology itself was partially responsible for this, although breakdown in the quality control system for raw materials compounded the problem, and resulted in declining performance by the factories.

Under current market conditions, it is not clear whether mechanized factories could be operated on a profitable basis by private companies. Furthermore, private firms presently considering alternative technologies are uncertain as to whether any new investments which they would have to make would be viewed favorably by government, given the latter's sunk investment in large-scale factories in almost every town in the southeast part of the country, for which there remains outstanding debt.

In the case of Kenyan dairy processing, the dominant firm Kenya Cooperative Creameries has been provided with government-backed donor loans to build medium-to-large-scale milk processing and storage facilities in major production areas and cities. The cooperative has been protected by a virtual monopoly in the markets for pasteurized and ultra-high temperature milk and the prevailing regulations have largely prevented the emergence of alternative, locally- or regionally-based systems involving cooperatives or private firms. Private firms have been restricted on what they could produce and where they could sell their products. Some donor-funded milk collection and processing facilities have enabled the Kenya Cooperatives Creameries to aggressively undermine the position of potential competitors. In recent years, the cooperative has operated at a low rate of capacity utilization and experienced levels of spoilage well above international standards. It has accumulated huge financial losses in meeting certain social objectives and produced relatively high cost products that are beyond the means of most Kenyans.

A wider review of the literature indicates that the above stories are not atypical for large-scale, parastatal food processing operations in Africa. Anecdotal evidence about poor technical efficiency and large operating losses for other African capital-intensive manufacturing facilities abounds.

The fiscal burden and inefficiencies of public enterprises have stimulated governmental and donor-supported efforts geared toward parastatal reform, with a varying admixture of structural and management reform on the one hand, and technical rehabilitation on the other.[86] The experience in most cases has been negative and since the mid-1980s there has been increasing emphasis on the liquidation or privatization of public enterprises. Over and above the general trend of encouraging privatization to minimize the fiscal burden on governments and encourage good management and commercially-oriented decision-making, the situation in many agro-industries has reached the point where these industries must be either privatized or abandoned.

There are strong arguments against abandonment. The foregone production and costs of imports to replace certain commodities on the domestic market would be considerable. Abandonment would also mean finally writing-off initial investments, whose loans nevertheless still have to be repaid. While overstaffing is certainly a widespread problem, the cost of laying off workforces in their entirety would also be large. On the positive side, with improved incentives and management, the assets of many public enterprises could be made to achieve satisfactory technical and financial results. In some cases, the economies that could be made through privatization and disaggregation are readily visible.

Despite these advantages and considerable donor pressure, the privatization effort has appeared to make little headway for a number of political, economic and technical reasons. In a recent review of Africa's privatization experience, Berg (1993) concluded that:

> Divestiture programs in Africa have made little progress . . . It is a hard and discouraging fact that in most of sub-Saharan Africa, sales of enterprises have been few in number and slight in economic weight, that the terms of sale have often been far from optimal, that many of the state owned enter-

---

[86] See Swanson and Wolde-Semait (1989). National reform programs in Niger, Madagascar, Senegal and Ghana are discussed in detail.

prises sold have gone out of business, and that the objectives of increased efficiency and stimulus to private sectors have been attained in only a few cases. The liquidation of state owned enterprises has been more vigorously pursued, but even here benefits have been small, partly because many of the liquidated enterprises had closed their doors years ago, partly because claims by workers and creditors absorb much of the receipt from asset sales. (p. 19)

The actual record of privatization in Africa is still unclear. Most studies on the subject merely provide a 'body count' indicating the number of liquidated or privatized enterprises, but offering little insight into the size and signifi- cance of such enterprises, the terms of their liquidation/privatization and the subsequent experience of the firm and its sub-sector. Some of the parastatals counted as 'dead' are merely firms included on some government list of privatization/liquidation candidates. Conversely, some 'dead' parastatals find their way back into public or semi-public ownership after failed privatizations. Too few detailed country and enterprise-level case studies exist to make any conclusive remarks.

According to Shaikh et al. (1993), between 1986 and 1992 there were 287 privatizations (including partial sales) in Africa, two-thirds of which took place in only four countries—Mozambique, Nigeria, Guinea and Ghana. Nearly one-third of all privatizations in Africa appear to have been of small retail outlets in Mozambique and Guinea. While Nigeria's privatization effort has been relatively well organized (with sales of several insurance companies, cement plants and other companies), total receipts from these sales were less than 1% of the book value of state-owned assets. By comparison, Guinea's privatization program was much more poorly executed. Many of the enter- prises were sold on the basis of single offers after non-transparent valuation exercises, and a large majority of the industrial enterprises never resumed business or failed within a few years of privatization. Similarly in Niger, privatized enterprises for groundnut oil processing, cattle marketing and groundnut and cowpea marketing were liquidated shortly after sale.[87]

Several factors have slowed the progress of public enterprise divestiture in Africa, as described by Berg (1993), Grouitch (1992) and others. The first is the *overall lack of public support* for privatization. In Africa, privatization is widely viewed by intellectuals and others as an externally imposed process which is often directed by foreigners for the benefit of foreigners. This feeling

---

[87] This experience is discussed by Berg (1993).

is re-enforced by the inclusion of privatization conditionality in donor support programs and by the frequency with which foreign investors do in fact acquire divested assets. The effects of divestiture on unemployment are also widely feared and can stimulate industrial unrest. Parastatal staff themselves form a powerful vested interest against privatization. Both governments and donors have done an inadequate job of convincing people that the benefits of privatization exceed the clear and immediate costs. Lack of transparency during negotiations and the undoubted tendency of some privatizations to benefit political elites have made privatization's public image even more negative.

The second factor that has slowed divestiture are *problems of defining and valuing enterprises* for transfer. Privatization can involve disaggregation of large enterprises and thus remedy diseconomies of scale or inappropriate mixes of activities. It may be difficult to compromise between the interests of potential buyers in acquiring well-defined profitable units and the interests of governments in not being left with the residual loss-making components. This is related to the question of valuation and whether governments remain liable for debts incurred by the enterprise during its public phase. If too many liabilities are left for governments, they will have little interest in pursuing privatization.

The last major factor is a *problem of finding willing and acceptable buyers.* Given the poor performance to date of the industries and difficulties with their valuation, in many cases it is difficult to find willing purchasers. The problem is more acute if there is opposition to the acquisition of divested enterprises by foreign investors, by local non-African groups or even by particularly active indigenous ethnic groups.[88] Weaknesses in capital markets have exacerbated this problem, by limiting the scope for 'acceptable' buyers to raise investment funds and by limiting the scope for diverse parties to pool investments.

The available information does not enable us to provide an in-depth analysis of privatization of high-value food processing and marketing enterprises. Limited data and information from a few countries provide the basis for only a preliminary generalization of patterns.

A first, tentative generalization is that privatization has often benefited

---

[88] A very particular case is when potential buyers are existing importers of a product, and thus suspected of a conflict of interest. This did not prevent the Malian tomato paste industry being sold to the leading importers (World Bank 1993).

foreign interests. In Mali, out of seven agro-industrial parastatals slated for the first and second phases of the privatization, it seems as if three will end up under the control of French or American interests.[89] Numerous other cases are cited in the literature. Sixty percent of the Office Camerounais de la Banane was sold to French private interests in 1990. The assets of Stalpeche, a joint Togolese Libyan parastatal venture in the fish sector, were sold in 1989 to a private company with 74% foreign, mainly French, shareholding. Government-owned pineapple plantations in Benin have typically become joint ventures between local businessmen and large French fruit distributors. A U.K.-based company took over management and 40% ownership of the Zambian Poultry Processing Company. A South African-owned company has taken over management of Mozambique's poultry processing plant and also sells the products through its own retail outlets.[90] In Uganda and Zaire some privatization has taken the form of restitution of confiscated assets to former nationals of Asian origin and former European settlers, respectively.

While there may be serious political arguments against divestiture to foreign buyers, as a trend it is in accordance with the economic argument presented throughout this report. International companies, or local interests closely bound to them, are much more likely than indigenous business interests in most countries to be able to undertake the financial commitments necessary to rehabilitate medium-to-large-scale agro-industries and manage the risks and transaction costs associated with export-oriented agricultural trade.

Some of the perceived problems of foreign ownership can be limited through joint ventures, with either the government or local entrepreneurs, or both, as local partners. Joint ventures in which the government retains some stake seem particularly common in Francophone Africa. In Mali in particular, enterprises have been privatized under complex equity arrangements involving foreign and local entrepreneurs, the Malian government and the French government. In one case, the fruit and vegetable company FRUITEMA, a local private company, has been able to increase its share gradually to 65%.

An interesting variation has been the involvement as equity holders of multilateral and bilateral finance organizations such as the International Finance Corporation, Britain's Commonwealth Development Corporation and

---

[89] World Bank (1993).

[90] In both of these cases, enterprise performance has improved markedly since the assumption of (foreign) private management. See FAO (1991, 1992).

France's PROPARCO.[91] Their involvement is useful in simultaneously assuaging government fears of irresponsible or exploitative private management and private sector fears of abrupt turnarounds in government policy leading to re-nationalization.

Our second preliminary generalization is that so-called non-traditional privatization has been more successful than the outright sale of assets to private parties. To test this, we can look at different forms of privatization, and problems that arise:[92]

1) *Classic sale of assets*: Outright sale of the entire concern is the most common and most straightforward form of privatization, but the one in which the problems outlined above can be felt most acutely; problems of valuation, lack of transparency, fears of foreign domination and lack of willing buyers. A specific problem is one of land tenure because land cannot be sold freehold, especially to foreign enterprises, in many African countries.

2) *Management contracts*: Many of the advantages of privatization can be achieved through management, technical or marketing contracts, generally with foreign companies, that do not involve the sale of assets.[93] Besides Cameroon, such contracts are widespread in Mozambique and Ghana. A management contract was the initial basis for Del Monte's entry into Kenya's pineapple canning industry. These contracts limit the investments, particularly fixed investments, required of private parties, avoid problems of land acquisition and are less vulnerable to political criticism of 'selling the country's heritage'. Problems arise when the rights and duties of the management company are left vague or experience slippage. The private partner can find itself either powerless to effect real reform or compelled to adopt a greater role than that specified in the contract.

3) *Leasing*: An alternative solution is the leasing of operations to private parties; a state holding company may retain ownership of some or all of the assets. Responsibilities for maintenance and replacement of fac-

---

[91] A semi-autonomous unit of the Caisse Française pour le Développement set up to assist the private sector in developing countries.

[92] Using a classification developed by Grouitch (1992).

[93] Or only involve a partial sale of assets, as in the case of the Zambian Poultry Processing Company referred to above.

tories have to be clearly specified. The advantages are largely the same as for management contracts, though a lessee would normally have more powers to effect reform. The problems lie in fixing a fair and attractive rent or rental formula, given fluctuating world markets for the product and in the fact that leasing requires less of a screening process than purchase. A lessee may turn out, once agreements have been finalized, to lack capital for reinvestment and operation.[94] Leasing appears to be the most viable solution to Tanzania's current white elephant problem regarding its large-scale cashew nut processing factories.

4) *Divestiture in favor of employees*: Management buy-outs and similar ideas fashionable in developed countries seem to have been little tried in Africa, or at least seldom admitted to. Although parastatal managers are becoming involved in private food-processing in Mali, this is by founding new companies, not by buying parastatal assets.[95] To the extent that privatization is aimed at reducing overstaffing or replacing unsuitably qualified managers (most often, generalist civil servants), the reluctance to try these approaches is understandable. Management may be more likely to become involved when relatively small units serving domestic markets are sold off individually, as Box 3.13 illustrates. It also illustrates some of the pitfalls.

These do not exhaust the types of divestiture possible. There are also, for example, hybrid forms involving a leasing or management contract for a fixed period followed by transfer of assets. The discussion does show that if divestiture is to be successful, the form it takes must be tailored to circumstances of the case and the country; and that transfer of ownership to the private sector is neither necessary nor sufficient for the successful running of an enterprise.

While much past government and donor attention was directed at the development of parastatal food processing ventures, the private sector plays an important role in the processing of high-value foods in many of the relatively large and commercially well-developed countries within the region. This can be seen in Table 3.7 which indicates the relative importance of private firms in various sub-sectors in a selection of ten countries. Private sector activity predominates in the formal processing of poultry, fish, oilseeds, fruits

---

[94] As happened in the case of a pineapple plantation in Guinea (see Grouitch 1992).
[95] CIRAD (1992).

TABLE 3.7: **Private Sector Involvement in 'Formal' (Medium/Large-Scale) Food Processing**

Industry	Kenya	Tan-zania	Zim-babwe	South Africa	Mada-gascar	Ghana	Nigeria	Côte d'Ivoire	Cam-eroon
Beef	2	4	2	1	1	—	1	3	—
Poultry	1	1	1	1	1	1	1	1	1
Dairy	3	3	3	1	1	1	1	1	1
Fish	1	2	1	1	1	2	1	1	1
Oil Palm	—	—	1	—	4	1	2	2	3
Oilseed	1	2	1	1	3	—	2	2	1
Fruit	1	1	1	1	1	1	1	1	1
Vegetable	1	1	1	1	1	—	1	1	1
Tree Nut	2	4	1	—	4	2	1	1	1

CODES:
1 Exclusive or Dominant (e.g. >60%) share of output by privately owned companies.
2 Important (e.g. 25–60%) share of privately owned companies.
3 Minor (<25%) share of privately owned companies.
4 No private sector participation
—No formal sector processing exists.

SOURCES: Literature Review; World Bank Agricultural Operations Staff.

Box 3.13: FROM MANAGERS TO PROPRIETORS: A CAUTIONARY TALE FROM MALAWI

In 1988 Malawi's Agricultural Development and Marketing Agency began to divest itself of unprofitable estates and activities. At least one of these, the Chirambe poultry and pig unit, was bought by a former senior manager of the agency, following a feasibility study by the IFC and using USAID and government finance.

The experience has not been successful. First, the government raised the price at the last minute, after the manager had committed himself. Then the 300 pigs attached to the unit died from swine fever, causing loss of revenue and wastage of a highly-specific asset. Lack of credit led to delays in importing feed, so some chickens died and others failed to reach their expected weight. By 1989 cash flow was so poor that the business was surviving on a week-to-week basis. Experience within a parastatal appears to have been inadequate for the technical demands of animal husbandry and the problems of a competitive business environment.

SOURCE: Marsden (1990).

and vegetables. In a few countries, it also predominates for beef and tree nut processing. The significance of public sector involvement tends to be highest for oil palm, dairy and tree nut processing where large-scale technologies have been employed with donor support.

Medium-to-large-scale private food processors have been engaged primarily in import-substitution activities, frequently aided by high rates of nominal protection. With relatively high unit costs (due to low capacity utilization, costly packaging, stringent labor laws and other reasons), most firms have not been competitive in international markets. There have been a couple of exceptions, including fish canning operations in parts of West and East Africa, meat processors in Kenya and Zimbabwe, and fruit and vegetable processors in several countries. Many, although certainly not all, of the successful export-oriented operations have been linked to major multinational corporations through ownership, management and long-term marketing agreements. For example, the tuna canning and export industries of Senegal, Côte d'Ivoire, Seychelles, Mauritius and Madagascar are all based on joint ventures with major French, Japanese and other international companies.[96]

Some industries have exhibited a dualism whereby most individual firms focus on serving the domestic market, while a limited number specialize in certain products for export. The Kenyan fruit and vegetable processing industry is one example. Here, the large majority of individual firms have operated multi-purpose processing plants, producing a broad range of products for the protected domestic market. These firms are entirely locally owned and managed. In contrast, a smaller number of firms have developed specialized operations, producing products for sale abroad. These firms have been owned and/or managed by multinational corporations and their sales have been incorporated into the wider international production and trading operations of the latter. The competitive advantage of firms linked to multinational corporations derives from their marketing expertise, rather than technology.[97] Table 3.8 summarizes this dualistic pattern among the industry's medium- and large-scale enterprises.

---

[96] ADB/Infofish Global Industry Update: Tuna (1989). Joint ventures also dominate Tanzania's and Uganda's emergent export-oriented fish processing industry at Lake Victoria (van der Hoeven and Budeba 1993).

[97] This dualism extends to crop procurement arrangements as well, with the domestic market firms relying primarily on seasonal surplus production, while the export-oriented firms have incorporated production activities via nucleus estates and contract farming schemes.

TABLE 3.8: **'Dualism' Among Kenya's Medium- and Large-Scale Fruit and Vegetable Processors**

Firm	Ownership	Management	Product Mix	Market Orientation	Export Earnings KL '000[a]	# of Employees[a]
Local Market-Oriented						
KO	Kenya Euro.	Local	Diverse	85% Local	<100	79
KC	Kenya Asian	Local	Diverse	90% Local	<100	55
Tru	Kenya Asian	Local	Diverse	95% Local	<50	65
KS	Kenya Asian	Local	Diverse	95% Local	<50	50
Export-Oriented						
KC	Foreign	Foreign	3 Products	98% Export	30,822	2500
NC	Kenya Asian	Foreign	1 Product	100% Export	2410	870
PAV	Foreign/Gov't	Foreign/Gov't	Limited Range	90% Export	813	240
KFP	Foreign/Gov't	Foreign	2 Products	85% Export	386	60

[a] 1985

SOURCE: Jaffee (1990).

Throughout the region, medium-to-large-scale food processing factories operate at relatively low levels of capacity utilization, due to a combination of raw material procurement problems, breakdowns in infrastructure (such as water and electricity), shortages of spare parts and weak market development. Although there are few individual country sub-sectors where reliable data are available for both private and public enterprises, the available data do suggest that private firms have achieved higher rates of capacity utilization than have parastatals (see Table 3.9).

There do not appear to be any systematic differences in the locational patterns of private and public food processing enterprises. Both tend to be highly concentrated in capital cities and one or two other major cities, as a consequence of the availability of infrastructure, the need for access to repair and maintenance facilities and the preferences of company management. For example, in the mid-1980s, thirty-eight of Senegal's forty-four food processing units were in the Greater Dakar area (Trouve 1984). Virtually all of Zimbabwe's formal sector food processing establishments are located in either Harare or Bulawayo. Kenya's food processing industry is heavily concentrated in four towns—Nairobi, Mombasa, Nakuru and Thika.

The experiences of formal, private sector processors with regard to choices of technology and product development are not well documented in the exist-

TABLE 3.9: **Rates of Capacity Utilization in Selected Food Processing Industries[1]**

Industry	Country	Cap. Util. (%)	Year
Fish Canning/Meat Processing	Ghana (Fish)	9	1992
	Nigeria (Fish)	12*	1990–91
	Senegal (Fish)	36*	1980
	Kenya (Pork)	52*	1990–92
	Zimbabwe (Beef)	54	1991–93
Dairy	Nigeria	12*	1990–91
	Tanzania	23	1987
	Kenya (Public)	36	1992
	(Private)	52*	1992
	Burundi	50	1988
Fruit, Vegetable and Nut Processing	Tanzania (Cashew)	5	1984–91
	Ghana (Fruit)	15	1991
	Burundi (Passion Fruit)	20	1988
	Nigeria (Fruit/Vegetable)	25*	1990–91
	Kenya (French Beans)	63*	Mid-80s
	Kenya (Pineapple)	83*	Mid-80s
Vegetable Oil	Gambia (Groundnut)	30	1984–88
	Nigeria (Oil/Fats)	50*	1990–91
	Cameroon (Oil Palm)	54	1988
	Senegal (Groundnut)	59	1987
	Burundi (Cottonseed)	60	1988

[1] Private sector industries marked with an asterisk (*).

SOURCES: Ndiaye et al. (1985; 1992); Hyman (1990); Jaffee (1990); Woodward et al. (1989); Lele and Christiansen (1989); Ross and Owusu-Sekyere (1992); Case Studies.

ing literature. The exceptions to this are for sugar processing, maize milling and *gari* processing, which all fall outside of our focus on high-value foods. Still, evidence from selected cases can be used to illustrate several points.

Within Kenya's dairy industry, there are several dozen small-to-medium-scale private firms producing cheeses, yogurt, ice cream, fermented milk, and pasteurized milk, either in competition with the dominant parastatal or targeting narrow niche markets (like the hotel trade). Most of the small, cottage industry-type firms employ less than twenty people and have concentrated on cheese, yogurt and fermented milk products, using simple batch technologies and makeshift equipment. The hygienic conditions in some of these processing units are quite good; in others, conditions are poor to the point of posing danger to the final consumer. A few medium-scale firms (employing twenty-five to fifty people) have sought to produce ice cream, tinned and pasteurized milk, and portion-sized cheeses and yogurt (for airline catering) using semi-mechanized flow technologies. Hygienic conditions are generally far higher in these operations. Most firms have sought to produce a wide range of products which are complementary from a technical and market point of view.[98] Some firms have also taken advantage of technical complementaries with other products or production processes, as in the use of whey as a feed for pigs and in the use of pasteurizing equipment for juice-making when supplies of raw milk are limited. Policy uncertainty and government restrictions on firm raw material production and sales strategies have deterred private firms from undertaking large investments in specialized technologies.

In Nigeria the recent expansion of soybean processing has been an interesting development. An export-oriented trade in unprocessed soybeans developed in Nigeria between the 1940s and 1960s. The local population was discouraged from using the seeds by colonial authorities who went so far as to tell them that the seeds were poisonous. Following the withdrawal of European companies and with the marketing board paying low prices to farmers, by the early 1970s this trade had fallen off precipitously. The availability of inexpensive imported soybean oil discouraged the development of a local processing industry. Because soybean production was low and limited to a few locations, by the mid-1970s the only commercial use for the seed was as a raw material for the traditional *daddawa* flavoring.

However, since the early 1980s, this situation has changed dramatically. Initial restrictions followed by complete bans on many imported foodstuffs and agricultural raw materials led processors to search for alternative, locally-produced raw materials, one of which was soybeans. Because of rapidly increasing prices for meat, milk and eggs, soybeans also proved to be a far cheaper source of protein. With the considerable support of the International Institute for Tropical Agriculture (based in Ibadan) as well as local researchers and food technologists, some forty Nigerian firms began to utilize soybeans as a replacement for other raw materials and as a basis for the development of entirely new products for the Nigerian market. In addition to using soybeans for oil and animal feed production, firms have produced and marketed a range of food products, including soy milk, soy-fortified flours and cassava products, soy-enriched cereals, biscuits and baby foods, and soy snacks.

---

[98] For example, producing low-fat yogurt and cream or producing full-fat cheeses and skimmed milk. Firms have produced cheeses of varying maturation in order to benefit from the higher prices of long maturity cheeses, while sustaining steady cash flow.

Collaboration between the private firms and researchers has been critical in product development and the design and adoption of technologies. It has also stimulated local demand for soy-based food products.

The wider experience in Nigeria's food processing industry indicates that the larger companies (affiliated with multinational corporations) which have integrated raw material production into their activities and which have focused on the production of packaged value-added food and beverage products targeted to middle- and upper-income groups have maintained or even increased their profitability in the wake of structural adjustment reforms. In contrast, many of the small-to-medium-scale firms which are dependent upon non-captive sources of raw materials and which are producing staple foods with lower levels of value added (such as vegetable oils, milk from powder, flour) have seen an erosion in their profitability since the mid-1980s.

Artisanal and Small-scale Food Processing[99]

In contrast to the mixed and frequently negative record of medium-to-large-scale food processing operations in Africa, the informal sector has been vital in supplying processed and ready-to-eat foods to domestic consumers, particularly in towns. Our discussion will focus on artisanal processing and trading to meet urban demand. Nonetheless, it is recognized that rurally based and rurally-oriented micro-enterprises are of considerable importance for high-value foods. This is especially true in the case of the edible oils sub-sector where great numbers of simple mechanical presses are operated across Africa by small or family businesses.[100]

Twenty-nine percent of the population of sub-Saharan Africa, or 142 million people, live in towns. This number has been growing by an average of 5.8% since 1970. It includes 36 million urban Nigerians, 23 million urban South Africans, and over a million people each in virtually every other African country.[101] Although there are small amounts of food cultivated in the backyards of urban residents, and some direct, non-commercial transfers of foodstuffs from relatives in home villages, most food consumed in towns must be bought.

---

[99] This section owes a considerable debt to the analytical perspective and Dakar case material presented in Bricas (1984).

[100] For oilseed pressing, see Gordon and Swetman (1990) for a general survey and Hyman (1993) for a Tanzanian case study. For artisanal palm oil pressing, see Devautour (1990) for Benin and Ay (1990) for Nigeria.

[101] World Bank (1993).

Evolving urban lifestyles result in an increased demand for processed and ready-to-eat foods. As urban women increasingly take paid employment, the time available for food preparation is reduced and second-generation urban women may never acquire traditional food-processing skills. Commuting, especially on crowded and poorly developed urban transport systems, further reduces the time available. Workplaces and schools are much less likely to have food canteens than their counterparts in developed countries.

It is clear that informal urban food supply systems have a huge potential market. This is borne out by quantitative information (by its nature approximate) on the importance of the sector. In Dakar the informal sector accounts for nearly all the supply, processing and distribution of traditional foodstuffs, most of the retail sale of industrial food products and all catering to workplaces. It is estimated to provide 12–15% of all urban employment, or 40–50,000 jobs, compared with 6800 jobs in industrial food-processing.[102] In Abidjan it is estimated that there are over 13,000 informal sector restaurants and food stalls. In Ile-Ife, Nigeria, in the early 1980s there was a woman preparing and selling street foods for every fifty-two people, and street food accounted for one third of the average household budget.[103] Recent survey work in Southern Africa found food and beverage processing to be the second most common line among micro- and small-scale manufacturers, trailing only textile apparel activities. While much of this activity relates to our focal commodities (for example, vegetable oil extraction, traditional cheese-making, fish drying and meat slaughtering), both grain milling and beer brewing were also important activities in the surveyed countries—Botswana, Lesotho, Malawi, South Africa, Swaziland and Zimbabwe.[104]

Besides the size of urban demand, the other determinant of the size of the informal sector are its relations to the formal sector, both public and private. These relations are complex and vary by country and sub-sector. Even in those cases where a formal sector (public or private) monopoly exists at the processing level, it is likely that the informal sector will undertake some of the retailing of these products. Other sub-sectors are almost exclusively controlled by the informal sector, such as domestically-traded fresh vegetables

---

[102] Bricas (1984). Only 4.8% of employment in Ghana's food and beverage manufacturing industries is in the large-scale sub-sector, a figure virtually unchanged between 1963 and 1984 (Steel and Webster 1991).

[103] CIRAD (1992).

[104] Liedholm and Mead (1993).

and fish in most African countries. In other sub-sectors there is clear market differentiation, with the formal sector providing an industrially-processed or imported product, usually well-packaged, for middle- and upper-income groups (and expatriate residents), and the informal sector providing a local product for the general population. In many countries, this is the case with fish, dairy products, and most notably, edible oil. Figure 3.1 below shows in simplified form the connections between the artisanal and industrial fishery sub-sectors and the dominance of the former in West Africa in terms of volume of fish caught and processed.

FIGURE 3.1: **Industrial and Artisanal Sub-sectors in the West African Fishing Industry** (tons per year)

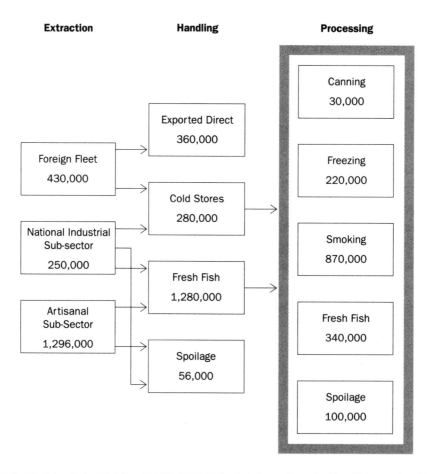

SOURCE: Adapted and simplified from UNIDO (1989). Estimated figures for entire West African region, Nigeria to Mauritania.

Box 3.14: INFORMAL MEAT TRADE IN SOUTH AFRICA'S TOWNSHIPS

Despite the heavy regulation of South African meat marketing, and the resulting concentration of trade and processing in the hands of three large private companies, informal meat trade in the black townships has continued for many years. Middlemen obtain sheep from auctions or through fixed arrangements with smallholders. They sell to butchers for high prices, seeking compensation for the risks now inherent in township trade, and the risk of disqualification from formal marketing channels. Township demand is for fatty meat considered inferior by the inflexible official grading system, so butchers pay more for this than the auction prices for the highest grade meat.

Meat moves quickly at the butchery stalls, clustered around public transport points through which black workers return to their outer-city residential areas. The butchers together with roadside steakhouses and female dealers in ready-cooked offal cater efficiently to urban needs and tastes.

SOURCE: Karaan and Myburgh (1992).

The advantages of the informal sector stem from prices, flexibility and taste preferences (Box 3.14). Prices will generally be lower because overhead costs such as rent are lower, labor is generally remunerated at lower rates and less (expensive) packaging is used. However, informal retailers of items produced by formal sector enterprises may still have to pass on high prices to consumers. The informal sector is flexible in its location; artisanal processes generally do not need specific sorts of premises and are less likely to depend on specific infrastructure provisions. Retail and the sale of street food are often carried out by mobile vendors who circulate in the markets and busy, central districts. Actors in the informal sector can also meet changing demand by dealing in different commodities and switching between retail and different sorts of processing as appropriate.

Taste preferences are one of the biggest advantages of employing artisanal processes. People have strong attachments to the foodstuffs that form part of their culture. Even when local foodstuffs can be industrially processed at a comparable cost to the consumer, the market for them is usually very small. This may be an ideological preference by consumers for a hand-processed

product, it may depend on differences in texture, or the greater variety presented by an artisanal product, or it may stem from easily verifiable differences in composition. For example, artisanally-processed red palm oil is greatly
preferred to industrial products by consumers throughout West Africa, because its higher proportions of free fatty acids give it a 'sharper' taste.[105]

Close integration with local consumption patterns and cultures is not syn-
onymous with economic or technological conservatism: those patterns and
cultures are themselves changing rapidly, especially in towns. Many of the
techniques now widespread, such as small mechanical oil presses or oil-drum
fish smokers, were themselves innovations earlier in this century, and the
sector still exhibits a characteristic openness to all sorts of innovation. Opportunities presented by new infrastructure (like electric refrigeration, cooking
on gas) will be exploited where costs permit. Technical innovations, like mechanized grinding or dehusking, are introduced as new components in the commodity chain and are often undertaken by service contractors who do not
assume ownership of the commodity, rather than by existing traders or processors. Some spontaneous development of products takes place: *gari* processors in Ghana and Nigeria may mix soy with the *gari* to give a 'milkier' taste
and add to its nutritional value. Traditional beer sellers in Benin, losing their
market to bottled beer, developed a weaker, sweeter product they could sell to
women and children.[106]

The chief constraint on innovation in the artisanal sector is its poor access
to outside research and development, both in terms of information and capital cost. Where useful new technologies are developed and carefully disseminated, the response can be impressive (see Box 3.15). Dissemination can be
through multiple channels: large donors, foreign or local NGOs, academic
institutions, missions.[107] Some innovations can be fundamental. In Senegal,
street food sellers successfully developed and sold new products when introduced to a Mexican technique of maize processing unknown in Africa.[108]

The artisanal food sector then accounts for a huge quantity of employment
and is vital in assuring adequate food supply to Africa's cities. It is flexible,
meets local demand and has the capacity to innovate. In light of this, it is

---

[105] Hyman (1990).

[106] RIO (1992), Devautour (1990).

[107] Tartanac and Treillon (1989) present a number of case studies, in which the roles of different
institutions in developing and disseminating technical innovations in food-processing are analyzed.

[108] Mestres and Ferre (n.d.).

important to emphasize its limitations. Throughout the literature it is emphasized that the urban informal sector, both generally and in food supply and processing, is characterized by survival rather than accumulation.[109] Its clientele and much of its workforce are the product of an urbanization process associated with sustained rural poverty and dislocation. With the formal sector unable to create employment, the informal sector functions as a safety net, and like most safety nets, makes a poor launching pad.

In other words, there is a low degree of graduation from the informal sector to the formal. This is now a widespread conclusion of work on the informal sector as a whole, and work on the urban informal food sector bears it out.[110] Collecting hard economic data is difficult, but it appears that most operators in the sector either do not save, or invest their savings in their children's education, social expenditures or remittances to rural relatives instead of in their businesses. Only entrepreneurs at the larger end of the informal sector, and formal entrepreneurs associated with it seem to be able to accumulate capital. These include transporters and wholesalers as well as bureaucrats and community leaders who invest in informal enterprises such as restaurants.[111]

Access to credit is perceived as a key constraint by many participants in the informal sector. Bureaucratic barriers and requirements for collateral prevent access to formal credit. Informal mechanisms are diverse. Rotating credit associations, Ghanaian *susus* and *tontines* in the francophone countries have received much attention. Yet, in most cases these are mechanisms for disciplined saving and carry little ability to make major productive loans. There are other mechanisms such as money lenders or hidden investment by bureaucratic or religious patrons, but these are often disadvantageous to the person operating the business. Even if the informal sector is not a launching-pad for the formal sector, its importance deserves attention in order to improve the availability of credit which will encourage increases in productivity and employment.

Prospects for accumulation in rural artisanal food processing may be somewhat better. The forced urbanization and safety net arguments do not

---

[109] Giri (1990), Marsden (1990); Bricas (1984).

[110] Liedholm and Mead (1987); Giri (1990); Onyeiwu (1992). Similar concerns are found in the literature on grain market liberalization where relatively few firms have gone on from primary (first-handler) to secondary (wholesale) marketing due to lack of resources, infrastructure and ability to bear the associated risks. Christiansen (1991) provides a useful discussion of this issue.

[111] Bricas (1984).

Box 3.15: NGO SUPPORT FOR SMALL-SCALE DAIRY ENTERPRISES IN KENYA

Since the late 1980s, U.S.-based NGOs Technoserve and Appropriate Technology International have worked with farmer groups, village-based societies, and family companies to develop small-scale milk processing enterprises in rural Kenya. The focus has been on the production of a cultured milk beverage ("mala milk"), using relatively simple facilities and a simple technology, developed initially by an expatriate visiting food technologist to the University of Nairobi. The cultured milk is very popular and is far less perishable than fresh milk as it can be stored for up to ten days without refrigeration.

The NGOs have provided assistance in market research, enterprise development, and training, and, in the cases of farmer groups, have made initial equity investments through a non-profit local trust. While there have been a few failed enterprises, most of the up-start processors have been highly successful and demand for the technical and managerial services of the NGOs by additional farmer groups in Kenya has far exceeded their capacity to respond.

---

apply, and there is a more natural progression from farming into small-scale processing to somewhat larger-scale processing on a custom basis or using outgrowers. It has been argued, for example, that village-level, camel-drawn sesame milling was a key rung up the economic ladder for many of Sudan's largest trading families.[112] Several of the 'success stories' featured in the FAO's (1982) *The Private Marketing Entrepreneur and Rural Development* come from among the class of rural artisanal processors. This area deserves further investigation.

STRUCTURAL FEATURES IN HIGH-VALUE FOOD MARKETING AND TRADE

This section highlights several prominent structural features of African private sector high-value food trading. It discusses a range of measures frequently adopted by private firms in order to overcome prevailing policy, infor-

---

[112] Mahmoud (1984).

mational and other barriers to trade. This material brings out the considerable importance of extra-market relationships in trade development and the often intertwined roles of formal and informal market institutions. Given the underlying weaknesses of infrastructure and market support services within the region, the economies of scale associated with certain trading functions and the relatively high risks and transaction costs faced in HVF trading, it is not surprising that the marketing channels for these commodities exhibit high levels of concentration, especially in export marketing. The evolution of HVF markets and marketing channels will be further examined in the individual case study chapters which follow.

The Private Sector Under State Domination

Private trade in agricultural commodities has shown a remarkable capacity to survive decades of government policies that have attempted to limit its role, exclude it from certain commodities or suppress it altogether. Paradoxically, the very adaptations that the private sector adopted in order to survive now limit its effectiveness in a new, liberalized context.

Many sub-sectors in numerous countries experienced little state intervention, particularly with domestically marketed foodstuffs not considered strategic. Thus, even in Congo, the first African 'People's Republic', the important domestic trade in vegetables and bananas remained private.[113] The most important national commodity sub-sectors, however, were subject to attempts at state control. These took two forms: bans on private trade in the commodity or limitation of the private sector by restricting the issue of trading licenses and maintaining official prices, which transformed private traders into 'licensed buying agents' (or some similar phrase). The first strategy was more often applied to staple foodstuffs or export beverage crops. It was also adopted by Tanzania for commodities such as cashews, and by Guinea for virtually all trade at points in its history. The second strategy, sometimes resulting from a partial liberalization of the first, has been used for a variety of export commodities within and outside the high value foods category and included groundnuts in Senegal, oilseeds in Sudan, and meat and dairy products in much of Southern Africa.

The effects of these two forms of state intervention on the private sector overlapped to a great extent. Ironically, the skills that the private sector was

---

[113] Ali-Gaye et al. (1989), Ma-Mfuka (1989).

forced to acquire and maintain were not those that would serve it in a liberalized market. Specifically,[114] there was a growth in corruption, as private entrepreneurs suborned officials to be allotted licenses, quotas or regional monopolies or for a blind eye to be given altogether to their operations. The incidence of this and other sorts of corruption was significant in most African states. In trades that had been prohibited, more private efforts were expended on the survival of enterprises, including bribes of officials, than on their growth and development. In licensed enterprises, efforts were directed to legal, borderline and illegal means of gaining patronage. In either case, the private sector collectively lost many of the skills necessary to 'normal' commercial operations, those of business administration and entrepreneurship.

In sub-sectors where private traders were enlisted as licensed buying agents, the competitive spirit of enterprise, of finding and defending new markets, was replaced by rent-seeking behavior as traders obtained quotas and regional monopolies and lived off of them. No value was placed on taking risk, and in systems where a state body provided advances to its private agents, there was no need to seek alternative sources of capital.

Government interventions also contributed to a climate of uncertainty; even during periods of liberalization, private operators have been uncertain whether policies favorable to them would be maintained or rescinded. Therefore, they have chosen low risk strategies, diversifying their source of income and avoiding large or long-term investment. Uncertainty has strengthened existing preferences for forms of savings that do not involve reinvestment in formal productive enterprise—gold, real estate, livestock, and social investment in consumption.

Some of these effects are illustrated in Chapter VI on the vanilla trade in Madagascar. Licensing has been the most important entry requirement into all levels of production, processing and trade, and most crucially into exporting. Only a dozen or so firms have been given export licenses. A small number of well-connected firms were awarded most of the export quota. In addition to bureaucratization and rent-seeking, the structure of incentives established by the state has led to the declaration of fictitious product stocks (whose costs are paid for by government) and the covert sale of such stocks at prices below the official rate.

Pockets of private enterprise can sometimes exist legally within state-

---

[114] To adapt a framework used by Terpend (1992).

controlled marketing chains. For example, in Zimbabwe between 1980 and 1989 a small and dynamic family firm was able to manufacture and develop new export markets for corned beef by a combination of buying from the parastatal Cold Storage Commission and importing meat.[115] Cases like this one and those of commodities that were never subject to state intervention are important for the lessons they can provide. Nonetheless, in many countries there has been a major distortion of the private sector such that many private enterprises are wholly unequipped to search for capital, raw materials and markets in a liberalized economy. They are even less capable of entering into competitive export trading.

Marketing Channels in Informal and Formal Export Trading Systems

Export marketing entails potentially quite significant transaction costs, given the considerable physical distance separating the exporter from the target market(s), differing cultural and business norms, potential language differences, and legal barriers to trade and effective contract enforcement. These transaction costs—related to communications, market assessments, legal and accounting fees, transport negotiations and quality claims—have proven to be among the most important barriers to export marketing by indigenous African firms who lack previous experience in international trade.

A common feature of successful and sustained export-oriented operations in Africa has been the development of extra-market trading networks which have economized on transaction costs, provided exporters with improved access to information, finance and other resources, and provided exporters with assurances of market outlets, even in unstable or declining markets. Extra-market networks have taken various forms and have involved both informal and formal systems.

The best examples of informal trading networks come from the trade in live animals, both the Sahelian and Coastal West African trade and that taking place in East Africa among producers and traders in Somalia, Kenya and Ethiopia.[116] The livestock trade is largely informal as it involves little institutional or judicial intermediation, except when a dispute cannot be settled within the social and trading community. Livestock trading channels are

---

[115] Riddell (1990).

[116] This discussion is based on Kulibaba and Holtzman (1990) and on the case study dealing with Somalia cattle marketing.

highly personalized and based on agreements and sanctions internal to the community. While certain ethnic or familial ties are found, ethnic solidarity tends to be less important than established trading networks involving producers, intermediaries, traders and final buyers (for example, butchers and processors). Various intermediaries including brokers play important roles in transmitting production and market information and in aggregating supplies. They also negotiate deals and provide assurance to buyers that animals are not stolen. These intermediaries shorten the transacting distance, if not the physical distance, between producers and final processors.

Within these trading networks, informal lines of credit tend to be far more important than commercial bank credit. Trust-based credit systems prevail in which traders or processors are required to make only partial or delayed payment for animals until the time that sales receipts are realized.[117] Social pressures and threats of future loss of reputation, business or access to animals contribute to relatively low default rates.[118]

Kenya's export trade in horticultural products has exhibited a blend of informal and formal trading arrangements which have been critical to that country's success (Chapter VII). Informal trading networks have been especially important in the fresh produce trade, where each of the leading firms has based much of its overseas trade on family ties or long-term personalized arrangements with selected firms (see Box 3.16). Relationships such as these have provided for superior access to reliable and up-to-date market information, reduced trading and price risks, and better flexibility in financial management. In contrast, a large number of firms which have been dependent upon arms-length, short-term marketing arrangements have been highly vulnerable to changes in market demand and to opportunistic behavior on the part of overseas market importers. The life-expectancy of firms who have conducted trade on a spot market basis has been extremely short, frequently less than one season.

For trade in processed fruit and vegetable products, the successful exporters have been those whose trade has been governed by intra-firm relations or long-term contractual ties. As noted earlier, export markets have only been

---

[117] This is discussed by Samatar et al. (1988) for Somalia and in Chapter IX.

[118] Although Kulibaba and Holtzman (1990) indicate growing problems of payment delays or default by West African butchers, partly as a result of structural adjustment programs and weakened consumer spending patterns.

Box 3.16: DEVELOPING A MARKET THROUGH PERSONALIZED TRADING NETWORKS

For the past quarter century, one of the core components of Kenya's expanding horticultural trade has been the export of nearly two dozen 'Asian vegetables' (including chilies, karela, okra, dudhi, etc.) to the United Kingdom to serve that country's expanding Asian minority communities. The development of this trade was built upon a series of highly personalized trading relationships, quite distinct from the mainstream U.K. fruit and vegetable marketing system.

Beginning in the 1960s and continuing through the 1970s, there was a rapid expansion in the U.K.'s population of individuals of South Asian ethnic origin. Fueled by immigration as well as relatively high birth rates, this population reached 550,000 in 1971 and over one million by 1980. Exhibiting a preference for certain traditional foods and lacking acceptable local substitutes for many of these foods, there developed a large un-met demand for a wide range of fresh vegetables which, for agro-climatic reasons, could not be grown locally. An import trade in 'Asian vegetables' first emerged in the early 1960s when several small-scale Indian merchants began receiving produce consignments from India and selling this produce from the parking lot of Heathrow Airport. Within a few years, Kenya would replace India as the primary 'Asian vegetable' supplier. Kenya's entry into this market was eased by the fact that most of that country's leading produce exporters were Asian-owned family companies with experience in the production and trade of 'Asian vegetables'.

By the early 1970s, some of the parking lot importers acquired vans and began making deliveries to London-based retailers; others developed wholesale distribution centers nearby to the primary mainstream wholesale markets. Still, the trade remained small and the market underdeveloped, especially outside of London. This would change in 1973, when a senior partner in Kenya's largest fresh produce company emigrated to the U.K. and established his own import/distribution company. This firm would re-shape the 'Asian vegetable' market by developing a network of secondary wholesalers and retailers within London and distribution networks within the major cities in the Midlands. The firm's family-affiliated supplier in Kenya responded to the market opening by rapidly expanding supplies. This integrated export-U.K. distribution operation soon became the leading actor in this market, setting the standards for quality and strongly influencing the levels of import and wholesale prices.

By the late 1970s, Kenya's other leading produce exporters also developed highly personalized, long-term trading arrangements with selected importer/distributors in the U.K. In some cases, the trading firms were linked by family ties; otherwise, connections were made through mutual friends and business associates. Both on the Kenyan and U.K. sides, the primary actors in this 'Asian vegetable' trade remained small-to-medium-scale Asian-owned family operations. Whether or not there were family ties, the typical framework for trade was seasonal contracts specifying the range of products to be traded, required quantities and delivery days, negotiated fixed prices, and payment arrangements. Most Kenyan exporters developed and maintained trade links to buyers based in several different cities so to achieve wider distribution and minimize direct competition among their buyers.

These personalized and long-term trading arrangements facilitated improved information flows, lowered exporter market risks and buyer procurement risks, reduced the risks faced by exporters of importer payment failure or false quality claims, enabled the firms to bypass exchange controls and otherwise take advantage of currency fluctuations, and enabled the firms to undertake joint efforts to test and promote new commodities. Secure exporter-importer ties provided the confidence to exporters to expand their trade and diversify their product range and the confidence of importers to search out new distribution channels, including those serving multiple-chain retailers.

the focus of foreign-owned and joint venture firms or firms which already have had contracts with foreign manufacturing and distribution companies. The Kenyan firms or subsidiaries have not been engaged in international marketing in the usual sense. Instead, Europe-based affiliates have been responsible for most decisions regarding product line, sales volume, delivery time, market destination and prices. Market research and development activities have been left to the European affiliates. So have the determination of distribution channels for the product and the negotiation of sales agreements with individual distributors and manufacturers.

While these integrated sales arrangements have led to concerns and allegations about transfer pricing and neglect for the financial profitability of the Kenyan enterprises, such ties have been critical to the success and sustainability of trade. Long-term and exclusive trading ties with major Europe-based firms have provided Kenyan and joint venture firms with immediate and continued access to markets, even those that are highly concentrated at import and wholesale levels or that have experienced stagnant or declining demand. These connections have improved flows of market and especially technical information and have reduced logistical problems. While these non-market trading ties have generated certain social costs (for instance, the failure to provide Kenyans with true international marketing experience), those fruit and vegetable processors who lacked strong ties with international firms have generally been unable to compete in European and Middle Eastern markets on the basis of cost and quality, and as a consequence, have not been able to develop sustained and profitable export trades.

A similar contrast is found in the recent market liberalization of cashew nuts in Tanzania (Chapter IV). Since 1991, more than ten private firms and cooperatives have sought to export raw nuts to India alongside the trade being conducted by the Tanzania Cashew Nut Marketing Board. A few of the private firms with prior international trading experience and experience serving the Indian market have developed successful trades over the past year that are based on links with affiliated companies overseas. The other workable alternative has been to engage trade brokers who have provided access to international sources of finance and obtained guaranteed purchase orders from individual Indian processors. These half-dozen successful exporters have not had to deal directly with Indian buyers or to handle the significant paperwork associated with trade between Tanzania and India.

In contrast, other Tanzanian exporters and cooperatives have entered the trade by negotiating deals with individual Indian buyers with whom they have had not prior business dealings. The results have been largely disastrous with regular cancellations of deals, large quality claims, 'missing' quantities of nuts in Indian ports, and other unexpected events which have resulted in losses for the Tanzanian exporters.

The Pyramidal Structure of Export Marketing Channels

Export marketing systems under the exclusive control of parastatal marketing boards have typically featured a pyramidal structure with significant numbers of licensed buying agents at the primary level, often a secondary level of cooperatives or other processors and transporters of the crop, and then the final level involving a monopoly exporter. With official producer prices, fixed trader margins and frequently exclusive trading zones, there was virtually no competition within such systems which would stimulate improved services to farmers and economies in marketing costs.

In parallel fashion, export marketing systems within the private sector have also tended toward pyramidal structures with numerous buyers or agents at the primary level and far fewer firms concentrated in export trade. However, except where strong government intervention remains (for example in the case of Madagascar vanilla trade), these exporting systems differ significantly from the parastatal-led systems because the oligopsonistic exporters and their primary level agents/buyers must compete for the business of farmers through price and non-price means.

Although market liberalization, exchange rate devaluation and foreign currency retention schemes have led large numbers of individuals and firms to enter into the export trade in unprocessed high-value agricultural commodities, most of these entrants operate on a very small, periodic or seasonal basis. Failure rates are high. In most of these industries, only a handful of firms tend to account for two-thirds or more of total trade (see Table 3.10). These are the core firms which not only remain in business but actually develop the trade through their investments in marketing facilities, investments in trading relationships and devotion of time and effort to lobbying government for improvements in services and the trade regime. While there are cases where trade oligopoly is a matter of government protection and rent-seeking, in the more typical scenario, trade concentration results from economies of scale, differences in management and marketing skills, and differences in access to (off-shore) financing and overseas marketing channels.[119]

Unfortunately, whether it is due to the ethnic characteristics of the leading firms, to objectives related to 'spreading the benefits' from particular trades or to other factors, these trade leaders are typically omitted in government and donor programs to expand and increase the competitiveness of non-traditional agricultural trade. Yet, at least in the short-to-medium-term, it is likely to be these firms which will underpin non-traditional export growth and provide the models in terms of products, markets, technologies, organization which other firms will seek to imitate.

---

[119] A recent review of major 'success stories' of HVF exports in Latin America and Asia similarly found high levels of concentration at the export stage, although in some industries there were large numbers of participants at the primary production and post-harvest stages (Jaffee and Gordon 1993).

TABLE 3.10: **High Rates of Export Concentration Among Private Firms**

Industry/Country	Share of Trade (%)	Number of Leading Firms
Horticulture		
Kenya Fruit/Vegetable	67	6
Senegal Fruit/Vegetable	81	5
Ghana Pineapple	63	6
Fish/Animals		
Nigeria Shrimp	74	3
Côte d'Ivoire Fish	>75	3
Somalia Cattle	70[a]	3
Spices/Nuts		
Tanzania Cashews	64[b]	3
Madagascar Vanilla	75	3

[a] For overseas trade from southern Somalia.
[b] Market share among private firms. Also public exports.

Cross-border trade

No study of private trade in Africa can ignore the existence of enormous unofficial flows of goods including high-value food commodities between African countries.[120] While accurate statistics are hard to collect, those who have studied the phenomenon have come up with astonishing estimates. In 1983 the total value of contraband between ECOWAS states was estimated at US$ 1.7 *billion*. Togo's unofficial trade with Ghana, valued at CFA 5.7 billion in 1983, was equivalent to 25% of its total official foreign trade. Gambia did not feature in Senegal's official trade statistics in 1985, but 45% of its actual foreign trade that year was with Senegal. Benin's official imports of sugar, which it does not produce, were less than the published consumption of its brewery.[121] The large flows of livestock between African countries are described in Chapter IX.

This trade appears in different forms from organized smuggling operations to local people trading with neighbors as they did until a national border was put between them. The extent to which such trade is explicitly illegal—or merely unrecorded—varies. In some cases, goods pass into an official export market through an intermediary country: coffee from Tanzania and Zaire has been known to enter Rwandan official marketing channels, and

---

[120] And in the case of Northeast Africa, between those countries and Saudi Arabia.
[121] Various authors cited in Coussy and Hugon (1985).

Gambian groundnuts to have been bought by Senegal's marketing organization. Even when the trade appears to be a local and traditional phenomenon, it is often very sophisticated: in markets in the area where Zaire, Uganda and Sudan meet traders deal in U.S. dollars and gold, as well as the three national currencies.[122]

Unofficial cross-border trade is generally explained as the consequence of government policies or as a straightforward manifestation of comparative advantage. The first argument is based on differences between parallel and official exchange rates (such as the former overvaluation of the Nigerian Naira and the Ghanaian Cedi against the CFA Franc) and on differences in prices due to official pricing and taxation policies. The latter argument is based on differences between a country with an interventionist marketing board and one with free trade in a commodity, or between two marketing boards, as in the case of Gambian and Senegalese groundnuts.

While it would be unwise to deny the relevance of these factors, arguments about them are often couched in extreme terms and become untenable. Barad (1990) cites 'conventional wisdom' as holding that:

> African states do not trade with each other because they all produce the same tradable goods. Unofficial transborder trade flows, if they are recognized, are usually explained as a response to price differentials induced by government policies.

Many obvious examples contradict this 'wisdom': for example, where unofficial trade flows in agricultural commodities are the result of the most straightforward form of comparative advantage: ecological differences. The huge flows of livestock from semi-arid zones to the coastal countries of West Africa, Egypt and the Middle East are a ready example of this, but there are others. There are also intermediate cases where the differentials between countries are in general levels of prosperity and purchasing power; this explains the export of fish over short distances from Tanzania and Uganda to Kenya.[123]

One significant feature of unofficial transborder trade is that entry barriers are usually lower than those to the official export trade. Potential buyers

---

[122] Meagher (1990).

[123] But not the export of dried fish (by bicycle) from Tanzania to Burundi, which seems much more specifically dependent on exchange rates. It is estimated that 20% of Tanzania's exports of nile perch are undeclared exports by boat or road (van der Hoeven and Budeba 1993).

are likely to be known through existing networks. When, as is so often the case, these are ethnic- or kin-based networks which span national boundaries, they provide pre-existing relations of trust and possibilities for informal enforcement of contracts. There is also more scope for small and irregular shipments, and fewer bureaucratic skills are required than with sea or air freight. These points are explored further in Chapter IX.

Commodity Diversification as a Trading Strategy

Multi-sectoral holding companies have played a prominent role in high-value foods processing and trading in certain African countries. These companies or groups have been able to spread their risks and better utilize their access to in-house or external financing. Their access to considerable infrastructural and managerial resources helps them gain a competitive advantage in the individual sub-sectors where they are active.

Commodity diversification is a prominent feature of medium-to-large scale private agricultural trade. This pattern contrasts sharply with the commodity specialization of most (export) marketing boards. Commodity diversification is common among private firms oriented to both domestic and foreign markets. Among the latter, one commonly finds exporters who use part of their foreign exchange earnings to legally (or illegally) import food, spare parts, appliances and other goods. This is especially common in intra-regional trade where the exporters import other items on the return trip and therefore do trade coming and going.

In many cases, this trade in imported products has been more profitable than the export trade. Oftentimes, it has been necessary simply in order to conduct export trade. Examples in this last category come from Guinea Bissau and Mozambique where the lack of basic goods and financial liquidity in the local economies led cashew nut exporters to pay farmers in the form of rice and other foods which the exporters imported. Also, in Somalia during the mid-1980s, trade liberalization provided profitable opportunities for the importation and distribution of vegetable oil, rice and other foodstuffs. The only firms which had the resources (and foreign exchange) to conduct this trade were the principal livestock exporters whose overseas trade was at the time only marginally profitable.[124] Policy reforms on exports and imports may thus have greater complementarity than sometimes realized.

---

[124] See Jaffee and Weli (1985).

Aside from this blend of export and import trading, trade diversification is widely practiced in order to counter the seasonality of individual crops, and thus to utilize more completely transport and other infrastructure. An additional factor may be a move to minimize policy-related risks related to possible government interventions in the marketing of any particular commodity.

Among our case studies, trade and investment diversification are quite common and usually provide for a complementarity of activities, products and market outlets. For example, many of the emerging private exporters of cashew nuts in Tanzania have been actively involved in trade in a range of non-traditional agricultural exports for many years. Each of these commodities, including various types of oilseeds and legumes, is storable and does not require specialized marketing facilities. These traders did not have to undertake any new investments to enter this trade. Since each of the crops has a different seasonal yielding pattern, the firms and their procurement agents have been able to engage in trade throughout the entire year and spread the investment costs for trucks and other infrastructure over a broad range of commodities. Revenues from other crop sales have provided working capital for these firms to make their initial cashew nut purchases.

Finally, commodity diversification has been an important ingredient in successful fruit and vegetable export marketing operations within the region. While a high-quality lead item is critical for initial penetration of particular markets, successful exporters have quickly diversified their product range so as to differentiate themselves from competitors and to spread their own commodity supply and market risks and to maintain steady clients of air freight carriers through both the peak and slow export seasons. By contrast, most of the enterprises who have failed in Kenya, Senegal, Mali and elsewhere have been totally dependent on only one or two commodities for their horticultural trade.

Product Promotion as a Marketing Strategy

As in much of the developing world, product promotion has something of a bad name in Africa. It has been argued that sophisticated product promotion has largely benefited affiliates of multinational firms and has served to marginalize local firms.[125] Memories of the breast milk vs. baby bottle for-

---

[125] See, for example, Langdon (1975), Mufson (1985), and Jouet (1984).

mula controversy, efforts to increase local tobacco use and similar campaigns by multinational firms to engineer a 'transfer of tastes' by introducing 'inappropriate products' from industrialized to developing countries have tarnished the image of advertising. Advertised products suffer by (negative) association.

While recognizing the social costs and frivolous nature of some promotion campaigns, it would be wrong to regard all food product promotion in Africa as anti-social and a mistake to ignore its potential advantages both in domestic market development and in exports of high-value foods. Yet, other than the horror stories, the literature on agricultural processing and marketing in Africa is virtually devoid of actual experiences in marketing or merchandising, including market research and product and brand name promotion. This applies to both public and private sector enterprises.

Advertising and product and brand name promotion are fairly significant in a number of African countries, especially Nigeria, South Africa, Zimbabwe, Côte d'Ivoire, Senegal and Kenya.[126] In Kenya, research in the early 1980s found that advertising for food and drink products exceeded Ksh. 10 million per year, and ranked fourth behind transport, personal care and household products in advertising expenditures. In both the food and drinks sectors, as well as more generally, many of the most heavily advertised products belonged to affiliates of multinational companies. Some local companies were also active.[127] More recent analysis of the marketing strategies employed by Kenya's small-to-medium-scale local private dairies reveals that few engage in media advertising. Yet, several do promote their products through in-store demonstrations and the distribution of samples at public events. Box 3.9 previously discussed the experience of one firm in Kenya in successfully promoting pork products among middle- and higher-income consumers. One of that firm's promotional devices are visits of "Bwana Sausage" to stores where he offers cash prizes to individuals who are seen ordering the company's products. Food product promotion hasn't only been directed at upper-income groups. In Nigeria, successful efforts have been made in recent years by research institutes and by small-to-medium-scale private firms to promote various types of soybean-based food products among all strata of income groups.

The available evidence does suggest that in many African countries, the most aggressive product promotion efforts are undertaken by affiliates of

---

[126] For Nigeria, see Newswatch (May 13, 1991). For Zimbabwe, see Katsande (1987). For Francophone West Africa, see Jeune Afrique Economie (December 1987).

[127] Jouet (1984), op cit.

multinational companies. This can be attributed to their experience, management and to the up-market clientele whom they serve. Local firms appear more inclined to sell non-branded products to institutional buyers or to rely upon longstanding links with retail outlets and chains to distribute their goods. In markets where competition is weak, there has been little perceived need to communicate directly to consumers or to listen to them. Such passive marketing strategies are likely to result in missed opportunities for local firms and relatively weak market development.

Product promotion is even more important (and less controversial) with regard to the export of high-value foods. Brand name recognition and promotion are prominent features of international trade in canned food products, and increasingly, fresh horticultural produce. For the most part, African exporters sell their products under somebody else's brand. With the exception of South Africa, nearly all of Africa's exports of canned fish, vegetables and fruit are marketed under the brand of a European, American or Japanese company. In many cases, these companies operate or are joint venture partners in the African firms.

Many African exporters of fresh horticultural produce have sought to establish a recognized brand name in European markets. These efforts have not been successful since few firms have been able to effectively promote their brand and to back it up with consistently reliable service and product quality. Thus, there are dozens of different West African brands for fresh pineapple, yet there has been little effective promotion of any of these brands for the past decade.[128] All of Kenya's more than one hundred fresh produce exporters have their own brand name, yet few of these are recognized by European distributors and consumers. Only South Africa's Outspan and Cape brand names (for fruit) are widely recognized in Europe.

---

[128] Afrique Agriculture (July 1993).

PART B:
CASE STUDIES

INTRODUCTION

Chapters IV through IX are case studies examining the development of and private sector role and performance in six commodity systems in five sub-Saharan African countries. Each study begins with an analysis of the techno-economic characteristics of the focal commodity and its production, processing and marketing. This yields insights into the potential risks, transaction costs and logistical problems which private processors and traders face as well as the potential barriers to their entry. In each case study, this analysis is followed by a brief overview of the importance of the focal commodity in the production, domestic consumption and international trade of sub-Saharan Africa. The background and historical development of the particular country commodity system is then outlined. The subsequent and core section of each chapter concerns the characteristics and operations of the private sector. The order of presentation of the studies relates to the *degree of government intervention* in the focal commodity systems, whether directly in trade and processing or indirectly through regulation and control of private activity. While in some cases governments have facilitated private sector investment and trade, at other times governmental controls and direct participation in markets have deterred private sector entry or undermined its performance.

Chapter IV examines the development of Tanzania's cashew nut industry, emphasizing the nature and apparent impact of recent policy changes which have liberalized the market and permitted private firms to participate in trade. For more than two decades this industry featured monopoly trading and processing operations by a parastatal enterprise. With the industry approaching almost complete collapse, the government moved in 1991 to liberalize cashew trading. The case provides insights into the *nature of private sector responses to policy reforms* in a still uncertain policy and market environment.

Chapter V examines the development of and private sector role in Kenya's dairy sector. While smallholder dairy development in that country has been a considerable success, *formal marketing of milk and other dairy products has been dominated by a government-controlled cooperative* which has used the powers of the state and donor financing to marginalize private and independent cooperative dairies. The case study examines the entry and *competitive difficulties faced by the private and cooperative dairies*, their strategies for coping in a constrained market environment, and their prospects under a liberalized market.

Chapter VI deals with Madagascar's vanilla sub-sector. It provides a case in which processing and trading functions have been conducted exclusively by private firms and individuals, yet within a highly controlled framework set by government. In recent years, excessive market controls and a short-sighted commercial policy have dulled producer and trader incentives, channeled private entrepreneurship into rent-seeking modes, and undercut the country's international market position. This case is illustrative of *circumstances in Africa where private firms have been forced to serve as mere agents of the state.*

Chapter VII deals with the case of Kenya's horticultural sub-sector, one of Africa's major success stories in non-traditional export development. This sub-sector has featured a dominant role for the private sector in processing and trade, although during its post-independence take-off stage the government facilitated a series of foreign investments which proved to be of strategic importance to the overall development of the sub-sector. The case study highlights the *diverse forms which private processors and traders take* and their varied linkages with producers and with overseas marketing agents. The importance of developing long-term crop procurement and marketing arrangements in this highly risky line of trade is emphasized.

Chapter VIII examines the case of Ghana fisheries, one of West Africa's largest and most influential fishery sub-sectors. The case highlights the *centrality of artisanal fishing and processing activities for domestic markets* and the *short-term adverse effects* which that country's *structural adjustment program* has had on the sub-sector, both its artisanal and industrial components.

Chapter IX deals with the case of cattle marketing in Southern Somalia prior to the breakdown of civil order in that country in 1992. The case illustrates the *importance of informal and often kinship-based trading networks in Africa's long-distance and cross-border trade* in live animals, as well as the responsiveness of private traders in the face of general economic and political instability.

IV.

Private Sector Response To Market Liberalization in Tanzania's Cashew Nut Industry

Steven Jaffee

INTRODUCTION

In the period between World War II and the early 1970s, Tanzania developed one of the world's largest cashew nut industries, accounting for some 30% of total world production and ranking among the leading exporters. Cashews became one of Tanzania's largest sources of foreign exchange and provided an important source of income for some 250,000 smallholder farmers. Although Tanzania's cashew nut trade was intitially developed by private traders, during the 1960s a multi-tiered marketing system—featuring local cooperative societies, regional cooperative unions and a national marketing board—was imposed, and the role of private traders marginalized and eventually removed entirely.

As analyzed by Ellis (1979, 1980, 1982), this multi-tiered marketing system failed to operate efficiently. Rising marketing costs together with declining real producer prices and the forced 'villagization' (a program of collectivization) of smallholder farmers greatly undermined the incentives to produce cashew nuts. From the mid-1970s the industry underwent a steady and dramatic decline. By the late 1980s, marketed cashew nut production was only 15% of the level it had reached in the early 1970s. Most government processing factories lay idle and Tanzania's reputation for a high quality product had been badly damaged.

In 1991 with the industry on the brink of complete collapse, the Tanzanian Government announced that the cashew nut market would be liberalized, and private firms permitted once again to undertake trade. It viewed liberalization of the cashew nut market as somewhat of a test case whose results would influence the speed and nature of institutional reforms in the processing and marketing of Tanzania's other major industrial crops, including coffee, cotton and tobacco.

This chapter examines the liberalization process within Tanzania's cashew nut industry over the past two years, placing particular emphasis on the nature of the private sector response to market reforms. What types of firms have been able to take advantage of the market reforms? How has the re-entry of private firms into the cashew trade affected the trade of cooperatives and the Tanzania Cashew Nut Marketing Board, and the welfare of farmers? How competitive is the liberalized market and what factors have constrained the emergence of a greater degree of competition? What residual market controls have remained, either officially or unofficially? To what extent has market liberalization placed the industry on a road to recovery? The liberalization experience within Tanzania's cashew nut industry offers useful insights for other sub-Saharan African countries where uncertainty remains about the appropriate role for marketing boards in liberalized markets, the ability of cooperatives to compete in such markets, and the ability of indigenous firms to take advantage of new trading opportunities.

This chapter is comprised of four sections. The first section examines important techno-economic characteristics of cashew nuts and their production and processing, noting possible implications for the organization of cashew nut processing and marketing. The second section reviews the world market situation for cashew nuts and the changing position of Tanzania and other sub-Saharan countries therein. The third section traces the rise and decline of Tanzania's cashew nut industry from the early 1930s until 1990. Finally, the last section examines the process of market liberalization which has taken place since 1991, emphasizing the nature and effectiveness of the private sector response.

Cashew Nuts: 'Poor Man's' Crop and 'Rich Man's' Food

The cashew (*Anacardium occidentale L.*) belongs to the Anacardiaceae family of plants, which also includes the mango, the pistachio nut, and the noxious poison ivy, poison oak, and poison sumac.[1] The cashew tree is an evergreen perennial found in many tropical areas. Native to northeast Brazil, in the

---

[1] The English word cashew is derived from the Portuguese *caju*, which in turn came from the Tupi-Indian *acuji*. This section of the case study is based on FAO (1969), Northwood and Kayumbo (1970), Rosengarten (1975), and Ohler (1979).

16th Century the cashew was taken by Portuguese colonists and missionaries to East Africa and Goa (India) where it thrived. The cashew has since spread to several dozen countries, primarily between latitudes 15 degrees north and south. Under favorable conditions, the tree can grow to a height of 40–50 feet.

While used for shading and anti-erosion purposes, the cashew tree is most valued for its fruit. The fruit is unusual in that it has two connected parts. One part is a fleshy, pear-shaped stalk, known as the 'cashew apple'. This apple is juicy and thin-skinned, from two to four inches in length. The second part of the fruit is a kidney-shaped nut, one to one and one-half inches long. The nut shell is smooth and oily and contains a toxic, resinous material. Contained within the nut is a white kernel—the cashew nut which is eaten—approximately seven-eighths of an inch in length.

While the cashew nut kernel is frequently the focus of commercial activities, various components of the cashew fruit as well as the cashew tree itself can be regarded as industrial raw materials. In this regard, the cashew is similar to the coconut tree. Having an astringent taste when eaten directly, the cashew apple has multiple potential uses in juices, jams, syrups and alcoholic beverages.[2] The vitamin C content of the apple is several times that of citrus fruit. The toxic liquid found in the nut shell, known as cashew nut shell liquid (CNSL), has been used in tropical medicines and has had various industrial applications (as a friction-modifying material in brake linings and as an ingredient in paints and varnishes). The cashew nut shell can be ground into a powder for use as an ingredient in building materials and pest-repellents. The wood itself provides excellent raw material for charcoal production and for the construction of boxes. Our discussion focuses attention on the cashew nut and kernel since these are the dominant commercial products within Tanzania's industry.

Cashew nuts (and kernels) have certain properties which may influence the organization of their trade. They are characterized by:

1) **Low perishability:** As long as the nuts are properly dried immediately after harvest (to a moisture content of less than 8%), they can be stored

---

[2] In most countries the cashew apple is wasted or discarded. In Africa, despite the fruit's very high nutritional properties, the 'apple' is used primarily to make alcoholic beverages. In contrast, both in India and Brazil the apple is widely used, contributing to increased farmer incomes and increased employment and value-added in industry. In India, a carbonated beverage and several types of alcoholic drinks are made from the apple; in Brazil, a wider industry has developed which uses the apple to produce juice, jam, chutney, etc.

without significant loss of quality for up to one year.[3] This implies that production and subsequent processing operations need not be tightly coordinated with one another as processors can conceivably maintain stocks of nuts to guarantee even throughput into their factories. Post-harvest drying involves a simple technique of placing the nuts on bamboo or metal sheets under the sun. Hence, unless the harvest period coincides with precipitation or very high humidity, there is no technical requirement for a rapid collection of the crop from farmers. Cashews can be stored in heaps or in bags and do not have special storage requirements. The kernels also have a long shelf-life as long as they are stored in air-tight containers or similar forms of packaging.[4]

2) **Bulkiness of the raw material:** Although cashew nut kernels are a very high value commodity (see below), the kernel makes up only 20–30% of the weight of the harvested raw nut. Given the presence of foreign matter, empty shells, and diseased or deformed nuts, the actual yield of kernel material from raw nuts is generally only 18–23%. Unless other by-products are to be used, the transport of raw nuts will involve movement of much wasted material. This indicates potentially large cost savings by locating processing facilities in close vicinity to major production areas.

3) **Wide quality variability in the raw nuts and kernels:** As a result of genetic, agro-climatic, and other factors, there are significant differences in the size and shape of raw nuts, in the thickness of the shell, and in the proportion of kernel material contained. These variations occur between locations, trees and even on the same tree. The quality (and size) of the kernel cannot be judged by the outward appearance of the nut, except when there is clear evidence of disease or deformities. Even though kernel size/quality is not necessarily linked to raw nut size and color, these crude indicators are frequently used to determine grades. Only by doing a cutting test on a sample of nuts can a trader detect the true quality of the nut. There is thus a likelihood for conflict and uncertainty over grading.

---

[3] Nuts which are not properly dried will develop mould or bacteria or experience irreversible damage to the kernel as a result of enzyme action.

[4] In contrast, the cashew apple is highly perishable and must be processed within 24 hours after being picked.

Wide quality variability also occurs for kernels. Major distinctions are between 'wholes' and 'brokens', between 'white' and 'scorched', and between different sizes of kernels. There exist international quality standards which provide the vocabulary for international trade. Very large price differentials exist between the different grades of whole and broken cashew kernels. It is the production and proper grading of high standard kernels which separates profitable from unprofitable processing operations.

The production and processing of cashew nuts have several characteristics which also influence organizational patterns:

4) **Cashews are tolerant of varied, marginal soil and climatic conditions:** Due to their extensive root system, cashew trees can grow in areas with relatively poor soils and with relatively low rainfall. Cashew can grow on poor or stony soils, although best results are obtained on well-drained sandy loam soils. It can set fruit where rainfall is as limited as 40 inches per year as long as there is a distinct dry period of two to four months. Its resilient properties have frequently led to its cultivation in areas where few other crops provide an economic return. Yet, although the tree will grow under adverse conditions, it will not reach its full productive potential and consequently yields in such regions are well below their genetic possibilities.

5) **Cashew production features relatively low entry costs and little intensity of cultivation or maintenance:** Cashews can develop in the wild through natural cross-pollination but are otherwise generally cultivated from selected or unselected seeds, rather than from purchased seedlings. Entry costs are minimal unless planted on a large scale. The fact that cashews can be intercropped with other crops (at least until the development of the tree canopy), does not lock the farmer into long-term monocrop cultivation of cashews. Few, if any, specialized production inputs are required for cashew cultivation. Tree maintenance, involving weeding and pruning, is less demanding than for most other tree crops. Depending on genetics and local conditions, the cashew will normally yield a commercially worthwhile crop by the third or fourth year and reach premium yields by the eighth to tenth year. The cashew has a very long productive life of thirty years or more.

6) **Cashews have a seasonal and uneven yielding pattern:** Cashew trees yield mature fruit (and nuts) during a distinct season, which lasts three

to four months. Effective storage is thus critical for continuous utilization of processing facilities. If the 'apple' is not being used, the grower can wait for the fruit to drop to the ground signifying its maturity. One problem is that the yielding pattern is very uneven with small quantities maturing initially, building up to larger quantities, and then dropping down to smaller amounts again. Under humid conditions or where harvesting coincides with precipitation (as in Tanzania), the harvesting must be very regular. The uneven yielding pattern creates barriers to efficient use of hired labor for this task. This, together with features (4) and (5) above partially explain the dominance of smallholder cultivation with family labor for cashews (and its nickname, the 'poor man's crop').

7) **Cashew nut processing is a complicated process not amenable to on-farm activity:** Cashew nut processing is more costly and difficult compared with that for other dessert nuts. The cashew nut shell is more difficult to break and requires conditioning, via humidification and roasting, before the kernel can be removed through decortication. This problem is exacerbated by the presence of the toxic, sulphur-containing CNSL. Physical contact with CNSL can result in severe burns or dermatitis. Care must also be taken to prevent the CNSL from coming into contact with the kernel and therefore contaminating it. Cashew nut processing thus requires some technical skill and careful management.

8) **There are a range of technologies available for cashew nut processing:**[5] Traditionally, the various functions of cashew nut processing were performed manually, using semi-skilled workers with experience. This remains the situation in India, the world's largest producer of cashew nut kernels. Since the 1960's, however, various mechanized processes and equipment have been introduced in several countries for roasting, CSNL extraction and decortication (deshelling). For the most part, raw material cleaning and sizing and kernel grading have remained very labor-intensive, manual operations. There are significant differences in investment requirements, labor skills (and health) requirements, and levels of efficiency between the Indian, largely manual technology and the various types of medium-to-large-scale mechanical and semi-me-

---

[5] The technologies of cashew nut processing are examined in FAO (1969) and in Ohler (1979).

chanical operations. In general, the Indian processing system involves lower investment and variable costs and achieves far greater efficiency in terms of kernel material yield and the proportion of whole kernels. Nonetheless, that system requires large numbers of experienced workers who work at unhealthy levels of exposure to the CNSL. The mechanized systems are more vulnerable to breakdown (due to shortages of spare parts, lubricating oils, etc.), require large quantities of nuts for efficient operations,[6] and operate well below manufacturer specifications wherever strict grading and sizing activities are not in place prior to the decortication process.

THE WORLD MARKET SITUATION FOR CASHEW NUTS

International trade in cashew nuts began from India after World War I. Following the introduction in the 1920s of improved packaging for long-distance transit, the trade expanded rapidly, especially between India and the United States. By World War II, cashew nuts had become the second most important traded dessert nut (after almonds). They have remained in this position for the past half century.

Although consumed in the countries of production, the cashew nut is widely regarded as a luxury snack food, chiefly destined for markets in countries with above average per capita incomes. Cashew nuts are the most expensive of the major dessert nuts with a unit value typically 40% higher than that of almonds and three times that of all nuts as a group.[7] Some 90% of cashews are eaten out-of-hand, in contrast to the pattern for other nuts which are more commonly ground down into paste or used for confectionery purposes. This explains the very large price differentials between whole and broken cashews and among whole nuts of different sizes.

World Production Trends

World production of cashew nuts grew rapidly during the 1950s and 1960s, reaching a peak of 510,000 tons (of raw nuts) in 1974.[8] Three countries—India, Mozambique, and Tanzania—accounted for the majority of this pro-

---

[6] Most of the major manufacturers have produced systems with a rated capacity of more than 3000 tons/year. There are a few manufacturers whose systems have rated capacities of 500 tons/year or less. It is the larger systems which have been put in place in Tanzania and Mozambique.

[7] Only macadamia nuts are more expensive than cashew nuts.

[8] Gill and Duffus Edible Nut Market Reports, various years.

duction, while smaller industries had developed in Brazil, Kenya and several other African countries. Beginning in 1975, however, and continuing through the mid-1980s, there was a sharp fall in world production, which contributed to a tight international market. Indian production remained stagnant, and the global fall can be attributed to the huge decline of production in Mozambique and Tanzania. Since the mid-1980s, there has been some recovery in world production due primarily to a significant expansion in Brazilian production. Table 4.1 summarizes major patterns in world production over the past two decades.

The table indicates that the share of sub-Saharan Africa in world production decreased from nearly 60% in 1969–71 to only 28% in 1989–91. A small recent expansion in West African production has not compensated for the extreme decline in Mozambique's and Tanzania's production levels. While in 1969–1971 Brazil's production was only 8% that of sub-Saharan Africa, by 1989–1991 Brazil's output exceeded than of the African continent.

World Trade Trends

Cashews are one of the many varieties of edible nuts traded worldwide. World trade in edible nuts has experienced relatively rapid growth, averaging about 2.7% per year since the early 1970s and increasing in value from $1.94 in

TABLE 4.1: **World and Country Cashew Nut Production, 1969–71 to 1989–91**

Country/Region	Average Annual Production (000 Tons)			Share of World Production (%)		
	1969–71	1979–81	1989–91	1969–71	1979–81	1989–91
India	**175.7**	**159.0**	**140.0**	**33.8**	**36.2**	**28.1**
Brazil	**24.1**	**71.3**	**145.5**	**4.6**	**16.2**	**29.2**
Africa	**311.1**	**174.9**	**140.4**	**59.9**	**39.8**	**23.2**
Mozambique	180.0	69.4	44.7			
Tanzania	108.4	54.2	27.0			
Kenya	16.2	15.8	11.5			
Nigeria	Na.	25.0	25.0			
Guinea Bissau	2.4	3.8	19.0			
Others[1]	5.0	6.7	13.2			
World	519.5	439.7	497.9	100.0	100.0	100.0

[1] Including Côte d'Ivoire, Madagascar, Angola, Benin, Togo, Mali and Zambia.
Na. Not applicable.

SOURCE: FAO Production Yearbooks, various years.

1980 to $2.84 billion in 1990.[9] Only seven varieties of nuts—groundnuts, almonds, cashews, brazil nuts, desiccated coconut, hazelnuts, and walnuts—account for 90% of international trade in edible nuts. While international trade in cashew nut shell liquid is not insignificant, the discussion here focuses on trade in raw cashew nuts and kernels.

International trade in **raw cashew nuts** has traditionally involved shipments from East Africa to India. India was the first country to build up a processing industry. Domestic production has been unable to meet the requirements of that country's hundreds of small-to-medium-scale processing factories. Government restrictions on internal movements of cashew nuts further constrained raw material supplies and necessitated imports from the emerging East African industries during the 1950s and 1960s. Peak levels of raw nut imports into India were reached in the early 1970s and exceeded 175,000 tons per year. The imports, generally concentrated over the December to May period, complemented the local harvest which begins in May and continues until July. Indian processors could thus operate over an extended period without having to maintain large stocks of raw nuts.

This trade declined when production in East Africa declined and as a result of periodic constraints on access to foreign exchange by Indian importers. Raw nut imports fell to as low as 20,000 to 30,000 tons/year during the early 1980s. Since then, import levels have increased due to greater supply availability, particularly from Southeast Asia. In the first six months of 1992, imports totaled over 80,000 tons with the largest supplies coming from Vietnam, Indonesia and Tanzania.[10] While Tanzania once obtained premium prices over those of other suppliers, this has not generally been the case in recent years due to growing uncertainty about the quality of Tanzanian shipments.[11]

World trade in **cashew kernels** is far better documented than is the trade in raw nuts. According to Gill and Duffus, world imports in 1990 totaled over $500 million, ranking cashews second (behind almonds) among dessert nuts. India has long been the world's largest supplier of kernels with its prices and quality setting the benchmarks or standards for the industry. At least in Europe, India has been the preferred supplier, with long-standing trading relationships based on confidence in product quality and on fast and regular deliveries. India has more than 150 cashew kernel shippers, many of which have offices in the United States and Europe.

---

[9] Such figures are for world exports as reported in United Nations, Yearbook of International Trade Statistics.

[10] *The Cashew*, October–December 1992 (Indian trade magazine).

[11] As reported by international cashew brokers and as indicated in the Indian import data.

Box 4.1: CASHEW NUT INDUSTRY DECLINE AND RECOVERY IN MOZAMBIQUE

Between World War II and the early 1970s, Mozambique emerged as the world's largest producer of cashew nuts, accounting for some 40–50% of total world production. Initially, private traders of Indian origin initially procured the crop and shipped raw nuts to India for processing. However, with a steady build up of local processing capacity after 1960, Mozambique began to export most of its production in kernel form, undercutting India's former monopoly of this trade.

After Mozambique's independence in 1975, things began to fall apart in the cashew nut industry. The decline was brought on by the exodus of experienced traders and factory managers, combined with civil war and severe shortages of foreign exchange and basic consumer goods. Security problems led farmers to flee from important production areas and restricted the overall movement of goods. Shortages of spare parts further hampered the transport of cashew nuts and forced many traders out of business.

Producer incentives also declined sharply. The export trade was brought under the control of a parastatal agency (although private traders continued to act as buying agents), and official producer prices and trading margins were set. From the mid-1970s through to the mid-1980s, real producer prices declined sharply. This and the overall shortage of consumer goods undermined incentives for producers to sell their nuts. Home consumption of cashew nuts increased sharply (to compensate for declining groundnut production) and much of the rural trade in cashew nuts came to be based on barter arrangements. Overall productivity declined as production support services deteriorated and the age of most trees extended beyond their productive years. Production which had averaged over 200,000 tons/yr. during 1972–1974 fell to only 25,000–30,000 during the mid-1980s. Nearly half of the country's cashew nut processing facilities were closed, and the others operated at well below capacity.

Starting in the mid-1980s, the industry began to recover. This process has been accelerated by the recent ending of hostilities in the main production areas. Private firms have once again been permitted to operate processing factories and conduct exports, and in 1992 they accounted for 35% of the value of trade. The parastatal Caju de Mocambique is presently being prepared for privatization. A World Bank-funded project is supporting the rehabilitation of cashew groves and marketing infrastructure. The improved security situation in the countryside has aided cashew collection. Marketed production recovered to 54,000 tons in 1991/92 and export levels are increasing from year to year. Cashews remain a very important crop for smallholder agriculture in Mozambique and the further recovery of the industry will be critical to the country's overall economic recovery.

SOURCES: Edible Nut Market Report; Austin (1991); Jaffee (1993); World Bank documents.

Through the early 1970s, Mozambique was also a major exporter. Its decline has been paralleled by a major expansion in Brazilian exports. While Brazil doesn't obtain the technical results which prevail in India's manual processing system, it has been competitive in the U.S. market due to lower transportation costs and the unique larger-sized variety of the nut produced there. Other suppliers, including Tanzania, Kenya and China have a reputation for irregular quality, contributing to substantial price discounts (of 25–30%) in international markets. Table 4A (see Annex at end of this chapter) traces the levels of kernel exports by the leading suppliers, while Table 4B (see annex) illustrates the substantial price premium obtained by Indian suppliers.

On the import side, the United States is by far the largest single market, accounting for more than 50% of world imports. The bulk of such imports are eventually marketed as a snack food under three main brand names—Planters, Eagle Snacks, and Fisher. Cashews are the only major dessert nut for which U.S. domestic production is negligible and the U.S. is in fact a major exporter of almonds, walnuts, hazelnuts and other varieties. Table 4C (see annex) indicates import levels of the other major import markets (Japan, Australia, Canada, the former USSR and several EEC countries). With the chief exception of the former USSR (which had previously been a large importer of lower quality nuts for confectionery use), import levels increased in these major markets during the 1980s.

Long-term trends in international prices in kernels are shown in Figure 4.1. The data refer to U.S. CIF prices per ton for benchmark size 320 whole kernels. Current prices have been deflated by the G-5 MUV index to obtain real prices. The graph shows that since the early 1970s, sharp increases in (nominal and real) prices were recorded during three periods—1976 to 1977, 1979 to 1982, and 1984 to 1987. Through most of the 1980s, real prices were higher than those which prevailed during the early 1970s.

FIGURE 4.1: **International Prices for Cashew Nut Kernals**

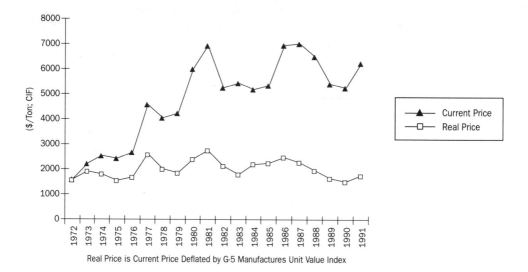

Real Price is Current Price Deflated by G-5 Manufactures Unit Value Index

THE RISE AND DECLINE OF TANZANIA'S CASHEW NUT INDUSTRY

Cashew nut production and trade has long played an important role in the Tanzania economy. Over much of the period since the early 1960s, cashews have been Tanzania's fourth largest source of foreign exchange, following coffee, cotton and sisal. Cashews are grown by more than 250,000 smallholder farmers. Although cultivated throughout the coastal area, cashew nuts have long been the most important source of farm incomes in the southern regions of Mtwara, Lindi, and Ruvuma. The decline of the industry has had a strong adverse effect on living standards in these regions.

The cashew was probably introduced into Tanzania from Mozambique in the 16th Century and was initially used to check soil erosion in the coastal areas. Cashew groves developed naturally and there is no evidence of any specialized production or commercial trade of the crop prior to this century. This section traces the early development and subsequent decline of the Tanzanian industry through four periods, namely:

1) 1930s to 1962—Private merchants and the development of trade

2) 1962 to 1974—Expansion and multi-tiered marketing system

3) 1974 to 1985—Industrialization and production decline

4) 1985 to 1991—Reversing the downward slide

Private Merchants and the Development of Trade (1930s to 1962)

A commercial cashew nut trade did not develop until the 1930s when plantings on Mafia Island and on sisal estates in Tanga yielded an export crop of 210 tons in 1938.[12] This trade was interrupted during World War II, but immediately afterwards there was an expansion in plantings, especially in the Mtwara and Ruvuma Regions in the southern zone. Both production and trade grew steadily and the rapid progression of exports is illustrated in Figure 4.2. This trade was entirely in raw nuts sent to India for processing. An attempt in the early 1950s to develop a small-scale processing operation at Mtwara was unsuccessful due to the instability in the available labor force.

While there were some cashew plantings on estates, including on lands leased by the Tanganyika Agricultural Corporation (famous for the failed groundnut scheme), most of the expanding production took place on small-holdings. Cashews fit into the traditional cropping system and often cashew was intercropped with cassava until the tree canopy developed. In parts of Newala District, the high population density and previous intensive cultivation had impoverished the soils so greatly that only cashews and cassava provided a reasonable return. A drought-resistant tree, the cashew has the

FIGURE 4.2: **Tanzania Raw Cashew Nut Exports, 1945–62**

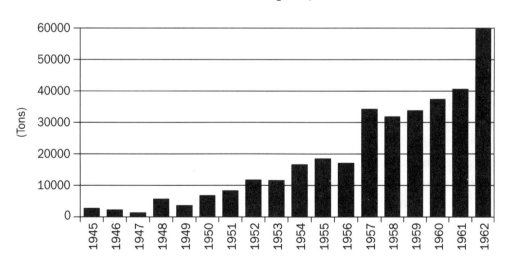

[12] This and the subsequent paragraph are based on Northwood (1962) and Tanganyika Trade Journal (1963).

unusual ability to flower and set fruit during the driest part of the year. This proved important in southern Tanzania where the dry season lasts as long as six months.

These early cashew plantings were encouraged by private traders (of Indian and Arab origin) who operated local shops or transport companies and who bought or bartered for the cashew crop. During the October–February harvest season, buying days were announced when traders would purchase the crop for cash. Some two dozen private traders and shippers stored and exported the crop out of Mtwara port to India, where they built up long-term trading relations with processors and brokers.

Expansion and Multi-Tiered Marketing System (1962 to 1974)

At independence in 1962, a Southern Region Cashew Nut Board was established with the mandate to stabilize prices and develop cooperatives in the region.[13] The Board was given sole authority to purchase the cashew crop and sell it to exporters at auction. The Board divided up the region into eleven procurement zones, appointing a main buying agent for each, who in turn appointed primary buying agents to deal directly with farmers. Initially, most of these buying agents were the private merchants already active in the trade. However, by 1963, 80% of the crop in the Mtwara and Rumuva Regions was handled by primary cooperative societies at the local level and newly-formed cooperative unions at the secondary level. In that same year, the functions of the Southern Regional Cashew Nut Board were taken over the Southern Agricultural Products Board. A year later, the latter would be superseded by the National Agricultural Products Board. Thus began the institutional roller coaster which has plagued the cashew nut industry up to the present.

The multi-tiered system operated satisfactorily through much of the mid-to-late-1960's, although the official producer prices set by the government were not adjusted upward. While available records suggest that both crop collection and payments to farmers took place on a timely basis, the cooperatives were apparently not effective in screening product quality. For example, in 1968 the National Agricultural Products Board lost large quantities of nuts due to improper drying and grading at the post-harvest stage. In response to this problem, the Board commandeered the agricultural staff as-

---

[13] This and the subsequent paragraph are based on Northwood and Kayumbo (1970), Ohler (1979), Annual Reports of Agriculture, and an interview with former cashew researcher A. Tsakaris.

signed to the southern zone, using them as cashew nut collection observers and graders.

While the pace of new plantings declined, the maturation of existing *shambas* (cashew trees) contributed to continued rapid growth in production and trade. This production peaked at over 145,000 tons in 1973/74, accounting at that point for nearly 30% of total world production (see Figure 4.3).

Smallholders continued to be the backbone of the expanding industry. One survey conducted in the mid-1960s found that 71% of cashew farmers had total holdings of less than four acres, with the majority of farmers owning less than fifty trees.[14] In the survey area (Lulindi in Masasi District) approximately 25% of the total land area was covered by mature cashew trees, with cashews accounting for 78% of the total cash income of the farmers. At this time, efforts were also made to expand cashew production in the Tanga Region along the coast in order to replace cotton cultivation. The official agricultural staff provided seedlings and technical assistance for this effort.[15] By 1972, the Agricultural Census reported national cashew plantings of 200,000 hectares, of which 139,000 hectares were monocrop and 61,000 hectares were intercropped with one or more crops.

During this period, a further attempt was made to develop a cashew processing capacity in order to increase value-added and to reduce the dependency of the industry on a single market—that of India for raw nuts. A government-sponsored study conducted in 1962 argued that uncertainties regarding the availability of labor in the south and shortages of skilled labor would prevent Tanzania from following the Indian model of manual cashew processing.[16] The study recommended that the country move toward mechanical processing. In 1965, an Italian company, Oltremare S.A. set up Tanzania's first mechanized cashew nut factory in Dar es Salaam with a 9000 ton raw nut capacity (later upgraded to 12,500 tons).[17] While the factory did begin to operate, its kernel exports were not profitable due to the generally low quality of raw nuts found in the Dar es Salaam Region. The factory's non-profitability also stemmed from its comparatively poor yield of kernel material per ton of raw nuts. In 1968, a second mechanized factory was set up in Mtwara by a Japanese company (Cashco). The factory had an 8000 ton capacity, al-

---

[14] Tsakaris (1967).

[15] Ministry of Agriculture, Annual Report 1966.

[16] Tanganyika Industrial Development (1962).

[17] This was by far the largest cashew processing factory in the world at that time.

FIGURE 4.3: **Marketed Cashew Nut Production, 1962–85**

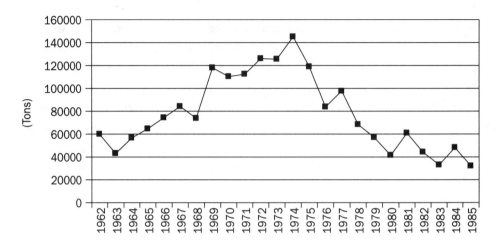

though equipment breakdowns and power shortages prevented it from operating for several years. By 1973, still less than 10% of the cashew crop was processed locally, and raw nut exports remained the dominant trade.

Industrialization and Production Decline (1974–1985)

In 1973, the Cashew Authority of Tanzania was created in order to promote the expansion and wider development of the cashew nut industry. The Authority would take over the crop buying functions of the NAPB and bypass the former exporters by selling the crop to foreign buyers on a tender basis. Its mandate was much broader, however, with plans outlined for the establishment of a cashew extension and grading service, the development of a cashew research program, an investment in a port storage facility for CSNL exports, and for further investments in large-scale cashew processing facilities. As the cooperative unions were phased out over the 1974–76 period, the Cashew Authority began procuring the crop directly from village societies and influencing the determination of official, pan-territorial producer prices.

In 1974, the initiation of a World Bank-funded project to construct five cashew processing factories with a total capacity of 36,400 pursued one of the Cashew Authority's main objectives. The factories, to be located in each of the main towns in Mtwara and Lindi Regions, were to contain 'state-of-the-art' (Oltremere) equipment for mechanical processing. Factory construction proceeded satisfactorily but the actual costs ended up being several times larger than the original estimate.[18] As a result, the research component of the project was dropped and large cutbacks were made in technical support services.

In 1976, with construction of the new factories still taking place, the Tanzanian government requested a second phase of the World Bank project. Concern was expressed about the lack of operational experience in the factories funded earlier and as to the overall economic viability of additional factories. At the time, there was also some evidence of a decline in cashew nut production, although greater weight was given to the Cashew Authority's optimistic projections for future production levels. Nevertheless, the second phase of the project was approved, and three more factories were built creating an additional capacity of 26,000 tons. Parallel bilateral financing for two more factories would bring the total processing capacity to 113,000 tons by 1980.

Before any of the new factories came on line, Tanzania's cashew production began to plummet. From the 1973/74 peak of over 145,000 tons, marketed production fell quickly to 84,000 tons in 1975/76 and then declined through the late 1970s and early 1980s to 31,100 tons in 1982/83. Thus, just as the new factories were being completed, total national production was only one-third to one-fourth of factory capacity.

Several factors were likely to have contributed to this pattern.[19] One of these was the villagization program mentioned earlier whose implementation in the southern zone began in mid-1974. This program involved the forced relocation of the rural population into villages which were then awarded priority in the allocation of land and the provision of social services. In the south, one of the results of the program was to separate smallholders from their cashew *shambas*, sometimes by considerable distances. This, together with new work responsibilities in the development of the new villages and communal plots, prevented many farmers from harvesting cashews and from properly maintaining these shambas. The latter was probably an important factor in the spread of a mildew disease among cashew trees in certain locations and a subsequent decline in yields.[20]

---

[18] Actual costs were 3.6 times original estimates.

[19] Ellis (1979, 1980). A detailed analysis of crop production problems did not feature in the supervision reports of the World Bank project until 1980, despite the critical importance of these problems for the economic viability of the Bank-funded investments. Instead, attention focused on the progress of factory construction and on management problems within the CATA.

[20] Although this mildew disease was first cited and diagnosed in the 1960s, it apparently began to have an important negative effect on yields only by the late 1970s.

These logistical and technical problems were exacerbated by the virtual collapse of support services for cashews at this time. With the Cashew Authority focusing on processing and trading activities, little research work was done, extension services deteriorated, and no system was put into place to detect and monitor farm-level production problems.[21]

Further undermining production incentives was a decline in the real producer prices of cashew nuts, together with a decline in cashew prices relative to those of other crops. This is illustrated in Tables 4.2 and 4.3. Table 4.2 shows the decline and then stagnation of real producer prices from 1971/72 through to the early 1980s. The table also shows the substantial decline in the producer's share of total export revenues during the 1970s, when it reached its nadir at 25–30% between 1978 and 1981. Cashew nut producers did not benefit from the significant increase in international prices for raw nuts and kernels which occurred from 1977 to 1982. Nor did they capture any of the benefits associated with the shift toward increased local processing which took place in the late 1970s and early 1980s.[22]

Examining trends in producer incentives during this period, Ellis (1980) found that increased international prices were absorbed by rapidly increasing operating costs (especially unit administrative costs) on the part of CATA. Significant increases in (real) producer prices were not implemented until the 1981/82, by which time world prices had fallen back somewhat. The result of these developments was a temporary sharp increase in the producers' share of export values and a corresponding large trading loss recorded by CATA.

Table 4.3 shows that while the real prices for other crops also declined over much of this period, cashew nut producers were most adversely affected by government price (and marketing) policies. By the mid-1970s, there was evidence of farmers not only neglecting their cashew *shambas*, but of displacing cashew nuts with short-cycle legumes, such as cowpeas, pigeon peas and various beans. In some places, farmers began to fell cashew nut trees for use in charcoal production.[23] The government's response to such developments

---

[21] Research was undertaken only after a bilateral grant provided by the Italian government became effective in 1979. Of the 344 extension assistants recruited under the World Bank project, only 32 had prior training in agriculture. The extension staff were largely involved in the procurement of raw nuts. In retrospect, it was unrealistic to expect the newly-created CATA to be able to effectively take on a wide range of marketing and support services all at one time.

[22] Just the opposite occurred as delays in processing and CATA losses in kernel exports weakened the financial structure in the cashew nut industry and resulted in the emergence of delayed payments to farmers.

[23] Havnevik (1979) reports on the situation in Rufiji District.

TABLE 4.2: **Producer Price Trends for Cashew Nuts, 1971/72 to 1983/84**

Season	Nominal Producer Price (TSh./kg.)[1]	Producer Price in Constant 1971/72 TSh./kg.	Producer Price as % of Export Unit Values[2]
1971/72	0.91	0.91	67.0
1972/73	0.91	0.84	67.0
1973/74	0.91	0.73	49.8
1974/75	1.03	0.67	54.5
1975/76	1.03	0.58	47.4
1976/77	1.07	0.55	36.5
1977/78	1.12	0.52	30.0
1978/79	1.64	0.65	40.2
1979/80	1.64	0.51	24.7
1980/81	1.78	0.44	30.9
1981/82	2.80	0.56	72.2
1982/83	4.70	0.70	65.8
1983/84	6.58	0.80	48.2

[1] Weighted value, assuming 80% Standard Grade and 20% Undergrade.
[2] Calculated as producer price % average unit value of all cashew export products (raw nuts, kernels, CNSL) on a raw nut equivalent basis. The methodology is similar to that used by Ellis (1979) except that the assumption here is a 20% kernel material recovery from the raw nut.

SOURCES: Calculated from Data provided in Marketing Development Bureau, Annual Review of Cashew Nuts, various years.

TABLE 4.3: **Comparative Trends in Producer Prices During the 1970s**
(% Increase or Decrease)

Crop	1969/70–1973/74		1973/74–1979/80	
	Nominal	Real	Nominal	Real
Export Crops				
Cashew	0.0	−38.4	91.2	−24.0
Coffee	7.2	−33.9	104.7	−18.6
Cotton	3.8	−36.0	157.3	+2.3
Tobacco	29.1	−20.5	58.1	−37.1
Domestic Crops				
Maize	17.9	−27.4	202.9	+20.4
Paddy	9.6	−32.5	163.2	+4.6
Groundnuts	25.0	−23.0	247.8	+38.3
Sunflower	31.0	−19.3	154.5	+1.2

SOURCE: Ellis (1982).

included: (1) a campaign to "teach" farmers the importance of maintaining their shambas, (2) road blocks and the banning of petty-trading and charcoal-making in the affected areas, (3) and various types of threats against producers who did not harvest and sell their cashew nuts.[24] Such interventions were not effective, and production and trade levels continued to decline.

---

[24] These efforts are discussed further by Msangi et al. (1987).

Shortages of raw materials were one of the main factors undermining the viability of the new processing factories. Even though more than half of the total production was locally processed between 1980 and 1982, this level of production was insufficient to operate more than a few of the factories. Two of the completed factories lacking access to reliable sources of water and power were never operated. Of the remaining ten factories, only four operated in 1982/83 and only two operated during the subsequent two seasons.

The availability of raw materials was not the only problem. Due to poor grading of raw nuts and with power and water interruptions, the quality of the finished product was uneven and generally below international standards. Tanzanian kernel exports thus brought price discounts of 35 to 50% from the Indian price.[25] This, together with the favorable prices for raw nuts imported by India, resulted in the Tanzanian factories accruing negative value-added in 1981 and 1982 and sustaining continued financial losses.

Reversing the Downward Slide (1985–1991)

In 1985, the Cashew Authority was replaced by the Tanzania Cashew Nut Marketing Board (TCMB) and the cooperative unions were re-established. From now on, crop procurement arrangements would resemble those prevailing during the early 1970s, where primary cooperative societies would procure the crop from farmers (paying official pan-territorial prices for the two grades), using funds supplied by cooperative unions. The unions would in turn transport the crop to the Tanzania Cashew Nut Board, which would then either process the nuts or export them as raw nuts. An inter-store price was negotiated between the cooperative unions and the Board, ostensibly geared toward enabling the unions to recover their procurement and wider operating costs.

At approximately the same time, the second Cashew Nut Development Project was restructured, with the remaining undisbursed funds going toward a pilot program of applied research, extension and training.[26] Under this program, the powdery mildew problem was investigated and farmers were encouraged to dust their trees with sulphur as a remedy. Such efforts were geared toward reversing the decline in production yields, thus stimulating farmers to harvest their crop. In addition to the technical measures, offi-

---

[25] Over the 1981–83 period.
[26] This was the Cashew Production Improvement Pilot Project.

cial producer prices were increased in real terms from the 1987/88 season onward.[27]

Such measures, however, were undermined by inefficiencies and graft in the marketing system. The cooperative unions lacked strong managerial capabilities and had only weak accounting systems. These were not effective in performing their administrative functions and they built up huge arrears on their bank loans.[28] Financial problems fed down through the system with cooperative societies unable to purchase the cashew crop on a regular basis and making payments to farmers only after several months.[29] In several years, large quantities of nuts remained unsold at the farm or village level at the end of the buying season. Between cooperative societies and unions, significant quantities of nuts 'leaked' out of the system. Inflation was also rampant in the system of grading, with more than 95% of nuts delivered during the late 1980s being classified as standard (that is, first) grade.[30]

Declining marketed production and problematic buying agents were important, yet these were not the sole factors constraining the operations of the TCMB during this period. Foreign exchange shortages led to shortages in spare parts and oil to operate the factories. At the same time, the factories were required to make employees permanent after only three months of work. This greatly added to labor costs for factories which operated only 100 days (or less) per year. Even in the procurement of nuts, the factories ran into barriers set up by local authorities who viewed the factories as local assets and thus sought to prevent local nuts from being transported to other factories for processing. Between 1985 and 1990, nine factories were closed entirely, while the three others operated only intermittently. The value added from processing was either negative or too low to cover processing costs. Raw nut exports also plummeted, dipping below 7500 in 1989/90.[31]

---

[27] The extent to which farmers realized these higher prices is not clear. During this period, local taxes (for education, building, and other funds) on cashew nuts, paid either by farmers or by cooperative societies, were increased significantly. One thing is clear, however. Farmers benefitted little or none from the large international price increase over the 1986–88 period, with windfall profits accruing to the TCMB.

[28] This analysis is based on Duncan (1988) and cooperative union records.

[29] Farmers were also directly taxed to cover for cooperative union losses via excessive deductions for 'shrinkages' between the farm-gate and cooperative union delivery to the TCMB.

[30] Historically, 80–85% of nuts were graded as standard grade.

[31] During this period, the TCMB began to mix nuts from different locations, completely undermining foreign buyer confidence in Tanzania's system of grading and weakening the tender system. Concerns were also expressed about the non-transparency of the tender system, with the possibility of private interests overriding public interest.

TABLE 4.4: **Indicators of Cashew Nut Industry Performance 1984/85–1990/91**

Indicator	1984/85	1985/86	1986/87	1987/88	1988/89	1989/90	1990/91
Marketed Production (Tons)	32,073	18,956	16,544	24,374	19,275	17,059	29,325
Producer Price (TSh./kg.) Nominal[1]	9.66	11.58	17.93	29.50	39.35	82.60	108.15
Constant (1984/85)	9.66	8.98	10.49	13.23	13.76	23.14	25.27
Producer Price as % of Unit Export Value[2]	71%	37%	25%	32%	38%	57%	56%
Cooperative Union Losses (TSh. Million)	Na.	94.6[3]	84.1[4]	95.9[4]	131.3[4]	135.6[4]	332.2[4]
TCMB Profits/(Losses) (TSh. Million)	Na.	Na.	488	386	72	(493)	Na.
Raw Nut Exports (Tons)[5]	13,853	13,379	13,871	14,004	7485	7429	19,000
Kernel Exports (Tons)[5]	518	0	0	1014	1711	1412	956
Processing Value Added (%)[6]	12%	Na.	Na.	–4%	–2%	12%	36%
Factory Capacity Utilization (%)[7]	2.1%	0	0	4.1%	8.4%	12.9%	4.3%

[1] Weighted Average, 95% standard grade and 5% undergrade.
[2] Takes into account exports of raw nuts, kernels, and CNSL.
[3] Aggregate for Unions for Lindi, Coast, Mtwara, and DSM Regions.
[4] Aggregate for (3) above plus Tanga Cooperative Union.
[5] For calendar year (e.g. 1985, 1986, etc.)
[6] Unit value of kernels and CNSL over and above raw nut export value.
[7] Utilization rate for total national capacity.
Na. Not available.

SOURCES: Marketing Development Bureau, Annual Report of Cashew Nuts, various years; unpublished Cooperative Audit report.

Table 4.4 provides various indicators of performance for the industry over the 1984/85 to 1990/91 period. Table 4D (see annex at end of chapter) summarizes the limited utilization of Tanzania's large-scale, state-of-the-art processing factories.

MARKET LIBERALIZATION AND PRIVATE SECTOR RESPONSE (1991–PRESENT)

As part of a structural adjustment program begun in 1983, the Tanzanian government began to liberalize the domestic marketing of grains and other food crops, moving away from the single channel system put into place in the mid-1960s. Private traders (who had continued to be active in parallel market trading) were first permitted to conduct trade across regional boundaries. Quantity restrictions were later relaxed and removed altogether. By 1988/89, private traders were allowed to purchase crops from primary societies and by 1990 all restrictions were lifted.

In the southern regions where cashews are the major cash crop, private traders successfully competed with cooperatives in the procurement of the liberalized crops. In general, private traders paid higher prices and paid cash, so farmers did not experience the same payment delays as with the cooperatives.[32] Private merchants were particularly active in the trades in sesame and cassava roots, for which sizable export markets have been developed. An illustration of the emerging major role of private traders in southern zone food marketing is provided in Table 4.5 which provides survey data from the East Makonde area concerning farmer market outlets for different crops. As the Table indicates, during the 1990/91 season only for cashew nuts did the cooperative societies continue to play a major role.

While domestic markets were liberalized, the marketing of traditional export crops remained confined to one channel, multi-tiered systems. Initial proposals to liberalize the cashew nut trading system were put forward in the late 1980s under the Cashew Nut Production Improvement Pilot Project. However, it was not until the 1990 Tanzania Agricultural Adjustment Programme that the government announced its intention to implement major policy and institutional changes in export crop marketing. This commitment was put in concrete form in Tanzania's Policy Framework Paper presented by the government in April 1991.

TABLE 4.5: **Proportion of Sales Transactions by Buyer and Crop in E. Makonde Plateau** (Percentage; 1990/91 Season)

Crop	Primary Society	Private Trader	Consumer
Cashew	100	0	0
Cassava	25	48	27
Sesame	25	75	0
Groundnuts	0	31	69
Pulses	10	31	59
Cereals	7	43	50

SOURCE: ODA Cashew Research Project (1992), *Household Agricultural Marketing Survey.*

---

[32] ODA Cashew Research Project (1992), *Household Agricultural Marketing Survey*, op cit.

The cashew nut industry would play the leading role in export crop market liberalization, beginning with the 1991/92 season. This industry was chosen in part due to the relative weakness of its cooperative unions (compared with those in the cotton and coffee industries). The industry was also in the most serious shape. A survey conducted during the 1990/91 season had found that, depending upon location, some one-third to one-half of farmers with cashew *shambas* were not harvesting nuts (see Table 4.6). Even those who did harvest faced severe sales problems. By July 1991 (some two to three months after the expected end of the buying season), 30% of the crop had still not been purchased due to cash shortages. The government needed to intervene with the banks to clear the crop. Especially in the southern zone, where cashew nut sales account for between 36% and 80% of total farmer crop incomes (depending upon location), the decline in production and the inefficiencies in marketing were contributing to a significant decline in living standards. At the same time, the government's huge investment in processing facilities was bringing minimum return, and most factories lay idle.

The government's original intention was for the Tanzania Cashew Marketing Board to retain a monopoly on export marketing, while liberalizing primary marketing. The Ministry of Agriculture issued its guidelines in July 1991, which left only three months for preparation before the beginning of the marketing season. These guidelines were vague and were announced only through the media (radio and newspapers). No official documentation was sent to the regional and district authorities who would be responsible for implementing and monitoring the structural changes. Local authorities thus were given no explanation of the rationale behind the policy changes and were largely unaware of the structural changes envisioned within the marketing system. Implementation of the guidelines was seemingly left up to the discretion of local authorities.

This ambiguous communication, combined with the conservative attitude of some local authorities and the vested interests of the cooperatives, caused a delay in the registration of private cashew traders and resulted in ad hoc procedures. In some regions, local officials viewed would-be private traders not as competitors with the cooperatives, but as supplementary actors in the procurement of the crop. Restrictions were placed on the locations where the private traders could operate and on the quantities which they could purchase. They were required to pay official prices and submit weekly sales returns to local authorities. The registration process was interpreted by some regional authorities as a fund raising exercise, with significant licensing fees

TABLE 4.6: **Importance of Cashews and Cashew Sales in Tanzania's Southern Zone**

Area	% of House-holds with Cashews	Of Those with Cashews, % Har-vesting in 1990/ 91 Season	Of Those With Cashew % Sold Cashews	Of Those With Cashews % Use Cashews for Food	Mean Cashew Income (TSh.)	Mean Total Income from Crop Sales (TSh.)	Cashew Sales as % of Total Crop Sales
E.Makonde	70	64	59	40	7436	12630	59
W.Makonde	96	83	75	80	24319	28988	84
S.Masasi	73	77	73	67	13531	21804	62
Tinduru	81	44	40	35	6880	19007	36
Lindi/Nach./ Nemasasi	73	60	53	45	6218	10244	61
Coastal Plain	75	65	61	29	7473	10937	68

SOURCE: ODA Cashew Research Project, Agricultural Marketing Survey 1991.

being charged.[33] Initially, private traders were required to sell the crop to Marketing Board. They argued that without the right to export (and retain foreign exchange), there was little incentive to participate. Only in April 1992, did the Board concede the right to private firms (and cooperatives) to export cashew nuts on their own account.

As a result of the uncertainties and official barriers, very few private traders were registered through December of 1991. By February of 1992, there were still only thirty-one registered traders, the majority of which were in Lindi (fifteen) and Mtwara (ten). In Coast and Tanga Regions, local authorities sought to protect the regional cooperative unions by greatly limiting the number of registered private traders. Only in the Lindi Region did private traders play a major role in the procurement of the 1991/92 crop. The regional cooperative union LIRECU was declared insolvent prior to the season and was thus unable to obtain a bank overdraft to procure cashews. Only late in the season did the Marketing Board provide LIRECU with funds in order to buy the crop in remote areas where the private traders had not ventured. In Lindi, private traders accounted for 77% of the purchased crop. The share of private traders nationwide was only 17.5% during the first season of liberalization.

Because of the pre-determined official prices and fixed margins and efforts

---

[33] One trader reports having to pay TSh. 20,000 for the right to purchase cashew nuts in a particular district.

to segregate the buying operations of cooperatives and private traders, no real competition emerged during this season. The only major distinction occurred with regard to grading. In contrast to the cooperatives, grading was taken seriously by private traders. As a result, nearly 30% of the nuts purchased in Lindi were downgraded to 'undergrade'.[34] In contrast, in neighboring Mtwara Region, the cooperative union (MARCU) purchased nearly 10,000 tons of nuts, only two tons of which were classified as undergrade.

Several private firms did try to export part of the 1991/92 crop. The results were generally disastrous.[35] Having procured much of their crop relatively late in the season, the firms had acquired stocks of mixed quality. Having been granted the right to export as late as April, the private exporters were not in a position to sell their crop until after the Indian domestic season had begun. As a result of these two factors, Indian buyers offered relatively low prices which several exporters rejected. These firms subsequently had to unload their stocks at even lower prices during the following season.[36]

A few cooperative unions also sought to directly export their crop. They too ran into severe difficulties related to product quality and experienced several cancellations in sales contracts. Shipments which were made by the cooperative unions were subjected to major quality-related claims, reducing actual sales values to less than $400/ton, compared with invoice prices of more than $600/ton.[37]

Despite all this confusion, marketed production did increase by 38% over the previous season, reaching 41,238 tons. Favorable weather, an increase in sulphur dusting in some locations (especially in Tinduru where a major government- and cooperative-directed campaign took place), higher producer prices, and prompt payments to farmers all contributed to a larger proportion of cashew owners actually harvesting their crop and probably to a higher

---

[34] Standard grade nuts are defined as those containing not more than 0.25% foreign matter and not more than 13% (by weight) of damaged, empty, immature, or old nuts. Moisture content should not exceed 13%. Undergrade nuts are those not meeting these requirements.

[35] Equally disastrous were initial private attempts to import and distribute sulphur and blowers for cashew tree dusting. With delays in sulphur shipments and trade documentation, the imported inputs arrived too late for use before the season, leaving the firms with the responsibility of maintaining large input stocks and incurring expensive finance charges.

[36] One firm which purchased about 600 tons during the 1991/92 season was still holding this (now deteriorated) stock in April 1993. A sizable loss was predicted on sales.

[37] For example, MARCU had a contracted price of $700/ton for 3500 tons, although realized sales earnings were only $394/ton.

level of output.[38] Although it exported most nuts in raw form, the Marketing Board did put two of its factories into operation and processed 9000 tons of nuts. Once again, however, this resulted in negative value added from processing as raw nut prices were favorable and Tanzania's kernel exports received price discounts. While providing employment opportunities, the Tanzania Cashew Marketing Board's processing operations generated losses as a result of high unit costs and relatively poor technical results.

The competitive disadvantage faced by the TCMB is illustrated clearly in Table 4.7 below. Its use of mechanical processing, together with the organization's poor technical efficiency in utilizing this equipment and weaknesses in the raw material grading system, have resulted in a situation where the kernel-based revenue per ton of raw nuts processed in Tanzania is nearly 26% lower than that obtained in India. This huge difference, stemming from Tanzania's lower yield of kernel material and much lower proportion of realized whole kernels, has been a major reason why India has been able to pay seemingly high prices for raw nuts and why the TCMB frequently achieves low or negative value added through processing.

The beginning of the 1992/93 season was characterized by uncertainty and confusion.[39] The experience of the prior season, together with pessimistic predictions about the Indian market for raw nuts, led private traders to delay their registration and buying operations. The uncertainty was compounded by mixed signals from the TCMB concerning whether or not it would buy nuts from private traders. If not, then private firms would need to depend entirely upon their own export channels. While the Lindi branch of TCMB announced that it would buy from private traders, it did not have funds at the beginning of the season and thus issued IOUs to traders. The Mtwara branch of TCMB waited until December to announce its intention to buy from private traders, a deliberate delay designed to protect the procurement interests of the regional cooperative union.

Uncertainty and confusion spread to the financing of crop procurement and to the prices which producers would be paid. Under pressure to recover

---

[38] The Cashew Farmer Practices Survey (1992), conducted by the ODA Cashew Research team, did show a greater propensity of farmers to harvest nuts.

[39] The analysis below is based on field work conducted by the author in March 1993. Interviews were conducted with government and commercial bank officials, with officials of the TCMB and several cooperative unions/societies, and with twenty-four private trading companies/individuals. The field work concentrated in the Mtwara and Lindi Regions and in Dar es Salaam. Tremendous assistance was provided by Commercial Unit of the Cashew Improvement Programme.

TABLE 4.7: **Comparative Cashew Processing Yields and Revenues**

Grade	Price ($/lb. FOB)[1]	Typical Production Breakdown		Revenue Breakdown for Composite Ton of Kernels ($ FOB)	
		Tanzania[2]	India	Tanzania	India
Wholes					
W210	3.09	1%	3%	34	204
W240	2.80	3%	7%	185	432
W320	2.70	27%	47%	1607	2797
W450	2.65	14%	14%	818	818
Scorched	2.62	3%	6%	173	346
Dessert	1.93	7%	6%	298	255
Sub-Total		55%	83%	3114	4852
Brokens					
Butts	2.09	9%	5%	415	231
Splits	2.15	14%	5%	663	237
Large White Pc.	1.82	17%	4%	681	160
Small While Pc.	1.71	5%	3%	188	113
Sub-Total		45%	17%	1948	741
Total Revenue Per Ton of Kernels				**5062**	**5593**
Total Revenue Per Ton of Raw Nuts				**962**[3]	**1296**[4]

[1] December 1991.
[2] Oltremere system.
[3] Assuming an average of 19% kernel yield from raw nuts. Likombe factory achieved 18.7% in 1990/91.
[4] Assuming an average of 23% kernel yield from raw nuts.

SOURCE: Modified from Agriconsult/AMEC (1992).

past loans and to weed out non-paying clients, the commercial banks (particularly the parastatal National Bank of Commerce) denied overdraft facilities to several of the cooperative unions and made loans to others contingent on agreements regarding guideline producer prices and inter-store TCMB buying prices. Negotiations on these matters were protracted and things were not sorted out until December, three months into the buying season.

While a few of the cooperative unions (including Ruvuma, Coast, and DSM) did obtain overdraft facilities, the others (including MARCU and LIRECU in the most important production areas) would need to obtain their financing through the TCMB, which finally obtained overdraft facilities in December and January. Relatively high inter-store TCMB buying prices of TSh. 182–190/kg. (depending upon region) were agreed to. In determining the guideline producer price, greatest consideration was given to the financial viability of the cooperative unions and their ability to repay loans to the banks. Hence, the sample budgets constructed for the unions built in a sum of TSh. 20/kg. for finance costs. At the agreed guideline producer price of TSh. 125/kg. for standard grade, it was expected that the unions would obtain net margins of 10 to 12% which they could direct toward repayment of arrears.[40]

The agreed guideline producer prices of TSh. 125/kg. for standard grade and TSh. 89/kg. for undergrade were lower than the official prices for the previous year (namely, TSh. 137 and 89/kg., respectively). They were also lower than the guideline prices which regional authorities had already announced in some areas (TSh. 140/kg. for standard grade in Lindi Region) and considerably lower than the prices which private traders were actually paying in the beginning of the 1992/93 season (namely, between TSh. 140 and 160/kg. for standard grade). While the lower guideline price was implemented in the north and in Lindi Region, it was rejected outright by farmers in parts of Mtwara Region, forcing the regional cooperative union to increase its procurement prices.

Figure 4.4 provides a flow chart for the industry during the 1992/93 season. Three main channels have emerged. One is organized by private exporters who have hired private traders or cooperatives located in major production areas to serve as their buying agents. The second channel features cooperative unions procuring nuts from cooperative societies and then trading on their own account. The third channel involves private traders and cooperatives selling to the Tanzania Cashew Marketing Board, which in turn exports the raw nuts. The discussion below focuses primarily on private trader activities.

Private Trader Activities

Despite initial entry delays (particularly among smaller traders), by January there were many private traders active in the market. Compared with the prior season, relatively few restrictions were placed on them other than the stipulations that they should buy the crop from cooperative societies (and not directly from farmers) and that they should pay certain local taxes. Some traders intended to buy only standard grade, and in several districts local authorities forced them to also buy the nuts under grade. Many of the smaller,

---

[40] Calculated from cooperative cost/revenue budgets.

FIGURE 4.4: **Cashew Nut Channels in Tanzania** (1992/93 Season)

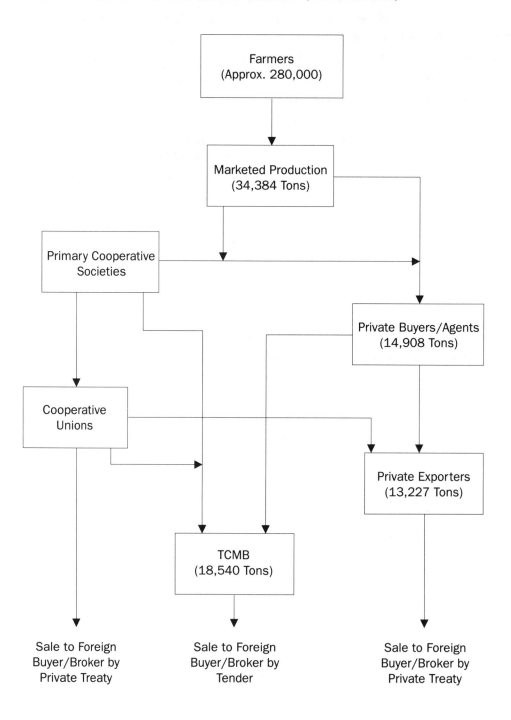

part-time traders didn't bother to register themselves with district authorities. The number of private traders buying at the local level probably numbered more than 200.

Three main types of private traders emerged this season as first handlers at the local or regional levels (Table 4.8). One type, referred to here as "petty traders", consists primarily of farmers and office employees who, with some limited initial savings, bought nuts from farmers in order to supply the TCMB. Although initially hesitant to enter the trade, these actors took the plunge once it was clear that the established inter-store TCMB price and the guideline producer prices afforded a comfortable margin. Such traders generally experienced problems in obtaining bank financing for their activities, despite having adequate security. As a result, they dealt in small quantities, relying on their sales turnover to generate funds for further purchases. Most of these traders made use of hired vehicles to transport the crop and many sought to avoid district and cooperative levies by dealing directly with farmers rather than with cooperative societies.

A second type, referred to here as "buying agents/stockists" consists of business people who were also attracted by the favorable margins available on sales to the TCMB. Such individuals/firms typically own a shop and run some sort of transport business. Quite a few of them have also become involved in stocking sulphur and blowers and/or providing spraying services on contract (in return for nuts). While some received limited overdraft facilities from Banks, most relied upon savings for initial purchases and on subsequent sales turnover to finance further purchases. These traders operated on a considerably larger scale than the first group, handling several hundred tons each during the 1992/93 season.

The third type of trader consists of family-based enterprises involved in wider commodity trading, transport and other ventures (e.g. petrol stations). These firms serve as cashew buying agents for Dar es Salaam-based exporters. The local traders are provided with money and instructed on the quantities and source areas preferred. Receiving a commission, these firms use their local knowledge to procure the nuts and often to manage loading and freight-forwarding from Mtwara port. Several of these firms have a history in the cashew trade, either with the present or former generation involved in similar procurement arrangements. These firms became active in trade in sesame, cassava, and other products in the late 1980s and found that cashew nuts fit well into their trading calendar, keeping both staff and vehicles employed.

TABLE 4.8: **Profiles of Three Types of Private Cashew Nut First Handlers**

Type	Main Activities	Typical Ethnic Origin	Source of Finance for Purchases	Quantities Handled (Tons)	Mode of Crop Transport	Prior Cashew Trading Experience	Market Outlet	Form of Remuneration
Petty Trader	Farming; Office Employee	Indigenous	Savings; Crop Turnover	< 25	Hired Vehicle	No	Other Traders; TCMB	Margin on Inter-store Price
Buying Agent/ Stockist	Farming; Inputs Stockist; Transport	Indigenous	Crop Turnover; Bank overdraft	50–400	Own Truck	No	TCMB	Margin on Inter-store Price
Commodity Trader/Agent	Commodity Trade; Freight-forwarding	Tanzanian Asian	Exporter; Bank overdraft	200–3500	Fleet of Trucks	Frequently	Private Exporter	Commission

TABLE 4.9: **Illustrative Trading Calendar of Multi-Commodity Trader**

Sept.	Oct.	Nov.	Dec.	Jan.	Feb.	Mrc.	Apr.	May	Jun	Jul	Aug
		Cashew Nuts ——————— >									
							Sulphur ——— >				
							Sesame ———>				
Yellow Gram ——— >											Beeswax – >
Cassava ——— >											
		Pigeon Pea									
Timber ——————————————————————— >											

At the first handler level, competition was still not strong during this second year of a liberalized market. Several factors contributed to this. One was the overall shortage of finance available. The number of traders in possession of cash present at any one time in the villages was limited to one or very few. A second reason is a common practice among traders to bypass villages where another private trader is known to be active. The reasons for this are not very clear. However, it is the case that private traders have sought to (and have apparently succeeded) 'buy' primary cooperative society secretaries through the payment of a small commission (e.g. TSh. 1/kg.) or through the provision of a gift such as a radio or bicycle. These cooperative officials seek to guarantee village supplies for the favored buyer by telling other would-be buyers that the local crop is already committed to another party.[41] Third, price competition was weakened by the announcement of guideline or indicative prices. Given the many years of government-directed prices, the notion of an indicative price is not well understood, and most traders and primary societies tended to settle on prices at or very close to the indicative prices. The fact that cooperative unions were paying the indicative price reinforced this notion of an official price.

While the majority of the local first handlers are indigenous traders, some of the larger traders and all of the exporter buying agents are long-established Tanzanian Asian trading companies. Table 4.10 provides a breakdown

---

[41] As one trader noted, the objective is to have the cooperative secretary tell would-be competitors that there are 'no vacancies' in the village for cashews.

TABLE 4.10: **Cashew Nut Suppliers to TCMB Lindi** (1992/93 Season)

First Handler/Supplier	Quantity Supplied	Proportion
Coop. Society/Union	293.6	6.5%
R.T.C. (Public Enterprise)	202.5	4.5%
Private Traders Of which:	3988.2	89.0%
Tanzanian Asian (14)	2048.6	45.7%
Indigenous (17)	1939.6	43.3%

SOURCES: Based on TCMB Lindi Buying Records; Lindi Regional Agricultural Staff.

of the suppliers to the Lindi branch of the TCMB during the 1992/93 season. It indicates that, at least for the trade directed through the TCMB, indigenous firms have been able to hold their own.

The pattern for private exporters is quite different. During the 1992/93 season, twelve private companies undertook (or were preparing) exports, accounting for about 40% of the country's raw nut trade. Nine of these exporters were interviewed, and their profiles are indicated in Table 4.11. By Tanzanian standards, each of these firms is quite large or is part of a larger group of companies. In contrast with the mixed pattern found for local buyers and traders, each of the exporters is owned and/or managed by Tanzanian Asians, typically family-based companies or partnerships. Only one firm concentrates on cashew nut trading, but even this firm is part of a conglomerate. Each of the other firms is active in trading of a wide range of commodities. Most are also active in the transport business and in agro-processing ventures. During the 1992/93 season, cashew nut trading accounted for 20% or less of the turnover of most of these firms. These firms are also among the country's largest traders of non-traditional agricultural commodities, including sesame and cassava roots.

Table 4.12 outlines the trade mix of one of the largest emergent cashew nut exporters. Notice both the extensive range of products and the diversity of markets served. These new cashew nut exporters are generally quite experienced in international trade or else have hired experienced managers from abroad to develop this business. Several of the new exporters had experience in cashew nut trading during the 1960s and 1970s.

TABLE 4.11: **Characteristics of Surveyed Private Cashew Nut Exporters**

Company	Year Established	Ownership	Fixed Assets ($ 000)	Cashew Export Volume (Tons)[1]	Cashew Turnover as % of Total Earnings	Prior Cashew Trading Experience	Source of Financing	Other Activities/Trading
TWD	1989	Tanzanian Asian Individual		3700		No	External	Commercial Import and Export
ETC	1992	Tan. Asian + U.K. Partnership	120	2800	20%	No	Own	Commodity Exports Relief Agency Sales
FDHN	1947	Tan. Asian Family	2500	2045	13%	Yes	Own + Bank	Commodity Exports Oilseed Milling
BDS	Na.	Tan. Asian Individual	500	2150 (1150)	20%	No	Own + External	Commodity Exports Seed Beans Transport
RPR	1989	Tan. Asian Family	170	2000 (1000)	20%	Yes	Own + Bank	Commodity Trade Textiles
AMKT	Na.	Tan. Asian Partnership	100	1300	50%	No	Own + Bank	Commodity Exports Gems Pharmaceuticals
KRSH	1991	Tan. Asian + U.S. Partnership	15	1200 (1200)	100%	Yes	Own + Bank	Part of Large Holding Company
ABTR	1973	Tan. Asian Family	2500	270	6%	No	Own	Commodity Exports Transport/Clearing Spare Parts
MENT	1983	Tan. Asian Family	4050	0 (600)	Na.	No	Own	Commodity Exports

[1] Figures in parentheses are tonnage of 1991/92 crop exported in 1992/93.
Na. Not available.

SOURCE: Author's Survey (March 1993).

TABLE 4.12: **Commodity Export Mix of Major Private Cashew Trader**
(1992/93 Season)

Commodity	Market Destination	Quantity (Tons)	Value ($ 000)
Cashew Nuts	India	2045	1496
Cotton Seed Cake	Western Europe	16,000	1436
Cocoa Beans	U.K.; Netherlands	670	589
Sesame Seed	Turkey; Japan	1026	540
Beeswax	Japan	152	413
Cassava Roots	Western Europe	3000	345
Yellow Gram	India, Ethiopia	1714	257
Pigeon Peas	India; U.K.	755	217
Castor Seeds	Europe; Japan	736	146
Miscellaneous Minor Items[1]	Pakistan; Zaire		219
		27,300	5658

[1] Including betel nuts, cardamom, copra cake, cooking oil, and gum arabic.

SOURCE: Based on Private Exporter Trade Records provided to author.

While several of the firms financed their cashew nut purchases out of their own funds, most obtained additional funding, either from local commercial banks or from external buyers or affiliated companies. Such external finance provided a strong competitive edge, since money was available on a timely basis and at interest rates below 10%, compared with the 27–31% interest rates on local overdraft facilities.

As noted above, the private exporters are generally not directly involved in the local-level procurement of the crop. They have instead relied upon private traders (or less commonly cooperatives) based in the main production areas to arrange crop collection, grading, farmer payments and the preparation of consignments for shipment. The buying agents are not strangers; several are linked through family, while others have previously dealt with the exporter with other commodities (e.g. sesame, cassava). Trust is essential in this type of trade, given the relatively large sums of money which the exporter provides the agent to make purchases, and given the fact that the exporter is simultaneously negotiating forward export contracts which the agent's supplies will help fulfill.

Similarly, export transactions are not conducted with strangers. Several firms direct their trade toward affiliated companies or through buyers/brokers with whom they have had past trading experience. Few of the firms deal directly with Indian processors. Instead, they rely upon offshore brokerage firms (based in places such as Singapore and the Virgin Islands) which provide reliable financial and shipping services and which guarantee product quality to the eventual buyer.

The interviewed exporters were asked to rate various potential problems on a scale of 1 to 5, with 5 signifying a 'major problem or bottleneck' and 1 signifying that the factor is not a problem faced by them in their procurement or sales. Table 4.13 aggregates the results of this exercise.

According to the exporters, the most significant problem is social infrastructure (telephones, roads) linking them or their buying agents with the main production areas. This raises overall transaction costs in crop procurement. Taxation is the next concern of significance, especially the (increasing) local taxes imposed by district authorities. In some locations, the sum of educational, building, and other funds totals up to TSh. 18/kg. While traders are normally required to pay part of the fees, these fees are in fact simply taxes on local producers.[42]

Exporters indicated that the storage and transport facilities which they own or lease are more than adequate for their present trading activities. In fact, not a single firm indicated that it needed to make any additional invest-

TABLE 4.13: **Private Exporter Assessment of Problems** (1 to 5 Scale; 1 = No Problem, 3 = Moderate Problem, 5 = Severe Problem)

Factor/Problem	Rank	Average Rating
Poor Communications to Producing Areas	1	4.2
Poor Roads	2	3.7
Taxation/Cesses	3	3.1
Availability of Cashew Nuts	4	2.8
Access to Short-Term Finance	5	2.7
Lack of Time/Conflicting Activities	6	2.7
Inflation/Price Instability	7	2.4
Lack of Market Information	8	2.3
Availability/Cost of Packaging Materials	9	2.3
Official Restrictions on Cashew Procurement	10	2.1
Inadequate Transport/Storage Facilities	11	2.0
Lack of Market Outlets	12	2.0
High Cost of Cashew Nuts	13	1.9
Unreliability of Buyers	14	1.8

SOURCE: Author's Field Survey (March 1993).

---

[42] Data on producer prices for cashews provided by the Marketing Development Bureau are thus misleading as they do not take into account these taxes. When taken into account, the share of farmers in the export value this past season was only 40–45%, depending upon location.

ment in order to enter into the cashew trade. In the southern zone, there is significant unused storage facilities, especially at the depots of the National Milling Corporation and at the idle cashew nut factories. Varied responses were given to the question about finance. This was not a problem for those firms who receive financing from overseas affiliates or buyers. Still, it was reported to be a costly and difficult barrier by those firms having to rely upon local commercial banks. The exporters do not see marketing (including market information, market outlets, and buyer reliability) as a serious constraint to the current trading activities.

Private exporters were asked about their potential interest (or emerging plans) to enter into cashew nut processing to replace or supplement raw nut exports to India. Several firms, each with external partners, have been engaged in discussions with the TCMB to lease one or more of the existing factories. At least one of these deals is expected to go through in time for operations during the 1993/94 season. A few other exporters expressed skepticism regarding the financial viability of the complete mechanical processing systems. They have been exploring alternative, semi-mechanized technologies whose operating scales are significantly lower than the existing factories. In March of 1993, no investments of this type were imminent. A third option, suggested by one of the firms, was to cannibalize a few of the existing factories, utilizing the best features from the Oltremere and Cashco systems, while building in less mechanized features for several processes.

Dimensions of Performance

During the 1992/93 season, the overall performance of the industry was mixed. Total marketed production declined to about 35,000 tons because of an unseasonal cold spell which damaged flowers and reduced fruit setting. There was some evidence of increased effort to combat the powdery mildew problem (through sulphur spraying) and rehabilitate cashew *shambas*.[43]

One of the major objectives beyond the market liberalization was to improve the reliability of the crop procurement system and to raise farmer incomes. To some extent, progress has been made. In contrast with past seasons when crop buying was not completed until April or later, this year virtually the entire crop was purchased by the end of February, and in some

---

[43] The evidence coming from surveys by the ODA Cashew Research team and from the loan applications of the commercial banks does indicate that it is primarily farmers with above average landholdings and other assets which are obtaining finance and making the investments to restore cashew productivity. The vast majority of smallholders have not made such investments.

areas, a month earlier. This occurred despite the delays in bank overdraft approvals. Furthermore, in contrast with past experience, this season farmers were paid on a timely basis, especially when private traders paid cash directly to farmers or to the cooperative societies. The activities of private traders undoubtedly put pressure on the cooperative unions and societies to improve their services to farmers.[44]

Relatively few farmers benefited from the higher prices (TSh. 140–160/kg. for standard grade) which private traders were offering at the very beginning of the season. While trade figures for the entire season were not finalized by the time that research field work was completed, the share of farmers in the export value is likely to have fallen back below 50% (see Table 4.14). Given the profit margins earned on exports (see below) and the level of producer prices prior to the announcement of guideline prices, it would appear that official interventions resulted in a transfer of income from farmers to private traders/cooperatives/banks amounting to some TSh. 525 million.[45] Direct taxes on producers, in the form of local cesses, amounted to about TSh. 350 million (that is, an average of TSh. 10/kg).

During the season, both farmers and traders did move cashew nuts across district and regional borders in order to counter or take advantage of differ-

TABLE 4.14: **Recent Trends in Producer Prices** (TSh./kg.)[1]

Season	Standard Grade	Undergrade	Weighted[2]	Share of Export Value
1989/90	84	56	82.6	57%
1990/91	110	73	108.2	56%
1991/92	137	89	132.2	66%
1992/93	120–140	80–90	110.0–127.5	47–54%[3]

[1] Does not take into account local cesses paid by farmers which vary significantly by district (e.g. between TSh. 2 and 18 per kg.)

[2] For 1989/90 and 1990/91 weighted 95% standard + 5% undergrade. For 1991/92 and 1992/93 the respective ratios are 90/10 and 75/25.

[3] Only raw nuts exported. Estimated average FOB value at $700/ton.

SOURCE: Marketing Development Bureau and Author's Field Work.

---

[44] One future difficulty is foreseen here. It is still the cooperative unions and societies which provide most of the input loans and inputs to farmers, with repayment coming through deductions on the delivered crop. With private traders taking an increasing proportion of the cashew crop (and other crops), input loan recovery may become a severe problem for the cooperatives.

[45] Given export prices and the shilling exchange rate, still very comfortable margins would have been earned by the private trade with a producer price of TSh. 140/kg. At this producer price, the cooperative unions who sold to the TCMB could have covered their finance charges and still had a modest profit to begin repayment of arrears.

entials in guideline/actual producer prices and in local cesses. This 'migration' of the crop also took the form of chasing the available cash because in some villages, districts and regions there were periods in which cooperatives, the TCMB, and locally operating private traders did not have cash to make purchases. As a result of these 'migrations' district-level figures for marketed production showed considerable anomalies with huge recorded increases in some areas and major declines in others.

Due to differential access to transport facilities, it was traders rather than farmers who were able to best take advantage of these inter-district price and tax variations. The available evidence suggests that local (that is, first handler) trader operations were quite profitable this season as a result of the set TCMB buying prices and the guideline producer prices. An indication of this is provided in Table 4.15. The first column is for a Masasi-based trader who procured nuts within a 25 km radius of the town and then sold to TCMB in Masasi. For this low risk operation, the trader obtained a margin of 12.8%. The second column concerns a trader in Nachingwea who transported nuts to Lindi to sell to TCMB at much higher inter-store price. The trading margin was considerably higher.

Overall, private traders accounted for about 43% of the crop procured directly from either farmers or cooperative societies and, by the completion of sales, probably accounted for a similar proportion of the export volume. However, with the TCMB and several of the cooperative unions not obtaining finance until December or January, the export-oriented private traders (through their buying agents) were able to procure most of the high quality nuts from the 1992/93 harvest. That is, all or a large proportion of the nuts from Tinduru and Nachingwea Districts (known for high-quality nuts) were eventually procured by private traders. In contrast, most of the nuts in Newala District (the quality of which is uneven or poor) were left for the TCMB and MARCU. While procurement was more or less equally divided between MARCU and eight private traders in Masasi District, the majority of MARCU's stock was classified as undergrade. Traders supplying both private exporters and TCMB tended to provide the former with standard grade nuts and the latter with undergrade (selling them as standard grade if possible).

While the TCMB was still negotiating with foreign buyers/brokers in March, most of the private exports were shipped by the end of February. Financially hand-cuffed by the banks, TCMB obtained a lower quality stock of supplies and it is likely that the average export prices it earned will turn out to have been considerably lower than those obtained by the private traders.

TABLE 4.15: **Private Cashew Trader Margins on Sales to TCMB (1992/93 Season)** (All Values are TSh./kg.)

Cost or Price	Masasi Trader Supplying TCMB in Masasi	Nachingwea Trader Supplying TCMB in Lindi
Producer Price	127.00	120.00
Levies/Cesses/Duties	14.40	9.40
Village Secretary Commission	Na.	1.00
Transport Costs	2.00	12.00
Packaging Costs	4.35	4.35
Finance Charges	Na.	3.60
Depreciation (On Vehicles)	Na.	4.10
Overhead, Labor, Insurance	1.70	5.50
Total Costs	149.45	159.95
TCMB Inter-Store Price	166.45	190.00
Trader Margin	19.20 (12.8%)	30.05 (18.8%)

SOURCE: Author's Trader Interviews.

As noted earlier, private trader efforts during the 1991/92 season to export were largely unsuccessful, with both product quality and buyer unreliability problems. Firms entering the trade during the 1992/93 season faired much better. FOB prices were mostly within a range of $675 to 715/ton. While these were lower than for the previous season (when average exports were $813/ton), the exporters benefited from a devaluation of the Tanzania Shilling from 290 per $1 in March 1992 to 345 per $1 a year later. Together with the lower producer prices, this provided comfortable trading margins (12–20%) for most exporters this season. The trading costs and earnings for two companies (two transactions) are illustrated in Table 4.16.

During the 1992/93 season, all processing factories were completely idle. Prior to the season, the large permanent work staff at several of the factories was let go. Both the TCMB and the cooperative unions were under pressure from the banks to repay their loans. Had they chosen to process the nuts themselves, this would have added several months' delay before the crop would be sold and thus before payments were received. Although discussions were held between several private firms and the TCMB about the possibility of TCMB performing custom processing services, no arrangements were ever implemented.[46]

---

[46] Neither private firms nor cooperative unions have much confidence in TCMB's ability to process nuts on an efficient basis. For its part, the TCMB was requiring firms to deliver a minimum of 1000 tons before it would consider custom processing activities.

TABLE 4.16: **Illustrative Exporter Trading Costs and Profits (1992/93 Season)**
(Figures in TSh./kg. or $/ton)

Cost or Price Item	Cashew Nuts Procured in Masasi in January and Exported via Mtwara Port in Late February	Cashew Nuts Procured in Tinduru in December and Exported via Mtwara Port in Late January
Price to Producer	127.00	130.00
Levies/Cesses	18.00	15.00
Commissions to Buying Agents and/or Cooperative Officials	6.00	6.50
Transport Costs to Mtwara	16.00	19.00
Packaging Materials	4.35	4.35
Weight Loss	1.40	1.50
Finance Charges	13.25	13.56
Overhead Costs	4.00	4.50
Port/Inspection/Handling	6.60	6.60
Total Costs	196.60 (at TSh. 345 = $1) $570/ton	201.01 (at TSh. 330.3 = $1) $608.8/ton
FOB Earnings[1]	$689.5/ton	$691.5/ton
Exporter Margin	$119.5/ton (20.9%)	$ 82.7/ton (13.6%)

[1] Assuming 1.5% weight loss in transit and $68/ton for freight and insurance.

SOURCE: Author's Field Interviews.

CONCLUSION

In the period between World War II and the early 1970s, Tanzania developed one of the world's largest cashew nut industries. By 1973/74 marketed production reached 145,000 tons (about 30% of total world production) and exports were among the highest in the world. Cashews were the country's fourth largest source of foreign exchange and provided an important source of income to some 250,000 smallholder farmers. During the 1960s a multi-tiered marketing system—involving local cooperative societies, regional cooperative unions and a marketing board—was imposed on what had been a trade carried on by private firms and private traders were removed from the marketing system.

The steady rise in production and trade during the 1950s and 1960s has been mirrored by a dramatic and steady decline of the industry since then. Despite a buoyant international market, Tanzania's cashew nut production fell to less than 17,000 tons by the late 1980s and its early reputation for a high quality product was badly damaged. Several factors contributed to this downward spin, including the country's 'villagization' program, a sharp and virtually continuous decline in real producer prices, and major inefficiencies in cooperative and marketing board crop collection and downstream activities. Government 'education' campaigns (and threats) were insufficient to counter the loss of farmer incentives due to declining services and incomes. The massive decline in production has not only had a sharp adverse affect on living standards in the southern regions, but has made most of the large-scale, donor-funded, government-owned, state-of-the-art processing factories into 'white elephants'.

With the industry on the brink of complete collapse, the Tanzanian government announced in 1991 that the cashew nut market would be liberalized and private firms permitted to undertake trade once again. The reform process has been confusing and full of irregularities, although there are signs that the industry may be set for a recovery. Whether by design or default, the policies of liberalization were poorly communicated by the central government, leaving local authorities to use their own discretion and ad hoc procedures in implementing the new set of rules regarding trade. The first year of the reform (1991/92) was largely a failure: few private traders were licensed, there was no competition, controls over prices and crop movements continued, and results were poor when private and cooperative enterprises sought to market cashew nuts outside of the TCMB.

The second season of the liberalized market featured some improvements, though considerable confusion still existed. Private traders were more widely licensed, yet there was little commercial bank finance available either to them, to cooperatives or to the marketing board. In order to insure that official loans extended to the cooperatives and marketing board were recovered, an agreement was reached between these parties and the regional governments to set 'indicative' producer prices at levels 10–15% lower than the previous season. Private firms, which had been paying farmers considerably higher prices at the beginning of the season, complied with the 'indicative' prices by reducing their own prices and pocketing the windfall. Government and commercial bank interventions thus resulted in a huge transfer of income from poor farmers to a combination of banks, cooperatives and private firms.

Despite these limitations, some positive trends are emerging. With the entry of private traders, crops are collected soon after harvest and farmers are being paid promptly (not only by private traders but also by cooperatives which are feeling the competitive pressure). This is leading farmers to harvest their cashews, rather than neglect them, and has led some of the better endowed farmers to rehabilitate their farms and plant new cashew seedlings.

During 1991/92 and 1992/93, marketed production averaged 37,000 tons and export revenues recovered to their level of the early 1980s.

More and more private firms are entering the trade. Collectively, they accounted for 43% of the purchased crop during the 1992/93 season. Most individual firms are very small and have undertaken the low risk activity of buying from farmers and selling to the TCMB at a guaranteed price. The larger players are firms which are active in domestic and export marketing of a wide range of non-traditional commodities. Some have excellent international trading contacts which they are using in developing their own cashew nut exports.

Due to uncertainty about government policies, private firms have not yet made investments in production or marketing infrastructure for cashews. They continue to utilize trucks, warehouses and infrastructure used for other commodity trade. With the confidence gained and profits earned during the 1992/93 season, this is likely to change. Some firms are likely to begin to establish their own cashew farms and develop closer links with producers. Several firms have expressed an interest in processing the nuts locally.

Under the current policy environment, and with considerable uncertainty as to whether Tanzania's highly-mechanized processing factories can be financially viable even if operated on a commercial basis by private firms, the most appropriate strategy is to enable interested private firms to lease selected TCMB factories. At the same time it is important to encourage these and other firms to investigate alternative, semi-mechanized technologies. Leasing of the large-scale factories for periods of one to five years would expand the resources available to the private sector without significantly increasing its exposure to policy reversal risk. This approach would signify the government's commitment to the continued liberalization of trade, plus provide the government with some return on its factory investments. The long-term competitiveness of Tanzania's industry will require changes in the technologies used toward a lower degree of mechanization and reduced dependence on fuel oil as an input. While some adaptions can be made within the existing factories or by combining certain features of the Oltremare and Cashco systems, it would be expedient for would-be processors to explore and test alternative technologies.

ANNEX TO CHAPTER IV

TABLE 4A: **Exports of Cashew Kernels by Major Producers** ('000 Tons)

Country	1975	1980	1985	1988–90 (Ave.)
India	58.0	37.4	31.6	34.9
Mozambique	24.4	17.1	2.5	3.2
Brazil	7.6	11.9	25.0	21.7
Tanzania	4.0	5.5	0.5	1.4
Kenya	0.0	2.7	1.9	0.5

SOURCE: Gill and Duffus, *Edible Nut Market Reports*, various years.

TABLE 4B: **Price Comparisons of Major Cashew Kernel Suppliers** (United States Import Values (FOB) All Grades; 1989–90 Averages)

Country	Quantity (Tons)	Unit Value ($/ton)	% of Indian Price	Comments
India	19,833	4835	100	Manual Processing; High Quality
Brazil	19,429	4205	87	Mechanical Processing; Medium Quality
Mozambique	2,845	3577	74	Mechanical Processing; Low Quality
Tanzania	1,332	3673	76	Mechanical Processing; Low Quality
China	744	3568	74	Manual Processing; Low Quality
Kenya	403	3262	68	Mechanical Processing; Low Quality

SOURCE: Agriconsult/AMEC (1992).

TABLE 4C: **Cashew Nut Kernel Imports into Major Markets** (Tons)

Country	1980–82 Average	1984–86 Average	1989–91 Average
United States	30,917	43,073	48,372
(Former) USSR	20,816	3302	3328
Netherlands	3080	2301	3669
Germany	2796	2736	3661
Canada	2666	3235	4309
United Kingdom	2638	2934	4919
Japan	2371	2717	4520
Australia	1535	3011	2930
Total	66,819	63,309	75,708

SOURCE: Gill and Duffus *Edible Nut Market Report*, various issues.

TABLE 4D: Operations of Cashew Nut Processing Factories

Factory	Date of Test Run	Source of Finance	Est. Maximum Capacity	Annual Raw Nut Throughput (Tons)						Total # of Days Operated Through Sept. 1991
				1985/86	1986/87	1987/88	1988/89	1989/90	1990/91	
Tanita	1965	GOT	10,700	0	0	218	2455	3000	1345	>1000
Mtwara	1968	GOT + ES	6800	0	0	0	0	0	0	?
Lindi	1978	WB	8600	0	0	0	0	0	0	301
Mbagala	1978	ES	10,700	0	0	0	0	0	0	?
Mtama	1979	WB	4300	0	0	0	0	0	0	358
Likombe	1980	WB	8600	0	0	2402	3144	6000	1473	>800
Kibaha	1980	WB	8600	0	0	1383	2536	3500	1345	720
Nachingwea	1981	WB	4300	0	0	0	0	0	0	95
Masasi	1981	WB	8600	0	0	0	0	0	0	91
Newala II	1981	WB	8600	0	0	0	0	0	0	116
Tinduru	Never	ES	8600	0	0	0	0	0	0	0
Newala I	Never	WB	8600	0	0	0	0	0	0	0

SOURCES: Agriconsult/Amec (1992); MDB Annual Cashewnut Report, various years.

V.

Perishable Profits: Private Sector Dairy Processing and Marketing in Kenya

Steven Jaffee

D airy products account for approximately 4% of the agricultural GDP of sub-Saharan Africa and 11% of the total value of food production in the region.[1] Dairy products provide an estimated 2% of calories and 4% of protein in the average diet in SSA, and these shares are considerably higher in the region's main producing countries.[2] Primarily for agro-climatic reasons, SSA is a large net importer of dairy products. In fact, for much of the past decade, the value of SSA's dairy imports exceeded the region's exports of all individual agricultural products other than coffee, cocoa and sugar.[3] The historical experience from many countries points to the importance of the dairy industry in agro-industrial development and in the structural transformation of agriculture. This has certainly been true in Kenya since Independence.

This chapter focuses on dairy processing and marketing in Kenya. Kenya is one of SSA's largest milk producers and has developed one of the region's most commercialized dairy industries. The industry has long been dominated by the private sector, unlike the situation in Zimbabwe and South Africa which have developed Africa's two other commercially advanced dairy industries. The Kenyan experience is illuminating for two reasons. First, much of the history of the industry has centered around the development of a large private cooperative which persistently sought to utilize the powers of the

---

[1] Mbogoh (1984); Walshe et al. (1991).

[2] Walshe et al. (1991). See FAO *Food Consumption Patterns* for dietary profiles of individual countries.

[3] FAO *Trade Yearbooks*, various issues.

state to protect its interests and minimize competition. In what amounts to an ironic historical twist, over the past decade this same cooperative has essentially been 'publicized' and now serves as a de facto parastatal. A second interesting feature of the sub-sector has been the attempts by other private firms and cooperatives to develop dairy processing operations on the geographical and competitive margins permitted by government and the dominant cooperative. With recent changes in governmental competition and pricing policies within the industry, these private and cooperative activities are expected to expand and be replicated in many parts of the country. Thus, the Kenyan experience can provide insights into the costs of market controls and the likely degree and forms of private sector response to market liberalization.

The chapter has three sections. The first section examines major techno-economic characteristics of dairy products and production, noting possible implications for entry into dairy processing and marketing and the forms this may take. The second part provides a concise overview of the scope and features of dairy production and markets in sub-Saharan Africa. The last part examines the Kenyan experience. It discusses the historical development of the industry and summarizes current patterns of operation by private enterprise engaged in dairy processing.

MAJOR TECHNO-ECONOMIC CHARACTERISTICS OF MILK AND DAIRY PRODUCTS

There are several techno-economic features of milk, milk production and dairy processing which generate risks as well as opportunities for dairy producers and marketing enterprises and which might be expected to influence the industrial organization of dairy commodity systems in Africa.[4] Among the inherent properties of raw milk itself are the following:

1) **High perishability:** Since milk provides a good medium for micro-biological development, quality deterioration is rapid unless the raw milk is cooled or processed within a few hours of 'harvesting'. Raw milk's perishability minimizes the scope for storage and places a premium on the development of a reliable milk collection and cooling system and on investments in equipment and processes which convert the raw product into less perishable forms.

---

[4] This discussion is based in part on Hopcraft (1978), Manchester (1983), Brown (1991), and Walshe et al. (1991), and on helpful comments by Cees de Haan.

2) **High bulkiness:** Since milk is 87% water, its valuable components (fat, proteins and casein) constitute only a small share. Together with the perishability factor, this presents major logistical problems. Raw milk carries relatively high transport costs per unit value, reducing the scope for economical long-distance trade and leading toward localized supply and distribution arrangements. When producing areas are distant from major markets, it may be profitable to convert the raw product into less bulky forms by separating the water from the valuable components.

3) **Wide quality variability** in terms of fat content, micro-biological quality and the presence of diseases and of antibiotic residues: Quality variations stem from differences or changes in animal breeds, climate, feed availability, animal health and the hygienic conditions during milking. Milk can also be adulterated by producers and traders. The quality of raw milk delivered by producers and traders can have major public health implications and influence the economics and product quality of dairy processing. This implies a need for quality standards and monitoring measures, as well as potentially significant benefits from measures to support animal husbandry and health at the farm level.[5]

In addition, the production of milk at the farm level has several generic properties which might be expected to influence the market structure for dairy products. These include:

4) **Relatively high entry and exit costs:** Lumpy investments must be made in specialized assets (grade cows, milk cans and perhaps milking machines and buildings) whose alternative uses yield far lower returns (for example, culling grade cows for meat). Even at the smallest scale, such as one or two milking cows, dairying entails a relatively significant fixed cost element and must be regarded as a long-term investment. Thus, smallholder entry will require credit facilities or significant savings from other activities. Prospective producers must consider the overall reliability of livestock support and dairy marketing services and the long-term remuneration of dairy market outlets.

5) **Relatively low short-term production elasticity:** Due to multi-year biological lags, relatively small adjustments in output can be made by

---

[5] While quality standards have public good properties, measures to improve milk quality (for instance, through production support) may be associated with externalities and the service supplier being unable to appropriate the benefits from the activity. See Umali, Feder and de Haan (1992).

changing the feeding regime. More significant output changes require either adding or culling cows. Significant production lags might be expected following changes in prices or other incentives. However, where only a small proportion of milk output is marketed, changes in the incentive system could result in a more rapid and significant supply response as shifts are made between household consumption and marketed supply.

6) **Continuous product harvest:** Cows produce milk throughout the year rather than during a limited season of a few weeks or months.[6] While this yielding pattern has the attraction of providing a continuous source of income for the producer, it requires that the milk collection and marketing system also be continuous and reliable. Otherwise, much milk will be wasted or the producer will be forced to utilize greater quantities than preferred.

7) **Seasonal variability in output:** This can lead to surpluses and shortages at the local and/or national levels with heavy pressure placed on transport, processing and other infrastructure during the 'flush season' and underutilization of such infrastructure during the 'dry season'. Because the demand for liquid milk has seasonal patterns which may not match those of production, the result can be wide swings in market prices from one season to the next. Production seasonality implies a need to offer incentives to producers to increase dry season production (through use of manufactured feeds, the timing of calving, etc.) and a need for processors to make special arrangements to procure sufficient raw materials during the season. Inherent trade-offs are faced between using milk for calf-rearing versus human use.

Finally, the processing, commercialization and demand for dairy products have distinctive features which might be expected to influence dairy system organizational patterns.

8) **Liquid milk can be consumed in its raw harvested form or preserved through pasteurization or fermentation.** Raw milk provides the cheapest source of milk-based nutrients and its direct supply to consumers avoids most of the coordination problems associated with other dairy processing and distribution modes. Raw milk consumption may entail health hazards although boiling the milk can destroy all

---

[6] In Kenya, harvesting is typically done two times per day—in the morning and evening.

pathogens. Raw milk can be treated and preserved for a few days through pasteurization and preserved for a longer period in liquid form either through exposure to ultra-high temperatures (UHT) and aseptic packaging or through fermentation. The costs of these processes and associated packaging vary significantly. This multiplicity of potential milk products offers considerable flexibility for dairy systems to adapt to local demand, infrastructure and technological conditions.

9) **Raw milk can be converted into numerous processed products,** including soft and hard cheeses, yogurt-based products, butter and butter oil (*ghee*), cream and skimmed milk, and powdered milk. The primary ingredients of raw milk can be disassembled and then recombined in different ways or mixed with other raw materials to yield different products. This again offers considerable flexibility in processing and marketing operations. Because of this technical as well as financial complementarity among certain products (that is, cream and skimmed milk, butter and butter oil, cheeses of different rates of maturity), one would not expect to find processors with single-product specialization.

10) **There are many technological options for the preservation or processing of most dairy products.** Both batch and continuous processes are available that utilize different degrees of mechanization and different (efficient) operating scales. Some products can be efficiently treated in rural areas on a small-scale basis using relatively simple non or semi-mechanized technology. This applies to fermented milk, butter, cream and most types of cheeses and yogurt products. Relatively little asset-specificity is involved—most of the equipment and inputs used (boilers, fuelwood, vats, refrigerators) can be used for other purposes. For these products, technical and financial barriers to entry are not expected to be significant, and subject to demand, many small producers are likely to be active.

Other products require more complex processes and higher investments in plant and equipment. Milk pasteurization can be done on a relatively small scale, although some economies of scale are realized in (semi-)mechanized continuous heating and cooling systems, and 'lumpy' investments in cold stores are required. Still, both pasteurizers and cold stores can be put to alternative uses (for example juice-making), limiting the degree of asset specificity. Where there is sufficient market demand (along with or instead of raw milk), one would expect to find several small-to-medium-scale milk pasteurizers and distributors serving each market center or urban area.

The production (and packaging) of UHT milk and evaporated powdered milk require more sophisticated, capital-intensive techniques and more specialized skills. The production of these products is associated with greater economies of scale and higher degrees of asset specificity. Due to its high-cost packaging, UHT milk might be expected to encounter relatively limited local demand in Africa in spite of the absence of household refrigerators. For these commodities one would expect relatively few, larger-scale producers.

11) **Sources and patterns of demand will vary significantly among products** with market segmentation being common. The highest valued ingredient in milk is fat. In Africa, products with a very high milk fat content are likely to face a relatively limited market, restricted primarily to middle-to-upper-income groups and tourists. In contrast, raw milk is likely to be the predominant dairy product sold in milk-producing rural areas for reasons of both logistics and purchasing power.

DAIRY PRODUCTION AND MARKETS IN AFRICA

The livestock sub-sector plays an important role in the economies of many sub-Saharan African countries. For the region as a whole, the sub-sector accounts for about 25% of agricultural GDP. This share exceeds 40% in several countries.[7] For the region as a whole, dairy products account for an estimated 20–25% of the value of livestock sector output.[8]

Dairy production and processing in Africa is based upon cattle, camel and small ruminant production. Dairy production data for the region should be regarded as 'guess-timates' since they are based on estimated herd sizes and very rough indicators of average yields. Data are especially tentative for camel and small ruminant milk production because this production occurs largely in poorly monitored arid and semi-arid areas, and in many cases, is primarily for subsistence purposes. Based on FAO data for cow and small ruminant milk production and on specialists' estimates of camel milk production, sub-

---

[7] Winrock International (1992).
[8] Walshe et al. (1991).

Saharan Africa's 1988 milk output of 15.2 million metric tons consisted of 9.62 million metric tons of cow milk (63%), 2.94 million metric tons of small ruminant milk (19%), and 2.68 million metric tons of camel milk (18%).[9] Cow's milk constitutes the bulk of local production in the vast majority of countries. Only in five countries (Somalia, Chad, Mali, Mauritania, and Niger) does estimated small ruminant and camel milk production exceed local cow milk production.[10]

Sub-Saharan Africa's production of cow milk in 1991 was 11.9 million metric tons, representing 2.6% of world production.[11] Due to agroclimatic and other reasons, this production is heavily concentrated in relatively few Southern and East African countries (Table 5.1). The three largest producers— South Africa, Sudan and Kenya—accounted for nearly 59% of the region's total reported cow milk production in 1991. Annual cow milk production on a per capita basis ranges from less than one kilogram for many West and Central African countries to nearly 100 kgs. for Kenya.

While reported cow milk production in sub-Saharan Africa grew rapidly during the 1960s, since the mid-1970s production has barely kept pace with average annual population growth of 3.1%.[12] Most of this expansion in production can be attributed to increased herd size, rather than improved pro-

TABLE 5.1: **Concentration of SSA's Reported Cow Milk Production**

Country	Production ('000 Metric Tons)	Share of SSA Total (%)	Cumulative Share of SSA Total (%)
South Africa	2515	21.1	21.1
Sudan	2299	19.3	40.4
Kenya	2189	18.3	58.7
Ethiopia	752	6.7	65.4
Somalia	497	4.2	69.6
Madagascar	472	4.0	73.6
Tanzania	463	3.9	77.5
Uganda	437	3.7	81.2

SOURCE: FAO *Production Yearbook* (1991).

---

[9] This calculation is based on Walshe et al. (1991, Annex 2) plus data on South African cow milk production from the FAO *Production Yearbook* (1990).

[10] Ibid. Sudan and Somalia account for about three-fourths of SSA small ruminant and camel milk production.

[11] This total SSA production is similar to the milk output of the Netherlands.

[12] This covers the period from 1975 to 1987.

ductivity.[13] With the exception of a few areas and production systems, milk production is based predominantly on low-yielding, yet disease-resistant, indigenous zebu stock. Excluding South Africa, the average annual cow milk yield in SSA is estimated at 353 kgs. per cow, compared to an average of 820 kgs. per cow for all developing countries as a group.[14]

The available data suggest that regional per capita dairy product consumption has remained steady since the early 1970s at slightly below 30 kgs. per annum. Most of this consumption—estimated at 90%—is of liquid milk, either fresh or in sour or fermented forms. Sour or fermented milk consumption is especially prominent in rural areas. Evidence from some countries indicates that most fresh milk is consumed in tea or in cooked meals rather than drank separately.[15] The remainder of dairy consumption is in the form of cheese, butter oil, butter and yogurt-based products. While FAO data for cheese and butter suggest stagnant production within the region over the past two decades, such data is highly questionable given that most production and consumption occur in rural areas and do not enter formal marketing channels. Such production is unlikely to be captured in national statistics.

Even though much of the available dairy production and consumption data may be underestimated, it is clear is that sub-Saharan Africa has become a large net importer of dairy products over the past two decades. Commercial imports of dairy products rose in value from $113 million in 1970 to $705 million in 1980. Although imports declined during the 1980s, they remained at $613 million in 1989.[16] Over this period, expanding quantities of skim milk powder and butter oil (for recombination to form liquid milk) were imported into Africa as part of food aid programs of the United States, the EEC and the World Food Program. In recent years, commercial and donated imports have accounted for 20–25% of total estimated dairy product consumption in the region.[17]

---

[13] Over the 1974–1989 period, the number of cows in SSA increased by 56% from 14.88 million to 23.24 million. Average milk yields increased only by 15.7% from 305 kg./head to 353 kg./head. (Shapiro et al. (1990, p. 50).

[14] FAO *Production Yearbook* (1989). Average yields in South Africa have exceeded 2500 kg./head in recent years.

[15] Walshe et al. (1991, p. 9) refer to 70% in Zimbabwe.

[16] Of which $499 million was of condensed/dry/fresh milk, $69.6 million was of butter, and $44.6 million was of cheese and curd (FAO *Trade Yearbook* 1989).

[17] Imports have been especially important in West Africa, where they accounted for 40–50% of total regional consumption during the mid-to-late-1980s. See Shapouri and Rosen (1990) for a country-by-country analysis of the importance of and growth in dairy imports.

Several factors contributed to the rapid growth in SSA dairy imports during the 1970s and their maintenance at significant levels in more recent years. On the supply side, price support and other incentive programs contributed to the development of large dairy product surpluses in North America and within the EEC. In the case of the United States, large quantities of surplus production were made available for bilateral and multilateral food aid programs. For the EEC, subsidies were provided which enabled producers to export at prices well below those of domestic prices. On the demand side, imports were stimulated by (1) overvalued exchange rates which made commercial imports even less expensive, (2) donor assistance in building large-scale milk reconstituting factories, and (3) rapid urbanization rates in some countries. Dairy imports into SSA have come predominantly from outside of the region. Only Kenya, Zimbabwe and South Africa have undertaken limited exports to other African countries.

Dairy systems in sub-Saharan Africa are characterized by dualistic production and marketing structures. Most production, trade and consumption occurs within traditional or informal systems. Here, production is derived from indigenous breeds of animals and either consumed by the producing household or sold locally. Production, processing and trade are generally conducted on a very small scale. Although constituting the bulk of dairy activity in the region, these traditional or informal systems are poorly documented and not well understood by outside analysts.

Modern or formal dairy sub-systems account for less than 10% of the milk production and flow in most SSA countries. This rises to slightly more than 25% in Kenya and over 50% in Zimbabwe and South Africa. These systems are based on grade or pure bred cattle, have a significant or predominant large farm component, and historically have featured dominant or monopsonistic national cooperatives and parastatals serving the urban markets. In many parts of East and Southern Africa, during the colonial period these formal systems were controlled by European settlers. In the period since independence, large state farms have played major roles in the formal sub-systems in both these countries and several others.

Past efforts to improve dairy product supplies and processing have involved the construction of large-scale processing and milk reconstituting plants to meet urban demand for liquid milk.[18] These efforts were influenced by the

---

[18] This discussion is based on Walshe et al. (1991), pp. 58–68.

availability of cheap or free imports of skim milk powder and butter oil and by an initial emphasis (particularly by UNICEF) in supplying pasteurized milk to children. Many of these investments were financed by donors whose technical advisors were most familiar with capital-intensive dairy systems.

These ventures have encountered substantial problems in developing efficient milk collection and dairy marketing systems. Some of these problems have stemmed from the general features of African production, infrastructure and demand including high ambient temperatures, highly seasonal rainfall (and hence production) patterns, low milk production densities, poorly developed and poorly maintained transportation systems, low per capita incomes, and relatively low rates of urbanization. Milk production densities in Africa are illustrated in Table 5.2. These patterns call into question the advisability of centralized, large-scale processing facilities, at least those based on a local production base.

Many of these dairy investments have also suffered from major institutional problems. Parastatal enterprises have operated most of the large-scale dairy processing facilities in Africa. They have typically experienced major managerial problems and have had little incentive to perform efficiently.[19] In many cases, they have been granted exclusive milk collection and marketing rights, thus limiting competitive pressures. Weak livestock support services, together with government pricing policies that have provided only minimal incentive for farmers to supply formal marketing channels and left processors and distributors with inadequate operating margins, have further inhibited dairy development. Dairy investment schemes have commonly resulted in low rates of factory capacity utilization, large financial losses and low levels of development of local milk supplies.

Africa's dairy potential remains far from being effectively realized. At the same time, a long-term strategy of meeting increased demand through imports will become increasingly more costly. Adjustments in dairy policy in North America and the EEC have already contributed to significant reduction in production surpluses and in the availability of dairy products on concessional or food aid terms.[20] World prices for non-fat dry milk powder have increased from $600–700/ton in the early-to-mid-1980s to $1750–2000/ton in 1989/90.

---

[19] See Nellis (1986).

[20] Donated dairy products declined from one million tons (liquid milk equivalent) in 1985 to 315,000 tons in 1988. (Shapiro et al. 1990, p. 52).

TABLE 5.2: **Comparative Milk Production Densities** (kgs./Km^2 per day)

African Patterns		Comparative Patterns	
East Africa	4.2	Netherlands	930
West Africa	0.7	Switzerland	256
Southern Africa	0.5	Ireland	247
Central Africa	0.2	New Zealand	82
Total SSA	1.5	India	28

SOURCE: Nell (1990), p. 37.

Among African governments and donor agencies, there has been a growing recognition of the costs and retarding effects of monopsonistic/monopolistic milk procurement and marketing systems and reliance upon centralized, large-scale processing facilities to meet diverse and expanding demand. The need to focus more attention on building up local production and supporting small-to-medium scale processing activities in rural areas and market towns has also been emphasized. In several countries, including Zimbabwe and Nigeria, there have been moves to privatize dairy enterprises and liberalize dairy marketing systems.

The Kenya dairy industry, the primary focus of this chapter, is in the midst of a transition away from a centralized, near monopolistic formal marketing system toward one featuring multiple participants and different models of milk procurement and dairy product distribution. The Kenyan experience is interesting because the firm which has dominated historically has remained, at least in its formal legal status, a private commercial enterprise while operating as a de facto parastatal since the late 1970s. Competing private and cooperative processors have been forced to operate on the geographical and consumer margins of the formal dairy marketing system due to government restrictions and anti-competitive behavior by the state-sponsored firm. The ongoing market liberalization will lead to significant structural changes as well as a likely reversal in the sub-sector's recent decline.

THE KENYA DAIRY SUB-SECTOR: BACKGROUND AND PRIVATE SECTOR DEVELOPMENT

Livestock production plays an important role in the Kenyan economy. In 1990, sales of livestock products, including meat, milk and hides accounted for 26% of agricultural GDP and nearly 7% of total GDP. Livestock production is especially important for Kenya's smallholder and pastoral populations as a source of food, income and employment, and as a form of savings.[21] The production and sale of dairy products have long comprised one of the most important segments of Kenya's livestock sector. Since independence, the dairy sub-sector has continued to account for some 30% of livestock product sales through formal marketing channels. The very large informal trade in dairy products adds to the sub-sector's importance.

In this section we provide an overview of the origins and evolution of commercial dairy production and marketing in Kenya. After summarizing current patterns of dairy production, consumption and distribution, we move to an examination of the background, operating characteristics and performance of private and cooperative dairy processors.

A Short History of the Development of the Dairy Sub-sector

The raising of cattle has traditionally been an important production and investment activity for many of Kenya's indigenous communities.[22] In these communities, milk has occupied an important place in the daily diet. While milk has been exchanged at the village level for many years, the indigenous zebu cattle generally provided little surplus milk over and above household requirements. Production was for subsistence rather than market purposes.

The development of commercial dairy production and trade in Kenya can be divided into five historical stages, namely:

1) the origins of export-oriented butter production (1900–1930s),

2) discovering the domestic milk market (WWII–mid-1950s),

3) dualistic development (late 1950s–1970),

4) market consolidation and the 'publicization' of the private sector (1971– early 1980s),

5) high cost expansion and creeping liberalization (mid-1980s–present).

The main developments of each of these stages are summarized here.[23]

---

[21] According to Kenya's Integrated Rural Survey (1), during the mid-1970s sales of livestock products accounted for 47% of smallholder agricultural sales earnings nationwide. Only in two Provinces—Nyanza and Eastern—were sales of crops more important than livestock product sales.

[22] Heyer (1976) discusses the traditional role of livestock production in Kenyan rural communities.

[23] This summary draws upon the work of Hill (1956), Klemm (1966), Hopcraft (1976), Raikes (1981), Minae (1981), Stoltz (1979), and DANIDA (1991). Readers interested in a more in-depth review of the historical development of the sub-sector should consult these sources.

The Origins of Export-oriented Butter Production

Commercial dairy production in Kenya originated with the import of pedigree dairy stock from Europe at the beginning of this century. These animals were cross-bred with indigenous stock on European settler farms and research and breeding stations.[24] Commercial butter production started in 1901. By 1908, a private cooperative called the Lumbwa Creamery was exporting the product to Uganda, and other small dairy processing units followed. During World War I the emergent industry was called into service and the entire Veterinary Department was called up. The government's breeding program was interrupted and large numbers of cattle were slaughtered to provide meat to the army.

Following the war, commercial dairy stock was rebuilt and butter production and trade grew steadily. The Lumbwa Creamery expanded production and many smaller makers of cheese, cream and butter emerged. Construction of a large cold store at Kilindi port by the government made possible exports of cheese and butter to London. In 1925, a group of large European farmers in the Naivasha and Nakuru areas formed the Kenya Cooperative Creamery to produce cheese, share technical information and pool sales revenues. Another group of European settler farmers formed the Nanyucki Cooperative in 1928. Periodic efforts by these three main cooperatives to set common prices and quality standards and to undertake joint export sales campaigns were not successful.

The Depression significantly reduced international butter and cheese prices and led to losses for Kenya's cooperatives and European dairy farmers. In order to protect their investments and markets, the three main dairy cooperatives merged in 1931 under the banner of the Kenya Cooperative Creamery (KCC). A year later, the KCC was the first company to register itself as a cooperative under the Co-operative Societies Registration Ordinance. In order to counter the effect of declining world prices, the KCC successfully lobbied the government to apply a levy on domestic sales of butter that would be used as a subsidy on exported butter.[25] Since two-thirds of KCC's sales were sales abroad, it was the smaller private producers which bore most of the cost of the subsidy.

---

[24] Much of this discussion on the early development of commercial dairying is drawn from Hill (1956).

[25] This was instituted under the Butter Levy Ordinance (1931).

Although KCC's membership, processing capacity, production and sales all grew steadily during the 1930s, the organization continued to face competition from smaller dairies and private milk dealers which sought supplies from members of the cooperative. These conditions, on top of widespread evasion of the Butter Ordinance, led the KCC to advocate the creation of a Dairy Control Board which would pool the marketing of all dairy products under a single direction. Underlying the proposed scheme was the KCC's assumption that it would be appointed as the board's sole marketing agent and that other private dairies would either be closed or merged into the KCC operation. Although the government did not create such a board, it did provide the KCC protection against competitive imports and restricted potential competition from African farmers.[26] KCC's advocacy of a Dairy Control Board marked the beginning of more than a half-century of efforts by the firm to use the legal powers of the state to create and maintain exclusive marketing rights within the domestic dairy products market.

Discovering the Domestic Market

During World War II, the Kenyan government and the British Ministry of Food contracted with the KCC to provide large supplies of butter and cheese. It was in serving the military forces and agencies responsible for feeding locally-held prisoners of war that the bulk of KCC's sales were directed at the local market for the first time. At the same time, rapid wartime population growth in Nairobi and Mombasa resulted in greater local demand for whole milk which the KCC and other firms sought to supply.

During the late-1940s and early 1950s, the commercial dairy sub-sector prospered in spite of periodic droughts, termination of the government bulk commodity purchase scheme, and political and security problems in parts of the highland areas. In 1950, the KCC began to market fresh milk on a pilot basis in Nairobi and Sotik. This proved profitable and milk marketing activities were extended to other locations. As in the 1930s, the KCC made another attempt to monopolize this expanding market.[27] The general manager of

---

[26] African farmers were discouraged by the Veterinary Department from acquiring grade cattle. Technical support to African livestock owners was limited to disease control programs. The only support for milk marketing was a scheme at the coast, distant from any KCC procurement or sales activity.

[27] After a feasibility study determined that it would not be profitable for the KCC to construct a large milk distribution depot in Nairobi, the organization proceeded to lobby the government to prevent any other firm or cooperative from making such an investment. This episode is discussed by Hill (1956).

Britain's Milk Marketing Board was invited by the KCC to advise it and the Kenyan Government on measures to improve dairy marketing. Not surprisingly, he recommended compulsory control over milk sales with a single sales agent—the KCC.

Although the government again rejected the scheme for monopolization of milk marketing, it did organize a voluntary milk marketing program involving the KCC and an association of other European private and cooperative dairy producers and traders.[28] A Milk Committee was created which would issue contracts to producers and firms to supply the Nairobi market. The Committee guaranteed minimum producer prices and channeled unsold milk to factories for dairy product manufacturing. The Committee would later extend its activities to other markets.

While the KCC continued to face competition from several local and regional suppliers, it retained its dominant market position. In 1954, it accounted for 77% of milk production by settlers from Europe and 90% of the European milk suppliers were members. The membership of the KCC continued to be exclusively Europeans. Expanding milk and *ghee* production by African farmers still did not enter formal marketing channels other than the government's milk program on the eastern coast and a few other isolated schemes for *ghee* marketing.

Dualistic Development

The period from the mid-1950s to 1970 witnessed rapid and steady development of smallholder dairy production and its initial incorporation into the formal dairy marketing system. During this period, the KCC continued its efforts to expand its operations and consolidate its dominant market position. Even though small farmers would come to account for about two-thirds of total national milk production, large farmers continued to form the backbone of this formal marketing system due to the discriminatory milk procurement and pricing policies employed by the KCC.

The expansion of smallholder dairy production stemmed from several sources. One set of stimuli was a series of government- and donor-financed programs following the development of the Swynnerton Plan and in the years just prior to and after Kenya's independence in 1963. Some of these programs, including the UNICEF-supported Rural Dairy Development Project

---

[28] This was the Kenya Dairy Cooperative Association.

and the USAID-supported Dairy Training Center, were geared specifically toward assisting smallholder dairy producers. Other initiatives, including a land titling program, the Smallholder Credit Project, a massive land transfer program from European to African owners and various settlement schemes, contributed to smallholder dairy development.

Smallholder dairying further benefited from the rapid growth in smallholder tea, coffee and pyrethrum production which took place in Central and Rift Valley Provinces during the 1950s and particularly the 1960s. This expanded cash crop production not only generated increased demand for milk (and other dairy products) in rural areas, it also provided the capital for smallholder purchases of grade cows.[29]

Because most smallholder producers had only one or very few cows and the expansion of smallholder production occurred simultaneously across many districts, the issue arose of how to develop a commercially viable milk collection system for such farmers. Parallelling concurrent developments in the coffee and pyrethrum sub-sectors, local dairy cooperative societies were formed. The first of these cooperatives was established in the mid-1950s. A decade later there were 125 of them with tens of thousands of members. Cooperative development benefited from infrastructure investments (especially in rural roads) and from a UNICEF-funded program which supplied milk cooling and other equipment.

In the late 1950s, the KCC began to procure, process and market milk provided by smallholder cooperatives. The portion of its milk supplies from cooperatives would remain very small, accounting for only 5% of the total volume procured in 1960.[30] By 1965, when smallholder and settlement farmers accounted for some two-thirds of total production, only 22% of KCC's supplies came from these farmers.[31] Perhaps as much as 75% of smallholder production was consumed by the farming households who produced it and much of the marketed milk was sold locally through informal channels.[32]

Several factors contributed to the limited incorporation of smallholders into the formal dairy marketing system. First, KCC's procurement arrange-

---

[29] This point is made by Raikes (1981) and Bates (1990). Some 80–90% of grade cow purchases by smallholders during this period were made with savings from off-farm employment and cash crop production. See Stolz (1979).

[30] World Bank (1963).

[31] Klemm (1966), p. 10.

[32] Hopcraft (1976), p. 2; Brown (1963).

ments for smallholder milk were largely passive rather than active.[33] The firm played no part in ongoing government technical support programs, provided no market information to smallholders, and left milk collection and financial matters to the cooperative societies. The KCC did not in fact have a presence in rural areas. The geographical scope of KCC's procurement and processing operations was limited to the central highland areas, leading farmers from other areas to face enormous transport bottlenecks and costs when supplying KCC plants.

Second, the system of procurement quotas and prices applied by KCC during this period offered little financial incentive for smallholders to supply the organization. In 1954, the KCC replaced the former contract system with a three-tier pricing structure which offered premium prices year round to those suppliers which could meet agreed upon dry season quotas ('quota milk'), next highest prices for 'contract milk' which would be used to produce manufactured products, and relatively low prices for 'separation milk' which would be used to produce cream and skimmed milk. In a typical year, prices paid for 'quota' and 'contract' milk exceeded those for 'separation' milk by 100% and 66%, respectively. Quota contracts were initially offered exclusively to large European farmers, based on their past deliveries and their access to irrigation facilities to meet dry season requirements. By the mid-1960s, these farmers still accounted for 70% of quota milk deliveries, whereas smallholders were largely paid at the lower price scales.[34] This is not surprising given that KCC's membership and management continued to be comprised mostly of European farmers.

As the KCC continued to consolidate its market dominance, smallholder farmers faced a dwindling range of alternative channels to market milk in urban areas. During the mid-to-late-1950s, the KCC built several new factories, expanded its product line (to include pasteurized cheddar cheese, ice cream, skim and whole milk powder, condensed milk, casein, *ghee* and butter), and was the first firm outside of Europe to adopt the Tetra Pak technology to extend product shelf life. The organization's in-take of milk and butter fat, stagnant at a level between 125,000 and 150,000 liters/year between 1955 and 1963, rose to 200,000 liters/year by the end of the 1960s. At that time the firm had an 88% share of the formal market for milk and butter. Throughout this period, the KCC operated at a profit.

---

[33] Minae (1981), op cit.
[34] Klemm (1966), p. 19.

In 1958, in the midst of a downturn in world dairy prices, and at the instigation of the KCC, a Kenya Dairy Board was established. The Board had a broad mandate to stabilize prices, improve milk quality, conduct market research, and implement regulations and support services which would aid the development of dairy production and marketing. From the beginning, the KCC dominated the Board, which relied on the cooperative organization's tax payments for most of its operating funds. The KCC used the Board's regulatory powers to restrict the activities of real and potential competitors. By the mid-1960s, the Dairy Board had withdrawn the licenses to sell milk in major urban areas independently of the KCC of all producers, cooperatives and retailers. Henceforth, such organizations would be permitted to sell milk only in smaller townships and rural areas.

Market Consolidation and the 'Publicization' of the KCC

In 1970, an official Dairy Working Party was set up to examine the state of the dairy industry, including issues related to competition and pricing. In the midst of spirited discussions among the Working Party members, the KCC announced the abolition of independent dairies and its monopolization of the urban dairy market. The KCC argued that it could provide the services of the independent dairies at lower cost and that its control of the market would lead to full compliance with product quality standards. The Dairy Board acquiesced to this intervention, which was one of its last actions before the Board's management was dissolved and its functions absorbed by the Ministry of Agriculture.

A year later, the three-tiered milk quota and pricing system was abolished. It was replaced by a system of uniform producer prices set by the government, with no differentials by season or location. The government also set consumer prices for pasteurized milk. Under the new rules, the KCC would be obligated to accept all milk delivered to its factories and depots, regardless of its ability to market the liquid milk. In effect, the KCC would become the 'buyer of last resort' for farmers who first sought potentially more remunerative local milk sales. As compensation, the KCC was given virtual veto power over the entry of competing dairy manufacturers and control over competitors' raw material procurement. Competing firms would be required to source milk in collaboration with the KCC and pay it an administrative fee for handling producer payments. Competing firms were restricted in the products which they could handle and the locations where they could sell.

The creation of a guaranteed market outlet, the significant short-term price increase (for formerly non-quota producers), and favorable weather patterns led to a large increase in KCC's milk intake in 1972 and 1973.[35] Compared to prior years, deliveries also showed much greater seasonality. This surge in supplies surpassed KCC's processing capacity during the rainy season and led to considerable waste, large inter-factory transfers of supplies and the need to convert large quantities of milk into storable products. For some of these storable products, including cheese and powdered milk, the KCC incurred large storage costs and sales losses. For the first time since the 1930s the firm recorded considerable financial losses. Thus, the requirement that the KCC purchase all (delivered) supplies at the higher official price brought about a financial crisis that was eased only by reduced production in 1974 and 1975 due to drought.

During the mid-to-late-1970s, (estimated) national milk production grew at a slower pace. KCC's milk intake varied from year to year in line with rainfall patterns and remained below the peak 1972–1973 levels. Most of the incremental production during this period was used for smallholder household consumption and informal rural market sales. By 1979, only one-half of all milk production was ever marketed. The KCC, holding a near monopoly on the formal dairy market, handled only 20% of national production. As Table 5.3 illustrates, by this time smallholder farmers had come to account for two-thirds of total production and 50% of marketed milk. However, because only a small proportion (11%) of smallholder production was channeled to the KCC, larger- (and medium-)scale farmers remained the backbone of its operation. Large farms alone accounted for 68% of KCC's milk intake.

By the late 1970s, the operational characteristics and financial structure of the KCC had changed so greatly that the organization could no longer be regarded as a private, commercially-oriented firm. This also occurred with several other national cooperatives during this same period. KCC's operations were increasingly affected by political intrusions which influenced its appointment and retention of managers, its patterns of investment, the services it provided and the parties with whom it could contract for supplies and services.[36] Despite incurring large financial losses, the KCC was required to

---

[35] For a detailed analysis of developments during the early to mid 1970s, see Hopcraft (1976).

[36] Other cooperatives and agricultural associations which were heavily politicized included the Kenya Farmers Association, the Horticultural Cooperative Union, and the Kenya Coffee Planters Union. I thank Shem Migot-Adholla for this point.

purchase milk supplies in excess of its marketing needs for conversion into powdered milk which would be maintained as a strategic reserve. When the KCC became the sole supplier of a new school milk program, the government (that is, the Ministry of Education) became one of the largest buyers of KCC products. Huge financial losses totally eroded the KCC's equity base and rendered it completely dependent upon government-backed loans and subsidies.[37]

High Cost Expansion and Creeping Liberalization

KCC's operations have undergone considerable expansion over the past decade. The firm has accumulated large financial losses as the returns to milk producers have declined and several private and cooperative enterprises have begun to chip away at its dominant market position. The KCC's expansion involved the extension and modernization of several factories, the construction of about a dozen milk collection and cooling centers in or near small

TABLE 5.3: **Kenya Milk Production and Usage (1979)** (Millions of Liters)

	Smallholders	Medium-Scale Farmers (20–50 Acres)	Large-Scale Farmers	Total
Total Production	769.0	192.8	195.6	1157.4
Of which consumed or fed to calves	436.4 (56.7%)	62.7 (32.5%)	14.8 (7.6%)	513.9 (44.4%)
Of which sold	295.4 (38.4%)	114.0 (59.1%)	177.8 (90.9%)	587.2 (50.8%)
Sold to KCC	87.7[a] (11.4%)	47.6[b] (24.7%)	160.1[c] (81.2%)	234.4 (20.3%)
Other disposal	37.3 (4.9%)	16.2 (8.4%)	2.9 (1.5%)	56.4 (4.9%)

[a] Residual after calculating medium- and large-scale farm supplies.
[b] As reported in Integrated Rural Survey (1976–79).
[c] Estimated at 90% of total sales.

SOURCE: Integrated Rural Surveys, 1976–1979.

---

[37] Over the 1977–79 period, cumulative losses totalled Ksh. 82.7 million. In 1978, the firm's ratio of net worth to net assets was −1.22 and its ratio of current assets to current liabilities was 0.76. Grosh (1987) provides data showing the KCC's dramatic financial deterioration during the 1970s.

towns in central Kenya, and the further extension of its product line. It was made possible by large, government-backed soft loans from bilateral donors.

With the collection stations providing improved smallholder (and cooperative) access to the KCC, milk deliveries to the organization increased substantially. From an average of 228 million liters/year over the 1980–1985 period, the KCC's milk intake surged to over 350 million liters/year in the late 1980s. Similar to what had happened in the early 1970s, this sudden expansion in milk purchases contributed to a financial crisis as the KCC accumulated large stocks of powdered milk which it sold at considerable loss. KCC's losses reached a cumulative level of nearly Ksh. 250 million by 1989. Mismanagement, declining product quality, delayed or no payment for milk supplied to the school milk program and increases in unit processing and marketing costs above the margins provided by official prices also further eroded its profitability.[38]

While most government and KCC attention was directed at building up the milk marketing infrastructure, Kenya's dairy production base suffered. Since the mid-1980s, official producer prices have not kept pace with production costs and overall inflation rates (Figure 5.1). This has reduced the profitability of dairy production and thus the available resources for animal maintenance and feeding. Many large-scale farmers whose sales have been almost entirely directed through the KCC have responded to declining profitability by slaughtering or selling parts or all of their dairy herds. Between 1981 and 1989, the number of dairy cows on large-scale farms declined from 167,800 to 110,200, thus reducing the available supply of high-quality breeding stock.[39] Over the same period, the quality of government livestock and dairy support services has declined significantly because most public research, extension and veterinary service institutions have increasingly suffered from shortages of funds and inadequate staff training and mobility.

Although the government supported the expansion of the KCC, at the same time it has announced a policy of promoting rural dairy processing activities. This was signaled in the National Livestock Development Policy (1980), which stated that, "Cooperatives will be helped to assume the major milk collection, cooling and transportation functions in those areas where the

---

[38] See the Dairy Master Plan, Technical Report #4 for an analysis of recent KCC operations and performance.

[39] Statistical Abstract, 1990.

FIGURE 5.1: **Nominal and Real Producer Prices for Milk**

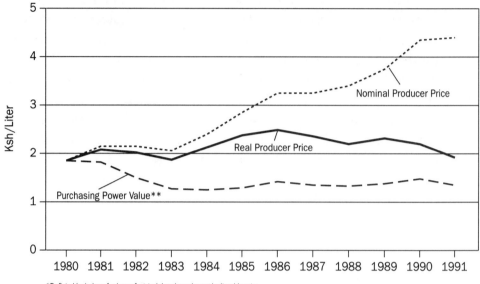

*Deflated by index of prices of material and service agricultural inputs
*Deflated by index of purchased consumer goods in rural areas
SOURCE: Economic Survey, Various Issues

KCC does not operate. Rural dairies will be developed and equipped with the necessary facilities." The Sessional Paper No. 4 of 1987 went further:

> The dairy cooperatives will be encouraged and assisted to establish rural small-scale dairy processing plants, particularly in surplus areas where KCC does not have processing factories. The paper recognizes the national role of KCC, but at the same time sees it necessary that KCC's development plans and those of rural dairies should be coordinated in order to harmonize milk collection, processing, and marketing for the benefit of farmers and the country.

In practice, government support for rural dairies has been very limited and selective. Only two cooperative investments, each involving substantial donor grant or soft loan components, have received financial or other support from the government. Both involved the construction and operation of UHT processing plants in locations formerly not covered by KCC operations. In spite of the relatively small-scale of these two ventures, KCC attempted to subvert them by establishing milk collection and sales depots in nearby loca-tions to compete for the local supplies and markets, and by refusing to purchase the surplus milk collected by these cooperatives. The government has provided little or no support to several other cooperatives and private firms which have sought to enter the market for processed fluid milk and other dairy products. License applications have been rejected or considerably delayed while firms which have engaged in processing have had their range of products and their market areas restricted by the Dairy Board.

Despite the growing financial burden of KCC's losses, the fact that many parts of the country are not served by the KCC infrastructure, and the apparent viability of small dairy processing operations even in the face of severe restrictions, the government has moved very slowly to liberalize the dairy market. Even after a high-level work group produced the Dairy Master Plan (1991)—which emphasized the inefficiencies of the present system and its unsustainability—reform measures were not introduced. Among the likely contributing factors for this inaction were: (1) concerns about the large sunk investments in KCC infrastructure and the need to repay government-guaranteed external loans; (2) strong vested interests in the prevailing system involving KCC staff and firms providing inputs and services to the KCC, and (3) concern that liberalization would result in a reduction in government control over the sub-sector while foreign or other non-indigenous firms emerged as new leaders.

Initial market liberalization was forced upon the government in early 1992. Drought in major production areas, a KCC liquidity crisis which led to delays in payments for three to four months, and the inability of KCC to reconstitute large quantities of imported powdered milk due to a lack of butter oil resulted in severe shortages of milk in urban areas over the February–May period. KCC milk purchases declined by some 35% during the first half of the year, compared with the previous year. With the KCC unable to meet urban demand for milk, the government was forced to relax controls on private milk distribution. This relaxation allowed raw milk to be brought into Nairobi and other major cities. The formal milk collection and marketing system had completely broken down and most producers, processors, and distributors scrambled to obtain non-KCC sources and outlets for their milk.

To counter the disarray, the government removed its controls on producer and consumer prices (on June 2, 1992). The KCC promptly increased its producer price from Ksh. 5.20 to 6.50 per liter and its price to retailers for pasteurized milk from Ksh. 9.50 to 13.10 per liter. Although the process of decontrolling prices was taking place in a legal and regulatory vacuum, it provided additional stimulus to private traders, cooperative societies and large farms to buy, process and sell milk throughout the country. In the two months following the price decontrol, the Dairy Board received over one hundred applications from prospective processors and traders of dairy products.

Nearly a year later (April 1993), very few of these applications had been acted upon. In the interim, multi-party political elections attracted most official attention and government decisions regarding the future direction of the dairy industry were placed in abeyance. Nevertheless, the price decontrol brought a significant response from informal sector traders of raw milk, who captured a major share of the urban market. Partially as a result of such raw milk sales, the KCC's sales of pasteurized and UHT milk in the Nairobi area fell from about 400,000 liters/day in early 1982 to less than 230,000 liters/day in early 1993.[40]

RECENT STATUS OF DAIRY PRODUCTION, CONSUMPTION, AND MARKETING

Dairy Production and Farm Economics

In 1990, Kenya had an estimated cattle population of 11.9 million. This herd consists of nearly 2.4 million high milk-yielding grade cattle (mostly crossbreeds of European breeds and indigenous zebu cattle) and some 9.5 million zebu cattle. While the indigenous cattle are heat tolerant and disease resistant, their milk yields are very low. Kenya has basically three dairy herds:[41]

1) The *pastoral herd* is estimated at 4.7 million head and composed entirely of indigenous stock. Milk is central to the pastoral diet. However, milk yields are less than 200 liters/year per lactating cow and output rarely enters the formal market. The pastoral herd accounts for an estimated 8% of total milk production.

2) The *smallholder herd* which numbers some 7.0 million head, of which 2.1 million head are grade cattle. Production systems vary from region to region and consist of open-, semi-zero, and zero-grazing feeding systems involving different levels of technology and use of purchased

---

[40] Staal and Shapiro (n.d.).
[41] This summary is based on Price Waterhouse (1991) and information provided by Tetra Pak.

inputs. The smallholder herd accounts for an estimated 69% of total production.

3) The *large-scale herd* presently numbers some 220,000 head of pure bred and grade animals. This herd is maintained on private, corporate and state-owned farms with relatively high levels of management and animal nutrition. Open-grazing supplemented by feed concentrates is the common feeding program. This herd now accounts for some 23% of total production.

While accounting for only 20% of the total cattle population, grade cattle account for some 69% of total estimated milk production and virtually all of the marketed milk production. They are kept in the country's high-altitude, high-rainfall areas, principally in Rift Valley (47% of the total herd), Central (31%) and Eastern (11%) Provinces.

According to available estimates, total Kenyan (cow) milk production has experienced a slow but steady increase since the early 1970s, with the exception of the drought years of 1975, 1976, 1978 and 1984. This is illustrated in Figure 5.2.

FIGURE 5.2: **Estimated Kenyan Milk Production** (Million Liters)

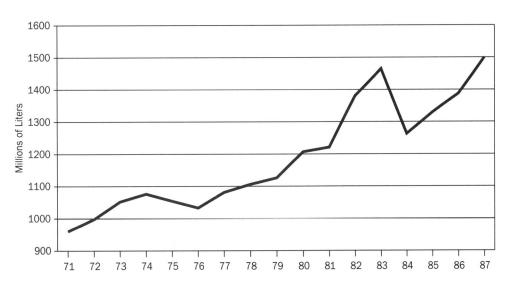

SOURCE: Agricultural Growth Prospects and Strategy Options p. 70. Vol. 3.

TABLE 5.4: **Profitability of Milk Production (1989)** (Ksh. per kg. of Milk)

Location	Production System	Production Cost	Payment from Coop #1	Payment from Coop #2	Official KCC Producer Price	Local (Informal) Market Price
Nakuru	L-S Open	2.86			3.63	4.00
	S-S Open	2.48	2.90	3.04	3.63	4.00
	S-S Semi-Zero	2.64	2.90	3.04	3.63	4.00
	S-S Zero	3.50	2.90	3.04	3.63	4.00
Nyeri	S-S Open	3.09	3.00	3.35	3.63	5.50
	S-S Semi-Zero	3.58	3.00	3.35	3.63	5.50
	S-S Zero	3.80	3.00	3.35	3.63	5.50
Kakamega	S-S Open	3.00	3.20	Na.	3.63	7.00
	S-S Zero	4.51	3.20	Na.	3.63	7.00

Costs per kg. for 1988/89 season (Sellen et al. 1990).
Average producer payments from area cooperatives (1989) MOCD.
Local prices paid by private buyers (1989) MOCD Survey.
L-S Large-scale.
S-S Smale-scale.

Historically, dairy production in Kenya has been quite profitable, especially for smallholders. However, the recent deterioration in livestock support services and decline in real producer prices paid by the KCC since the mid-1980s have weakened production incentives. In several important production areas, payments made by the KCC and local cooperatives did not cover production costs (Table 5.4). Only farmer milk sales in local markets provide significant profits in these locations. In Nyeri and Kakamega, smallholder milk production generated little or no profit when milk was supplied to local cooperatives or sold directly to the KCC. Only local market sales through informal channels provided large profit margins. In Nakuru, large-scale open-grazing systems were minimally profitable for sales to the KCC, considering the added costs for transport and various taxes. Smallholder sales through local cooperatives similarly yielded relatively small profit margins. Formal market prices were inadequate to cover the additional labor and other costs incurred in production under zero-grazing.

Table 5.5 illustrates that the returns to labor in smallholder milk production are generally below those for other crops and below the prevailing rural daily wage. These figures make clear that the sustainability of smallholder dairy production has required incentives over and above those provided by formal marketing channels. These added incentives have included: (1) household consumption needs, (2) remunerative, informal (rural) market outlets

TABLE 5.5: **Returns to Labor from Milk Production and Competing Activities (1990 Prices)**

Milk Production		Competing Uses	
Open-grazing in Rift Valley with herd of 5 improved Cows	20.8	Daily rural wage	20–25
Semi-zero grazing in Central and Eastern Provinces with herd of 2 cows	17.8	Tea	47.4
Open-grazing in Western Province with herd of 5 improved cows	17.3	Maize	22.6
Zero-grazing in Central and Eastern Provinces with herd of 2 cows	8.4	Coffee	20.0

SOURCE: Kenya Dairy Master Plan.

for some part of production, (3) use of by-products from dairy animals (for example, manure and hides), and (4) the use of cattle as a form of investment.

Consumption, Demand and Prices

Only rough estimates can be made about current levels of milk consumption and demand for marketed dairy products in Kenya. The most recent surveys recording information on milk consumption and expenditures date back to 1983 (Rural Household Budget Survey—1981/82 and Urban Budget Household Survey—1982/83). The authors of the Dairy Master Plan drew upon this information, updated population estimates and other data to project forward dairy demand to 1990.

According to the 1981 survey, out of total national milk production of 1.28 billion liters, about 52% (668 million liters) was consumed by the farmers who had produced it. Some 191 million liters were sold to the KCC and 290 million liters sold through other channels, with the remainder used to feed labor and livestock. In certain areas, especially in parts of Rift Valley, Central and Western Provinces, part of the household consumption was probably 'forced', since it is higher than what it would have been normally if adequate marketing infrastructure and market outlets had been available. The 1982 and 1983 surveys indicate per capita milk consumption of 64 kgs./yr. and 125 kgs./yr. in rural and urban areas, respectively.

Table 5.6 provides the Dairy Master Plan's estimated distribution pattern of milk consumption in 1990. The table shows that while urban areas accounted for only 13% of the national population, they accounted for 24% of total milk consumption and 50% of the marketed milk. The higher urban consumption rates can be attributed to several factors, including higher disposal incomes, better developed food distribution infrastructure, greater access to refrigeration, and demand from the hotel and catering trades. Although 76% of milk is consumed in rural areas, less than one-third of this milk is purchased, either from formal or informal distribution channels.

The 1983 survey found that overall milk expenditure patterns were highly skewed. While the 58% of the urban population which comprises the lowest income category accounted for only 8% of milk expenditures, the highest income group, representing only 2% of the population, accounted for 45% of expenditures. High-income groups accounting for 19% of the population made 75% of milk expenditures. These patterns suggest that it has been the relatively wealthy who have benefited most from the government's controls on pasteurized milk prices. Milk expenditures in rural areas are much less skewed as a result of lower income disparities and the fact that many of the more wealthy rural households own cows and thus do not need to purchase milk. Using survey data, one recent study calculated the income elasticity of milk expenditure to be 1.01 in rural areas and 0.58 in urban areas.[42]

Some 10–15% of milk (and other dairy product) consumption in Kenya occurs outside of the household. This distribution comes through various institutions such as hospitals, the army, schools, hotels and restaurants/canteens. The largest of these outlets is the School Milk Program. Some 38 mil-

TABLE 5.6: **Milk Consumption Patterns (1990)**

Area	Popu-lation	Per Capita Consump-tion (Liters)	Consumption (Million Liters)	Proportion of Total Con-sumption (%)	Proportion Marketed Milk (%)
Nairobi + Mombasa	2.4	125.0	300.5	19.7	41.3
Other Urban	0.5	125.0	62.5	4.1	8.6
Rural	18.9	61.6	1165 of which:	76.2	50.1
			365 (purchased)	23.9	
			800 (own production)	52.3	
Total	21.8	70.1	1528	100.0	100.0

SOURCE: Based on Dairy Master Plan, Technical Report #1, Tables 1 and 3.

[42] World Bank (1990).

lion liters of milk were distributed through this channel in 1990, although in the past two years delayed government payments (to the KCC) have undermined the program. The hotel and catering trades have also absorbed increasing volumes of milk and other dairy products as Kenya's tourist industry has undergone a major expansion. Holiday and business visitors doubled during the 1980s from 336,000 to 696,000.[43] It is tourists, together with expatriate residents and Kenya's middle- and upper-income population, who are the primary consumers of cheese, yogurt and other high-value products.

The bulk of milk consumed in Kenya is raw milk which is neither processed nor packaged. Raw milk is normally boiled before use and in many areas, the largest proportion of consumption is as a whitener in tea or an ingredient in cooking. More than 90% of the milk consumed in rural areas is raw milk, including milk retained on the farm and milk purchased locally. Little is known about the quantities or proportion of marketed milk in urban areas which is sold in raw form, as this is illegal. A recent, limited household survey in Nairobi did indicate that raw milk may account for 10–20% of total purchases.[44]

In 1990, consumer and institutional sales of pasteurized milk totaled about 180 million liters. Sales of long-life UHT milk totalled about 105 million liters. Most sales of pasteurized milk were in urban areas, with the Nairobi and Mombasa metropolitan areas together accounting for some 75% of the total. In contrast, 82% of packaged UHT milk is sold in rural areas.[45] The school milk program took another 38 million liters of pasteurized and UHT milk. The milk-equivalent consumption of fermented milk and high-value manufactured dairy products did not exceed 80 million liters.[46] Therefore, the remaining 1.1 billion liters of consumption was of raw milk.

Prices

Since 1971, consumer prices for pasteurized milk have been controlled by the government. During the 1970s and through to the mid-1980s, price adjustments were made in line with overall inflation levels. However, between 1987 and early 1992, official consumer prices did not keep pace with overall rates

---

[43] Visitor numbers are drawn from the Statistical Abstract, 1990.

[44] Unpublished survey sponsored by Tetra Pak (Kenya).

[45] Price Waterhouse (1991), Annexes 18 and 19.

[46] The total Kenyan market for cheese is only about 800 tons per year, while sales of other high-value dairy products are considerably lower.

FIGURE 5.3: **Retail Prices for Pasteurized Milk**

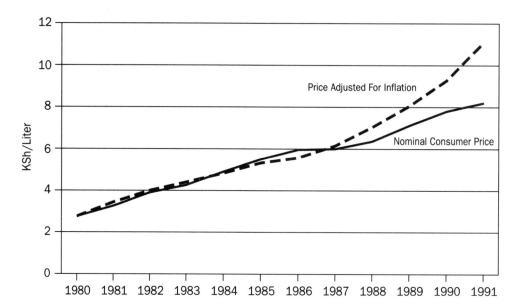

of inflation (Figure 5.3). By the early 1990s, consumer prices for pasteurized whole and semi-skimmed milk in Kenya were considerably below those found in several other African milk-producing countries, including Zimbabwe, South Africa and Tanzania.[47] In 1992, Kenyan retail prices for pasteurized milk were considerably lower than import parity prices.[48] Consumer price controls have been one of the contributing factors to KCC's poor financial performance. For example, over the 1988–90 period, KCC's cumulative loss for pasteurized market milk sales was Ksh. 42.6 million, accounting for about 20% of the firm's total losses.[49]

Consumer prices for other types of fluid milk and for manufactured dairy products are not determined by government, except when the government is the buyer (the School Milk Program, supplies for the army). Time series data on prices for such products are not available. In recent years, consumer prices for UHT milk have been 25%–33 higher than for pasteurized milk as a result

---

[47] This is one of the findings of a survey conducted by Tetra Pak (Kenya).
[48] Staal and Shapiro (n.d.).
[49] See Dairy Master Plan, Technical Report #4, p. 32.

of higher packaging costs and the absence of government price controls. This has led to a recent expansion of KCC's UHT production, despite its higher cost to consumers.

The price for raw milk sold in rural areas is generally well below that for processed milk due to lower transport costs and the absence of packaging costs. This is illustrated in Table 5.7 which compares KCC milk prices with the average local prices reported by cooperatives in several districts in Central, Rift Valley, and Western Provinces.

Milk Collection, Processing, and Marketing Channels

A substantial proportion of smallholder milk production is retained on the farm, whether by choice or because of transport or other marketing bottlenecks. According to the Dairy Master Plan, 52% of smallholder production was retained nationwide, with this rate ranging from 32% to 68% among different provinces. In contrast, less than 15% of milk produced on large-scale farms is retained for domestic consumption.

Some milk is sold by producers directly to consumers, institutions and private processors. Part of these sales have been illegal, especially those taking place in or near urban areas. Several thousand smallholders and the vast majority of large farmers deliver their milk directly to KCC processing plants and cooling centers, using their own vehicles, tractors and bicycles.

Most milk sales however occur through intermediaries. For smallholders, the most important outlet has been primary cooperative societies. In 1990, there were 183 registered cooperatives with nearly 120,000 members who had dairy marketing as their main activity. However, 105 of these coopera-

TABLE 5.7: **Average Consumer Prices for Processed and Raw Milk**
(Ksh. per Liter)

Source or Location/Type of Milk	1988	1989	1990
KCC Pasteurized	6.90	7.20	7.80
KCC UHT	Na.	Na.	11.00
Nyeri (Raw; Local)	5.00	5.50	6.00
Kirinyaga (Raw; Local)	4.00	4.60	6.07
Eldava Ravine (Raw; Local)	4.00	4.00	4.80
Busia (Raw; Local)	5.50	6.50	7.10
Kakamega (Raw; Local)	5.80	7.00	7.00

Na. Not available.
SOURCES: Kenya Cooperative Creameries; Ministry of Livestock Development Cooperative Survey.

tives were either dormant or under liquidation and there were tens of thousands of non-active members. A few dozen other cooperatives, registered as 'multi-purpose' cooperatives, do undertake a significant level of dairy marketing. There has been considerable volatility among Kenya's cooperatives with frequent start-ups and liquidations and widespread management and financial problems.

Dairy cooperatives have organized milk collection systems, generally using their own vehicles. In most cases, milk collection is done only in the morning and members need to consume, sell or otherwise dispose of the previous evening's milk. Although the Rural Dairy Development Project provided milk coolers for evening milk to close to sixty cooperatives, more than 50% of the coolers were either misplaced, never used or used only occasionally.[50] Few cooperatives perform milk quality checks, providing little incentive for farmers to improve quality.

The cooperatives sell milk directly to local consumers and institutions, to the KCC, and in recent years, to private processors. In milk deficit areas and in areas with difficult or long distance transport to a KCC factory or cooling center, most cooperative sales occur locally with only seasonal or periodic surpluses being directed to the KCC. On a national level, probably no more than 25% of the milk collected by cooperative societies is sold to the KCC.

Transportation is a major bottleneck and the leading cost item for cooperatives. Smallholder milk supplies are greatest during the rainy season when rural roads are in their worst condition. Some roads are simply impassable, even with tractors. One multi-district survey in the early 1980s found transport costs to account for 70% of total cooperative costs and more than 22% of the cooperative milk sales prices.[51]

KCC is the predominant dairy processor in Kenya. With ten active processing plants, the KCC has the capacity to handle up to 700 million liters per year for fluid milk processing. During the 1980s, the KCC accounted for some 98% of the milk processed by formal organizations. The company produces seventeen products, the most important being pasteurized, UHT and dehydrated milk in whole or semi-skimmed forms, fermented milk, cheese and butter.

---

[50] Dairy Master Plan, Main Report, p. 2.15.
[51] Ministry of Livestock Development data as reported in Price Waterhouse (1991).

Until recent years, the volume of KCC purchases has been closely associated with levels of annual rainfall in major producing areas—and hence the production surplus available for household and rural consumption needs (see Figure 5.4). It reinforces the notion that the KCC has long been a residual buyer of smallholder (surplus) production. The 1986–1987 break in this association between rainfall and KCC purchases can be attributed to the large increase in the official producer price in 1986 and to the start-up of operations for several KCC milk buying centers.

Two cooperatives, the Meru Cooperative Union and the Kitinda Dairy Farmers' Society, have UHT processing plants with capacities of 15.8 million liters/year and 7.9 million liters/year, respectively. The Kitinda plant was inoperative in mid-1992 due to management and other problems. Both cooperatives have utilized an expensive technology supplied under a bilateral donor program. There are approximately fifty private enterprises involved in dairy processing. Most of these are backyard, cottage industry-type operations, with only a dozen or so firms being formally registered. Most of these

FIGURE 5.4: **KCC Milk Purchases and Rainfall, 1971–1989**

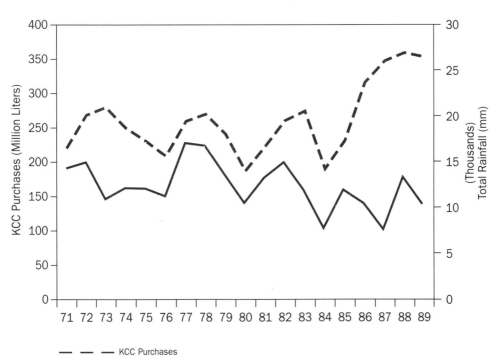

SOURCE: Sellen et al. 1990.

firms produce a range of high-value products, including cheeses, yogurt products, cream and ice cream. Some also produce or specialize in fermented milk products. Very few produce packaged pasteurized milk which has remained a protected preserve of the KCC.

Due to the KCC's recent financial problems, along with the creeping liberalization process, KCC's dominance of the formal market has begun to erode. In mid-1992, private and cooperative processors handled about 8% of the milk intake of the formal processor industry, an increase from only 2–3% a year or two earlier. If aggregate milk intake levels remain at this level and the KCC emerges from its current financial crisis, then new investments by the private and cooperative sectors will likely increase their market share to 20% by the end of 1993.

Figure 5.5 summarizes the main marketing channels for milk and other dairy products with estimates provided for 1991 flows. The figure illustrates that while the KCC occupies an important place in the system, other flows, largely of an informal nature, are dominant. The figure also illustrates the marginal position which cooperative and private processors have been placed in by KCC interventions and government restrictions on their operations.

Private and Cooperative Dairy Processors

In the beginning of 1992, there were approximately fifty private and cooperative processors of dairy products in Kenya. Several of these firms are not formally registered; many others handle very small quantities of milk (<100 liters/day) or primarily buy and sell raw milk. At the time of the field work, there were seventeen firms which had been producing high-value dairy products on a commercial scale for two years or more. Interviews were completed with ten of these firms and basic information gathered on four others from secondary sources. Some fifteen to twenty firms and farms held licenses to process and sell fluid milk products, while many other firms were at various stages in the licensing process.[54] Interviews were held with eight firms already engaged in or on the verge of investing in milk processing and sale. This small sample included the largest private and cooperative actors in this area, together with a few firms contemplating significant investments.

---

[54] The exact number of licensed processors is uncertain. Kenya Dairy Board lists of licensed firms makes reference to 'whole', 'fresh', and other types of milk, sometimes providing confusion over whether the firm is licensed to sell only raw milk instead of processed milk.

FIGURE 5.5: **Milk Flow Channels in Kenya (1991)** (Million Liters)

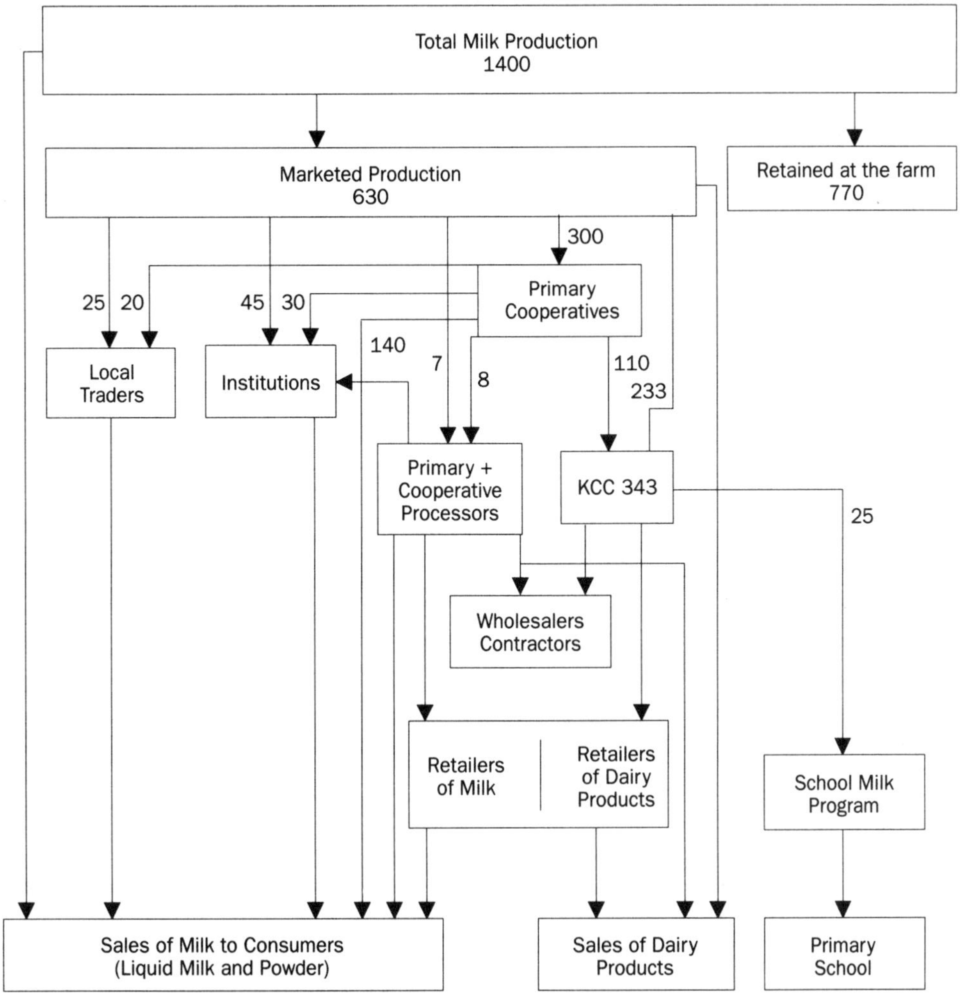

SOURCE: Estimates Based on Information from KCC, Ministry of
Cooperative Development and Non-KCC Processors

Structured interviews were held with eighteen current or prospective dairy processors, in addition to interviews with the KCC and several important packaging and distribution companies. The interviews covered the background and ownership of the firms, their milk procurement arrangements, product line, processing technologies and marketing arrangements, as well as aspects of performance.

Background and Characteristics of Processors of High-Value Products

Table 5.8 provides a profile of Kenya's private manufacturers of high-value dairy products. The information is complete only for the ten firms interviewed. Most of these enterprises have emerged only during the past decade and their development has paralleled the significant recent growth in Kenya's tourist industry. Only three of the firms represent a continuation of pre-independence dairy processing activities.

All of these firms have majority local ownership, with foreign participation being limited to the ownership and/or management role of a few individuals. The small market size and past restrictions on new entry have inhibited foreign investment. Nine of the fourteen firms are family companies owned by Kenyan Africans. Most of these are very small-scale cottage industry type operations. In contrast, several of the leading firms in this industry are either joint ventures (managed by non-Kenyans) or owned by members of Kenya's small European and Asian communities. Among this sample of firms, Kenyan African family companies accounted for only 29% of the total milk intake (during the 1992 'flush' season) and an estimated 35% of 1991 dairy product turnover.

Most of the firms in this industry are small in scale, with only one firm having sales exceeding $500,000 and most having annual sales of less than $100,000. With only one exception (in which a relative manages the firm), each of these firms is self-managed. Again, with only one exception, these firms employ less than twenty people in dairy operations, which usually include only one to three people with formal training or prior experience in dairy processing or food science.

The backgrounds of the entrepreneurs are varied. Many are professionals with a business or academic background who view dairying and dairy processing as either a second career, a source of supplementary income or as a worthwhile hobby for themselves and their spouse. Among the proprietors of these firms include several former university teachers and administrators, a former World Bank and government economist, and a Minister of Agriculture. In several cases, these entrepreneurs have had academic training and prior experience in marketing or one of the social sciences which has proven useful in developing their dairy business. Only in the case of the largest firm has the owner-manager had many years of dairy processing experience.

Nearly all of the cheese and yogurt makers have investments in additional agricultural ventures, most commonly in pig farming, beverage crops and horticulture. Pig farming can be well integrated with cheese-making because the whey makes excellent pig feed. One firm spreads the costs from its pasteurizing and cold storage equipment by also producing a range of fruit juices. Only six of the firms rely on sales of dairy products for 50% or more of their income, and only two family companies are totally specialized in this field.

Most of these firms have built up their operations slowly, ploughing back earnings to acquire additional pieces of equipment or to upgrade technologies. Batch, rather than flow, process technologies are used and most operations are manual or semi-mechanized. The majority of firms have relied upon locally produced or reconditioned equipment. The limited introduction of sophisticated technologies in this industry is a function of several factors: the small size and uncertain growth of the product market; the high cost of imported machinery; limited capital resources; and a generally conservative business development attitude in the face of potential reactions or intrusions by the KCC.

Most of these firms produce a range of dairy products in order to make maximum possible use of the fat content of milk and to spread their market risk and production over time. The seasonality of both the available milk supplies and the demand for high-value products (linked to peak tourist and slow seasons) is one important reason why firms produce many different types of cheeses with varied maturity and storage periods. KCC actions and pressures have at times hindered the private processors from fully developing their product lines. For example, for many years registered processors were restricted from marketing their own cheddar cheese in competition with the KCC's product. Uncertain KCC supplies of dehydrated milk inhibited private investments in ice cream production. If there were no restrictions on milk marketing, many of the firms would also have sought to integrate production and sales of whole and skimmed milk into their operations.[55]

Most of these cheese and yogurt makers are based in rural or peri-urban areas, with the largest clusters located on the outskirts of Nairobi and Nakuru.[56] This locational pattern contrasts sharply with that of the KCC's processing factories which are all urban-based. Given the bulkiness and rapid

---

[55] A few firms have by-passed market restrictions, meeting special orders for skimmed and whole pasteurized milk from hotels and others.

[56] The largest private processor is, however, urban-based. This firm has had long-term linkages with the KCC and has been dependent upon the latter's nearby milk collection/processing plant for its raw materials.

TABLE 5.8: **Private Producers of High-value Dairy Products (Cheeses, Cream, Yogurt Products) in Kenya**

Company	Year Started	Ownership	Source of Finance	# of Employees	Other Ventures	Dairy Share of Total Turnover[1]	Dairy Products	1991 Dairy Product Turnover (Ksh. Mill.)	Milk In-take (Lts./day)[2]
DL	1964	K.European 80%, Employees 11%, Foreign 9%	Savings	45	Pig Farming, Meat Canning	A	Many Cheeses, Tinned Milk, Ice Cream	20.0	11,000
KMP	1952	K. Asian Partnership	Other Ventures	17	Hardware, Paints, Paper Products	D	Many Cheeses, Yogurt	5.5	6000
ABD	1984	K. Afr. Family	Savings	15	None	A	Many Cheeses	6.5	4200
EF	1976	K. Afr. Family	Savings	15	Fresh/Frozen Vegetables; Pig Farming; Meat Products	B	Yogurt, Cream, Soft and Cottage Cheeses, Skimmed Milk	8.5	2500
SNP	1982	K. European Family	Savings	16	None	A	Soft Cheeses, Cream Cheese	7.0	1600
BFD	1990	K.Asian/Foreign Partnership	Savings + Commercial Loans	20	Grain Milling; Agro-industry consulting	B	Flavored Yogurt	9.0	700
EDV	1984	K. Afr. Family	Savings	7	Poultry, Eggs, Fruit Juices	B	Cream, Yogurt, Milk	3.0	560
MLS	1972	K. Afr. Family	Savings/AFC	3	Tea, Flowers, Beekeeping	D	Cream, Yogurt, Dip bases	1.5	250

[1] A = 75–100%, B = 50–74%, C = 25–49%, D = Less than 25%.
[2] Peak season supplies (1991 or 1992).
Na. Not available.

TABLE 5.8: **Private Producers of High-value Dairy Products (Cheeses, Cream, Yogurt Products) in Kenya** (continued)

Company	Year Started	Ownership	Source of Finance	# of Employees	Other Ventures	Dairy Products	Dairy Share of Total Turnover[1]	1991 Dairy Product Turnover (Ksh. Mill.)	Milk In-take (Lts./day)[2]
KWG	1986	K. Afr. Family	Savings	4 PT	Consulting	Cheddar Cheese	D	0.5	150
LDW	1982	K. Afr. Family	Savings/AFC	3 PT	Tea, Flowers	Yogurt, Cream	D	0.75	100
Firms Not Interviewed									
CT	1980s	K. Afr./Foreign Partnership	Na.	Na.	Tea	Soft Cheeses, Mala Milk	D	7.0 (Est.)	1500
GA	Na.	Kenya African	Na.	Na.	Coffee, Trade, Industrial Investments	Yogurt, Cream, Mala Milk	D	3.0 (Est.)	500
TK	1980s	K. Afr. Family	Na.	Na.	Politics, Cereals	Soft Cheeses	D	1.5 (Est.)	250
MP	1980s	K. Afr. Family	Na.	Na.	Na.	Yogurt	Na.	1.5 (Est.)	250

[1] A = 75–100%, B = 50–74%, C = 25–49%, D = Less than 25%.
[2] Peak season supplies (1991 or 1992).
Na. Not available.

perishability of milk, rural and decentralized placement of dairy manufacturers is more appropriate. Yet, the KCC's main cheese-making factory, at Dandora just outside of Nairobi, has generally processed milk transported over distances of 100–300 kilometers.

Background and Characteristics of Fluid Milk Processors

Table 5.9 provides basic information on nine existing or prospective private/cooperative fluid milk processors. Eight of these firms were interviewed. At the time of field work, the Kitinda Farmers Dairy Society was inoperative and problems of security prevented access. The interviewed firms are representative of the wider set of firms already active or preparing investments in this area.

The table shows the varied profiles of these firms. Some are large mixed farms with significant dairy and beef herds. These firms have sought to add value to their output and to by-pass the KCC and deal directly with quality-conscious consumers or institutions. Others are cooperatives which have obtained the financial and technical backing of international donors and equipment supply companies. The 'BD Company' is representative of about a half-dozen small firms which have undertaken the production of fermented milk with the technical and financial support of an American PVO (Technoserve).[57] Several multinational companies, including two interviewed for this study, are considering major investments in a liberalized Kenyan milk market. Most of the interviewed firms have diverse agricultural and other interests. Dairy-related sales are not their dominant source of income. Only small firms producing fermented milk had specialized in this area.

Unlike the pattern for cheese and yogurt makers, none of these firms are small family companies. Until now, entry into the fluid milk market has required either political muscle or external sponsors, neither of which apply to small family companies.

The pattern that is slowly emerging is one where large farms, larger companies and cooperatives undertake the production and sale of pasteurized, UHT or powdered milk, while smaller companies and cooperatives focus on fermented milk products. This follows directly from the differential investment requirements for the different products and the differential capacities

---

[57] Some of these firms are owned by individuals while other are owned jointly by groups of small farmers and run on a cooperative basis. The latter firms are registered as private companies rather than cooperatives in order to avoid intrusions by the Ministry of Cooperative Development.

TABLE 5.9: Characteristics of a Sample of Actual and Prospective Private and Cooperative Milk Processing/Market Enterprises

Company	Year Started Processing	Ownership	Source of Finance	(Intended) Dairy Products	Dairy Product Sales (Ksh. Million)	Other Ventures	Dairy Share of Total Turnover[1]	Milk In-take in Liters/day[2] (Planned)
KLF	Early 1960s	K. Euro. Family	Savings	Pasteurized Milk, Cream, Butter	20.0 (1991)	Sisal, Beef	B	8500
NGK	1978	K. African	Other Ventures	Pasteurized Milk	Na.	Coffee	D	1000
Meru Co-operative Union	1982	Cooperative	Concessional Foreign Loan, Gov't Grant, Member Contrib.	UHT Milk	26.4 (1990/91)	Coffee, Maize Milling, Animal Feeds	D	20,000 (50,000)
Kitinda Farmers Dairy Coop.	1987	Cooperative	Donor Grant; Member Contributions	UHT Milk	14.7 (1989)	None	A	
Buit Dairy Co.	1990	PVO/K. African	PVO Equity Finance, Member Contributions	Mala and Raw Milk	0.8 (1990/91)	None	A	1000
MNE	1992	K. European	Company Savings	Pasteurized Milk, (Yogurt)	12.0 (1991)	Cereals, Beef, Stockbreeding, Tourism	D	8000 (24,000)
Limuru Dairy Farmers Co-operative	Planned	Cooperative	To be Determined Donor Concessional Loan likely	(UHT and Fermented Milk, Yogurt)	38.5 (1989/90)	Agricultural Inputs, Post Office	A	34,000 (50,000)
EAT	Planned	Foreign	To be Determined	(Pasteurized Milk, Cream, Butter)	Na.	Pig Farming, Animal Feeds, Part of Conglomerate	D	4000 (10,000)
NST	Planned	Foreign	To be Determined	(Powdered Milk)	Na.	Weaning/Baby Foods, Confectionery	Na.	(80,000)

[1] A = 75–100%, B = 50–74%, C = 25–49%, D = Less than 25%.
[2] Current peak season in-take or farm production. Planned in-take for new or expaned facilities is in parentheses.

to service regional or national markets. Fermented milk is popular in rural areas and small townships. Relatively simple, batch-process technologies can be used to produce fermented milk and the product can be kept for more than one week without refrigeration. In contrast, in the production of pasteurized, UHT and powdered milk, both cost economies and improved hygiene can be gained by adopting mechanized or semi-mechanized flow-process technologies. Marketing pasteurized milk requires refrigerated storage, while marketing UHT milk requires use of sophisticated, high-cost packaging materials.

Given the relatively large market potential, actual and planned producers of pasteurized, UHT and powdered milk are considering milk intake levels which are much higher than even the largest processor of high-value dairy products. Simply for the firms listed here, planned processing capacity would exceed 200,000 liters/day, a figure which is several times larger than the total processing capacity of all high-value product manufacturers.

Enterprise Development: Registration, Technical Information, and Finance

To register a dairy processing enterprise and comply with other official operating regulations, a firm must obtain a wide range of licenses and certificates. In addition to the initial company registration, a firm has to obtain a manufacturer's license, a Kenya Dairy Board license, a food and drug license, a health certificate, a Kenya Bureau of Standards certification, a VAT license, and for marketing, a wholesaler's license. Acquiring these licenses and certificates is costly. Depending upon whether the licenses are for single or multiple years and the level of side payments made to licensing officials, the annual costs are reported to be Ksh. 8000–15,000.[58]

Even more important than the actual costs are the delays from rejected applications and the restrictions placed on company operations. Delays of between one and three years have been the norm for obtaining the Kenya Dairy Board license, caused by KCC efforts to deter or limit potential competitors. The Kenya Dairy Board license restricts what the holder can produce and where the product can be sold. In general, licenses also restrict the quantity of production and sales. The usual delay for receiving health, food and drug licenses is between six months and a year. Bureaucratic inefficiency and bribe-seeking behavior account for this delay.

---

[58] The firms report that proprietors or senior managers must spend two to three weeks at the beginning of the year procuring the necessary licenses/certificates.

Manufacturers of dairy products are not permitted to obtain wholesalers' licenses. Instead, they are required to use the services of a commissioned trading agent. This regulation, applied throughout the manufacturing sector, was instituted during the 1960s in order to encourage the development of indigenous trading companies at a time when the manufacturing sector was dominated by foreign and Kenyan Asian companies. The KCC has been exempt from this law and has developed its own sales depots. By contrast, the largest private cheese-maker has been prevented from wholesaling its products, placing it at a competitive disadvantage vis-a-vis the KCC because of the additional 20% commission fees charged by distributors. Other private dairy firms have been able to bypass this regulation, either by setting up sister companies (usually run by relatives) to perform distribution tasks or by dealing directly with hotels and caterers for a large proportion of their sales.

The established and emergent dairy processors have had several sources of technical information available to develop product ideas and recipes and to make decisions about processing technology. For the recently developed high-value product producers, the most important sources of technical information have been: local and visiting dairy specialists at the University of Nairobi and Egerton College, representatives of equipment supply companies, foreign country trade representatives, personal visits and short training courses abroad, and technicians and food specialists from hotels and from a private company which provides food services to international airlines (for example, the National Airline Service). The technology for fermented milk production, developed and initially tested at the University of Nairobi, was later extended to several small companies by a private voluntary organization.

None of the firms who were interviewed mentioned any public, non-university source of technical information, though several firms do have staff who attended courses at the Dairy Training Center. The weakness of public services applies also to the area of quality control. Most firms complain that the Kenya Bureau of Standards lacks qualified staff. Results from Bureau tests take months to arrive and are said to be incomprehensible at times. In contrast, the quality inspection and advisory services of both hotels and the private airline service are universally praised.

Among the producers of high-value products, the dominant source of finance for investment and working capital has been savings from employment and agricultural activities. Of the ten firms interviewed, only one had obtained a commercial loan to develop its processing factory. Two others had received loans from the Agricultural Finance Corporation to purchase their farms. Several firms report being rejected for long-term loans for dairy processing investments.[59]

The cooperatives which have invested in milk processing plants have financed their projects through a combination of concessional loans and grants from external donors, small Kenyan government grants and contributions received from members. The external concessional loans or grants were linked to the purchase of equipment and technical service contracts with companies from the donor country. In the case of the Kitinda Cooperative, 85% of the initial investment was a grant from a foreign government.[60] The Meru Cooperative will complete the construction of a large new UHT processing facility in 1993 with tied bilateral donor funds. Several schemes to produce fermented milk, including that of the Buit Dairy Company, have involved a joint venture between a PVO (registered locally as a foundation) and a group of small farmers, the plan being to sell the PVO's equity shares to the farmers over time.

Raw Material Procurement Arrangements

Restricted product sales and KCC controls on all milk flows within the formal sector have prevented private processors from developing sustained raw material procurement arrangements which best match their needs in terms of both quantity and quality. At the time of field work, just after the decontrol on producer prices had been announced, raw material procurement arrangements were in a state of flux. Both farmers and processing firms were just beginning to develop new types of linkages.

Impending changes seem most apparent in the milk procurement arrangements of processors of high-value product processors. Until early 1992, the two largest producers were required to obtain their milk supplies from the KCC. The system involved direct deliveries by (primarily) large-scale farmers to the plants, invoices were made on a KCC account and payments passed from the firms to the KCC and then to the farmers. Farmers were paid the prevailing official KCC prices and the factory paid the KCC an 'administrative fee' for its bookkeeping. In recent years, this administrative fee was Ksh.

---

[59] At least for cheese-makers this has created cash flow problems given the time needed for the product to reach maturity and thus yield income.

[60] This is discussed by Tribe (1989).

0.50 per liter, representing a tax on processors of more than 10% of the prevailing official procurement price. While this procurement arrangement was generally satisfactory during the 'flush' season, whenever there were shortages of milk, the KCC would seek to ration supplies to the processors in order to increase the utilization of the KCC's own processing facilities. Mid-1992, these firms were in the process of breaking their link with the KCC and forming direct procurement channels. Kenya Milk Products Limited reported developing a collection system for a network of forty large-scale suppliers and some 150 smallholders. The firm was also considering supplying private veterinary services to its farmers at cost.

The moderate size processors (those handling 1000–5000 liters/day) have relied upon local cooperative societies for the bulk of their raw material needs, supplemented by clandestine deliveries from large-scale and other neighboring farmers. The common practice has been to make bi-weekly or monthly pre-payments to the cooperatives and then to draw down the accounts through deliveries. These processors have been favorable outlets for the cooperative societies, because they offer a steady and fairly sizeable market outlet, pay prices slightly above KCC rates and feature lower transaction costs than those incurred when dealing with the KCC. Not only is payment more prompt, the cooperatives also do not encounter the milk intake congestion which is common at KCC collection stations during the 'flush' season. For their part, the processing firms have found these arrangements to be acceptable, although all complain about periodic quality problems. Due to the presence of antibiotics in some deliveries, the firms have generally relied upon their own small dairy herds for starter culture. The procurement of milk directly from farmers had been fraught with risk until the recent decontrol with fines, bribes and threats of or actual confiscation of milk containers occurring regularly. The smaller cottage industry firms have relied mostly on their own dairy herds for milk, supplemented by supplies from neighboring farmers.

Among the existing and prospective fluid and powdered milk processors, there are varied procurement arrangements and plans. One model integrates large-scale dairying activities with milk processing. These farms have herds numbering 500 or more milking cows. Animal feeding and calving is undertaken or timed either to maintain steady year-round supplies or to target supplies for the dry season when market prices are higher. These farms indicate that they will buy supplies from other (large) farms in order to supplement their own production and reach desired levels of capacity utilization. As these farms are seeking to tap the premium quality end of the milk market, preparations are being made for extensive quality checks of both own-farm and out-supplier milk.

Successful, relatively large-scale dairy cooperative societies and unions have developed extensive milk collection and service systems for their members. The Meru Cooperative Union and its affiliated primary cooperative societies have an extensive milk collection network. The Union provides credit to members and sells them feeds, agro-chemicals and many other production inputs at cost. The Limuru Dairy Cooperative Society has gone further and provides its members with private artificial insemination and clinical services, charged at cost. A similar, multi-dimensional procurement system is being considered by Nestlé, should it invest in a dehydration factory. The firm will likely concentrate its milk procurement activities in one high-potential region, offering a full range of services within the framework of a contract farming scheme. This would be similar to those operated by Nestlé in other countries.

Marketing Arrangements

The Kenyan market for cheese, yogurt, cream and other high-value dairy products remains small due to the limited purchasing power and lack of an acquired taste for such products by most of the population. As noted above, consumers of these products are mostly tourists, expatriate residents and Kenya's relatively small middle- and upper-income population. Therefore, distribution of these products is primarily through hotels, restaurants and up-market grocers and chain stores.

There has been relatively little supplier promotion of high-value dairy products, whether by the KCC or by private companies. For many years, the KCC has produced cheese largely as a means of using surplus milk and serving large institutional needs (military, hospitals). Private firms have also been very cautious, producing only types and quantities of products for which they have firm orders or know that they can sell. Only a few firms have advertised their products in magazines or on television or conducted promotions in stores, through clubs or at public events. While all products sold through stores have company or brand labels, only in the past few years have firms recognized the importance of product presentation and invested in higher quality packaging and labeling.

For most dairy processors, market research has consisted only of discussions with hotel and restaurant chefs and supermarket managers about current demand. A few firms, with the cooperation of hotel chefs, have test marketed their products in hotel buffets. Two firms have benefited from marketing advice provided by a specialized distribution company which carries their products.

The sales strategies and channels generally differ between the cottage industry type firms and the larger firms. The former companies direct most of their sales to hotels and up-market shops, without using distribution agents and without paying the required value added tax on sales. These firms tend to channel their products to buyers in only one or two major towns. In contrast, the larger firms combine sales to hotels and restaurants, sales at the farm and factory gate or through affiliated companies, and sales to shops. Some firms, particularly those operating under proper hygienic conditions, also supply the National Airline Service. The larger firms tend to use commission agents for some sales, especially for distant markets. Most serve Nairobi and Mombasa and selected other sites. Their preferred outlets are hotels and the airline service since they get immediate feedback on quality and advice from them, there is no risk of returned unsold items, and the processors can escape paying VAT on such sales. Sales are on a cash basis to stores and a credit basis to hotels. Although prices are negotiated, it is generally the buyers which have the final say, especially in the cases of five-star hotels, the airline service and large retail chain stores. For cheddar cheese, the high-value product with the largest market volume, private company prices (and overall profitability) have been kept down by KCC sales of the product at or below its variable production costs. The KCC has consistently shown losses on this product.

Although the market for fluid milk is far larger than that for high-value products, Kenya Dairy Board restrictions on sales quantities and locations and the predominance of KCC is certain areas have handicapped marketing efforts by private and cooperative firms. While Kenya Dairy Board restrictions have been less aggressively enforced in recent years, their presence has still prevented firms from establishing long-term distribution arrangements outside of their licensed market areas. Whenever their own target market areas have been temporarily saturated, these firms have had to develop ad hoc sales arrangements in other areas. Some lucrative market outlets, such as the School Milk Program, the Army and other public institutions have been monopolized by the KCC.

The cooperatives engaged in milk processing have generally sold both raw and processed milk. Their sales, made at cooperative society depots and factory gates and through local shops and distribution agents, have been concentrated in close vicinity to the factory. Surplus quantities have been sent to distant major cities, such as Nairobi or Kisumu. In contrast with the pan-territorial sales prices for KCC milk, these cooperatives employ different price schedules by location and type of buyer. Previously prevented from doing so, several of the large cooperative processors are now assessing the feasibility of setting up large wholesale depots in Nairobi to compete directly with the KCC in that market.

Indicators of Performance

Both private and cooperative dairy processors have faced official restrictions in their milk procurement arrangements, choice of products and areas and channels to or through which they could market these products. At the same time, these firms have faced aggressive efforts (in milk collection, marketing, and pricing) by the KCC designed to weaken or limit the growth of its competitors. Not surprisingly, these constraints and aggressive intrusions have undermined the sales and financial performance of private and cooperative processors and greatly limited the extent to which private firms could support farm-level milk production.

Table 5.10 examines rates of capacity utilization for the KCC and for private and cooperative processors for which data (or estimates) are available. (Private firms are indicated by initials.) For fluid and fermented milk producers, the indicated utilization levels are for peak production years and/or for 1992, and based on one-, two- or three-shift operations. For cheese and yogurt makers, the estimates are for the peak production season during 1992, with all calculations based on an assumption of two shifts. In practice, most of these firms operate for only one long shift of 9–10 hours, but conversions are made to render utilization rates comparable to those of fluid milk processors. The table does not include some of the small, cottage-industry firms, whose processing capacity is difficult to estimate and which lack records on monthly or quarterly milk intake.

The table shows capacity utilization rates varying between 26% and 75%. The KCC's capacity utilization rates in its peak production year (1989/90) were higher than comparative rates among private and cooperative milk processors. However, with reduced milk purchases, KCC's average capacity utilization fell below 36% in 1992. The average figures for the KCC do not reveal

TABLE 5.10: **Rates of Capacity Utilization in the Dairy Sector**

Fluid Milk Processors					Cheese/Yogurt Makers	
Company	Year	Product	# of Shifts	% Capacity Utilization	Company	% Capacity Utilization
KCC	1989/90 (Peak)	Pasteurized Milk	2	61	DL	56
			3	55		
		UHT Milk	3	69		
	1992	Powdered Milk All Products	3	36		
Meru Coop.	1988	UHT Milk	2	26	KMP	40
Kitinda Coop.	1989	UHT Milk	2	30	ABD	57
	1992		1	5		
KLF	1992	Pasteurized Milk	2	51	EF	75
MNR	1992 (Aug–Dec.)	Pasteurized Milk	1	75 (est.)	SP	57
Buit	1992	Fermented Milk	1	40	BFD	35
Average	1992			38	Average (Weighted)	52

SOURCES: DANIDA (1991); company interviews and financial data.

the very low rates of capacity utilization at some of its factories. These factories, in a state of disrepair and experiencing major congestion at intake points during the peak season, have been used in recent years primarily as collection points for milk to be transferred to operational factories several hundred kilometers away. Only three of KCC's factories—at Kitale, Kiganjo, and Nyahururu—process large quantities of milk produced from within a 75 kilometer radius.

Neither Meru nor Kitinda has ever achieved annual utilization rates above 30%, due to the seasonality of milk supplies, periodic factory and infrastructure-related breakdowns, profitable cooperative society sales of raw milk, and aggressive KCC milk collection and sales programs in nearby locations. Nevertheless, with the support of an external concessional loan, the Meru Cooperative is presently completing construction of a new factory with more than double the capacity of the existing factory.[61] The relatively low capacity utili-

---

[61] A recent consultant report claims that neither Meru nor Kitinda have been able to produce UHT milk with the equipment that they have. The shelf life of their product has been about five days, and both cooperatives receive back up to 10% of their output returned to them (spoiled) from distributors (Avezard 1992).

zation for the Buit company stems from shortages of water (for cooling the heated milk) and the profitable diversion of some raw milk supplies to fresh market sale. While the Kilifi Plantation could nearly double its milk intake, its market area has been restricted by the Dairy Board.

Among the larger cheese and yogurt-makers, average capacity utilization rates during the 'flush' production season are about 50%, given the assumption that there should be two operating shifts. The limited market size and its seasonality (because of tourist arrivals), past restrictions on milk procurement arrangements, and the narrow management and labor supervision base of all of these firms have prevented more complete capacity utilization even during the 'flush' production season. For similar reasons, most of the cottage-industry processors operate only a few hours per day.

Table 5.11 indicates recent patterns in the sales and financial performance of the KCC, the two leading cooperative processors and the two largest private high-value product processors. The table highlights the large and continued financial losses incurred by the KCC. Operational inefficiencies, official price controls and huge losses incurred in converting seasonal surplus milk supplies into storable products have been the major contributing factors to its negative balance sheet. KCC losses have been covered by increased borrowing, especially from the government. Still, liquidity problems have resulted in delayed payments of several months to farmers, cooperatives and other input and service suppliers.

TABLE 5.11: **Sales and Financial Performance in the Dairy Sector**
(Ksh. Millions)

Company	Indicator	1987/88	1988/89	1989/90	1990/91
KCC	Sales	2,203.9	2,644.4	2954.3	3031.6
	Profit (Losses)	(159.1)	(57.1)	(103.2)	(66.7)
	Accumulated Profit (Losses)	(191.1)	(248.2)	(351.4)	(418.1)
Meru Coop.	Sales	22.6	23.5	22.6	26.4
	Profit (Losses)	(2.5)	0.8	(0.1)	(0.02)
	Accumulated Profit (Losses)	(11.7)	(10.9)	(11.0)	(11.0)
Kitinda Coop.	Sales	13.3	14.7	16.9	12.0
	Profit (Losses)	(0.4)	(0.6)	(0.9)	(1.1)
	Accumulated Profit (Losses)	(0.8)	(1.4)	(2.3)	(3.4)
DL (Private)	Sales	Na.	17.6	19.0	20.0
	Profit (Losses)	Na.	0.3	0.4	0.4
KMP (Private)	Sales	4.3	4.2	5.1	5.5
	Profit (Losses)	0.4	0.5	0.5	0.6

SOURCES: DANIDA (1991); Company financial statements.

TABLE 5.12: **Payments to Producers as a Share of Sales Turnover**

Company	1988	1989	1990	1991
KCC	55.1	54.3	53.2	47.7
Meru Coop.	65.6	55.7	54.4	49.1
Kitinda Coop.	54.3	62.3	63.1	Na.
Buit Mala Co.	Na.	Na.	Na.	52.4
Engineer Mala Co.	Na.	Na.	Na.	51.4

SOURCES: DANIDA (1991); Company financial statements.

In addition, both Meru and Kitinda Cooperatives have exhibited unsatisfactory sales and financial performance in recent years. As with the KCC, their accumulated losses have been covered by government and external donor grants. The private firms listed in the table have generated steady, if modest profits, yet sales turnover has increased only moderately in recent years.

Table 5.12 provides a comparison of the share of company sales paid out to producers by the KCC, the two main cooperative milk processors, and two small private fermented milk producers which obtain milk directly from company shareholders/members. Similar calculations are not possible for firms converting milk into high-value products. Since the cooperatives and small companies have sought to increase their payout to members in order to minimize tax liabilities, we would expect to find higher producer shares of final realized sales for these firms. The table indicates that the small-to-medium-scale processing cooperatives have indeed had a larger share of their sales earnings paid out to milk producers. The payout to producers from the KCC has fallen below 50% in recent years.[62]

Table 5.13 compares the cost/price structure for UHT milk produced by the KCC and the Kitinda cooperative in 1990. KCC milk is packed in multi-layered Tetra Pak containers, and Kitinda milk packed in plastic sachets. The table shows lower net costs for Kitinda, largely due to the high cost of Tetra Pak packaging and KCC's relatively high overhead costs. These extra costs more than compensated for Kitinda's higher unit distribution and labor costs. Because of the KCC's higher transport cost and the high import content

---

[62] The share was 48% in 1992. For comparison, Eriksen (1992) found that farmers received 60% of the value of dairy processor sales to retailers in Morocco. He also reported that among urban northeast dairy plants in the United States, the relevant farmers' share was nearly 62%.

TABLE 5.13: **Cost/Price Structure of UHT Milk in Kenya** (1990, Ksh/Litre)

	Kitinda Coop. (plastic sachets)	KCC (Tetra Pak)
Net Farm-gate Price	3.31	2.98
Transport to Collection Station and Factory	0.75	0.84
Cooperative Society Expenses	0.30	0.30
Taxes/Dairy Development Cess	0.34	0.32
Cost Ex-factory	**4.70**	**4.44**
Processing Costs		
Salaries/Wages	0.69	0.26
Power and Fuel	0.27	0.19
Machinery Repair	0.14	0.22
Depreciation	0.67	0.12
Packaging	1.20	2.75
Other Costs	0.24	0.22
Sub-total	**3.21**	**3.76**
Distribution Costs		
Transport	0.27	0.33
Selling Costs	1.00	0.47
Returns and Leakages	0.30	0.11
Sub-total	**1.57**	**0.91**
Overhead Costs	**0.44**	**1.71**
Total Costs	**9.92**	**10.82**[1]
Retail Sales Price	**11.00**	**11.00**

[1] KCC receives milk with 3.5% butter fat and sells milk containing 2.3% butter fat. Taking this into account the unit costs for production are reduced by Ksh. 0.30/litre.

SOURCE: FAO (1991).

of Tetra Pak packaging (for the materials and machinery rental), the foreign exchange costs for KCC milk are considerably higher than those for Kitinda, Meru and private milk processors.

CONCLUSIONS

Although milk exhibits several technical properties which constrain production and distribution, it can be consumed in many different forms and be preserved or processed using a range of different technologies with varied efficient operating scales. The organizational patterns and technologies adopted for dairy processing and marketing should reflect the structure and location of farm-level milk production, as well as the nature of demand for dairy products. For many years, the development of Kenya's dairy industry has not followed this dictum. While Kenya's dairy industry is one of the largest and most commercialized in sub-Saharan Africa, its recent pattern of development has been poorly suited to the structure of local production and demand. As a result, the majority of Kenya's producers and consumers have benefited little from major government-backed dairy industry investments and have in fact opted out of the formal dairy marketing system.

Throughout much of the colonial period, dairy industry development was largely geared toward serving the interests of its producers who were settlers from Europe. Local consumers were taxed to subsidize loss-making exports and most African farmers were discouraged from undertaking dairy production. The Kenya Cooperative Creamery, a commercial cooperative with largely European membership, used the powers of the state to protect its members' interests and to thwart the activities of competitors.

Following Kenyan independence, smallholder dairy production was successfully promoted. Yet, smallholders were incorporated into the KCC's milk procurement system on highly disadvantageous terms. This, together with the limited geographical spread of KCC operations, the absence of direct KCC linkages with smallholder farmers and of services to assist them, led most of the latter to consign the bulk of their production to household use and informal rural area sales. After formal market competition for the KCC was suppressed (in the 1960s) and the KCC itself transformed into a "public" entity (in the 1970s/80s), a single model of dairy processing began to emerge. With the backing of external donors, the government and the KCC undertook a large investment program featuring urban-based, medium-to-large-scale processing facilities. These facilities operated at well below their capacity and generated a stream of products affordable to only a small proportion of the local population. Most producers and consumers have continued to rely upon the informal market for much of their sales outlets and consumption needs. The KCC has experienced worsening problems of management, product quality and illiquidity.

Despite policy pronouncements to the contrary, many past efforts to develop competitive small- and medium-scale private or cooperative processing facilities have been discouraged, if not directly prevented. Facing delays or rejections for license applications, subsequent restrictions on raw material sources, products, and market areas, and periodic or sustained anti-competitive measures by the KCC, private and cooperative processing and marketing activities have been pushed to the margins of the formal market in terms of both product line and geography. Enmeshed in a web of controls, these firms have encountered difficulties developing effective long-term arrangements for milk procurement and downstream product sales. With the partial exception of a few cooperatives, these firms have also been unable to fill the vacuum created by a deteriorating system of official livestock support services.

A climate of change appears to be emerging. The Kenya Dairy Master Plan, produced in 1990/91 by a high-level team of local and foreign consultants, argued strongly that the centralized, KCC-dominated system was both inefficient and unsustainable and that measures needed to be taken to liberalize the dairy market and stimulate additional private and cooperative processing and marketing activities. There is considerable interest within the country in undertaking such ventures. The potential participants in a liberalized market are very varied, as are their intended operational scales, products and linkages with dairy producers. Such new ventures could complement as well as compete with a re-organized, decentralized and commercially-oriented KCC.

In future programs to support Kenya's dairy industry it should be recognized that no single model or operating system can meet the diverse production support, processing and consumption needs of the country. A healthy, restructured dairy industry would combine:

a) *rural small-scale processing units* (perhaps linked to NGOs),

b) *regional cooperative processors offering a range of production support and marketing services* to their members,

c) *large farms doing their own milk pasteurizing and processing*, perhaps providing production and marketing services to nearby farmers (who supply them),

d) *small-to-medium-scale private firms producing and selling a range* of processed dairy products to middle- and upper-income population groups and tourists,

e) *large processing firms with integrated or contracted milk supplies and serving both* domestic and international markets for processed dairy products, and

f) *a reconstituted Kenya Cooperative Creamery* competing in the major urban markets and redeveloping export sales.

Each of these enterprises will have to compete with the raw milk market, both in the procurement of supplies and for consumer custom. In the absence of government price controls, competition from this source will likely drive up producer prices and put significant pressure on processors to increase their operating efficiency and alter their product mix (for example, away from costly UHT products) to attract consumers from the lower income strata.

VI.

Market Imperfections and Government Failures: the Vanilla Sector in Madagascar

Benoît Blarel and Diane Dolinsky

INTRODUCTION

Vanilla is the second most expensive spice traded on the world market.[1] After dominating the world market with more than 95% of total supplies, sub-Saharan Africa is in the process of rapidly, and perharps permanently, losing its dominant position to more competitive and commercially aggressive countries in the Pacific Basin. By 1991, SSA's share of the expanding and promising world market for vanilla had already fallen to about 50%. If the last ten years' trends were to continue unchanged, SSA would cease exporting vanilla by the year 2000, foregoing potentially large export revenues from a US$ 100 million market.

This dramatic loss of competitiveness cannot be explained by an unfavorable cost structure. Madagascar, which alone accounts for about three quarters of all SSA vanilla exports, produces vanilla for a third of the cost of its most direct competitor, Indonesia. It cannot be explained either by a production of sub-standard quality. According to the world's largest user of vanilla, a U.S.-based flavor manufacturing house, the vanilla produced in Madagascar continues to constitute, quality-wise, the reference for the flavor industry worldwide. The explanation for this loss of competitiveness lies elsewhere.

---

[1] This case study is based on the results of a background paper on the international vanilla market prepared for the World Bank by Thomas J. Payne Market Development (1990), and on field work conducted by the World Bank, in February/March and July 1991, for the preparation of a vanilla sector report (World Bank, 1991). Besides the main author of the present paper, Messrs Thierry Aube, Francis Masson, Andriantsoamiraho Rasolojaona and Velonjara participated in the World Bank mission.

The cause for the decline of Madagascar on the world market lies in a sectoral organization and policy which are proving inflexible and unable to react to a fast changing world market. Yet the same sectoral organization and policy were also the main factors behind Madagascar's past successful achievements on the world vanilla market. Until 1960, the market was small, stagnant, highly unstable and prone to speculation. This can be traced back to the numerous, structural market imperfections and failures which characterize both the supply and demand for vanilla. After independence, the Government of Madagascar quickly intervened to establish an orderly domestic vanilla market which would promote consistency and reliability in production and quality among the tens of thousands of small-scale vanilla growers, and would take the necessary collective action to develop external markets. Public sector interventions to overcome market failures were necessary and initially very successful: in about 15 years, Madagascar export volumes increased sixfold and export earnings fivefold. Madagascar was also able to maintain a dominant share of an expanding world market, as well as to sustain the highest quality standards.

However, Government intervention in the vanilla market eventually proved counter-productive. The organization and policies governing the Malagasy vanilla sector since 1960 were too rigid and heavily biased towards direct Government intervention rather than relying on more market-based instruments, and on greater private sector involvement in the management of collective market institutions. The resulting incentive structure has generated myopic and collusive behavior on the part of a handful of exporters and an over-powerful public administration. After the mid-1970s, Madagascar made increasing use of its monopoly power on the world market by exacting an ever increasing price from its world buyers. Vanilla growers, however, did not reap any gains from the dramatic increase in monopoly rents which Madagascar extracted from the world market.

Despite important technical barriers to entry into vanilla production, Indonesia rapidly expanded its production capacity and became increasingly successful at overcoming the same market failures which Madagascar had faced in the past. Indonesia has now supplanted Madagascar to become the world's largest vanilla exporter and is starting to challenge Madagascar in the quality of its production. The myopic and collusive behavior resulting from the Malagasy sectoral organization has so far proved unable to adapt to the competitive situation it helped establish on the world market.

The Madagascar vanilla example offers an almost perfect illustration of a number of instances where African countries have lost their world market shares and competitiveness as a result of policy failures. The private sector continues to perform all commercial functions, yet under the pervasive control of Government policies. This case study is also illustrative of numerous instances where the private sector's initiatives, operating under the heavy control of Government policies, engages in rent-seeking activities rather than developing markets and product quality. Finally, it is a good example of an apparent need for collective action to overcome multiple market failures and imperfections. Such collective action, when it is dominated by Government and too distanced from market signals, can lead to even greater inefficiencies and inequities, as this case study will show.

In the second section of this case study we review the technical characteristics of the product and show how they contribute to market imperfections and failures. In the third section we analyze the structure of world vanilla demand and supply and identify the corresponding market failures and imperfections. In the fourth section we describe the technical and economic characteristics of vanilla production in Madagascar, at each of its three stages (growing, curing and packing), and derive for each level the nature of the possible market failures and imperfections which may emerge. In the fifth section we review the successive policy regimes (free market, orderly market, and government managed) which have governed the organization of the vanilla sector in Madagascar until today, and how these relate to the failures identified previously. In the sixth section we assess the impact of these different policy regimes on the performance of the Malagasy vanilla sector using both economic efficiency and equity criteria. We then conclude by drawing out the main policy implications of this case study.

TECHNO-ECONOMIC CHARACTERISTICS OF VANILLA

Vanilla has **low perishability,** at least once it is cured.[2] Processors can hold cured vanilla beans in stock for years if the beans have been harvested at the

---

[2] An explanation of terminology is necessary. Production of the vanilla beans actually consists of three stages—vanilla growing, curing and packing. At the growing stage, vanilla beans are referred to as "green", and need to undergo the curing process to acquire their flavor and aroma characteristics, hence providing them with their commercial value. They are then referred to as cured vanilla. The packing stage consists of the sorting, grading, conditioning and storage which are necessary before exports.

appropriate time, and the curing has been carried out properly. If either of these two conditions is not met, there is heightened risk of mold. The spread of mold is checked by examining beans periodically during conditioning and storage to permit removal and treatment of infected beans. As long as there are regular inspections, low perishability permits packers to maintain stocks for sale at optimal times.

It is **low in bulkiness,** and **high in unit value.** Vanilla beans are compact in size and easy to pack together. Vanilla beans have high unit value, and after saffron, are the second highest priced spice on the world market, with an average world FOB price of US\$ 53/kg. in 1991. While vanilla beans accounted for only 0.5% of U.S. imports of spices and herbs in volume terms, their share of value was as high as 16%. Vanilla beans' low bulkiness and high unit value make distribution over long distances feasible and highly profitable. Because of its high value, the vanilla trade is also prone to speculation.

There are **many dimensions to the quality** of a vanilla bean. The major quality components are: flavor profile, natural vanillin content, bean length, moisture content, appearance, color, and presentation. Flavor profile is the most important quality characteristic of a vanilla bean, and differs greatly from one variety of vanilla plant to another.[3]

Differences in quality make the **substitution between vanilla beans from different origins difficult.** At least, four major types of vanilla beans can be distinguished:[4] the Bourbon vanilla (grown in Madagascar, Comoros and Réunion), the Java vanilla (grown on the island of the same name in Indonesia), the "Bourbon-like" vanilla (mainly grown on the island of Bali in Indonesia), and the Mexican vanilla. They differ in flavor profile, organoleptic and analytical properties as a result of variations in growing conditions (e.g., quality and age of the vine, number of fertilized flowers per inflorescence), harvesting and curing practices.[5] Malagasy vanilla ranks top in terms of quality, a result of improved and well-established production, harvesting and curing

---

[3] Three species of vanilla plants are commercially grown throughout the world. *Vanilla fragrans* cultivated in the Indian Ocean (Madagascar, Comoros, Réunion), Mexico and Indonesia dominates the world supply with over 95%. Two other varieties are grown in French Polynesia (Tahiti) and in Guadeloupe, respectively. They do not directly compete with the *V. fragrans* since they are used mostly in the perfume industry.

[4] McCormick & Company (1992).

[5] McCormick & Company (1992).

practices. As the world leader, it sets the standard for the industry. Vanilla grown in Indonesia ranks fourth (after the three Bourbon-producing countries) because of lower natural vanillin content and less attractive flavor profile (the result of premature harvesting practices and poor curing techniques).

Some of the **quality characteristics are not directly observable,** and grading standards help reduce transaction costs and the level of uncertainty for buyers. The flavor profile and natural vanillin content are not directly measurable without special testing equipment. There is a small degree of correlation between the natural vanillin content and other more easily observable characteristics such as the length of the vanilla bean, whether the bean is split or not, its appearance, etc. Experienced vanilla specialists can detect appreciable differences in the quality of vanilla beans. To manage these wide quality differences, grading standards have long been elaborated in Madagascar and are schematically represented in Table 6.1. All producing countries follow some sort of grading system, although these may differ greatly.

Because important quality characteristics are not directly observable and are largely determined by growing conditions, time of harvest, and the curing process, there is scope for **marketing externalities at the production** (farm, curing, packing) **level.** Together, vanilla growers financially benefit from following similar growing, harvesting and curing practices which safeguard consistency and high quality (flavor profile and vanillin content). This reduces uncertainty and risks for the buyer, potentially raising the demand for and market value of vanilla beans. Because direct observability of intrinsic qual-

TABLE 6.1: **Madagascar Vanilla Export Grades Standards of Vanilla Beans**

1st Quality		2nd Quality		3rd Quality		4th Quality	
Whole	Split	Whole	Split	Whole	Split	Whole	Split
		Good Flavor Length > 14 cm Tan Brown Uniform Color				Broken or Cut Length < 14 cm	
Supple Full No Spot No Scratch Moisture Content 38%		Supple Some Spots & Scratches Moisture Content 38%		Supple or Dry Spots & Scratches Moisture Content 30%		Moisture Content 25%	

SOURCE: Ministere du Commerce, Direction de la Qualite et de la Metrologie Legale.

TABLE 6.2: **Technico-Economic Characteristics of the Vanilla Product and Relationships with Market Imperfections and Failures**

	Low Perishability	High Unit Value	Quality Characteristics:	
			Multi-dimensional	Limited Observability
Market Imperfections and Failures: 1) Market Instability (speculative market)	X	X		
2) Marketing externality: —Transaction costs			X	X
—At production level				X

ity characteristics is difficult, individual growers and/or curers can be tempted to free-ride.[6]

THE WORLD MARKET FOR VANILLA

Structure and Composition of the World Demand[7]

The world market for vanilla beans is **small.** Aggregate global demand for vanilla is estimated at about 2,000 tons a year. Over the period 1965–1989, world consumption of vanilla beans has grown at the average annual rate of about 2% (see Annex Table 6A). Between 1980 and 1989, demand expanded rapidly, in particular in the U.S. where it grew at 7% a year (in volume terms). In Europe, the rate of progression was more modest at 2–3%. The growth in aggregate demand has not matched the rates of income and population growth in developed countries, despite the fact that the demand for vanilla is associated with highly income-elastic demand for end-products[8] (e.g., ice creams, colas). The advent of synthetic vanilla (vanillin) whose production has been booming[9] helps to explain this phenomenon. On the other hand, a number of factors have strengthened the demand for vanilla beans over the

---

[6] To follow stringent growing, harvesting and curing practices increases quality but also tends to reduce production levels; e.g., the number of vanilla flowers pollinated on an individual vine raises production, but can also lower quality.

[7] This section draws heavily on Thomas J. Payne Market Development (1990).

[8] Purseglove, Brown, Green and Robbins (1981.)

[9] Synthetic vanilla production in the U.S. increased by 135% between 1984 and 1988.

past decade: increased health awareness for natural products, escalating consumer demand for processed foods (which use new flavors and spices), and an explosion in popularity of gourmet ice creams (which tend to use exclusively pure natural flavors).

The world market for vanilla beans is **highly concentrated** in a few, rich countries. Three countries only (U.S., France and Germany) account for about 80% of world imports, the U.S. absorbing 50–60%, France and Germany between 10 and 15% each (see Figure 6.1). These three countries are also major re-exporters of both vanilla beans and processed vanilla products.[10] Other industrialised countries are significant minor importers.[11]

There are a **very small number of importers** of vanilla beans,[12] which makes for **limited competition,** although they cater to the need of a much larger, diverse and competitive food industry. Vanilla beans are imported by brokers specializing in the spice business who sell them to flavor manufacturers and extractors for further processing. Vanilla bean brokers provide a variety of services to their clients: they ensure the necessary consistency in quality and in supplies by keeping inventories, they offer quality control services, they select the beans according to their quality requirements, and they maintain close commercial contacts with suppliers in producing countries, often providing technical assistance and expertise to the packers. Reputation, exclusivity and technical expertise on the part of the brokers lower transaction costs which, more than financial constraints, act as important barriers to entry in the vanilla importing business. The marketing policies of Madagascar, Comoros and Réunion have voluntarily restricted the number of buyers. This policy is not being pursued by other exporting countries, such as Indonesia, which may sell to a larger number of brokers or directly to the food industry. However, it is believed that most imports from these sources are

---

[10] Germany only consumes 30–40% of its imported beans, and its re-exports are by far the most significant, reaching approximately 135–210 metric tons per year in the late 1980's and early 1990's. France's annual re-exports were equalled 70–120 tons, while the United States' re-exports were 40–60 metric tons.

[11] Canada, Japan, and Switzerland each import about 35–60 tons each, the Netherlands, United Kingdom, Denmark, Italy, and Saudi Arabia 18–35 metric tons each, and Brazil, other EC countries and Australia between 10 and 20 metric tons each. Highest per capita consumption is found in Denmark (4.5 grams), the United States (3.85 grams) and France (2.5 grams).

[12] In the U.S., there are only two major importers of vanilla beans produced in the Indian Ocean, with a third representing a small and declining share of U.S. imports. In France, there were seven importers of beans from the Indian Ocean islands in 1990–1991, although the two larger ones account for about half of all imports. In Germany, only two dealers import vanilla beans from the Indian Ocean islands.

FIGURE 6.1: **Share of World Vanilla Beans Imports** (1989–91)

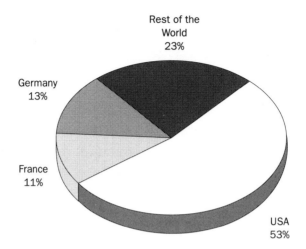

Rest of the
World
23%

Germany
13%

France
11%

USA
53%

still being imported (in particular in the large consuming countries such as the U.S. and France), by the same dealers/brokers who also enjoy exclusivity contracts from Madagascar (and Comoros and Réunion).

Vanilla beans are primarily used as an **ingredient in the food industry.** The corresponding **demand assumes special characteristics** peculiar to the food ingredients market. Besides price, quality standards and consistency, reliability in supply, technical characteristics of the product, changes in food technology, regulations pertaining to food labelling and technology are all major determinants of the demand for vanilla beans. In the United States, over 95% of the vanilla beans are processed into extracts sold to flavor manufacturers or to the retail trade. Some extract processors are vertically integrated with flavor manufacturers. Three types of vanilla extracts and flavors are manufactured: pure vanilla extracts, vanilla with other natural flavors, and vanilla flavors which may contain artificial substances. Only a small proportion of vanilla beans are consumed directly by consumers, except in France where the proportion is about 20%. The dairy industry (e.g., ice cream, frozen desserts) is the largest consumer of vanilla extracts and flavors,[13] the confectionery, baking, and beverage industries (e.g. cola) the other major industrial users.

---

[13] 44% of all vanilla extracts in the U.S. are used in the production of ice creams.

Asymmetric information between buyers (the food industry and its brokers) and sellers of vanilla beans may arise. Confidentiality about quality and technical characteristics of the vanilla bean and its processed products, because of formulation secrets and proprietary processes in the food industry, is of paramount importance in the commercial relationship of the food industrialist and the vanilla broker. This provides the vanilla buyer with superior knowledge and information about the true demand for vanilla, resulting in the possible presence of asymmetric information.

Vanilla is the spice most subject to competition from **imperfect substitutes** (low-cost artificial flavorings). **Aggregate demand for vanilla** beans therefore remains concentrated on the upper quality end of the vanilla flavoring market, where it is fairly **price-inelastic,** hence creating the potential for an unstable market. Four types of substitutes exist to date: synthetic vanillin, ethyl vanillin, other natural flavors, and tissue culture products. Synthetic vanillin accounts for more than 90% of the U.S. vanilla flavoring market and about 50% of the French market, the lowest national share. Synthetic vanillin costs one-hundredth the price of the natural product and serves not only to substitute for vanilla, but also to supplement or adulterate vanilla extracts.[14] Technological changes in the food, extract and flavor industry are major determinants of the extent to which these substitutes can compete with vanilla beans.[15]

Competition from substitutes, and the significance of technological change in the food and ingredient industries on the demand for vanilla beans, strongly suggest the presence of **marketing externalities at the demand level in three areas: generic promotion and advertising, food product and production research, and food regulations.** Generic advertising and promotion directed to the food and ingredient industries, as well as to consumers, could increase the demand for natural vanilla, at the expense of substitutes.[16] To be effective, programs of generic advertising and promotion require substantial and sustained investments which are too large for most individual producers and

---

[14] When vanilla extract is made from inferior quality vanilla beans, the resultant may contain less than the required percentage of vanillin content. In order to raise the latter, synthetic vanillin is often mixed with the extract, thereby keeping a lid on the cost of the mixture.

[15] For a more detailed discussion of these technological considerations, see Thomas J. Payne Market Development (1990).

[16] In addition, the scope for generic advertising and promotion—i.e. for the same country of origin—is underscored by the technical characteristics of the commodity: flavor profile tends to be similar within a same country of origin, and quality characteristics are not always directly observable.

exporters of vanilla beans. An individual exporter's financial incentives to invest in such generic advertising and promotion programs are also reduced because other exporters from the same country of origin may benefit from the investment. These problems associated with economies of scale and free-riding give rise to marketing externalities that result in inefficiencies in a free market (i.e. too little generic advertising and promotion programs). A similar marketing externality prevails in the case of funding of research to increase potential uses of vanilla beans in the food and ingredients industry, or of extract certification to detect adulterations. As a result, in a free market, potential uses of vanilla beans in the food and ingredients industry are not being fully exploited, and increased competition from substitutes is not being addressed to the extent possible.

Another example of marketing externality arises in the case of food regulations. In major consuming countries (U.S., EC), vanilla is the only spice which benefits from a *Standard of Identity* which helps shield vanilla beans from competition by substitutes. These regulations govern both food labelling and vanilla extract production. Food labelling regulations, which differ markedly in the U.S. and EC, determine the ease of substitution between natural vanilla beans and artificial substitutes in the food industry. In the U.S. and EC, food labelling regulations that impose specific labelling rules for vanilla flavored food products, allow for a clear distinction between food products that contain natural vanilla and those that contain synthetics. Current U.S. food labelling regulations offer a positive regulatory environment for vanilla beans. By contrast, the supra-national European Community food labelling regulations are less protective than some of the national regulations now being superseded (e.g. France), but are clearly more favorable than others (e.g. Italy).

Extract regulations influence the **scope for substitutability between vanilla beans of different origins and quality,** as well as the potential for market segmentation. French regulations on extracts stipulate the minimum percentage of natural vanillin content rather than the method of extraction. This favors high quality vanilla beans (those beans with a high vanillin content). By contrast, U.S. standards, by making possible the use of lower quality vanilla beans (i.e. with low vanillin content), encourage price competition and market segmentation in the largest world market for vanilla beans.

Madagascar increasingly faces a price-elastic demand for its vanilla beans. Improved farming and curing practices recently adopted in Indonesia have enhanced the flavor profile and overall quality of its vanilla beans, in particular those grown in Bali, Celebes and Sumatra islands. As a result, there has been a marked convergence of quality, and concurrently, of importer's preferences between Indonesian and Bourbon vanilla.[17] The Malagasy and top-of-the-line Balinese beans are increasingly seen as substitutes by the major world users of vanilla beans. Balinese output has been characterized by the world's largest producer of vanilla extracts and flavors as "Bourbon-like" in reference to the world standard.[18] With increased substitution possibilities between Madagascar and Indonesia, the individual demand for Malagasy vanilla is becoming increasingly price-elastic.[19]

To summarize, world aggregate demand for vanilla beans is small, highly concentrated, and relatively price inelastic. Conditions for an unstable market prevail as a result of vanilla beans' high value and inelastic demand. Vanilla beans are primarily used in the food industry as a food ingredient. The nature and characteristics of this demand for vanilla beans are such that competition among importers is limited, and there are potentially severe problems of asymmetric information between vanilla producers and users. These demand characteristics also lead to marketing externalities at the demand level. Finally, the scope for price competition among vanilla beans of different quality and origins varies from one consuming country to another, and appears to be much more important in the largest world market for vanilla beans (U.S.) than in France. These distinctive features of the demand for vanilla give rise to potential market imperfections and failures, which are being summarized in Table 6.3.

---

[17] Technical and organizational efforts at the production stage (quality of vines, agronomic practices, time of harvest), and at the curing stage are being successfully undertaken in Indonesia, especially on the islands of Bali, Celebes and Sumatra.

[18] McCormick & Company (1992).

[19] In addition, the ability of Madagascar to charge a premium for its aromatic and other sensory traits tends to diminish at least proportionately with its decline in world trade. The share of high quality vanilla beans produced in Indonesia is extremely difficult to know, but estimates provided by vanilla dealers indicate that, by 1991, at least a third of total Indonesian exports were of good to excellent quality. The continuous improvement in quality of the Indonesian vanilla is reflected in the observed increase of the average price of the vanilla imports from Indonesia, in particular between 1988 and 1992 when the average import price increased from US$ 19/kg. to US$ 31/kg. (see Annex Table 6C). It is also reflected by the much later introduction of the Indonesian vanilla bean on the French market (1986) than on the U.S. (at least since 1980), where a high vanillin content is required on the former market but not on the latter as a result of differences in extract regulations (see above). It is also reflected by the much smaller average import price differential between the Malagasy and the Indonesian vanilla beans in the French than in the U.S. market (35% as opposed to 82% in 1988).

Structure and Composition of World Supply

Competition on the supply side is limited, and two countries—Madagascar and Indonesia—dominate the world supply of vanilla beans (see Figure 6.2 and Table 6.3). This leads to a situation of market power by the producing countries on the world vanilla market. Market power, when combined with a price-inelastic demand, potentially gives rise to **significant instability on the world market.** It also provides countries possessing market power with the ability to extract **monopoly rents** from the world market. This concentration of vanilla production in a handful of countries partly results from the exacting agro-climatic conditions its cultivation requires, limiting entry by new countries.[20] Madagascar is by far the largest vanilla bean producer, with an average production of 1,200 tons per year over the period 1980–1990. Madagascar has until recently dominated the world market for vanilla, supplying at least 70% of world demand until 1980, and as much as 90% in the early 1970s. After a spectacular boom during the 1980s, Indonesia has now become the world's largest vanilla supplier, its exports jumping from 80 tons in 1980 to 666 tons in 1991,[21] surpassing total exports from Madagascar (644 tons in 1991). Comoros ranks third in production and exports, its exports averaging 140 tons over the period 1980–1990, but with large fluctuations from one year to another. The French island of Réunion was the fourth largest producer and exporter, but its exports have been steadily declining from 58 tons in 1965 to only 13 tons in 1991, and it is now being overtaken by Tonga. Other minor producing countries include Mexico (13 tons exported in 1991), French Polynesia (Tahiti), Costa Rica, and more recently (since 1993) Uganda.

Vanilla **production is highly unstable.**[22] Instability in production partly results from agronomic and climatic factors that make vanilla highly susceptible to disease, rainfall and wind patterns. Unstable production of a high-

---

[20] The vanilla plant, a member of the orchid family, originates from Central America and only thrives in areas located within 25 degrees on either side of the equator, and also requires rich soils. It needs certain elevations and rainfall patterns to survive. It grows best in areas sheltered from strong winds, on gently sloping land, and supported by trees that offer shade. It is highly susceptible to pests and diseases under conditions of excess moisture and overcrowding. In addition, because vanilla production is highly labor-intensive with limited scope for mechanization, it is rarely produced in countries where wage levels are high. This may help explain the production decline in the French island of Réunion.

[21] No production data are available, but Indonesia keeps virtually no stocks.

[22] For instance, the coefficient of variation of commercialized vanilla production in Madagascar stood at 15% between 1961 and 1979, and 41% between 1979 and 1990.

FIGURE 6.2: **Share of World Vanilla Bean Exports in Volume**
(Re-exports excluded)

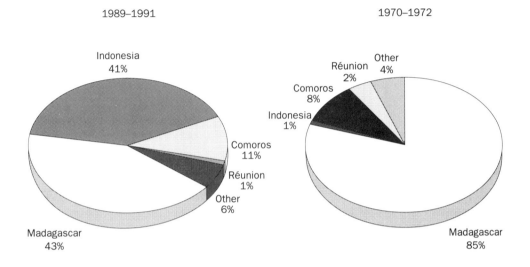

TABLE 6.3: **Characteristics of the International Demand for Vanilla and Relationships with Market Imperfections and Failures**

	Inelastic Aggregate Demand	Highly concentrated Demand	Technical barriers of entry at import (e.g., exclusivity, confidentiality, reliability)	Food Ingredient market characteristics: Technological change, quality, reliability, etc.	Imperfect substitutes
Market Imperfections and Failures:					
1) Limited Competition		X	X		
2) Market Instability	X				
3) Asymmetric Information			X	X	
4) Marketing Externality: —Promotion and Advertising				X	X
—Food Product Research				X	X
—Food Regulations				X	X

valued commodity, combined with a price-inelastic aggregate demand and significant market power by a few supplier countries, provide all the necessary ingredients for a highly unstable market.

Costs of production vary considerably among the three major producing countries. As indicated by Table 6.4, Madagascar is the lowest-cost producer. Its official cost of producing vanilla beans, curing and packing them for export is less than $US 15/kg.; the spread between its official cost and the official FOB price (US$ 74/kg.) is entirely accounted for by export taxes and the stabilization levy. This cost compares favorably with direct competitors, such as Indonesia—whose estimated production costs range from US$ 20/kg. to US$ 35/kg., depending on quality—and Comoros where official costs are the highest (US$ 44/kg.).

Finally, **pricing and trade policies vary markedly** among the three largest producing countries. In Madagascar and Comoros, all domestic prices are officially set by the Government, and exports are subjected to export taxes, particularly steep in the case of Madagascar (82.8% of the FOB price, equivalent to 450% of the official guaranteed export price in 1990). In addition, high export prices and small quotas are set by the *Alliance de la Vanille* or Vanilla Alliance (an informal cartel association created in 1962 which groups Madagascar, Comoros and Réunion as well as the major vanilla dealers from the importing countries). These export prices and quotas are strictly enforced by the Governments of Comoros and Madagascar. By contrast, in Indonesia the vanilla sector is free from any Government interference: no export taxes are being levied, no domestic prices are officially set, and export prices and volumes are the result of market forces.

To summarize, the supply side is characterized by unstable production, largely for natural reasons, and a very small number of countries who enjoy large market power. This, combined with an aggregate price-inelastic demand, provides the necessary conditions for a highly unstable and speculative vanilla market. After having been dominated by Madagascar, the world vanilla market is now characterized by a dual oligopoly situation shared by Madagascar and Indonesia. This dual oligopoly situation is resulting in fierce competition between the Indian Ocean vanilla producers organized as a cartel, dominated by Madagascar and pursuing a monopolistic strategy (high export prices, low export volumes) on the one hand, and Indonesia pursuing an aggressive commercial strategy on the other. The market imperfections

TABLE 6.4: **Cost of Production in Major Producing Countries in 1990/91** (US$/kg.)

	Madagascar[1]	Comoros[2]	Indonesia[3] Low Quality	Indonesia[3] High Quality
Producer Price (Cured vanilla equivalent)	6.17	35.71	13.70	27.50
Curing and Packing Margins	6.91	7.93	6.90	6.90
Total Cost	13.08	43.64	20.60	34.40

[1] Issued from 1990/91 Differentiel; Source: VSF Madagascar.
[2] Issued from 1990/91 Differentiel; Source: Ministry of Agriculture, Comoros.
[3] Industry sources in Bali, 1991.

and failures arising out of the characteristics of world vanilla supply are summarized in Table 6.5.

CHARACTERISTICS OF VANILLA PRODUCTION IN MADAGASCAR AND THE ORGANIZATION OF THE PRIVATE SECTOR

The technical and financial requirements of vanilla bean production have important repercussions on the organization of the vanilla sector in Madagascar, from cultivation to marketing. They give rise to possible market failures and imperfections. Several steps are involved in the production and marketing of vanilla beans which will be reviewed and briefly described below: the green production stage, the curing process, and the packing and exporting stage.

The Green Production Stage

Production of "green" vanilla beans (i.e. freshly harvested and not yet cured) at the farm is characterized by a set of technical and financial requirements which influence the structure and organization of production. These include the following:

1) The cultivation of vanilla bean is **highly labor intensive,** requiring careful crop husbandry. Total labor requirements for a 1 hectare plot have been estimated at 261 man-days during establishment (the first year), and average 460 man-days between year 4 and 8 when the plant reaches full maturity. This includes pollination, weeding, pruning and

TABLE 6.5: **Characteristics of the World Supply for Vanilla and Relationships with Market Failures and Imperfections**

	Technical Barriers to Entry (e.g., agro-climatic requirements)	Unstable Production	Cost Comparative Advantage	Trade & Commercial Policy
Market Imperfections and Failures: 1) Limited Competition	X			
2) Duopoly Market Structure	X		X	X
3) Market Instability	X	X		
4) Market Power	X		X	

harvesting, but hand pollination and harvesting consume a large chunk of the most taxing work.[23]

2) There are relatively **low entry and exit costs at the farm level.** Vanilla vines are grown from cuttings that can be readily propagated. They are grown in rainfed areas with little to no purchased inputs. Vanilla can be successfully inter-cropped with other cash and food crops, thereby diversifying risks, provided appropriate shading is maintained. Given such low entry requirements and minimal fixed costs, a grower can readily enter into vanilla production or switch to other crops. However, because vanilla production requires exacting agro-climatic conditions, its production is often restricted to a limited region within a country.

3) The vanilla vine is a perennial, implying a **supply elasticity smaller in the short-term than the long-term.** The vanilla plant will start producing after 3 years, and reaches its peak production in year 6. Its average longevity is 6 to 8 years, and maximum longevity 10 to 12 years.

---

[23] Hand pollination is extremely labor intensive not only because each flower must pollinated by hand and a single vine may yield 2 to 10 clusters where approximately 10 flowers need to be pollinated, but also because the time for pollination is staggered among flowers. Each vanilla flower opens for a half a day or so, and if not pollinated at that time, no beans will be produced. This requires the cultivator to check and recheck the vines continuously over the three months of flowering. Similarly, harvest takes place over a three month period, requiring daily inspection of the vanilla vines so that the beans can be harvested at the most appropriate time to achieve the highest quality.

It is therefore not surprising to observe that vanilla growing is almost exclusively performed by small-scale farmers in Madagascar. European traders introduced the production of vanilla in Madagascar in 1870, but quickly relied on the more efficient smallholder producers for most of their supplies. The authors are aware of only one vanilla packer-exporter in Madagascar who is still managing a large vanilla plantation using hired labor. In Madagascar, the number of vanilla growers has been estimated at about 60,000 and the area under vanilla at approximately 28,600 hectares in 1989 (0.48 ha per vanilla grower). With a total production estimated at 7,730 tons of green vanilla, it represents an average of about 130 kg. of green vanilla production per vanilla grower. Actual levels of production vary considerably from one grower to another. Vanilla growing is restricted to the northeast coast of Madagascar, primarily around the cities of Antalaha, Sambava, and to a lesser extent Andapa and Vohemar. Insignificant quantities of lower quality vanilla beans are also being produced in the North on the western coast, near Ambanja and on the island of Nosy-Be, as well as further south on the East Coast, closer to the main port of Toamasina.

The Curing Process

Vanilla beans require a **long, complicated curing process.** The curing process is crucial in determining the commercial quality of the cured vanilla bean. When vanilla beans are picked, they are both tasteless and odorless. The flavor and aroma which consumers associate with vanilla develop over several months as a result of the curing process. The curing process is very delicate and requires a great deal of technical skill.[24] The whole curing process takes about three to four months, is fairly labor intensive, and subject to the vagaries of weather. The potential for economies of scale in the curing process is minimal.

---

[24] Curing entails dipping the beans in near-boiling water, then starting an enzymatic reaction by alternate heating and sweating. In Madagascar, this involves boxing the beans, taking them out and exposing them to sunlight, and then re-boxing them. They must be wrapped in blankets with each move. This process is repeated for eight to twenty days until the beans are supple, possess a uniform, dark color, and smell strongly of vanilla. The subsequent step involves slow drying for about 2–3 months by exposure to ambient temperature (usually outdoors), during which the beans loose about two-third of their moisture. A possible alternative technology to the slow, sun drying process consists of the use of hot air dryers. This alternative technology involves placing the vanilla beans on trolleys which transit through a dryer which can be operated continuously. Although this method accelerates and simplifies the curing process, providing scope for economies of scale, it requires larger investments and a reliable source of energy, and quality seems more difficult to control. Only three such dryers exist in Madagascar, and are rarely used. See Theodose (1973) and Bennett & Woods (1992).

The risks involved in the curing process, the technical skills and labor intensity required, the cash outlays for green vanilla which need to be mobilized for three to four months result in some **barriers of entry** at the curing stage, although they remain moderate.

Asymmetric information between the vanilla grower and the curer in charge of the curing process arise because it is at the curing process that the true quality characteristics develop. This creates strong financial incentives for the individual vanilla grower to vertically integrate into the curing process. This incentive is however frustrated by the conflicting labor requirements between growing and curing vanilla that compound otherwise existing barriers of entry at the curing stage. This asymmetric information also creates strong financial incentives for the packer to vertically integrate upstream in the curing process, since the packer also enjoys privileged information about demand requirements (see below).

Only a relatively small share (about 15–25%) of the vanilla beans produced in Madagascar have historically been prepared by the vanilla growers themselves. In fact, vanilla beans are predominantly prepared by the packers (60 to 65%), the balance (15–20%) being prepared by independent curers who have specialized in the business of curing vanilla beans. The actual number of independent curers varies quite significantly from one year to another, following closely the level of green vanilla production (see Table 6.6), strongly suggesting that barriers of entry into the curing activity are indeed relatively minor.

The predominance of packers in the curing activity confirms their strong financial incentives to vertically integrate the curing stage into their packing operation by capturing the rents arising from the presence of asymmetric information at the curing stage and their superior knowledge of market demand. At the time of independence, as a result of the conflicting interests between vanilla growers and packer-exporters under a colonial regime, vanilla grower cooperatives were promoted, and a few were successfully developed. These grower cooperatives were primarily designed to collectively handle the curing process and so overcome the problems of asymmetric information and barriers of entry faced by individual growers in entering the curing business. However, these cooperatives quickly disappeared in the mid-1970s following lack of technical support and important changes in government policies. We will come back later to these policy changes.

TABLE 6.6: **Madagascar Vanilla Entry and Exit at the Curing Stage**

	1986	1989	1990
Production of Vanilla:			
Green (tons)	2650	4147	3569
Commercialized (tons)	695	1681	N.D.
Number of Curers	619	1045	517

NOTE: Commercialized production refers to cured vanilla production purchased by packers.

SOURCE: GNIV.

The Packing and Exporting Stage

Once cured, the vanilla beans need to be sorted, graded, tied in small homogeneous bunches of 250 grammes, wrapped in paraffin paper, packed in small aluminum boxes, and stored to develop their flavor, before they are exported. Throughout storage, vanilla beans require weekly inspection. Madagascar is virtually the only country which provides for the storage of vanilla beans, and the average storage time is about two years. Other producing countries, in particular outside the Indian Ocean, generally export their entire crop and keep no stocks. Packers perform all these functions, including exports; however, not all packers are involved in the export of vanilla beans. The packing process requires a fair amount of technical experience and knowledge about vanilla beans which act as barriers to entry.

Importers of vanilla beans maintain close and permanent contacts with their vanilla suppliers (the packers) which are developed and nurtured over long periods, and a vanilla importer often maintains exclusivity contracts with one or several packers. As suggested earlier, reliability in volume and quality, as well as confidentiality, are vital to developing and maintaining demand for vanilla beans. Hence, the ability to consistently satisfy these requirements is a highly valued and sought-after quality among packers. These close marketing relationships between buyers and packers represent an additional and important **technical barrier to entry** into the packing and exporting business.

Financial requirements and risk also represent another important barrier to entry at the packing stage. They stem in part from the important mobilization of financial resources involved in the buying and the storage of the high-value vanilla beans, and the risks involved in storage (e.g., mold) as well as in the external markets.

The intimate and superior knowledge about demand requirements by the packer provides a further basis for **asymmetric information** between the vanilla packer and the vanilla grower. This gives the packer strong financial incentives to integrate vertically into curing in order to best satisfy his customers and capture associated rents.

Virtually all packers are family-owned and managed businesses, most of which have been involved in the vanilla industry for a long time. Packers are all local Malagasy companies. There have been no foreign-owned companies, or even foreign joint ventures, since the time of independence and subsequent socialist revolution (1972) when all ex-colonial vanilla export companies left Madagascar. For historical reasons, packers of Chinese origin have been particularly active in the vanilla industry, accounting for about a third of all packers. They have the reputation of being among the longest established and most experienced packers. More often than not, vanilla packers are also involved in the export of cloves, coffee and raffia which are also grown in the vanilla region. The number of employees varies by packer depending on their level of stocks, and also throughout the year. Packers have a core of permanent employees who handle their stocks throughout the year and prepare shipments for exports. They also hire large number of temporary employees at the time of the vanilla marketing and curing season, when vanilla beans are being cured, and need to be sorted, graded, and packed. The vanilla industry is by far the largest employer of the vanilla-growing region.

In 1992, there were about forty-five packers almost equally distributed between Sambava and Antalaha, with a few in other towns (e.g., Toamasina, Andapa, Vohemar). There is a great deal of variation in size among packers, as reflected by their respective levels of stocks ranging from about 300 tons to less than a ton (a few packers no longer hold any stocks). Together, the five largest packers hold close to 50% of all vanilla beans stored in Madagascar, indicating a highly concentrated industry at the packing stage. Among the five largest packers, stocks are more equally distributed, each holding between twelve and eight percent of total stocks.

The level of concentration among packers is even greater at the exporting stage which is increasingly dominated by a single packer-exporter. There is also a large instability in the market share of the secondary packer-exporters. Over the period 1985–1990,[25] there were less than fifteen active exporters,

---

[25] Historical data on the distribution of exports by packers were available only for the period 1985–1990.

with 75% of all exports from Madagascar met by only three to six exporters, depending on the year. In 1989/90, among the thirteen active exporters, three firms controlled more than two-thirds of exports. The top packing-export business held an average of 40% of the exported volume from 1985–1990. Its market share seems to be rising, reaching close to 60% in 1988/89 and again in 1992/93. The second ranked firms (the identity of which changed from year to year) generally accounted for a much smaller share, varying between 10 and 14% of total exports. While the top packer-exporter has been successful in maintaining its dominant position on the export market, other packer-exporters are therefore significantly smaller (in terms of market share). Among these smaller packer-exporters, important changes have occurred between 1985 and 1990: the (relatively) larger ones in 1985/86 have become marginalized and supplanted by new packer-exporters who have significantly increased their market shares over the period.

Most of the losers have been packers from the Chinese community which were gradually pushed out of the export business. More than 40% of the active packer-exporters are ethnic Chinese firms. While collectively they exported close to 22% of aggregate exports in 1985/86, this share dropped by a third to less than 14% in 1989/90.[26] Historically, their share was even higher than in 1985. Instead, the gainers appear to benefit from close contacts with Government and the public administration, and the headquarters of these successful packers are often established in Antananarivo, the capital city, located hundreds of miles from the vanilla region. The top packing-export business is a special case. It is part of a much larger business entity which deals with a wide range of import, export and local business activities (motorcycle, car, truck, farm and earth-moving machinery imports, beer brewery, etc.); by contrast, other packer-exporters are largely specialized in agricultural exports (coffee, cloves, raffia). This firm is among the largest one in Madagascar, was originally created by a French settler during colonial times, and has remained within the same family ever since.

While barriers of entry and presence of asymmetric information at the packing stage may explain this pattern of increasing concentration of storage and export activities over time, the policies governing the organization of the vanilla sector in Madagascar have played an even greater role. Before describing the nature and impact of these policies on the vanilla sector, we need

---

[26] The ethnic Chinese share of the market had historically been even higher than 22%.

TABLE 6.7: **Characteristics of Vanilla Production, Curing and Packing and Relationships with Market Failures and Imperfections**

	Farm Level		Curing Level		Packing-Export Level		
	High Labor Intensity	Low Barriers to Entry	Moderate Barrier to Entry	Superior Knowledge About Quality	Technical Barrier to Entry	Financial Barrier to Entry	Superior Knowledge about Demand
Market Imperfections and Failures:							
1) Limited Competition					X	X	
2) Asymmetric Information				X			X

to complete the exposition of the vanilla sector in Madagascar with a brief presentation of the arrangements for raw material procurement.

Raw Material Procurement Arrangements

Two channels of procurement for vanilla beans can be identified: the procurement for green vanilla, and that for cured vanilla. The market for green vanilla is by far the greater one: about 75–85% of all vanilla production is being procured on that market. The procurement for cured vanilla can be further separated into two distinct sub-markets: between the curers and the packers, and between the packers themselves. What distinguishes these two sub-markets is the fact that, in the second, the vanilla beans have already been sorted-out, graded, and conditioned. A schematic representation of the procurement system in Madagascar is given in Figure 6.3.

The Market for Green Vanilla

Historically, about 80% of the green vanilla production has been marketed; the balance being cured by growers themselves. The Government of Madagascar (GOM) officially designates the location of the market places where transactions between vanilla growers and buyers can take place, and also specifies the opening of the marketing season for green vanilla in an effort to prevent the harvesting and marketing of immature beans. Over time, as the next section will explain in further detail, there has been a marked effort on the part of GOM to formally organize and regulate the marketing of green vanilla with the view to improving market transparency, quality of vanilla beans, and equity between growers and buyers.

There is no grading for vanilla beans at the green stage, except for the maturity of the beans since immature beans are not officially allowed to be sold and should be destroyed on the spot. As we will see in the next section, since the early 1960s, the policies governing the market for green vanilla compel the buyers to purchase all the green vanilla that is offered on the market at the minimum and unique (i.e. irrespective of quality) official price. As a result, it is far from clear whether the buyers purchase all the green vanilla, irrespective of its apparent quality, or whether there is some kind of selection process. It is probable that the actual price paid to growers varies according to the quality of the green vanilla, although this possibility is not explicitly recognized by government policy.

Similarly, the extent to which the minimum official price has been effectively applied in the past is not known with certainty. It is likely that the actual price varied depending on the forces of supply and demand, although price controls appeared quite stringent, at least according to the prevailing legal and regulatory framework. Since the mid-1980s, it is clear that the minimum official price has not been paid by the buyers as a result of the increasing excess supply on the domestic market.

To our knowledge, there does not seem to be any formal contractual arrangements for procurement between packers and vanilla growers. It is probable, however, that packers in order to secure reliable supplies and consistency in quality, buy from the same vanilla growers each year, in effect building-up some type of preferential and informal procurement arrangement.

FIGURE 6.3: **Channels of Vanilla Procurement Channels in Madagascar**

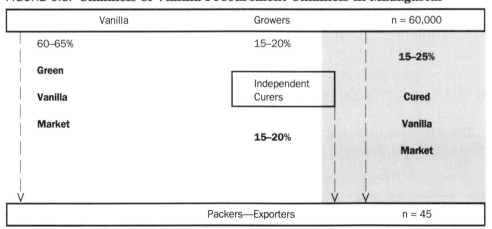

The Market for Cured Vanilla

Two sub-markets for cured vanilla can be identified: between the curers (including the grower-curers) and the packers, and among packers. The market for cured vanilla beans between curers and packers is quite small: only 35% of vanilla production has historically been procured on this market. However, since the mid-1980s, as a result of large disruptions in the vanilla sector, the market for green vanilla has shrunk significantly, increasing the supply of cured vanilla by curers (including grower-curers). These disruptions have indeed compelled packers to purchase and cure much less green vanilla than in the past, hence forcing growers to cure and store their own vanilla in the hope of finding a potential buyer at some later date.

GOM regulates the marketing of cured vanilla beans by officially specifying the location of the markets and the start of the marketing season. GOM also sets a minimum and unique (i.e. irrespective of quality) official price for the cured vanilla. Again, the extent to which this official price has been applied, and whether the actual price has been differentiated by quality, are unknown. Since the mid-1980s, it is clear that the official price for cured vanilla has not been followed and that market forces have been determinant in setting the actual price.

The second market for cured vanilla is between the packers themselves. This market is also regulated by GOM policies. Corresponding transactions are to take place at the officially set price for conditioned and cured vanilla, and to be reported to the existing marketing institutions overseeing the vanilla sector. The size and extent of this market is not well known, but believed to be fairly small, at least until recently. The increasing dominance by a single packer contrasts with the more equal distribution of stocks between packers, and may result in more frequent and greater transactions between the inactive packers and the largest packer.

POLICIES GOVERNING THE ORGANIZATION OF THE VANILLA SECTOR IN MADAGASCAR

A Brief History of Vanilla and Past Policies: Motivation for Policy Changes (1870–1960)

Vanilla has a long history in Madagascar. When Cortez invaded Mexico in the 16th century, the vanilla plant had already been cultivated by indigenous people. It was soon introduced to Europeans who provided an avid market.

Around 1793, the vanilla vine was smuggled from Mexico to the Island of Réunion.[27] Commercial production was undertaken there beginning in the mid-19th century, and introduced to Madagascar in 1870 where it found an ideal location for its development once the riddle of pollination had been solved.[28]

Early this century, vanilla production, cast in the context of a colonial economy, responded vigorously to the strong demand from the metropole, but production and prices were highly unstable. Malagasy production grew from 15 tons to more than 1091 tons in 1929, at which point Madagascar enjoyed an 80% market share of world supply. As incomes fell during the Great Depression, so did demand for this luxury product. In 1933, the colonial government introduced quality grades for vanilla exports to counteract falling quality, overcome marketing externalities and re-ignite demand. During World War II, Indian Ocean producers were cut off from their markets, causing inventories to accumulate. After the war, the government employed price controls and selective destruction of stocks in order to stabilize the market, but these actions fell short of their goal. Intermittent cyclones in the 1950s also impeded cultivation and orderly markets. A Price Support Fund, established by the government in 1953, constituted an initial attempt to enhance the profitability of the vanilla sub-sector, but it failed. Until 1963/64, exports from the Indian Ocean islands of Madagascar, Comoros and Réunion oscillated widely with no discernible trend.[29] Export FOB prices exhibited even larger fluctuations.[30]

Until 1963, the world vanilla market was subjected to great instability which spilled over into the domestic market. To a large extent, this instability can be traced back to the numerous market imperfections and failures characterizing the vanilla market identified in the previous sections. This market instability, combined with the inability of growers, marketers and consumers

---

[27] Réunion was then a French protectorate called Ile de Bourbon. The term Bourbon vanilla was subsequently applied to any vanilla beans grown in Madagascar, Comoros, Réunion.

[28] In Mexico, vanilla flowers are pollinated naturally by bees. When the vanilla vine was smuggled out of Mexico, however, the complementary bee was left behind, making it impossible for vanilla production to develop in other parts of the world until the technique of hand pollination was first discovered (1836) and perfected (1870). It is also interesting to note that the systematic cultivation of vanilla began in Indonesia almost at the same time as it began in Madagascar.

[29] 550 tons in 1953, 350 tons in 1955, 550 tons in 1957, 380 tons in 1960, 700 tons in 1961 and 1962, 500 tons in 1963.

[30] US$ 7/kg. in 1953, US$ 20/kg. in 1954, US$ 9/kg. in early 1956, US$ 30/kg. in 1959, US$ 11/kg. in 1962 and 1963.

to deal with these risks, limited the development of vanilla demand in consumer countries. The world market instability spilled over into the domestic market preventing a steady expansion of production, both in volume and in quality, resulting in recurrent periods of excess supply and conflicts of interests between the packers and the vanilla growers. Since the vanilla sector was operating under a colonial regime until Madagascar gained independence in 1958, equity concerns for the growers were minimal. Growers received low prices and were highly exposed to the instability of the market.

Establishment of an Orderly Market (1960–1973)

Dissatisfied with recurrent market instability, disappointing performance, and an inequitable distribution of the benefits and costs in the vanilla sector, the Government of Madagascar (GOM) intervened soon after independence in the sector's organization. GOM intervention paralleled actions by growers to organize themselves in 1959 in order to counter the dominance of the packers grouped in a cartel. Recognizing the peculiarities of the vanilla sector, GOM attempted in its interventions to reconcile the interests of the various economic agents by organizing a collegial approach to the management of the vanilla sector. Its intervention did not attempt, at first, to do away with the private sector and the operation of the market, nor to by-pass the experienced packer-exporters and foreign buyers. Instead, the GOM attempted to establish the conditions for an orderly market that would continue to rely on the private sector and preserve its role. A series of legislative texts were enacted to establish policy instruments and marketing institutions which were developed in consultation with representatives of Malagasy producers, curers, packers, as well as overseas buyers. It represented a determined effort on the part of the Government to bring order to the vanilla trade, which had been torn by instability and conflicts between producers and traders.

Starting in 1960, the GOM began to establish the legal and regulatory foundations of an orderly vanilla market. This process was eventually completed in 1966 with the creation of the *Groupement National Interprofessionnel de la Vanille* (GNIV), the interprofessional vanilla organization. The legal and regulatory framework sought to: increase the efficiency of the vanilla market by overcoming market failures and imperfections, reduce or eliminate market instability, and achieve a more equitable distribution of the gains from trade between the growers, the curers, the packers and the State. In the following paragraphs, we will review briefly the nature of these market instruments and institutions established between 1960 and 1966, ranging from production to export, that govern the organization and operation of the vanilla sector in Madagascar until today.

Regulations at the Production Stage

The presence of marketing externalities in production (growing, curing and packing stages) have motivated the elaboration, implementation, and enforcement of strict harvesting, curing and conditioning standards in Madagascar. Through a series of legal and regulatory texts, GOM has attempted to overcome the marketing externalities prevailing at the growing stage, mainly by the registration of vanilla growers (valid for three years), the branding of vanilla beans by individual vanilla growers, and the regulation of the marketing season for green vanilla. The registration of vanilla growers enables GOM to control the expansion of vanilla production into regions less favorable for vanilla production, with the view to maintaining high production standards. It also potentially gives the possibility of monitoring and enforcing production standards at the grower level. This possibility does not seem to have been widely used. The branding of vanilla beans[31] together with the regulations on the marketing season for green vanilla also aim at protecting the quality of the crop by preventing immature harvesting and vanilla theft.

Regulations at the Curing Stage

Curers of vanilla beans are also subjected to registration. The registration is associated with several duties; failure to comply with these duties could lead to the withdrawal of the registration card and legal disqualification from performing the curing activities. The main duties are: to follow minimum quality standards in the curing process; not to purchase and cure immature vanilla beans or stolen vanilla; and to comply with the official prices set by the Government. Again, the primary objective of these regulations is to enforce consistency in the curing of the vanilla beans with a view to overcoming the marketing externality at the curing stage. Although a potentially important impediment to competition at the curing stage, registration does not

---

[31] Branding is accomplished with pins stuck in a cork to introduce the grower's distinctive imprint into the bean during the sixth or seventh month of growth. The pin identification remains visible on the surface of the bean at harvest (8–9 months), and even after it has been cured (McCormick & Company 1992).

appear to be binding as suggested by the wide variation in the number of curers from one year to another depending on the level of green vanilla production (see Table 6.6).

Regulations at the Packing-Exporting Stage

Packers-exporters are also subjected to yearly registration by a licensing committee. The licensing committee and procedures (including possible recourse) are described in the supporting legal texts. The licensing committee is composed of representatives from the public administration overseeing the vanilla sector and quality control, the vanilla inter-professional organization (GNIV), the Vanilla Stabilization Fund (VSF), and exporters. The composition of this licensing committee reflects the collegial spirit and cooperative stance between the public administration and the private sector that characterized the early organization of the sector and its corresponding legal and regulatory framework.

The right to perform the packing and exporting operations is accompanied by several obligations with which the packer-exporter must comply. The most important are to: (i) purchase all vanilla beans offered on the domestic market; (ii) store all the purchased vanilla; (iii) submit stocks and exports to quality control by the GOM-run Quality Control Department; (iv) follow minimum standards in the sorting, grading, packing and storing of vanilla beans set by the GNIV; (v) report stocks to the GNIV and the VSF on a bi-weekly basis; (vi) comply with the minimum official prices (for green vanilla, cured vanilla, and cured and conditioned vanilla) set by GOM; and (vii) to follow export instructions from the VSF.

The packer-exporter registration with its assorted privileges and duties, by controlling entry at the packing and exporting stages on the basis of a priori professional standards, clearly intends to limit competition, to ensure and maintain quality, to safeguard the reputation of Madagascar vanilla production and confidence with foreign buyers, as well as to reduce the potential for speculation. This registration has been an effective, albeit rigid, instrument for maintaining high quality standards in the profession.

Regulations of the Green and Cured Vanilla Markets

Strict regulations were also issued on the operation of the domestic markets for green and cured vanilla beans. Official markets are specifically designated by the GOM, and regulations defining and controlling the nature of the transactions on these official markets are issued such as: the start of the marketing season, quality inspection for each market transaction performed by an agent remunerated by the GNIV, sanctioning of buyers (registered curers, packer-exporters, or their agents), method of payment, compliance with the minimum official price, etc. Failures to comply with these market regulations by any economic agent would be pursued by the GNIV, entrusted with the authority to petition the GOM for remedial actions. These market regulations aim at providing order and transparency in domestic transactions as well as promoting quality. They are also necessary to ensure compliance with official prices.

Official Prices in the Domestic Market

All domestic prices are set annually by the GOM and, together, are commonly referred to as the *differentiel* (see Annex Table 6D). This *differentiel* sets all official prices: the producer price for the green vanilla, the producer (and curer) price for the cured vanilla, and the price for cured and packed vanilla (also referred to as the guaranteed export price to the packer-exporter); as a result of this cost-plus pricing system, it also sets all marketing costs and margins in the vanilla sector: from the curer all the way to the point of export. The *differentiel* is officially announced by GOM at the beginning of each marketing season on the basis of the recommendations made by the GNIV.

The original objective was to ensure a certain, stable and remunerative pricing environment at all stages in the domestic vanilla sector and, by the same token, provide the incentives for consistency in production volume and quality.

The Vanilla Stabilization Fund

The Vanilla Stabilization Fund (VSF), a public entity with financial autonomy from the GOM, was legally created in 1961 and replaced the largely ineffective Price Support Fund, with the following operational objectives: (i) to stabilize the producer price; (ii) to elaborate and implement the measures designed to stabilize and promote the development of external markets; and (iii) to execute all programs designed to improve productivity.

The VSF is managed by a committee made-up of GOM-appointed representatives of the Ministries of Finance and Agriculture (two members), the vanilla growers (two members), and the packers (two members). The grower and packer representatives are proposed by their respective professional organizations. Decisions from the managing committee are implemented by the managing director, nominated by the Finance Minister.

To fulfill its first objective, the VSF supports a minimum official producer price (for green and cured vanilla) by (i) paying monthly storage fees to the packers for the storage they are compelled to undertake (on the basis of their bi-weekly storage declarations), and (ii) paying the guaranteed export price to the packer-exporters at the time of exports. Storage financing and guaranteed export pricing by the VSF to the packer-exporters provide the necessary financial counterparts to the latter's obligation to purchase all vanilla produced domestically at the minimum official producer price, to store it, and to export only when authorized to do so by the VSF. The storage policy, financed by the VSF, together with official prices, constitute the central instruments for stabilizing the domestic and external markets.

To achieve its second objective, the VSF, via its Sales Committee (established in 1966), authorizes and controls the exports of vanilla beans by the registered packer-exporters. The Sales Committee is composed of the managing director of the VSF, one representative from the public administration, and two packer representatives nominated by the GNIV. The VSF also finances generic advertising and market promotion campaigns, production, marketing and product research programs in the consuming countries.

It should be noted that, in 1968, Madagascar, Comoros and Réunion, decided to create, in association, Univanille and the Vanilla Information Bureau, two marketing organizations whose purpose was to execute these generic advertising and market promotion campaigns in the major consuming countries (U.S., France and Germany). Univanille and the Vanilla Information Bureau were financed by a cess (e.g., US\$ 1.5/kg. in 1990) to be paid directly by the importers.

To accomplish its third objective, the VSF finances vanilla production research programs in Madagascar, the results of which are disseminated by the Ministry of Agriculture extension agents, also financed by the VSF.

The VSF's own finances derive from a stabilization levy on exports. This stabilization levy is equal to the difference between the actual FOB price, and the sum of the export taxes levied by GOM and the guaranteed export price to the packer-exporter. The proceeds from the stabilization levy accrue to the VSF which uses them to cover its operating costs, the various research and promotion programs, and the storage fees (see Annex Table 6E); in addition, the balance is set aside and saved so that the accumulated savings can be used to guarantee stable prices and an outlet (storage and/or export) for all the domestic production to vanilla growers, curers and packer-exporters in the event that export prices or export volumes fall. In practice, until 1975, it was the packer-exporters who actually paid the stabilization levy out of their export proceeds upon notification by the VSF. By 1989/90, the VSF had accumulated FMG 125 billion (equivalent to about US$ 80 million) of net savings for stabilization purposes.

By assuming all financial risks involved with the storage of vanilla, coupled with the control of all domestic and export prices as well as export volumes, the VSF virtually eliminates all price risks and uncertainty facing the private operators of the vanilla sector in Madagascar.

The Vanilla Inter-Professional Organization (GNIV)

The GNIV, officially created in 1966, is composed of representatives of: vanilla growers, curers and packer-exporters. The GNIV's role is to: ensure that all market transactions are performed according to the official rules (quality, official prices, etc.), to elaborate and submit each year a new set of official prices and storage fee schedules to the GOM for its approval, to represent and defend the interests of the sector with the GOM, and to assist the GOM in its conduct of vanilla sector policies. The operations of the GNIV are financed by a fee levied at the time of exports, and paid out by the VSF. The GNIV, expression of the private sector, was intended to play an important and complementary role in the collective management of the vanilla sector.

The Vanilla Alliance and the Export Marketing Arrangements

A third marketing institution was created in 1962 to handle marketing arrangements on the world market. Its mandate is to provide for additional stability on the external market by establishing quotas and prices. The Vanilla Alliance holds meetings at least once a year, between representatives from the three Indian Ocean producing countries (Madagascar, Comoros and Réunion) and selected dealers/importers of vanilla beans. During those meetings, marketing plans for the coming marketing year are established which (see Annex Table 6F): (i) distribute export quotas among the three exporting countries, (ii) distribute import quotas among the vanilla dealers, and (iii) set an official FOB price for vanilla.

Besides setting country-specific export and import quotas, the Vanilla Alliance also voluntarily restricts the number of dealers/importers in an effort to provide for increased stability and confidence between exporters and importers. The marketing plans are explicitly intended to provide for increased stability in the export market by ensuring world buyers that their needs will be satisfied at a known and stable price. Initially, not all parties involved seemed to agree to the need for such drastic measures in order to provide for market stability and renewed confidence between exporters and importers, in particular in view of their own domestic anti-trust regulations.[32]

As in any cartel organization, these marketing plans have no legal value and cannot be enforced, and consequently free-riding abounds. This is confirmed by the fact that, at the time of sharp excess-demand such as that experienced in the late 1970s–early 1980s (as a result of devastating cyclones in the producing countries), exporting countries could not respect their export quotas and vanilla export prices sky-rocketed to more than US\$ 100/kg. In fact, the 1979/80 marketing plan was actually canceled, and not re-introduced until the 1981/82 marketing plan. Similarly, importers often do not purchase all their import quotas, in particular since the mid-1980s as a result of increased production and competition from Indonesia.

Despite its obvious shortcomings, the Vanilla Alliance has been a powerful instrument for providing stability in the world vanilla market at the risk, however, of inflexibility. The Vanilla Alliance was also instrumental in the development and implementation of export grading standards consistent across the three exporting countries. Following an agreement reached by the Vanilla Alliance, shipments do not need to be composed of a single grade; they can be composed of different grades according to pre-specified rules.[33]

In Madagascar, the realization of the Vanilla Alliance marketing plan was supervised nominally by the VSF, at least until 1973–75. Once the Madagascar export quota is established, the private sector takes the lead in exporting. In fact, the private sector may be said to enter the picture even before the Vanilla Alliance acts, because it is the packer-exporters themselves who make the initial contacts with counterparts overseas. This outreach occurs within the regular conduct of business, as Malagasy export companies enjoy long-

---

[32] It is apparent that importers in the United States did not wish to be held to strict allocations set by the Vanilla Alliance. According to an unclassified cable from the Department of State, Tananarive office (June 17, 1965), members of the Vanilla Bean Association of America proposed a system of increased flexibility to their African partners, but Malagasy officials were averse to unlimited exports.

[33] For example, an export shipment of "second-quality and below" is composed of 25% second quality and whole, 25% third quality and whole, 25% fourth quality whole, 20% fourth quality split, and 5% cuts.

standing relationships with importers to whom they sell year after year. Although the packer-exporter is the active marketing partner, the VSF has the last word regarding exports. For example, exporters negotiate directly with buyers for contracts, which must then be approved by VSF (the application is officially passed through regional offices of the GNIV, but this has been merely a formality since 1974).

SUMMARY: The above described policy instruments, market regulations and marketing institutions were explicitly designed by GOM to overcome the market failures and imperfections characterizing the vanilla market through to the early 1960s. Table 6.8 indicates which policy instruments and marketing institutions were developed to attempt to overcome the most important problems.

This sector framework is clearly authoritarian, rigid and heavily biased towards direct government intervention in the sector rather than relying on more market-based instruments, in particular with regard to both internal and external trade policies, the allocation of the export quotas among the packer-exporters, and the setting of import quotas among individual importers. It is a powerful instrument for managing Madagascar's market power. However, it is prone to promote a myopic management of the vanilla sector by the GOM, and in the process undermine the effectiveness of the overall sectoral organization in meeting its initial objectives. Because of its lack of transparency and absence of a market-based mechanism for distributing the annual export quotas among packer-exporters, this framework is prone to promote rent-seeking activities by exporters. Similarly, the lack of transparency or a market-based mechanism for setting the import quota among individual importers is prone to lead to rent-seeking activities by the public officials in charge of annual negotiations of the marketing plans. An additional and important weakness of the vanilla sector framework stems from the very limited role granted to GNIV in the management of the collective marketing institutions. By remaining unconnected from the reality of the world market and lacking the appropriate channels of information, the GNIV cannot be an effective countervailing power to that of the Government in the management of the sector. Nor can the GNIV be an effective institution for resolving efficiently and equitably the conflicting interests between the growers and the packers.

Despite these weaknesses, the overall vanilla sector framework provided, at least initially, for an important role for the private sector, not only in the

TABLE 6.8: Policy Instruments and Marketing Institutions to Counter Market Imperfections and Failures

	Regulations at		Domestic Market Regulations	Official Domestic Prices	Vanilla Stabilization Fund				Vanilla Alliance		
	Growing, Curing & Packing	Grading Standards at Export			Storage Policy	Marketing Programs	R&D	GNIV	Export Price	Export Quota	Designated Buyers
Market Imperfections and Failures:											
1) Limited Competition				X							
2) Duopoly Market Structure									X	X	X
3) Market Power					X				X	X	X
4) Market Instability				X	X				X	X	X
5) Assymmetric Information		X	X	X							
6) Marketing Externality:											
—Transaction Costs	X	X	X								
—At Production Level	X		X				X				
—Promotion & Advertising						X	X				
—Food Product Research						X		X			
—Food Regulations						X					
Equity Considerations				X							

physical handling of all vanilla-related operations from the farm to the point of exports, but also in the commercial relationships with external buyers, as well as in the collegial management of the marketing institutions (GNIV, VSF, and even the Vanilla Alliance) and instruments (*differentiel*, storage fee, commercial and trade policy, quality standards) governing the vanilla sector. In addition, despite an already dominant position on the world market, Madagascar through the Vanilla Alliance did not exploit its monopoly powers unduly by exacting a high price on the world vanilla market. Instead, it used its monopoly power to build-up confidence and trust with its few selected buyers; to reduce uncertainty by elaborating with them (and Comoros and Réunion) yearly marketing plans with the view to satisfying their needs at a pre-announced and stable export price; to build-up, maintain and finance important stocks (about a year worth of production, or 1,000 tons) with the view to discouraging speculation and preventing supply shortages in the event of production shortfalls. As we will see in the next section, this framework for collective action and a cooperative stance between the public and the private sector was extremely successful in promoting quality in production and growth in external demand, in triggering a formidable expansion of vanilla exports from Madagascar, as well as in distributing fairly the gains from trade between the growers, the packers and the State. Before turning to the analysis of the performance of the vanilla sector, we need to briefly describe the important policy changes that took place in the management of the vanilla sector, and the underlying reasons for these changes.

From Orderly Market Organization to Perverse Government Control: 1975–1992

Important policy changes in the vanilla sector started to take place in 1975 which perversely affected its performance, and were foremost in causing Madagascar's rapid loss of competitiveness on the world vanilla market and dismal performance since the mid-1980s. To a large extent, these changes have been triggered by events, political and macroeconomic, that are largely exogenous to the vanilla sector. However, the internal weaknesses and inconsistencies of the (internal and external) trade policies and marketing institutions have facilitated, if not precipitated, these changes.

It is important to underscore from the outset that between 1975 and 1992, minimal changes have been made to the legal and regulatory framework and to the (internal and external) trade policies governing the vanilla sector. What changed dramatically, however, was the selective interpretation and use which was made of the policy instruments and marketing institutions by the GOM over time. This points at the structural weaknesses of the vanilla policy framework, in particular the lack of flexibility and market-based mechanisms in the trade policy instruments, and the limited involvement of the GNIV in the management of collective actions by the marketing institutions, which could have provided a safeguard against perverse intervention either by Government or individual private sector agents. Three major changes were implemented which transformed a sectoral organization predicated on the long term goals of achieving economic efficiency and equity in the sector, to one that was predicated on the short term goals of surplus extraction from both producers and consumers.

Progressive Crowding-out of the Private Sector

The private sector was progressively marginalized, and its collective role in the management of the sector virtually disappeared. Starting in 1975, the GNIV became progressively defunct in its policy advisory role to the GOM; its recommendations with regard to the official prices and storage fee schedules were progressively ignored by GOM; the export levy financing the GNIV remained unchanged in nominal terms, and payments came increasingly late if ever, starving the GNIV of resources. Instead, the GNIV became a simple extension of the GOM apparatus for distributing growers' registration cards and other similar administrative functions. The management and strict quality and price controls of the official domestic markets by the GNIV were abandoned, and replaced by administrative and nominal controls performed by local administration officials.

Between 1975 and 1982, the Vanilla Stabilization Fund lost entirely its financial and management independence from the GOM, becoming a mere extension of the Ministry of Commerce which was overseeing all external trade operations. By contrast with the pre-1973 period, export quotas are now rigidly allocated by the GOM in an increasingly non-transparent manner, and this is confirmed by the abolition of the Sales Committee in 1982. It was during the 1980s that the concentration of exports among fewer exporters and, eventually, the dominance by a single packer-exporter took place. Similarly, the private sector as a group played a lesser role in the annual preparation and discussions of the Vanilla Alliance marketing plans, which become increasingly dominated by GOM representatives. The above noted weaknesses of the trade regime and marketing institutions, together with its resulting incentives, played a large part in this concentration of exports among a few packer-exporters, with the collusion of the GOM.

To some extent, the socialist revolution explains the increasing reluctance of the new GOM to share its prerogatives with a poorly trusted private sector, in particular the packer-exporters. Surprisingly, even the vanilla grower co-operatives which had been actively promoted by the earlier administration, were also marginalized and quickly disappeared.

Macroeconomic events also explain these important policy changes, and their acceleration in the early 1980s. In 1975, the GOM import-substitution, public sector-led industrialization development strategy required important public financial resources. The vanilla sector, as well as other traditional exports (coffee, cloves), became obvious targets for nationalization. In the case of vanilla, however, the GOM did not proceed with the nationalization of the packer-exporters. It did not need to, since the already established marketing institutions (the VSF, the GNIV, the Vanilla Alliance) and instruments simply needed to be brought under its tighter and exclusive control to achieve the same goals. In the early 1980s, as a result of the financial, foreign exchange and macroeconomic crisis unfolding in Madagascar, further financial and management control of the VSF by the GOM was implemented. In particular, in 1982, the GOM instituted a new system whereby the nationalized commercial banks distributed the proceeds from vanilla exports between the VSF (by crediting it with the stabilization levy), the packer-exporters (by paying them the guaranteed export prices), and the exchequer (corresponding to the export taxes); this completed the total loss of financial and management autonomy by the VSF. This loss is best exemplified by its inability to fulfill its financial obligations, in particular the payment of the monthly storage fees to the packers since January 1990 despite (nominal) accumulated financial surpluses amounting to at least FMG 125 billion in 1989/90, and a (nominal) budget amply covering the estimated storage expenditures.

Since the mid-1980s, following a stabilization program, Madagascar has embarked on a program of structural adjustments, liberalizing its domestic and external trade, lowering its import tariffs, and gradually lowering and eventually abolishing all export taxes, including coffee and cloves export taxes in 1992. The vanilla sector, however, has remained untouched by these structural reforms: GOM continues to set all domestic and export prices, export taxation is persistently high, and export quotas are still set and allocated by the GOM.

Increasing Domestic Taxation

Since 1975, the GOM has increased dramatically its taxation of the vanilla sector. This was done in two complementary ways: by explicitly levying new and additional export taxes (e.g., in 1977 and again in 1985), and in 1982 by implicitly absorbing the annual revenues generated by the stabilization levy as well as the operating surpluses accumulated by the VSF into the GOM budgetary revenues. In other words, the stabilization mechanism increasingly became a pure instrument of taxation rather than stabilization. As soon as the accumulated surpluses were controlled and absorbed by the GOM, the VSF effectively ceased to provide any stabilization function.

The share of overall taxation in the actual export price (i.e. combining both explicit export taxes and implicit export taxes accruing from the stabilization levy) increased from 45% in 1975 to 82% in 1989 and 1990 (see Annex Table 6D and Figure 6.4).

Reflecting the increasing weight of taxation, vanilla growers and packers have seen their share of the actual export price drop sharply. While vanilla growers still received a third of the actual export price in 1975, they only received (officially) about 8% of the actual export price in 1990. In practice,

FIGURE 6.4: **Evolution of the Vanilla FOB Price and its Distribution**

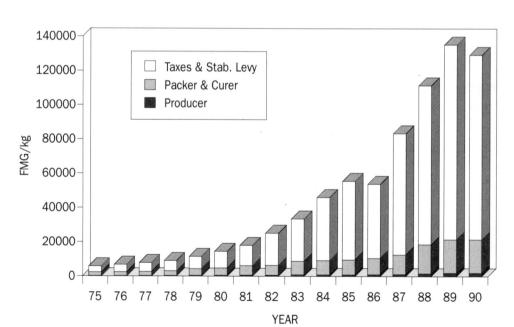

FIGURE 6.5: **Evolution of the Official Producer Price and Packing-curing Margins in Real Terms**

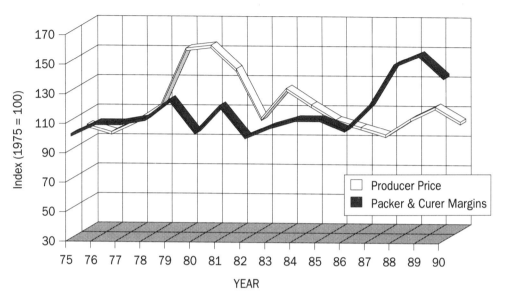

vanilla growers in 1990 were receiving a still lower price for their vanilla beans. Similarly, while packers-exporters received 27% of the actual export price in 1975, their share plummeted to less than 10% in 1990. In practice, most packers did not even receive this price since the overwhelming majority of them were not allowed to export; they only received the monthly storage fees, at least until January 1990 when the GOM ceased to make the monthly payments. It is interesting to note that vanilla growers were even more discriminated against than packers. Producer prices in real terms remained constant between 1975 and 1990,[34] while packers' margins increased by 40% over the same period (see Figure 6.5 and Annex Table 6G). Clearly, the objective of the stabilization fund had evolved from providing stable producer prices to providing stable **and** low producer prices. The stabilization fund had become a powerful instrument of agricultural taxation.

---

[34] The official producer price improved significantly between 1979 and 1981, a period when vanilla was in short supply on the world market (vanilla was then traded on the world market at about US$ 100/kg.).

Monopoly Rent Extraction from the External Market

As illustrated by Figure 6.4, GOM made increasing use of its monopoly power on the world market and extracted large monopoly rents. The official export price, established for each marketing plan by the Vanilla Alliance, was first kept basically constant at about US$ 10/kg. between 1963/64 (the first such marketing plan) and the 1974/75 marketing plan, Madagascar making little use of its already existing monopoly power on the world vanilla market. Between the 1974/75 and the 1978/79 marketing plans, the official export price jumped from US$ 14.50/kg. to US$ 30/kg., a 100% increase in only four years. By the 1984/85 marketing plan, the official export price was further increased to US$ 70/kg., a 133% jump in six years. By the 1989/90 marketing plan, the official export price had reached US$ 74/kg. level, where it has stabilized since.

As illustrated by Figure 6.4 and all of the successive increases in taxation (multiple export taxes and stabilization levy) by Madagascar were passed on into higher export prices, made possible by its monopoly position. The rate of overall taxation jumped from 45% of the actual export price in 1975 to 82% in 1990. This policy was highly successful: Madagascar vanilla exports in value terms more than quadrupled in a decade, jumping from about US$ 20 million in the mid-1970s, to close to US$ 90 million in 1987, its highest level ever reached (see Figure 6.6 and Annex Table 6H). Most if not all of these rents accrued to the Government in the form of (gross) overall revenues, either as export taxes or stabilization levy, increasing by 700% in real terms over the same period, from about FMG 1 billion in 1975 to FMG 70 billion in 1990.

PERFORMANCE OF THE VANILLA SECTOR: IMPACTS OF SECTORAL POLICIES

The Vanilla Export Boom: 1960–1975

After 1960, the vanilla sector entered a "take-off" period, with Madagascar vanilla export volumes increasing fivefold between 1960 and 1974. The progression was steady, growing from 270 tons in 1960 to close to 1400 tons in 1973, even reaching a historical maximum of 1700 tons in 1977. Total value of vanilla exports tripled between 1960 and 1974, increasing from US$ 6.70 million in 1960 to US$ 20 million in 1974, and reaching US$ 35 million in 1977.

FIGURE 6.6: **Madagascar Vanilla Exports in Value** (US$ Million)

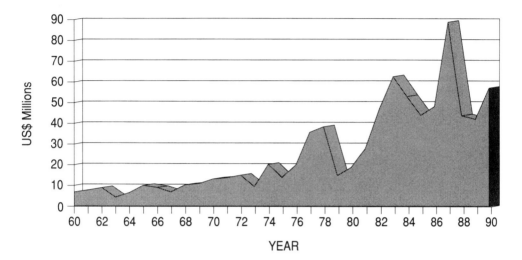

The sectoral organization instituted by GOM, despite its weaknesses, was therefore successful in overcoming some of the major market imperfections and failures which hindered the development of the vanilla market. Reliability and consistency in volume and quality provided the needed incentive for demand in the consuming countries to expand. Complementary programs of generic advertising and market promotion (e.g., a vanilla label was created and developed on both the U.S. and European markets during that period), as well as lobbying efforts to elaborate and adjust food and extract regulations were simultaneously launched in the major consuming countries (U.S., France, Germany) with obvious and positive results on the consumption side. Total world demand increased steadily from 1500 tons in 1965 to 2700 tons in 1977; Madagascar was also successful in establishing itself as the quality standard on the world market, building a positive brand image and reputation for providing high and consistent quality to its clients, which enabled it to maintain a dominant share of the expanding world market (75% on average between 1965 and 1975, even reaching 87% in 1971 and 1972).

On the domestic market, the sectoral policies were also successful since Madagascar was clearly able to respond to an increasing demand without jeopardizing its quality standards. It was also successful in extending the gains from trade to the vanilla growers. As suggested by the almost equal share of the export price between growers, packers and GOM/VSF in 1975

FIGURE 6.7: **Madagascar Vanilla Exports in Volume** (Tons)

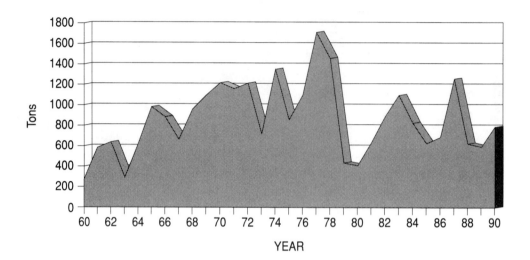

(33.3%, 27.4% and 39.4%, respectively), an equitable distribution of income seemed to have been achieved. In addition to being equitable, results also suggest that the distribution was also economically efficient since vanilla growers responded positively: in terms of increased levels of production, but also in terms of maintained high quality production. The latter suggests that the more equitable distribution of income may have helped lessen the inefficiencies resulting from asymmetric information between the growers and packers; other interventions may have also contributed to lessening these inefficiencies, such as the extensive market regulations designed to promote and enforce quality standards, and the extension efforts undertaken at the growers' level; the extent to which the promotion and training aspects were more effective than the regulations and enforcement remains difficult to ascertain.

Efficiency and Equity Losses: 1975–1992

The policy changes initiated since 1975 triggered dramatic reactions on the world market, both on the demand and the supply side, which eventually percolated into the domestic sector only to result in a full-blown crisis of the vanilla sector. The costs, both on efficiency and equity grounds, were extremely large, which Madagascar, the tenth poorest country in the world, could ill-afford.

Efficiency Losses on the External Market

On the external market, the policy changes induced an extreme loss of competitiveness for the Malagasy vanilla. As illustrated by Figure 6.8, reactions on the world market to the monopoly and inflexible pricing strategy (FOB prices are indicated by the solid line in Figure 6.8) pursued by Madagascar since the mid-1970s, throughout the 80s and until 1993, were swift. Although Madagascar supplied 87% of the world vanilla market in 1971, its market share was reduced by more than half to only 31% in 1991. Export volumes fell dramatically from its historical maximum of 1700 tons in 1977 to only 640 tons in 1991. This spectacular fall in market share and in export volume was for a long time masked by the equally dramatic progression in export earnings caused by the steadily escalating export prices through the mid-1980s. Notwithstanding the spike in export receipts in 1987, vanilla export earnings (in nominal terms) reached their maximum as early as 1983 and declined ever since. Export earnings in 1991 and 1992 are no higher (in nominal terms) than they were ten years earlier.

Reactions from the Supply Side

Competitors were fairly quick in their reactions given the relatively low short-term elasticity characterizing vanilla production, and the natural, agro-cli-

FIGURE 6.8: **Vanilla Export Performance**

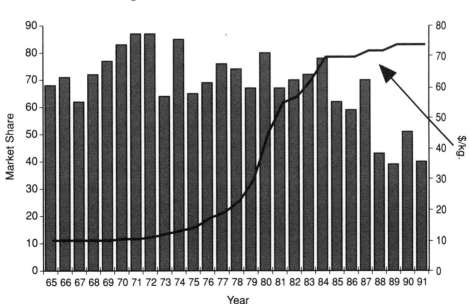

matic constraints on it. The major gainer was Indonesia whose total exports jumped from 80 tons in 1980 to 666 tons in 1991, becoming the world largest exporter in 1989 and again since 1991. It is interesting to note that Indonesia's exports had already progressed in the second-half of the 1970s but collapsed in 1979 (17 tons) and 1980 (80 tons), most probably as a result of a production crisis. This suggests that the international price and market stability introduced by the Vanilla Alliance since the first marketing plan of 1963/64 benefited other non-Vanilla Alliance producing countries as well, prompting them to increase their own production. The marketing policy pursued by the Vanilla Alliance (pre-announced quotas and prices, stability) permitted Indonesia to plan production levels, develop a marketing strategy, and estimate revenues. Indonesia seized the opportunity to implement an aggressive commercial strategy based on under-cutting the price of Bourbon vanilla. The high pricing policy pursued by Madagascar since the mid-70s increased even further the incentives for Indonesia to expand its production, accelerating Madagascar's decline.

The marketing strategy pursued by Indonesia on the world market is important to detail because it carries important implications for the future of Madagascar's vanilla exports. Indonesia's marketing strategy consisted of the following elements: (1) growth in production, (2) progressive and selective extension of geographic coverage by first entering the U.S. market followed by the European market; (3) progressive improvement in quality; (4) market segmentation by price, according to quality and country; and (5) distribution through a large number of buyers without quota. Following this marketing strategy, Indonesia first targeted the U.S. market where, as a result of favorable extract regulations, low quality vanilla beans could easily enter the market and where price competition was promoted. As indicated earlier, Indonesia progressively took the necessary technical and organizational measures on its domestic market to start improving the quality of its vanilla beans, and gradually moved up-scale within the U.S. market segments, as well as eventually into the European market where high quality (high vanillin content) imposed by the extract regulations constituted an important barrier to entry and to competition. As illustrated by Annex Table 6C and Figure 6.9, Indonesian vanilla exports concentrated first on the U.S. market, where it became the largest exporter since 1989; Indonesia started to export to the German market in 1984, and to the French market in 1986, its market share rapidly expanding over time in these two countries.

FIGURE 6.9: **Evolution of U.S. Market Shares**

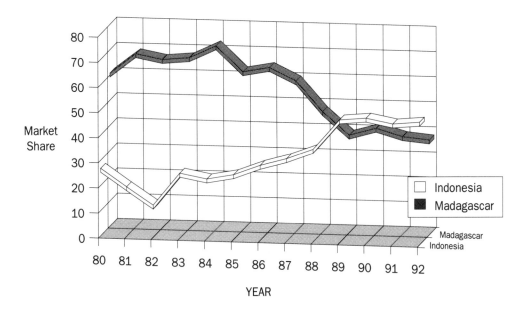

As a result of Indonesia's ability to gradually satisfy increasing quantities of the many quality segments of the vanilla market in the main consuming countries, Madagascar is not only losing its overall market share. It is also becoming a residual exporter which no longer enjoys a monopoly position on the world market. Its exports are now only confined to the highest quality segments of the world market: Madagascar can now only export its highest quality beans (longer than 14 cm in length) at the request of its buyers, whereas it used to be able to export all its grades, including the vanilla beans below 14 cm and even its cuts. Even within these highest quality segments, Madagascar faces increasing competition from Indonesia which will continue to expand as long as Madagascar does not modify its own export trade policy. Madagascar has until now been able to maintain a hand in world trade due to constraints on Indonesia's production capacities and in improving its production and curing capabilities (the same market failures Madagascar had been facing). Thus, unless it changes its commercial strategy, Madagascar's export future in vanilla increasingly depends on the climatic uncertainties and other production shortfalls in Indonesia, and Indonesia's difficulties in overcoming its supply problems.

REACTIONS FROM THE DEMAND SIDE. In addition to the above reactions on the supply side, Madagascan policy also triggered significant reactions on the demand side. The first and obvious reaction on the demand side was to induce a change in the consumption patterns away from Bourbon vanilla and towards Indonesian vanilla. This is extremely damaging for Madagascar's future since it implies that Madagascar has lost its quality edge, no longer being the standard of reference in a market where quality considerations are paramount. The demand for vanilla faced by Madagascar has therefore become increasingly price-elastic over time as well as subject to price competition by Indonesia, making its monopolistic policy even more incongruous.

In addition to triggering lasting changes to the shape of its individual vanilla demand curve, Madagascar's monopolistic and inflexible policy has also accelerated, or at least facilitated, the development of vanilla substitutes (synthetic vanillin, vanilla with other natiral flavors, and bio-technology products). The development of these substitutes in the course of the 1980s may have resulted in reducing the aggregate demand for natural vanilla, as well as in making the aggregate demand for vanilla more price-elastic.

Recent econometric estimation[35] of the vanilla demand curves faced by Madagascar and Indonesia would appear to confirm the increasing price-elasticity of the demand faced by Madagascar, as well as the greater substitutability and competition from Indonesia vanilla. The econometric results suggest that, for the individual demand curve faced by Madagascar, the own-price elasticity is becoming larger (in absolute value) over time, jumping from –0.0477 in 1974 to –0.954 in 1986, and becoming larger than unity by 1988; the cross-price elasticity of Indonesia vanilla also increases over time, from 0.096 in 1966 to 2.88 in 1996. The econometric estimation of the individual demand curve faced by Indonesia indicates an own-price elasticity of –0.071 in 1966 and of –2.13 in 1996, becoming larger than unity by 1981; and a cross-price elasticity of Madagascar vanilla equal to 0.09 in 1966 and to 2.7 in 1996.

Efficiency Losses on the Domestic Market

Madagascar's loss of competitiveness on the world market is also having important efficiency repercussions on the domestic market: export earnings are falling, the domestic stabilization mechanism has collapsed, yields from va-

---

[35] See de Melo, Olarreaga & Takacs (forthcoming).

nilla taxation are plummeting, the framework for safeguarding quality has disappeared, and the domestic sector is now being dominated by a single packer-exporter.

FALLING EXPORT EARNINGS. The fall in export earnings is even more damaging to Madagascar in that, following the successive collapse of the clove and coffee markets during the 1980s (its former two main exports), vanilla has become its largest export earner. Except for shrimp, non-traditional exports do not yet represent a viable alternative until major efforts are made by Madagascar to rehabilitate its basic infrastructure and to attract foreign investments.

COLLAPSE OF THE STABILIZATION SCHEME. While exports dwindled, domestic production remained high as a result of the stabilization scheme which, by maintaining a low but stable producer price, sheltered domestic producers and packers from the lack of performance on the world market. This excess-supply naturally resulted in an impressive stock build-up throughout the 1980s, reaching close to 4,000 tons in 1992 (see Figure 6.10) at enormous financial costs to the Vanilla Stabilization Fund and the exchequer (see Annex Table 6I).

Escalating stocks imply huge financial outlays for the VSF, whose mandate is to pay storage fees to the packers. Storage costs exploded from FMG 10 million in 1979/80 to more than FMG 9 billion in 1989/90, a 17,860% increase in real terms in only ten years, accounting for an ever increasing share of the VSF operating budget. Eventually, the system collapsed in January 1990, when the GOM simply ceased to make any further monthly storage fee payments to the packers. From that point on, free market forces fully resumed their course on the domestic market, and actual prices to the growers dropped dramatically (to, at best, less than 50% of the official price).

The FMG 125 billion accumulated surpluses by the VSF until 1989/90 had long been spent, and the GOM was financially unable to face its contractual obligations with the packers as well as the vanilla growers who had been financing the VSF since its inception. By 1990, the vanilla stabilization scheme had therefore ceased to perform the functions for which it was initially mandated (guaranteed price and market/storage outlet), although it continued to restrict exports and to levy a 50% stabilization tax on vanilla growers.

Even before its financial collapse in 1990, the VSF was unable to provide for stability on the domestic market throughout the 1980s. The increasing gap between export and production levels implied that fewer packers were permitted by GOM to export. Packers became increasingly dissatisfied with their inability to export and therefore to receive the guaranteed export price for their vanilla. For the large majority of packers who could no longer export, their only source of income became restricted to the monthly storage fees only. This increased the pressure for illegal exports,[36] leading in turn to more coercive measures by GOM to maintain its monopolistic strategy on the world market, as well as to increasing instability and disruptions on the world market. Packers who could no longer export faced increasing financial constraints from the commercial banks, and had no choice but to reduce and adjust their level of purchases to the level of credit they were able to obtain. Increasingly, a situation of excess-supply developed on the domestic market and domestic prices adjusted downward accordingly, the packers no longer complying with official prices. Vanilla purchases by packers became increasingly erratic as Figure 6.10 clearly illustrates (the coefficient of variation, an indicator of instability, in the volume of officially commercialized production jumped from 15% over the period 1961–1979, to 41% over the period 1979–89). The VSF attempted to remedy the situation by buying back about 800 tons from packers in 1986/87, but the solution was short-lived since it did not address the root cause of the problem, namely the loss of external competitiveness.

FALLING YIELDS FROM VANILLA TAXATION. In addition to the above efficiency costs, vanilla taxation is also becoming less and less attractive for the GOM. The explosion in the costs of the stabilization scheme associated with storage costs means that the net returns and yields from the taxation imposed on the vanilla sector are falling rapidly. While taxation yields were as high as 91% in 1983, they had fallen to 54% in 1990. In real terms, the net returns to the GOM from the vanilla taxation system were no larger in 1989 and 1990 than they were in 1983. The financial implications for the GOM are significant since vanilla taxation represents its single largest source of revenues: 14% of total budgetary revenues in 1989, but only 8.8% in net terms once the costs of the stabilization scheme were deducted. This helps explaining why the GOM ceased all storage fee payments since 1990.

---

[36] See in Annex Table 6H the gap between theoretical stocks and officially reported stocks.

FIGURE 6.10: **Escalating Stock Levels**

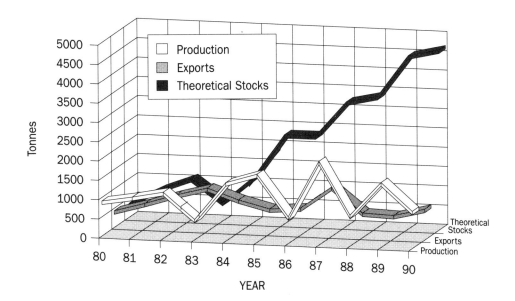

DISINTEGRATION OF THE SECTORAL ORGANIZATION. The disappearance of both a guaranteed price and a guaranteed outlet, combined with that of any quality control and enforcement (for domestic markets as well as for curing and storage practices and even at export) led to a total collapse of the sectoral organization designed to maintain high quality standards at all levels in the sector. Independent curers and even sometimes packers can no longer afford the neccesary material to ensure quality curing; agricultural extension services are no longer being provided to growers, no new planting material is being introduced to rejuvenate the vanilla vines. Quality is therefore deteriorating and consistency in quality can no longer be maintained, making it increasingly difficult for Madagascar to satisfy the needs of the high quality segment of the world market it has restricted itself to. The development of illicit exports, more often than not of poor quality, also undermines the confidence of foreign buyers by damaging the reputation of Madagascar.

DOMINANCE BY A SINGLE PACKER-EXPORTER. An additional loss of efficiency results from the fall in exports. Rather than sharing more equally the shrinking export volumes among packers in order to maintain a semblance of competition within the private sector, GOM instead has promoted the concentration of the domestic vanilla sector into the hands of a single packer-exporter, effectively supporting the creation of a monopsonist[37] who is at the same time a monopolist.[38] This concentration does not result solely from a vastly superior technical efficiency on his part. Instead it is consistent with the lack of transparency and perverse incentives inherent in the trade policies which result in a collusive behavior between the large exporter(s) and GOM. As a result of such a privileged position, efficiency losses for the sector are potentially large since the monopsonist can extract huge rents from the vanilla growers. Additional efficiency losses may also result for Madagascar if the monopolist-monopsonist uses its dominant position to capture rents from the external market which would otherwise accrue to the State/VSF as taxation revenues.

Equity Losses on the Domestic Market

In addition to the above efficiency losses, the disintegration of the vanilla sector organization in Madagascar also carries important equity implications. Clearly, the vanilla growers have suffered the most from a system which was originally designed to protect them from market imperfections and failures. They paid a high price to finance the VSF by accepting a small and declining share of the value of their production, and received no return from their investment. The VSF has virtually ceased to exist, no longer able to guarantee a minimum price and a market outlet for their production. For example, in 1992, in a desperate political effort to defuse the mounting social and economic crisis in the vanilla growing region, GOM almost doubled the official producer price without taking the other necessary steps to make that price effective (e.g., paying the overdue storage fees, radically changing its commercial policy on the world market in order to boost exports and reduce the excess supply on the domestic market). At the same time, GOM announced unilaterally that, from now on, only vanilla beans of at least 14 cm in length will be "supported" by the VSF, introducing new restrictions which never existed before.

Despite the high taxation levels extracted by the GOM from the vanilla region, little was ever plowed back into the region. The vanilla region, despite

---

[37] A single buyer of green and cured vanilla on the domestic market.
[38] A single exporter of vanilla on the world market.

its wealth and agricultural potential, is virtually isolated from the rest of the country; there are no operating phones, little in terms of public services, and local roads are in extremely poor conditions; the only possible means of communication are either by boat or plane.[39]

The current dominance of the vanilla sector by a single packer-exporter also carries important equity implications, besides the welfare costs imposed on vanilla growers by the virtual monopsonistic structure of the domestic vanilla sector. The interests of the dominant single packer-exporter are now at odds with the interests of the sector as a whole. It is in the economic interest of the dominant packer-exporter to pursue an inflexible monopolist commercial strategy on the world market, to maximize and capture rents (from both the external and domestic markets) in the short-to-medium-term, investing the profits in other activities. Instead, it is in the economic interests of the sector as a whole to radically change its commercial policy on the world market, in order to re-establish the conditions for a *sustainable* source of revenues and income.

CONCLUSION

More often than not, market failures and imperfections pervade agricultural markets. The vanilla case study provides such an illustration. There are multiple solutions for dealing with such market failures and imperfections, which were presented in a more general context in Chapter II. The respective outcome of each of these solutions will differ in their efficiency and equity impacts.

The solution to these supply problems, adopted by Madagascar at the time of Independence, consisted of creating an orderly market that would rely on collective actions between the growers, packers, Government and importers. Initially, these marketing institutions and policy instruments were successful in achieving a more efficient and equitable market outcome. Exports multiplied several fold, both in value and volume, high quality standards were attained, stability and consistency in supplies provided the needed stimulus

---

[39] A General Equilibrium Model developed for Madagascar (Dorosh 1993) also points to the fact that increased Government revenues and spending worsen rather than improve income distribution, favoring urban areas at the expense of rural areas, and within urban areas the higher income groups, further questioning the economic and social justification of the high level of taxation imposed on the vanilla growers.

for demand to expand, Madagascar's dominant position on the world market was managed in a sustainable fashion, and the gains from trade were equitably distributed domestically between growers, packers and Government.

Very quickly, however, the marketing institutions and policy instruments previously so successful were progressively diverted by the Government from their original objectives. The instruments of collective action were no longer used to serve long-term efficiency and equity objectives, but became increasingly a powerful instrument in the hands of the Government and a handful of packer-exporters for rent extraction from both growers and the world market. This diversion can be traced back to Government failures in setting these marketing institutions and policy instruments. As the Madagascar vanilla case study illustrates, these Government failures have resulted in large efficiency and equity costs to its vanilla sector as well as its economy.

Five main Government failures in its intervention on the vanilla market can be identified. Combined together, these Government failures have contributed to the myopic over-exploitation of Madagascar monopoly power on the world market, and to the concentration of exports among a handful of exporters. First, because the external policy regime is over-determined (since it sets both the export price and the export quota), it provides for little flexibility in the face of changing external conditions on the world vanilla market. The latter could result from structural (and/or random) changes either on the demand side (e.g., changes in price-elasticity, shifts in demand), or on the world supply side (e.g., development of competition). Second, the lack of market-based mechanisms (such as an auction system) for setting and allocating both the individual export and import quotas promotes rent-seeking activities among the packer-exporters and Government officials. Third, the vanilla price stabilization scheme through its collective storage policy, by delinking the domestic market from external market conditions, magnifies the development of structural imbalances between domestic supply and external demand. Fourth, the price regime (i.e., unique prices irrespective of quality) does not provide any financial incentives for improving quality, undermining the effectiveness of other complementary measures (e.g., market regulations; quality grades; production, curing and packing standards). Fifth, because Government of Madagascar increased, rather than decreased, its exclusive role in the conduct of the marketing institutions (GNIV, VSF, Vanilla Alliance) designed to play a central role in the collective management of the vanilla sector, the voicing of protest by different interest groups (growers, packers, importers) became virtually impossible. Consequently, there was no countervailing mechanisms for correcting the growing inefficiencies and inequities of the vanilla sector policies.[40]

Market failures or imperfections often impede the efficient and equitable development of agricultural markets. Failures in Government interventions may also be as, if not more, damaging. What the Madagascar case study indicates is that Governments should be cautious, selective and flexible in their market interventions, and to the maximum extent rely on market-based intruments as well as the articulation of interests in organizations (such as trade associations, professional or inter-professional organizations). Conversely, when contemplating the liberalization of agricultural markets (or the promotion of agricultural diversification), policy analysts should be aware of the often genuine concerns of Governments for the efficiency and equity impacts of market failures and imperfections, and the design of efficient solutions to these supply problems should be addressed.

---

[40] For a full treatment of market and non-market mechanisms, and their complementarity, for addressing conduct and performance issues in economic systems, see Hirschman (1970).

ANNEX TABLE 6A: World Vanilla Imports (Tons)

Year	North & Central America				Europe				South America	Asia			Africa	Oceania	World
	USA	Canada	Other	Sub-Total	France	Germany	Other	Sub-Total		Japan	Other	Sub-Total			
1965	1008	29	0	1037	160	76	99	335	11	10	79	89	1	14	1487
1966	864	39	0	903	156	95	125	376	11	13	4	17	1	21	1329
1967	591	38	0	629	171	103	129	403	15	14	6	20	4	12	1083
1968	1017	41	2	1060	175	126	134	435	14	17	9	26	7	18	1560
1969	840	43	2	885	233	118	132	483	17	22	8	30	13	19	1447
1970	1016	53	1	1070	234	118	124	476	10	40	11	51	5	20	1632
1971	923	45	2	970	245	113	111	469	8	30	6	36	6	20	1509
1972	991	47	2	1040	263	111	104	478	8	27	6	33	6	20	1585
1973	1056	54	3	1113	296	114	153	563	19	38	16	54	10	20	1779
1974	977	47	4	1028	277	160	176	613	19	40	32	72	12	30	1774
1975	963	50	35	1048	199	125	141	465	15	23	18	41	24	25	1618
1976	1014	65	1	1080	325	192	161	678	14	62	19	81	13	17	1883
1977	1554	183	0	1737	417	266	213	896	14	57	7	64	13	18	2742
1978	1185	43	33	1261	459	291	182	932	30	75	59	134	20	24	2401
1979	497	40	38	575	302	164	132	598	32	52	48	100	9	28	1342
1980	343	26	2	371	133	124	130	387	17	34	69	103	9	8	895
1981	640	19	29	688	248	183	169	600	30	21	79	100	20	9	1447
1982	884	30	18	932	301	182	134	617	21	19	8	27	1	5	1603
1983	977	29	10	1016	261	200	144	605	19	42	9	51	6	13	1710
1984	841	31	2	874	202	175	165	542	5	36	73	109	12	7	1549
1985	743	31	2	776	154	137	135	426	1	40	31	71	2	7	1283
1986	1001	28	1	1030	199	190	166	555	3	60	13	73	3	7	1671
1987	1387	58	4	1449	220	256	163	639	12	38	66	104	5	6	2215
1988	1224	71	5	1300	267	203	195	665	5	79	59	138	8	10	2126
1989	1107	36	13	1156	253	232	189	674	23	48	65	113	37	15	2018
1990	975	110	15	1100	220	294	218	732	8	59	116	175	16	16	2047
1991	1311	56	18	1385	245	279	216	740	17	60	49	109	13	29	2293

SOURCE: FAO Trade Yearbook.

ANNEX TABLE 6B: **World Vanilla Exports** (Tons)

	North & Central America				Europe		Asia		
Year	Mexico	Other	Re-exports	Sub-Total	Re-exports	South America	Indonesia	Re-exports	Sub-Total
1965	39	2	0	41	46	0	59	5	64
1966	22	1	0	23	40	0	56	4	60
1967	70	0	0	70	62	0	108	0	108
1968	54	0	0	54	67	0	86	4	90
1969	18	0	0	18	102	0	15	1	16
1970	22	0	0	22	80	0	15	1	16
1971	23	0	0	23	83	0	15	4	19
1972	18	0	0	18	77	0	15	4	19
1973	19	0	0	19	109	0	317	7	324
1974	15	0	0	15	118	0	53	3	56
1975	0	0	0	0	122	0	237	7	244
1976	0	0	0	0	161	0	334	0	334
1977	0	0	0	0	239	0	420	0	420
1978	2	0	0	2	334	0	389	11	400
1979	1	0	0	1	285	0	17	25	42
1980	0	0	0	0	150	0	80	24	104
1981	0	0	0	0	192	0	138	81	219
1982	0	0	0	0	205	0	116	0	116
1983	0	0	0	0	222	0	234	3	237
1984	24	0	0	24	245	0	154	1	155
1985	1	0	0	1	199	0	175	7	182
1986	0	0	0	0	222	0	298	10	308
1987	30	1	8	39	252	0	410	77	487
1988	27	0	67	94	296	0	506	16	522
1989	36	20	31	87	290	0	677	32	709
1990	14	0	78	92	338	11	607	23	630
1991	13	2	92	107	333	0	666	6	672

SOURCE: FAO *Trade Yearbook*.

ANNEX TABLE 6B: **World Vanilla Exports** (Tons) *(continued)*

Africa				Oceania					World Excl. Re-export
Mada-gascar	Comoros	Réunion	Sub-Total	FR. Poly-nesia	Tonga	Re-Exports	Sub-Total	World	
984	167	58	1213	132	0	0	132	1496	1445
885	134	16	1046	115	0	0	115	1284	1240
666	145	18	837	59	0	0	59	1136	1074
961	138	25	1132	67	0	0	67	1410	1339
1097	207	32	1344	55	0	0	55	1535	1432
1218	144	26	1392	33	0	0	33	1543	1462
1160	73	31	1269	27	0	0	27	1421	1334
1215	100	21	1341	25	0	0	25	1480	1399
720	34	21	775	19	0	0	19	1246	1130
1353	160	4	1517	12	0	0	12	1718	1597
858	211	8	1077	8	0	0	8	1451	1322
1101	124	19	1244	7	0	0	7	1746	1585
1713	100	13	1826	7	0	0	7	2492	2253
1459	117	9	1585	3	0	0	3	2324	1979
436	170	23	629	3	0	0	3	960	650
410	13	8	431	1	0	0	1	686	512
635	160	15	810	1	0	0	1	1222	949
887	259	11	1157	1	0	0	1	1479	1274
1099	177	10	1286	5	0	0	5	1750	1525
827	26	19	872	2	13	0	15	1311	1065
628	181	28	837	3	4	8	15	1234	1020
689	150	21	860	4	8	0	12	1402	1170
1260	63	14	1337	4	14	0	18	2133	1796
625	247	20	892	3	17	1	21	1825	1445
594	164	16	774	4	26	1	31	1891	1537
829	127	7	963	7	36	2	45	2079	1638
644	240	13	897	6	37	13	56	2065	1621

SOURCE: FAO *Trade Yearbook*.

ANNEX TABLE 6C: **Respective Performance of Madagascar and Indonesia Vanilla Exports on the Main Consuming Markets**

	1980	1981	1982	1983	1984	1985	1986	1987	1988	1989	1990	1991	1992
U.S.													
Total Volume (T)	343	640	884	977	841	743	1048	1387	1217	1107	975	1308	1262
Average CIF Price ($/kg.)	54	49	51	52	59	64	58	56	51	42	49	53	52
Madagascar													
Volume (T)	205	438	580	651	602	462	672	820	576	421	398	493	471
% Total	60%	68%	66%	67%	72%	62%	64%	59%	47%	38%	41%	38%	37%
Average CIF Price ($/kg.)	50	52	55	60	65	69	67	70	69	59	72	74	74
Indonesia													
Volume (T)	90	123	102	240	192	184	306	443	432	526	482	616	602
% Total	26%	19%	12%	25%	23%	25%	29%	32%	36%	48%	49%	47%	48%
Average CIF Price ($/kg.)	42	35	22	28	43	50	37	28	19	21	26	32	31
France													
Total Volume (T)	133	249	301	261	201	154	198	219	247	219			
Average CIF Price (FF/kg.)	350	317	380	479	581	646	517	410	391	Na.			
Madagascar													
Volume (T)	92	147	167	202	149	79	92	148	165	84			
% Total	69%	59%	55%	77%	74%	51%	46%	68%	67%	38%			
Average CIF Price (FF/kg.)	588	661	512	409	390	Na.							
Indonesia													
Volume (T)	0	0	0	0	0	0	1	11	9	55			
% Total	0%	0%	0%	0%	0%	0%	1%	5%	4%	25%			
Average CIF Price	0	0	0	0	0	0	451	298	256	Na.			
Germany													
Total Volume (T)	125	183	182	200	185	165	199	265	181	234			
Madagascar													
Volume (T)	100	136	143	175	151	137	177	213	130	141			
% Total	80%	74%	79%	88%	82%	83%	89%	80%	72%	60%			
Indonesia													
Volume (T)	0	0	0	0	2	0	1	11	11	43			
% Total	0%	0%	0%	0%	1%	0%	1%	5%	8%	30%			

SOURCE: U.S. Spice Trade, TJP Market Development.

ANNEX TABLE 6D: Madagascar Vanilla Official Domestic Prices, Actual Export Prices and Government Proceeds from Export Taxes and Stabilization Levy

	Official Producer Price			Official Guaranteed Export Price to Packer-Exporter				Proceeds from Export Taxes & Stabilization Levy	
					Packing & Curing Margins as % of:		FOB Price		
		% of:							
Year	(FMG/ kg.)[1]	FOB	Guar- anteed Export Price	(FMG/ kg.)[2]	FOB[3]	Guar- anteed Export Price[3]	(FMG/ kg.)[4]	Billion FMG[5]	as a % of FOB[6]
1975	250	33.3	54.9	2096	27.4	45.1	3457	1.17	39.4
1976	250	26.8	51.7	2226	25.0	48.3	4299	2.28	48.2
1977	280	25.2	53.6	2402	21.8	46.4	5109	4.64	53.0
1978	330	25.6	55.4	2739	20.6	44.6	5925	4.65	53.8
1979	500	32.2	59.8	3849	21.7	40.2	7140	1.43	46.1
1980	600	28.7	64.8	4260	15.6	35.2	9622	2.20	55.7
1981	700	27.3	58.4	5518	19.5	41.6	11,797	3.99	53.2
1982	700	17.1	56.4	5711	13.3	43.6	18,795	11.61	69.6
1983	1000	18.6	59.0	7801	12.9	41.0	24,760	18.64	68.5
1984	1000	12.5	55.6	8275	10.0	44.4	36,759	23.56	77.5
1985	1000	10.0	53.2	8640	8.8	46.8	45,868	23.38	81.2
1986	1100	11.7	53.7	9431	10.1	46.3	43,280	23.32	78.2
1987	1200	7.8	48.6	11,365	8.3	51.4	70,821	74.92	84.0
1988	1700	8.4	46.3	16,893	9.8	53.7	92,850	47.47	81.8
1989	2000	8.1	47.1	19,525	9.1	52.9	113,704	55.94	82.8
1990	2000	8.5	47.1	19,525	9.6	52.9	107,749	69.70	81.9

[1] Official Producer Price for green vanilla; 4.6 kg. of green vanilla yields 1 kg. of cured vanilla.
[2] Official Guaranteed Price for Cured, Packed & Conditioned Vanilla to the Packer-Exporter.
[3] Packing & Curing Margins = [Official Guaranteed Price to the Packer-Exporter] – [Official Producer Price, Cured vanilla equivalent].
[4] Unit Export Value.
[5] Proceeds = {[FOB price] – [Official Guaranteed Price to Packer-Exporter]}*[export volume].
[6] = {[FOB price] – [Official Guaranteed Price to Packer-Exporter]}/[FOB price].

SOURCES: Annual Differentiels VSF, BDE.

ANNEX TABLE 6E: **Madagascar Vanilla Financial Results of the Vanilla Stabilization Fund**

	1979/80	1980/81	1981/82	1982/83	1983/84	1984/85	1985/86	1986/87	1987/88	1988/89	1989/90
I. Operating Budget	0.400	0.550	0.210	0.660	0.820	0.990	0.138	0.132	0.348	0.203	0.206
II. Market Promotion Budget	0.640	0.190	0.130	0.356	0.450	0.427	0.436	1.811	0.882	1.493	0.000
III. Stabilization Budget:	2.141	2.039	3.555	3.886	1.010	1.158	2.759	4.401	4.275	7.421	9.409
Storage	0.100	0.160	0.320	0.651	1.010	1.156	2.759	4.401	4.275	7.421	9.409
Transfer to GOM	2.101	2.023	3.235	3.235	0.000	0.000	0.000	0.000	0.000	0.000	0.000
IV. Other	0.534	0.590	0.100	−0.350	−0.398	−0.416	−0.395	0.880	0.143	0.395	5.071
V. Total Expenditures	2.779	2.172	3.590	4.273	1.144	1.268	2.938	6.432	5.648	9.512	14.686
VI. Total Receipts from Stabilization Levy	3.158	1.530	1.592	11.886	15.563	17.543	11.287	19.850	35.848	26.495	31.066
VII. Annual Surplus		−0.821	−1.997	9.570	14.992	15.337	7.491	13.749	30.193	15.894	15.040
VIII. Surplus from Previous FY		5.800	4.979	2.982	12.552	27.544	42.881	50.372	64.121	94.314	110.208
IX. Cumulated Surplus	4.979	2.982	2.982	12.552	27.544	42.881	50.372	64.121	94.314	110.208	125.248

Madagascar Vanilla: Proceeds from Export Taxes

	1981	1982	1983	1984	1985	1986	1987	1988	1989	1990
DROITS DE SORTIE	0.9	2	3.27	3.65	4.0	5.0	12.0	7.6	8.6	9.9
TAXE CONJONCTURELLE	0.66	1.47	2.39	2.68	3.0	3.0	9.0	5.8	8.5	7.2
PRELEVEMENT SPECIAL	0	0	0	0	1.3	1.3	7.0	4.7	2.3	5.7
TOTAL	1.6	3.5	5.7	6.3	8.3	9.3	28.0	18.1	19.4	22.8

NOTE: The fiscal year for the VSF runs from May 1 to April 30.

SOURCE: VSF, Ministry of Finance.

ANNEX TABLE 6F: **Madagascar Vanilla Marketing Export Plans**

Plan Number	Year	Export Quotas U.S. (T)	Europe (T)	Other (T)	Total (T)	FOB Price (US$/kg.)	Volumes Actually Exported U.S. (T)	Europe (T)	Other (T)	Total (T)
2	1963/64					10.20	261	28		289
3	1964/65					10.20	579	49		628
4	1965/66					10.20	821	163		984
5	1966/67					10.20	533	175	4	712
6	1967/68					10.20	428	217	15	660
7	1968/69					10.20	685	270	20	975
8	1969/70					10.70	745	331	20	1096
9	1970/71					10.70	780	413	25	1218
10	1971/72					11.30	810	317	33	1160
11	1972/73					12.40	771	407	36	1214
12	1973/74					13.40	680	390	22	1092
13	1974/75					14.50	740	450	31	1221
14	1975/76					17.50	400	400	40	840
15	1976/77					19.30	776	437	61	1274
16	1977/78					23.00	950	600	50	1600
17	1978/79					30.00	720	384	5	1109
18	1979/81					45.00	495	266	28	789
19	1981/82					55.00	420	238	8	666
20	1982/83					57.00	566	300	43	909
21	1983/84					62.50	575	300	44	919
22	1984/85	404	211	35	650	70.00	461	211	46	718
23	1985/86	659	367	87	1113	70.00	556	243	50	849
24	1986/87	456	209	88	753	70.00	735	315	50	1100
25	1987/88	770	331	83	1184	72.00	698	336	50	1084
26	1988/89	421	166	56	643	72.00	460	268	50	778
27	1989/90	330	165	136	631	74.00	375	237	50	662
28	1990/91	420	244	80	744	74.00	450	256	50	756
29	1991/92	500	305	100	905	74.00	400	210	40	650

Marketing Plan runs from April 1 to March 31.

SOURCE: Vanilla Stabilization Fund.

ANNEX TABLE 6G: **Madagascar Vanilla Official Producer Prices, Marketing Margins and Government Proceeds from Export Taxes and Stabilization Levy in Real Terms** (Index 1975 = 100)

Year	Official Producer Price	Official Marketing Margin (Curing & Packing)	Proceeds From Export Taxes & Stabilization Levy
1975	100	100	100
1976	95	108	145
1977	103	108	183
1978	114	111	202
1979	152	124	184
1980	154	102	253
1981	138	120	227
1982	105	99	360
1983	125	106	390
1984	114	111	597
1985	104	111	712
1986	99	104	560
1987	94	121	852
1988	105	148	862
1989	113	155	980
1990	103	140	831

SOURCE: Differentiel VSF, BDE.

ANNEX TABLE 6H: **Madagascar Vanilla Production, Exports in Volume and Value Terms Theoretical and Officially Declared Stocks**

Year	Commer-cialized Production (tons)	Exports Volume (tons)	Export Value (US$ Million)	Export Unit Value (US$/kg.)	Export Value (FMG Million)	Export Unit Value (FMG/kg.)	Theo-retical Stocks (tons)	Declared Stocks (tons)
1960		270	6.70	24.80	1642	6081		
1961		585	7.69	13.14	1885	3222		
1962	650	640	8.82	13.78	2161	3377	10	
1963	1050	292	4.27	14.64	1048	3589	768	
1964	856	628	6.46	10.28	1583	2521	996	
1965	850	984	9.94	10.10	2437	2477	862	
1966	950	885	8.95	10.11	2216	2504	927	
1967	983	666	6.81	10.22	1672	2511	1244	
1968	654	961	10.23	10.64	2530	2633	937	
1969	1310	1097	10.84	9.88	3013	2747	1150	
1970	1330	1218	13.07	10.73	3610	2964	1262	
1971	1508	1160	13.64	11.76	3565	3073	1610	
1972	1690	1215	14.91	12.27	3819	3143	2085	
1973	660	720	9.41	13.07	2217	3079	2025	
1974	800	1353	20.13	14.88	4475	3307	1472	
1975	764	858	13.84	16.14	2966	3457	1378	
1976	859	1101	19.82	18.00	4733	4299	1136	
1977	847	1713	35.62	20.79	8751	5109	270	
1978	726	1459	38.31	26.25	8644	5925	−463	
1979	772	436	14.74	33.81	3113	7140	−127	
1980	900	410	18.67	45.53	3945	9622	363	
1981	1034	635	27.79	43.77	7491	11,797	762	
1982	1195	887	46.97	52.95	16,671	18,795	1070	
1983	526	1099	62.45	56.83	27,211	24,760	497	
1984	1508	827	52.82	63.86	30,400	36,759	1178	
1985	1761	628	43.80	69.74	28,805	45,868	2311	
1986	695	689	48.02	69.69	29,820	43,280	2317	
1987	2164	1260	88.75	70.43	89,235	70,821	3221	2194
1988	804	625	43.61	69.77	58,031	92,850	3400	2552
1989	1681	594	41.94	70.61	67,540	113,704	4487	2019
1990	972	790	56.97	72.11	85,122	107,749	4669	3256

NOTE: Commericalized production refers to cured vanilla production purchased by packers.

Theoretical stocks in year t are assumed to equal to: stocks in year (t-1) plus, the difference between production and exports in year t; it is also assumed to start from zero stock level in 1962.

SOURCE: Vanilla Stabilization Fund, BDE.

ANNEX TABLE 6I: **Madagascar Vanilla Gross, Net Proceeds and Yields from Vanilla Taxation System**

	1981	1982	1983	1984	1985	1986	1987	1988	1989	1990
Gross Proceeds (FMG billion): [FOB price— Official Guaranteed Export Price to Packer]	3.99	11.61	18.64	23.56	23.38	23.32	74.92	47.47	55.94	69.70
Net Proceeds: Current FMG (billion)	0.3	5.3	17.0	21.4	21.0	18.9	47.2	43.5	35.0	32.8
Constant 1980 FMG (billion)	0.1	2.9	9.2	10.4	9.3	7.1	14.9	11.9	8.2	6.9
Yields: Net Proceeds/ Gross Proceeds	9	46	91	91	90	81	63	92	63	54

NOTE: Net proceeds = [proceeds from export taxes] + [annual surplus from VSF].

SOURCE: VSF, Ministry of Finance.

VII.

The Many Faces of Success: The Development of Kenyan Horticultural Exports

Steven Jaffee

O ver the past two decades, international trade in horticultural products, such as fresh and processed fruit and vegetables, cut flowers and other ornamental foliage, has been one of the most dynamic components of international agricultural trade, featuring a 10% average annual increase in value.[1] With this growth in horticultural trade and the stagnation or decline in world trade for many other agricultural commodities during the 1980s, the value of fruit and vegetable products imported by OECD and developing countries now exceeds those for any other category of agricultural products, including cereals, oilseeds, fish products, meats and tropical beverages.

Many developing countries have participated in this expanding trade in horticultural products. Some countries have based their trade on high volume commodities such as bananas, pineapples and citrus fruits; other countries have targeted niche markets for high value, low volume specialty items and OECD market 'off-season' produce. Developing countries have competed well in many horticultural product markets. While the share of these countries in total world agricultural trade declined between the early 1960s and mid-1980s, their share of world horticultural trade increased, reaching nearly 37% by the end of this period.[2]

Many sub-Saharan African countries have a potential comparative advantage in the production of fresh and processed horticultural products as a

---

[1] GATT (1990); Islam (1990).
[2] Islam (1990), p.17.

result of their agro-ecological conditions, location and relatively low labor costs. Very few African countries and entrepreneurs, however, have effectively translated these resource advantages into competitive and profitable horticultural trades with Europe, the Middle East or other regions. The reason is that most African countries lack the physical infrastructure and the technical, managerial and marketing skills necessary for competitive horticultural export development. For the vast majority of SSA countries, nascent horticultural export industries have floundered due to weak production support systems, international transport and other infrastructural bottlenecks, ineffective marketing institutions, and poor trade linkages with overseas distribution systems. The potentially high risks and transaction costs associated with trade in highly perishable and quality-variable horticultural products have frequently been exacerbated by the underdeveloped transport and communications infrastructure and weak contract enforcement mechanisms found in many countries. Despite the considerable interest among African entrepreneurs, governments and external development agencies in horticultural exports as an engine of growth or source of trade diversification, there are few cases of successful and sustained development.

Kenya is one of the very few SSA countries that have emerged as major participants in international horticultural markets. Compared with the other successful exporters (which include South Africa, Côte d'Ivoire and increasingly Zimbabwe), Kenya's horticultural trade has been far more diverse in terms of the range of products traded, the participants and the institutional arrangements which have emerged to govern the trade. From a narrowly based trade in the 1960s with a few dominant products and small numbers of participating farmers and firms, Kenya's horticultural export sub-sector now delivers some seventy-five products to more than a dozen markets. The production base ranges from very small farmers to large plantations. The trade passes through a dense network of traders and processors of varied origins and diverse operational characteristics.

This chapter examines the development of Kenya's horticultural export sub-sector. Kenya's case is of interest for several reasons. First, this sub-sector has always featured a dominant role for the private sector, which contrasts to the general historical pattern of agricultural development in Kenya whereby the government has either monopolized trade through marketing board operations or strictly controlled the functioning of the market through controls on prices, crop movements, market entry, etc.[3] Kenya's horticultural export experience illuminates the complex relationship between the state and private sector development and the changes in that relationship as the industry matures. Second, the case clearly illustrates the diverse forms of organization which may emerge in African agro-industries, and the influence of technical, economic and political factors on the emergence and sustainability of these different organizational forms. Finally, Kenya's long experience in horticultural exports offers both positive and negative lessons for entrepreneurs, governments and donors interested in promoting horticultural exports in other SSA countries.

This chapter is composed of five sections. The first section reviews the major techno-economic characteristics of horticultural products, their production and trade. On the basis of this review, we develop hypotheses regarding organizational patterns to be found within Kenya's private sector-dominated horticultural sub-sector. The second section summarizes the patterns of participation of SSA countries in global horticultural products trade. Section three traces the historical development of Kenyan horticultural exports and identifies the major roles played by the private and public sectors, the importance of foreign investment in the sub-sector, and the various factors contributing to growth and stagnation in the exports of particular commodities. Section four examines the ownership characteristics of Kenya's horticultural traders and processors and reviews their institutional linkages, both backward toward production and forward to overseas markets. The last section offers lessons that can be drawn from Kenya's experience.[4]

---

[3] See Mosley (1983) and Bates (1990). Bates' critical stand against the alleged "miracle of the market" in the Kenyan context is greatly compromised by his failure to examine the only major agro-industry in that country where private firms and individuals have been largely permitted to develop their own institutional arrangements and respond to international market signals—the horticultural industry.

[4] This chapter is based on field and desk research conducted by the author during the mid-1980s, supplemented by a brief field visit to Kenya in 1992. The initial field work included interviews with forty-four exporters and processors (who at the time accounted for 97% of trade), interviews with farmers, extension workers, transport agents and others in Kenya, as well as interviews with a sample of importers, wholesalers, and retailers of horticultural commodities within the United Kingdom and the Netherlands. This chapter draws heavily from Jaffee (1990, 1991).

MAJOR TECHNO-ECONOMIC CHARACTERISTICS OF HORTICULTURAL COMMODITIES

Horticulture is defined as "the science and art of growing fruits, vegetables, flowers and ornamental plants". There are hundreds of different horticultural crops, rendering dubious any attempt to define generalized characteristics for these crops and their production. The considerable variability among horticultural crops with regard to certain techno-economic characteristics actually provides a basis for an interesting set of hypotheses regarding the emergence of different organization forms to govern horticultural production and trade. In this section, an effort is made to identify several 'general tendencies' among the broad range of horticultural crops and to compare Kenya's most important horticultural export crops according to the identified criteria. It applies elements of *transaction cost economics* to predict the organizational forms which one would expect to emerge in Kenya's horticultural sub-sector. In later sections, the actual institutional patterns within this sub-sector are discussed and analyzed.

In comparison with most other agricultural crops and commodities, the broad range of horticultural crops can be characterized by:

1) **High rate of perishability:** They experience rapid quality deterioration, severely limiting their marketable life as a fresh commodity and the period of time during which they can be used as a raw material for processing. Even under optimal post-harvest conditions, the marketable life of many horticultural crops is only several weeks or even several days.[5] Horticultural crops continue to ripen after harvest and this process can be slowed or delayed only slightly. Rapid perishability gives rise to high risks of product and revenue losses and puts a premium on effective post-harvest treatment and handling, transaction speed, and close coordination within the marketing and logistical chain. While perishability helps to clear the market of surpluses, it also affects the bargaining or power relationships within the marketing chain as growers and other sellers cannot afford to hold the product waiting for higher prices or other more favorable terms. Rapid perishability implies especially high transactional risks in long distance and international trade,

---

[5] The rate of perishability of horticultural crops stems not only from their own physiological properties, but also from their stage of maturity at harvest, the handling and storage procedures used, and the prevailing post-harvest environmental conditions (e.g. temperature, humidity).

as suppliers are vulnerable to erroneous quality claims and protection-ist inspection or clearance delays at ports of entry or other destination points.

2) **High variability of quality** from unit to unit and from one supply pe-riod to another: This heterogeneity derives from many factors, includ-ing the numerous different biological varieties which exist for most horticultural crops, variations in production and post-harvest practices, and the impact of climatic or other environmental factors. The hetero-geneity of horticultural crops is compounded by the fact that the qual-ity of such produce is very complex, meaning that it is typically associ-ated with many individual attributes. For example, commercially important attributes of fruit and vegetables may include such physical characteristics as color, shape, size, weight and texture, and such chemi-cal characteristics as moisture, sugar or acidic content. With cut flow-ers, fragrance is also a valued quality attribute.

Some of these attributes may be hidden or otherwise difficult to measure (for example, freshness), weakening the informational value of grades and complicating the language of trade.[6] Quality variability and complexity create uncertainty on the part of suppliers and buyers and can be a major source of conflict between them. While much qual-ity-related information must change hands, this normally needs to be supplemented by other measures, including direct observation of pre-shipped produce and/or the intervention of buyers in the production process through the provision of inputs, technical advice and so on. It is not surprising that reputations are a central element in the fresh pro-duce trade, serving as a close proxy for (expected) quality and overall reliability. Product heterogeneity implies that those pursuing a strat-egy of market segmentation can earn higher returns.

3) **High seasonality of production and demand:** Harvests and sales fre-quently need to be carefully scheduled in order to maintain high, stable input levels for processing facilities or to take advantage of 'market window' opportunities in the fresh produce trade. Seasonality in horti-cultural production is partly a result of seasonal differences in sun-

---

[6] As *Produce Business* columnist Max Brunk observes (September 1989), "Everyone talks about quality, [but] when asked, few people can come up with a consistent answer. Two traders speaking on the telephone can be talking about quality with little or no understanding because each trader has a different point of reference in mind. This is a cause of much conflict in marketing."

light, temperature and other environmental conditions which exhibit greater variability in higher latitudes. By breeding new varieties or employing certain techniques, it is possible to alter or extend natural production seasons to some degree, although this may be costly (for example, use of heated greenhouses) or lead one to sacrifice on certain quality or other objectives. One consequence of natural seasonality is wide seasonal variations in prices, with potentially lucrative 'market windows' for suppliers with less or counter seasonal patterns of production. As some horticultural crops provide aesthetic in addition to consumptive value, demand frequently shows strong peaks near particular holidays.[7] Seasonality of production combined with rapid perishability raises problems for processors and traders in obtaining steady suppliers of particular commodities/raw materials, generally requiring them to diversify their product mix and their sources of supply.

4) **Long gestation periods or extended production cycles of** many horticultural crops (including most fruit crops and many flowers): These expose producers to long-term market entry (and price) risks, lower the elasticity of supply faced by processors and traders, and frequently lead both sides to seek supply and purchase assurances.

5) **Labor intensiveness and need for careful crop husbandry.** While some horticultural crops do feature production activities amenable to mechanization, many do not and labor requirements, especially for planting, weeding and harvesting, are as high or higher than for most other agricultural crops. Most horticultural crops also require particularly careful husbandry with close attention given to the timing of specific cultivation and post-harvest tasks. These characteristics generate certain diseconomies of scale at the production level. Centralized, large-scale production systems frequently encounter high costs associated with labor recruitment, training, supervision and maintenance.

6) **High level of technical and management skills required and need for specialized production and post-harvest inputs:** The cultivation and post-harvest care of many horticultural crops require a level of

---

[7] This is especially the case for cut flowers, for which demand in the United States and parts of Western Europe is especially high at the times of Christmas, Easter, Mother's Day, and Valentine's Day. Varietal and color preferences also differ considerably at different times of the year.

technical and managerial skill which is greater than that for most other agricultural ventures due to the high environmental sensitivity of these crops, the strong influence of varietal choice and cultural (and post-harvest) practices over eventual market value, the potentially high benefits (as well as costs and risks) associated with particular techniques, and the characteristics of perishability, heterogeneity and labor intensiveness noted above. The quality of some horticultural crops and the timing of their harvest and availability is enhanced by the use of specialized chemicals, irrigation facilities and other purchased inputs and equipment. This implies potentially high barriers to entry for less skilled and less well-endowed farmers in the absence of effective channels for credit, inputs and technical advice.

7) **Economies of scale in some post-harvest and processing operations:** There are many types of marketing infrastructure—including produce collection stations, pack houses, cold stores and transport vehicles—which require 'lumpy' investments. Their appropriate scale will vary by circumstances. 'Lumpiness' and economies of scale also apply to international freight arrangements where a certain minimum level of trade is necessary to attract sufficient, competitive sea or air freight services and relatively high and predictable trade volumes are needed to enter into special freight chartering arrangements. While there are many technologies to process fruits and vegetables, most of the standard technologies for producing canned, frozen and dehydrated for international sale are fairly standardized and exhibit economies of scale associated with the full utilization of major pieces of equipment. There is scope for joint marketing, common use investments and coordinated negotiation of and allocation of transport services. Potential economies of scale in processing operations as well as in certain quality control and transport operations can be realized only through close coordination of production and downstream activities, whether through private or collective action.

Descriptions of techno-economic characteristics of agricultural commodities (and their production) are a useful starting point for surmising expected organizational forms within private agribusiness. To do so, one can draw upon and apply certain concepts from the expanding literature of *transaction cost economics.*[8] This literature focuses on the organization of transactions or, more broadly, exchange relationships. It demonstrates that there does not exist any single institutional structure which is superior to all others on efficiency grounds. Rather, different institutional arrangements are shown to have particular advantages and disadvantages. Their relative suitability depends on the actual operating conditions surrounding the trading relationship. In defining the operating conditions, emphasis is given in the literature to two main elements:

1) **Asset-specificity**—For any particular production and trading operation, individuals may undertake either generalized or specialized investments. Certain types of plant, equipment, materials and knowledge have potentially generalized use across a broad range of products or trades. Other assets are highly specialized for a particular product or trade outlet and have little or no alternative use or value outside of this product or trading area. Examples of asset specificity in horticulture include crops with extended gestation periods or production cycles (such as fruit trees), large-scale specialized processing and post-harvest facilities, and use of highly specialized production inputs and technical knowledge.

2) **Uncertainty**—In any particular trading context, the degree of uncertainty may vary—uncertainty regarding the availability of supplies or market outlets, the quality of the products on offer, the timing of supply and demand, the trading terms being offered, possible political interventions, and so on. Such uncertainties tend to be more pronounced in agriculture than in industry because of the important influence of changing weather conditions and the wider geographical dispersion of primary producers and intermediate users.

In the literature of transaction cost economics, it is postulated that spot market exchange, long-term contracts and vertical integration will each be

---

[8] In contrast with traditional microeconomic analysis where institutions are exogenously determined, transaction cost economics, together other branches of the so-called "New Institutional Economics", seeks to explain the origins or current existence of institutions, to account for the particular forms which they have taken, and to examine the efficiency and distributional properties of alternative institutional forms. The major elements and propositions of transaction cost economics are provided in Williamson (1975, 1985), Langlois (1986), and Bromley (1989). John (1980) and Reve (1980) apply transaction cost concepts to the study of industrial marketing channels. See Bardhan (1989) of applications of elements of transaction cost economics to the study of agrarian institutions in developing countries.

efficient modes of organization, defined in terms of economizing on a combination of production and transaction costs under different degrees of asset-specificity and uncertainty. The table below summarizes the hypothesized relationships.

The theory contends that under conditions of high asset-specificity, the most efficient mode of organization is the vertical integration of the two adjacent stages of production or marketing. The firm investing in specialized assets, particularly those which are durable and involve large sunk costs, will be highly vulnerable to opportunistic bargaining on the part of suppliers or buyers since they will know that this investor has little or no alternative use for such assets and thus must come to terms unless it is in a monopolistic or monopsonistic position. Vertical integration is also viewed as an effective means of countering high levels of operational uncertainty, since a central management gains control over the different stages and direct supervision can be introduced.

On the other hand, when asset specificity is moderate to low, other institutional arrangements are viewed as more suitable than vertical integration since they tend to provide greater flexibility of action, have lower 'start-up' costs, and do not incur the heavy overhead costs associated with integrating separate operations. Long-term contracts enable buyers and sellers to counter market uncertainties by offering mutual assurances and supplementing price signals with other informational devices related to the quantity, quality and timing of expected deliveries and purchasing requirements. Where both asset specificity and uncertainty are low, spot market arrangements may be most

TABLE 7.1: **Operating Conditions and Appropriate Institutional Arrangements**

| | | Asset-Specificity | | |
		High	**Medium**	**Low**
Uncertainty	**High**	Vertical Integration	Vertical Integration	Long-term Contract
	Medium	Vertical Integration	Long-term Contract	L-T. Contract or Spot Market
	Low	Vertical Integration	Long-term Contract	Spot Market

efficient since they give the participants greatest flexibility of action and immediate signals about performance. It is generally easier (and less costly) to negotiate an adjustment in price levels than to agree upon and implement changes in trading rules or lines of command.

In order to operationalize the insights of transaction cost economics for the purpose of developing and testing hypotheses regarding the organization of crop procurement systems, we have developed proxy indicators for both asset specificity and uncertainty for which quantitative or qualitative measures can be obtained in Kenyan horticulture. These proxy indicators and the rating system employed for our empirical analysis are as follows:

ASSET-SPECIFICITY:

1) *the length of the crop production cycle* or gestation period between the initial planting of the crop and the first commercial harvest: A production cycle of six months or less will be rated as short, one of six to twelve months will be rated medium, while one of over twelve months will be rated long.

2) *the scope for scale economies* in processing and post harvest operations. In this case, qualitative assessments of low, medium, and high are based upon the minimum efficient scale for the most restrictive processing activity, the needs for post-harvest treatments (for example, cleaning and waxing), and the advantages of cold storage.

3) *the degree of specialization of material production inputs and technical knowledge*: A high rating signifies that important inputs or cultivating techniques are used exclusively for the particular crop in Kenya. A medium rating indicates that important inputs (and techniques) have few alternative applications in Kenyan agriculture. A low rating indicates general applicability of material inputs and technical knowledge used.

UNCERTAINTY:

1) *the degree or rate of commodity/raw material perishability*: A high rating signifies that the crop maintains its quality before deterioration (under appropriate storage conditions) for less than one week. A medium rating is assigned for crops maintaining their quality for one to three weeks, while a low rating is assigned for crops maintaining their quality for more than three weeks after harvest.

2) *the degree of specificity in the commodity / raw material quality required*: A high rating indicates that quality must meet exacting (high) standards. A medium rating indicates that quality standards are set within a specified range, while a low rating indicates that quality standards are not tightly defined and simply minimum permissible standards are set.

3) *the degree of specificity in the timing of harvests and crop deliveries*: A high rating indicates that harvests and deliveries must be timed to meet daily or two-day processing/marketing requirements. A medium rating indicates that harvests and deliveries must be timed for bi-weekly to weekly procurement requirements, while a low rating indicates that more flexible harvesting and delivery patterns are acceptable to the processor/exporter.

Expected Organizational Forms in Kenyan Horticulture

Table 7.2 rates Kenya's most important horticultural export crops/commodities according to the above criteria and indicates the expected mode for organizing the link between exporter/processors and farm producers of the crop. As there is no *a priori* way of weighting the different proxy variables, we take a crude average of the ratings for the three variables under each heading when making predictions about institutional arrangements.

The table indicates that on the basis of technical crop characteristics, production characteristics and demand-based pressures for product quality and the timing of crop deliveries, one would expect the linkages between Kenyan producers and processors/traders to be governed predominantly by long-term (seasonal or other) contracts and vertical integration of production and downstream activities. Spot market sales and purchases are expected to occur primarily as supplementary, market-clearing devices and not to be a primary mode of sale/procurement for any of these major crops, with the possible exceptions of french beans and chilies for the fresh market.

SUB-SAHARAN AFRICA IN INTERNATIONAL HORTICULTURAL TRADE

Many countries and entrepreneurs in sub-Saharan Africa have attempted to develop horticultural export trades. Some have sought to supply the expanding West European and Middle Eastern import demand for a range of high-

TABLE 7.2: **Asset-Specificity, Uncertainty and Kenya's Major Horticultural Crops**

Commodity	Asset-Specificity			Uncertainty			Expected Mode of Coordination
	Production Cycle	Inputs/ Technical Specificity	Scale Economies in Post/Harvest/ Processing	Perishability	Quality Specificity	Timing Specificity	
Pineapple (for processing)	Long	Med	High	Low	High	Med	Vertical Integration
Mango	Long	Low	Med	Med	Med	Low	Long-Term Contract
Passion Fruit (for processing)	Med	Med	Med	Low	Low	Low	Long-Term Contract
Strawberry	Med	High	Low	High	High	High	Vertical Integration
French Beans:							
Fresh market	Short	Low	Low	Med	Med	Med	Spot Market/L.T. Contract
For processing	Short	Low	Med	Med	High	Med	Long-Term Contract
Chilies	Med	Low	Low	Med	Med	Med	Spot Market or Long-Term Contract
Carrots (for processing)	Med	Low	High	Low	Med	Med	Long-Term Contract
Carnation	Short	Med	Med	Med	High	Med	Long-Term Contract
Chrysanthemum	Short	High	Med	High	High	High	Vertical Integration
Statice	Med	Med	Med	Med	High	Med	Long-Term Contract

value temperate, sub-tropical and tropical fruits, vegetables and cut flowers; others have developed trade within the African region for lower value and less perishable commodities. On an aggregate basis, the performance of sub-Saharan Africa's horticultural export trade can be considered satisfactory, especially in comparison with the stagnation and decline in Africa's exports of more traditional agricultural commodities over the past decade or two. Table 7.3 indicates that between 1976 and 1989, sub-Saharan Africa's horticultural exports increased two and one-half times from $636 million to more than $1.5 billion. To put this in perspective, the listed cluster of horticultural products would rank third among agricultural exports within sub-Saharan Africa, trailing only coffee and cocoa. In recent years, the region's horticultural exports have been two and a half times (in value) its exports of either cotton or tobacco, and nearly four times its exports of tea. These are all major traditional exports and have been the focus of considerable attention in analyses dealing with SSA's agricultural trade.

While the rate of growth in Africa's horticultural trade has been slower than that experienced by developing countries in either Latin America or Asia, the region has not experienced the same precipitous decline in world market share as it has for some of its major traditional exports (including coffee, cocoa, and cotton). As Table 7.4 indicates, SSA's world market share increased between 1973 and 1989 for fresh fruit/nuts and for cut flowers. It was maintained (at a very low level) for preserved vegetables and declined for fresh vegetables and processed fruit products. Over this period, a small aggregate decline in market share was recorded.[9]

While SSA's horticultural export performance has been satisfactory on an aggregate basis, country-level patterns have been highly divergent. Only three countries—South Africa, Côte d'Ivoire and Kenya—have developed sizable trades, enabling them to become major participants in international horticultural markets. These three countries accounted for 79% of the region's horticultural export value in 1988 and for nearly 82% of the value of EEC horticultural product imports from sub-Saharan Africa in 1992. Several other countries

---

[9] See Islam (1990, Chapter 3) for a comparison between rates of change in African versus other regional exports of horticultural products. Islam's very negative assessment of Africa's performance stems partly from his inclusion of North African countries whose horticultural trade has declined (i.e. Morocco; Algeria), his non-inclusion of cut flowers in the basket of horticultural products, and his reliance upon FAO data which appear to underestimate the horticultural exports of many minor exporting countries. On the significant decline in SSA's world market shares for major traditional commodities, see Svedberg (1991).

TABLE 7.3: **Expansion of sub-Saharan Africa's Exports of Horticultural Products** (US $ Millions; F.O.B. Value)

Product Category	1976	1980	1989
Fresh Fruit + Nuts	307.5	659.1	1025.0
Processed Fruit	207.7	277.4	284.0
Fresh Vegetables	97.3	122.8	117.1
Preserved Vegetables	11.2	14.9	18.1
Cut Flowers	12.6	18.0	67.6
Totals	636.3	1092.2	1511.8

SOURCE: Data from United Nations, *Yearbook of International Trade Statistics*, various years.

including Cameroon, Zimbabwe, Swaziland and Ghana have experienced an expansion of horticultural exports in recent years, although such trade remains relatively small.

Most other African countries have either experienced a stagnation in their traditional fruit and nut export industries (for instance, banana exports in Somalia; cashew nut exports in Tanzania and Mozambique), or have encountered significant production, transport and marketing problems which have severely limited the development of trade in non-traditional products (Mali, Burkina Faso, Senegal, Uganda, Zambia and Ethiopia). Surveys of European fresh produce importers consistently indicate the perception of high transaction costs in dealing with African suppliers and high degrees of uncertainty regarding product quality, continuity and reliability of supply, provision of information, and the exporters' overall familiarity with the requirements of the trade.[10]

TABLE 7.4: **Sub-Saharan Africa's World Market Share for Horticultural Product Exports**

Product Category	1973	1989
Fresh Fruit + Nuts	5.4%	6.2%
Processed Fruit	12.6	4.2
Fresh Vegetables	3.1	0.9
Preserved Vegetables	0.6	0.5
Cut Flowers	1.0	3.0
Total (Weighted)	4.3	3.6

SOURCE: Based on data from United Nations, *Yearbook of International Trade Statistics*.

---

[10] The survey results of Hormann and Will (1987), covering fifty importers in six West European countries, is indicative of broad perceptions of the hazards of doing business with African suppliers.

Only a few of the successful SSA horticultural exporting countries have developed a broad-based trade, which includes a range of different products and market outlets. This pattern appears to apply only to South Africa, Kenya and Zimbabwe. The horticultural trades of these countries consist of a range of fresh and processed fruits and vegetables and cut flowers. In contrast, the horticultural exports of Côte d'Ivoire, Cameroon and Swaziland are dominated by only one or two commodities/products. Their trade is either linked to preferential treatment in particular European markets (for example, Ivoirian and Cameroonian banana exports to France) or an outgrowth of the exporting industry of a neighboring country (for example, the linkages between the industry of Swaziland and that of South Africa).

Hence, for different categories of horticultural products, a limited few countries account for the bulk of SSA's trade. As indicated in Table 7.5, only two countries account for 77% of the region's fresh fruit and vegetable exports to the EEC, nearly 87% of processed fruit and vegetable exports, and 81% of cut flower exports to the EEC.

THE HISTORICAL DEVELOPMENT OF KENYA'S HORTICULTURAL EXPORTS

This section examines the development of Kenya's horticultural exports over the past half century. It traces changes in the organization of production and trade, the forms and intensity of government interventions, the international

TABLE 7.5: **Concentration of SSA Horticultural Exports to the EEC (1992)**
(Value and % Figures Pertain to EEC Imports; CIF $ Millions)

Country	Fresh Fruit and Vegetables		Processed Fruit and Vegetables		Cut Flowers		Totals	
	Value	% of African Total	Value	% of African Total	Value	% of African Total	Value	% of African Total
South Africa	627.7	56.7	133.4	56.5	8.3	8.0	769.4	53.2
Côte d'Ivoire	226.6	20.5	1.9	0.8	1.8	1.7	230.3	15.9
Kenya	55.6	5.0	71.2	30.1	56.1	53.9	182.9	12.6
Cameroon	88.2	8.0	1.6	0.7	—	—	89.8	6.2
Zimbabwe	13.6	1.2	1.5	0.7	28.4	27.3	43.5	3.0
Swaziland	15.1	1.4	14.5	6.1	—	—	29.6	2.0
Other	79.4	7.1	11.8	5.0	9.5	9.2	100.7	7.0
Total	1106.2	100.0	235.9	100.0	104.1	100.0	1446.2	100.0

SOURCE: Eurostat Data Base.

market environment faced by Kenya's exporters, and the levels and composition of trade.

Early Origins and Development Through World War II

The historical origins of Kenya's horticultural export trade date at least as far back as 1500 when traders in the coastal ports of Kilwa and Malindi provided fruit and vegetables to Portuguese ships sailing to and from India. In a more recent era, Indian and Arab traders based in coastal towns included fruits and vegetables among the various agricultural commodities sent to Zanzibar during the late 1800s. Small quantities of tropical fruits continued to be exported from the coastal ports on into the early decades of the twentieth century.[11]

During British rule in Kenya, first as a protectorate (in 1895) and later as a colony (from 1920), relatively little attention and investment was directed to the production and trade of horticultural products. Prior to World War II, the horticultural sub-sector was characterized by an absence of modern marketing facilities, nation-wide marketing organizations, well-recognized grades and standards for fresh produce, and research and advisory services. Although small export trades in potatoes and passion fruit juice were developed by private firms during the inter-war years, the bulk of local fruit and vegetable production was of very low quality and Kenya remained a net importer of horticultural products.

Other than a few backyard jam- and juice-making units, the only commercial processing plants were four small factories constructed during the 1930s to extract juice from passion fruit for export to South Africa and Australia. Raw materials for the factories came from about one hundred European farmers based in Western Kenya who had planted passion fruit to supplement depressed incomes from cereals production. A Passion Fruit Board provided technical support to growers and regulated the competition between the factories. Although this trade was interrupted during World War II, the war-time restrictions on non-essential imports stimulated investment in import-substituting fruit and vegetable processing operations. These companies would subsequently benefit from high post-war tariffs on competing imported products.

---

[11] This coastal trade is discussed by Martin (1973).

Box 7.1: LOSING AND GAINING GROUND: A TALE OF TWO COUNTRIES

The recent experiences in Côte d'Ivoire and Zimbabwe illustrate the widely divergent trends taking place in horticultural exports within SSA. During the 1970's, Côte d'Ivoire emerged as a major, and then dominant, source of fresh pineapples to the West European market. It benefitted from both indigenous and foreign investments and high levels of integration into European distribution channels, particularly in France. The country's close proximity to Europe and the development of strong infrastructure for produce grading and sea shipment enabled it to undercut prices of more distant suppliers (e.g. Kenya, South Africa and Southeast Asian countries). Pineapple exports increased from 17,440 tons in 1970 to 157,700 tons in 1980. These exports peaked in 1985 at 196,000 tons, at which time Côte d'Ivoire accounted for nearly 93% of EEC imports. Since then, rapidly rising costs, an overvalued currency, the restructuring of the industry and the collapse of the country's pineapple processing companies reduced production and caused an overall decline in competitiveness of the industry. During the early 1990s, exports had fallen to below 120,000 tons per year and the country's EEC market share had fallen by nearly one-third to 63%.

In sharp contrast, Zimbabwe has experienced a rapid expansion in horticultural exports since the mid-1980s, rising from U.S $3.5 million in 1985/86 to $39.0 million in 1992/93. The initial impetus behind this expanding trade were efforts by some large-scale commercial farmers to diversify away from crops which had strict price, quantity and marketing controls. Recently, the implementation of broad economic policy reforms has considerably increased the incentives and competitiveness of Zimbabwean (horticultural and other) exporters. Much of the expansion in exports has occurred for cut flowers (especially roses) as several hundred commercial tobacco farmers have diversified into flower production, drawing upon technologies and advice provided by private sources from the Netherlands and Israel. Within a seven year period, Zimbabwe has emerged as a major player in the European cut flower market. There has also been considerable investment in citrus orchards in the past few years. Large quantities of marketable fruit are expected to be harvested by the mid-1990s. Investments are currently being made in post-harvest handling and transport facilities. The country's export trade in fresh vegetables is also expanding, and there have been several recent investments in factories to process fruits and vegetables for export.

Probably the most significant development during the war years was the implementation of a Dried Vegetable Project by the Agriculture Department. The project was dedicated to providing the Kenyan army and Allied troops in East Africa with supplies of dehydrated vegetables for use in soups and other foods. In 1942, dehydration factories were constructed at Kerogoya and Karatina in the center of the country. African smallholder farmers in surrounding areas were contracted to grow potatoes, carrots, cabbages and other vegetables to supply the factories.

Although many of the farmers had prior experience growing vegetables for the local fresh market, the project offered participating farmers access to high-quality seeds and technical advice, a guaranteed outlet for their entire production at remunerative prices, and exemption from recruitment into military labor service. A special unit of agricultural officers was assigned to the project. Supplementing smallholder outgrower production was production from factory nucleus estates on land leased from local farmers and production on collectively farmed swamp areas, where small irrigation systems were constructed. While initially encountering organizational and weather-related problems, by 1945 the project was a major success, involving over 13,500 farmers, an agricultural and factory staff of more than 3500 people, and deliveries of more than 22,000 tons of produce to the factories. The project was by far the largest food processing operation involving African farmers in Kenya to that date.[12]

When the war ended so did the military's need for dehydrated vegetables. Still, the closure and subsequent dismantlement of the factories created considerable controversy. The institutional and technical features of the project would influence later developments in smallholder agriculture in Kenya.[13] For example, the project represented the first widespread use of irrigation in African farming in Kenya. The experience gained in irrigated cultivation and irrigation management would prove important in later irrigation schemes. The scheme also demonstrated that an expansion in smallholder cash crop production could be achieved over a relatively short period. In this regard, the project anticipated subsequent programs to expand smallholder coffee, tea, pineapple and pyrethrum production during the 1950s. In addition, the

---

[12] In the food processing industry, only the Mumias sugar scheme developed in the 1970s and the Njoro Canners french bean scheme developed in the 1980s have featured larger numbers of smallholder outgrowers.

[13] Some of these points are noted by Moris (1973) in his analysis of the background to the Mwea irrigation scheme.

project's use of a specialized extension service and input distribution system for a targeted set of crops and locations anticipated innovations built into later smallholder contract farming schemes in Kenya. The project would also serve as a model for post-independence program to increase the incomes of farmers settled under the Million Acres Settlement Scheme.

Post-World War II to Kenyan Independence

Following the war, the British Government maintained restrictions which it had imposed on food imports from the United States and other dollar countries. Since the United States was the leading supplier of many canned fruit and vegetable products to the U.K., the import restrictions resulted in major shortages of these products. The colonial government of Kenya viewed this trade regime as an opportunity to expand the colony's exports. The Agriculture Department soon set up a horticulture section, whose initial mandate focused on experimental research into fruit and vegetable varieties suitable for canning and advisory services to farmers on cultivation practices and post-harvest procedures. Fruit and vegetable canning was also an area in which the government sought to promote foreign investment through tax relief and other incentives.

These research, advisory and investment promotion efforts were valuable contributions to the establishment of a pineapple canning industry. In 1948, two British companies in collaboration with European settler farmers set up canning factories to supply the U.K. with processed pineapple products. They got off to a very slow start and over the next fifteen years, these firms would experience a continuous stream of problems related to raw material procurement, transport, and intermediate input (e.g. cans, sugar) which weakened their competitiveness in international markets and generally resulted in financial losses. Although exports reached over 9000 tons by the early 1960s, the Kenyan product was largely a 'filler' when supplies from more preferred sources were inadequate. This was reflected in the far lower unit value of the Kenyan product compared with that of its competitors.[14]

The pineapple canning industry survived during this period due in large measure to interventions by government, including price guarantees for (European) farm producers, technical and financial support for African smallholder outgrowers, taxes imposed on pineapples sold in the fresh market, the enforcement of exclusive crop buying zones for firms, duty exemptions on im-

---

[14] The early history of this industry is discussed by Kay (1965) and Swainson (1980).

ported inputs, negotiations for improved international freight rates, and other measures. While the industry had initially been based on raw material supplies from a limited number of large-scale European settler farmers, by the early 1960s, some 75% of factory supplies came from smallholder farmers. A program undertaken by the Agriculture Department to provide technical advice and inputs (on credit) to smallholders was a major factor in the availability of raw materials (albeit of uneven quality) to the factories.

During the period between the war and Kenyan independence, export trades were also developed or redeveloped for other processed fruit and vegetable products. This was initially on a very small scale. In the case of passion fruit juice, Kenya's trade remained at tiny levels through much of the 1950s due to a decline in European farmer plantings of the crop, frequent outbreaks of plant diseases in the main producing areas and increased competition in world markets. Beginning in the late 1950s the Agriculture Department launched a program to encourage smallholder production in parts of Nyanza District. The result was a recovery of production and trade to pre-war levels. On a similarly small scale, other Kenyan companies entered into contracts to supply European manufacturers with canned vegetable products (e.g. green beans and tomato paste). Government support was also important in these ventures. The varieties used had been selected from among those tested by the Agriculture Department, and the farmers in the government-backed Perkerra Settlement Scheme were an important source of raw materials for the factories.

An export trade in fresh fruit and vegetables was also initiated during this period. In 1955, a local (Asian-owned) farming and trading company began to send consignments of lettuce, tomatoes and other temperate zone vegetables by sea to Aden in order to supply ships calling at that colony and oil companies operating in the Persian Gulf. Over the next two years, small trades in fresh vegetables were conducted with buyers in Djibouti and Somalia. In 1957, the Horticultural Cooperative Union (HCU) sent small quantities of high-quality produce by air to the U.K.[15] While the East African-Near East

---

[15] The Horticultural Cooperative Union was created in 1952 to provide marketing services to European growers. During its first decade of operations, the HCU became the largest wholesaler and exporter of fresh produce in East Africa and the most important distributor of imported horticultural seeds and temperate fruits in Kenya. It entered the export market only after several years of local market experience and investment in marketing infrastructure. While some African primary cooperative societies were brought into the Union, the HCU's senior management was entirely European and 80% of its sales was of produce from European farmers.

trade represented an extension of the earlier regional trade in potatoes, the air-freighted trade was an entirely new development, made possible by the initiation of passenger air carrier links between East Africa and Western Europe.

The fresh produce trade with the U.K. initially consisted of small volumes of strawberries, mangoes, pineapples, green beans and chilies, produced by European farmers and directed to a single wholesaler in London's Covent Garden Market. The air-freighted supplies were very expensive and sold only through 'up-market' restaurants, hotels and department stores during the winter months. Although this 'off-season' fresh produce market was as yet undeveloped, the U.K. demand for Kenyan produce far exceeded the latter's supply capability throughout the late 1950s and early 1960s. Kenya's annual exports were limited to a few hundred tons, primarily as a result of the very limited availability of air cargo facilities. The colonial government played a very minor role in the development of this air-freighted trade, regarding it as having prestige value for Kenya, yet little growth potential. While the government did provide the initial financing for the establishment of the Horticultural Cooperative Union, its support for the export trade was limited to research on packaging materials and quality assessment trials on fruit shipped by sea to Europe.

A very small commercial trade in cut flowers was also developed during this period, with a limited number of European settler farmers participating. One nursery company, started by a retired British Army officer, developed an export trade in carnations and sent consignments to neighboring countries as well as to the U.K. Another producer/exporter specialized in more exotic flowers such as orchids and strelitzia. Cut flower production among African smallholders also began, although this was limited to a few locations and only involved sales to Nairobi hotels and florists.

At Independence, Kenya's horticultural exports were relatively insignificant, amounting to about 1.2 million Kenyan Pounds or 2.8% of Kenya's total exports in 1963. The country's horticultural exports were dominated by an unstable pineapple canning industry which required extensive government support and whose future commercial viability was in doubt. While the European market for fresh horticultural produce appeared to provide Kenya with significant trading opportunities, the country lacked the level of production and infrastructure required for economical sea shipment of produce and its trade in highly perishable commodities was restricted by limited air freight facilities. The minor significance of horticultural exports at independence and the limited regard given to its future development were reflected in the World Bank's *Economic Survey Mission Report (1963),* which devoted only two paragraphs to the horticultural sub-sector and did not mention it in its extended series of conclusions and recommendations.[16]

First Decade of Independence

The first decade of Kenyan independence witnessed a moderate expansion and considerable diversification of Kenya's horticultural exports. Major structural changes occurred in the sub-sector as a result of new foreign investment, major financial and managerial problems encountered by a 'Kenyanized' Horticultural Union, and the entry of additional firms into the fresh produce trade. By the early 1970s the sub-sector would have the infrastructure and international market linkages to begin a rapid expansion in production and trade. During this period, the government directed very few resources to the further development of broad-based production support services, marketing infrastructure or regulatory mechanisms within the sub-sector. Instead, the it intervened primarily by facilitating and sometimes by directly participating in specific projects involving foreign investment.

Horticultural production support services were badly neglected during this period. With respect to crop research, most of the activities previously undertaken at the National Horticultural Research Station and its various sub-stations were terminated after independence as a result of severe shortages of qualified staff and financing. A joint Kenyan Government/FAO research project was initiated in 1971, but the work undertaken focused on varietal testing, largely duplicating work done during the 1950s. No field tests or post-harvest research were undertaken. While the Development Plan 1966–1970 indicated government intentions to establish a specialized horticultural extension service, no unit was ever formed and the number of extension agents with specialized horticultural training remained very limited. Throughout this period, no official research and advisory capability was developed for cut flower production.

Similarly, very limited public resources were directed toward developing the infrastructure for horticultural marketing. Studying the domestic marketing system for horticultural crops in the late 1960s, Wilson (1971) found

---

[16] The mission's main comment regarding horticulture was to warn that the exports of fresh pineapples to Europe was 'uneconomic'. Actual Kenyan experience proved this to be incorrect. In fact, fresh pineapples served as the 'growth leader' in Kenya's fresh produce trade during the 1970s, enabling firms to penetrate European continental markets.

that only two of Kenya's five largest urban areas had separate wholesale market facilities and that the transport facilities in major fruit and vegetable producing areas was very inadequate. By the early 1970s, the Nairobi airport still lacked a cold storage facility and had inadequate numbers of loading platforms and trolleys to handle the country's fresh produce exports. Despite previously successful trials in sea shipment of fresh produce, when the government expanded and re-equipped the port at Mombasa, it did not invest in cold storage, handling or loading facilities for horticultural produce.

During this period, little official attention was given to developing a proper regulatory framework for horticultural production and trade. In 1967, a Horticultural Crops Development Authority was created and endowed with an extremely broad yet vague set of powers. The Authority was in fact given little authority. It would operate under the direction of the Ministry of Agriculture, which provided it with few operating funds and little policy guidance. As a result, the Horticultural Development agency was for many years unable to build up a competent staff and experienced frequent changes in senior management. Instead of performing regulatory functions, the agency was initially used by the ministry as a conduit for channeling foreign donor resources into specific projects. The agency's support to the export trade was limited to operating a small shed at the airport, convening meetings between exporters and air freight suppliers, and instituting common standards for produce packaging.

Foreign Investment in Fruit and Vegetable Processing

The recovery of West European economies during the 1950s and the growing incomes and demand for convenience food that resulted from it produced a major increase in international trade in a wide range of processed fruit and vegetable products. This lasted throughout the 1960s and until the mid-1970s recession. Accompanying this expanding demand and trade was a partial relocation of processing operations for temperate fruits and vegetables away from Northern Europe and toward sites in Southern and Eastern Europe and a relocation of tropical fruit industries away from high-income countries (e.g. United States and Australia) and toward sites in developing countries. This relocation trend, stimulated partly by labor cost-saving objectives, was a prevalent strategy of European and U.S. multinational corporations.[17] Kenya would participate in this industrial relocation, becoming the site for foreign invest-

---

[17] This trend was discussed by Mackintosh (1977) and Groosman (1982).

ments in several product lines. In each case, the Kenyan government would make substantial resource commitments either in the form of equity holdings in a joint venture operation or through the provision of land, technical staff and financial support to expand raw material supplies.

One of the major foreign investments concerned the dehydration of vegetables for export. The initial investment took place in 1964 and was a joint venture between a British agricultural trading company and the parastatal Development Finance Company of Kenya. For the British company, the establishment of a small dehydration factory at Naivasha represented a pilot project to examine the technical, economic and market prospects for a larger venture. The firm had no prior experience with vegetable dehydration, but wished to retain a presence in Kenya following its ouster from the country's pyrethrum trade at independence. For the Kenyan Government, social and political objectives were paramount. The project would be used as a vehicle for enhancing the agricultural skills and incomes of smallholder farmers who were being resettled under the so-called Million Acres Settlement Scheme. By targeting support services to these farmers and by controlling the resultant crop (via a contracting arrangement), the government would be in a better position to recover its land purchase loans and strengthen its administrative control over the settlement area.

Many of the project's components were modeled on the war-time dried vegetable project. A targeted farmer advisory unit was set up, seeds and other inputs were provided on credit, and guaranteed prices were offered. The dehydration factory was also to receive raw material supplies from larger European farmers who had irrigation facilities and were otherwise producing for the fresh export market.

While the smallholder outgrower component largely achieved company and government objectives, no other dimension of the venture had any measure of success. Large farm supplies were less than expected because the fresh produce market offered more remunerative prices. Overall, raw materials supplies to the factory were highly seasonal, leading it to operate at less than half of its capacity. The factory itself was poorly equipped and managed and its final product was a low quality carrot powder, exported to the U.K. at a loss. In 1968, the Kenyan Government rescued the bankrupt company, paying off its past debts and buying out the former owners. Over the next few years, the company continued to struggle and required cash infusions from the Treasury. Despite very favorable international market conditions for dehydrated vegetables, the Kenyan company achieved only modest increases in production and trade. Because of the uneven quality and generally low value of its product mix, it accumulated financial losses annually.

In 1970, a Working Party on the Horticultural Industry criticized the vegetable dehydration company for its failure to develop a commercially sound, long-term plan to develop its trade and to utilize experts in its product field. The Working Party argued that in the longer run, the profitability of the industry was dependent upon a linkage being formed with a major European or U.S. company which would provide finance, technical know-how, and a secure distribution outlet. After several aborted contacts, the government did enter in a joint venture partnership in 1972. The venture would involve the construction of a large modern factory at Naivasha and a shift toward higher value crops and more reliance upon large-scale production, perhaps on nucleus estates. While the government would have a majority equity share holding, a key element of the project would be a management and marketing contract with (and minority shareholding for) Germany's largest manufacturer/distributor of dehydrated vegetables.

The pineapple canning industry was also transformed during this period via a government-supported foreign investment. In 1964, the firm Kenya Canners approached a parastatal financing company for a loan to expand the capacity of its factory. This was agreed to on the condition that Kenya Canners develop a strategic link with an international canning company. A year later, a management and marketing contract was entered into with the California Packing Company (Del Monte), giving the latter a low cost and low risk opportunity to assess the potential for diversifying its international production base. In addition to being awarded sole marketing rights to Kenya Canners' product and an option to purchase a majority of the company's equity, the American company received a commitment from the Kenyan government to expand its smallholder production support program. It also leased 5000 acres of land to the company so that they could examine the potential for developing a nucleus estate.

In the first few years under Calpak management, Kenya Canners continued to face major problems with raw material supply, in both quantity and quality. An extended drought in 1965–1966 and the sale of some former European estates were the proximate causes. Moreover, in the main pineapple-growing areas, smallholders were finding coffee production more remunerative and were scrambling to plant coffee before the International Coffee

Organization's ban on additional plantings was effectively applied. Faced with this situation, Kenya Canners proposed to the government that further expansion of the industry be based on estate production. This proposal encountered opposition from smallholder producers and their parliamentary advocates. Yet, the government agreed to it and purchased and then leased an additional 18,000 acres of land to Kenya Canners. The government also agreed to a Calpak demand giving Kenya Canners a ten-year monopoly on local pineapple processing and providing the firm with reductions on rail, wharfage and handling charges.[18]

Soon afterwards, Kenya Canners undertook a major investment program to develop its nucleus estate and construct a modern factory with an annual processing capacity of 170,000 tons, five times that of the existing factory. Still, through 1972 the company continued to operate at a loss with its volume of trade remaining at or below that at Independence. The official program of smallholder pineapple support was phased out and the government had to write off a large part of the loans provided to farmers. By 1974, outgrower supplies were totally phased out and the Kenya Canners operation was based entirely on estate production.

A joint venture involving foreign participation was also developed in the passion fruit juice industry soon after Independence. This joint venture, formed in 1965, involved an Australian firm (Cottees Limited) which was experienced in the exotic fruit juice industry and the Kenyan parastatal Agricultural Development Corporation. The new company, Kenya Fruit Processors Limited, modernized an existing factory, developed an extended fruit collection system and raised producer prices considerably. This stimulated increased plantings, but a plant disease wiped out much of the crop.

When Cottees quickly abandoned the project, its place was taken by a Swiss company, Passi AG, one of Europe's leading distributors of exotic fruit juices. Passi would blend the Kenyan product with passion fruit juice supplies from other sources. The firm's entry into Kenya necessitated little financial investment, yet it obtained sole control over marketing and received a commitment from the Kenyan government to provide financial and technical support to increase smallholder production of passion fruit. During the late 1960s and early 1970s, Kenya Fruit Processors' production and trade ex-

---

[18] These developments were reviewed by Kaplinsky (1979) and Swainson (1980). Both writers argued that the Kenyan Government was ill-advised to provide significant investment incentives to Del Monte and enable the firm to develop a nucleus estate for pineapple production.

panded rapidly, leading Kenya to emerge as one of the leading international suppliers of passion fruit juice. Expecting a major growth in market demand, the company undertook the construction of a large modern factory in 1972 and launched an expanded production support scheme.

Foreign Investment in Flower Production

During the 1960s, commercial cut flower production in Kenya expanded. Most of the increased production which came primarily from small European-owned companies, was directed to the domestic market. Growing numbers of African smallholders, particularly in the Limuru and Tigoni areas west of Nairobi, began to experiment with flower production. Kenya's earlier flower trade was diversified to include chrysanthemums, alstromeria, molecella and other flowers. However, the limited local investment in post-harvest facilities and lack of local marketing expertise limited Kenya's cut flower exports to only 75 tons in 1969.

This cottage industry was transformed by a multi-million dollar investment in 1969 by a Danish firm, Dansk Chrysanthemum Kultur (DCK), then the world's largest producer of chrysanthemum cuttings and a major player in the European market for other types of flowers. While DCK had initially concentrated its operations in northern Europe, in the 1960s the firm began to develop production sites in the Mediterranean and other areas in order to extend its product range and supply season and to take advantage of lower labor costs.

As in the case of the foreign investors in Kenya's fruit and vegetable processing industry, DCK was offered highly favorable terms to invest in Kenya. For example, the Kenyan Government provided the firm with a long-term, low-cost lease of a 15,000 acre estate (at Masongaleni), exclusive growing and trading rights for several types of flowers for eight years, extensive work permits for expatriate workers and a twenty-five year *status quo passus* with regard to changes in the laws about foreign investor taxation and profit repatriation. The Danish Government reduced the start-up costs for DCK by providing a cash grant equivalent to about one-third of the initial investment costs.[19]

---

[19] While the investment did offer significant employment and foreign exchange earning potential, the very favorable investment terms accorded to DCK may also have stemmed from the fact that the Kenyan Government's primary negotiator and signatory for the investment was a high-ranking official who had initially invited DCK to Kenya and who later became a Director in its Kenyan subsidiary.

Within a few years, the Dansk Chrysanthemum Kultur Production Company (Kenya) had some 100 hectares under chrysanthemums and other flowers/foliage at the Masongaleni estate and had purchased two additional farms. The Masongaleni operation featured relatively advanced production and post-harvest technologies (including an advanced irrigation system, shaded netting and a large grading and cold storage unit) and employed some 1600 people. One of the firm's newly acquired farms, a 3000 hectare estate on the shores of Lake Naivasha, was developed to grow carnations, a flower whose European market was then expanding at a very rapid pace. The third farm, at Updown near Nairobi, was used by the firm primarily as a nursery and experimental station. Although DCK (K) initially experienced major technical production problems, by 1973 large increases in both the quantity and quality of production were recorded. Kenya's cut flower exports that year were nearly 1500 tons, with DCK accounting for some 90% of the total.

Expansion and Diversification in the Fresh Fruit and Vegetable Trade

During Kenya's first decade of independence, the market conditions within the European fresh produce market were highly favorable for new as well as established suppliers. West European import demand for 'out-of-season' and 'exotic' produce, though still small compared with imports of more traditional commodities (for example, citrus fruit, bananas), expanded rapidly as a result of increased incomes, greater consumer awareness of tropical products, growing health awareness, and expanding European populations of 'guest workers' and immigrant communities from the Mediterranean, Asia and other origins. Kenya faced relatively few competitors in the product markets during the seasons in which its supplies were concentrated. Its competitive position was enhanced by duty free access to the U.K. market, tariff reductions which accompanied the Agreement of Association between the East African Community and the EEC, and relatively low, Kenyan government-directed air freight rates for exported produce.

Kenya's ability to service the growing European market was further enhanced by investments in production infrastructure and the expanded availability of air-freight facilities. During the 1960s, several investments in irrigation systems were undertaken on large farms around Lake Naivasha. The development of the nucleus estate at Kenya Canners also made available to the fresh market trade small quantities of very high quality pineapples, which came to serve as the 'product leader' of this trade. The increased availability

of air-freight chartering facilities in the late 1960s and the subsequent introduction of wide-bodied carriers for passenger air traffic between East Africa
and Western Europe facilitated the flow of greatly increased volumes of trade.
Kenya's fresh fruit and vegetable exports increased from only 1400 tons in
1968 to 8600 tons in 1973.

During this period Kenya's fresh produce trade not only expanded in size,
it also became increasingly diversified. More than two dozen different commodities were exported on a seasonal or more extended basis. These included
tropical and sub-tropical fruits (pineapples, mangoes, avocado and passion
fruit), temperate zone vegetables (french beans, sweet peppers and zucchini),
and a broad range of 'Asian vegetables' (chilies, okra, karela and dudhi).

Kenya's trade was concentrated in the U.K. market, although some commodities found a profitable market on the European continent. Trade was
oriented to specialty markets or the high-quality end of more mainstream
markets. The rapidly expanding trade in 'Asian vegetables' was directed to
the South Asian (immigrant) communities in London, whose population was
growing due to immigration and whose dietary habits included a preference
for traditional fruits and vegetables. Kenya's growing trade in fresh pineapples consisted of large fruit with large crowns which were used as well for
ornamental purposes.

While three companies accounted for the bulk of this growing trade, a
large number of companies began to involve themselves in the fresh produce
trade on a seasonal or full-year basis. By 1973, there were thirty-six registered exporters. Entry into this trade came from two major sources. One set
of new entrants were domestic wholesalers and/or retailers of fresh produce.
These firms acquired experience in grading and packing, established trading
relations with producers and built up their storage and transport facilities
prior to entering the export trade. The second set of new entrants consisted of
medium-scale farmers integrating trading into their operations in order to
circumvent existing exporters. During this period, the Horticultural Cooperative Union's position in the trade was eclipsed due to internal financial and
managerial problems and the Union's politicization. Despite the growth and
product diversification of the fresh produce export trade, this trade still had a
very limited base with only about 150 to 200 (medium-to-large-scale, non-
African) farmers accounting for the bulk of supplies.

Horticultural Export Development Since 1974

Over the past two decades, the horticultural export sub-sector has developed
into an important component of the Kenyan economy, providing a major source
of foreign exchange earnings as well as substantial employment and farm
income opportunities. During this period when Kenya's exports of many 'traditional' commodities either declined (sisal, meat, pyrethrum) or fluctuated
greatly from year-to-year (coffee, tea), the aggregate volume and value of
horticultural exports increased substantially and virtually continuously,
mounting into double-digit rates most years. As Table 7.6 indicates, horticultural exports have increased nearly five-fold in volume and thirteen-fold in
dollar value terms since 1973. By 1991, the value of horticultural exports—at
$133 million—accounted for 12% of Kenya's total merchandise exports.

While the sub-sector has achieved substantial and virtually continuous
export growth, the trade patterns for particular (categories of) commodities
have varied considerably. Such variations and the factors contributing to them
are examined below.

Fresh Fruit and Vegetables

Table 7.7 traces the progression of Kenya's export trade in fresh fruit and
vegetables. The most rapid growth in this trade occurred between 1974 and
the early 1980s, with aggregate exports doubling from about 10,000 tons to
more than 20,000 tons. Since then, trade has expanded at a slower pace, and
except for one year in which there were unusual circumstances (1988), it has
remained more or less stagnant in volume and value terms since 1987. While
maintaining a diverse product mix (spanning some fifty different commodi-

TABLE 7.6: **The Growth of Kenya's Horticultural Exports[a], 1973 to 1991**

Year	Volume (000s Tons)	Value (Millions of Kenyan Pounds)	Value ($ Millions Equivalent)	Average Unit Value ($ Per Ton)
1973	27.4	3.6	10.4	380
1976	47.3	13.2	31.8	672
1980	66.3	23.1	61.0	920
1984	90.0	51.6	65.4	727
1988	111.1	99.9	107.4	967
1991	125.1	187.3	133.4	1066

[a] Includes fresh and processed fruits and vegetables; cut flowers. Does not include nuts for dried leguminous vegetables.

SOURCES: Kenya Customs and Excise Reports; Horticultural Crops Development Authority.

ties), Kenya's fresh produce trade is dependent upon only a few items for the bulk of its turnover. For example, in 1990 a single commodity—french beans—accounted for more than half of the value of fresh fruit and vegetable exports, while four commodities—french beans, mango, avocado, and chilies—accounted for three-fourths of the total.

Kenya's trade performance for many fresh fruits has lagged far below the country's potential. Kenya's fresh pineapple trade, having served as the lead product for the penetration of continental European markets in the early 1970s, succumbed to competition from less expensive, sea-freighted supplies from Côte d'Ivoire during the 1980s. A lack of public and private investments prevented Kenya from developing its own sea-freight capacity for pineapples and other less perishable fruits until the late 1980s, by which time major markets in Western Europe and the Middle East were well supplied from competing sources. Kenya's fresh pineapple trade was also inhibited by the Kenyan Government's restrictions on Kenya Canners (the dominant pineapple producer) in making sales to the fresh market. Only in the late 1980s was Kenya Canners given a license to export fresh pineapples. Although sales boomed in 1988, the subsequent restructuring of the parent Del Monte company (and the sale of its fresh produce marketing division) reduced the incentive for the company to begin exporting and it refocused solely on canning.

Kenya's trade performance for mangoes, avocadoes and passion fruit has also been disappointing. The country has failed to take advantage of the major expansion in European (import) demand for the former two during the 1980s, and Kenyan exporters and their downstream distributors have failed to more fully develop the European market for passion fruit. Lacking the major varieties preferred by European traders and consumers, much of Kenya's mango trade has been directed to Middle Eastern countries where the Kenyan product is used primarily for juicing rather than for direct consumption. Although Kenya's avocado exports have increased steadily, trade volumes remain trivial compared with booming European import levels which have exceeded 100,000 tons in recent years. The Kenyan product has served merely as a supplement or gap filler for shipments from Europe's more preferred suppliers (Israel and South Africa). Trade in other fruits, including 'off-season' supplies of strawberries and melons, and limited supplies of apple, bananas and various exotic fruits have performed somewhat better.

Kenya's trade performance for fresh vegetables has been more favorable. Trade expansion through the mid-1980s was broad-based. Since that time,

TABLE 7.7: **Fresh Fruit and Vegetable Exports** (Tons)

Commodity(s)	1974	1976	1978	1980	1982	1984	1986	1988	1991
Fresh Fruits									
Pineapple	2445	1878	3717	1882	517	807	864	16,745	580
Avocado	281	407	717	654	963	1400	2151	3753	4193
Mango	674	718	878	1308	1735	2472	2941	3485	1745
Passion Fruit	80	101	138	264	324	425	646	733	619
Other Fruit[a]	123	202	772	486	432	816	665	1728	833
Total Fruits	3603	3306	6222	4594	3971	5920	7267	26,444	7970
Fresh Vegetables									
French Beans	921	2324	3187	4964	6306	7524	9674	12,269	14,855
Asian Vegetables[b]	3741	4811	5953	7079	8051	9050	10,102	8582	9230
Sweet Pepper	854	573	497	111	50	81	16	37	14
Courgette	758	881	787	780	891	814	231	54	20
Other Vegetables[c]	159	294	1096	950	1003	949	761	787	956
Total Vegetables	6433	8881	11,520	13,884	16,307	18,418	20,679	21,729	25,075
Total Fruit and Vegetables	10,036	12,187	17,742	18,478	20,278	24,338	27,946	48,173	33,035

[a] Includes strawberry, melon, papaya, lime, banana, and several other minor items.
[b] Includes about twenty-five different vegetables, the most important being chilies, okra, karela and eggplant.
[c] Includes bobby beans, tomatoes, carrots, and other temperate vegetables no specified elsewhere.

SOURCE: HCDA Trade Statistics.

virtually all growth has come from expanded shipments of french bean, supplemented by small incremental gains for chilies and okra. Survival in the increasingly competitive markets for these items has been dependent upon exporter moves to upgrade their product through customized pre-packing for individual retail chains. Bulk consignments (in cartons) of these and many other vegetables are now only marginally profitable for Kenyan exporters. Kenya's trade in the broader range of 'Asian vegetables' has been stagnant since the mid-1980s as a result of increased competition from other countries and the adverse effects of increased air-freight costs on profitability. Kenya's once significant trade in sweet peppers and courgettes has fallen victim to competitive products from within Europe and the Mediterranean region.

These divergent patterns in trade development can be linked to several sets of factors:

- Rising air-freight costs and persistent air-freight bottlenecks have contributed to a long-term shift in Kenya's product mix away from relatively low-value commodities to those with higher unit values. Exporters facing limited freight allocations have sought to maximize sales turn-over by adjusting their product mix.

- Belated and limited investments in horticultural research and advisory services, belated and limited arrangements for planting material propagation, and official barriers on imports of planting material have greatly constrained the long-term development of competitive exports for several commodities, including most fruit. Weakness in official horticultural support services proved to be less important in the case of french beans and many 'Asian vegetables' since the older varieties grown in Kenya continued to be accepted by European consumers.

- Most of Kenya's fresh produce exporters are small-to-medium-scale trading companies whose overall size and limited, sometimes intermittent, involvement in fresh produce exports have prevented them from investing in proper post-harvest packing and storage facilities. Together with the failure to develop common use packing and cold storage facilities, these factors have constrained the development of trade in highly perishable or easily damaged commodities (such as strawberries and papaya). Another institutional factor is that much of Kenya's fresh produce trade is undertaken by ethnic minority-owned firms whose political vulnerability has undoubtedly weakened their incentive to make long-term investments in marketing facilities or produce crops with extended gestation periods (for example, many fruits). With only a few exceptions, most of the leading exporters have concentrated their trades on crops which mature rapidly, require less intensive post-harvest treatment and are relatively less costly to produce.

- The differential trade results also reflect the intensity and sources of competition which Kenya's exporters have faced. For fresh fruits and vegetables, Kenya has not been successful when it has tried direct competition with suppliers from within Europe and the Mediterranean region. The declining fate of Kenya's trade in courgettes, sweet peppers and other 'off-season' temperate vegetables is a testament to this. For mainstream commodities, Kenya's trade has largely been based on supplementing supplies of leading competitors (e.g. for avocado) or in supplying narrow 'market windows' (e.g. for strawberries in December/January). In contrast, for high-quality french beans and for many 'Asian vegetables', Kenya's primary competitors have been African and Asian suppliers whose transport costs are comparable to those of Kenya and whose production and marketing systems are frequently less well developed than those of Kenya.

The expansion of Kenya's fresh produce trade has been accompanied by, and is in many ways dependent on, the entry of many new participants, especially at the production level. While in the early 1970s only a few hundred smallholders produced for the fresh export market (accounting for some 10–20% of supplies), by the mid-1980s some 15,000 smallholders were active in this trade, accounting for nearly half of its volume. More recent information is not available. Table 7.8 provides a breakdown of the estimated numbers of smallholder producers of selected horticultural crops and their estimated share of export volumes.

Expanded smallholder production and sales have been a major component of Kenya's increased exports of french beans, 'Asian vegetables' and several fruits. In the case of vegetables, this expanded production came in response to a rapid increase in foreign demand during the 1970s and was stimulated by competitive pressures within Kenya which led exporters to extend and diversify their sources of supply. Smallholder adoption of these crops was facilitated by informal technical advice provided by larger farmers in several locations and the production support services offered by several exporters. The fact that several crops have technical production characteristics which are quite similar to more traditional smallholder crops further eased their introduction.

In the case of the avocado, the main stimulus for smallholder production came not from the encouragement or support of exporters, but from a seedling propagation program undertaken at the National Horticultural Research Station. During the late 1970s and early 1980s, NHRS employees distributed avocado seedlings free to farmers in nearby areas and provided them with informal technical advice. This informal assistance contradicted a stated government policy that official support for avocado production go only to farmers planting a minimum of five hectares. Once the smallholder plantings matured, the government, through the Horticultural Crops Development Authority, was obliged to collect and market the crop since there was inadequate demand on the part of private exporters.

Several other changes have taken place in the structure of production underpinning the fresh produce trade. Over the past decade, large-scale corporate farms owned by foreign companies or private local firms have become increasingly important for this trade. In most cases, the firms involved have

TABLE 7.8: **Smallholder Participation in the Fresh Produce Export Industry**
(Estimates for the Mid-1980s)

Crop(s)	Estimated Number of Smallholders	Estimated Share of Export Volumes (%)	Main Locations	Typical Plantings of the Crop
French Beans[a]	4000–4500	40	Embu, Kikuyu, Athi River	1/8 to 1/2 acre
Asian Vegetables[a]	2750–3000	50	Matuu, Mtito Andei, Kibwezi	1/2 acre
Mango[b]	1500–2000	65	Malindi, Lower Tana River area	1/2 to 1 acre
Avocado[c]	2000–2250	50	Kandara, Kangema	1/2 acre
Passion Fruit[d]	3000–4000	40	Embu, Kirinyaga	3/4 acre
Sub-Total[e]	13,250–15,750	50		

[a] Information based on Hormann (1981), District Annual Reports, interviews with MOA officials, and field visits to major production areas.
[b] Participating in export marketing channels only. Based on Retief and Tucker (1985) and interviews with exporters.
[c] Central Province only and producing only Hass and Fuerte varieties. Based on Muranga District Avocado Census (1984), interviews with exporters and MOA officials, and field visits to major production areas.
[d] Based on information provided by Kenya Fruit Processors and fresh produce exporters.
[e] Limited numbers of smallholders are also producing other fruits and vegetables for export.

also had extensive interests in other lines of agriculture, with horticultural production serving as a diversification away from less or non-profitable coffee, cattle and/or sisal operations. Another important change relates to the ownership and management of medium-scale horticultural farms. Such farms, especially those at Naivasha and Thika, were the backbone of the fresh produce trade until the late 1970s. Until that time, the vast majority of them were owned and managed by Kenyan Asians and Europeans. However, in the wake of the late 1970s coffee price boom and more recently, a large number of African entrepreneurs and civil servants have leased or purchased farms near Nairobi or Naivasha in order to grow vegetables for export.

The structure of export trade has also changed at the entry level. After the government relaxed its licensing policy, enabling all interested locally-owned firms to register as exporters, the number of licensed exporters increased from thirty-six in 1973 to eighty by 1978 to over one hundred by the mid-1980s. Fresh fruit and vegetables were among the very few major agricultural commodities whose marketing had not been controlled by parastatal marketing boards or well-established multinational corporations. The fresh produce trade thus offered what was perceived to be the easiest access by local firms into international markets and the foreign exchange which accrues through this trade.

Processed Fruit and Vegetables

Like the fresh fruit trade, Kenya's trade performance for processed fruit and vegetable products has been uneven. Following the major joint venture investments in the early 1970s, production and export levels expanded rapidly and substantially, going from just over 10,000 tons in 1974 to more than 49,000 tons in 1977. Over the next five years, exports remained in the 45,000 to 50,000 ton/year range before increasing again to 55,000–60,000 tons/year during the mid-1980s.

Over much of this period, a single firm—Kenya Canners—whose expansion of canned pineapple exports and subsequently pineapple juice exports has more or less dominated the broader trends within the industry, has accounted for 80–90% of Kenya's processed fruit and vegetable exports. The boom in processed fruit and vegetable product exports during the mid-to-late-1970s can primarily be attributed to Kenya Canners' success in building up its integrated nucleus estate/factory operations and its effective linkage with Del Monte's European marketing operations. This success made Kenya the leading source of canned pineapple to Western Europe in some years. As the West European market for canned pineapple became increasingly saturated during the 1980s, and the fresh fruit juice market showed greater vibrancy, Kenya Canners undertook to expand its own production and exports of pineapple juice.

Kenya's broader experience in processed fruit and vegetable product exports has been more varied and generally less successful. The joint venture operation at Naivasha for vegetable dehydration experienced a build-up of trade levels in the mid-to-late-1970s, but subsequently faltered due to raw material procurement problems, frequent breakdowns in factory operations and the high cost of intermediate inputs (especially fuel). Financial losses were persistent and the company eventually passed into receivership in 1982.

Similarly, the performance of Kenya's longstanding passion fruit juice industry has been poor. Raw material supply problems as well as management problems prevented the major joint venture company from fully utilizing its modern processing plant and taking advantage of the large expansion in world trade which took place between the mid-1970s and mid-1980s. For a broad range of other processed fruit and vegetable products, poor quality and high production and intermediate input costs have prevented Kenyan firms from being competitive in international markets.

The only non-pineapple product for which the industry has achieved some sustained success in export development has been canned french beans. During the 1980s, the basis for this expansion was a joint venture between a local firm and a major French manufacturing/distributing company. While the European market for canned green beans has generally been stagnant or in decline, the Kenyan venture has generated a superior quality product which has filled a particular niche in the market, especially in France. Kenya's labor cost advantages (over European producers) have compensated for the higher packaging and other intermediate input costs faced by the firm. In the past few years, there have been several additional investments in french bean canning and freezing operations by local and joint venture companies.

Flower Production and Trade

The production and trade of cut flowers has been one of the most dynamic components of Kenyan agriculture over the past two decades. This industry has experienced several new medium-to-large-scale investments, a secondary yet substantial growth in smallholder production, and a considerable diversification in the mix of crops produced and marketed. Two major stimuli are responsible for this expansion and diversification of production and trade. One has been the large and steady expansion in West European use and trade of cut flowers since the early 1970s and the sustained interest on the part of European flower trading companies in broadening their product range and their supply sources. The second stimulus was the successful example provided by DCK(K) during the early to mid-1970s. When employees left the firm to strike out on their own, the technical and marketing experience they had gained there served them in good stead.

Rapidly expanding its production and exports during the early to mid-1970s, the DCK venture was plunged into a financial crisis in 1976 when the company's major shareholder suddenly pulled out of the project. The DCK farms were passed into Kenyan ownership and the Updown Farm branched off as a separate company. Following two seasons of continuing financial and managerial problems, ownership of the estates changed hands again. Brooke Bond acquired the Naivasha and Masengoleni Estates, while the Agricultural Development Corporation acquired the Updown Farm.

While Brooke Bond had no prior experience in flower production or trade, it was able to retain the services of several of DCK's expatriate production specialists. The company soon closed down the flower operation at Masongaleni, absorbing many of its 2500 workers in the company's tea estates. At Naivasha, the company (under the name Sulmac) soon undertook to expand carnation production. By the early 1980s, Sulmac had approximately 120 hectares planted under fifty different varieties of carnations, making this the largest operation of its kind in the world. Since then, Sulmac has diversified its flower mix to include roses and gypsophilia and the company has remained Kenya's dominant flower company.

When Updown Ltd. branched off in 1976, a cabinet-level government decision was made to develop a smallholder outgrower scheme for flowers. Within two years, Updown had some 425 outgrowers and a list of 1200 others waiting to join the project. Although the outgrower project collapsed soon after Updown was purchased by the Agricultural Corporation who dismissed its expatriate staff, many of the farmers who had learned floricultural skills under the project continued to produce cut flowers for commercial purposes. Some have formed marketing cooperatives, while others have sold flowers to one or more of the private firms which were established by former expatriate staff of DCK or Sulmac.

The experience of DCK and Sulmac and the efforts of particular individuals have contributed to the development of additional foreign investments in Kenya's flower industry. The largest such investment has been that of the Oserian Development Corporation, which is owned by a Dutch family now based in Kenya. The Oserian Estate, located adjacent to the Sulmac Farm at Naivasha, diversified into cut flower production (from vegetable production) during the early 1980s with the technical and marketing support of former DCK employees. Within a few years, the scale (although not the value) of Oserian's cut flower operations rivaled that of Sulmac, with production including many different types of flowers (such as delphinium, roses, dille, statice). The Oserian flower project has subsequently given rise to several other spin-off investments in flower production and trade. A former DCK employee was also instrumental in a mid-1980s investment by Yoder Brothers (U.S.) for the production and export of chrysanthemum cuttings.

In the past five years, there have been several additional investments in flower production and trade. Most involve either joint ventures or efforts by fruit and vegetable export companies to diversify into flower production and

TABLE 7.9: **Kenya's Exports of Cut Flowers**

	1975	1978	1980	1982	1984	1986	1988	1990	1991
Volume (Tons)	2746	3214	3499	4194	6941	8264	9809	14,423	16,405
Value ($ Millions)	8.9	8.3	8.1	6.4	8.9	15.3	35.8	37.8	Na.
Unit Value $/Ton	3241	2582	1743	1526	1282	1851	3650	2621	Na.

SOURCE: Central Bank of Kenya.

trade. Much of the new investment has been for rose production and other relatively high value crops, the result being dramatic recent growth in the value of Kenya's cut flower exports. Table 7.9 traces the expansion of Kenya's cut flower exports since the mid-1970s.

PRIVATE SECTOR CHARACTERISTICS AND THE ORGANIZATION OF THE SUB-SECTOR

Over the past two decades, participation in Kenya's horticultural export sub-sector has broadened considerably, with growing numbers of smallholder and other producers providing commodities and raw materials and with increased entry into trade, especially for fresh produce exports. Nevertheless, a close analysis of published and unpublished trade statistics indicates that only a few individual firms continue to account for the bulk of Kenya's horticultural exports and that firms owned by Kenyan Africans account for only a tiny proportion of this trade. These patterns (for 1991) are summarized in Table 7.10.

The last column of the table indicates that while some seventy-six companies did export horticultural products in 1991, three companies accounted for more than half of the trade. The six largest exporters accounted for nearly three-fourths of the $133 million trade.[20]

The table also shows that foreign-owned companies (including joint venture companies in which multinational firms have controlling shares) pres-

---

[20] Such a concentration of trade is not atypical for horticultural-exporting developing countries. For example, between three and six firms account for the majority of exports within the Colombian cut flower, Brazilian frozen concentrated orange juice, Chilean temperate fruit and Mexican fresh vegetable export industries.

TABLE 7.10: **Competitive and Ownership Structure of Kenya's Horticultural Exports, 1991**

	Fresh Fruit and Vegetables	Cut Flowers	Processed Fruit and Vegetables	Combined
Number of firms	47	17	13	76
Proportion of trade:				
3 Leading firms	57%	81%	92%	55%
6 Leading firms	75%	93%	98%	71%
Export shares for Foreign vs. Local Firms:				
Foreign-owned	7%	69%	89%	58%
Private-Locally owned	93%	31%	11%	42%
of which:				
Kenyan Asian	64%	2%	9%	24%
Kenyan European	17%	25%	0%	13%
Kenyan African	11%	4%	1%	5%
Parastatal	0%	0%	1%	0%
Total	100%	100%	100%	100%

SOURCES: Based on unpublished HCDA data and personal communications (for cut flowers and fresh fruit and vegetables) and data provided in UNIDO (1992) (for processed fruit and vegetables).

ently account for about 58% of Kenya's horticultural export earnings, with most of the remainder accounted for by firms owned by Kenyan Asians (24%) or Kenyan Europeans (13%). African-owned enterprises accounted for only 5% of the trade in 1991. This represented only a small improvement over their 3% share of trade during the mid-1980s.

There has been widespread entry into *the fresh produce trade* over the past two decades. This trend has given rise to some degree of trade fragmentation and firms have competed with each other for the available air-freight space. Kenyan produce continues to be sold under a number of different brands. Overseas buyers have been able to play off one Kenyan exporter against another and negotiate export prices downward. The same dominant core of firms have accounted for the majority of the trade over the past twenty years. Since 1970, there has not been a single year in which the ten leading firms accounted for less than 80% of the fresh produce trade, and in most years this share exceeded 90%. Most of the other players in this trade have conducted small and highly seasonal trading activities and have generally not remained in business for more than a year or two.

Over half of the leading firms are Asian-owned family companies or partnerships. Most had considerable experience in fruit and vegetable production and trade in the domestic market before entering the export trade. Most have their own wholesale and/or retail establishments and farms; some also have complementary interests in freight forwarding and transport. Several of the leading exporters benefit from having relatives in Europe with whom they conduct a significant proportion of their trade. These operating features have significantly reduced the risks and transaction costs which such firms have faced when trading in highly perishable and heterogenous horticultural commodities.

Much of the new entry into the trade in the past decade has been by African-owned firms. Despite their having preference in government-sponsored trade fairs and training programs and periodic preferential access to the air-freight facilities of Kenya Airways, there has been a very high failure rate among African owned firms and only a few of the survivors have achieved sustained trade growth. Of twenty-two licensed exporters with 50% or more African share ownership in 1979, only four remained in business by 1985. Several factors have contributed to the high failure rates of new African-owned trading companies:

1) **Most of the African entrepreneurs entering this field had no prior experience in horticultural trade or in international marketing *per se*.** They have instead relied upon 'learning by doing', a strategy which is very risky in the field of horticultural marketing where information, contacts, and trader reputations are key components of competitive advantage and disadvantage.

2) **Most of these entrepreneurs have maintained diverse business and other professional interests which have little or no relation to horticultural marketing,** yet which have tended to consume a great deal of their attention and resources. As most such horticultural trading companies are single proprietorships or family enterprises, the diversion of management attention to other, unrelated activities has undermined trading effectiveness.

3) **Most of these African-owned firms have sought to operate only on a small-scale or part-time basis** in the form of commercial clearing houses. They have sought to operate without investing in post-harvest treatment, packing and storage facilities. Their scale and seasonality of

operations has given them virtually no bargaining power vis-a-vis medium-to-large-scale growers and air freight carriers, while their lack of
marketing infrastructure has weakened their capacity to supply produce of high and uniform quality.

4) **Most of these firms have focused their trade on only one or relatively few commodities.** This has exposed such firms to considerable
crop procurement and market risks and has given their trade a high
degree of seasonality. Their concentration has rendered them far less
attractive to potential overseas buyers and distributors than is the case
for Kenya's exporters carrying a broad product mix.

Over many years, selected politicians and others have contended that the
dominant position in the fresh produce trade by a few firms and the high
failure rates of new entrants can be attributed to anti-competitive practices
on the part of the former, including predatory pricing, bribery of airfreight
officials, and various forms of 'exploitation' of farmers (such as non-payment,
under-weighing, and false grading). Accompanying such arguments have been
accusations of under-invoicing and failure to repatriate foreign exchange earnings. Such practices have at times occurred although their use has certainly
not been restricted to the leading export companies. Over the years, many of
the new entrants into this business had as their primary objective gaining
access to and retaining foreign currency, in circumvention of existing foreign
exchange control laws. Some of the small, unstable companies have been
particularly delinquent in their relationships with small-scale farmers.

The above allegations, together with the vested interests of particular government officials, have led to various proposals and interventions geared toward restructuring the fresh produce trade in order to provide Kenyan Africans with a greater share. Promotional measures have been taken, such as
the provision of technical support to African-owned firms and the prominent
featuring of their products at trade fairs. Other measures have given preferential treatment to Kenyan Africans, such as the reservation of Kenya Airways freight space exclusively for African-owned firms. At times, Asian-owned
firms have been harassed and 'encouraged' to take on African partners who
in most cases turned out to be prominent government officials. While the
market share of African-owned firms is higher today (11%) than it was during the mid-1980s, this expansion can be attributed to the continued development and growth of a few individual firms, rather than to any positive impact

of racially preferential policies. Many of the people who have benefitted from preferential policies have been government officials active in the fresh produce trade.[21]

In the case of *cut flowers*, the government has long recognized the need for foreign investment and technical support but never developed an official system of floricultural research and extension other than on an ad hoc, project-level basis. Many more firms are active today than a decade ago. Yet Kenya's cut flower exports continue to be dominated by Sulmac and Oserian, whose combined export share was 74% in 1991. Several African-owned companies have developed successful floricultural operations, and many have strong technical and marketing linkages with an overseas company. However, most of these companies are small and African-owned firms accounted for only 4% of cut flower exports in 1991. Kenya Government efforts to promote the 'Kenyanization' of this industry have historically been limited to some direct floricultural investments by the parastatal Agricultural Development Corporation and to pressures on foreign companies to limit the size of their expatriate staffs and provide training to Kenyans.

Kenya's exports of *processed fruit and vegetable products* are even more concentrated and dominated by foreign-owned companies. Kenya Canners, a subsidiary of Del Monte, has accounted for 80% or more of such exports over much of the past two decades. The only other processing firms which have been oriented primarily to export markets have also featured the involvement of a foreign company, either in a joint venture with a Kenyan parastatal or private company or within the framework of a management and marketing contract with a local firm. All operations have been linked into the global production and marketing operations of major multinational corporations.

The Kenyan government has sought to increase 'Kenyan control' in this industry by entering into joint ventures with foreign partners. However, such local control has generally been illusionary as the local partners have typically been 'sleeping partners' (that is, equity holders without influence), while most fundamental production, marketing and financial decisions have been made by the foreign partners and their overseas parent companies.

---

[21] For example, during the mid-1980s, among those active in the fresh produce trade were high-ranking officials in the ministries of Agriculture and of Lands and Settlement, in the Horticultural Crops Development Authority, in the Agricultural Finance Corporation, and several Members of Parliament.

In contrast, the vast majority of locally-owned fruit and vegetable processing companies have focused on serving the Kenyan domestic market, a strategy made profitable due to strong tariff and non-tariff barriers on imports of competing products into the country. These firms did service the neighboring markets of Tanzania and Uganda under the tariff umbrella of the East African Community. However, after the dissolution of the Community in 1977 and the subsequent political and economic crises in these neighboring countries, these exports declined substantially. Most such locally-owned firms have not been cost or quality competitive in international markets.

The structure of ownership in Kenya's trade has both positive and negative elements. On the positive side, without the technical skills and marketing expertise and links of foreign companies, Kenya's horticultural trade, especially that for cut flowers and processed fruit and vegetables, would have been considerably lower. A few foreign investments have had a demonstration effect (especially for cut flowers) and encouraged local entrepreneurs to make similar investments in production and post-harvest facilities. On the negative side, such an ownership pattern poses potential political problems. This sector is now one of the fastest growing components of the Kenyan economy and concerns about the distribution of benefits from this trade continue to be expressed. The government has experienced problems in monitoring and regulating the pricing and financial practices of firms which are trading with subsidiaries or associated firms overseas. From a long-term development perspective, this structure of trade has also served to provide relatively little experience for Kenyan Africans in the international marketing of Kenya's horticultural crops, experience which could be applied to other agro-industrial areas. It is ironic that the government's most persistent attention to the 'Kenyanization' issue has been directed toward a component of the horticultural trade—the export of fresh fruit and vegetables—in which Kenyan-owned firms have long accounted for more than 90% of sales.

Institutional Linkages Between Producers and Processors/Exporters

In the discussion in the first section dealing with the techno-economic characteristics of horticultural crops, it was hypothesized that due to problems of risk, transaction costs and logistics, the coordination of horticultural production with downstream activities in Kenya would be governed more by contractual ties and vertical (ownership) integration than by spot market purchasing arrangements. Here the actual vertical linkages in the Kenyan sub-sector are summarized. These institutional arrangements are classified into five categories along the following continuum from open market arrangements to internal organization:[22]

>	>	>	>	
Spot	Market	Forward	Interlinked	Vertical
Market	Reciprocity	Market	Factor and	Integration
Purchase	Agreement	Contract	Market Contract	
>	>	>	>	

On one end of the spectrum are *spot market purchases*. Here the processor or exporter purchases requirements from the market at a particular time at market prices. The firm may buy from farmers, local merchants or truckers. In this institutional framework, the processor or exporter will play no role in the production process itself. On the other end of the spectrum is the *vertical integration* of production and subsequent processing and marketing activities. Here the marketing firm develops its own farm and flows of information and resources for production are internalized within the firm.

In between these two extremes are various intermediate arrangements. For example, there may be *market reciprocity agreements*. These are informal, yet highly personalized repeat trading ties in which some degree of loyalty is built up between the exporter and a certain sub-set of growers. Still, produce is exchanged at the current market price and the exporter is not involved in the production process. Two types of intermediate contractual arrangements are indicated. Crop procurement can be made via *forward market contracts* which feature formal commitments to buy and sell specified quantities and qualities of produce at particular times. Prices may be agreed to in advance or at the time of actual exchange. A more intensive arrangement combines these forward purchase and sale commitments with buyer promises to provide specified production inputs and technical advice on credit and farmer agreement to follow the buyer's instructions regarding production. Such *interlinked factor and market contracts* are frequently referred to as contract farming.[23]

---

[22] This section draws heavily on Jaffee (1994).

[23] Along the continuum from spot market purchases toward vertical integration, the relationship between the exporter/processor and the crop producer changes in several fundamental ways. For example, i) decisions regarding production and sales become more centralized in the hands of the exporter or processor, ii) the relationship between producer and buyer becomes more formalized, iii) the terms of exchange become more extended into the future, and iv) the role of market prices in coordinating production and marketing is reduced and progressively supplemented by operating rules and direct supervision.

TABLE 7.11: **Institutional Arrangements Governing Private Processing and Trader Crop Procurement** (Percentage Share of Raw Material/Commodity Volume, 1985/86)

Crop/Industry	Alternative Institutional Arrangements					Consistent With Expectations Based on Techno-Economic Characteristics
	Spot Market	Market Reciprocity	Forward Market Contract	Inter-linked Factor and Market Contract	Vertical Inte-gration	
Fresh Produce and Cut Flowers Trade						
French Beans	20	20	30	20	10	Yes
Asian Vegetables	30	20	20	20	10	Yes
Avocado	40	40	0	0	20	No
Mango	35	40	20	0	5	No
Strawberry	10	0	90	0	0	No
Carnations	0	5	0	0	95	No
Chrysanthemum	0	0	0	0	100	Yes
Other Cut Flowers	0	15	0	5	80	Na.
Fruit/Vegetable Processing						
Pineapple	0	0	0	5	95	Yes
French Beans	5	0	0	95	0	Yes
Passion Fruit	60	0	20	20	0	No
Carrots[a]	0	0	0	95	5	No
Orange	80	0	20	0	0	Na.

[a] For 1980.

SOURCE: Author's Field Survey.

Table 7.11 depicts the actual institutional arrangements by which private processors and traders procured horticultural commodities and raw materials during the mid-1980s. The data, obtained from interviews with processors, exporters and other sources, indicate the proportion of the exported or processed volume which was procured via the various institutional linkages with growers.

The table indicates that there are great variations in the procurement arrangements used for different horticultural crops, although some of the patterns are not consistent with our expectations based solely on the crops' techno-economic characteristics. Other factors, including the capacities and experience of companies, the (non-)availability of official technical support services, geographical, logistical, political and historical factors have also influenced the emergence and evolution of institutional arrangements linking growers, processors and exporters.

The table represents the institutional patterns at a single point in time. The earlier discussion of the historical development of the sub-sector indicated that while institutional patterns have gradually evolved in the case of the fresh produce trade, there occurred more sudden and significant shifts in institutional arrangements within the cut flower and fruit and vegetable processing industries. These typically resulted from foreign or joint venture investments which brought with them not only new capital but also new forms of organization and new strategies for crop procurement.

Several interesting patterns can be observed from the table. One is that contrary to expectations, spot market linkages between growers and downstream firms have been quite prominent, even for mango and avocado in the fresh trade and in some components of the processing industry. These arrangements were thought to entail too high a level of risk for the producer and too much uncertainty with regard to product quality, supply continuity and timeliness for the processor/exporter. What is interesting is that exporters (and some processors) have tended to deal with smallholder farmers on an open market basis, while gaining most of their supplies from medium-to-large-scale producers governed by seasonal or longer term contractual and ownership ties.

Instead of having direct ties with smallholder farmers, most exporters have relied upon selected local farmers and merchants who serve as intermediaries. These appointed agents have fulfilled a number of functions including: (1) identifying and 'recruiting' farmers, (2) communicating short-term information to farmers regarding exporter quantity and timing requirements and regarding expected prices, (3) informing the exporters about local supply and competitive conditions, (4) distributing packaging materials to farmers, and (5) issuing payments to farmers. These agents typically have a shed or store to which farmers deliver their crop. The exporter's vans and trucks pass on these pick-up points on their collection rounds. For their services, the local agents are paid a commission based on the volume of sales. Based on instructions from exporters (who must contend with fluctuating availability of air freight space and fluctuations in the deliveries of medium-to-large-scale farmers), and the extent of competition from other exporters and agents, the local agents may adjust upward or downward the quality standards sought and the prices offered to farmers.

Reliance upon local agents has enabled exporters to economize on the infrastructural and transaction costs which would ordinarily be associated with procuring produce from large numbers of individual smallholders. By using local agents, exporters need not establish collection stations of their own within the smallholder areas. Rather than attempt to communicate and negotiate directly with dozens or hundreds of smallholders, exporters need only deal with a limited number of agents who have superior knowledge of local conditions and people. The residence of agents in the producing areas facilitates a continuous, if somewhat superficial monitoring of the crop.

The buying procedures used also provide great flexibility and enable exporters to shift at least part of the transport and market risks which they face back to the growers. In the face of unexpected cutbacks in air freight allocations, downturns in market prices or surplus supplies from larger farmers, exporters and their buying agents can adjust their purchases from smallholders and farm-gate prices to them so as to minimize stocks and prevent losses on sales. The typically poor communication links between Nairobi and major smallholder producing areas creates an information asymmetry which is used to their own advantage by exporters and their agents.[24]

For many farmers and processors/exporters, spot market linkages have proven to be a sub-optimal arrangement. Yet, the adoption and maintenance of alternative institutional arrangements have been constrained by difficult logistics, weak bargaining power, competition and other factors. For smallholder farmers, spot market linkages have not provided a context for enhancing or even maintaining farm-level productivity as little or no technical advice is available. Such arrangements have also provided little basis for improving product quality because the quality standards for several crops are either poorly defined or highly variable. Sometimes, spot market prices are completely divorced from quality considerations. High levels of waste have also occurred as a result of poor coordination between growers and downstream buyers. In the early-to-mid-1980s, some 25% of the smallholder crop of avocadoes, french beans, and 'Asian vegetables' remained unharvested or

---

[24] There are of course limits to the opportunistic manipulation of information and adjustment of quality standards by exporters and their agents. Competitive pressures provide one restraint on behavior with different firms and agents acquiring reputations for reliability and fairness. Opportunistic behavior is also restrained by the need to obtain the loyalty of at least a core set of growers so that the agent can economize on his own search costs and consistently fulfill the exporter's product requirements. Pressures from local politicians and from HCDA officials also restrain opportunistic behavior.

unsold as a result of seasonal production gluts and short-term exporter reductions in crop purchases due to transport or other bottlenecks.

Processing companies which have relied primarily on spot market purchases of raw materials have tended to operate at very low rates of capacity utilization. For example, the country's largest producer and exporter of passion fruit juice had an average capacity utilization rate of 29% during the late 1970s and early 1980s. In the previous decade, that firm had developed a very successful contract farming scheme involving some 4500 smallholder farmers. However, with increased overseas demand for fresh passion fruit and growing demand from the local hotel and catering trade, the firm was unable to effectively compete for the crop, and most of its contracted producers abandoned it except for the part of the year when there was a market glut. Unable to maintain control over product flows, the processing company cut back on its technical assistance and input supply program and became increasingly dependent upon highly seasonal spot market purchases from wholesalers/transporters.

Another interesting pattern is the wide variability of institutional arrangements used to procure individual commodities. This is most evident for french beans (for the fresh trade and for processing) where the prevailing arrangements span the full institutional spectrum. A more detailed analysis of the procurement arrangements for this crop indicates close positive associations between the quality standards and total volume required by the buyer and the intensity of the buyer's involvement in the production process. Firms requiring mostly or solely beans of the highest quality grade (that is, 'extra-fine') have tended to involve themselves in the production process via seasonal contracts and the provision of inputs and technical assistance to farmers. For example, Njoro Canners, whose target market is the French market for premium quality beans, has developed a highly intensive and hierarchically-organized contract farming scheme with smallholder farmers which features:[25]

1) close controls on farmer participation in the project, strict limits on the planted area for any contracted farmer, and close controls on the timing of bean plantings;

---

[25] This case is examined in greater depth in Jaffee (1990, 1994).

2) the organization of farmers into distinct groups to which specific company staff are assigned. The company's field staff has numbered more than 500 people;

3) the provision of a mandatory and standardized package of production inputs;

4) the close specification and supervision of each stage of the french bean production process;

5) the specification of fixed procurement prices and input costs; and

6) strict quality standards, below which beans are subject to rejection.

Other companies with lower quality standards need far lower volumes of beans, have fewer technical and financial resources and have developed far less intensive linkages with french bean producers.

Institutional Linkages Between Kenyan Exporters and Overseas Buyers/Distributors[26]

The organization of the Kenyan horticultural export sub-sector has also featured diverse patterns in the institutional arrangements linking Kenyan exporters with overseas buyers, agents and other distributors. Table 7.12 summarizes the main patterns from the mid-1980s. Trading relations are classified as being governed by consignment transactions, long-term contracts and vertical integration.

At least for the main products, Kenya's exports of processed fruit and vegetables were governed almost entirely by intra-firm trade or long-term contractual arrangements. While exports of canned french beans and dehydrated vegetables were technically governed by annual or longer-term marketing contracts, all or nearly all trade was conducted through European firms which also played important management and technical roles in the Kenyan operation. Ninety percent of passion fruit juice sales were made through the majority shareholder of Kenya's leading producer. Kenya's exports of pineapple products have been handled exclusively by a U.K.-based subsidiary of Del Monte.

While actual product shipments have been made from Kenya to more than one country or final buyer, in each of the above cases practically all

---

[26] A more detailed analysis of this such institutional patterns and their implications for the development and growth of trade is provided in Jaffee (1991).

marketing activities have been orchestrated by the Europe-based affiliate and nearly all exports are invoiced to them. In each case, it has been the Europe-based affiliate and not the Kenyan firm which has been responsible for short- and long-term decisions regarding product lines, sales volumes, delivery times, market destinations and prices. Hence, rather than speak of 'export marketing arrangements', it is more appropriate to regard Kenya's major processed fruit and vegetable exports as elements of the international product supply and trading operations of major multinational food corporations.

Not all of Kenya's processed fruit and vegetable exports are carried out via exclusive trading links with ownership- or management-affiliated firms. Kenya's smaller processors, including those which are oriented primarily to servicing the domestic market, sell their products to several African and Middle Eastern buyers, usually on the basis of periodic purchase orders at agreed prices.

Kenya's trade in cut flowers has similarly been dominated by intra-firm trade or long-term contractual arrangements with particular companies. For many years, Kenya's exports in carnations were made almost exclusively under a long-term contractual arrangement with a subsidiary of Europe's largest flower distributor. The marketing contract, which was renewed several times between the mid-1970s and mid-1980s, provided the importer/distributor with full control over the marketing of Sulmac's carnations and potential veto power over additional elements of Sulmac's production and trade operations.[27] While Kenya's exports of chrysanthemum cuttings have been undertaken through a single vertically-integrated operation, the bulk of Kenya's sales of other cut flowers have occurred within the Dutch flower auction system. In the mid-1980s only one Kenyan exporter was consigning its flowers directly to particular auctions. Other companies had either subsidiaries or partners in Holland to whom flowers would be invoiced or sold before the Dutch partner sold the flowers within the auctions or direct to other buyers.

Kenya's fresh produce trade has featured greater variability of exporting arrangements. Various forms have been used for the sale of individual crops and individual firms have diverse sales strategies depending upon their products, markets, contacts and experience. Still, even here, a majority of trade is governed either by long-term contracts or vertical integration. In this case,

---

[27] Sulmac has since diversified its marketing channels.

TABLE 7.12: **Institutional Arrangements Governing Export Sales**
(Percentage Share of Trade)

Crop/Industry	Institutional Arrangements		
	Consignment Transactions	Seasonal or other Long-Term Contracts	Vertical Integration
Processed Fruit and Vegetables			
Canned Pineapple and Pineapple Juice	0	0	100
Canned French Beans	0	100	0
Dehydrated Vegetables	10	90	0
Passion Fruit Juice	0	10	90
Fresh Produce			
French Beans	40	40	20
Asian Vegetables	30	30	40
Avocado	85	0	15
Weighted Average for all Fruit/Vegetables	43	31	26
Cut Flowers			
Carnations	0	100	0
Chrysanthemums	0	0	100
Other Cut Flowers	15	30	55

vertical integration involves trade between members of the same family. Many exporters, both Asian and African, have family members resident in the U.K. or elsewhere with whom trade is conducted.

The development of long-term contractual arrangements with overseas buyers and the prominence of intra-family and intra-firm trade has played a critical role underpinning the sustained development of Kenya's horticultural exports. Such institutional arrangements have:

1) provided 'Kenyan' firms with immediate and continued access to markets, even those which are highly concentrated at the import and wholesale levels;

2) facilitated the deeper penetration of Kenyan products within the targeted import markets, enabling the Kenyan suppliers to continue trade or even gain market shares during periods when market demand was stagnant or declining;

3) provided some Kenyan firms with access to a continuous stream of technical and market information, enabling them to better match their product mix, quality, packaging, etc. to the tastes and requirements of consumers and end users;

4) reduced the transaction costs faced by Kenyan suppliers, by reducing company exposure to opportunistic quality claims, sales misreporting, and payment delays, and as the overseas partner organizes the downstream distribution and sale of product to potentially quite diverse buyers;

5) improved logistics and quality control, with the overseas partner maintaining some product stocks, providing quality control information, doing re-processing or re-packing were necessary, and helping to organize or negotiate international freight arrangements; and

6) provided Kenyan and foreign companies with considerable scope to manipulate export and production input prices and to by-pass currency, tax, and other provisions in order to best meet their own financial objectives.

CONCLUSIONS

While many African countries have a potential comparative advantage in the production of fresh and processed horticultural products, few such countries have been able to develop competitive and profitable horticultural trades to the markets of Europe and the Middle East. For the vast majority of African countries, nascent horticultural export subsectors have exhibited little or no growth over the past decade, despite favorable international market conditions for many commodities. Weak technical support systems, international transport and other infrastructural bottlenecks, inappropriate marketing institutions, and poor international trade linkages have been among the common constraints.

With the possible exception of South Africa, Kenya has developed the most diversified and successful horticultural export trade within sub-Saharan Africa. However, even for Kenya, trade development patterns have been very mixed, both among commodities and individual firms. In the processing industry, export success over an extended period has only been achieved by a limited number of firms which developed strong ties with major multinational corporations either through joint ownership or through long-term technical, management and marketing contracts. Strong long-term technical, managerial and marketing linkages between Kenyan and foreign firms have also been essential to the development of Kenya's cut flower export industry. In both industries, critical 'infant-industry' support was provided by the colonial, and then the independent, government of Kenya during the 1950s and 1960s.

In the fresh fruit and vegetable trade, profitable and sustained export growth has been achieved by less than a dozen of the several hundred firms which have entered this trade over the past quarter century. For the most part, the successful firms had long experience in domestic horticultural trade and production before entering the export market. They thus had an understanding of the quality control, storage, packaging and more general risk elements associated with horticultural production and marketing before searching out export opportunities. Most of these firms initiated exports during the 1960s or 1970s, a period in which the European market for exotic and 'off-season' fruits and vegetables was just developing. The successful Kenyan firms built up long-term trading links, sometimes with family relations, which enabled them to more completely understand the requirements of the trade, reduce their risks and transaction costs, and achieve greater penetration of their products in foreign markets.

In stark contrast, the large majority of entrepreneurs who have entered the horticultural trade have done so on a part-time, highly seasonal basis. Large numbers of businessmen, civil servants and politicians have entered this trade as a leap in the dark. Lacking both technical knowledge of horticulture and relevant trading experience, the tenure of such entrepreneurs in the horticultural trade has typically been quite short.

For African countries and entrepreneurs seeking to replicate aspects of Kenya's horticultural development experience, several lessons can be drawn from that experience. First, while many African countries share with Kenya some ecological, locational and labor cost advantages in the production of certain horticultural crops, few such countries are well endowed with the additional technical, financial, infrastructural and managerial assets which are critical for developing a competitive horticultural trade. In the absence of foreign investment or a considerable initial investment by government and/or the local private sector in horticultural research, training and marketing infrastructure, the development of horticultural exports will be a very slow process in Africa with a high incidence of failure among individual firms.

Second, and relatedly, the development of African trade in many horticultural commodities will require the attraction of foreign investment or at least the development of long-term technical and marketing contracts between domestic and foreign firms. This may be especially important in commodity lines requiring highly specialized knowledge and inputs, featuring rapid technical and market changes, and featuring highly concentrated international markets. Governments need to improve the incentives for foreign investment and the legal and informational basis for the development of complex contractual relations between local and foreign companies.

Third, 'learning by doing' may no longer be a viable means of developing a horticultural export trade in light of the intensification of competition in European and other markets and the increased requirements for quality, supply continuity, and product variety in these markets. Prospective exporters would be advised to gain experience first in the domestic market, perhaps by developing crop procurement and distribution arrangements to supply high-quality produce to restaurants, hotels and 'up-market' retail outlets. In encouraging new entry into horticultural exports, attention should focus on private firms and cooperatives currently active in domestic fresh produce wholesaling, large individual growers, and firms or individuals which currently carry out exports of other agricultural or manufactured products and thus have market contacts and an understanding of the risks and mechanics of international trade.

VIII.

Fish Mammies and Tuna Conglomerates: Private Sector Fish Processing and Marketing in Ghana

Geoff Ames and C. J. Bennett

O ver 4.01 million tons of fish were landed in sub-Saharan Africa in 1989.[1] Fish provides up to 25% of the protein in the diet in some countries,[2] and fishing and fisheries related industries such as boat-building, net-making, fish processing and marketing provide employment and income for large numbers of people. While certain East African and Indian Ocean countries have fishing industries, and while fish is an important item of domestic consumption in the inland countries adjoining the great lakes of Africa, it is West Africa that accounts for most of African fish production and employment in fisheries.

This case study focuses on fish processing and marketing in Ghana, which presents several interesting features. Despite its short coastline (536 km), Ghana has a very prolific fishery, ranking about 35th in the world's fish catches. It also has one of the highest per capita fish consumption figures in Africa. Ghana has a wide range of fishing operations, with large-scale industrial and artisanal marine fisheries, and also inland fishing. Most fish processing and marketing is done by the private sector, with minimal inputs by official organizations. Women play a major role in both processing and marketing, and in fishing itself, as they own many of the fishing boats, even at the industrial level. Ghana's fishing industry has considerable regional importance, as much of the fish landed in other West African countries is caught

---

[1] FAO (1990).
[2] Essuman (1992).

by Ghanaian fishermen. They operate for short and long periods from countries as far away as Senegal and The Gambia. Finally, the Ghanaian case vividly illustrates the impact of an ongoing Structural Adjustment Program on the fisheries sector.

The case study has three sections. The first section examines major techno-economic characteristics of fish production, noting possible implications for entry into different forms of fish processing and marketing. The second section provides a short overview of the scope and features of fish production and markets in sub-Saharan Africa. The third and core section examines the Ghanaian experience, with particular reference to the negative effects of Structural Adjustment policies on both parastatal and private industrial fisheries, and the relative resilience of the artisanal sector. The latter is distinguished by the persistence of traditional methods and traditional marketing relationships, and by the continued dominance of female fish buyers, the "fish mammies".

GENERAL CHARACTERISTICS OF FISH, FISH PRODUCTION AND FISH MARKETING

Fish as a commodity, together with fish production and marketing, have certain techno-economic characteristics which influence the incentives and risks of undertaking activities in this sector, as well as the organizational patterns that are adopted.

Techno-Economic Characteristics of Fish as a Commodity

Perishability: Fish is very perishable: at ambient temperatures in the tropics, and without some form of preservation, serious spoilage of small fish occurs within 6 to 8 hours. Small fish become putrid within about 12 hours, and even large fish are of poor quality within a day. Packing fish in ice is a very effective means of preserving fish, which retains its natural appearance, flavor and texture, all qualities favored by consumers. However, in many areas ice is expensive. Also, many artisanal fishing boats are not equipped to take ice to sea, which limits the distance over which they can operate if the fish is to be landed in marketable condition.

Fish can often be sold un-iced at landing sites, and trade in un-iced fish can be significant in some major coastal cities. However, most fish has to be iced or preserved in some other way. When fish is intended for export to developed countries it may be frozen, but the scarcity of frozen storage, distribution and marketing facilities, and the cost of operating them, mean that there is little sale of frozen fish in most developing countries. (There are exceptions, such as Ghana, where much fish is frozen, either for smoking out-of-season, or for sale while thawing.) The other alternative is curing, that is reducing the moisture content so that the spoilage processes in the fish are greatly reduced.

Mixed species catches: Whatever kind of net is used will retain all the fish inside it, other than those small enough to escape through the mesh. This is a minor problem with pelagic (near-surface) fish, which tend to move in single species shoals. Trawling, on the other hand, tends to retain all the species living near the bottom, resulting in a very mixed catch. This is a major factor in shrimp trawling, where the non-target species, referred to as by-catch, can make up as much as 95% of the catch. The need to use available space for the much more valuable shrimp catch generally leads to this by-catch being thrown back, representing an economic loss to the country as a whole.

Characteristics of Fish Production

Glut catches are the most important characteristic of the production process, occuring in many marine fisheries. It is very unusual for catches to be evenly distributed throughout the year. Weather conditions such as high seas or monsoons may make fishing difficult or impossible for a substantial part of the year. Often the fish can only be caught at a particular season for climatic or oceanographic reasons. This applies particularly to pelagic fish such as sardines, anchovies and mackerel. In the period July–September each year, off the coast of Ghana, there is a huge upswelling of cold water rich in minerals. This leads to a sudden proliferation of plankton and of the fish which feed on it. Large quantities of fish are caught over a short period, far in excess of the current consumer demand, and putting pressure on processing and marketing facilities. Such a seasonal production peak is in many ways analogous to the harvest of annual crops, but is given extra importance by the very high perishability of fish.

Common access aggravates the problems of glut catches. A characteristic feature of marine fisheries (and some inland lake fisheries) is that the resource is not owned by any individual or group. In principle the fish are available to anyone who can catch them. To some extent common access is

limited by Exclusive Economic Zones where nations limit fishing by licensing, but this is not usually relevant to artisanal fishermen. In some cases
access is limited by agreement between groups, for example where canoes
fish in a coastal zone up to 10 km. out, small boats operate in the next zone,
and bigger boats further offshore. However, even within these groups there
will inevitably be competition between individuals. Every fisherman will want
to land as much fish as possible while he can do so. It will rarely be possible
for any fishermen to defer catching fish, to avoid a glut in the hope of a price
rise; someone else is likely to catch those fish.

Risks are inevitable in anything related to fisheries. First, fishermen have
to find the fish. In an industrial fishery, this is less difficult, with modern
technology. At the artisanal level, much depends on the acquired skills of the
fishermen. The resource itself is uncertain. Pelagic fish especially are greatly
affected by climatic and other changes. With a change of only a few degrees in
the temperature of the water near the surface, pelagic fish may disappear,
perhaps to deeper water or to a completely different area. Allied to this, risk
within the marketing system due to the high degree of perishability, means
that fishing has often remained a marginalized activity, financed by the informal sector and under-valued by government. Fishing communities are often transient, lacking in secure land tenure and alternative income sources,
and considered low status.

The unpredictable supply of fish creates risk for fish processors. They have
to decide when to buy, knowing that at any time large quantities of fish may
be landed, causing a sudden drop in price. Alternatively, if little fish is landed,
prices may rise equally quickly. Processors and traders will have to judge the
price consumers will be prepared to pay for cured fish many months ahead.

Formal information systems are very rare in fisheries. Hence, informal
sources and forms of information are critical to the functioning of many fish
marketing systems and in linking producers, processors and traders.

High initial fixed capital costs; these include large single payments for
nets, boats and increasingly, motors. Due to the unpredictable nature of fishing income streams, repayment of loans for such investments can be problem-
atical. This explains why the financing of the sector, especially the artisanal
fishery, is commonly characterized by informal financial arrangements between boat operators/owners and shore-based money lenders and middlemen/
women who will lend where other institutions are reluctant to do so (formal
credit systems among fishing communities have a poor record). This financ-

ing role is likely in many areas to be taken by those involved in the processing and marketing of fish. Considerable economies of scale are available in the fisheries sector. Larger vessels can have greater catch per unit effort and longer times at the fishing grounds, reducing the unit cost of travelling to and from these grounds.

Fish Processing

Value added products from fish are not very important in Africa. In South East Asia, for example, there is a big market for products such as fish sauces, fish soups, fish crackers, etc. In Africa the consumer requirement is for fish in its wet state or cured. Cured fish cannot properly be described as a value-added product. Its price per kg. or per ton may be higher than that of wet fish, but that overlooks the fact that 1kg. of cured fish is obtained by removing water from up to 3 or 4kg. of wet fish. In terms of value per unit of dry matter or food value, cured fish is a lower value product than wet fish. Almost always, consumers want wet fish and many will pay more for it when they can get it. Therefore, fish is cured not to increase its value but to preserve it during marketing and distribution.

Cured fish is usually produced by sun-drying or smoking, often after preliminary treatment with salt. Salting reduces the moisture content of the fish, retarding the processes involved in spoilage. More moisture can then be removed by sun-drying or smoking, depending mainly on the size of the fish, and whether it is oily. Small fish such as triggerfish (*Balistes*) can be sun-dried readily. Small oily fish such as anchovies can be sun-dried directly, but usually they are salted first to remove some of the water and to reduce the rancidity of the final product. Large fish can be difficult to sun-dry, as the surface hardens as it dries, preventing moisture from within the fish evaporating; the outside may be dry while the inside continues to spoil. Large fish can instead be hot-smoked, heated in a kiln or oven so that it is cooked and dried at the same time. Salting before smoking can accelerate the drying process. Depending on the extent to which it is dried, cured fish can be kept for periods of many months.

Glut processing is a convenient term to describe the problem which arises from the combination of glut catches with the need to process most of the catch. Demand for labor and utilization of processing capacity are both highly seasonal. In artisanal processing, family labor including women and children is utilized to spread, turn, collect, and pack the product. Fish smokers are limited by the capacity of their kilns, and have to consider that the capacity needed at glut seasons will not be used for most of the year. Options for speeding up processing, or making it less-labor intensive, are limited and tend to require more fuel, or larger-scale operations. Attempts to create complementary forms of non-fisheries employment in fishing communities have not generally been successful, partly because such communities often lack secure access to land.

In the industrial sector, besides a similar tendency to seasonal employment patterns, there are serious problems of low overall utilization of processing capacity, and of the difficulty in predicting returns to capital, especially returns to scale.

Fish Marketing

Low entry costs are typical of artisanal level fish marketing and processing. However, this statement should be balanced by noting that income in this sector is also low, inflating potential capital investment as a proportion of overall financial resources. Processing (salting, drying, smoking or curing) tends to require low levels of technology and inputs. Fixed capital costs in the industrial sector are high, and demand high utilization of available catch. Additionally, canneries are commonly dependent upon imported packaging materials and must compete with imported processed products.

Vertical ties are the norm among artisanal fish marketing systems and are common in industrial fisheries. This mitigates risk and develops patron-client linkages between buyer and seller. In the face of variable and sometimes unpredictable supplies, these ties provide some degree of assurance to both sellers (assured markets, ad hoc loans, etc.) and buyers (first rights to available supplies and a means to guard against short-term price fluctuations). Fishermen need to know where to land their catch, which will depend on market requirements and processing facilities in each area. Fishermen usually manage to avoid landing fish for which there is no outlet, resulting in a complete loss.

At the industrial level, integration is common. Fleet owners often develop processing and marketing facilities to maximize returns on investment in ships. At the artisanal level, integration within family and cultural groups is common with family labor often divided between fishing, processing and marketing. Cooperative marketing is not typical of fisheries and many attempts to implement such schemes have failed. In the authors' experience, mutual trust exists among fishing families and between buyers and sellers of fish products with strong patron-client links; less so between fishing households.

ROLE AND IMPORTANCE OF FISH IN SUB-SAHARAN AFRICA

Fish and meat are the two main sources of animal protein in Africa, and are nutritionally superior to vegetable proteins. Their relative importance varies throughout SSA. Key factors are the length of coastline and/or the amount of inland water which is available and the quantity of fish available in those waters.

While many African countries are major cattle producers and meat is much more important in the diet than fish, fish may be a much cheaper source of animal protein than meat. For example in Zambia and Zimbabwe fish production is much smaller than that of meat, but the fish which is produced sells very readily as demand exceeds local supply at prevailing prices. Fish, especially cured fish, is much cheaper than meat in many African countries. In many countries fish provides much of the animal protein of low income groups.

In a substantial number of SSA countries, fish is a very important food for most or all levels of society. This applies particularly to the coastal states with rich off-shore fisheries such as Côte d'Ivoire, The Gambia, Ghana and Senegal. It also applies to some inland countries such as Uganda, where fish from lakes provides much of the nation's protein food. Fish consumption data for selected countries are given in Table 8.1.

Fish catches and landings for SSA countries are shown in Figure 8.1. There is a huge variation in production levels, ranging from only 40 tons in Lesotho to more than 500,000 tons in South Africa and Nigeria. The available data indicate no clear pattern of change over recent years. As noted above, catches fluctuate substantially. This is particularly true for the pelagic fish species which represent the greater part of all the principal countries' catches.

Employment in fish production is substantial, but difficult to define and measure. Some countries produce data for the number of fishermen. For example, in 1990 Ghana claimed to have 91,400 fishermen whilst Nigeria had 164,870.[3] UNIDO (1991) estimated that Ghana employed 83,000 full-time

---

[3] From Infopeche (1990).

TABLE 8.1: **Fish Consumption in Selected African Countries and Regions**

Country	Per capita consumption (kg/year)	Fresh (%)	Cured (%)	Fish products as share of protein supply %
Chad	8.5	10	90	9.9
Côte d'Ivoire	17.7	35	65	8.7
Gambia	16.4	30	70	Na.
Ghana	26.4	20	80	18.7
Mali	7.1	10	90	3.5
Senegal	20.7	70	30	9.8
Sudan	2.0	70	30	0.5
Uganda	13.0	45	55	7.2
West Africa	10.0	Na.	Na.	Na.
Central Africa	13.2	Na.	Na.	Na.
East Africa	6.0	Na.	Na.	Na.

SOURCES: Essuman (1992), (protein figures (1990) from World Bank 1993).

and 58,000 part-time fishermen in the capture fisheries sector, and 30,000 in post-harvest support industries. Seasonality and the wide geographic spread of employment in the artisanal sector makes estimation difficult and may lead to underestimation in the post-harvest sector. Employment in pre-harvest support industries such as boat-building and net-making plus fish processing and marketing mean that the total number of people employed as a result of fish production is many times the number of actual fishermen.

It is difficult to generalize about African external trade in fisheries. Some countries import and export similar quantities, but these can be high-value frozen shrimp for export and low-value dried fish as imports. Increasingly, there are exports of high quality iced fish, such as the export of Nile perch to Europe from Kenya, Uganda, and Tanzania. Table 8.2 gives some idea of the complexity of import and export patterns.

Most of the trade within sub-Saharan Africa is in wet or cured fish to neighboring countries. Examples are Chad, which exports nearly all its fish to Nigeria, and Malawi, which exports dried fish to Zambia. Uganda and Tanzania export substantial quantities of cured fish to Rwanda and Burundi, although a growing proportion of their trade is of fresh and frozen fish to European countries.

Intra-regional trade is widespread but unmeasured. Much is unofficial and related to traditional migration and ethnic linkages. Migration of peoples along the African coastline over a period of many centuries has produced vast socio-economic spaces which were only later constrained by territorial limits

FIGURE 8.1: **Fish Production in sub-Saharan Africa, 1989** (000's Tons)

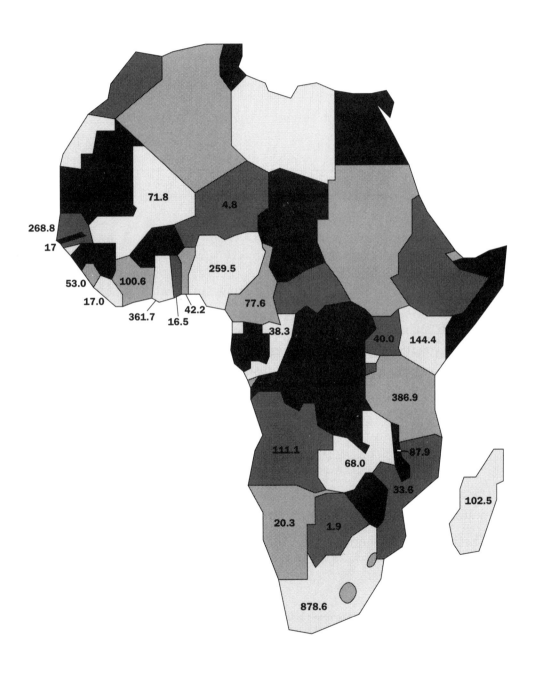

SOURCE: FAO (1990).

TABLE 8.2: **International Trade in Fisheries Products from Selected African Countries, 1991**

Country		Imports	Exports
Angola	V	49,502	5896
	Q	45,289	1224
Côte d'Ivoire	V	114,947	173,067
	Q	186,444	109,405
Ghana	V	31,320	15,916
	Q	32,630	16,490
Nigeria	V	191,460	15,590
	Q	492,580	5815
Senegal	V	38,635	233,400
	Q	50,316	123,143

V = value in US$ '000, Q = quantity in tons.

SOURCE: FAO (1991).

superimposed by colonial powers.[4] People migrate to catch, process and market fish.[5]

Short term migration to trade in fish seems widespread.[6] This trade is commonly conducted by women and is primarily export oriented. Recent studies[7] suggest a number of constraints to such trade. These include:

- high costs of intra-regional transport;
- high import duties;
- poor infrastructure (i.e. lack of cold-chains);
- non-tariff barriers (i.e. complicated import-export procedures);
- devaluation of currencies; this has, to some extent worked in Ghana's favor since the Cedi has been devalued considerably against the CFA.

The Ghanaian fisheries sector has considerable regional advantages in terms of skills. Currency devaluation and reduced trade restrictions have

---

[4] See Jean Pierre Chauveau's paper in Haakonsen (ed.) 1991 for an attempt at periodization of the regional fishery migration.

[5] Migration is defined here as the movement of peoples to seek profit or employment outside their traditional area of abode.

[6] See for example the map of the international cured fish trade in the West African sub-region in Infopeche, 1990, Appendix 1:88.

[7] INFOPECHE (1992, 1993).

allowed them to exploit these advantages more fully. Further benefit would accrue from improved intra-regional communications and reduced bureaucracy at borders.

The Policy Environment

Policy within the fisheries sector has reflected both the worsening economic predicaments of some African countries and the changing agendas of the international donors. In the post-independence period there was a general development focus on industrialization. As the private sector was weak in this area, governments played a significant role in enterprise development through the formation of state-run fishing and fish processing enterprises.[8]

Four successive approaches to intervention in the fisheries sector can be seen. In the 1950s the focus was on large-scale, vertically integrated projects aiming to increase food supply and employment. These projects were mainly in the industrial fisheries sub-sector and designed to exploit unused resources. Lack of expertise in the private sector meant that much of this activity was channelled through parastatals. Added impetus was given to these national programs by the extension of the 200 mile national exclusive fishing zone in the 1970s.

This policy continued into the 1960s and 1970s with an additional emphasis being on resource assessment and institution building. By the 1970s it had been realised that artisanal fisheries played a much greater role in food supply and employment than previously thought.

By the 1980s evidence that fishery resources were nearing full exploitation switched the emphasis from the pre-harvest aspects of fisheries to the post-harvest aspects in an endeavor to increase the value of existing resources and reduce losses. Most recently, support has reflected a more general switch to holistic approaches to rural development with national and regional integrated community development projects.

THE FISHERIES SUB-SECTOR IN GHANA

General Characteristics

Ghana is one of Africa's major fish producers. In view of its small coastline it must be the world's largest fish producer in terms of catch per unit area of its

---

[8] This section is based mainly on Campbell et al. (1993, 30–35).

Economic Zone.[9] Fish is the major source of animal protein in Ghana, and a relatively sophisticated fish processing and marketing system operates almost entirely within the private sector, despite early governmental policies of promoting public sector enterprises.

Artisanal fishing in Ghana has been a traditional activity since before recorded history.[10] The traditional fishing vessel is a large dugout canoe as wood is plentiful in the coastal areas. The most significant change in the artisanal sector for the purposes of the present discussion occurred in the 1970s, when outboard motors became available. This enabled the canoes to travel further, and take advantage of better fishing grounds. It also led to a considerable increase in the number of canoes. Meanwhile, industrial and semi-industrial fishing industries were developing, both in the public and in the private sector. For the purposes of describing the operational framework of Ghanaian fisheries, industrial and artisanal fisheries can be considered as two separate but interacting sub-sectors.

Industrial fishery refers to all fishery propelled by inboard engines. This implies larger, more sophisticated vessels requiring relatively high initial investment and operational costs but needing low per unit fishing effort. In Ghana's case, this relates mainly to inshore wooden hulled vessels, distant-water steel hulled purse-seiners and trawlers, and tuna vessels.

Artisanal fishing boats use out-board engines or sails for propulsion. This implies small vessels, often built of traditional materials, and fishing short distances from the shore with relatively low initial investment and operational costs but high per unit fishing effort. Canoes are the main vessel in this category in Ghana. In addition, land-based fishing systems (i.e. beach netting) are included in this category as entirely artisanal in character because of their low use of capital goods. The entire inland fishery, in the rivers and the Volta Lake, is artisanal in nature, and accounts for about 20% of total national catch by weight.

The relative economic importance of the two sub-sectors in the Ghanaian economy is shown in Table 8.3. For the purposes of this study of the private sector, data for marine and inland artisanal fisheries have been combined. All inland capture fishery is artisanal in character. Especially in the artisanal sector, the number of fishermen cited here does not exhaust the number of

---

[9] Excepting countries such as North Korea which catch most of their fish in distant waters.

[10] For a review of the early history of coastal fishing in West Africa see Chauveau in Haakonsen (ed.) (1991).

TABLE 8.3: **Comparison of Artisanal and Industrial Fishing Sub-Sectors**

Sector	Total catch 1991		Vessels 1988 (No.)	Fishermen 1988 (No.)
	Tons	%		
Artisanal	272,850	80	14,372	138,000
Industrial	68,400	20	346	4460
Total	341,250	100	14,718	142,460

SOURCES: Department of Fisheries Statistics for catch, UNIDO (1991) for vessels and fishermen.

people employed in fisheries. There is considerable, but declining, employment in boat building, boat repairing and net-making, as well as in the downstream activities of processing, marketing and distribution.

Figure 8.2 attempts to indicate some of the interactions and linkages between the two sectors in their production, processing and marketing systems. Once fish enters the domestic marketing chain, distinctions between industrial and artisanal products become less well defined.

Recent Trends

The recent history of private sector fisheries and fish-processing will be discussed below. At this point it is worth discussing the broader context of fisheries development in Ghana, in particular the relevant policies of the Ghanaian Government, and the effects on fisheries of the Structural Adjustment Program initiated in 1982.

Government intervention in fisheries became significant in the 1960s and 1970s. A State Fisheries Corporation (SFC) was set up, originally in 1961 using a Norwegian company to manage a fleet of deep sea vessels. At that time a separate company, Ghana Cold Store, bought the fish and marketed it. The price of the products was determined by the Prices and Incomes Board and was based purely on input costs, in the manner of centrally planned economies. During this period prices were commonly set below operating costs. The fishing and marketing companies merged in 1974 to form the SFC itself. At this time it was operating twenty-five large trawlers in Angolan waters. The SFC set up forty cold stores in various places in Ghana.

A second government intervention was the establishment in 1973 of the Tema Food Complex Corporation (TFCC). This consists of a single large-scale integrated food processing plant with fish canning, smoking and freezing operations sharing the site with a flour mill (the core activity), an animal feed mill, an oil mill and a fish meal plant.

FIGURE 8.2: Interactions Between Artisanal and Industrial Fisheries in Ghana

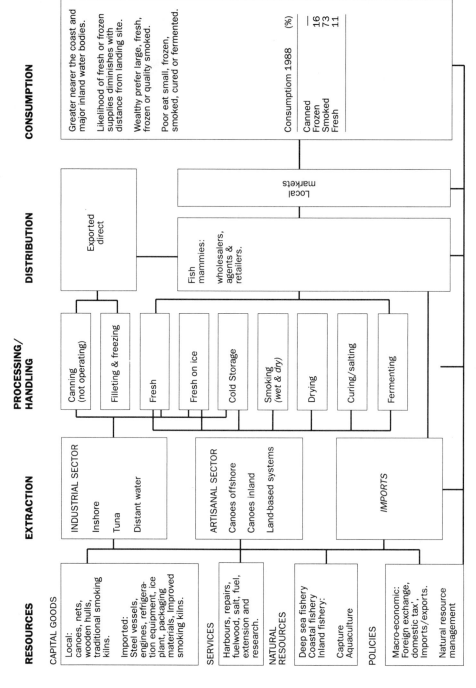

NOTE: Based on UNIDO (1991, p.8).

The main reason for setting up the TFCC facilities seems to have been to take advantage of the hydro-electricity available from the Volta Lake development. It is not clear whether the facilities were ever fully utilized. The TFCC started large scale fish smoking, mostly of sardines but also of tuna, croakers and mackerel. It processed canned sardine and mackerel, using fish imported from Senegal and South Africa. The fish meal plant processed some cannery waste but mainly sun-dried anchovies, purchased locally.

The SFC and TFCC are still in existence, but with a greatly reduced role. When other African countries set up Exclusive Economic Zones, the SFC trawlers' catches declined, from a peak of 33,000 tons per year to none now. Despite the end of fishing activities, staff were kept on. In 1986 the Corporation had 11 boats and 3,000 employees. Now it has 530 employees. In 1987 the SFC was placed on the Government's divestiture list, where it remains to date. This effectively prevented the SFC from raising further loans from the formal sector. To continue operation the current Chairman has organized a consortium of fish mammies[11] who provide working capital in return for free cold storage.

Total SFC cold storage capacity is 12,000 tons in 40 cold stores spread around Ghana. Some, like those in Tema harbor, are potentially highly profitable. Others, many in remote inland areas, are not. About 8,000 tons (66%) is operational at present. Profitability is low due to lack of a fast freezing facility, rigid operating arrangements, poor operating standards, a heavy debt burden and aging plant. Some inland cold stores have been rehabilitated using capital borrowed from fish mammies in return for rent free use. Lack of income from these stores is leading to problems with covering key recurrent costs such as electricity and staff salaries. Opportunities exist for the importation of frozen fish, but lack of liquidity and an inability to borrow prevent the company benefiting from this.

The SFC also owns a flake ice plant, recently rehabilitated with donor assistance. This lies idle because demand for ice from the inshore fishing fleet has collapsed.

As a result of trade liberalization, the TFCC has found it very difficult to compete with cheap imports of canned fish. This problem has been compounded by the widespread provision of canned fish as food for work as part of donor

---

[11] The term 'fish mammie' is widely used in West Africa to describe women involved in fisheries. It includes all women traders of fish: wholesalers, retailers, agents, processors and financiers.

assisted structural adjustment amelioration programs. Cold storage capacity
at the TFCC is surplus to needs and poorly situated for use by private fish
traders. Seasonal demand for cold storage means that the cold stores may not
be economically viable on their own. The TFCC fish smoking plant has a
capacity to produce twenty tons per day. This is far in excess of the demand
likely from any individual traders. Furthermore, the high cost of firing the
kilns means that they can only be used "to order". At present the canning
plant is reaching 9% capacity utilization.

A review of the Corporation in 1992 showed that trading losses have been
incurred due to lack of raw materials, an inability to find markets for its
products, a lack of investment in machinery and maintenance and the high
cost of inputs, such as aluminium cans, due to currency devaluation. TFCC
staff themselves point to a number of bureaucratic and non-commercial management practices that have hindered profitable operation and reinvestment.

The decline of the two parastatals is a result both of the over-centralized,
statist policies that set them up in the first place, and the Structural Adjustment policies that have replaced them. An Economic Recovery Program was
adopted in Ghana in 1982, with the support of the IMF, to reverse negative
growth rates and reduce massive budget deficits, by measures including an
increase in agricultural producer prices, withdrawal of subsidies on consumer
prices, and devaluation. It has also entailed the withdrawal of support from,
and government divestiture of parastatals. In the short- and medium-term it
has undoubtedly had some negative effects on many sub-sectors, including
both artisanal and private-sector industrial fishing.

Some of the effects of Structural Adjustment policies on the economy are
indicated by the figures in Table 8.4. Whilst inflation has been largely controlled, there has also occurred a credit squeeze and a reduction in the purchasing power on the part of many consumers. This has had very damaging
effects on an industry heavily dependent on imported fuel, and, especially for
the industrial sub-sector, on imported spare parts. Devaluation of the Cedi
has been the primary cause of this, though constraints on the money supply
have also had their effects in terms of poor access to credit and diminished
demand for fish.

Interest rates during this period have often been negative, falling behind
the current rate of inflation between 1988 and 1990. However, access to the
formal banking system is so limited by other barriers, that credit cannot be
said to be effectively rationed by the interest rate. Rates for borrowing in the
informal sector are much higher than those in the formal sector.

TABLE 8.4: **Inflation Rate, Exchange Rate and Indicative Interest Rates**

Year	Inflation (%)	Cedis per US$	Lending Rates[1]
1980	50	1.02	—
1981	117	1.15	—
1982	22	2.75	—
1983	123	20.33	—
1984	40	35.99	—
1985	10	54.37	—
1986	25	89.21	—
1987	40	162.37	—
1988	31	202.35	23.0–30.0
1989	25	270.00	22.5–30.0
1990	37	326.33	22.5–29.5
1991	18	367.78	19.5–31.5

[1]Lending rates are for agriculture, forestry and logging.

SOURCE: Statistical Services (1992).

While the Government of Ghana's policies for fisheries[12] now implicitly include assistance to the private sector, both artisanal and industrial, this has tended to concentrate on provision of equipment and infrastructure for the industrial fisheries.[13] Recent reviews[14] have noted the absence of integrated support to the artisanal fisheries sector, especially with regard to credit provision, post-harvest losses and resource management.

Consumption and Prices

Fish is Ghana's most important source of animal protein. Official statistics suggest consumption per capita ranges between 14kg. and 21kg. per annum, well above the average for West Africa. Consumption is much higher in the south of the country than in the north where poor communications make marketing fish more problematic.

Neither quantitative nor qualitative market research into fish consumption patterns in Ghana exists. Anecdotal evidence, and discussion with key informants, suggest the following:

1) Meat (including poultry) is preferred to fish. The widespread availability of cold chains in urban and peri-urban Ghana has encouraged the development of markets for frozen meat and poultry. The authors' ex-

---

[12] As described in UNIDO (1991, pp.10–11).
[13] With the notable exception of work on the Chorkor kiln.
[14] FAO (1989), UNIDO (1991).

perience in other countries suggests that higher income groups will switch from fish to meat and poultry unless fish products of better quality (usually this means fresh fish) are available. While it is often believed that fish are effectively the last resort for poor income families, such families often in fact choose meat as a low-cost protein source. It can be purchased in smaller quantities and is perceived to result in less waste, to be more filling and very versatile.

2) Fresh and frozen fish are (jointly) preferred to cured fish. Generally, wealthier consumers prefer larger, fresher fish for which they are prepared to pay a premium. Less wealthy consumers tend to buy less fresh fish, and of a smaller size. The cheapest fish available is that which has deteriorated, or "stink fish". Poorer consumers buy smoked fish that has been re-smoked, is broken into smaller pieces by over-handling, or subjected to attack by mould and/or insects.

3) Consumer preferences between freshwater and marine fish are hard to define. Migration of people from areas of traditional freshwater fish consumption to cities in the south of Ghana has led to a significant trade in fish between these areas. Similarly, since large freshwater fish can be sold profitably in the south, the gap in the market is often filled by marine fish, either smoked or recently frozen. However, in areas distant from sources of supply, for example northern Ghana, choice is limited and demand for some types of fish products, such as fresh and frozen fish, goes unfulfilled.

4) In Ghana, unlike most countries, there is no consumer resistance to frozen fish as compared to fresh fish. Fresh fish statistics quoted in much of the literature actually refer to recently de-frosted fish. No premium is available for fresh or iced fish (with the possible exception of the catering trade which makes its own arrangements for fresh supply). Frozen fish is also thawed for subsequent smoking, and is also the basis of the increasingly popular dish of fish fried in vegetable oil, cooked in roadside restaurants and valued as a present from travellers.

5) Niche markets exist for crustaceans, snails, eels, bivalves, shark fins, crabs and numerous other aquatic products. These items are generally more readily available in the markets of more populous areas where a strong demand exists.

FAO[15] estimated the demand for fish in Ghana in 1990 to be between 30.6 and 36.2 kg. per capita, implying a shortfall in supply of 50%. This might have been met by imports but a shortage of foreign currency caused fish imports to decline to a low of 22,000 tons in 1987 from a peak of 50,000 tons in 1977. Subsequent devaluation has led to a recovery in this business with about 34,000 tons being imported in both 1992 and 1993. It is suggested that imports may now have peaked as consumer purchasing power has not kept pace with the increase in prices of imports.

One of the consequences of the Structural Adjustment policies[16] was that inflation has been higher than the growth of nominal incomes of a large part of the population. By July 1993, the average per capita consumption of about 20kg. fish per annum, if supplied by frozen mackerel, could cost 11,000 Cedis or 4% of a typical laborer's annual income.

Loss of consumer purchasing power may have been to the benefit of fisherfolk because there seems to be some degree of substitution between fish protein and other more expensive sources of protein such as beef or pork. Various studies by researchers affiliated to Cornell University[17] show that changes in income result in a high degree of substitution between the different calorie sources of the varied Ghanaian diet. There is, however, other evidence that, despite diminished real incomes consumers are spending more on meat and poultry. While data on animal offtake (and thus meat availability) were not available for the present study, the national populations of sheep, goats and pigs have increased markedly since 1987 (the poultry population has also increased, while cattle numbers have remained static). The advantages of meat over fish perceived by lower-income groups, as detailed above, may be a factor here. Information on the division of consumption between income groups and in different geographic areas might reveal more about the impact of Structural Adjustment on fish consumption patterns.

Seasonal price fluctuations are determined by market forces. Fish supply peaks in August/September, and the glut of pelagic species depresses the whole market. In addition, the price of fish is determined by the supply of alternative protein sources such as chicken and beef. Fish are sold either whole or by the piece making comparisons of unit prices and assessment of

---

[15] FAO (1990).
[16] As noted by FAO (1989).
[17] Alderman (1990) and (1992), Alderman and Shively (1991) and Alderman and Higgins (1992).

relative marketing margins difficult. Retail and wholesale price information is therefore limited.

Fish prices exhibit all the characteristics of trade uncertainty and fluctuating supply. Prices can change fourfold in a day depending on the size of landings. Marketing margins appear considerable, but transaction costs and risks (due to perishability and irregular supply) subsumed by marketing agents are relatively high compared with other commodities. Prices reflect seasonal supply variability and physical distance from the source of supply.

The State of the Resource

There are three areas of resource constraint in the Ghanaian fisheries sector, that of the fish itself, the timber required to construct the fishing boats, and the biomass needed to process the fish once landed. Evidence for the pressure on existing marine fish stocks is limited, though anecdotal evidence suggests that catch per unit of fishing effort is decreasing and that the use of illegal fishing methods (i.e., reducing the mesh size of nets) is also increasing.[18] Fishermen and middlewomen alike talk of increasing proportions of juvenile fish in the catch. In recognition of this problem, and to prevent exploitation of the resource by industrial fishermen from other countries, the Government of Ghana has taken several measures.

Ghana declared an Exclusive Economic Zone of 200 nautical miles through the Territorial Waters and Continental Shelf Act (amended) of 1977. Other important regulations effecting fishing are as follows:

1. licences are required to fish in Ghanaian waters;
2. tuna vessels registered in Ghana are required to land at least 10% of their catch in Ghana;
3. importation or construction of new fishing vessels (this applies especially to trawlers) is only allowed as replacements for existing ones;
4. minimum mesh size is specified for different types of gear;
5. at least half the crew of each vessel must be Ghanaian.

These and other regulations effecting the production and marketing of fish are not effectively enforced because insufficient provision has been made for monitoring, surveillance and control.

---

[18] For example, many canoe operators now find it economic to use ice on board their vessels to reduce spoilage and to allow them longer over the fishing grounds. This is a sign that they are travelling further out to sea and spending longer meeting catch targets.

A similar situation occurs in the lake fishery, though this is protected from over-exploitation for the time being by large trees which were covered when the lake was constructed and which effectively prevent trawling. Anecdotal evidence suggests that fishing for fresh-water fish is highly profitable and that large numbers of fishermen have migrated to the lake from the coast to exploit this resource. There, however, is no research available to support this contention.

The use of large forest trees for canoe construction is traditional in Ghana. The great expansion of the canoe fleet during the 1970s and 1980s with the development of motorized fishing, coupled with a tendency to develop larger canoes which can go further to reach more productive fishing grounds, has meant that canoe carvers now have to travel considerable distances to find suitable trees. This is reflected in the increased costs of commissioning canoes (around Cedi 2 million each).[19]

Use of wood to smoke fish, hitherto not considered a great problem in Ghana, is potentially a severe resource constraint for the future. In areas of intensive smoking, forest wood has become scarce and must be purchased from the hinterland, representing a significant recurrent cost for fish smokers who must pay at the beginning of the peak season in cash. Discussions with traders from the Volta Lake suggest that wood for smoking is becoming scarce on the lake islands where this activity is carried out and wood must now be purchased and transported from the mainland.

Monitoring and control of open access resources such as fisheries and forests is not easily managed in the private sector. However, despite commitments by the Government of Ghana to police resource use, no action has been taken. The issue of resource management requires further attention.

Current Production, Imports and Exports

Recent catch data for Ghana are given in Table 8.5. These clearly show the fluctuation in anchovy catches, with catches varying from 15,200 tons in 1986 to nearly 88,000 tons the following year. Cured fish production is described in Table 8.6 and imports and exports of fish and fish products are given in Table 8.7.

What these figures represent, partial as they are, is the Ghanaian fisheries sector in a state of stagnation relative to the rapid growth of the 1960s

---

[19] See the innovative paper by Chevas in Haakonsen (ed.) (1991, pp. 233–242).

TABLE 8.5: **Fish Production in Ghana, 1985–1992** (tons)

Fishery	1985	1986	1987	1988	1989	1990	1991
Marine							
Canoe	159,230	190,200	262,380	244,560	220,880	242,020	215,850
Round Sardine	54,070	45,490	45,670	75,850	Na.	Na.	Na.
Flat Sardine	22,230	16,630	25,480	10,450	Na.	Na.	Na.
Anchovy	27,590	15,210	87,890	75,900	Na.	Na.	Na.
Inshore	17,980	21,890	14,930	7410	12,660	9250	7360
Round Sardine	9430	5510	1740	70	Na.	Na.	Na.
Flat Sardine	1830	2090	1700	100	Na.	Na.	Na.
Distant waters	56,340	57,060	53,640	51,470	55,740	68,120	66,460
Shrimps	—	—	—	—	380	730	780
Tuna	34,410	34,270	33,470	35,430	32,290	40,800	37,790
Total Sea Fishery	233,550	269,150	330,950	303,440	289,280	319,390	289,670
Total Inland Fishery	55,000	57,630	57,660	58,000	57,000	Na.	Na.

SOURCE: Department of Fisheries, personal communication.

and early 1970s. This stagnation is particularly marked in the industrial subsector, where some indices of production are actually declining. What accounts for the stagnation in fish production: is it a supply side constraint or is it demand led? The evidence seems to suggest that both forces are at play. On the supply side, the down-turn in the industrial fisheries as a result of reduced resources (i.e. the imposition of EEZs) and higher costs (i.e. a result of currency devaluation) has not, it seems, been reflected in radically higher prices for landed fish. Furthermore, though imports have risen (see Table

TABLE 8.6: **Ghana: Cured Fish Production** ('000 tons)[a]

Year	Dried[b]	Smoked
1981	6.8	44.0
1982	6.3	43.2
1983	6.5	44.5
1984	6.2	48.8
1985	6.5	49.6
1986	8.3	58.1
1987	8.3	44.0
1988	8.6	46.1
1989	8.6	46.1
1990	8.7	46.4

NOTES:
a) 1 ton of cured fish is derived from 3 to 4 tons of wet fish.
b) Freshwater dried fish only.

SOURCE: FAO (1984, 1991).

TABLE 8.7: **Ghana: Fish Imports and Exports**

Year		1987	1988	1989	1990
Imports					
Fresh, chilled, frozen	Q	21.7	33.1	30.4	31.0
	V	14.0	26.5	24.6	30.0
Dried, salted, smoked	Q	0.7	0.4	0.1	0.1
	V	1.5	1.0	0.4	0.3
Exports					
Fresh, chilled, frozen	Q	20.7	24.9	12.7	12.4
	V	14.2	20.1	11.4	19.7
Dried, salted, smoked	Q	0.3	0.4	0.2	1.0
	V	0.1	0.2	0.2	0.5
Crustaceans, molluscs	Q	0.4	0.3	0.5	0.7
	V	0.9	0.7	1.6	2.7

Q = quantity in '000 tons, V = value in million US$.

SOURCE: FAO (1991).

8.7), production growth still lags behind the expansion in population. This suggests that in addition to increased input costs, Ghana fisheries have suffered from the deflationary fiscal and monetary policies of the Ghanaian Government during the period of Structural Adjustment. Consumers' willingness or ability to buy fish has been limited by declining real income growth.

Most of these imports are of low value small frozen pelagic fish from Northern Europe, though some tinned fish (mainly mackerel and tuna) is also imported. Traditionally, frozen fish is imported to meet the fish supply shortfall outside the main local fish catching season. It is believed that little or no fish is imported into Ghana from other West African countries at present, though historically, some Ghanaian migratory fishermen have returned their catch to home. Also it is said that fresh water fish used to be imported from Mali to Kumasi.

Marketing

Fish production, processing and marketing in Ghana[20] can be considered as four distinct systems, shown schematically in Figures 8.3–8.6. These are:

1) Artisanal: canoes and beach seines, often processed and marketed by immediate family members.

---

[20] The most comprehensive review of fish marketing in Ghana is contained in Infopeche (1990). Descriptions in DANIDA (1988), FAO (1989) and UNIDO (1991) are also useful.

2) Inshore: larger wooden hulled vessels with inboard motors, product usually marketed by an immediate family member.

3) Industrial (deep sea and tuna fishery): Ocean going vessels, product usually marketed by a middlewoman with strong financial ties to the boat owner.

4) Freshwater fishery: canoes using nets and traps on the Volta Lake system selling through family members to middlewomen from the same ethnic group.

FIGURE 8.3: **Market Chain for the Marine Artisanal Fishery**

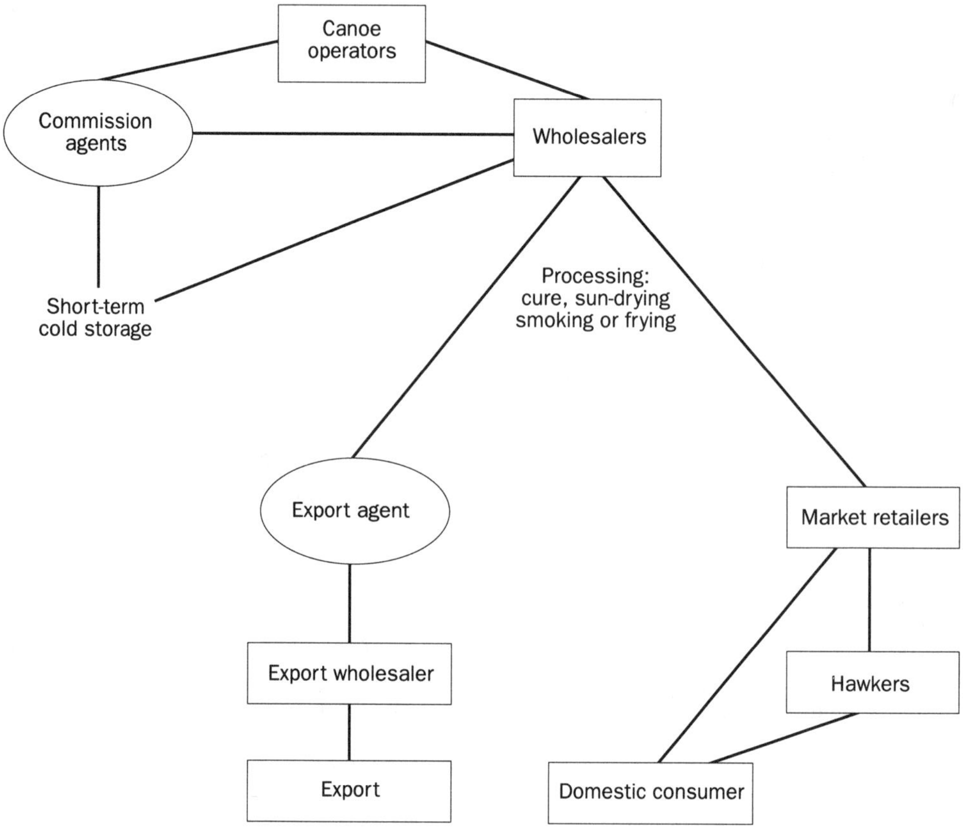

NOTE: A box denotes transfer of ownership.
A circle denotes other physical movements not involving transfer of ownership.
Unboxed denotes a process or activity.

FIGURE 8.4: **Market Chain for the Marine Inshore Fishery**

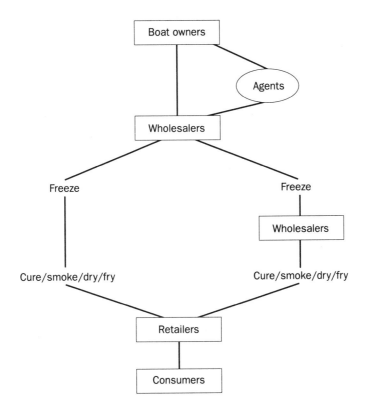

NOTE: A box denotes transfer of ownership.
A circle denotes other physical movements not involving transfer of ownership.
Unboxed denotes a process or activity.

In addition, there are fisheries imports and domestic exports which link into these systems. Fish mammies may conduct a variety of marketing activities. For convenience these have been disaggregated in the diagrams into specific marketing functions such as wholesaling, retailing, commission agents etc.

Artisanal Sector Marketing and Processing

The great majority of domestically produced and imported frozen fish (as much as 80%, estimated by the Department of Fisheries) is processed into traditional products. Fresh fish at landing sites is sold to fish mammies, who may be wives of the fishermen, and who may be owners of the boats, or creditors of the fishermen.

Fish mammies may act as buyers on their own account, or as agents selling to wholesalers, in which case they do not take title to the fish, but take a commission on its sale. In either case, fish mammies often have a financial interest in the fishing operation. Transactions between wholesalers and retailers are often done on credit with wholesalers deferring payment until after on-sale has been achieved.

On the whole, the marketing chain is relatively short, with fish changing hands about twice before purchase by the consumer. In the case of dried fish travelling to distant rural markets, two or three wholesalers may be involved before retail.

Fish is bulked up and wholesaled in large baskets (of dried or smoked fish) or packaged blocks (of frozen fish). A considerable ancillary trade in the supply of baskets, packaging material and packaging exists, centered around

FIGURE 8.5: **Market Chain for the Tuna Fishery**

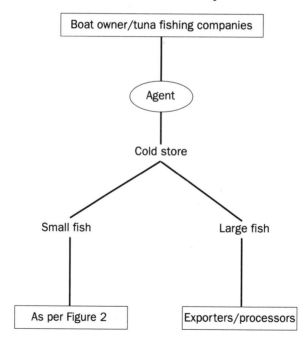

NOTE: A box denotes transfer of ownership.
A circle denotes other physical movements not involving transfer of ownership.
Unboxed denotes a process or activity.

FIGURE 8.6: **Market Chain for Freshwater Fishery**

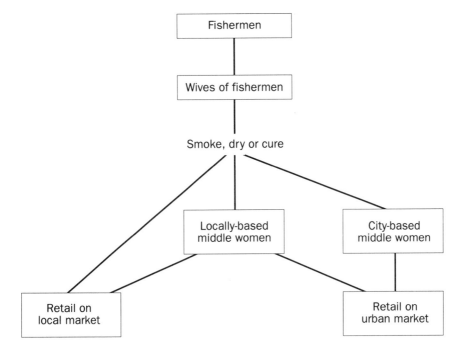

NOTE: A box denotes transfer of ownership.
Unboxed denotes a process or activity.

major producing areas and markets. Fish landed at Tema fishing harbor is auctioned in wooden crates.

Transportation involves hiring a truck or pick-up. Groups of wholesalers often combine to rent a truck. Transport costs reflect the increasingly high cost of fuel. For example, a trader in Kumasi market pays C1,000 ($1.61) per 20kg. carton of frozen fish for transport from Tema, a distance of about 110 kilometres. This represents around 12% of the purchase price of C8,500 per carton.

Processing is conducted at the major landing centres like Tema, Elmina, Chorkor etc., and also in the main inland consumption/marketing centres such as Kumasi. Cured fish in its various forms is the main fish product in Ghana. Only low-cost technology is used, or needed. Salting can conveniently be carried out in tanks built of concrete or baked brick. Sun-drying can be done on the sand or earth, though it is better to use racks made from wire netting, reed slats, or old fishing nets supported by a wooden frame and resting on wooden poles, to reduce contamination with dirt and animal excrement. The fish is then raised above ground where there is more wind, and moisture loss can take place on both sides of the fish. Drying is often done on a tarmac road, where the hard surface serves as a barbecue.

Smoking fish is the most common method of processing fish in Ghana.[21] Two methods are practiced, hot-smoking and smoke-drying. The former has a higher moisture content and therefore reduced (2–3 days) shelf life in comparison with smoke-dried fish. Sardinella, horse mackerel, mackerel, snapper, threadfin bream, croaker, grouper, seabream, barracuda, tuna, catfish, sharks and rays are the most common fish which are hot-smoked.

Smoking is carried out by fish mammies both at the landing sites and inland. For inland smoking, frozen fish is brought from cold stores at the coastal landings and transported to the smoking area. Once smoked, fish is either sold directly to retailers or taken to weekly markets and sold in bulk to wholesalers both from Ghana and neighboring countries. The Tuesday market in Chorkor village and the Thursday market in Djemeni are good examples of wholesale markets for smoke-dried and hot-smoked fish.

Retailers of the relatively perishable hot-smoked fish must re-smoke the product regularly to prevent deterioration. In Kumasi, an ancillary trade in transporting fish from the Central Market back to the smoking areas for re-smoking has developed. Quality and therefore price declines with each re-smoking.

Smoke-dried fish can last up to nine months. Anchovies, shrimp and most freshwater fish are smoke-dried. Mackerel and sardines can be processed in either way.

Fish were formerly smoked in primitive kilns, mud-brick or dug-out, as still used in other parts of Africa. Soon after international trade in oil developed it was found that forty-four gallon oil drums could conveniently be used as fish smoking kilns. With both ends cut off, and holes pierced in the sides to take rods to support the fish, and set on blocks over a wood fire, an oil drum serves as an effective kiln. In 1970 the FAO introduced an improved, fuel-efficient kiln made mainly of mud-bricks, known as the Chorkor kiln after the fishing village where the project was based. This has become very popular in some areas, but requires a larger investment than oil-drum kilns, and is only efficient with large quantities of fish. Many oil-drum kilns, more effi-

---

[21] Koranteng (1992).

cient with smaller quantities, are still in use, alongside or instead of the improved kiln.

The establishment by SFC and TFCC of cold stores throughout the country had a marked effect on fish marketing and processing. In most tropical countries fish is frozen only when it is intended for export. The lack of retail outlets with freezers prevents the local sale of any significant quantity of frozen fish. However in Ghana glut catches of fish are frozen and stored until the slack season, when it is thawed, either for direct sale to consumers (in a part-frozen state, for immediate use) or for smoking. As far as the authors are aware, there are no similar operations in any other country.

Fish-drying occurs in two forms: sun-dried and salt-dried. These processes take up to three days, involve minimal capital outlay and are therefore commonly practised during gluts. Salt-drying is a preferred method of processing Tilapia.

Fermented products are used mainly as flavor enhancers in the Ghanaian diet. Fermented fish, often referred to as "stink fish", is usually made with fish that has deteriorated beyond a marketable stage.

Ethnicity, Gender and Traditional Marketing Methods

While ethnicity and gender are not irrelevant to industrial sector fisheries, it is in the artisanal sector that they are most clearly seen as structuring the division of labor, and they are therefore best discussed at this point.

A number of different ethnic groups are involved in fishing activities. There are a number of cases in which identifiable ethnic groups work in fisheries outside their home areas, or where markets are divided along ethnic lines. For example:

(a) Ga women in Winneba migrate seasonally to Elmina, a predominantly Fante area, to smoke fish;

(b) Ewe women from Volta Region smoke fish on the coast and market it in their home towns, whilst fresh water fish smoked in Volta Region is marketed in Accra and on the coast, also by Volta people;

(c) Women traders in Kumasi use family members resident in Tema to purchase and ship frozen fish for processing and sale.

Using family members or fellow-members of an ethnic group is a way of reducing the high transaction costs in both the artisanal and the industrial sectors. Such costs are increased by poor communications, undeveloped financial systems, uncertainty and insecurity. Middlewomen complain that huge amounts of cash are required to conduct business as a result of inflation and devaluation. This is both inconvenient and insecure. Banks have begun to issue Cedi travellers cheques, but banking hours do not generally fit well with trading activities and few small-scale fish mammies have bank accounts.

An example of traditional marketing methods is the communication of price information between family members in the fish marketing chain, from landings to inland marketing areas. Beans or stones tied in a piece of cloth are sent with the fish denoting the purchase price and expected sale price. Individual families have their own codes which are passed on through generations. Women, many of whom are illiterate, often group together to share transport costs, and an elaborate system of markings has evolved using specific knots, cloth strips, leaves or painted symbols to distinguish baskets and parcels on arrival.

Women are involved at all levels of Ghana's fishery, both artisanal and industrial, pre-harvest and post-harvest. Given the unique position of women in organising and financing private fish trading in Ghana, this would seem to be an under-researched area.[22]

It has been estimated[23] that, including fuel and food supplied to crew, pre-financing of fishing activities, processing and markets, women manage 40–60% of the cash flow of artisanal fisheries in West Africa. In Ghana this may be an underestimate. Increasingly, women pre-finance fishing operations in order to ensure continuity of fish supply. Another estimate is that up to 90% of marine produce is distributed by fish mammies in Ghana.[24]

In a typical artisanal fishing community, men harvest fish and sell the product to their wives or other local women.[25] Individual fishermen sell their whole catch to a single fish mammy. Fish mammies are often also entitled to shares of the catch because they are owners or part-owners of boats, or are entitled to buy at low prices because they have loaned money for nets, outboard motors and fuel.

Husbands and wives pursue their own separate objectives and maintain their own budgets in these transactions, even when they deal with each other.

---

[22] But studies by the FAO (d'Assise 1992 and Randall n.d.) and IDAF (Haakonsen (ed.) 1991 and IDAF 1991) provide the main background.

[23] D'Assise (1992).

[24] Randall (n.d.).

[25] Note that fishing itself is not an exclusively male domain in Ghana. Particularly in the inland fishery and coastal land-based fishery, women also participate.

But it is difficult to discern how and by whom prices are fixed, and how this varies with the degree of kinship between fisherman and fish mammy. Fishermen see fish mammies, through their power as creditors, as fixing purchase prices below going market rates. Discussion with a number of fish mammies suggests that prices are usually fixed by the husband/male family member in an arbitrary manner at what is considered a "fair" price for that day. The woman is then expected to sell at a price over that figure. This is not always possible and many women complained that they were forced to loan money to their husbands whether they had made a profit or not.

The likelihood of immediate kinship links between fish mammies as buyers and fishermen as sellers seems to diminish with the scale of operation. In canoe fishing, processing and marketing is typically conducted within an extended family group. Sales of the catch to unrelated fish mammies occur but are not considered as mutually beneficial as those within family groups.

Fish mammies operate on several levels and considerable vertical mobility exists. Women often start out as retailers of fish supplied by related wholesalers, or assistants to processors in the same kinship group. With experience it is possible to accumulate capital quite rapidly and enter the long distance smoked and frozen fish wholesaling trade.

Discussion with fish mammies travelling long distances to buy fish gives the impression that the effort and hardships involved in this type of trade are considerable. Women traders from Togo, for example, must spend three or more days travelling day and night to markets in coastal Ghana. Since many fish markets commence at dawn, particularly at landing sites, it is common for women traders and their children to sleep in the market. In some markets, such as Chorkor village, businesses have developed to cater for this, by providing secure places for visiting traders with large amounts of cash to sleep. Farther away from main trading centres where roads are poor, fish mammies must travel for several days to buy fish and return in time for regular village markets. For example, traders from Tamale in the north of Ghana travel to Kumasi, Tema and Elmina on the coast to get supplies of smoked fish. It should be remembered that the work of fish mammies is combined with child rearing, small-scale farming and household management.

Women also play a major role in the industrial fisheries of West Africa. Ghanaian fish mammies own or manage a considerable proportion of the inshore fleet. Many of these individuals have invested profits from earlier pre-financing activities in larger vessels, or have taken over management due to accumulated debts. Many, even at this level of operations, are illiterate and do not keep accounts. Nevertheless, they have continued operations despite rising input costs and increased competition from deep-sea trawlers in Ghanaian waters. As far as the authors are aware, this group has not been directly involved in donor funded activities to date and very little is known about their scale, scope or operating patterns.

Industrial and Semi-industrial Fisheries

The story of industrial fisheries in Ghana is one of unabated decline (with the notable exception of the tuna fishery) since the introduction of Structural Adjustment measures in 1983. To some extent this decline is disguised by the statistics, especially those for number of vessels, because they do not describe the sea-worthiness of the ships, which has declined drastically. Several of the larger companies now have fleets of trawlers which are unable to put to sea because they need repairs or because they are the subject of legal action with regard to unpaid debt.

There are three main types of industrial sea fisheries in Ghana: the inshore fleet (coastal purse-seiners and trawlers), the distant water fleet (deep-sea refrigerated trawlers and purse-seiners) and the tuna fleet.

The **inshore fleet** is characterized by locally constructed, wooden, multipurpose vessels. Small vessels (9–12m in length) operate from Mumford, Elmina and Sekondi and were designed to harvest trigger fish. Larger, more sophisticated vessels (12–23m in length) operate from Tema. The FAO (1989) observes that the relatively high level of technology adopted by this latter group (i.e, echo-sounders, sonar) does not seem to have been justified and is not currently in use.

In 1987 only 257 of the 388 vessels registered at Tema were operating, and fishing effort was low except during the sardine season. This reflects the poor economics of this fishery. Although up-to-date figures are unavailable, discussions held with boat owners and boat builders in Elmina reiterate the pattern of decline experienced in Tema. Respondents mentioned longer periods at sea necessary to reach target catches, high input costs, heavy debt burdens and the disappearance of the trigger fish as the causes of decline.

The inshore fleet contributed 8% (21,890 tons) of the total marine catch in 1986, its peak year. Subsequently it has declined to 3% (7,360 tons) in 1991. This is a result of intensified competition from vessels that used to fish in distant waters, increased input costs and declining catch per unit effort.

Characteristics of the inshore fleet which may constrain further development include: aging boats, a decline in fleet size, high indebtedness and lack of bargaining power. There is increased hegemony of fish mammies who hold debt, though this is not necessarily a problem as many are related to boat owners and therefore have vested interests in maintaining production. They are also often on-lending down the marketing chain to wholesalers, retailers and cold-store operators. The dramatic example of the State Fisheries Corporation raising working capital from fish mammies has already been mentioned.

Distant water fishing (outside Ghanaian waters) was effectively curtailed by the imposition of the EEZ in 1979. In the 1960s and 1970s the Ghanaian fleet ranged along the coast of west and south-west Africa from Mauritania to Namibia. In 1989 there were twenty-eight vessels registered of 30–70m in length, of which ten were out of service and eleven were only used irregularly. A number of even larger vessels are owned by the State Fisheries Corporation and a few companies in Tema: all are unserviceable and few if any will ever put to sea again.

The experience of one company involved in distant water fishing is illuminating. Kaleawo Fishing Company purchased eight trawlers from Poland in 1969 at a time when fish prices were fixed by the Government of Ghana and all duties on inputs had been waived, making industrial fishing financially very attractive. Under a joint venture agreement, the vessels were skippered by expatriates and crewed by Ghanaians. All fish were landed and sold in Ghana. The bank loan for these vessels was paid off in full by 1974. Between 1974 and 1983 these vessels earned high rates of profit for the company.

Structural Adjustment measures introduced in 1983 had two immediate effects: firstly, the company suddenly found itself unable to extend its credit at the bank to pay for day-to-day operational costs due to the anti-inflationary credit squeeze. Secondly, rationing of foreign exchange meant that the supply of spare parts for their foreign built ships dried up. By 1983 only five of the eight original vessels were operating. Subsequently, these vessels too had to be abandoned. To maintain activities, the company diversified into cold storage whilst at the same time undertaking a joint venture to fish with a Soviet fishing company. This fizzled out with the collapse of the former Soviet Union.

As of July 1993 the company had only one serviceable boat wholly under its own name. This boat does not operate, but is incurring harbor dues (a common problem). The company is buying a shrimper under a hire-purchase agreement with a Greek company; the Greeks provide officers and the vessel in return for 70% of the catch. Kaleawo dispose of the remainder of the catch locally to pay for inputs and the salaries of the expatriate officers. Under the joint venture agreement, 30% of the foreign exchange earned by the operation can be repatriated to Greece and 70% must stay in a foreign exchange account in Ghana to pay for inputs. Kaleawo claim that of the original loan of US$176,000 over five years, none of the principal has been repaid (after two years) due to the inflated cost of inputs as a result of devaluation of the Cedi.

The tuna fishery was developed in the early 1960s using Japanese, Korean and US vessels selling to Starkist Foods for export to the United States. Domestic companies started fishing in 1973, and by 1987 the fleet consisted of thirty-six vessels.

The history of Mankoadze Fishing Company illustrates well how companies became involved in this sector and the problems they have encountered maintaining viability in the wake of both Structural Adjustment and the greatly reduced fishing area available since the imposition of the EEZ.

Mankoadze started shortly after the end of World War II in a small fishing village using canoes. The original capital was provided by the family of the owner, a retired army officer who was well connected in the village and within Government circles. This proved helpful in expanding the fleet during the early 1950s when various Government schemes were available for boat building. In the late 1950s when distant water fishery was expanding, the Company got loans from U.K. financial institutions to build distant water vessels in the U.K. for use in Ghanaian waters.

In the 1960s, the Company began a series of joint ventures with American, Japanese and Korean companies to catch tuna for canning in the company's recently opened canning factory for both re-export and domestic sales. This business continued successfully throughout the 1970s, but in the 1980s the American company (Starkist) pulled out due to the poor security situation in Tema harbor, and Structural Adjustment measures changed the economics of the activity: fuel and spares became expensive and foreign debt grew alarmingly. Eventually the canning operation had to be closed down because the cost of importing cans was prohibitive.

Efforts to diversify the business included setting up a farming enterprise in the mid 1980s. In a sense this was vertical integration, because the main objective was to provide food for fishing crews, an important variable cost.

They also built repair shops for their boats to reduce reliance on government yards which were perceived to be expensive and inefficient, cold storage facilities to reduce reliance on the State Fisheries Corporation facilities, and warehousing facilities to store inputs which had to be purchased in large quantities when available due to supply uncertainties.

Thus, in order to maintain efficient supplies of inputs and continue regular operation, the company had to tie up capital in operations which contributed little to overall profitability. The motivating force behind this diversification and integration was to ensure maximum time at sea to enable its fleet to cover its fixed operating costs. The net result was a large and cumbersome company with a wide variety of interests and top-heavy administration.

In the late 1960s Mankoadze had thirty-two boats. In 1973 it built a canning plant, and in 1981 it purchased eight large vessels from Norway. By July 1983 only seven of these vessel were serviceable. Of the 2100 workers employed in 1989, 500 remain.

The existing operation is based upon three vessels fishing for herring in Senegalese waters. The catch is landed in Dakar, frozen and trans-shipped to Ghana, where it is held in store and sold to fish mammies for distribution. The company used to freeze in Tema, but finds it cheaper and easier to do it in Dakar. The company's remaining boats are engaged in tuna fishing, selling about 20% of the catch locally through fish mammies and the remainder to Starkist for export.

The contribution of tuna fishing to the total Ghana catch has remained fairly stable, peaking at 15% (34,410 tons) of the total marine catch in 1985. Tuna production has averaged roughly 13% of marine fish production during the period 1985–1991. Demand for tuna for export has been relatively stable. The ability of the product to earn hard currency has partially hedged the sector as a whole against currency devaluation which has hit the rest of the industrial fishing industry so severely, but high input costs have still left the fleet in a very poor state. As illustrated by the case study, individual businesses have struggled to survive under the conditions of the Structural Adjustment program, partly because of problems inherited from the previous period when the economy was centralized, and partly due to the changes in cost structure resulting from currency devaluation.

A poor **herring/sardine** catch during the 1992 season has led many to believe that this resource is in decline, although this could be the result of a single-year fluctuation in sea temperatures—the 'El Nino effect'—or other factors. For a number of reasons the industrial fishery would have problems responding to an upturn in its fortunes such as improved catches and enhanced prices. High levels of debt to indigenous banks and to foreign donors and investors will make getting further loans or re-capitalizing the industry problematic. Boats are lying idle. Plant is out of date and needs replacing. Overmanning is widespread, especially in what remains of the public sector. Banks lack confidence in existing management capability.

The single largest element of operating costs for all industrial fisheries is fuel, possibly accounting for up to 70%.[26] Fuel costs, therefore, are the largest single determinant of profitability. Industrial fisheries have been exempted from a recent 60% increase in taxation on fuel. Anecdotal evidence suggests anyway that many in the semi-industrial sector are still buying fuel at sea from tenders bringing fuel from other West African countries, notably Nigeria. In July 1993 marine diesel cost US$220/ton in Tema harbor but was available for between US$185–190/ton off-shore. Fuel purchased off-shore must be bought in US Dollars. Despite the apparent free convertibility of the Cedis, this is still considered to be a problem since the banks periodically face shortages of US dollars.

Industrial Processing and Marketing

The tuna export market is dominated by one U.S. company (Starkist) which buys the great majority of large landed tuna for re-export in frozen form. Some is converted to frozen loins. The price variation with fish size is considerable. For export, a premium is paid for large fish (see Table 8.8), but for domestic fresh consumption and smoking/curing, heavy competition has bid up the price for smaller fish (less than 3 lb) to C476/kg.

Starkist will shortly commence construction of a 100 ton per day canning plant for tuna in Tema. They have negotiated highly beneficial conditions for this plant with the Government of Ghana, including tax holidays and tariff exemption. They plan to conduct a bonded operation[27] using locally landed fish, imported cans and imported soya oil. The product will be exported to the U.S. and particularly the European Community, where it will not incur im-

---

[26] This figure is disputed by a World Bank Report of 1989 as an exaggeration, putting the figure nearer 50%, which is still significant. However scrutiny of one company's annual balance sheet during the field work for this report adds credence to the 70% figure.

[27] The term bonded means that goods imported into the factory and re-exported will not be counted as imports and exports and will not, therefore, be liable for duty.

TABLE 8.8: **Indicative Landed Tuna Prices, July 1993**

Weight (lbs)	Landed Price (Cedi/kg.)
>20	600
7.5–20	600
4–7.5	600
3–4	278
<3	118

NOTE: C630 = US$1, June 1993.

SOURCE: Starkist International.

port duty due to Ghana's status as a signatory of the Lomé Convention. Existing total landings will not meet this demand for some years to come.

The project is a joint venture with a large local fishing company which has experience in managing a canning operation. The operation will be vertically integrated from the canning plant onward, with Starkist's international marketing operation being used to distribute the product. Within Ghana it will not be integrated, but will rely on either buying tuna under contract from boat owners or through fish mammies.

Potential benefits to the Ghanaian economy of the development of this large canning operation will be: firstly, the creation of 370 jobs, mainly for women manual workers; secondly, the increased use of currently over-supplied electricity utilities; thirdly, increased demand for locally landed tuna using locally owned vessels and crew. Finally, the additional supply of fish waste from the factory will be sold locally providing a valuable input of protein meal into local animal feed ingredients which have decreased in quality and increased in price in recent years.

Potential draw-backs of this approach to inward investment include: firstly, that profit will be held in US dollars and will probably be repatriated rather than re-invested; secondly, the quality of employment created will be low and transient, i.e. low skilled, low waged, on a day-to-day basis; thirdly, that the investment may not be as long-term as it appears. Canning operations are easily moved. Starkist has moved its operation in Ghana to Côte d'Ivoire in the past when it was not happy with conditions in Tema. Finally, the additional demand for tuna may result in a reduction in fish available for domestic consumption, though tuna canneries demand large fish and the domestic market is for small ones.

Starkist have a long track record in the Ghanaian tuna fishing industry, know their local partners well, dominate demand for tuna, have assured markets for their finished products and are being offered highly advantageous terms for setting up this business. In the present, stable, open business environment in Ghana, they might be expected to do very well from this enterprise. The only potential cloud on the horizon is the future supply of tuna, the state of the resource being the subject of considerable debate, though Starkist believes that supply is "nearly in-exhaustable".

Credit

Access to and the cost of credit are key issues in any discussion of fish production and marketing. Fishing using motors requires considerable working capital for fuel which must be financed before fishing commences. Demands for fixed capital at irregular intervals are considerable. Fishermen's income is, as stressed earlier, highly unpredictable. In the marketing system, selling processed fish involves bulk transactions with relatively small margins requiring a high degree of liquidity on the part of the middle-person.

Credit provision can be divided clearly between formal and informal systems. The former consist of Development Banks and Cooperative Societies and usually entail compliance with certain criteria on the part of the borrower such as provision of surety, collateral, evidence of savings and testimonials. Informal credit is made up of a wide range of credit arrangements between relatives, ethnic groups, buyers and sellers characterized by their lack of formal fixed terms and conditions and often repaid in kind.

The experience of the formal sector in providing credit to fisheries over the decades since Ghana's independence has not been favorable.[28] Recovery levels on loans to artisanal fisherfolk for canoes, nets, motors and working capital for one bank are still only running at 50% of total disbursements. For the inshore fishing sector, recovery rates are even lower and the banks have pulled out, because fishing in this sector is no longer economically viable.

To improve recovery rates, banks in Ghana have tended to increase the stringency of requirements for loans. For example, the Agricultural Development Bank requires applicants for loans to undertake the following:

- Provide evidence of their "background" i.e., be known to the bank;
- Have their existing assets valued by bank valuation officers to offset against potential default;

---

[28] Neither has its experience with agriculture—see Obben (1991).

- Have savings deposited with the bank which are greater than the value of the loan;
- Have documentary evidence of ownership of property for collateral;

In lieu of this last requirement, the bank will, under exceptional circumstances, accept a personal guarantor as surety for a loan. Effectively however, these requirements exclude the majority of artisanal and industrial fisherfolk from bank loans at discounted rates.

In the past banks have lent money to middlewomen for marketing and processing purposes. Usually this involves lending money at the beginning of the herring season to be paid back over the following eight months. However, very few of these loans are still undertaken. In one case all the borrowers in this sector defaulted, it is believed because they on-lent the loan to their husbands for fishing activities instead of investing in trading. The issue of fungibility of loans has yet to be resolved.

Even when formal sector companies need credit, the smooth functioning of the credit market can be obstructed by traditional values and expectations. Large capital assets, be they companies, land or fishing vessels are often felt to be owned "in trust" for family members of the next generations.[29] While the kinship system allows companies access to loans, often interest free, from within the family group, it can limit a company's ability to raise outside equity to fund capital expenditure. For example, banks now request borrowers seeking loans for family concerns to provide collateral in the form of real estate. In interviews boat owners revealed that they either had no proof of ownership of their family land or were not prepared for the social stigma associated with "mortgaging" their children's birthright.

It also means that companies with excessive liabilities and debt may be unwilling to file for bankruptcy and recommence more profitable working free from debt. The deep-sea fishing fleet in Ghana is a case in point. One company invested heavily in trawlers from Europe and then found that the economics of trawling had changed, making it uneconomic to put to sea. Devaluation of the Cedi during the past decade has massively increased the Cedi cost of financing the debt of the trawlers which are now unseaworthy. The net effect is that the company is unable to raise capital from formal

---

[29] Companies are registered either under Sole Proprietorship laws, or as 'exempt companies' registered by a restricted number of extended family members. In this way, traditional family businesses can enjoy limited liability protection. There are few public companies in Ghana, and none in fisheries.

institutions, or to spread its equity base to finance potentially profitable new areas of businesses because creditors are fearful of their liability position. Owners are reluctant to allow businesses to go bankrupt and the absence of an enforceable insolvency law compounds this situation.

All the Ghanaian banks have been involved in the donor-funded program of concessional loans for outboard motors. Default rates on these loans were high and collateral requirements minimal. Borrowers experienced further problems with spare parts especially when the Cedi was not freely exchangeable for other currencies. A second tranche of donor money made available in 1987/88 for engines was handled more circumspectly but the collapse of the trigger fish catch effectively made repayment of these loans impossible.

One new area in which most banks have become involved is the financing of construction of cold stores. These are mostly used for the storage of imported frozen herring and sardines for sale during the low season.

Informal Credit Provision

The loaning of money (or deferment of payment of accounts) is an important part of informal sector fisheries and fish marketing. Of particular interest are the credit relationships between individual members of fishing families. These have been discussed above, in terms of the relations between artisanal fishermen and fish mammies, but are also important in industrial fisheries.

Anecdotal evidence suggests that, with the increasing costs of both artisanal and industrial fishing, the levels of indebtedness within families and between fisherfolk and middlewomen is increasing. Traditionally, there has always been a degree of debt, but of late, with the devaluation of the Cedi and reduced resource base, this system has been placed under further stress. When fish prices fall sharply, this can occasionally result in a loss on the part of the fisherwomen causing considerable family tension. Little is known about the impact of these changes on fishing societies and particularly on income distribution within family groups.

There exist a number of different informal credit and savings arrangements between groups of individuals. An example is the susu or revolving credit and savings union which accepts regular savings from members who each in turn receive a lump sum equivalent to their total expected savings over the period.[30] There exist a number of informal fish mammies associa-

---

[30] For a comprehensive study of informal credit systems with many references to West Africa see Adams and Fitchett (1992).

tions which collect savings from members, provide health insurance and give loans. One such association in Kumasi (the Kumasi-Mopti Cooperative Fish Marketing Society) has nearly 2,000 members who are shareholders. Credit is provided by some societies. Others will stand as guarantors for loans from the formal sector.

CONCLUSION

Because fisheries are an extreme example of an open-access resource, there will always be an important role for government in regulating exploitation. Ghana has seen heavy public-sector involvement in fisheries, through the establishment of two large parastatals, but it is debatable whether this core function has been performed effectively in the past, still more so after the withdrawal of government from fisheries production and processing. There is therefore a threat to the resource base behind the rest of the story presented here, the differential effects of Structural Adjustment policies on artisanal and industrial fisheries.

In Ghanaian fisheries family and kinship units are involved in various activities from production through processing to marketing. The ability of these units to benefit from intra-family vertical linkages in both the artisanal and industrial sectors is demonstrated by their capacity to survive the severe economic cleavages of the 1980s and early 1990s. However, within these units there has been a continued but unmeasured transfer of debt, mainly from male household members to female household members. Direct results of Structural Adjustment policies, such as high input costs, constrained consumer demand and competition from imports, combined with increasing competition for a finite resource, seem to have changed the economics of fishing in Ghana. Generally this has been in the favour of the artisanal sector.

Traditional, informal linkages in processing and marketing fish products have proved more robust than large-scale industrial integration (in both private and public enterprises), though the objectives of the two sectors differ. The ability of the artisanal sector to respond to the inherent uncertainties of fish production (i.e., risk, product variability, supply fluctuation, perishability etc.), contrasts markedly with the managerial and institutional problems that the large public sector enterprises, and even larger private sector enterprises, have had.

Methodological Note and Acknowledgements

The research for this chapter consisted of two elements: a study of existing literature and data sets on Ghana fisheries, and a field trip to investigate the fishery first hand.

Major sources of secondary data have been indicated throughout, but of particular use for the section on industrial fisheries were a series of sector reports completed during the last five years for various international donors considering rehabilitation of the industrial sector (UNIDO 1991; World Bank 1989; FAO 1989; DANIDA 1988 and CTA 1987).

The field work was divided roughly equally between key informants in the production, marketing and processing of artisanal and industrial fisheries. For individual fisherfolk, middlewomen and processors, a purposive sampling system was necessitated by the brevity of the period of research. Interviews were, in the main, semi-structured, to cover the key issues while allowing additional insights to be pursued. Where possible, key informants were sought, such as chief fishermen, "Queen" fish mammies and heads of cooperative trading and processing bodies. Key informants in the industrial private sector and managers of fisheries parastatals were also interviewed about their businesses. The bias inherent in this approach is recognised by the authors. Other potential sources of error/bias are the lack of a seasonal perspective on the fishery and the necessity to seek informants in accessible areas of Ghana.

A number of key informants in Government institutions and agencies as well as donor agencies and universities were also interviewed in order to gain a wider perspective on the framework within which the fisheries sector operates.

The authors wish to express their gratitude to the following individuals and institutions without whom this report could not have been completed.

John Manful and Lawrence Abbey of the Food Research Institute, Accra. Florence Lamptey, Department of Fisheries, Accra. Andrew Wilson, British High Commission, Accra. Ernest Tettey, Infopeche, Abidjan.

We would like to thank all the informants, both in the private and public sectors.

In July 1993 US$1 = 640 Cedis

IX.

Merchants and Middlemen in the Cattle Trade of Southern Somalia[1]

INTRODUCTION

This case study of cattle marketing in Southern Somalia focuses on the unofficial cross-border trade with Kenya and demonstrates the inter-relatedness of domestic trading and official and unofficial exports. The analysis reveals that the orientation of export trade is highly contingent on economic and political factors that have led at times to reversals in trade flows. The relationships between different types of traders and their diversification strategies are examined in detail.

Conditions of market uncertainty, macroeconomic decline and political instability have reached extreme proportions in Somalia during the last few years. Those traders who have become agents of large, export-oriented merchants focusing on a single market have suffered the most, whereas traders who are based in small villages and involved in both domestic and export markets have sometimes prospered. The unofficial trade in livestock to neighboring countries has allowed certain groups of Somali traders to withstand an environment of extreme economic and political volatility that is exceptional even in the African context.

The chapter begins by discussing the volume and general characteristics of trade in livestock from the arid and semi-arid countries of Northeast Africa and the Sahel. After discussing the historic precedents of market crisis and instability in southern Somalia, it goes on to suggest that: (1) dyadic and multiple relationships among livestock traders, often based on some form of material exchange, are the norm during periods of both economic decline and

---

[1] This is an edited version of "Traders, Brokers and Market 'Crisis' in Southern Somalia" previously published in *Africa* 62 (1), 1989. John Morton edited the paper for re-publication and contributed additional material on the dimensions and general characteristics of the livestock trade in Sahelian and Northeast Africa.

relative prosperity; and (2) economic differentiation among livestock merchants makes it difficult to generalize about trader behavior without paying attention to differences in scale, access to markets and position in the market chain. Market channels are distinguished spatially and sociologically in order to demonstrate that certain groups of traders are associated with particular patterns of trade and geographic location. The chapter concludes with a discussion of the importance of social relations in marketing and the responses of traders to macroeconomic changes.

The countries of the Sahel and the Horn of Africa all export large numbers of livestock on the hoof either to neighboring African countries or to the Middle East. In each country there are large arid and semi-arid areas where livestock production by traditional pastoralist methods or agropastoralism is the most rational land-use strategy. Contrary to some stereotypes, most pastoral societies have customarily and systematically sold live animals and animal products to agricultural societies near or distant.[2] They have engaged in animal trade because there existed an external market for animals as meat, as a means of transport or for social reasons,[3] because the terms of trade frequently allowed pastoralists to obtain more calories than they could through the direct consumption of animal products, and because male animals could be sold without endangering herd reproduction.

Prior to the advent of modern freezing and chilling technologies, there were few alternatives to taking live animals to market.[4] Before motor transport, they were necessarily trekked overland. Because the international markets for Sahelian and Northeast African livestock are relatively close,[5] live animals continue to be exported. Now, they can be taken by truck or train or trekked in the traditional manner according to cost considerations that vary by time and place. The continued use of trekking through sparsely inhabited areas allows many livestock exports to bypass frontier controls and avoid associated taxes and duties.[6] In many cases, the trade existed long before the frontier. This element must be factored into official export figures for livestock from the countries.

---

[2] Kerven (1992).

[3] This refers principally to the use of animals as bridewealth.

[4] A traditional meat-drying technique appears to have allowed a longstanding trade in meat from Northern to Southern Nigeria (Silverside 1992).

[5] By comparison with Southern Africa, where end markets for exports are in Europe.

[6] This is not to say that unofficial exports of livestock are not in some cases effected by truck or by boat; livestock are shipped unofficially by dhow to Saudi Arabia from both Sudan and Somalia (Morton 1989; Jaffee and Weli 1985).

While governments are involved in export of livestock, particularly by sea, the trade has remained in private hands throughout the Sahel and Northeast Africa. Several studies[7] suggest that trader profits are not excessive, and that the apparent involvement of large numbers of intermediaries in many marketing systems is in fact an efficient response to the difficulties inherent in the nature of livestock as a commodity.

CHARACTERISTICS OF LIVESTOCK AS A COMMODITY

Animals on the hoof, particularly those raised by pastoralists or agropastoralists, have distinctive characteristics that affect marketing patterns.

1) **Livestock are both a commodity and a form of capital.** There is no clear division in pastoralist economies between 'capital', 'inventory' and 'surplus'.[8] While under optimal conditions, pastoralists will sell only surplus males, in times of stress even reproductive females can be sold, eventually leading to the pastoralists' destitution. Traders can continue to be active, even or especially when the productive system is in crisis.

2) **High 'perishability':** Livestock on the hoof are much less perishable than meat, but need considerably greater care than many harvested crops. Livestock must continue to be fed and watered, and in some cases, protected against disease. Care involves trade-offs between transport costs, labor costs, speed of marketing and animal condition. For instance, before the advent of large-scale trucking of livestock in Nigeria, the necessity of trekking stock quickly from the semi-arid zone through the trypanosomiasis belt to the end markets resulted in significant weight loss (and therefore lower prices) but was judged preferable to mortality en route.

3) **Scattered supply:** Livestock are necessarily produced on natural rangelands at low population densities. As a result, time and transport costs in collecting together marketable herds of livestock are high. These may fall on the producers or the first traders in the marketing chain.

---

[7] Usefully reviewed in Sandford (1983).

[8] It is partly because of this that pastoralists are sometimes alleged to display a 'perverse supply response', a debate which need not be entered into here. See Sandford (1983).

4) **Individual variability:** Livestock vary individually by a number of criteria, all of them relevant to market value. These include weight, age, sex, proportion of fat and presence of parasites or diseases.[9] As a result, a great deal of time must be invested in examining animals and negotiating prices. In many markets there are brokers who perform this function on behalf of larger merchants without necessarily taking ownership of the stock.

5) **Multiple uses:** Animals have multiple uses to pastoralists: milk, meat, manure, transport, social uses. How they are ranked will vary in different situations. Once animals enter the marketing chain, there is also at least a theoretical choice (depending on the infrastructure of the countries in question) between keeping them on the hoof, or having them slaughtered and marketed as red or frozen meat.[10] Marketing livestock on the hoof involves continuous decision-making, more so than marketing an agricultural surplus (assuming the choice of crop has been made).

6) **Livestock production entails relatively low requirements for purchased inputs:** Even though there is increasing use of purchased fodders (such as oilseed cake), medicines and veterinary services, pastoralists in Africa still purchase very little of what could be considered a production input. Traders are therefore less likely to become providers of credit than are crop traders, although they may provide credit to pastoralists for grain and other necessities for household maintenance.

7) **Skill requirements:** Considerable knowledge is necessary to keep stock healthy, as well as docile and tractable, during transit to market. Such knowledge is acquired through experience, which largely accounts for the high degree of ethnic specialization in long-distance livestock marketing.

8) **Varied investment requirements:** Market systems are typically made up of many levels with widely differing entry requirements in terms of capital. Because of the demand for skilled animal handlers and brokers, there is some scope for people to work in the trade with no

---

[9] Where stock-raiding or theft is a problem, the legitimacy of the seller's title may also have to be verified.

[10] There is some specialized export of animals that are not to be slaughtered at all, for instance the trade in riding camels from Sudan to the Gulf. There is little information on this, and it is unlikely to be significant compared with the trade in animals destined for slaughter.

capital at all. A few may later graduate to become small traders in their own right. Especially if motor transport is involved, however, there are likely to be levels of trade with heavy investment requirements, namely, the capital (or at least the credit) to purchase one truckload of animals and prepay for truck hire. Such an investment is less than that required for industrial processing equipment in many other sectors, but more than that required for artisanal processing or simple trade in those sectors. It is also likely to be permanently beyond the reach of ordinary pastoralists, even if they enter the trade at lower levels.

9) **Non-financial entry requirements:** Traders who export officially require ability to deal with bureaucratic procedures. Even where livestock leaves one country unofficially, there may be bureaucratic procedures necessary at the end market. For example, in Nigeria a requirement for veterinary clearance certificates is successfully enforced, even on livestock unofficially exported from Niger.[11] Bureaucratic procedures are likely to be more cumbersome where livestock are shipped rather than trucked or trekked.

10) **Seasonality in trade:** Marketing of livestock by pastoralists may show some seasonality due to both supply and demand factors. On the supply side, animals are in their best condition at the end of the rainy season. Pastoral migrations and road conditions may make it is easier to take them to market at another time of year. Demand may exhibit seasonality with maximum consumption occurring at religious festivals and other holidays.[12] Yet, seasonal peaks in sales are unlikely to be as sharp as they are for many annual crops, and under certain conditions sales can take place at any time of year.

11) **Possibility of "back-haul trade":** Pastoralist producers living in zones poor in other productive possibilities are likely to present permanent markets for a variety of commodities: grain and other basic foods, sugar, beverages and stimulants, cloth. In many, but by no means all, situations these commodities are *imported* from the countries to which livestock are *exported* by the same merchants using the same means of transport.

---

[11] Kulibaba (1991).

[12] This is complicated by the fact that Muslim festivals move forward against the Western calendar every year.

EXPORT MARKETING, COMPETITIVE STRUCTURE AND GOVERNMENT INTERVENTION

The export systems under consideration divide generally into overland trade, whether official or unofficial, and trade by sea. In overland trade, governments are not heavily involved, except by taxing traders and ensuring health standards.[13] Overland trade is likely to be relatively open to competition, even at the highest levels, and one is likely to find successful enterprises in both exporting and importing countries. Even where the trade is completely official, enterprises will be characterized by a degree of informality with integration of the marketing chain achieved by kinship, ethnic or client ties— 'agreements and sanctions internal to the community'[14]—rather than by formal contract or partnership.

In the case of trade by sea, governments have become more involved, and there is greater tendency for a small number of firms to dominate export marketing. In Ethiopia the parastatal ELIMCOR has accounted for over 70% of all sheep exports in recent years.[15] In Somalia, official exports of cattle to Yemen and Egypt during the mid-to-late 1980s were dominated by three companies that were set up under government supervision. Trade with Egypt took place under a specially negotiated agreement between the two governments.

The reason for the differences is fairly obvious. Shipping involves more bureaucratic procedures—letters of credit, bills of lading—than even official overland export is likely to. These are unavoidable costs of using international shipping and represent potentially large economies of scale. In addition, when pre-existing links to end markets are not established, there will be high costs involved in searching for a purchaser and enforcing contracts. Finally, overland trade usually involves countries sharing the same currency (for example, the CFA Franc), or countries for which there is an easily accessible parallel currency market. This is less likely to be the case where countries do not have a land border.

---

[13] There were attempts to set up parastatal livestock companies with both production and marketing functions in the Sahel in the 1970s, but these failed or have been dissolved in the course of Structural Adjustment programs. See Kulibaba and Holtzmann (1990).

[14] Kulibaba and Holtzmann (1990).

[15] FAO/World Bank (1993). ELIMCOR dominates official exports for all species, but only for sheep is official export more important than unofficial.

Export Volumes and Trends

The FAO now attempts to include unofficial livestock exports in its annual trade statistics (Table 9.1). These figures, together with data from other sources on Ethiopia and Somalia, give an indication of the volume and importance of livestock exports from the Sahelian and Northeast African countries. The table makes no attempt to quantify marketing of livestock within the countries concerned; yet, there are major flows of stock to urban centers for consumption in all the countries listed. Both Côte d'Ivoire and Nigeria, men-

TABLE 9.1: **Live Animal Exports from Sahelian and Northeast African Countries**

Country	Exports ('000 head)	Destination	Exports as % of National Export Earnings
Mauritania	70 cattle 450 small stock	Senegal, Middle East	Na.
Mali	190 cattle 470 small stock	Côte d'Ivoire and other coastal countries	26
Burkina Faso	81 cattle 92 small stock	Côte d'Ivoire and other coastal countries	6
Niger	100 cattle 170 small stock	Nigeria	Na.
Chad	40 cattle 160 small stock	Cameroon and elsewhere	19
Sudan	600 small stock 14 cattle	Saudi Arabia. No official export of cattle or goats since 1986. Substantial unofficial exports of sheep to Saudi Arabia and camels to Egypt and Libya	18
Ethiopia[1]	176 cattle 359 sheep 266 goats	Official cattle exports only to Yemen, small stock to rest of Middle East. Unofficial exports to Kenya and Somalia	3
Somalia[2]	68 cattle 734 small stock	Official cattle exports to Egypt and Yemen, small-stock to Saudi Arabia. Unofficial cattle exports to Kenya	41

[1] Ethiopia: 1987/88 figures including estimated unofficial exports; 85% of cattle, 28% of sheep, 75% of goats. Export earnings figure based on official exports only.
[2] Somalia: 1987 official figure for cattle, plus estimated 40,000 unofficial exports. 1984 official figures for small stock.

SOURCES: Export figures from FAO Trade Yearbook 1991, except Ethiopia (FAO/World Bank 1993), Somalia (Little 1989; Jaffee and Weli 1985). Export earnings figures all from FAO Trade Yearbook 1991.

tioned above as importers, both also produce large quantities of livestock in their northern regions which are trucked south to the cities. Domestic and import/export marketing systems may be organized by the same merchants or may compete for livestock supply and markets. The table excludes meat exports, which are generally small yet growing in some countries.

Livestock exports from the countries under consideration have proved vulnerable both to demand factors—non-economic barriers and international competition in the importing markets—and supply factors. There is a legitimate fear that imports of livestock on the hoof may infect the national herd, but policies based on such fears have sometimes been taken to extremes by Saudi Arabia and the other Gulf states. A Saudi ban on Somali cattle to prevent the spread of rinderpest has been in force since 1984, despite the lack of evidence of rinderpest in Somalia.

Livestock from the countries under consideration now has to compete in export markets with stock or meat from developed countries. Despite high transport costs, ranched livestock from Australia is taking over markets in the Gulf states because a reliable supply which meets health requirements is more assured. The European Community exports subsidized meat to West Africa and Egypt, which has serious effects on inter-African trade.

Supply of livestock has been affected by the drought and environmental degradation that has taken place in the arid and semi-arid zones in the last two decades. It is hard to find reliable data or to distinguish short-term from long-term trends within it. Livestock numbers in the Sahelian and Northeast African countries all declined in aggregate over the 1980s, but much of this was due to a sharp fall in 1984–85. At that point, exports from Mali, Burkina Faso and Sudan (three countries for which data is at hand) peaked sharply, probably because distress sales by pastoralists were converted into exports. While one might expect a long-term decline in exports, the relationship between desertification (itself a controversial concept), herd numbers and livestock marketing remains extremely complex and does not simply spiral downward.

Another supply problem is that of political instability in exporting countries. Somalia is the worst case here. The present case study will show the resilience of trading networks up to around 1990, but there has probably already come a point where trading networks have been broken up. On a smaller scale, political instability may affect livestock production and export in other countries of the region.

THE LOWER JUBBA REGION OF SOMALIA

The Lower Jubba Region[16] in the far south of Somalia consists of a semi-arid plain, in which most cultivation is carried out in the immediate vicinity of the Jubba river and in scattered settlements along the coastal plain to the south of Kismayo town. Approximately 25% of this population is classified as pastoral nomadic, 30% as urban, and 45% as settled agropastoralist or agriculturalist.[17] Average rainfall is 560 mm, much lower in the west, and falls mainly between April and June, with uncertain 'short rains' between October and December. Compared to other regions of Somalia, the lower Jubba is a relatively favorable rainfall area.[18] The seasonal floodplain of the Jubba River and the Lag Dera basin are important dry-season grazing resources. The former support the highest concentration of cattle in any region of Somalia, which is among the highest in eastern Africa.[19] The Lag Dera basin was developed as a grazing resource by the World Bank which financed the Trans-Jubba Livestock Project from the mid-1970s. Larger export-oriented herders and traders were among the chief beneficiaries, and the project was discontinued in 1986 amid local conflicts and environmental controversy.

The other important geographical feature of the region is its 150 kilometer coastline and Kismayo port, in particular, which is the third largest port in Somalia and serves as a major livestock export facility. The port provides access to lucrative international livestock markers for nomadic herders and local traders. Their counterparts elsewhere in the pastoral regions of sub-Saharan Africa are not similarly endowed.

The characteristics discussed above help explain the importance of the livestock sector (particularly cattle) to the regional economy. In most years Somalia derives more than 80% of its export earnings from the livestock sector. Largely because of its excellent water and range resources, the Lower Jubba Region has the largest population of cattle in the country (approximately 860,000) and also a sizable camel population (estimated at 222,000).[20] These represent about 22% and 4%, respectively, of Somalia's cattle and camel

---

[16] The Region is subdivided into four administrative districts. Fieldwork concentrated on two: Kismayo and Afmadow.

[17] Evans et al. (1988).

[18] Hubl (1986), Conze and Labahn (1986).

[19] Murray Watson, personal communication.

[20] Hubl (1986).

populations. In the aggregate, livestock numbers seemed to stabilize in the late 1980s after a rapid expansion of herds, especially of cattle. It is estimated that from 1952 to 1983/84, regional cattle and camel herds grew annually at rates of 7.9 and 5.2%, respectively. At these rates, herds of cattle would have doubled approximately every nine years, and camel herds every thirteen years.[21] Growth in regional herds during this period was related to: (1) growth in human populations due in part to in-migration of herders (and herds); (2) development of export markets for cattle; (3) establishment of water points in underutilized parts of the region, which allowed cattle to use these areas regularly; and (4) improvement in veterinary health services and the eradication of such animal diseases as rinderpest.

Families of the region now have cattle herds that are well above the country's average and among the highest in East Africa.[22] Ownership of both camels and cattle in the region is highly skewed. Among a sample of forty-two households owning camels, the richest 12.5% control an estimated 52% of these animals. While ownership of cattle in the lower Jubba is not as skewed as this, considerable differences do exist. The richest 12.5% of households own 39% of total cattle, while the bottom 50% of cattle herders control only 15% of the herd. Such inequalities in livestock ownership are not unusual for pastoral economies.[23]

In most years the Lower Jubba Region, because of Kismayo port, accounts for 35 to 40% of the country's total overseas exports of cattle and about 20% of its camel exports. The unofficial export of cattle to neighboring countries, especially to Kenya, has been even more significant. During the 1980s, the Lower Jubba Region was exporting about 30,000 cattle a year to Kenya on the unofficial market, or approximately 60% of Somalia's total exports to that country.[24] During 1987 and 1988, unofficial sales to Kenya exceeded official exports from Kismayo port by a factor of six. Because of the recent civil war

---

[21] Hendy (1985).

[22] See Schneider (1979) for general East African comparisons, and Ensminger (1984) and Grandin (1988) for particularly cattle-rich groups. Lower Jubba herds are also well above averages recorded in West Africa; see Sutter (1987) and Swift (1986).

[23] Sutter (1987); Little (1985).

[24] It is obviously very difficult to estimate the annual volume of unofficial trade to Kenya. Cassam (1987) conducted research in both Kenya and Somalia to derive his estimate of about 50,000. Using this figure, with the estimated herd sizes of the Lower, Middle and Upper Jubba Regions and the author's market data, it can be estimated that some 30,000 cattle, or 60% of the total, originate from the Lower Jubba Region.

TABLE 9.2: **Average Herd Size and Composition Among Herder Households**

Livestock	Kismayo District	Afmadow District	All
Cattle	42.98	74.74	58.14
Camels	22.37	1.73	12.52
Sheep/goats	6.54	8.26	7.36

SOURCE: Author's survey of forty-six households in Kismayo District and forty-two households in Afmadow District, 1987–88.

in the country, the differential has probably increased since official exports of livestock have virtually halted since 1990.

Livestock production systems in the region exhibit substantial variability that relates to both environmental and social variables. Major differences in livestock production systems occur between Kismayo and Afmadow Districts, for example, the most important being the significance of camels in Kismayo as opposed to cattle in Afmadow (see Table 9.2). The average number of camels controlled by herders in Kismayo District is more than ten times that of Afmadow herders who, in turn, own considerably larger cattle herds than do Kismayo households. Neither district holds large numbers of goats and sheep, a finding that further distinguishes the Lower Jubba Region from most other areas of Somalia where small stock—especially sheep—are so important.[25]

Environmental parameters partially explain interdistrict variation in the ownership of cattle and camels: Afmadow, particularly its southern half, contains larger expanses of perennial pastures suitable for bovine production than does Kismayo, which has a browse/shrub environment suitable for camel pastoralism. These production differences also correlate loosely with the clan structure of the region. The area's two most important subclans, the Maxamed Zubeer of the Ogadeen clan and the Herti, are found in Afmadow and Kismayo Districts, respectively. There are significant differences in their production systems. The Maxamed Zubeer, who inhabit most of Afmadow District and a territory extending more than 100 kilometers inside the Kenya border, are closely associated with cattle pastoralism. The Herti, residing mainly in Kismayo District, focus considerably more attention on camel pastoralism. In addition, many Herti are actively engaged in commerce (including livestock trade) and control many of the businesses in Kismayo town. The Maxamed

---

[25] See Samatar (1989).

Zubeer are more strictly pastoral, and their commercial activities are limited mainly to small retail trade and minor roles in the overseas export trade.

While clan is not the only social factor determining regional production relations and systems, it is, along with such variables as class and territory,[26] critical to understanding relationships among traders and between traders and herders. The current chaos in Somalia has solidified clan relations, and most of the regional political and military movements are based on particular clans.

Both the Maxamed Zubeer and the Herti migrated to the Lower Jubba Region last century. The major influx of Maxamed Zubeer was in the 1870s and 1880s after they and other subclans of the Ogadeen clan were pushed by the expanding Ethiopian Empire and a series of inter-clan conflicts.[27] During approximately the same period, Kismayo began to grow as a commercial center and attracted Herti families from northeastern Somalia who moved there to trade and settle in the hinterland as pastoralists.[28] The Herti were experienced traders who had been involved with northern Somalia's trade of livestock and other products to the Arabian peninsula. This commerce predates the export trade from Kismayo. The Herti were able to adapt to a settled lifestyle, and by the latter part of the nineteenth century they had become "the dominant group of petty traders along the coast between the Jubba and Tana Rivers".[29]

The influx of the Herti clan brought them into direct confrontation with the Ogadeen over control of the lower Jubba. In the 1880s the Herti "were engaged in a struggle for political supremacy and control of local commerce with elements of the neighboring Maxamed Zubeer clan." The Maxamed Zubeer clan along with other Ogadeen subclans controlled caravan movements in and out of Kismayo town.[30] While livestock and livestock products assumed some significance in the caravan commerce, the most important

---

[26] See Samatar (1989).

[27] For more detail on the history of different groups in the Jubba area, see Dalleo (1975), Menkhaus (1989), and Turton (1970, 1975).

[28] Menkhaus notes that the Herti traders "were accompanied by clansmen who relocated in the region with their herds, in part to offset competition for control of local land and trade from the Muhammad Subeyr sub-clan of the Ogadeen clan" (1989).

[29] Cassanelli (1982). The Herti also were to become strong allies of the British colonial state, serving as policemen, clerks, and even "spies" for the administration (see Turton 1970, 1972). This close association further strained their relationship with Ogadeen groups in the region.

[30] Cassanelli (1982), see also Dalleo (1975).

commodity was ivory. The export of cattle and other products from Kismayo became more important in the 1880s and 1890s with Herti merchants playing a major role. Today, the region's most prosperous export trader traces his roots to this period when an earlier member of his family moved to Kismayo to establish an export business.[31]

A few of these northern traders eventually moved out from Kismayo into smaller centers like Afmadow in order to establish market alliances with the Ogadeen nomads and to be closer to sources of supply. A small number of Herti merchants married Maxamed Zubeer women. The town-based merchants and large middlemen[32] often extended credit to herders and small middlemen, developing a network of market alliances in the area that extended into what is today northeastern Kenya.[33] When the cattle trade was focused on Kenyan rather than Somali markets, the Ogadeen nomads and middlemen who occupied much of northeastern Kenya, as well as the lower Jubba of southern Somalia, played a greater role in the commerce. Market networks of this type continue today and are crucial to understanding how traders have responded to recent economic and political crises.

Historical Context of Market Crisis and Instability

The decade of the 1980s was a period of devastating political and economic decline in Somalia that took its toll on the livestock sector. Since the mid-1980s, the national economy has gone from bad to worse. As of 1989 the value of annual imports was about twice the value of Somalia's annual exports, while more than 70% of the annual operating budget of the government was directly paid out of foreign aid. The market value of the Somali shilling declined from 37 SSh = $1.00 in 1983[34] to about 1500 SSh = $1.00 in 1989. Annual inflation in the late 1980s exceeded 300%. Even before the most recent crisis, Somalia's economy exhibited "most of the major symptoms of African underdevelopment, for example, growing food imports, balance of payment problems, declining agricultural production, malnutrition, and starvation."[35]

---

[31] Cassanelli (1982).

[32] While women traders dominate the milk and other agricultural markets (Herren 1990), virtually none are involved in the cattle or camel trade.

[33] See Hjort (1979).

[34] Samatar and Samatar (1987).

[35] Samatar (1987, p. 356).

The current national political situation in Somalia, in which clan-based political factions control different regions, hardly needs further description here.[36] Even prior to the overthrow of the Siad Barre regime in January 1991, the southern-based Somali Patriotic Movement controlled most of the Lower Jubba region with the exception of Kismayo town. Major armed clashes between Barre's forces and the Somali Patriotic Movement, who are mainly drawn from the Ogadeen clan, took place as early as August 1989. The state, weak even during periods of relative stability, had effectively lost sovereignty over most of the lower Jubba by the end of 1989.

During the decade of the 1980s the livestock sector–the country's most important economic specialty–declined dramatically after more than fifteen years of rapid growth in livestock exports. During the 1970s the dominance of Saudi Arabia as a market for Somali cattle had grown rapidly, and by the early 1980s it accounted for more than 95% of the external market. In volume alone, the expansion of the Saudi market was a dramatic departure from the past. Cattle exports from Kismayo increased more than threefold from the late 1960s to the late 1970s. The amount of revenue also increased dramatically since Saudi importers were willing to pay relatively high prices to guarantee meat for their burgeoning domestic market. This growth in Saudi demand correlated with the general oil boom of the 1970s and early 1980s that drove up Arabian incomes.

The period 1983 to 1989 saw a reduction in total animal exports to Saudi Arabia. Fierce competition from Australia and other countries for the lucrative Saudi Arabian market reduced the volume of sheep exports to that country. The export of Somali cattle was also hurt by other actions that were only marginally market-related. In 1983 Saudi Arabia imposed a ban on cattle imported from Somalia in response to fears of rinderpest in southern Somalia. The immediate effects of the ban were catastrophic: annual cattle exports declined from 157,000 in 1982 to less than 8,000 in 1984 (Figure 9.1). While an international team from the FAO verified early on that the area's cattle are not infected by rinderpest—nor were they in 1983—the ban on cattle exports to Saudi Arabia remains in force.

The loss of the Saudi market was particularly disastrous to the economy of the lower Jubba region because of its dependence on cattle exports. In two

---

[36] It is not surprising that current political factions draw much of their support from the clan structure, since the Siad Barre regime reinforced "clanism" by strategically manipulating one group against the other.

years (1982 to 1984), annual cattle exports from Kismayo declined from approximately 51,000 to less than 1,000. This hurt certain merchants more than others and resulted in a redirection of the cattle trade to Kenyan markets.

New markets in Egypt and Yemen partially compensated for the loss of the Saudi market, but annual exports from Kismayo in 1985 and 1986 remained at only 50% of the 1982 volume. The next few years brought evidence that these new export markets might also prove volatile. From 1985 to 1987 annual cattle exports from Kismayo declined from 26,213 to 4,168 and prospects for 1988 looked only marginally better. Although trade to Yemen may continue, Egypt has stopped importing cattle from Somalia, including Kismayo, and is unlikely to resume imports in the near future. The civil unrest in Somalia has also reduced exports, the major port of Berbera being closed since mid-1988. As a result, the total value of livestock exports from Somalia fell from US $51 million in 1987 to US $22.4 million the following year. During much of 1989, the last year of reliable data, no official exports of cattle from Somalia took place. The trade situation could only have become worse in 1990 and 1991.[37]

For the Lower Jubba Region, the Kenya market proved to be the most reliable during this period. While Kenyan cattle had been exported overseas via the Kismayo port during the Saudi boom period, the trade was now reversed. As of 1989, Somali cattle were being sold at Kenyan markets and Kenyan cattle were no longer being sold at Kismayo.

How unusual is this sort of political and economic instability? Although the current situation is an extreme case, turbulent conditions have characterized the region for much of the past century. The cattle trade, for example, was disrupted by colonial policies of both the British and Italian governments, policies that included regulation of livestock movements, imposition of quarantines and restrictions on foreign currencies. It was also affected by warfare: in the 1890s and early 1900s between the Maxamed Zubeer and the British, in the 1930s between the Italians and Ethiopians, in the 1940s between British and Italian troops, and in the 1960s between Somalis and the Kenyan government. Severe droughts have occurred during almost every decade of this century. Fighting among local clan factions flares up periodically. Ambiguity and risk have surrounded livestock trade in the region during much of this century. Dalleo examines the structural transformation of the

---

[37] See Woodward and Stockton (1989) for export figures and prospects, and Greenfield (1991) for an update after the end of the Barre regime.

livestock trade in the 1920s due to of the imposition of a 20-year long ban on exports of Somali cattle to zones of Kenya settled by Europeans. The policies of the fascist Italian state also added to the uncertainties surrounding regional livestock trade:

> In July of 1936, Italian officials at Bardera [in the Jubba valley] gave a five day quit notice to the Somali who had been waiting there to sell their livestock. The Italian action put the Somali at a disadvantage because the water pools necessary for the safe return of their livestock to Wajir [in Kenya] had already dried out. The Italians purchased the Somali cattle at 'cutthroat prices'.[38]

Several times during the past century reversals in the flow of cattle between Kenya and Somalia occurred, depending on political and market conditions in the two countries. The shift toward Kenyan markets since the mid-1980s is only the latest in a series of transitions. During the periods of approximately 1890–1910, 1921–1940, 1945–1950 and 1968–1983, the cattle trade went mainly from northeastern Kenya to southern Somalia, especially to Kismayo. By contrast, during the periods 1910–1920, 1941–45, 1951–1967 and 1984 to the present, movements of cattle went mainly from Somali markets to Kenyan markets in the Northern Frontier Province, and then eventually to Kenya's commercial ranching areas and towns.

These market trends were not absolute, and during any given year cattle flows could be reversed or go in both directions, depending on seasonal and local market conditions. For example, the lack of water points in northeastern Kenya restricts movements of cattle to its markets during the dry season, even when prices are more favorable there than in Somalia. At any rate, the risks associated with cattle trade, regardless of their origins, have always required astute merchants to maintain multiple relationships with other traders on both the Kenyan and Somali sides of the border.

Overview of Different Markets

The rapid expansion in cattle exports from 1970 to 1983 resulted in two important changes. First, it inserted into the region a class of very large export traders from Mogadishu and other areas to the north. These traders

---

[38] Dalleo (1975, pp. 171–172).

FIGURE 9.1: **Cattle Exports—for Kismayo Region and National Total Exports from 1980 to 1988**

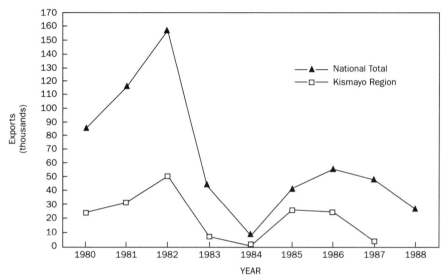

Based on Cassam (1987); Woodward (1989).

were not associated with the pastoral sector of the Lower Jubba,[39] and depended on large brokers and middlemen to procure their animals. The growth in cattle exports and the insertion of large outside traders in turn altered local and regional market relations, as local middlemen and brokers began to serve as agents for the large traders. In lower Jubba this resulted in a scale of trading enterprise and specialization not characteristic of earlier periods.

The contemporary cattle trade is essentially focused on four types of markets which account for about 90% of the region's sales. First is the regional domestic market, concentrated in regional towns like Kismayo, Jamaame and Jilib. This trade is for local consumption and rebuilding of local herds, and it involves both low-quality, low-priced cattle and young heifers or bulls (less than 3–4 years). On the consumption side, it is centered on local butcheries and accounts for an estimated 40% of cattle sales in the area. This figure includes purchases by local herders to replenish their own herds, but not animals bought for eventual resale in other markets.

---

[39] Of the more than 100 registered companies in Somalia involved with livestock exports, none are from the Kismayo area.

The second market is the national domestic market located in Mogadishu, Somalia's largest city; it requires the trekking of cattle over a distance of more than 300 kilometers. The Mogadishu market is growing rapidly along with the city's population, and cattle prices there tend to be about 20–25% higher than in the lower Jubba. Herti merchants are strongly involved in this trade and usually have partners in Mogadishu on whom they rely. The Mogadishu market is the final destination for approximately 16% of cattle sold in the region.

The third and fourth market channels in the lower Jubba involve international export trade. In the case of the Kenya market, animals are sold and moved unofficially across the border to Kenyan markets, particularly to Garissa. This trade accounts for about 25% of cattle sales. Because the trade is controversial and not officially sanctioned, its importance has probably been understated by traders. Ogadeen middlemen and traders are heavily involved, and those Herti who participate usually have forged some type of alliance with an Ogadeen middleman.

This trade is seasonal: during the dry season (January–March), virtually no cattle move from the lower Jubba to northeastern Kenya. This is the trade that has captured the bulk of cattle exports since the ban on Saudi Arabian imports. The Kenyan trade involves medium- to high-quality male and female animals, which are used for fattening and eventual slaughter in urban centers and for restocking and breeding purposes on commercial ranches in the Rift Valley. The sale of Somali cattle to European-owned ranches in central Kenya began early in this century and frequently took place illegally even during periods of market quarantine. At least part of the reason for the recent Kenyan market boom was the 1984 drought, which devastated approximately 50% of Kenya's national cattle herd. The result was a surge in demand for cattle in Kenya, and the country's herders have been rebuilding their herds through unofficial imports from Tanzania, Ethiopia and Somalia.[40]

The fourth market, the overseas export trade, is very different from the other three channels, and it is the only livestock business in which the largest merchants and companies are involved. In 1988, it accounted for fewer than 8% of the cattle sold, but because it involved high-quality animals, this trade was responsible for about 15% of the aggregate value of marketed cattle. The

---

[40] Cassam (1987).

overseas export trade entails the grafting of a modern contractual system of marketing onto a customary pattern of trade. The export traders who are typically registered members of a company (see below) have contracts with a private importer, usually from a Middle Eastern country, to supply a specified number of high-quality animals at an agreed price. The contract indicates the party responsible for shipping costs and the vaccination and quarantine requirements. When the Somali trader has written proof of an order, he can request a letter of credit from the state-owned Somali Commercial and Savings Bank and receive half of its value in local currency.

Until the mid-1980s the state's role in this trade was minimal, except for providing financial, shipping and veterinary services. Since then, however, the government has assumed a more active posture. It has implemented legislation requiring individual exporters to cooperate and form companies and has negotiated government-to-government contracts on behalf of the commercial sector. Sales of cattle to Egypt, which were very important for Kismayo during 1985 to 1988, resulted from a negotiated contract between the governments of Somalia and Egypt which the private sector has implemented. The Somali government took these actions because Somalia was losing market share in its traditional export markets (especially in the Middle East), and competition by export traders for cattle in Somalia was boosting local prices too high, thus allegedly reducing traders' profits and competitiveness at the international level.[41]

The formation of companies was a way to reduce competition by limiting the local arena to a smaller number of actors—in this case, companies. However, competition has not been reduced since most of the companies are dominated by two or three large traders who operate essentially as individual merchants rather than as members of a collective. They procure their own contracts and register them in the name of the company, but keep the proceeds from sales for themselves. After the export crisis of the 1980s, cooperation among export traders declined even further, as larger merchants sought to attain a bigger slice of a diminishing trade by forcing out smaller competitors and consolidating their own market advantage.

Some of the individual contracts in the 1970s were for as many as 10,000 cattle over a period of 18–24 months. One of the largest traders in Kismayo town exported 47,000 cattle and 18,000 camels to Saudi Arabia between 1971

---

[41] Samatar (1987).

and 1983. Other traders had contracts in excess of 2,000 cattle that had to be met within five or six months. Because formal credit is usually only extended for a period of two to three months, the exporter must procure the animals within that brief period. When the Saudi trade was in place, many Somali exporters received private financing from their Saudi Arabian contacts. Without it, they must depend on local informal credit or government sources and they count on herders accepting payment only after the final sale is made which amounts to obtaining a form of credit from them.[42] The need to purchase large numbers of cattle in a relatively short period of time further distinguishes the overseas export trade from other markets.

The local system of procurement for overseas trade is essentially the same as that used for other markets with a few important distinctions. First, overseas traders usually do not purchase animals at local market centers but rely instead on their own chain of middlemen and agents for supplies. Second, export traders often employ some full- or nearly full-time people whose function it is to procure animals. Third, in contrast to other markets, the overseas commerce is restricted to young male cattle aged four to seven years. Female cattle may not be exported, and only the largest males, those that exceed 275–300 kg. live weight, are purchased. Finally, because of the sheer size of their orders, exporters are forced to procure animals throughout the year and to employ hired herders to manage the animals. Exporters usually keep only their head herders employed throughout the year. Other herders are hired as needed. To manage a herd of 100 cattle, one head herder and three temporary employees are required.

The benefits and costs of these different market channels vary considerably. While there are increased risks with the overseas trade, the largest net returns for traders take place in the overseas export trade, followed closely by the Kenya trade (see Table 9.3). Time-series data are not available on trader profitability in the overseas trade, but profits are likely to have declined since the imposition of the Saudi ban. While the FOB price of US$950 per live weight ton for cattle changed very little between 1984 and 1988, costs for veterinary and other inputs for traders increased considerably during this period. That cattle exporters still received a relatively favorable return in 1988 strongly implies that profits were likely to have been very high before 1983.

---

[42] See Samatar et al. (1988).

TABLE 9.3: **Cattle Trader Margins and Net Returns** (Somali Shillings per Head of Cattle)

	Overseas Trade	Kenya Trade	Mogadishu Trade	Kismayo Town Trade
Traders				
Final Price	38000	30000	17500	10592
Purchase Price	(23000)	(21000)	(13029)	(8820)
Trader Margin	15000	9000	4471	1772
Trader Costs	(8135)	(3758)	(2298)	(905)
Net Return	6865	5242	2173	867
As Percent of Final Price	18.07	17.47	12.42	8.19
Middlemen[a]				
Selling Price	23000	21000	13029	data
Purchase Price	(19000)	(16000)	(10620)	not
Middleman Margin	4000	5000	2409	available
Middleman Costs	(2225)	(1985)	(1324)	
Net Return	1775	3015	1085	
As Percent of Selling Price	7.72	14.36	8.33	

[a] This reflects a case where the middleman buys directly from a herder and then sells to a larger trader. In many cases, however, the middleman may be buying from smaller middlemen ("bush traders") who in turn purchased the animal from the producer. The table has been greatly simplified and does not take into account the full range of market transactions that occur.

Average exchange rate during 1987 to 1988 (until February 1988) is calculated at 130 SSh=US $1.00.

SOURCES: Author's data, and Stockton (1987) for overseas trade.

The lowest profits among traders are found in the regional/Kismayo town trade, which is based predominantly on sales of low-value animals. Since the costs of engaging in this trade are considerably below those of other markets, it is open to most small-scale traders. To a lesser extent, the same can be said for the Kenya and Mogadishu markets (see Table 9.4). Not surprisingly, the highest trader costs are associated with the overseas export commerce, where in 1988 the operation costs per animal were 31,135 Somali shillings (including the purchase and other costs). The scale of investment per head of cattle, even though the exporter often has credit, precludes most traders other than the wealthiest from participating at the upper levels of this market. In comparison to other trade channels, the overseas trade in cattle is particularly distinctive in its volume and types of transaction costs.

The net returns of middlemen, on the other hand, vary according to the different markets, but they tend to be highest for the Kenya trade. Middlemen acting between a Kenya-based trader and the producer can earn net returns equivalent to 10% of the sale price in Kenya, or about 3,015 Somali shillings per animal. By 1988, the net returns per head of cattle for agents involved in the overseas trade were about 40% below those of middlemen in the Kenya trade, and were equivalent to about 4.5% of the FOB price at Kismayo. Because the Kenya trade is so lucrative for local middlemen and traders, they are directing most of their efforts to it rather than to other markets. This pattern, coupled with the general decline in overseas markets, has made the official export trade from Kismayo increasingly problematic.

Trade in other animal species—such as camels, goats, and sheep—reveals neither the complexity nor the volume that cattle marketing does. The marketed volume of cattle exceeds regional sales of small stock and camels by factors of three and fifteen, respectively.[43] An examination of the figures in Table 9.1 shows why this might be so: average cattle herds in the region are considerably higher, especially in Afmadow District, than those of other livestock types. Despite this discrepancy, some camels and small stock are exported from Kismayo to the Middle East, though it is likely that many of the camels for export originate from the Middle and Upper Jubba, not the Lower Jubba. Neither animal type is exported from the region to Kenya. Camel markets are poorly developed in Kenya and relative demand for the animal there is low. Exports of sheep and goats to Kenya are inhibited by the adequate supplies of the animals in the country. Regional trade in small stock is almost strictly oriented to local markets, especially those in the larger towns. With the collapse of the overseas cattle trade, merchants who were involved at least partially in the trade of small stock or camels were better prepared to confront the market crisis of the 1980s.

Traders

Several types of actors are involved in livestock trade, distinguishable by market, scale and location in the market chain. Local terms are used to define some of the roles in the different markets, but many of these terms have been redefined as market conditions have changed. Cattle merchants, in particular, can be classified into five general types although distinctions among certain types may be blurred at times.

Recognizing social and economic differences among traders is important

---

[43] Little (1989).

TABLE 9.4: **Estimated Costs Incurred by Cattle Traders** (Somali Shillings per Head of Cattle)

Expenditure Item	Overseas Trade	Kenya Trade	Mogadishu Trade	Kismayo Town Trade
Traders[a]				
Water	180	90	45	90
Local Transport	200	300	663	
Vet Costs	100	34	30	60
Hired Labor	450	271	35	200
Fodder	150	200	100	25
Feed-Related Costs	1000			
Risk/Loss	690	1050	261	265
Broker Fee	140	525	326	265
Tax/Fees	591		438	
Credit	445	600	300	
Insurance	534			
Ship Agency	630			
Port Charge	10			
Kenya Tax		688		
Market Broker Fee	575			
Association Fee	100			
Quarantine/Holding	840			
Fee	500			
Communications	1000			
Trucking Costs	23000	21000	13029	8820
Purchase Price	31135	24758	15327	9725
Total Trader Costs				
Middlemen[a]				
Water	90	90	90	
Fodder	50	25	25	data
Tax	575	525	266	not
Risk/Loss	570	480	212	available
Broker Fee	475	400	266	
Vet Costs	60	60	60	
Hired Labor	405	405	405	
Purchase Price	19000	16000	10620	
Total Middlemen Costs	21225	17985	11944	

[a] These categories do not reflect the full range of traders and middlemen involved in cattle trade (see discussion of traders later in the article). The costs included here are based on estimates from a sample of 27 traders and are only illustrative. Average exchange rate during 1987 to 1988 (until February 1988) is calculated at 130 SSh=US$1.00.

SOURCES: Author's data, and Stockton (1987) for overseas trade.

for understanding the Somali livestock marketing system. At one end of the scale are the largest traders, those involved in overseas commerce who usually have offices in Mogadishu or another large town. Their operations involve substantial expenditures of capital on veterinary services, office and communications equipment, and in some cases, trucks. At the other end of the spectrum are bush traders, who may account for no more than twenty cattle sales annually. These are usually indistinguishable from the herders. Certain traders, especially in the major market centers, serve only as brokers (called *dilaal*), while some act both as *dilaal* and trader. Brokers match buyers with sellers and charge a percentage of the sale price or a fee per animal for their service. As with most commodity market systems, the level of competition among traders diminishes as one moves further up in the market chain. Market concentration at the highest levels of the system seems to have increased with the steep decline in the volume of overseas exports. In the case of Kismayo, three large traders accounted for more than 70% of overseas cattle exports in 1987.

Approximately half of the traders interviewed specialized in buying and selling only one animal type, usually cattle. From their discussions, it appears that this sort of specialization has increased in the past 20 years. Among the twenty-seven traders in the sample, 30% traded both cattle and camels, 39% traded only cattle, 13% traded only camels, and 17% traded in all animal species. More than 30% of livestock traders owned water points (usually surface ponds) in the pastoral areas, and sometimes they provided water to herders in exchange for the right to purchase cattle at a price below market level.

Part-time Bush Traders

The smallest traders or 'bush traders' are the most numerous and usually are involved in the regional domestic or Kenyan trade rather than in the overseas trade. They are distinguished from other local traders and middlemen by their small scale—frequently they buy only twenty to twenty-five cattle a year—and their lack of full or nearly full-time commitment to trade. Many of these traders started in the livestock business by first accumulating some capital through trading in goats and then moving into the cattle trade. This category of trader operates in the more remote areas of the region, buying animals to sell to larger traders and middlemen such as those represented in Tables 9.3 and 9.4. They frequently buy from small- and medium-scale herders rather than larger ones and they pursue a pastoral lifestyle that is indistinguishable from local herders. Many of these traders are young (under thirty-five years) and they use profits earned from livestock trade to build up their own herds and marry. Their position in regional livestock trade has improved as the Kenyan market has grown. They reside in the interior of the Lower Jubba Region at some distance from the large towns but often close to the Kenya border.

Jeeble Traders

The term *jeeble* can only roughly be equated with the concept of a middle-man.[44] The scale of *jeeble* enterprises varies considerably. Approximately 70% of middlemen sold animals to exporters during 1986 to 1988, but fewer than 20% did so on a regular basis. Middlemen frequently cooperate with two or three other *jeeble*, pooling resources and assisting each other with purchases. Seventy-one percent of middlemen have trading ties with other middlemen, usually of the same clan. Some of these relationships endure for years. The larger middlemen buy from smaller middlemen and then sell directly to export traders. These larger middlemen are likely to be involved in at least one of the export trade channels. Among the larger middlemen, who handle more than 250 cattle per year, 83% are associated with the overseas trade, the unofficial trade with Kenya or both.

It has been noted in the literature that the role of *jeeble* has changed in response to the internationalization of the Somali livestock trade. In discussing the livestock trade in northern Somalia, where it is considerably more developed than in the south, Samatar and his co-authors suggest that middlemen became more important as the overseas export trade grew and exporters increasingly relied on them to procure animals in a timely fashion, especially during the pilgrimage season when demand in the Middle East is at its maximum. In northern Somalia by the 1970s, the system of depending on brokers (*dilaal*) to procure animals "was incapable of collecting livestock from thousands of pastoralists in time for delivery during the Haj [pilgrimage] season." *Jeeble* were needed to augment the supplies that export traders could obtain from their own agents and brokers.[45] In southern Somalia the situation seems to have had a similar development, although *jeeble* clearly were prominent in the Kenyan trade before the growth in overseas exports. In the Kismayo region the roles of both *jeeble* and broker (*dilaal*) assumed more importance

---

[44] By definition, a middleman in the cattle trade is not involved in final transactions, but rather is a person who buys and then sells to agents of large traders or to the large traders themselves. *Jeeble* however refers to any type of petty trader, whether a middleman or not, and thus, it represents the most ambiguous category of traders. In the cattle trade of the lower Jubba, the term is used for most traders except for brokers and export traders. In the export trade, a *jeeble* is clearly a middleman, operating between the producer and the export trader, but in other market channels a *jeeble* may be involved in final transactions. In the overseas trade, some *jeeble* have begun to provide brokerage services to exporters, rather than actually buying and selling export-quality animals. For the purposes of this analysis, the terms *jeeble* and middleman will be used interchangeably.

[45] Samatar, Salisbury and Bascom (1988).

with the expansion of the overseas export trade. Yet, the supply of livestock to Saudi Arabia during the period of pilgrimage never assumed the importance in the south that it did in the north.

Market Brokers (dilaal)

Cattle brokers are found in each of the major market towns, and in the large towns they are often required to be registered with the local government. They provide a market service to buyers by directing them to potential sellers and negotiating a price. At the smaller markets, it is the broker that guarantees to the buyer that the animal is not stolen and thus will not be reclaimed at a later date.[46] In the past, the broker was usually from the local area and knew the herders and townsmen well, but this has not always been the case since the growth in the overseas trade.

What is the difference between a *jeeble* and a *dilaal*? Some *jeeble* also serve as *dilaal*, but this was recorded in only 15% of cases. The major difference between the two is that unlike the *jeeble*, the broker does not actually buy or sell the animal; rather, brokers match buyers with potential sellers. Usual fees are 2.5% of the value of the animal, or a per animal fee of around $2.00 to $3.00. Although the broker merely performs a minimal service— pointing out a potential seller to a buyer, for instance—traders in towns almost always use a broker for procuring cattle since that is a way of sanctioning the sale and provides a measure of insurance that the animal is not stolen. The number of brokers in a market varies according to its size. The largest numbers are active in Kismayo and Afmadow towns (in excess of fifteen in each).

Over the years, individual traders have built up strong associations with certain brokers, using particular *dilaal* for procuring animals. Export traders especially rely on brokers, and some brokers work for only one large trader. By the late 1970s certain brokers and middlemen had begun to specialize in procuring cattle for only one or two export traders. The growth in the export trade resulted in some middlemen turning to brokerage activities full-time where they served as agents in the export trade. In providing brokerage services, middlemen do not have to spend large amounts of money to procure cattle themselves. Since purchase prices of export-quality cattle (US $150 to

---

[46] Brokers are frequently found in livestock markets in Africa: see Dupire (1962); Cohen (1969); Manger (1984).

$200 each) are often 200% or more above prices of other bovines, outlays for cattle would be substantial.

Agents of Large Traders

Agents of large traders are middlemen and brokers who have attached themselves to a large export trader (or traders). The agent position is a direct result of the growth in the overseas export trade, and reflects the movement of certain *jeeble* into procurement for export traders on a full-time basis. During the Saudi boom period, agents profited more than other local traders.

Since it is less costly for export traders to deal with *jeeble* than with brokers, *jeeble* more often serve as agents. They remain middlemen despite the fact that many would prefer to be paid a brokerage fee rather than to buy and sell animals. It is in the interest of the export trader, however, to force the *jeeble* to be responsible for purchasing the cattle. Under the brokerage system, the export trader has to pay a fee and account for the actual purchase. In dealing with a middleman, he avoids responsibility for lower-level transactions. It is the *jeeble*, then, who has to make arrangements for buying from smaller traders or directly from herders. In most cases the seller is paid at least half the price at the time of sale, and the remainder when the animal is exported. It is only after the exporter receives his money that the *jeeble* is paid in full and he in turn can pay off the herder. Even in cases where the full price of the animal has been paid to the herder, the middleman may be paid only 30–40% of the price until the animal is exported. Because these outlays are costly, only the larger *jeeble* can afford to deal with overseas exporters, and even these try to pass on the costs to herders by delaying their payments. After transaction costs are calculated, in 1988 middlemen earned a return of about 8% in the overseas export trade as opposed to approximately 14% in the Kenyan trade (see Table 9.3).

Another reason why export traders prefer to deal with *jeeble* rather than with brokers is because they can shift responsibility for the management of the animals to the *jeeble*. Because profits have been increasingly squeezed in the overseas export trade, export traders have delayed purchases from middlemen so as to force them to incur more of the production costs. Once the animal is purchased, labor, water, veterinary and other production costs must be met. If the date for export is delayed or postponed, as was common in the late 1980s, the costs of maintaining large, high-quality cattle can bite deeply into a trader's profits. Not surprisingly, many *jeeble* have resisted these tactics by entering into the less restrictive trade to Kenya where possible.

Most of the middlemen who moved toward the status of full-time agents for the export trade were from the major towns of Kismayo and Badhaade Districts, rather than from the smaller towns of Afmadow District. While there are important exceptions, many of those who are tied into the overseas export trade are Herti. Agents are frequently from the same clan as the exporters, or from a related clan. Yet, clan relationships do not eliminate the possibility of domination and exploitation by export traders. The manipulation of clan ideologies by larger traders disguises to some extent what are markedly class-based relations. In an activity as risky as livestock trade, it should not be surprising that family- and clan-based ties permeate many aspects of the business. This is a pattern in trading enterprises that is not unique to Somali, Africa or even to the developing countries.[47]

Another reason for Herti involvement in the overseas trade is that they live in or near the port of Kismayo and historically have been closely associated with the town's commerce. On the other hand, the Maxamed Zubeer and other Ogadeen sub-clans do not usually reside in Kismayo town or its immediate environs, and thus, they are less likely to be involved in the overseas export trade.

Export Traders

In the 1970s, several large-scale traders and trading companies from outside the area opened branches in Kismayo to take advantage of increased cattle exports. Most of them operated a diversified trade, using all three of Somalia's major ports (Berbera, Mogadishu, and Kismayo) for animal exports. Capital requirements for the trade were such that very few locally based traders became exporters (see Table 9.4).

The overseas export traders operate procurement systems based on their own networks of agents. On average, export traders employ three to four agents full-time or nearly full-time throughout the year, as well as several middlemen on a part-time basis. Those exporters who do reside in the area live in Kismayo town, the only regional center that provides some of the banking and communications facilities required for the export trade. They do not maintain strong links to the nomadic sector or to smaller traders, but work instead through a small number of large brokers and middlemen. When interviewed in Mogadishu, many export traders had little familiarity with

---

[47] See Clark (1988).

the actual day-to-day operations of their enterprises. Specific information about numbers and names of local traders with whom they worked had to be obtained from their employees in Kismayo.

The overseas export trader buys cattle throughout the year, but restricts his purchases of large numbers until he has a contract from an importer specifying price, volume and date of export. He relies on middlemen to incur at least a portion of the costs of managing the herd. Since letters of credit from the Somali Commercial Bank are granted for only two to three months, the export trader cannot pursue much speculative buying prior to export. However, once the merchant receives information on a definite export date and number of cattle, large-scale buying begins.

Despite the recent slack in external markets, traders often cannot meet their contract terms because time constraints are too restrictive and cattle may have migrated away from the main purchase areas or, as in 1987, may be in very poor condition. Even reliance on local brokers and middlemen has not always allowed exporters to meet the conditions of contracts. For example, when representatives of an Egyptian import company came to Kismayo in May 1987 to check on the progress of their agreement with a Somali exporter, they found that their allotment of cattle had not been procured. The date of export had to be postponed for several months. At least part of the 1987 decline in cattle exports can be traced to difficulties in procuring cattle, especially since some *jeeble* have reoriented their trade to Kenyan markets. The time limitations on letters of credit make it difficult, costly and risky to procure large numbers of export-quality animals several months prior to export.[48] In recent years traders have depended on buying cattle from outside the region (for example, in the Lower Shebelle) to meet quota levels.

Unlike the overseas exporters, traders who deal with the Kenya market are from the smaller towns such as Libooye and Afmadow. The logistical requirements for this trade are minimal, differing very little from those needed to sell animals to Mogadishu or any other domestic market. Thus, a merchant of this type is not likely to differ from local traders in the region and usually will orient a portion of his business toward regional and national domestic markets as well. The overseas export trader, on the other hand,

---

[48] When the Saudi Arabian ban was imposed, one exporter had more than 7500 cattle in the lower Jubba awaiting export. The trader claims to have lost almost 5000 of these during the severe dry season of 1984.

differs considerably from these traders in terms of both scale of enterprise and degree of market specialization.

Social Relations of the Cattle Trade

Credit in a variety of forms permeates all levels of cattle markets in the region. Ironically, it is producers and middlemen of more modest means who provide credit to wealthier traders in the overseas export trade, a phenomenon that also occurs in northern Somalia.[49] Because they do not receive full payment until after their animals are exported, local middlemen and herders are providing credit to the export trader. Whereas in other livestock markets, traders often provide some form of credit to herders. Moreover, in these latter markets herders are usually paid in full at the time of sale, which is why many pastoralists prefer to trade with Kenya rather than overseas. *Jeeble* who own retail stores may advance maize flour, sugar and other necessities to herders. The same is true for traders who own water points and provide this resource to herders before sales are consummated. Credit is also provided by Kenyan traders who regularly buy cattle in the lower Jubba. These loans to local middlemen may not involve a direct interest charge, but they usually obligate the borrower to sell cattle to the trader at a price equal to or below market levels.

A large *jeeble* may have dozens of credit relationships outstanding at any given time, supported by few or no formal credit instruments. The practice has been referred to as a 'trust-based credit system'.[50] In the lower Jubba region, it may equal the amount of credit provided through the formal credit system (that is, the government bank). In the absence of formal contracts in the 'trust-based system', the credit relationship is often reinforced by clan or kinship ties. The informal system works because relationships are not based on financial exchange alone. Even where clan is not a binding mechanism, local traders invest in activities that are not strictly commercial yet that reinforce market alliances. These can be as small a gesture as when a trader donates a few cattle to help a herder's son to marry or pays the Koranic school fees of a local community member.

The overseas export trader taps into these relations by working through a small number of local brokers and middlemen who have strong ties to the community. Because most of the export traders are non-Ogadeen and their

---

[49] Samatar, Salisbury and Bascom (1988).
[50] Ibid.

business is focused on the Kismayo port, they recruit agents from among the local population. It is then up to local agents to invest in the relationships they need to ensure a regular supply of cattle.

Dealing with a Market Crisis

The disintegration of the overseas trade and the subsequent collapse of the Somali economy left exposed the export traders and those local merchants and middlemen who had become agents in the overseas trade. Although exporters lost a substantial source of revenue, they were able to shift their emphasis from Kismayo to begin exporting from Berbera and Mogadishu and to focus on small stock and camels, rather than cattle. A number of export traders had already diversified into urban real estate and other business, using revenues derived from animal exports; these were additional buffers against the effects of the decline in cattle exports.

This is not to imply that export merchants did not incur considerable losses because of the closure of the Saudi market. Nonetheless, it was the local traders and brokers who had invested most of their efforts and social capital into maintaining market channels for the export trade who suffered most. Because their alliances, including those with herders,[51] were geared to the overseas trade (and to a lesser extent the Mogadishu trade), many of these local merchants and middlemen have not benefited from the unofficial trade to Kenya. In fact, they have been hurt by it because it has made it more difficult for them to procure animals. Nor do they have supplementary investments on which to rely. Two examples of local traders demonstrate the injurious effects of recent changes (Box 9.1).

Neither trader A nor B, both of whom are Herti, has been able to capitalize on the booming unofficial trade to Kenya. They do not have the ties— either with middlemen in Kenya and Somalia, or with Ogadeen herders —that would enable them to take advantage of opportunities in the Kenyan trade. Moreover, they are older traders, unlikely to want to endure the rigors of the Kenyan trade, which frequently requires moving animals long distances over poorly watered areas of the lower Jubba and northern Kenya.

In contrast to these traders, the changes in the cattle trade have placed many small-scale bush traders and Afmadow *jeeble* in favorable positions.

---

[51] Large herd owners in particular benefit from the overseas trade because they are the ones most likely to own export-quality steers.

Box 9.1: MISSED OPPORTUNITIES

Trader A, approximately 55 years old, is among the largest middlemen in Kismayo District involved in the cattle export trade. He is an agent for a single export company which is owned by town-based relatives, and supplies cattle directly to it. He started to participate in the export trade in 1967, but did not specialize in it until the mid-1970s. Merchant A has business relationships with six small middlemen in Kismayo and Badhaade Districts who purchase animals for him. These trade relations endured throughout most of the 1970s and early 1980s. He often advanced them money and could delay full payment to them until after the animals had been exported. With the collapse in cattle exports at the end of 1983, he continued to export a small number of camels but this was a limited business. During 1986 to 1988 he neither bought nor sold cattle and has traded less than 10 camels per year on average. Thus, his revenue from the animal trade dropped considerably since the mid-1980s, and he now spends most of his time managing his small retail store rather than trading livestock.

Trader B, who is 50 years old, has concentrated his efforts on the overseas trade during the past 15 years, while maintaining some trade in the relatively small domestic market in Kismayo town. He serves as an agent for five export traders (three of them based in the Mogadishu area) rather than only one, as was the case for trader A. When the export trade was good, he worked with four small middlemen in Kismayo district who supplied him with cattle. His revenue has been hurt by the loss of overseas markets, but not to the extent that trader A's has. From 1986 to 1988 he bought and sold only 40 cattle, but traded more than 300 goats to supply domestic markets in the Kismayo region. Unlike trader A, he has maintained ties with middlemen and herders oriented toward the Kismayo domestic market and thus has been able to avoid the full effects of the loss of the overseas trade.

The changes have also helped those Kismayo-based traders who had maintained strong ties to various markets and to Afmadow herders. Most Afmadow middlemen participated in the Kenya and Somalia domestic trade, even if at times they were selling to the agents of overseas exporters. Very few concentrated entirely on supplying animals for the overseas export trade. In contrast to Kismayo District, where 75% of *jeeble* sell to overseas exporters or to their agents, only 40% of Afmadow traders have market links, mainly of an intermittent nature, to the overseas trade. Whereas the overseas export trade is essentially urban-based, the Kenya trade is rural-based and focused on small towns that became thriving centers of unofficial commerce in the late 1980s.[52]

An interesting aspect of the recent growth in the Kenyan trade is that younger traders at lower levels of the market chain are benefiting from it. Young traders rarely can procure the high-quality cattle required for the overseas trade, but they do have good access to other types of bovines that are in demand in Kenya along with costlier animals. In the overseas export trade they were geographically and economically disadvantaged (that is, distant from Kismayo port and small-scale with poor linkages to exporters). Thus, even when they did supply animals for overseas export, they received a low percentage of the FOB price.

Another outstanding feature of the changes in export markets has been the new prominence of small and medium-sized *jeeble* based in the small towns along the Kenya border. Participating in the overseas export trade only as distant suppliers, these *jeeble* have nonetheless been in a favorable position to capitalize on the Kenya trade because many of their market alliances (often based on clan) were already oriented in this direction. Currently, cattle markets at small border towns like Libooye (population of c. 2500) are more active and experience higher prices than those in the region's largest town Kismayo (population c. 70,000). In 1987 and 1988 even overseas exporters were forced to concentrate on buying cattle along the Kenya border where markets were more active than elsewhere in the region. Buying at these distant markets cut into their profits because they were compelled to compete with Kenya traders who paid relatively good prices and to pay them the high transport costs from these areas to Kismayo port.

Profiles of two traders who have benefited from the Kenyan trade provide an informative contrast to traders A and B (Box 9.2). Both traders C and D have benefited from the overseas export crisis in the area, although D will be vulnerable to future market swings unless he seeks market diversification. So far, Kenyan officials have not discouraged unofficial imports of cattle from Somalia but this could change at any time, especially if any serious disease breaks out in southern Somalia. The middlemen currently involved with the Kenyan trade are profiting more than most other traders. In 1988 *jeeble* of

---

[52] See Little (1992).

Box 9.2: CAPITALIZING ON CRISIS

Trader C is 40 years old and his trading activities are based in Afmadow town. This individual sells animals for the domestic markets of Kismayo and Mogadishu and for the Garissa market in Kenya. He has never bought animals for the overseas export trade. He works with three other middlemen based in the Afmadow area and with traders based in Kenya and Mogadishu. He has been active in livestock trade since 1977, focusing first on camels that he brought in from Kenya. However, he is no longer involved with camel trade.

When the cattle trade shifted from the overseas to the Kenyan market, he was ideally located. Trader C's sales to Kenya have grown steadily since 1985, making him one of the largest middlemen in Afmadow. In 1987 he bought and sold 400 cattle, mainly to supply the Kenyan market. He and his associates frequently buy directly from nomads along the Kenya border and sell to traders on the Kenya side. Much of his profit comes from lucrative foreign exchange transactions stemming from the Kenya trade. When he receives Kenya shillings, he often sells them to wholesale and retail merchants who use the currency to import goods from Kenya. Taking advantage of the rapid devaluation of the Somali shilling, in early 1988 trader C earned as much as a 33% return by holding Kenya shillings for six months before selling them. (In 1989 a trader could earn even higher returns from this strategy because the decline in the value of the Somali shilling during this period was even greater.)

Trader D is a small bush trader who works in the Afmadow area. He is 26 years old and has only been engaged in cattle trade since 1985. He began trading because of the growth in exports to Kenya, and by 1987 was supplying annually more than 170 cattle to markets in Garissa and Garsen, in Kenya. He deals only with the Kenya trade, but has an association with one other middleman. In contrast to trader C, trader D transports the animals himself from Afmadow to the Kenya markets, and sells them without using a middleman in Kenya. Trader D is a good example of a bush trader who has become a nearly full-time *jeeble* because of the growth in the Kenyan trade.

Afmadow District who sold to Kenya as their prime market had average annual sales of 278 cattle. In contrast, those few who were still selling to overseas export traders had average annual sales of around 160 cattle in 1988 (this figure was probably substantially reduced in 1989 and 1990).

Because the Kenya market is more diverse than the overseas market with regard to animal type (that is, it buys more than just four to seven year old steers), smaller traders and herders can participate. Traders who are either Ogadeen themselves or who have maintained strong ties to the Ogadeen herders and middlemen in Afmadow District—including alliances based on marriage—have been able to capitalize on the Kenya trade.

CONCLUSIONS

The materials on Somalia presented here demonstrate the difficulties in generalizing about the effects on traders of a market crisis. By distinguishing among four different markets and five types of market actors, the analysis has attempted to unravel the complexities of livestock trade in southern Somalia and to differentiate the categories of traders that have benefited from those that have been hurt by recent changes. Those who have benefited are the small (bush) and medium-sized middlemen of Afmadow District who have capitalized on the growth in informal exports to Kenya.

On the other hand, the large *jeeble* of Kismayo District who lost their traditional overseas markets have suffered. These traders who became agents in the export trade have been squeezed from both the upper and lower ends of the market. As profits in the cattle export trade have declined, large exporters have moved the burden of transaction and production costs increasingly onto their agents, and have delayed payments to them as well in order to protect their own margins. The agents who have been involved in the overseas export trade cannot easily enter the informal trade to Kenya because Afmadow and Kenyan middlemen dominate this trade. Instead, they have been forced to accept more and more unfavorable terms from the overseas export traders or to withdraw to other activities (the case of Trader A).

At the lower end of the market chain, Kismayo agents have been squeezed by smaller traders who have made it difficult for them to procure cattle at reasonable prices. The smaller middlemen have been scrambling to take advantage of market opportunities in Kenya, and to a lesser extent Mogadishu, while they diversify away from the overseas trade. These *jeeble* are in a favorable position because they have more options and can demand higher prices from the agents. In contrast to the export-oriented traders of Kismayo, they do not compete with the larger middlemen in the Kenyan trade, and thus, can enter it as suppliers to the latter. Because it is the agent of the exporter, rather than the export trader himself, who usually procures the cattle, agents have disproportionately absorbed the added costs of higher local prices which they have not been able to pass along to the export trader. Thus, while the agent is effectively controlled by the exporter, he has difficulty influencing the behavior of the small traders on whom he has depended.

Additional conclusions about market behavior in the face of change can be drawn from the Somalia materials. First, while livestock export markets in Kismayo existed in the past, the steep rise in exports in the 1960s and 1970s represented a departure from earlier patterns. The growth in cattle exports from the lower Jubba region set in motion the following changes: (1) the insertion of a class of large export traders of a scale not previously known in the region; (2) transformations in regional production practices, where wage labor for herding and the development of private water points grew in importance; and (3) the emergence of local agents who specialized in supplying cattle for the overseas trade. While precursors of these trends were found prior to the late 1960s,[53] they grew in magnitude during the 1970s and 1980s.

Second, the Somali materials point to the limitations of the current cattle marketing system in meeting the demands of international trade. Prior to the collapse of overseas markets, Somali exporters had difficulties in procuring local supplies of cattle in sufficient quality and volume and in a timely fashion.[54] In many cases, exporters and their agents remained dependent on the activities of other traders and herders who may be only loosely tied to the overseas export trade. Because the latter are not vertically linked to the exporters, either through contracts or other mechanisms, they can exercise their options to sell in other markets. The experience since 1985 has shown this to be true.

Third, traders in Somalia have always invoked social relations to gain access to markets, whether during periods of prosperity or decline. The volatility of the region during the past century has shown that investment in social relations, as well as in market diversification, is a prudent strategy. These activities are usually pursued through an idiom of clanship or clientelism, yet they can be as manipulative as they are beneficial for small traders. "Clanism" did not always deter exploitative behavior on the part of export traders, especially during the waning years of the overseas trade. The demands of the official export trade, however, were sufficiently different from

---

[53] And considerably earlier elsewhere in Somalia; see Samatar (1989).
[54] Samatar (1987) has found a similar pattern among sheep exporters in northern Somalia.

other trade patterns that the major actors could not easily pursue market diversification while at the same time participating in the overseas trade. At the upper end of the market exporters were separated from the pastoral community and their agents were left to maintain the supply channels that allowed them to meet their contractual obligations. Like export-oriented producers and traders elsewhere in Africa,[55] they were seriously disadvantaged when markets collapsed and the state began to disintegrate.

Finally, the Somali materials show that even under so-called crisis conditions, certain traders and producers do quite well. Although those involved in the overseas trade were hurt by economic and political changes in the late 1980s, emerging opportunities in the unofficial trade sector seem to be beneficial to local and regional economies.[56] The loss of the overseas export trade represented a collapse of the so-called formal economy. The informal economy, which is considerably more important to most Somalis including traders[57] survived up to around 1991. It is much harder to be optimistic about the informal sector or any economic activity whatsoever in the intensified chaos that has followed the fall of the Barre regime.

METHODOLOGICAL NOTE AND ACKNOWLEDGEMENTS

The analysis above is based on data collected in the Lower Jubba Region over a fifteen month period during 1987 and 1988. Information on marketing was gathered from seasonal surveys of eighty-eight herder households, structured interviews with a random sample of twenty-seven livestock traders in the region, weekly monitoring of livestock sales in four markets and secondary data.

The fieldwork for this chapter was completed prior to the massive political and civil unrest that has characterized Somalia since 1990. Immense political and economic problems loomed in 1987 and 1988, but they were minor compared to the upheavals of 1990 and 1991. The situation as of 1991 was still in considerable flux and subject to almost daily perturbation. Efforts were made to keep the paper as current as possible up to its original publication in 1992. Some reliable data are available for 1989, but for subsequent years the infor-

---

[55] See Bunker (1987) for a Ugandan case.
[56] Little (1988).
[57] Jamal (1988).

mation often is anecdotal and based on very little systematic data collection. However, in terms of the livestock trade—the topic of this chapter—much of the crisis in this sector had already set in by the late 1980s.

The research for the paper was carried out under the auspices of the Institute for Development Anthropology and Clark University Cooperative Agreement on Settlement and Natural Resource Systems Analysis. The author acknowledges the support of his colleagues on the larger rural-urban study: Abdulkhadir Khalif Abdulle, Hugh Evans, Michael Cullen, Avrom Bendavid-Val and Yusuf Said Hersi. He also acknowledges the support of the staff of the Livestock Marketing and Health Project in Mogadishu, who allowed him to have access to the market data that they had gathered in the lower Jubba. Dr. Alex Dickey of LMHP was particularly helpful in this respect. He also would like to thank Paul Baxter, Michael Horowitz, Murray Last, and Abdi Samatar for their helpful comments on earlier drafts of the manuscript. The above institutions and individuals, of course, are not responsible for the content of the paper.

X.

Reflections

Across much of sub-Saharan Africa, macroeconomic and agricultural sector policy reforms are now being implemented, with a view toward increasing production and investment incentives and improving the efficiency of factor and product markets. While the implementation of these policy reforms has been mixed within the region, it is evident that the expected surge in private sector activity has yet to materialize. The analysis and case studies in this book demonstrate that the private sector in agricultural trade has been inadequately understood, and that policies have frequently been adopted without strong empirical evidence on private sector processing and marketing institutions and experience.

During the 1970s and 1980s, academics and donors alike focused much of their analysis on the operations and deficiencies of parastatal marketing boards and directed little attention to the private sector. It was generally assumed that private entrepreneurs would respond quickly and efficiently to policy reforms. Competitive market structures would presumably replace single-channel, price-controlled systems. Even if privately organized markets would be marred by imperfections, it was assumed that such arrangements would still be more efficient than systems dominated by parastatals.

In most countries, the actual supply response by private agribusiness to market and other reforms has been slower and more narrowly based than expected.[1] Several reasons account for this. One widely-recognized reason is the incomplete nature of the policy reform process. In most African countries, official and unofficial restrictions on private investments and trade persist. In some countries, private firms expect (or have already experienced) slow implementation or reversal of policies. Some policy changes, including aspects of

---

[1] The primary exceptions are in cases where there has been long-standing parallel market private activity (for example in the trade of staple grains in parts of East and Southern Africa) or where special circumstances—such as the end of a war or the recovery from a major drought—provided unusually large opportunities for a quick supply response.

the privatization of public enterprises, have not been transparent, causing suspicion and uncertainty. Such conditions have deterred investors, especially in ventures which entail high fixed costs and do not offer the potential for quick returns.

A second reason is that some of the reforms which are implemented under structural adjustment programs—including the retrenchment of public employees, the reduction or elimination of food subsidies, and devaluation of the domestic currency—have brought about a short-term reduction in the effective purchasing power of large numbers of rural and urban people. This in turn has weakened the demand for a broad array of products, including several of the high-value foods covered in this study. Declining demand together with higher costs for intermediate inputs have tended to squeeze the operating margins of formal and informal sector firms. Such circumstances have weakened their interest and financial ability to invest in facilities or equipment to meet future market opportunities.

Our study reveals clearly a third reason for the limited private sector response. These policy reforms have done little or nothing to alleviate structural, supply-side weaknesses and the high risks and transaction costs which the private sector faces as a result of these structural inadequacies. Existing and potential private investors and traders continue to face an operating environment characterized by inadequate and poorly maintained transport, communications and other physical infrastructure, weak financial intermediation, and weak or politicized formal legal structures. In most African countries, the scope and effectiveness of (public and private) agricultural and business support services are also quite limited by international standards. Hence, the costs of gathering information, the risks of physical losses during product transformation and movement, and the difficulties in ensuring transactor compliance with business agreements continue to be higher in Africa than elsewhere. In some respects the budgetary and civil service cuts implemented under structural adjustment programs have exacerbated the long-standing deficiencies in the provision of public goods in Africa. Yet, it is exactly these public goods related to infrastructure, information, and law which are critical to the development of efficient markets and a vibrant private sector.

The case studies and other empirical evidence provided in this book point to great variability in the nature and performance of private sector trading and processing activity for high-value foods. The private sector in Africa exhibits such variation in terms of enterprise size, mode of operation, and technology as to raise questions about the analytical and practical usefulness of any broad concept of 'private sector development'. In some contexts, it is difficult to make distinctions between the private and public sectors—given the frequency of hybrid organizations combining public and private ownership and management, the ability of some larger private firms to determine the competitive rules by which they operate, and the frequent participation of public officials in private ventures.

The performance of private traders and processors is also quite varied, both among formal and informal enterprises. Firms have been identified which have been very successful in adopting/adapting new technologies, diversifying their product lines, and gaining entry into competitive international markets. Many small traders and artisanal processors were found to be very responsive to consumer taste preferences and be able to provide nutritious foods at affordable cost. Still, few informal enterprises are able to acquire resources sufficient for them to expand and upgrade their technologies, most medium-to-large-scale processors operate at well below their capacity, and relatively few indigenous entrepreneurs have been successful in developing internationally competitive trading or processing operations.

In the uncertain and weakly supported market environment faced throughout sub-Saharan Africa, it is not surprising that many of the more successful private ventures, both recent and long-standing, have been based on some form of extra-market institutional arrangement. The most common forms have been kinship links, intra-family transactions, long-term (trading and/or management) contractual ties, horizontal conglomerate structures, and vertical integration of production and downstream activities. Such continuous and often complex institutional arrangements have enabled firms and entrepreneurs to compensate for deficiencies in the enabling environment by internalizing flows of information, finance, and physical commodities, and thereby lowering certain risks and economizing on transaction costs.

This recourse to extra-market relationships is observed in many domestic market contexts, where trade and finance are commonly linked. Such relationships have been even more important in cross-border and other international trade where domestic policy and other problems are exacerbated by greater physical (and cultural) distance, weak legal integration, and the complexities of foreign currency transactions. Most of Africa's intra-regional trade in live animals, whether from the Sahel to the West African coast or between the countries of northeast Africa, is governed by longstanding trading networks whose participants are associated by kin or area of origin. The bulk of Africa's exports of processed fish and horticultural products is governed by joint ventures, management/marketing contracts, exclusive distribution arrangements, or other forms of long-term collaboration between African and foreign companies or among affiliates of the latter.

Most small-scale trading and processing of high-value foods in Africa is undertaken by indigenous entrepreneurs and firms, with women entrepreneurs frequently playing a central role. In larger-scale processing and in long-distance domestic and international trade, certain ethnic minorities and foreign-owned or managed companies typically play a prominent, if not dominant role. Social, political and historical factors have contributed to these patterns. The framework of institutional economics provided here also offers useful insights into the observed patterns of specialization and the relative success of certain groups or types of enterprises.

Otherwise quite distinct groups such as the Bamileke in Cameroon, the Chagga in Tanzania, the Lebanese in parts of West Africa, and various 'Asian' groups in East Africa, share a number of common features which have contributed to their relative commercial success. Those highlighted in this study include their development of informal information-sharing mechanisms, mutual trust (and credit), association or longstanding experience with particular commodities, and strong international contacts. International trading and agribusiness companies generally have access to cheaper finance and a broader array of information sources than do African-based firms and entrepreneurs, and typically have more experience than the latter in the physical logistics and official formalities of conducting international trade. While structural adjustment programs have increased the incentives to export, they have done little (or nothing) to equip African entrepreneurs to meet international product and service standards and to compete against more experienced firms.

This study has emphasized that the potential advantages of developing complex forms of contracting, organization, and collective action depend at least in part on the inherent techno-economic characteristics of commodities and those of their production, processing, and trade. Though differing in degree, most of the high-value foods studied here are highly perishable in their raw form and exhibit considerable variability in their quality. These characteristics generate procurement and market risks, put pressures on logistical and quality control systems, and inhibit many forms of bulk marketing.

However, for most of these HVFs initial post-harvest activities do not require sophisticated skills or investments in specialized and expensive capital equipment. For most HVFs, there exists an array of processing technologies, with some relatively small-scale technologies yielding products of acceptable or even very high quality. Many HVFs are marketed and consumed in different forms (e.g. fresh, dried, frozen, canned, etc.) Hence, in a favorable economic environment, there may be considerable opportunities for small companies, farmer groups and similar enterprises to engage in the processing and domestic trade of HVF products. More advanced forms of HVF processing (e.g. fish canning; vegetable dehydration, pasteurization or dehydration of milk) and the export marketing of certain HVFs do require high levels of technical or marketing skill and investment (in specialized facilities and equipment). Where high levels of asset-specificity apply, investors will be driven to adopt more complex contractual ties with input suppliers and downstream marketing agents in order to lower their own risks and transaction costs.

The mixed experience of private sector HVF processing and trade and the generally slow supply response to macroeconomic and sectoral policy reforms, call for policy-makers to look beyond policy reforms *per se* and address many of the additional constraints faced by the private sector. While no grand strategy for supporting private agribusiness activity is proposed here, the following are suggested areas for policy-makers to consider.

AVOID 'GREAT LEAPS FORWARD' IN THE DESIGN OF AGRICULTURAL DIVERSIFICATION STRATEGIES: Facing poor market prospects for major traditional agricultural exports (e.g. beverage crops; tobacco) and searching for new sources of agricultural growth, African decision-makers and donors have begun to explore options for promoting agricultural diversification led by the private sector. There has been particularly strong interest in the prospects for developing export-oriented production and trade in high-value horticultural commodities. The positive experience of Kenya is widely cited to illustrate the considerable trade growth potential.

Although international market trends in these commodities have indeed been favorable, only a small number of developing countries have been able to take advantage of the market opportunities. The vast majority of African countries and private enterprises are poorly placed to compete in this area due to the exacting demands for quality and marketing services as well as the stiff competition faced in these markets from both developing and industrialized countries. While African suppliers might have certain sources of comparative advantage (e.g. relatively low labor costs; counter seasonal availability of supply), most African countries are at present poorly endowed with the infrastructure and technical, organizational, and marketing know-how required for internationally competitive fresh horticultural trades. In the light of the skills required, the development of fresh horticultural exports is more akin to industrial export development than it is to agricultural development. It is therefore not surprising that the bulk of developing country horticultural exports (other than bananas and pineapple) has been by countries which have also been successful exporters of industrial products (e.g. Brazil, Chile, Mexico, Colombia, Taiwan, and Thailand).

In Africa, three countries—South Africa, Côte d'Ivoire, and Kenya—account for more than 85% of the region's exports in fresh and processed horticultural products. Although firms in many other African countries have entered this trade, only those in Zimbabwe and Cameroon appear to have established a considerable presence in the European market. Kenya's relatively successful experience illustrates the many pitfalls and the long time horizon involved in horticultural development. That case illustrates the importance of both foreign investment and the presence of a local merchant class with considerable international trading experience. Despite concerted efforts by government, a broad expansion of the sub-sector to include large numbers of farmers and traders did not take place until ten to fifteen years after the initial post-Independence take-off in exports.

Thus, a broad-based agricultural diversification strategy should not be centered upon exports of exotic or off-season perishable commodities. There will be opportunities for individual products and firms, especially those which can form linkages with European trading companies. Yet, both past experience and considerations of risk and logistical barriers indicate that it will be many years before emerging horticultural export subsectors effectively incorporate large numbers of producers and traders. This is not to suggest that this sector should be neglected—there is a strong rationale in some countries to provide research and infrastructural support to emerging trades. It does imply the need for a downward adjustment in expectations about likely growth and developmental impact of horticultural exports in Africa.

The case studies and other experience presented here suggest that many of the more immediate and viable opportunities for private sector-led diversification lie in domestic, regional or international markets for animal and fish products, oilseeds/vegetable oil, spices/flavorings, and less perishable (including processed) fruit and vegetable products. There is growing demand for these products in rural as well as urban areas and among different income strata. International market demand is also generally favorable. There are multiple opportunities for developing new products and adding value to raw materials using a diverse array of technologies. Opportunities exist at the artisanal as well as larger, formal sector level. There is much unrealized potential in servicing particular market segments in domestic and regional markets and in deriving new products and uses from existing raw materials. Some of this production would be import-substituting, either directly or for products which serve similar dietary/culinary requirements; other production would be for export. Instead of promoting leaps into the unknown, greatest attention should be given to assessing the scope for and modalities of natural extensions of existing activities through vertical and horizontal diversification.

This view is consistent with the experience of many of the noteworthy success stories of high-value food exports in Latin America and Asia.[2] These were not isolated industries which arose out of thin air in response to the pull of the market or the push of policy reform. Instead, many of these export-oriented operations built upon pre-existing infrastructure or complementary industries (e.g. wheat marketing facilities for soybean, feed supply for poultry, vegetable canning facilities for fish canning) and featured the prior or parallel development of domestic markets for the focal commodities. The latter has been particularly important, not only as a source of demand or safety valve for non-exportable production, but also in enabling firms to acquire expertise in packaging and marketing prior to venturing abroad to more discriminating markets. While the domestic market for some high-value foods is small in many African countries, each country does have an urban middle-income population and/or tourist segment which entrepreneurs can initially target. It is the quality, not the quantity of the learning experience which is important.

IMPROVE THE PROVISION OF IMPORTANT PUBLIC GOODS: Governments can facilitate improved performance on the part of private entrepreneurs by providing a range of basic public goods. One critical area is investments to develop or improve physical infrastructure, including roads, ports, electricity, telecommunications, and water supply. Another is support for or direct provision of research, training and advisory services on agriculture, post-harvest

---

[2] Jaffee and Gordon (1993).

techniques and food technology. Yet another is the adoption and enforcement of standard weights and measures and (in collaboration with the private sector) the development of grades, packaging standards and quality control procedures. In some cases, publicly supplied market intelligence and other information services can enhance private agribusiness performance.

ADOPT MEASURES TO BOOST PRIVATE SECTOR CONFIDENCE: Macroeconomic reform programs and sectoral level initiatives have begun to increase private sector confidence. However, in many countries, doubts persist regarding the government's commitment to reform, its actual capacity to implement announced policies, its ability to deliver basic social and support services, and its ability to protect property and help enforce contracts. Greater attention needs to be given to measures and procedures to boost the confidence of the private sector. These might center around an expanded role for private sector representatives (e.g. from manufacturer, trade, or producer associations) in policy-making discussions, increased transparency in the implementation of policy changes (e.g. pertaining to import, export, and trade licensing), greater consistency between announced government policies and local-level implementation, increased transparency in the bids and negotiations pertaining to the privatization of public enterprises, and improved public relations vis-a-vis the private sector. Public mistrust for private activities persists in some countries and efforts are needed to improve the understanding of public officials regarding the environment faced by and the behavior of private traders and processors. This might involve a combination of training programs and workshops involving private-public sector interaction.

SUPPORT DEVELOPMENT OF LOCAL MARKETING MANAGEMENT SKILLS: Past support for agricultural marketing in Africa has centered around the construction and rehabilitation of physical facilities (e.g. marketplaces, factories, abattoirs) or the development of market information systems. Relatively little attention has been given to developing local skills in marketing management—encompassing such topics as market research, product development, logistics management, market segmentation and channel selection, promotion, and pricing strategies. Skills in these areas are not especially critical when trade involves storable, largely homogeneous commodities or when trade is largely conducted via large-scale auctions. However, for many high-value food products, the lack of skills in such areas is an important barrier to effective market development.[3] Based on assessments of present and future needs, there is scope for beneficial programs of training, internships and technical assistance in this area, either on a country or sub-regional basis. Short-term training schemes focusing on export marketing procedures and methods might also be useful.

MAINTAIN SUPPORT FOR SMALL-SCALE PROCESSING ACTIVITIES: Valuable work is being done by a variety of institutions, both in Africa and in industrialized countries, to improve the technologies used in artisanal and small-scale industrial food processing. Such improvements can enhance the productivity of small enterprises while retaining the advantages of the informal sector in terms of its receptivity to consumer preferences, its lower costs and investment requirements, its capacity to provide employment, and its geographically decentralized nature. Donors should continue to support the development and extension of new and improved technologies through research institutes, universities, private firms, and NGOs. Given the importance of women in the informal sector, their requirements should be given particular attention and their possible displacement in the course of technological upgrading carefully monitored.

SUPPORT MORE COMPLEX FORMS OF CONTRACTING, ORGANIZATION, AND COLLECTIVE ACTION: The design of policy changes pertaining to market liberalization in Africa has frequently centered around measures to improve the functioning of spot markets for commodities and inputs. While this approach is suitable in markets for storable, relatively low-value homogenous commodities (e.g. staple grains), it is less appropriate for many perishable, high-value food commodities which need more complex forms of contracting and association in order to control for quality and to stimulate and coordinate specialized production, trading and processing activities. Support for HVF and similar agro-industrial development thus needs to include assistance in properly structuring and implementing more complex forms of contracting and organization. This applies at various commodity system levels and would

---

[3] Because African entrepreneurs frequently lack such skills, they have depended upon foreign firms to perform marketing services for them and typically have had little input into the design of marketing strategy. More independent novices have taken the precarious road of learning by doing in international markets. The absence or weakness of these skills has also hindered the development and profitability of intra-regional and domestic market sales and placed local firms at a distinct disadvantage vis-a-vis larger firms which utilize more sophisticated marketing techniques.

include contractual arrangements governing outgrower schemes, franchising agreements for food processors and distribution outlets, management/ marketing contracts between local and foreign firms, joint venture agreements, agreements for local use and production of patented or protected technologies (e.g. seeds, processing equipment), the formation of producer, manufacturer, and trade associations, and other mechanisms to bring about collective action (e.g. in product promotion, market research, quality control, etc.). African governments need to provide the legal framework for such arrangements and provide impartial arbitration of disputes arising from them. Training programs could be provided as could information on the legal, financial, and other ramifications of different contractual arrangements.

PROMOTE FOREIGN COLLABORATION IN AFRICAN HIGH-VALUE FOOD SECTORS: Although the potential for increased foreign direct investment in Africa is modest at best, the opportunities may be better now than they were through much of the 1980s. African governments have begun to welcome foreign investment, making adjustments in their investment codes and developing easier procedures for investment approvals. However, the image of many African countries abroad remains poor. In order to attract new investments, governments are likely to require the support of multilateral agencies and industrialized country agencies which have already developed institutionalized programs of investment promotion.[4] Common promotion methods have included information and match-making services, support for feasibility studies, investment missions to individual countries, and support for project development and start-up. These programs could be utilized to attract foreign investment in high-value food sub-sectors in individual African countries or in certain sub-regions (e.g. Southern Africa).

It should be recognized that forms of foreign collaboration other than direct investments are likely to be more important for the foreseeable future. The perceived high risk of operating in Africa, coupled with the trend among many international agribusiness companies to move away from primary production and toward emphasis on value-adding processing and distribution are among the contributing factors to the prominence of non-equity forms of foreign participation in African economies. In many countries, both private

---

[4] Belot and Weigel (1991) review and evaluate a range of industrial country and multilateral programs to promote foreign direct investment in developing countries.

firms and African governments will require advice and information on alternative forms of foreign collaboration, including joint ventures, management/marketing contracts, equipment supply, and agency relationships.

BE PRAGMATIC RATHER THAN DOGMATIC: A pragmatic approach is needed to develop African food markets and support private agribusiness activity. In all such efforts, considerable attention needs to be given to the actual objectives, constraints, and operating characteristics of Africa's diverse private sector. This means that policy makers must consult with representative private traders and processors and work with them in the design of policies and programs. All available marketing and agribusiness management skills need to be marshalled. This means that social objectives should be pursued via positive incentives and support services (i.e. training), rather than through discriminatory restrictions on the activities of particular groups. African agro-entrepreneurship needs to be nurtured and strengthened, rather than suppressed as was all too common in the past.

About the Authors

GEOFFRY AMES recently retired as Head of the Fisheries and Aquatic Section of the Natural Resources Institute, Chatham, United Kingdom. He has a Ph.D. in Organic Chemistry from London University.

C.J. BENNETT is a Senior Research Officer in the Social Sciences Group of the Natural Resources Institute, Chatham, United Kingdom. He is currently seconded as Marketing Specialist to the Philippines Small Island Agricultural Support Services Program.

BENOÎT BLAREL has a Ph.D. in Agricultural Economics from the University of Wisconsin-Madison. He is presently Sector Economist in the India Operations Division of the World Bank.

DIANE DOLINSKY has a M.A. in International Affairs from Columbia University. Until recently she was a Trade Analyst in the Foreign Agricultural Service of the U.S. Department of Agriculture.

STEVEN JAFFEE has a D.Phil. in Agricultural Economics from Oxford University. He is presently an Economist in the Southern Africa Department of the World Bank. This book was prepared while he was a Consultant in the World Bank's Agriculture and Natural Resources Department.

PETER LITTLE has a Ph.D. in Anthropology from Indiana University. He is Senior Research Associate at the Institute for Development Anthropology and an Associate Research Professor in the Department of Anthropology, Binghamton University.

JOHN MORTON has a Ph.D. in Social Anthropology from the University of Hull and is with the Social Sciences Group of the Natural Resources Institute, Chatham, United Kingdom.

Bibliography

Abbott, J. *Agricultural Marketing Enterprises for the Developing World*. Cambridge: Cambridge University Press, 1987.

Adams, D. W. and D. A. Fitchett, eds., *Informal Finance in Low-income Countries*, Boulder, CO: Westview Press, 1992.

Africa Watch. "Somalia: A Government at War With Its Own People." London, 1990.

Agriconsult/AMEC. "Study Report on the Best Possible Utilization of the Currently Idle Cashew Nut Processing Plants." Consultancy report to Ministry of Agriculture, Livestock Development and Cooperatives, Dar es Salaam, 1992.

"Agricultural Diversification and Intensification Study." Report by Food Studies Group (Oxford) and Department of Rural Economy (Morogoro, Tanzania). Oxford, September 1992.

Ahmed, R. and C. Donovan. *Issues in Infrastructural Development: A Synthesis of the Literature*. Washington, D.C.: International Food Policy Research Institute, 1992.

Akiyama, T. and D. Larson. "Recent Trends and Prospects for Agricultural Commodity Exports in Sub-Saharan Africa". World Bank PPR Working Paper #348. Washington, D.C., 1989.

Alderman, H. "Nutritional Status in Ghana and Its Determinants," Cornell Food and Nutrition Policy Program, Working Paper no. 1. Ithaca: Cornell University, 1990

————. "Incomes and Food Security in Ghana," Cornell Food and Nutrition Policy Program, Working Paper no. 26. Ithaca: Cornell University, 1992.

Alderman, H. and G. Shively. "Prices and Markets in Ghana," Cornell Food and Nutrition Policy Program, Working Paper no. 10. Ithaca: Cornell University, 1991.

Alderman, H. and P. Higgins. "Food and Nutritional Adequacy in Ghana," Cornell Food and Nutrition Policy Program, Working Paper no. 27. Ithaca: Cornell University, 1992.

Ali-Gaye et al. "Analyse des Filieres de Commercialisation des Produits Maraichers a Brazzaville (Congo)". Paper presented at the Xeme Seminaire d'Economie Rurale des Regions Chaudes. Montpellier, France. September, 1989.

Allen, G. "Development of the Mumias Company," *Oxford Agrarian Studies*. Vol.12 (1983),pp. 63–93.

Anand, A. and A. E. Smith. "The Market for Vanilla." Report no. G198. London: Tropical Development and Research Institute, July 1986.

Anonymous "Boom in a Buyer's Market, but . . .: Focus on the Advertising Industry," *Newswatch* (13), 1991, pp.37–40.

Arhin, K., P. Hesp, and L. van der Laan. *Marketing Boards in Tropical Africa*. London: KPI, 1985.

Arrow, K. *The Limits of Organization*. New York: W.W. Norton, 1974.

_____. "Vertical Integration and Communications," *Bell Journal of Economics*: 1975, pp. 173–83.

Arthur, H., J. Houck, and G. Beckford. *Tropical Agricultural Structures and Adjustments—Bananas*. Boston: Harvard School of Business Administration, 1968.

Asian Development Bank and Infofish. *Global Industry Update: Tuna*. Abidjan, 1990.

d'Assise A. F., "Role of Women in Fisheries Development in West Africa," *Bonga*, no.16, April 1992.

Austin, J. "Cashew Exporting from Mozambique: Companhia Do Caju De Nacala." Unpublished mimeo, 1991.

Avezard, C. "Programme for the Identification, Preparation and Promotion of Industrial Investment Projects in Kenya in the Food Industries Sector". Report prepared for the Government of Kenya. Vienna: UNIDO, 1992.

Ay, P. *Women in Food Processing*. Ibadan: UNDP/ILO/FDARD, 1990.

Baker, J. "The Gurage of Ethiopia: Rural-Urban Interaction and Entrepreneurship" in J. Baker and P. Pedersen (eds.) *The Rural Urban Interface in Africa: Expansion and Adaptation*. Uppsala: Scandinavian Institute of African Studies, 1992.

Barad, R. "Unrecorded Transborder Trade and Its Implications for Regional Economic Integration" in *The Long-Term Prospective Study of Sub-Saharan Africa*. Background Papers Volume 4. Washington, D.C.: World Bank, 1990.

Bardhan, P. ed., *The Economic Theory of Agrarian Institutions*. Oxford: Oxford University Press, 1964.

Barthelemy, J.C. "Le Cas De Madagascar." In *Offre de Biens Manufacturés et Développement Agricole*. Paris: Centre de développement de l'OCDE, 1988.

Barton, C. "Credit and Commercial Control in South Vietnam," Paper for USAID. Washington, D.C., 1974.

Bates, R. *Beyond the Miracle of the Market*. Cambridge: Cambridge University Press, 1990.

Bates, R. *Markets and States in Tropical Africa*. Berkeley: University of California Press, 1981.

Baumol, W., J. Panzar, and R. Willig. *Contestable Markets and the Theory of Industry Structure*. San Diego: Harcourt, Brace and Jovanovich, 1982.

Benchley, B. "Will Vanilla Join The 20th Century?" *Dairy Field*, October 1985.

Bennett, A. and R. Woods. "Study Tour Report: Vanilla Production in Madagascar." ODA Technical Report no. TR 92/2. London: ODA, 1992.

Berg, E. "Obstacles to Liberalizing Agricultural Markets in Developing Countries," in *Agricultural Marketing Strategy and Pricing Policy*. D. Elz (ed.) Washington, D.C.: World Bank, 1987.

_____. "The Liberalization of Rice Marketing in Madagascar," World Development, Vol. 17, no.5 (1989), pp.719–28.

_____. "Privatization in Africa: Results, Prospects and New Approaches". Draft Report for the World Bank. Bethesda: Development Alternatives Inc., 1993.

Billings, M. "Contract Poultry Farming in Senegal". Contract Farming in Africa Project Working Paper #5. Binghamton: Institute for Development Anthropology, 1987.

"Biotech Vanilla's Promise Still Remains Down the Road." *Chemical Marketing Reporter*, March 19, 1990.

Blanchfield, R. "Technological Change in Food Manufacturing and Distribution," in *The Food Industry: Economics and Policies*. J. Burns, J. McInerney, and A. Swinbank (eds.). London: Heinemann, 1983.

Boumedouha, S. "Adjustment to West African Realities: the Lebanese in Senegal," *Africa*, Vol.60, no.4 (1990), pp. 538–49.

Bowbrick, P. "The Economic of Grades," *Oxford Agrarian Studies*. Vol. XI (1983), pp. 65–92.

Breimyer, H. *Economics of Product Markets in Agriculture*. Ames: Iowa State University, 1976.

Brenner, G. et al. "Les Entrepreneurs Bamilekes de Douala et leurs Enterprises". Rapport de Recherche, Ecole des Haute Etudes Commerciales, Montreal, 1990.

Bricas, N. *Dynamique et Roles de l'Artisanat Alimentaire a Dakar*. Massy/Paris: Altersial, 1984.

Bromley, D. *Economic Interests and Institutions*. Oxford: Basil Blackwell, 1989.

_____. "Markets and Agricultural Development: The Promise and the Challenge". Binghamton, NY: Institute for Development Anthropology, 1986.

Brown, J. (ed.), *Agroindustry Profiles*. EDI Working Papers, Agriculture and Rural Development Division. Washington, D.C., 1991.

Brown, L. "Agricultural Change in Kenya, 1945–1960." Palo Alto: Food Research Institute, 1968.

Bryceson, D. *Liberalizing Tanzania's Food Trade*. Geneva: UNRISD, 1993.

Buch-Hansen, M. and J. Kieler. "The Development of Capitalism and the Transformation of the Peasantry of Kenya," *Rural Africana*, Vol. 15–16 (1983), pp.13–39.

Bunker, S. *Peasants Against the State: The Politics of Market Control in Bugisu, Uganda, 1900–1983*. Urbana: University of Illinois Press, 1987.

Campbell, D. "Voluntary and Compulsory Cooperative," *Canadian Journal of Agricultural Economics*. Vol. 5, no.2 (1967), pp.26–37.

Campbell R., S. Sen and B. Uyttendaele. "Evaluation Study on Private Initiative in Artisanal Fisheries Projects in Africa South of the Sahara." CEC Evaluation Series no.4. Brussels: Commission of the European Communities, Directorate General for Development, 1993.

Carlton, D. "Vertical Integration in Competitive Markets under Uncertainty," *Journal of Industrial Economics*, Vol. 28, no.3 (1979), pp.460–68.

Carney, J. "Contract Farming in Irrigated Rice Production: Jahaly Pacharr Project, the Gambia". Contract Farming Working Paper. Binghamton, N.Y.: Institute for Development Anthropology, 1987.

Cassady, R. *Exchange by Private Treaty*. Austin: Graduate School of Business, University of Texas, 1974.

Cassam, M. "The Kenya Beef Industry: Prospects for Somali Cattle Exports." Mogadishu: Livestock Marketing and Health Project, 1987.

Cassanelli, L. *The Shaping of Somali Society: Reconstructing the History of a Pastoral People, 1600–1900*. Philadelphia: University of Pennsylvania Press, 1982.

Casson, M. *The Entreprenuer*. Oxford: Martin Robertson, 1982.

_____. "The Theory of Vertical Integration," University of Reading, Department of Economics Discussion Paper #150. Reading, U.K., 1984.

_____. "Contractual Arrangements for Technology Transfer: New Evidence from Business History." Mimeo. Reading: University of Reading, Department of Economics, 1987.

Caswell, J. and D. Padberg. "Toward a Comprehensive Theory of Food Labels," *American Journal of Agricultural Economics*, Vol. 74, no.2 (1992).

Christiansen, G. "Towards Food Security in the Horn of Africa: The Private Sector in Domestic Food Markets," Food Studies Group Working Paper #4. Oxford, 1991.

Chuke, G., T. Banta, and S. Abdulsalami. "Utilization of Soyabeans as "Daddawa" in Parts of Kaduna State: Results of a Preliminary Survey," Paper presented at the 5th Annual Meeting of Nigerian Soybean Scientists, IITA, Ibadan. February 4–5, 1985.

CIRAD "La Valorisation des Produits Vivrieres dans les Pays d'Afrique Humide et Sub-Humide". Report for the World Bank Special Program for Agricultural Research in Africa. Montpellier: CIRAD, 1992.

Clark, G., ed. *Traders Versus the State: Anthropological Approaches to the Study of Informal Economies*. Boulder, CO: Westview Press, 1988.

Clark, G. "Price Control of Local Foodstuffs in Kumasi, Ghana," in G. Clark (ed.) *Traders versus the State*. Boulder: Westview Press, 1988.

_____. "Flexibility Equals Survival," *Cultural Survival Quarterly*, Winter (1992).

Cleaver, K. "A Strategy to Develop Agriculture in Sub-Saharan Africa and a Focus for the World Bank," World Bank Technical Paper No. 203. Africa Technical Department Series. Washington, D.C.: World Bank, 1993.

Coase, R. "The Nature of the Firm," *Economica*, (1937), pp. 386–405.

_____. "The Problem of Social Cost", *Journal of Law and Economics*, Vol. 1, no.1 (1960), pp. 1–44.

Cohen, A. *Custom and Politics in Urban Africa*. Berkeley: University of California Press, 1969.

"Coke Adds Life to Vanilla Bean Market With Some New Plantations in Mexico." *Chemical Marketing Reporter*, December 1, 1980.

Coleman, W. "Agricultural Policy and the Associations of the Food Processing Industry," in W. Grant (ed.) *Business Interests, Organizational Development and Private Interest Government.*, pp.151–65. Berlin: Walter de Gruyter, 1987.

Comanor, W. "Market Structure, Product Differentiation, and Industrial Research", *Quarterly Journal of Economics*, Vol. 81 (1967), pp. 939–57.

Commons, J. *Institutional Economics*. Madison: University of Wisconsin Press, 1934.

Conze, P. and T. Labahn, eds., *Agriculture in the Winds of Change*. Saarbrucken-Schafbrucke: epi Verlag GmbH, 1986.

Cormier–Salem, M. "Diversite de Dynamisme des Systems Techniques Locaux de Transformation du Poisson en Casamance". Paper presented at Journees Scientifiques, Montpellier, November, 1992.

Correll, D.S. "Vanilla—Its Botany, History, Cultivation and Economic Import." *Economic Botany*, Vol 7, no.4, October–December, 1953.

Coulter, J. and P. Golob. "Cereal Marketing Liberalization in Tanzania," *Food Policy*, 17, no. 6 (1992), pp.420–30.

Coussy, J. and P. Hugon. "Note sur les Echanges Interafricains non Officiels du Produits Agro-alimentaires". Mimeo. Montepellier: CIRAD, 1985.

Cuevas, C. et al. "Case Studies of Enterprise Finance in Ghana". Final Report for World Bank Regional Program on Enterprise Development. Columbus: Cuevas International, 1993.

Dalleo, P. "Trade and Pastoralism: Economic Factors in the History of the Somali of Northeastern Kenya, 1892–1948." Ph.D. Thesis, Syracuse University: Syracuse, New York, 1975.

DANIDA. "Kenya Dairy Master Plan." Nairobi, 1991.

DANIDA. "Thematic Evaluation of Industrial Scale Fisheries Development Projects: Ghana, Socio-economic Case Study." Draft Interim Report (mimeo) no.2, Accra, 1988.

Daniels, L. and A. Ngwira. "Results of a Nationwide Survey of Micro, Small, and Medium Enterprises in Malawi. Bethesda: USAID GEMINI Project, 1993.

Davis, J. and R. Goldberg *A Concept of Agribusiness*. Boston: Harvard School of Business Administration, 1957.

Delgado, C. "Why Domestic Food Prices Matter to Growth in Semi-Open West African Agriculture," *Journal of African Economies*, Vol. 1, no.3 (1992), pp.446–471.

Demsetz, H. "The Exchange and Enforcement of Property Rights," *Journal of Law and Economics*, Vol 4., no.1(1964), pp.11–26.

_____. "Barriers to Entry," *American Economic Review*, Vol. 72, no.1 (1982), pp. 47–57.

Devautour, H. "Etudes des Systemes Techniques: Application a l'Artisanat Alimentaire au Sud-Benin". Doctoral Thesis, Ecole Nationale Superieure Agronomique de Montpellier, 1990.

Dongmo, J-L. "L'Approvisionnement Alimentaire de Yaounde". Mimeo. Faculte des Lettres et Sciences Humaines, Universite de Yaounde, 1983.

Dorosh, P. "Structural Adjustment, Growth and Poverty in Madagascar: A CGE Analysis." Cornell Food and Nutrition Policy Program. Washington D.C., 1993.

Due, J. and M. White-Jones. "Differences in Earning, Labor Inputs, Decision-Making and Perception of Development Between Farm and Market: A Case Study of Zambia," *East African Economic Review*, Vol. 5, no.2 (1989).

Duggleby, T., E. Aryeetey, and W. Steel. "Formal and Informal Finance for Small Enterprises in Ghana." Industry and Energy Department Working Paper. Washington, D.C.: World Bank, 1992.

Duncan, I. "Tanzania Cashew Nut Marketing." Report for Cashew Nut Production Improvement Pilot Project, April 1988.

Dupire, M. *Peuls Nomades*. Paris: Institut d'Ethnologie, 1962.

Economic Commission for Europe. *Food Processing Machinery*. New York: United Nations, 1991.

Economist Intelligence Unit. "EIU Country Report: Madagascar, Mauritius, Seychelles, Comoros." Various quarterly bulletins, 1991, 1992.

Ellis, F. "A Preliminary Analysis of the Decline in Tanzanian Cashewnut Production, 1974–1979: Causes, Possible Remedies and Lessons for Rural Development Policy." Report no. 79.1. Dar es Salaam: Economic Research Bureau, University of Dar es Salaam, 1979.

_____. "Marketing Costs and the Processing of Cashewnuts in Tanzania: An Analysis of the Marketing and the Potential Level of the Producer Price." Report no. 79.2. Dar es Salaam: Economic Research Bureau, University of Dar es Salaam, 1980.

_____. "Agriculture Price Policy in Tanzania." *World Development*, Vol. 10, 1982, pp. 263–83.

Elz, D. "Agricultural Marketing Policies and Development," in *Agricultural Marketing Strategy and Pricing Policy*. D. Elz (ed.) Washington, D.C.: The World Bank, 1987.

Ensimnger, J. "Political Economy among the Pastoral Galole Orma: The Effects of Market Integration." Ph.D. Thesis, Northwestern University: Evanston, Illinois, 1984.

Eriksen, J. "Observations on Morocco Dairy Processing Enterprises in 1992." Unpublished consultancy report. Washington, D.C.: the World Bank, 1992.

Essuman, K.M. "Fermented fish in Africa." FAO Fisheries Technical Paper no. 329. Rome: FAO, 1992.

Evans, H., M. Cullen and P. Little. *Rural-Urban Exchange in the Kismayo Region of Somalia*. Binghamton, NY: Institute of Development Anthropology, 1988.

"Export Mix Is the World's Most Fragrant." *African Business,* October 1986.

FAO. "Cashew Nut Processing." Agricultural Services Bulletin no. 6. Rome, 1969.

_____. *Food Consumption Patterns*. Rome 1991.

_____. *The Private Marketing Entrepreneur and Rural Development*. Rome: FAO, 1982.

_____. *Food Balance Sheets, 1984–86 Averages*. Rome: FAO, 1991.

_____. "Kenya: Pig Sector Development Project". Report # 153/91 ADB-Ken. Rome: FAO, 1991.

_____. "Mozambique: Women's Cooperative Development in Maputo Green Zone". Report # 110/91 AF-MOZ. Rome: FAO, 1991.

_____. "Zambia: The Agro-Industrial Sector". Report #49/92, ADB-Zam. Rome, 1992.

_____. *Production Yearbook*. Rome, various years.

_____. *Trade Yearbook*. Rome, various years.

_____. "Sector Study, Ghana: Fisheries Sector Review." FAO/World Bank Cooperative Programme Investment Centre. Report no. 10/89 CP-GHA 22 SR. FAO, Rome.

_____. "Utilization of Tropical Foods: Sugars, Spices and Stimulants." Food and Nutrition Paper no. 47/6, Rome, 1989.

_____. *Yearbook of Fishery Statistics,* various years.

_____. "Kenya Dairy Development Project: Initial Preparation Mission." Rome, 1991.

_____. "Mid-Term Review." Mimeo. February 1993.

FAO/World Bank, "Ethiopia Livestock Sector Development Project Preparation Report." Rome: FAO, 1993.

Faruqee, R. "Private Investment in Sub-Saharan Africa: An Exploratory Analysis". Africa Regional Series Internal Discussion Paper. Washington, D.C.: World Bank, 1992.

GATT *International Trade.* Geneva, 1990.

Geertz, C. "The Bazaar Economy: Information and Search in Peasant Marketing," *American Economic Review.* Vol. 28 (1978), Papers and Proceedings.

Giri, J. "Formal and Informal Enterprises in the Long-Term Future of Sub-Saharan Africa," in *The Long-Term Perspective Study of Sub-Saharan Africa.* Background Papers Volume 2. Washington, D.C.: World Bank, 1990.

Glover, D. and K. Kusterer. *Small Farmers, Big Business: Contract Farming and Rural Development.* New York: St. Martin's Press, 1990.

Goldberg, R. *Agribusiness Coordination: A Systems Approach to the Wheat, Soybean, and Florida Orange Economies.* Boston: Harvard School of Business Administration, 1968.

_____. *Agribusiness Management for Developing Countries—Latin America.* Cambridge, Mass.: Ballinger, 1974.

Goldberg, V. "Toward an Expanded Theory of Contracts," *Journal of Economic Issues,* Vol. 10, no.1 (1976), pp.45–61.

Gordon, A. and A. Swetman. "Report on a Visit to Tanzania, Malawi, Ghana, and Burkina Faso to Carry Out a Baseline Study of Small-scale Oilseed Processing". Chatham, U.K.: Natural Resources Institute, 1990.

Government of Tanzania, Marketing Development Bureau. "An Assessment of the New Cashew Nut Marketing System 1991–92." Dar es Salaam, 1992.

_____. *Review of Cashewnuts.* Dar es Salaam, various years.

Grandin, B. "Wealth and Pastoral Dairy Production: A Case Study from Maasailand." *Human Ecology* 16(1988): 1–21.

Greeley, M. *Postharvest Technologies: Implications for Food Policy Analysis.* EDI Development Policy Case Series, #7. Washington, D.C., 1991.

Greenfield, R. "Siad's Sad Legacy." *Africa Report*, March/April (1991): 14–18.

Grisson, M. "Une Application Simplifee du Concept de Filiere en vue de la Definition des Politiques Agricoles". Paper presented at the Xeme Seminaire d'Economie Rurale des Regions Chaudes. Montpelier, France. September, 1989.

Groosman, A. "Fruit and Vegetable Processing in the New International Division of Labor." Development Research Institute Occasional Paper no. 14. Tilberg, Netherlands, 1982.

Grosh, B. *Public Enterprise in Kenya.* Boulder: Lynne Rienner Publishers, 1987.

Grouitch, Y. "Reflexions sur la Privatisation des Agro-Industries d'Afrique Francophone." Draft Report for the World Bank. Washington, D.C., 1992.

Haakonsen J. M., ed., "Recent Developments of the Artisanal Fisheries in Ghana," FAO/DANIDA/Norway Project report no. IDAF/WP/21. Cotonou, Benin: FAO, 1991.

Haaland, G. "The Jellaba Trading System," in L. Manger (ed.) *Trade and Traders in the Sudan.* Bergen: Department of Social Anthropology, University of Bergen, 1984.

Hart, K. "Informal Economy," in J. Eatwell, M. Milgate, and P. Newman (eds.) *The New Palgrave: A Dictionary of Economics.* London: Macmillan, 1987.

Havnevik, K. "Charcoal and Cashewnut Production in Rufiji." Paper 79/13, Dar es Salaam: Bureau of Resources and Land Use Planning, University of Dar es Salaam, 1979.

Hayek, F. "The Use of Knowledge in Society," *American Economic Review*, Vol. 35 (1945), pp. 519–530.

Hendy, C. *Land Use in Tsetse Affected Areas of Southern Somalia.* Surbiton, UK: Land Resources Development Centre, 1985.

Henry, A. et al. *Tontines et Banques au Cameroun: Les Principes de la Societe des Amis.* Paris: Karthala, 1991.

Herlehy, T. "New Approaches to Growth: Systemic Development of Agricultural Marketing in Uganda, 1987–1992," USAID, Africa Bureau, Washington, D.C, 1993.

Herren, U. "The Commercial Sale of Camel Milk from Pastoral Herds in the Mogadishu Hinterland." ODI Pastoral Development Network Paper #30a. London: Overseas Development Institute, 1990.

Heyer, J. "The Marketing System," in *Agricultural Development in Kenya: An Economic Assessment*, edited by J. Heyer, J. Maitha and W. Senga. Nairobi: Oxford University Press, 1976.

Hill, M. *Cream Country: The Story of Kenya Cooperative Creameries Ltd.* Nairobi: East African Standard Ltd., 1956.

Hirschman, A.O. *Exit, Voice and Loyalty: Responses to Decline in Firms, Organizations and States.* Cambridge: Harvard University Press, 1970.

Hjort, A. *Savanna Town: Rural Ties and Urban Opportunities in Northern Kenya.* Stockholm: University of Stockholm Press, 1979.

Holtzman, J. and Collaborating Authors. *Agribusiness Development in Sub-Saharan Africa: Suggested Approaches, Information Needs and an Analytical Agenda.* Washington, D.C.: Abt Associates, 1992.

Hoos, S.(ed.) *Agricultural Marketing Boards: An International Perspective.* Cambridge: Ballinger Publishing Company, 1979.

Hopcraft, P. "Milk Pricing in Kenya: the Case of a Bulky, Perishable Commodity with Seasonally Varying Production Costs." Discussion Paper no. 266. Nairobi: Institute for Development Studies, 1978.

_____. and G. Ruigu. "Dairy Marketing and Pricing in Kenya: Are Milk Shortages the Consequence of Drought or Pricing Policies?" Discussion Paper no. 237. Nairobi: Institute for Development Studies, 1976.

Hormann, D. "Export Oriented Horticulture in Developing Countries—Kenya." Working Paper no. 31. Hannover, Germany: Institute for Horticultural Economics, 1981.

_____. and M. Will. "The Market for Selected Tropical Fruits from Kenya in Western European Countries." Working Paper no. 57. Hannover, Germany: Institute for Horticultural Economics, 1987.

Horton, J. "Characteristics of Horticultural Export Enterprises Utilizing Contract Farming in Senegal." Contract Farming in Africa Project, Working Paper. Binghamton, N.Y.: Institute for Development Anthropology, 1987.

Hubl, K. "The Nomadic Livestock Production Systems of Somalia," in *Agriculture in the Winds of Change* edited by P. Conze and T. Labahn, 55–72. Saarbrucken-Schafbrucke: epi Verlag GmbH, 1986.

Hyman, E. "Prospects for the Palm Oil Industry in Cameroon", *Oleaginaeux*, 1990.

_____. "Production of Edible Oils for the Masses and by the Masses: the Impact of the Ram Press in Tanzania," *World Development*, Vol. 21, no.3 (1993), pp. 429–443.

IDAF. "Fishermen's Migrations in West Africa." FAO/DANIDA/Norway Project Report no. IDAF/WP/36. Cotonou, Benin: FAO, 1991.

"Industrial Processing Opportunities," in *Tanganyika Industrial Development*, 44–52, 1962.

INFOPECHE. "Improvement of Post-harvest Utilization of Artisanal Fish Production in West Africa: Marketing of Artisanal Fish Products." Abidjan, 1990.

_____. "Transport of Cured Fish from Mamprobi (Ghana) to Cotonou (Benin): Trade Formalities and Constraints." Dr. E. O. Tettey and K. Klousseh. *Bonga Reportage*, vol. I, Abidjan, 1992a.

_____. "Cured Fish Export Trade from Gunjur (Gambia) to N'zerekore (Guinea): Challenges and Opportunities." Dr. E. O. Tettey and M Mjie. *Bonga Reportage*, vol. II, Abidjan, 1992b.

_____. "Intra-African Trade in Fish and Fishery Products." Report to the 3rd meeting of the Inter-African Committee on Oceanography, Sea and Inland fisheries in Cairo, 12–17 April 1993.

International Trade Centre UNCTAD/GATT. *Spices: A Survey of the World Market, Volume I: Selected Markets in Europe*. Geneva 1982.

_____. *Trade Development Opportunities For Selected Essential Oils and Spices From The Least Developed Countries*. Geneva 1982.

International Finance Corporation "An Evaluation of IFC's Experience in the Agricultural Processing and Storage Sub-sector". Washington, D.C. December 31, 1987.

_____. "Report on the Activities of the Africa Enterprise Fund". Washington, D.C., March 3, 1993.

International Road Transport Union. *World Transport Data*. Geneva, 1990.

Islam, N. "Horticultural Exports of Developing Countries: Past Performances, Future Prospects, and Policy Issues." Research Report no. 80. Washington, D.C.: International Food Policy Research Institute, 1990.

Jaeger, W. "The Effects of Economic Policies on African Agriculture," World Bank Discussion Papers, Africa Technical Department Series. Washington, D.C., 1992.

Jaffee, S. "The Organization of Agricultural Export Sub-sectors". Technical paper for USAID/ Bureau of Science and Technology. Washington D.C., 1986.

_____. "Case Studies of Contract Farming in the Horticultural Sector of Kenya". Binghamton, N.Y.: Institute for Development Anthropololgy, 1987.

_____. "Alternative Marketing Institutions for Agricultural Exports in Sub-Saharan Africa with Special Reference to Kenyan Horticulture." Unpublished D.Phil Thesis, University of Oxford: Oxford, 1990.

_____. "Marketing Africa's Horticultural Exports: A Transaction Cost Perspective." Paper presented at the Workshop on the Globalization of the Fresh Fruit and Vegetable System at the University of California, Santa Cruz, December 6–9, 1991.

_____. "How Private Enterprise Organized Agricultural Markets in Kenya," in *Food Security and Food Inventories in Developing Countries* edited by P. Berck and D. Bigman. Wallingford, U.K.: CAB International, 1993.

_____. "Mission Report on Export-oriented Agroindustries in Mozambique." World Bank, Agriculture and Environment Division, Southern African Department, 1993.

_____. "Contract Farming in the Shadow of Competitive Markets: The Experience of Kenyan Horticulture," in *Living Under Contract: Contract Farming and Agrarian Transformation in Sub-Saharan Africa* edited by P. Little and M. Watts. Madison: University of Wisconsin Press, 1994.

_____. and A. Weli. "The Marketing of Livestock and Livestock Products." Working Paper no. 4, Somalia Agricultural Sector Survey. Washington, D.C.: World Bank and Government of Somalia, 1985.

_____. and P. Gordon. "Exporting High-value Food Commodities: Success Stories from Developing Countries." World Bank Discussion Paper no. 198. Washington, D.C.: World Bank, 1993.

_____. and J. Srivastava. *Seed System Development: The Appropriate Roles of the Private and Public Sectors.* World Bank Discussion Paper #167. Washington, D.C., 1992.

Jamal, V. "Somalia: Understanding an Unconventional Economy." *Development and Change* 19 (1988): 203–265.

Jensen, M. and W. Meckling. "Theory of the Firm: Management Behavior, Agency Costs, and Capital Structure", *Journal of Financial Economics*, Vol. 3(1976),pp. 305–60.

Jesse, E. *Social Welfare Implications of Federal Marketing Orders for Fruits and Vegetables*. USDA Technical Bulletin #1608. Washington, D.C., 1979.

John, G. "Interorganizational Coordination in Marketing Channels: An Investigation of Opportunism and Involvement Orientation as Mediators of the Process." Unpublished Ph.D. thesis, Northwestern University: Chicago, 1980.

Jones, W. *Marketing Staple Food Crops in Tropical Africa*. Ithaca, NY: Cornell University Press, 1972.

Jouet, J. "Advertising and Transnational Corporations in Kenya," *Development and Change*, Vol.15 (1984), pp.435–456.

Kane, J. "Contracting Animal Protein Production." Contract Farming Project Working Paper #6. Binghamton, N.Y.: Institute for Development Anthropology, 1987.

Kaplinsky, R. "Export-oriented Growth: A Large International Firm in a Small Developing Country." *World Development* Vol. 7, 1979, pp.825–34.

Karaan, A. and A. Myburgh. "Food Distribution Systems in the Urban Informal Markets: the Case of Red Meat Marketing in the Western Cape Townships and Informal Settlements," *Agrekon*, Vol. 31, no.4 (1992).

Katsande, K. "Food Marketing Strategies in Public Enterprises in Developing Countries: The Case of Milk Marketing in Zimbabwe," *Public Enterprise*, Vol. 7 (1987),p p.273–87.

Kay, D. "A Review of World Production of and Trade in Canned Pineapple." London: Tropical Products Institute, 1965.

Keddie, J. and W. Cleghorn. "The Choice of Technology in Food Processing: Some Case Studies," in C. Baron (ed.) *Technology, Employment, and Basic Needs in Food Processing in Developing Countries*. Oxford: Pergamon Press, 1980.

Kerdellant, C."Bataille pour le marche africain," *Jeune Afrique Economie*, December 1987, pp.66–71.

Kerven, C. *Customary Commerce: a Historical Reassessment of Pastoral Livestock Marketing in Africa*. London: Overseas Development Institute, 1965.

_____. "The Role of Milk in a Pastoral Diet and Economy: the Case of South Darfur, Sudan," ILCA Bulletin #27. Addis Ababa: ILCA, 1987.

Kilby, P. "An Entreprenuerial Problem," *American Economic Review*, Vol. 73, no.2 (1983), pp.107–11.

Kindleberger, C. "Standards as Public, Collective, and Private Goods," *Kyklos*, Vol. 36, no.3 (1983), pp. 377–96.

Klemm, H. "Some Aspects of Milk Marketing in Kenya," Discussion Paper #21. Nairobi: Institute for Development Studies.

Klitgaard, R. *Controlling Corruption*. Berkeley: University of California Press, 1988.

Kohls, R. and J. Uhl. *Marketing of Agricultural Products*. New York: Macmillan. Sixth Edition, 1985.

Koranteng, K. A. "Distribution of Cured Fish in Ghana." Draft mimeo of paper presented at the Sub-Regional Workshop on Tariff and Non-Tariff Barriers to Cured Fish Trade, Lome, Togo, 13–15 April 1992.

Koutsoyiannis, A. *Non-Price Decisions: The Firm in a Modern Context*. London: Macmillan, 1982.

Kulibaba, N. "Livestock and Meat Transport in the Niger-Nigeria Corridor." Report for USAID AMIS Project. Bethesda MD: Abt Associates, 1991.

_____. and J. Holtzman. "Livestock Marketing and Trade in the Mali/Burkina Faso-Côte d'Ivoire Corridor". Report for USAID AMIS Project. Bethesda MD: Abt Associates, 1990.

Lall, S., G. Navaretti, S. Teitel, and G. Wignaraja. "Technology and Enterprise Development in Ghana," for the Africa Technical Department, World Bank. Regional Program on Enterprise Development, 1993.

Lamb, G. and L. Mueller. *Control, Accountability, and Incentives in a Successful Development Institution: The Kenya Tea Development Authority*. World Bank Staff Working Paper #500. Washington, D.C., 1982.

Landa, J. "A Theory of the Ethnically Homogeneous Middleman Group: An Institutional Alternative to Law," *Journal of Legal Studies*, Vol. X (1981), pp.349–61.

Lang, M. "Vertical Coordination and Vertical Coordination Mechanisms: Analysis and Case Studies". NC117 Studies of the Organization and Control of the U.S. Food System. Working Paper #12, 1977.

Langdon, S. "Multinational Corporations, Taste Transfer, and Underdevelopment: A Case Study from Kenya," *Review of African Political Economy*, Vol. 1 no.2 (1975).

Langlois, R. *Economics as a Process: Essays in the New Institutional Economics*. Cambridge: Cambridge University Press, 1986.

Leblebici, H. "Transactions and Organizational Forms: A Re-Analysis," *Organization Studies*, (1985),pp. 97–115.

Le Guennec-Coppens, F. "Social and Cultural Integration: A Case Study of the East African Hadramis", *Africa*, Vol. 59, no.2(1989), pp. 185–95.

Lehrman, S. "Splicing Genes, Slicing Exports?" *The Washington Post*, 27 September 1992.

Lele, U., N. van de Walle, and M. Gbetibouo. "Cotton in Africa: An Analysis of Differences in Performance." MADIA Series Working Paper. Washington, D.C.: World Bank, 1989.

_____ and R. Christiansen. "Markets, Marketing Boards, and Cooperatives in Africa: Issues in Adjustment Policy," Managing Agricultural Devlepment in Africa, Discussion Paper #11. Washington, D.C.: World Bank, 1989.

Levay, C. "Agricultural Cooperative Theory: A Review," *Journal of Agricultural Economics*. Vol. 34, no.1 (1983), pp.1–44.

Liedholm, C. and D. Mead "The Structure and Growth of Micro-Enterprises in Southern and Eastern Africa: Evidence from Recent Surveys." Bethesda: USAID GEMINI Project, 1993.

Little, P. "Social Differentiation and Pastoralist Sedentarization in Northern Kenya," *Africa* 55(1985): 242-261.

_____. "Preliminary Observations of Rural-Urban Linkages in Southern Somalia." *Development Anthropology Network* 6(1988): 4–10.

_____. "The Livestock Sector of the Kismayo Region, Somalia: An Overview." Working Paper no. 50. Binghamton, NY: Institute for Development Anthropology, 1989.

_____. "Seasonality and Rural-Urban Linkages in Southern Somalia," in *The Rural Urban Interface in Africa: Expansion and Adaptation* edited by J. Baker and P. Perdersen. Uppsala, Sweden: Scandinavian Institute of African Studies, 1992.

Ma-Mfuka, A. "Etude de la Filiere de la Banane Douce dans la Region du Mayombe". Paper presented at the Xeme Seminaire d'Economie Rurale des Regions Chaudes. Montpellier, France. September, 1989.

Macauley, S. "Non-contractual Relations in Business: A Preliminary Study," *American Sociological Review*. (1963), pp.55–67.

Mackintosh, M. "Fruit and Vegetables as an International Commodity." *Food Policy* (December 1977): 277–92.

Macneil, I. "A Premier of Contract Planning," *Southern California Law Review*, (1975), pp.627–705.

Mahmoud, F. *The Sudanese Bourgeoisie: Vanguard of Development?* London: Zed Press, 1984.

Manchester, A. *The Public Role in the Dairy Economy: Why and How Governments Intervene in the Milk Business*. Boulder: Westview Press, 1986.

Manger, L., ed. *Trade and Traders in the Sudan*. Bergen, Norway: Department of Social Anthropology, University of Bergen, 1984.

Marion, B. "Application of the Structure-Conduct-Performance Paradigm to Subsector Analysis". NC117, Working Paper #7, 1976.

_____ and the NC117 Committee. *The Organization and Performance of the U.S. Food System*. Lexington, Mass.: D.C. Heath and Company, 1986.

Marsden, K. *African Entrepreneurs: Pioneers of Development*. IFC Discussion Paper #9. Washington, D.C.: International Finance Corporation, 1990.

Martin, E. *The History of Malindi*. Nairobi: East African Literature Bureau, 1973.

Matthews, R. "The Economics of Institutions and the Sources of Growth," *Economic Journal*, Vol. 96, no.12(1986), pp. 903–16.

Mbogoh, S. "Dairy Development and Internal Dairy Marketing in sub-Saharan Africa: Performance, Policies, and Options." Working Paper no. 5. Addis Addaba: International Livestock Centre for Africa.

The Vanilla Book. Huntsville, Maryland: McCormick & Company, 1992.

Mead, D. "Of Contracts and Subcontracts: Small Firms in Vertically Disintegrated Production/Distribution Systems in LDCs," *World Development*, Vol. 12, no.11/12 (1984).

Meagher, K. "The Hidden Economy: Informal and Parallel Trade in Northwestern Uganda", *Review of African Political Economy*, Vol. 47 (1990).

Mebrahtu, S. and N. Hahn "Daddawa: Indigenous Soybean Processing in Southern Kaduna, Nigeria". Ibadan: Institute of African Studies, University of Ibadan, 1986.

Meillassoux, C. (ed.) *The Development of Indigenous Trade and Markets in West Africa*. Oxford: Oxford University Press, 1971.

de Melo, J., M. Olarreaga and W. Takacs. *Pricing Strategy Under Eroding Monopoly Power: The International Vanilla Market*, forthcoming.

Menkhaus, K. "Rural Transformation and the Roots of Underdevelopment in Somalia's Lower Jubba Valley." Ph.D. dissertation, University of South Carolina: Columbia, South Carolina, 1989.

Menz, K. M. and E. M. Fleming. "Economic Prospects for Vanilla in the South Pacific." ACIAR Technical Report no. 11. Canberra: Australian Centre for International Agricultural Research, 1989.

Mestres, C. and T. Ferre "La Nixtamalisation au Senegal". Mimeo. Montepellier: CIRAD, (no date).

Mighell, R. and L. Jones. *Vertical Coordination in Agriculture.* Economic Research Service, USDA. Washington, D.C., 1963.

Minae, S. "Evaluation of the Performance of the Marketing Boards: The Small Farmer Milk Marketing System in Kenya." Unpublished Ph.D. dissertation, Cornell University: Ithaca, 1981.

Minot, N.W. *Contract Farming and Its Effect on Small Farmers in Less Developed Countries.* Working Paper no. 31. Michigan State University, Department of Agricultural Economics: Lansing MICH, 1986.

Moris, J. "The Mwea Environment." In *Mwea: An Irrigated Rice Settlement in Kenya* edited by R. Chambers and J. Moris. Munich: Weltforum Verlag 1973.

Morrissey, J. *Agricultural Modernization Through Production Contracting: The Role of the Fruit and Vegetable Processor in Mexico and Central America.* New York: Praeger, 1974.

Morton, J. "Descent, Reciprocity and Inequality among the Northern Beja." Ph.D. dissertation, University of Hull: UK 1989.

Mosley, P. *The Settler Economies.* Cambridge: Cambridge University Press, 1983.

Msangi, J., C. Griffiths and W. Banyikwar. "Man's Response to Change in the Coastal Zone of Tanzania." Department of Geography, University of Dar es Salaam, Tanzania, 1987.

Mufson, S. "Don't Thank Us, Pepsi; We Just Talked With a Few Bean Buyers" in *The Wall Street Journal,* 17 July 1985.

_____. "Smoking Section: Cigarette Companies Develop Third World as a Growth Market," *Wall Street Journal,* July 5, 1985, p.1.

Natural Resources Institute. COSCA Phase I Processing Component. Collaborative Study of Cassava in Africa, Working Paper #7. Chatham, U.K.: NRI, 1992.

Ndiaye, C. et al. *The Food Industry in Senegal, with Particular Reference to the Processing of Grains, Fisheries Products and Milk Products.* Geneva: UNCTAD, 1985.

_____. *Report on the Agro-Industrial Sector and the Framework for Technology Transfer in Burundi.* New York: UNCTAD, 1992.

Nell, A. "An Overview of Dairying in sub-Saharan Africa," in *Dairy Marketing in sub-Saharan Africa*, edited by R. Brokken and S. Seyoum. Addis Addaba: International Livestock Centre for Africa, 1990.

Nellis, J. "Public Enterprises in sub-Saharan Africa." World Bank Discussion Paper no. 1. Washington: World Bank, 1986.

Nelson, R. and S. Winter. *An Evolutionary Theory of Economic Change.* Cambridge, Mass.: Harvard University Press, 1981.

Newberry, D. and J. Stiglitz. *The Theory of Commodity Price Stabilization.* Oxford: Clarendon Press, 1981.

Nielsen, C., Jr. "The Story of Vanilla." Waukegan, Illinois: Nielsen Massey Vanillas Inc., 1992.

North, D. "Three Approaches to the Study of Institutions," in D. Colander (ed.) *Neo-Classical Political Economy: An Analysis of Rent-Seeking and DUP Activities.* Cambridge, Mass.: Ballinger, 1986.

Northwood, P. "Cashew Production in the Southern Province of Tanganyika." *East Africa Agriculture and Forestry Journal* Vol. 28(1962): 35–39.

_____ and H. Kayumbo. "Cashew Production in Tanzania." *World Crops* (March/April 1970): 88–91.

N'sangou, A. "La Contribution des buy'em sell'em au Developpement," in J-C Barbier (ed.) *Femmes du Cameroun: Meres Pacifiques, Femmes Rebelles.* Paris: ORSTROM/Karthala, 1985.

Obben J, "Some Aspects of the Ghanaian Rural Banking Scheme, 1976–87." *African Review of Money, Finance and Banking* no.2 (1991): 147–164.

ODA Cashew Research Project. "A Household Agricultural Marketing Survey in the Six Main Cashew Growing Farming System Zones in the Southern Zone of Tanzania, 1991." Mtwara 1992.

_____ "Cashew Farmer Practices Survey 1992." Mtwara, Tanzania, 1992.

ODA and World Bank. *Uganda: Developing the Private Sector through Supporting Markets*. London 1991.

Ohler, J. *Cashew*. Amsterdam: Koninklijk Institute voor de Tropen, 1979.

Ommeh, M. "An Investigation into the Kenyan Cashew Nut Industry. Unpublished Msc. Thesis, University of Nairobi, 1984.

Onyeiwu, S. "Graduation Problems Amongst MSEs in Eastern Nigeria," *Small Enterprise Development*, Vol. 3, no.4 (1992), pp. 45–50.

Perlez, Jane. "Two Months After Ousting Despot, Somalia Faces Life as an Abandoned Pawn." *New York Times Daily Newspaper*, 4 April 1991.

Peters, H. "Trade and Industry Logistics in Developing Countries: A Strategy for Improving Competitiveness in Changing International Markets". Unpublished paper, World Bank, 1992.

Platteau, J-P. "The Food Crisis in Africa: A Comparative Structural Analysis," in J. Dreze and A. Sen (eds.) *The Political Economy of Hunger*, Volume 2. Oxford: Clarendon Press, 1990.

Posner, R. "A Theory of Primitive Society, with Special Reference to Law". *Journal of Law and Economics*. Vol. 23, no.1 (1980).

"Potential of the Cashew Nut," *Tanganyika Trade Journal* Vol. 1 no. 5 (1963): 28–29.

Price Waterhouse. "The Kenya Dairy Sector: Facts and Figures," Nairobi, 1991.

Purseglove, J.W. and E.G. Brown, C.L. Green, S.R.J. Robbins. *Spices, Volume 2*. Essex, UK: Longman Group Ltd, 1981.

Raikes, P. *Livestock Development and Policy in East Africa*. Uppsala: Scandinavian Institute of African Studies, 1981.

Randall, P. "Women in Fish Production". Special publication of the FAO Regional Office for Africa. Accra, (no date).

Reve, T. "Interorganizational Relations in Distribution Channels: An Empirical Study of Norwegian Distribution Channel Dyads." Unpublished Ph.D. dissertation, Northwestern University: Chicago, 1980.

Rhee, Y. et al. "Firm-Level Study of Supply Sources of Potential Foreign Industrial Catalysts for Sub-Saharan Africa". Private Sector Development Department. Washington, D.C.: World Bank, 1993.

Richardson, G. *Economic Theory*. London: Hutchinson and Co., 1964.

Riddell, R. "Cote d'Ivoire," in R. Riddell (ed.) *Manufacturing Africa*. London: Overseas Development Institute, 1990.

Riverson, J., J. Gaviria, and S. Thrisutt. "Rural Roads in Sub-Saharan Africa: Lessons from World Bank Experience". World Bank Technical Paper #141. Washington, D.C.: World Bank, 1991.

Rosengarten, F. *The Book of Edible Nuts*. New York: Walker and Company, 1975.

Ross, J. and K. Owusu-Sekyere. "Agribusiness and Public Sector Collaboration in Agricultural Technology Development and Use in Ghana: A Study of Postharvest Technology for Fruits and Vegetables". AMIS Project sponsored by USAID. Washington, D.C.: Abt Associates, 1992.

Rottenberg, S. and B. Yandle. *Quality Controls of Traded Commodities and Services in Developing Countries*. World Bank Discussion Paper #38. Washington, D.C., 1988.

Rural Investments Overseas. "Small-Scale Agribusiness: Brong Ahafo and Central Regions". Report for ODA and Republic of Ghana. Stroud, U.K.: RIO, 1992.

Rusike, J. "Trader Perceptions of Constraints on Expanding Agricultural Input Trade Among Selected SADCC Countries," Department of Agricultural Economics and Extension Working Paper 5/89. University of Zimbabwe, 1988.

Ruttan, V. and Y. Hayami. "Toward a Theory of Induced Institutional Innovation," *Journal of Development Studies*. Vol. 20, no.4 (1984), pp.203–23.

Samatar, A. "Merchant Capital, International Livestock Trade and Pastoral Development in Somalia." *Canadian Journal of African Studies* 21(1987): 355–374.

_____. *The State and Rural Transformation in Northern Somalia, 1884–1986*. Madison, WI: University of Wisconsin Press, 1989.

_____ and A.I. Samatar. "The Material Roots of the Suspended African State: Arguments from Somalia." *Journal of Modern African Studies* 25 (1987): 669–690.

_____, L. Salisbury and J. Bascom. "The Political Economy of Livestock Marketing in Northern Somalia." *African Economic History* 17(1988): 81–97.

Sandford, S. *Management of Pastoral Developmnent in the Third World*. London: John Wiley with Overseas Development Institute, 1983.

Schatz, S. "Laissez-Faireism for Africa?" *Journal of Modern African Studies*, Vol. 25, no.1 (1987), pp. 129–38.

Schelling, T. *The Strategy of Conflict*. Cambridge: Harvard University Press, 1960.

Schiavo-Campo, S. et al. "The Tortoise Walk: Public Policy and Private Activity in the Economic Development of Cameroon". AID Evaluation Special Study #10. Washington, D.C.: United States Agency for International Development, 1983.

Schluter, M. "Policies to Increase Production of Commodities with Export Potential to Oil Exporter Markets," Working Paper No. 406. Institute for Development Studies, University of Nairobi, 1984.

Schneiberg, M. and J. Hollingsworth. "Can Transaction Cost Economics Explain Trade Associations," in M. Aoki, B. Gustafsson, and O. Williamson (eds.) *The Firm as a Nexus of Treaties*. London: Sage Publications, 1990.

Schneider, H. *Livestock and Equality*. Bloomington, IN: Indiana University Press, 1979.

Schreider, G. "Informal Financial Groups in Cameroon: Motivation, Organization and Linkages." Masters thesis, Ohio State University, 1989.

Sellen, D. et al. "Dairy in Kenya: Issues in Agricultural Policy." Policy Analysis for Rural Development Project. Working Paper no. 8. Egerton University, 1990.

Sen, L. K. "Development Prospects and Export Potential of Indonesian Vanilla: A Case Study in the Global Context." Unpublished thesis, Harvard Institute for International Development: Cambridge, 1985.

Shaffer, J. "Thinking about Farmers' Cooperatives, Contracts, and Economic Coordination". Michigan State University, Department of Agricultural Economics.Mimeo, (no date).

Shaikh, H. S. Kikeri and D. Swanson. "Privatization and Public Enterprise Reform in Africa." Background paper for *Adjustment in Africa: Reforms, Results and the Road Ahead*. World Bank: Washington, D.C., 1993.

Shapiro, K., E. Jesse, and J. Foltz. "Dairy Marketing and Development in Africa." *Dairy Marketing in sub-Saharan Africa,* Addis Addaba: International Livestock Centre for Africa, 1990.

Shapouri, S. and S. Rosen. "Dairy Imports in sub-Saharan Africa." *Dairy Marketing in sub-Saharan Africa,* Addis Addaba: International Livestock for Africa, 1990.

Siemens *International Telcom Statistics*. Geneva, 1992.

Silverside, D. "Report on a Visit to Nigeria to Study the Marketing of Dried Meat." Chatham, UK: Natural Resources Institute, 1992.

Smith, L. and A. Thomson. *The Role of Public and Private Agents in the Food and Agricultural Sectors of Developing Countries*. Rome: FAO, 1991.

"Spices: Attention Turns to Domestic Markets." In *SPORE*, No.42 (1992). Technical Centre for Agricultural and Rural Cooperation, Netherlands.

Staal, S. and B. Shapiro. "The Effects of Price Liberalization on Kenyan Peri-Urban Dairy." Draft paper prepared under the aegis of the International Livestock Centre for Africa, Addis Adaba, no date.

Staatz, J. "A Theoretical Perspective on the Behavior of Farmers' Cooperatives". Unpublished PhD. Dissertation, Michigan State University, 1984.

Statistical Services. *Ghana in Figures: 1992*. Accra, Ghana, 1992.

Stevens, C. "Nigeria," in R. Riddell (ed.) *Manufacturing Africa*. London: Overseas Development Institute, 1990.

Stigler, G. "The Division of Labor is Limited by the Extent of the Market," *Journal of Political Economy*, Vol. 59(1951), pp. 185–93.

Stockton, G. "The Case for the Development of the Private Livestock Export Infrastructure in Somalia." Mogadishu, Somalia: Livestock Marketing and Health Project, 1987.

Stotz, D. "Smallholder Dairy Development in Past, Present, and Future in Kenya." Unpublished Ph.D. thesis, University of Hohenheim: Germany, 1979.

Sutter, J. "Cattle and Inequality: Herd Size Differences and Pastoral Production Among the Fulani of Northeastern Senegal," *Africa* 57(1987): 196–217.

Svedberg, P. "The Export Performance of sub-Saharan Africa." *Economic Development and Cultural Change* April (1991): 549–66.

Swainson, N. *The Development of Corporate Capitalism in Kenya, 1918–77*. London: Heinemann, 1980.

Swift, J. "The Economics of Production and Exchange in West African Pastoral Societies." In *Pastoralists of the West African Savanna* edited by M. Adamu and A. Kirk-Greene. Manchester: Manchester University Press, 1986.

Tartanac, F. and R. Treillon. *La Cause de l'Innovation Tome 2: Innovations et Transferts Technologiques en Agroalimentaire: quelques etudes de cas*. Montpellier and Paris: CIRAD and ALTERSYAL, 1989.

Terpend, N. "La Promotion du Secteur Prive: Experiences of Development in the Last Ten Years". Report for the FAO Agricultural Services Division. Rome: FAO, 1992.

Theodose, R. "Traditional Methods of Vanilla Preparation, Improvement of These Techniques, and the Antalaha Station." *Spices*. London: Tropical Products Institute. Proceedings of the Conference on Spices, held at the London School of Pharmacy, 1972.

Thillairajah, S. "Development of Rural Financial Markets in sub-Saharan Africa." World Bank Discussion Paper no. 219. Washington, D.C.: World Bank, 1994.

Thomas J. Payne Market Development. Madagascar Vanilla International Marketing Study. Washington, D.C. Consultancy Study for the World Bank, 1990.

Thompson, A. "The Promotion of the Private Sector: Approaches and Methodologies". Report for FAO Agricultural Services Division. Rome: FAO, 1992.

Tovo, M. "Micro-Enterprises Among Village Women in Tanzania." *Small Enterprise Development*, Vol. 2, no. 1, March 1991, pp. 20–30.

TransExpert "Facilitation des Exportations Agricoles en Cote d'Ivoire". Report for the World Bank and the Ministere de l'Agriculture et des Ressources Animales, Cote d'Ivoire. Montreal: TransExpert, 1993.

Tribe, L. "Developing Small-scale Agro-processing in Kenya: Lessons from a Post-Implementation Review." Bradford University New Series Discussion Paper, 1989.

Tropical Development and Research Institute and Centre d'études et d'actions sociales maritimes. "Evaluation of Fish Wastage in West Africa." Report commissioned by the Technical Centre for Agricultural and Rural Cooperation, Ede-Wageningen, Netherlands, 1986.

Tsakaris, A. "Cashew Nut Production in Southern Tanzania, Part 2—A Survey of Peasant Holdings at Lulindi." *East Africa Agricultural and Forestry Journal* 22(1967): 35–39.

Turton, E. "The Pastoral Tribes of Northern Kenya, 1800–1916." Ph.D. Dissertation, University of London, UK, 1970.

_____. "Somali Resistance to Colonial Rule and the Development of Somali Political Activity in Kenya 1893-1960." *Journal of African History* 13(1972): 117–143.

_____. "Bantu, Galla and Somali Migrations in the Horn of Africa: A Reassessment of the Juba/Tana Area." *Journal of African History* 16(1975): 519–537.

Umali, D., G. Feder, and C. de Haan. *The Balance Between Public and Private Sector Activities in the Delivery of Livestock Services*. World Bank Discussion Paper, no. 163. Washington, D.C.: World Bank, 1992.

UNCTAD *Handbook of International Trade and Development Statistics*. Geneva, 1991.

UNECA "Survey in Zambia, Cameroon and Ghana on Women as Small-Scale Entrepreneurs". Addis Ababa, 1987.

UNICEF. *A Practical Guide to Improved Fish Smoking in West Africa*. New York, 1983 p. 34.

UNIDO. *Fish Processing*. UN Development Fund for Women, Food Cycle Technology Source Book no. 4. Vienna, 1988.

_____. "The Integrated Development of the Fisheries Industrial Systems of Benin, Gambia, Sierra Leone and Togo: a Programme Implementation Proposal." Vienna, 1989.

_____. "Programme Proposal for the Integrated Development of Fisheries Industrial System, Ghana." UNIDO/FAO Report Vol. I, draft mimeo, 1991.

_____. "Kenya's Fruit and Vegetable Processing Industry." Vienna, 1993.

United Nations Development Program *Human Development Report 1993*. New York: UNDP, 1993.

_____ and World Bank. *African Development Indicators*. New York, 1992.

United Nations. *Yearbook of International Trade Statistics*. New York, various years.

United Republic of Tanzania, "Agricultural Division Annual Report, Ministry of Agriculture and Cooperatives." Dar es Salaam, various years.

U.S. Department of Agriculture/Foreign Agricultural Service (FAS). Unclassified cable from U.S. Embassy/Nairobi to FAS/Washington. 19 May 1964.

_____. Unclassified cable from U.S. Embassy/Tananarive to FAS/Washington. 9 July 1964.

_____. Unclassified cable from U.S. Embassy/Tananarive to FAS/Washington. 17 June 1965.

_____. Unclassified cable from U.S. Embassy/Tananarive to FAS/Washington. 19 August 1965.

_____. Unclassified cable from U.S. Embassy/Nairobi to FAS/Washington. 19 May 1966.

_____. "U.S. Spice Trade." Washington, D.C.: Circular Series FTEA 1-93. 1993.

United States Department of Agriculture. *World Agriculture Trends and Indicators, 1970–89*. Economic Research Service. Statistical Bulletin #815. Washington, D.C., 1990.

Valentine, J. "Natural Vanilla Is Making a Comeback, Aided by Its Use in Gourmet Ice Creams." *The Wall Street Journal*, 8 September 1987.

van der Hoeven, J. and Y. Budeba. "A Marketing Study on the Tanzanian Part of Lake Victoria," UNDP/FAO Regional Project for Inland Fisheries Planning Development and Management in Eastern, Central, and Southern Africa. Bujumbura, 1993.

van der Laan, L. *The Lebanese Traders in Sierra Leone*. The Hague: Mouton, 1975.

_____. "Marketing West Africa's Export Crops: Modern Boards and Colonial Trading Companies," *Journal of Modern African Studies*, Vol. 25, no.1 (1987), pp. 1–24.

"Vanilla Breakthrough May Herald Biotech Revolution in Flavor Area." *Chemical Marketing Reporter*, 9 May 1988.

"Vanilla Extract Production Now Has CO_2 Process Option." *Chemical Marketing Reporter*. 15 October 1990.

"Vanilla Is Target for Product From Genetic Engineering Labs." *Chemical Marketing Reporter*, 29 June 1987.

Varangis, P., T. Akiyama, and E. Thigpen. "Recent Developments in Marketing and Pricing Systems for Agricultural Export Commodities in Sub-Saharan Africa," International Economics Department. World Bank Working Paper #431. Washington, D.C., 1990.

Von Pischke, J.D. *Finance at the Frontier: Debt Capacity and the Role of Credit in the Private Economy*. Economic Development Institute. Washington, D.C.: World Bank, 1991.

Walshe, M., J. Grindle, A. Nell, and M. Bachmann. *Dairy Development in Sub-Saharan Africa*. World Bank Technical Paper no. 135. Washington, D.C.: World Bank, 1991.

Waters-Bayer, A. "Dairying by Settled Fulani Women in Central Nigeria and Some Implications for Dairy Development". ODI Pastoral Development Network Paper #20c. London: Overseas Development Institute, 1985.

_____. "Soybean Daddawa: An Innovation by Nigerian Women" ILEIA Newsletter, Vol. 4, no.3 (1988), pp. 8–9.

Watts, M., C. Mock, M. Billings, P. Little, and S. Jaffee. *Contract Farming in Africa*. Study Conducted for the U.S. Agency for International Development. Binghamton, N.Y.: Institute for Development Anthropology, 1988.

Williams, S. and R. Karen. *Agribusiness and the Small-Scale Farmer: A Dynamic Partnership for Development*. Boulder: Westview Press, 1985.

Williamson, O. *Markets and Hierarchies: Analysis and Antitrust Implications*. New York: Free Press, 1975.

_____. "Transaction Cost Economics: The Governance of Contractual Relations," *Journal of Law and Economics*, Vol. 22 (1979), pp. 233–62.

_____. *The Economic Institutions of Capitalism*. New York: Free Press, 1985.

Wilson, F. "Some Economic Aspects of the Structure and Organization of Small-scale Marketing Systems," Discussion Paper no. 176, Institute for Development Studies, Nairobi, 1971.

Wilson, J. "Application of Uncertainty and Small Numbers Exchange: The New England Fresh Fish Market," *Bell Journal of Economics*, (1980), pp.491–504.

_____. "The Political Economy of Contract Farming," *Review of Radical Political Economics*. Vol. 18, no.4 (1986), pp.47–70.

Winrock International. *Assessment of Animal Agriculture in Sub-Saharan Africa*. Morrilton, Arkansas, 1992.

Wolde-Semait, T. and D. Swanson. "Africa's Public Enterprise Sector and Evidence of Reforms". World Bank Technical Paper # 95. Washington, D.C.: World Bank, 1989.

Woodward, D. and G. Stockton. "Somalia: A Study of the Profitability of Somali Exports." Washington, D.C.: Abt Associates, 1989.

_____., D. Hughes, and G. Posschelle. "Gambia: Study of the Privatization of the Gambia Produce Marketing Board". Report of Agricultural Marketing Improvement Strategies Project under contract with USAID. Washington, D.C., 1989.

World Bank*The Economic Development of Kenya*. Baltimore: Johns Hopkins Press, 1963.

_____. *Accelerated Development in SubSaharan Africa*. Washington, D.C., 1981.

_____. *Tanzania Agricultural Sector Report*. Washington, D.C., 1983.

_____. *World Development Report*. Washington, D.C., 1986.

_____. *Ghana: Prospects for Selected Export Products*. Draft Report no. 7307-GH. Washington, D.C.: World Bank, 1989.

_____. *Agricultural Growth Prospects Study*. Agricultural Operations Division. Eastern Africa Department, 1990.

_____. *Agricultural Marketing: The World Bank Experience, 1974–85*. Operations Evaluation Department. Washington, D.C., 1990.

_____. *Le Secteur de la Vanille: Analyse des Problèmes et Recommandations*. Report no. 10002-MAG, 1991.

_____. *Tanzania Economic Report: Towards Sustainable Development in the 1990s*. Washington, D.C., 1991.

_____. *World Development Report 1992*. Washington, D.C., 1992.

_____. *Commodity Trade and Price Trends*, 1989–91 Edition. Washington, D.C., 1993.

_____. *World Development Report 1993*. Washington, D.C., 1993

_____. *Adjustment in Africa: Reforms, Results, and the Road Ahead*. World Bank Policy Research Report. Washington, D.C., 1994

Zusman, P. *Individual Behavior and Social Choice in a Cooperative Settlement*. Jerusalem: The Magnes Press, 1988.

Index